INTRODUCTION

Learning a new language is an exciting ~~~~.
However, it can also sometimes seem confusing and
difficult. Feeling secure and at ease in using a
bilingual dictionary is essential to the building of
confidence in understanding and using a foreign
language.

This dictionary has been specially written for students
who are preparing for exams. We have paid particular
attention to making the dictionary as user-friendly as
possible. With the help of colour headwords, easy-to-
follow signposts and examples, the right translation
can quickly be found. Spanish verbs on both sides of
the dictionary are numbered to take the student
straight to the appropriate pattern in the centre pages
of the dictionary.

We have adopted a simplified version of traditional
bilingual entry layout. This means that the dictionary
is ideal for learning basic dictionary skills, which can
subsequently be built upon as the student moves
towards larger, more sophisticated dictionaries. We
have done our best to make this dictionary a practical,
easy-to-use tool for learning and understanding
Spanish.

Throughout the writing of this dictionary we have
worked in close consultation with students, teachers,
inspectors, and examining boards. We gratefully
acknowledge the cooperation of the Northern
Examinations and Assessment Board, the Southern
Examining Group, the Midland Examining Group,
London Examinations and the Associated Examining
Board.

HOW A BILINGUAL DICTIONARY WORKS

A bilingual dictionary is a dictionary that has two languages in it. When you look up a word in one of the languages, the dictionary gives the translation for that word in the other language. The two languages in this dictionary are English and Spanish. This dictionary is divided into two halves separated by blue-edged pages in the middle. In the first half you look up Spanish words to find out what they mean in English and in the second half you look up English words and find out how to say them in Spanish.

The words you look up are in blue and in the first half of the dictionary you will find **Spanish** words in alphabetical order from a to z and in the second half **English** words from a to z. In a dictionary, these are called **headwords** because each one of them comes at the **head** of an **entry**. In the **entry** you can find not only **translations** but also other sorts of information which you can use to make sure you get the correct translation. The different sorts of information are printed in different ways to help you see clearly which is which. Here is a guide to the different things you will find printed in an entry:

headword	headword: words you look up in the dictionary
translation	the translation of the headword or of an example; translations are the only things that are in 'ordinary' type in the dictionary. They are *always* printed like this, and something which is printed in a different way can *never* be a translation
noun	part of speech: tells you whether the word you are looking up is a noun, a verb, an adjective, or another part of speech. One headword can have more than one part of speech. For instance, **book** can be a noun *(she was reading a book)* or a verb *(I've booked the seats)*
(signpost)	helpful information: to guide you to the right translation, to show you how to use the translation, or to give you extra information about either the headword or the translation
example	a phrase or sentence using the word you have looked up. If these appear in the entry you are looking at, you should read through them carefully to see if they are close to what you want to understand or say
M	gender: after a Spanish noun to tell you that it is masculine
F	gender: after a Spanish noun to tell you that it is feminine
●	indicates a phrasal verb
★	shows an idiomatic expression such as *to be over the moon*
[27]	verb number – tells you which verb pattern to look at in the centre of the dictionary

You can think of a dictionary entry as being made out of different sorts of building bricks. In the entries below, you can see how they fit together to help you to find what you need. The more you use your dictionary the more confident you will feel about finding your way around it.

SPANISH–ENGLISH

headword in blue for easy look-up

verb number: shows you which pattern to look at in the verb tables in the centre of the dictionary

typical examples of use in Spanish

part of speech

informal word or expression

gender

feminine form for easy look-up

helpful additional information

catarro *noun* M cold; **coger un catarro** to catch a cold.

catear *verb* [17] (*informal*) to fail; **he cateado las mates** I've failed maths; **me han cateado en inglés** I've failed English.

catedral *noun* F cathedral.

categoría *noun* F **1** category; **2 de primera categoría** first class; **un hotel de mucha categoría** a top-quality hotel; **un restaurante de poca categoría** a second-rate restaurant.

católico/católica *noun* M/F *adjective* Catholic.

catorce *number* **1** fourteen; **tiene catorce años** he's fourteen (years old); **2** fourteenth (*in dates*); **el catorce de mayo** the fourteenth of May.

A STEP-BY-STEP GUIDE TO FINDING THE TRANSLATION YOU NEED

Finding a word in the dictionary

You will be using this dictionary to do one of the following things:

1 look up a Spanish word or phrase to find out what it means
2 look up an English word or phrase to find out how to say it in Spanish.

1 Finding out what a Spanish word means

Look for the word in the first half of the dictionary, where you can find the Spanish words and expressions with their English translations. You will see that the top of every page is marked like this.

Suppose you want to find out what Spanish word **mostaza** means. Flick through the pages until you get close to the word you are looking for. The word at the top left of the left-hand page and the word at top right of the right-hand page show you the alphabetical range of words which appear on these two pages. So if you look at pages 174–175, you will see that the words on these pages run from **montón** to **muerda** and in the right-hand column of the left-hand page you will find the alphabetical range which includes **mostaza**.

> **mosca** *noun* F fly; ★ **por si las moscas**
> (*informal*) just in case; ★ **¿qué mosca le
> ha picado?** (*informal*) What's got into him?
> (*literally: 'what fly has bitten him?'*).
>
> **mosquito** *noun* M mosquito.
>
> **mostaza** *noun* F mustard.
>
> **mostrador** *noun* M 1 counter (*in a shop*);
> 2 bar (*in a pub*); 3 check-in desk.

You can now see that **mostaza** means **mustard**. You can also see that it is a noun and because all nouns are either masculine or feminine in Spanish, you are given the gender F (F = feminine gender, M = masculine gender).

It often happens that a Spanish word has more than one translation in English. If you look at the entry for **comida** you can see that there are 3 different translations, each of which is numbered

> **comida** *noun* F **1** food; **tenemos suficiente comida** we have enough food; **2** lunch; **a la hora de la comida** at lunch time; **3** meal; **cuatro comidas al día** four meals a day; **mi comida fuerte es a medio-día** my main meal is at midday.

So **comida** can mean **food**, **lunch**, or **meal**. You will need to look at all the translations and decide which one fits best in the sentence you are trying to understand.

Most adjectives in Spanish have a masculine form and a feminine form. Both of these are given as headwords, so if you are trying to find out what **complicada** means, you will be able to find it easily:

> **complicado/complicada** *adjective* complicated.

2. Finding an English word and how to say it in Spanish

You can see that once you know how the dictionary works it is quite easy to look up a Spanish word and find out what it means. Students usually find it harder to use the dictionary to find out how to say something in Spanish. This dictionary is written specially to help you do this and to make it easy to find the right way of saying things in Spanish.

Suppose you want to know how to say garden in Spanish. Look up the word in the second part of the dictionary where the top of every page is marked like this.

You will find the entry **garden** in its place in the alphabetical sequence:

> **gangster** *noun* gángster M/F.
>
> **gap** *noun* **1** (*hole*) hueco M; **2** (*in time*) intervalo M; **a two-year gap** un intervalo de dos años; **3 an age gap** una diferencia de edad.
>
> **garage** *noun* garaje M.
>
> **garden** *noun* jardín M.
>
> **gardener** *noun* jardinero M, jardinera F; **he's a gardener** es jardinero.

Now you can see that the Spanish word for **garden** is **jardín**. But if you want to make a sentence using a noun such as **jardín** you need to know whether it is masculine or feminine. The **M** after **jardín** tells you that it is masculine so *in the garden* is **en el jardín**.

It is not always easy to work out which Spanish word you need. When the dictionary gives you more than one translation, it is very important to take the time to read through the whole entry. If you look up **hall** the entry looks like this:

> **hall** *noun* **1** (*in a house*) entrada F; **2** (*public*) salón M; **the village hall** el salón de actos del pueblo; **3 a concert hall** una sala de conciertos.

You can see that **1** tells you that the Spanish word for a **hall** in your house is **entrada**, **2** that the word for a public place like a **village hall** or a **school hall** is **salón**, and **3** that the phrase for a **concert hall** is **sala de conciertos**.

Remember that the information which is in brackets and italics is there to guide you to the right translation but will never be the translation itself.

Often it is not enough to find the translation of one single word. In the case of frequently used words, the dictionary also gives you a selection of common phrases you will want to use. In the entry **hair** you can see how the translation works in different expressions:

> **hair** *noun* **1** pelo M; **to have short hair** tener [9] el pelo corto; **to brush your hair** cepillarse [17] el pelo; **to wash your hair** lavarse [17] el pelo; **to have your hair cut** cortarse [17] el pelo; **she's had her hair cut** ce ha cortado el pelo; **2 a hair** (*from the head*) un pelo; (*from the body*) un vello.

How to use the verb table numbers

On the [SPANISH–ENGLISH] side of the dictionary all the headwords which are verbs look like this:

> **cerrar** *verb* [29]

On the [ENGLISH–SPANISH] side of the dictionary all the verbs given as translations of English verbs look like this:

> **frighten** *verb* asustar [17].

If you look at the pages edged in blue in the centre of the dictionary, you will find tables showing you how to use the different types of Spanish verbs. The verb **cerrar** above has the number **29**. If you look up number **29** in the verb tables you will find the tense patterns for this verb. The same is true for verb numbers after Spanish verbs in the English-Spanish side of the dictionary.

A a

a *preposition* (*note that 'a + el' becomes 'al'*) **1** to; **iremos a Italia** we'll go to Italy; **tuerce a la derecha** turn right; **voy a casa** I'm going home; **2 está a la izquierda** it's on the left; **sentados a la mesa** sitting at the table; **siéntate al sol** sit in the sun; **estaban a mi lado** they were by my side; **3** at; **a las diez** at ten o'clock; **a media noche** at midnight; **se casó a los treinta años** she married at thirty; **¿a qué hora termina?** what time does it finish?; **4 hoy estamos a dos de enero** it's the second of January today; **5 está a diez kilómetros de aquí** it's ten kilometres from here; **la vi a lo lejos** I saw her in the distance; **6 dos veces al día** twice a day; **están a cien pesetas el kilo** they're a hundred pesetas a kilo; **a ochenta kilómetros por hora** at eighty kilometres an hour; **7 ir a pie** to go on foot; **hecho a mano** handmade; **escrito a mano** handwritten; **a lápiz** in pencil; **8** to; **se lo di a Laura** I gave it to Laura; **le mandé un regalo a mi madre** I sent a present to my mother; **le da clases de piano a mi hermana** he gives my sister piano lessons; **9** (*not translated after certain verbs when followed by a person*) **no se lo dije a Mar** I didn't tell Mar; **vi a tu madre** I saw your mother; **10 voy a hacer los deberes** I'm going to do my homework; **nos fuimos a dormir** we went to sleep; **se han ido a nadar** they've gone swimming; **salimos a pasear** we went out for a walk; **11** (*in commands*) **¡a dormir!** go to sleep!; **¡a callar!** shut up!; **¡a comer!** food's ready!

abadía *noun* F abbey.

abajo *adverb* **1 aquí abajo** down here; **allí abajo** down there; **2** downstairs; **hay otro piso abajo** there's another flat downstairs; **los vecinos de abajo** the downstairs neighbours; **3 el piso de abajo** the flat below; the bottom flat.

abalanzarse *reflexive verb* [22] **abalanzarse sobre alguien/algo** to leap on somebody/something; **se abalanzaron hacia la ventana** they rushed towards the window.

abandonado/abandonada *adjective* **1** deserted; **2** abandoned; **sentirse abandonado** to feel abandoned; **3** neglected.

abandonar *verb* [17] **1** to leave; **abandonó a su familia** he left his family; **2** to abandon; **abandonar el barco** to abandon ship.

abanico *noun* M fan.

abarrotado/abarrotada *adjective* packed; **un bar abarrotado de gente** a bar packed with people.

abecedario *noun* M alphabet.

abedul *noun* M birch.

abeja *noun* F bee.

abejón, abejorro *noun* M bumble-bee.

abeto *noun* M fir.

abierto/abierta *adjective* **1** open; **la puerta está abierta** the door's open; **abierto al público** open to the public; **abierto de par en par** wide open; **siempre dejas el grifo abierto** you always leave the tap running; **2** open-minded; **mis padres son muy abiertos** my parents are very open-minded.

abochornado/abochornada *adjective* embarrassed.

abogado/abogada *noun* M/F **1** lawyer; **2** solicitor.

abolladura *noun* F dent.

abollar *verb* [17] to dent.
abollarse *reflexive verb* [17] to get dented.

abonar *verb* [17] **1** to pay (*a bill*); **2** to fertilize (*a field or plant*).
abonarse *reflexive verb* [17] **1** to subscribe; **abonarse a una revista** to subscribe to a magazine; **2** to buy a season ticket.

abono *noun* M **1** fertilizer; **2** a season ticket.

abordar *verb* [17] **1** to tackle (*a problem*); **2** to raise (*a subject*).

aborrecer *verb* [35] to detest.

aborto *noun* M **1** abortion; **2** miscarriage.

abotonarse *reflexive verb* [17] to do your buttons up; **me abotoné la chaqueta** I did my jacket up.

abrasado/abrasada *adjective* **1** burnt; **murieron abrasados** they burned to death; **2 estoy abrasada** I'm boiling.

abrasador/abrasadora *adjective* burning.

abrasar *verb* [17] to burn.

abrazar *verb* [22] to hug.
abrazarse *reflexive verb* [22] to hug each other.

abrazo *noun* M hug.

abrebotellas *noun* M (*does not change in the plural*) bottle opener.

abrelatas *noun* M (*does not change in the plural*) tin opener.

abreviatura *noun* F abbreviation.

abridor *noun* M **1** bottle opener; **2** tin opener.

abrigar *verb* [28] to be warm (*a jumper or coat*).
abrigarse *reflexive verb* [28] to wrap up warmly.

abrigo *noun* M **1** coat; **2 ropa de abrigo** warm clothes.

abril *noun* M April.

abrir *verb* [46] **1** to open; **abre la ventana** open the window; **abrió la boca para hablar** he opened his mouth to speak; **no abrió la boca en**

toda la tarde she didn't say a word all afternoon; **abrir algo de par en par** to open something wide; **2** to turn on (*a tap*); **abrir el agua** to turn the water on; **3 ¡abran paso!** make way!

abrirse *reflexive verb* [46] to open; **la puerta se abrió** the door opened.

abrocharse *reflexive verb* [17] **1** to do up your buttons; **abróchate la chaqueta** do your jacket up; **2** to fasten (*a seat belt*); **abróchense los cinturones** fasten your seat belts.

absoluto/absoluta *adjective* **1** absolute; **2 en absoluto** not at all; **'¿te importa?'** – **'en absoluto'** 'do you mind?' – 'not at all'.

absorbente *adjective* absorbent.

absorber *verb* [18] to absorb.

abstracto/abstracta *adjective* abstract.

absurdo/absurda *adjective* absurd.

abuelo/abuela *noun* M/F **1** grandfather/grandmother; **2 mis abuelos** my grandparents.

aburrido/aburrida *adjective* **1** boring; **2** bored; **estar aburrido/ aburrida** to be bored.

aburrimiento *noun* M boredom; **¡qué aburrimiento!** how boring!

aburrirse *reflexive verb* [19] to get bored.

abusar *verb* [17] **1 abusar (de)** to take too much/many (*alcohol or pills, for example*); **2 abusar de** to take advantage of; **están abusando**

de tu amabilidad they are taking advantage of your kindness.

abuso *noun* M **1** abuse; **el abuso del alcohol** alcohol abuse; **2** outrage; **¡esto es un verdadero abuso!** this is really outrageous!

abusivo/abusiva *adjective* **1** excessive (*price*); **2** unfair (*a law or rule, for example*).

aC *abbreviation* (*short for: antes de Cristo*) BC, before Christ.

acá *adverb* here; **¡ven acá!** come here!

acabado/acabada *adjective* finished.

acabar *verb* [17] **1** to finish; **aún no he acabado de leer el libro** I haven't finished reading the book yet; **¿has acabado con el lápiz?** have you finished with the pencil?; **2** to be over; **cuando acabó la fiesta** when the party was over; **3** to end; **la palabra acaba en 'r'** the word ends in 'r'; **la historia acaba bien** the story has a happy ending; **4 acabar de hacer** to have just done; **acabo de hablar con él** I've just spoken to him; **acaban de llegar** they've just arrived, **acabábamos de terminar** we had just finished.

acabarse *reflexive verb* [17] **1** to be over (*a party or film, for example*); **cuando se acabó la clase** when the class was over; **2** to run out (*money or food, for example*); **se ha acabado el pan** we've run out of bread; **se me acabó el dinero** I ran out of money.

academia *noun* F school; **academia de idiomas** language school.

académico/académica *adjective* academic.

acampada *noun* F **ir de acampada** to go camping.

acampar *verb* [17] to camp.

acantilado *noun* M cliff.

acariciar *verb* [17] **1** to caress (*a person*); **2** to stroke (*a cat or dog*).

acaso *adverb* **por si acaso** just in case.

acatarrado/acatarrada *adjective* **estar acatarrado/ acatarrada** to have a cold.

acatarrarse *reflexive verb* [17] to catch a cold.

acceder *verb* [18] **1 acceder a algo** to agree to something; **2** to access (*information or a file*).

accesible *adjective* **1** accessible (*a place, for example*); **2** affordable.

accesorios *plural noun* M accessories.

accidental *adjective* accidental.

accidente *noun* M accident; **tener un accidente/sufrir un accidente** to have an accident; **un accidente de circulación** a road accident.

acción *noun* F **1** act; **una buena acción** a good deed; **2** share (*in a company*).

aceite *noun* M oil; **aceite de oliva** olive oil.

aceitoso/aceitosa *adjective* oily.

aceituna *noun* F olive.

acelerador *noun* M accelerator; **pisar el acelerador** to put your foot down (*accelerate*).

acelerar *verb* [17] to accelerate.

acento *noun* M **1** accent; **tener acento andaluz** to have an Andalusian accent; **casi no tienes acento** you have hardly any accent; **2** accent (*on a letter in written Spanish*); **un acento agudo** an acute accent.

acentuarse *reflexive verb* [20] to have an accent; **se acentúa en la última sílaba** it has an accent on the last syllable.

aceptable *adjective* acceptable.

aceptar *verb* [17] **1** to accept (*an invitation or apology, for example*); **2 aceptar hacer** to agree to do; **aceptaron dejármelo** they agreed to lend it to me.

acera *noun* F pavement.

acerca de *preposition* about.

acercar *verb* [31] **1 acerqué la silla a la ventana** I moved the chair nearer the window; **acércame un poco la lámpara** bring the lamp closer to me; **2** to pass; **acércame ese libro** pass me that book; **3 acercar a alguien a** to give somebody a lift to; **me acercó a la oficina** she gave me a lift to the office.

acercarse *reflexive verb* [31] to come/ go near; **acércate más** come/get closer; **se acercó a la ventana** she went over to the window.

acero *noun* M steel.

acertado/acertada *adjective* right (*decision or answer*).

acertar *verb* [29] 1 to be right; **¡has acertado!** you've got it right!; 2 **acertar algo** to get something right; 3 **acertar en el blanco** to hit the target.

ácido *noun* M acid.

acierto *noun* M 1 correct answer; 2 good decision; **ese regalo ha sido un acierto** that present was a good idea.

aclaración *noun* F explanation.

aclarar *verb* [17] to make clear.
aclararse *reflexive verb* [17] (*informal*) to understand; **aún no me aclaro** I still don't understand.

acné *noun* M acne.

acoger *verb* [3] 1 to receive (*news or a proposal*); 2 to take in (*refugee*).

acompañar *verb* [17] 1 to go with; **la acompañé al dentista** I went with her to the dentist's; **te acompaño a tu casa** I'll see you home; 2 to keep company; **el perro me acompaña mucho** the dog keeps me company.

aconsejar *verb* [17] to advise.

acordarse *reflexive verb* [24] to remember; **no me acuerdo** I don't remember; **acordarse de algo** to remember something.

acorde *noun* M chord.

acordeón *noun* M accordion.

acortar *verb* [17] to shorten.

acostarse *reflexive verb* [24] 1 to go to bed; **¿a qué hora te acuestas?** what time do you go to bed?; 2 **acostarse con alguien** to sleep with somebody.

acostumbrado/acostumbrada *adjective* **acostumbrado/ acostumbrada a algo** used to something.

acostumbrarse *reflexive verb* [17] **acostumbrarse a algo** to get used to something.

acróbata *noun* M/F acrobat.

actitud *noun* F attitude.

actividad *noun* F activity.

activo/activa *adjective* active.

acto *noun* M 1 act; 2 **en el acto** immediately.

actor *noun* M actor.

actriz *noun* F actress.

actuación *noun* F performance (*in a play or film*).

actual *adjective* present, current; **la situación actual** the present situation; **el actual presidente** the current president.

actualidad *noun* F 1 **en la actualidad** at present, at the moment; **en la actualidad viven en Madrid** at present they're living in Madrid; 2 nowadays; **en la**

actualidad es más fácil viajar
nowadays it's easier to travel.

actualmente *adverb* **1** at present;
actualmente trabaja en un banco at
present he's working in a bank;
2 nowadays; **actualmente se
fabrica con máquinas** nowadays it's
done by machine.

actuar *verb* [20] to act.

acuarela *noun* F watercolour.

acuario¹ *noun* M aquarium.

acuario² *noun* M/F Aquarius; **soy
acuario** I'm an Aquarius.

Acuario *noun* M Aquarius.

acudir *verb* [19] **acudir a** to attend.

acuerdo *noun* M **1** agreement;
llegaron a un acuerdo they reached
an agreement; **2 estar de acuerdo
(en algo)** to agree (on something);
están de acuerdo en la fecha they
agree on the date; **no estoy de
acuerdo** I don't agree; **ponerse de
acuerdo** to come to an agreement;
3 ¡de acuerdo! okay!

acusación *noun* F accusation.

acusar *verb* [17] to accuse; **acusar a
alguien de algo** to accuse somebody
of something; **me acusó de mentir**
he accused me of lying.

acústica *noun* F acoustics.

adaptador *noun* M adaptor
(*electrical*).

adaptar *verb* [17] to adapt.
adaptarse *reflexive verb* [17]
adaptarse a to adapt to.

adecuado/adecuada *adjective*
1 adecuado/adecuada para
suitable for; **2 el momento
adecuado** the right moment.

a. de C. *abbreviation* (*short for:
antes de Cristo*) BC, before Christ.

adelantado/adelantada
adjective **1** advanced; **2** fast (*a clock
or watch*); **tu reloj va adelantado**
your watch is fast; **3 pagar por
adelantado** to pay in advance.

adelantamiento *noun* M
overtaking.

adelantar *verb* [17] **1** to bring
forward (*a date or trip*); **2** to
overtake (*when driving*);
3 adelantar el reloj to put the clock
forward.

adelante *adverb* **1** forward; **ir hacia
adelante** to go forward; **2 seguir
adelante** to go on; **3 más adelante**
further on; **4** later; **5 ¡adelante!**
come in!

adelgazar *verb* [22] to lose weight;
he adelgazado tres kilos I've lost
three kilos.

además *adverb* **1** besides; **además,
no es mi problema** besides, it's not
my problem; **no ayuda y además se
queja** he doesn't help and on top of
that he complains; **2 además de**
apart from; **además de eso, no
sabes conducir** apart from that, you
can't drive; **además de estos tres,
tengo cinco más** besides these
three, I've got five more; **son tres,
además de la madre** there are three,
not counting the mother.

adentro *adverb* inside, in; **vete adentro** go inside.

adicto/adicta *adjective* **adicto/ adicta a** addicted to.

adiós *exclamation* **1** bye!; **2** hello! (*when passing somebody in the street*).

aditivo *noun* M additive.

adivinanza *noun* F riddle.

adivinar *verb* [17] to guess.

adivino/adivina *noun* M/F fortune-teller.

adjetivo *noun* M adjective.

adjuntar *verb* [17] to enclose.

adjunto/adjunta *adjective* enclosed.

admirable *adjective* admirable.

admiración *noun* F **1** admiration; **sentir admiración por alguien** to admire someone; **2 signo de admiración** exclamation mark.

admirador/admiradora *noun* M/F admirer.

admirar *verb* [17] to admire.

admitir *verb* [19] **1** to admit; **admitió su responsabilidad** she admitted her responsibility; **2** 'no se admiten perros' 'no dogs'; 'no se admiten devoluciones' 'goods cannot be exchanged'.

adolescente *noun* M/F adolescent.

adonde *adverb* where; **la ciudad adonde iban** the city where they were going.

adónde *adverb* where.

adoptar *verb* [17] to adopt.

adoptivo/adoptiva *adjective* **1** adoptive (*parents*); **2** adopted (*child*).

adorar *verb* [17] to adore.

adorno *noun* M ornament; **los adornos de Navidad** Christmas decorations.

adquirir *verb* [47] to acquire.

adrede *adverb* on purpose.

aduana *noun* F customs; **libre de derechos de aduana** duty-free.

adulto/adulta *noun* M/F *adjective* adult.

adverbio *noun* M adverb.

advertencia *noun* F warning.

advertir *verb* [14] to warn; **quedas/ estás advertido** you've been warned; **le advertí que no llegase tarde otra vez** I warned him not to be late again.

aéreo/aérea *adjective* air (*traffic*); **el puente aéreo** the shuttle.

aerobic (*plural* **aerobics**) *noun* M aerobics.

aeropuerto *noun* M airport.

aerosol *noun* M aerosol.

afán *noun* M eagerness; **tienen afán de aprender** they are eager to learn.

afectar *verb* [17] to affect.

afecto *noun* M affection; **tenerle afecto a alguien/sentir afecto por alguien** to be fond of somebody.

afectuoso/afectuosa *adjective* affectionate (*person*); **recibe un afectuoso saludo** kind regards (*in a letter*).

afeitarse *reflexive verb* [17] **1** to shave; **hoy no me he afeitado** I haven't shaved today; **2** to shave off (*a beard or moustache*).

afición *noun* F interest, hobby; **¿qué aficiones tienes?** what are your interests?; **por afición** as a hobby.

aficionado/aficionada *adjective* **ser aficionado/aficionada a algo** to be fond of something.

aficionado/aficionada *noun* M/F **1 para los aficionados a la cocina** for those who like cooking; **un aficionado al jazz** a jazz lover; **un aficionado al rugby** a rugby fan; **2** amateur; **un grupo de aficionados** a group of amateurs.

aficionarse *reflexive verb* [17] **aficionarse a algo** to become fond of something.

afilar *verb* [17] to sharpen.

afinar *verb* [17] to tune (*an instrument*).

afirmación *noun* F **1** statement; **2** yes answer.

afirmar *verb* [17] **1** to state; **afirmó que era de su familia** he stated that it belonged to his family; **2 afirmar con la cabeza** to nod.

afirmativo/afirmativa *adjective* affirmative.

aflojar *verb* [17] **1** to loosen; **2 aflojar la marcha** to slow down.

afónico/afónica *adjective* **estar afónico/afónica** to have lost your voice.

afortunado/afortunada *adjective* fortunate.

África *noun* F Africa.

africano/africana *noun* M/F *adjective* African.

afuera *adverb* outside; out; **salimos afuera** we went outside.

afueras *plural noun* F **las afueras** the outskirts.

agachar *verb* [17] **agachar la cabeza** to lower your head.

agacharse *reflexive verb* [17] **1** to bend down; **2** to duck.

agarrar *verb* [17] to grab.

agarrarse *reflexive verb* [17] to hold on; **se agarró a la barandilla** she held on to the handrail.

agencia *noun* F agency; **agencia inmobiliaria** estate agent's; **agencia de viajes** travel agency.

agenda *noun* F diary.

agente *noun* M/F **1** agent; **agente inmobiliario** estate agent; **2 agente de policía** police officer.

agitar *verb* [17] to shake.

agosto *noun* M August.

agotado/agotada *adjective* **1** worn out; **estoy agotado** I'm worn out; **2** sold out; **3** flat (*a battery*).

agotador/agotadora *adjective* exhausting.

agotarse *reflexive verb* [17] **1** to wear yourself out; **2** to sell out (*goods*); **3** to go flat (*a battery*); **4** to run out (*reserves or supplies*); **5 se me está agotando la paciencia** my patience is running out.

agradable *adjective* nice.

agradecer *verb* [35] **1 agradecerle algo a alguien** to be grateful to somebody for something; **te agradezco tu ayuda** I'm grateful for your help; **2** to thank; **te lo agradezco** thank you; **¡y así nos lo agradeces!** and that's all the thanks we get from you!

agradecido/agradecida *adjective* grateful; **le estoy muy agradecido** I'm very grateful to you.

agradecimiento *noun* M gratitude.

agresión *noun* F aggression.

agresivo/agresiva *adjective* aggressive.

agricultor/agricultora *noun* M/F farmer.

agricultura *noun* F **1** agriculture; **2** farming; **agricultura biológica** organic farming.

agrio/agria *adjective* sour.

agua *noun* F water; (*even though 'agua' is a feminine noun, it is used with 'el' and 'un'*) **el agua está fría** the water is cold; **agua mineral con gas** sparkling mineral water; **agua mineral sin gas** still mineral water; **agua potable** drinking water; **agua corriente** running water; **agua de colonia** eau de cologne; ★ **estar más claro que el agua** to be crystal

clear (*literally: to be clearer than water*).

aguacate *noun* M avocado.

aguacero *noun* M downpour.

aguafiestas *noun* M/F (*does not change in the plural*) spoilsport.

aguanieve *noun* F sleet.

aguantar *verb* [17] **1** to hold; (*an object*) **aguanta esta caja un momento** hold this box for a minute; **2** to bear (*pain or heat*); **no aguanto este calor** I can't bear this heat; **3** to take; **no aguanto más** I can't take any more; **4 aguantar la respiración** to hold your breath; **aguantar la risa** to stop yourself laughing.

aguantarse *reflexive verb* [17] **tendrás que aguantarte** you'll have to put up with it.

agudo/aguda *adjective* **1** high-pitched (*a voice or sound*); **2** acute (*pain*); **3** acute (*an accent*); **4** stressed on the last syllable (*a word*).

aguijón *noun* M sting.

águila *noun* F eagle; (*even though 'águila' is a feminine noun, it is used with 'el' and 'un'*) **vimos un águila** we saw an eagle.

aguja *noun* F **1** needle (*for sewing or knitting*); **2** hand (*of a watch or clock*).

agujero *noun* M hole.

agujetas *plural noun* F stiffness; **tengo muchas agujetas** I'm really stiff.

ahí *adverb* **1** there; **ahí están** there
they are; **ponlo ahí** put it there;
2 tenemos que ir por ahí we have to
go that way; **dejó las llaves por ahí**
she left the keys somewhere.

ahijado/ahijada *noun* M/F
1 godson/goddaughter; **2 mis
ahijados** my godchildren.

ahogado/ahogada *adjective*
1 morir ahogado to drown; **2 morir
ahogado** to suffocate.

ahogarse *reflexive verb* [28] **1** to
drown; **se ahogó en el río** he
drowned in the river; **2** to suffocate.

ahora *adverb* **1** now; **¿qué vas a
hacer ahora?** what are you going to
do now?; **de ahora en adelante** from
now on; **ahora mismo** right now;
2 nowadays; **3** in a moment; **ahora
vuelvo** I'll be back in a moment;
ahora lo hago I'll do it in a moment;
ahora viene he's coming; **4 por
ahora** for the time being.

ahorcar *verb* [31] to hang (*execute*).
ahorcarse *reflexive verb* [31] to hang
yourself.

ahorrar *verb* [17] to save.

ahorros *plural noun* M savings;
todos mis ahorros all my savings.

ahumado/ahumada *adjective*
smoked.

aire *noun* M **1** air; **al aire libre** in the
open air; **teatro al aire libre** open-
air theatre; **mis hijos disfrutan
jugando al aire libre** my children
enjoy playing outdoors; **aire
acondicionado** air conditioning;
salir a tomar el aire to go out for
some fresh air; **2** wind; **hace mucho
aire** it's very windy; **3 tiene un aire
interesante** he looks interesting;
llegó con aire preocupado she
arrived looking worried.

aislado/aislada *adjective*
isolated.

ajedrez *noun* M chess; **jugar al
ajedrez** to play chess.

ajillo *noun* M **al ajillo** with garlic;
gambas al ajillo garlic prawns.

ajo *noun* M garlic; **un diente de ajo** a
clove of garlic; **una cabeza de ajo** a
head of garlic.

ajustar *verb* [17] **1** to adjust (*a seat
or safety belt*); **2** to fit.

al ('*al*' is what '*a + el*' becomes; look
under '*a*' for more examples)
1 fuimos al colegio we went to
school; **se lo di al camarero** I gave it
to the waiter; **2** (*with infinitive*)
when; **al salir nos encontramos con
Marta** we met Marta when we were
leaving; **tengan cuidado al bajar del
autobús** be careful when leaving the
bus.

ala[1] *noun* F (*even though '*ala*' is a
feminine noun, it is used with '*el*' and
'*un*'*) **1** wing; **el ala del avión** the
wing of the plane; **el pájaro batió las
alas** the bird beat its wings; **el
hospital tiene dos alas** the hospital
has two wings; **2** brim (*of a hat*).

ala² *noun* M/F winger.

alabanza *noun* F praise.

alabar *verb* [17] to praise.

alambre *noun* M wire; **alambre de púas** barbed wire.

alargador *noun* M extension lead.

alargar *verb* [28] **1** to lengthen; **voy a alargar esta falda un poco** I'm going to lengthen this skirt a bit; **2** to extend (*a visit or holiday, for example*); **el presidente ha alargado su visita** the president has extended his visit; **3** to stretch out (*an arm*); **alargué el brazo para alcanzarlo** I stretched out my arm to reach it.

alargarse *reflexive verb* [28] **1** to get longer; **los días se van alargando** the days are getting longer; **2** to go on; **la conferencia se alargó mucho** the conference went on for a long time.

alarma *noun* F alarm; **alarma contra incendios** fire alarm.

alarmante *adjective* alarming.

albañil *noun* M **1** builder; **2** bricklayer.

albaricoque *noun* M apricot.

albergue *noun* M **1** hostel; **albergue juvenil** youth hostel; **2** refuge (*in the mountains*).

albóndiga *noun* F meatball.

albornoz *noun* M bathrobe.

alborotar *verb* [17] **alborotar a los niños** to get the children excited.

alborotarse *reflexive verb* [17] to get excited.

alboroto *noun* M racket; **¡qué alboroto!** what a racket!

álbum *noun* M album; **un álbum de fotografías** a photograph album; **el mejor álbum del grupo** the group's best album.

alcachofa *noun* F artichoke.

alcalde *noun* M mayor.

alcaldesa *noun* F mayoress; mayor (*woman*).

alcanzar *verb* [22] **1** to reach; **la temperatura alcanzó los cuarenta grados** the temperature reached forty; **no alcanzo a la ventana** I can't reach the window; **2** to catch up with; **no pude alcanzar al resto del grupo** I couldn't catch up with the rest of the group; **3 alcanzarle algo a alguien** to pass somebody something; **¿me alcanzas las tijeras?** can you pass me the scissors?

alcohol *noun* M alcohol.

alcohólico/alcohólica *noun* M/F *adjective* alcoholic.

alcoholismo *noun* M alcoholism.

aldea *noun* F village.

aldeano/aldeana *noun* M/F villager.

alegrar *verb* [17] to cheer up; **verla les alegró un poco** seeing her cheered them up a bit; **me alegra saberlo** I'm glad to know.

alegrarse *reflexive verb* [17] to be happy; **me alegro mucho por ellos** I'm very happy for them; **¡cuánto me alegro!** I'm so happy!; **se alegró de venir** he was glad to come; **me alegro de haberte llamado** I'm glad I phoned you; **me alegro de verte** it's nice to see you.

alegre *adjective* 1 happy; **una cara alegre** a happy face; 2 cheerful; **soy una persona muy alegre** I'm a cheerful kind of person; 3 bright (*a colour*).

alegría *noun* F happiness; **¡qué alegría veros!** it's great to see you!; **¡qué alegría me das!** that makes me really happy!; **saltar de alegría** to jump for joy.

alejar *verb* [17] **alejar algo de alguien** to move something away from somebody.
alejarse *reflexive verb* [17] to move away; **¡aléjate del fuego!** move away from the fire!

alemán[1] *noun* M German (*the language*).

alemán[2]**/alemana** *noun* M/F *adjective* German.

Alemania *noun* F Germany.

alergia *noun* F allergy; **tener alergia a algo** to be allergic to something; **alergia al polen** hayfever.

alerta *noun* F alert; **en estado de alerta** on the alert.
adverb on the alert; **estar alerta** to be on the alert.

alfabeto *noun* M alphabet.

alfarería *noun* F pottery.

alféizar *noun* M **el alféizar de la ventana** the windowsill.

alfiler *noun* M pin.

alfombra *noun* F 1 rug; 2 carpet.

alfombrilla *noun* F mat; **alfombrilla de baño** bath mat.

alga *noun* F seaweed.

algo *pronoun* 1 something; **algo así** something like that; **¿te pasa algo?** is there something wrong?; 2 anything; **¿has cogido algo de aquí?** have you taken anything from here?; 3 some; **algo de leche** some milk; 4 any; **¿tienes algo de leche?** do you have any milk?
adverb a bit; **estoy algo cansado** I'm a bit tired.

algodón *noun* M cotton; **una camisa de algodón** a cotton shirt.

alguien *pronoun* 1 somebody, someone; **vino alguien preguntando por ti** somebody came asking for you; 2 anybody, anyone; **¿has hablado con alguien?** have you talked to anybody?

algún SEE **alguno/alguna**.

alguno/alguna *pronoun*
1 **alguno/alguna** one; **alguno de vosotros** one of you; **tiene que haber alguno aquí** there must be one here; **para alguna de sus hijas** for one of her daughters; 2 **algunos/algunas** some; **faltan algunos** there are some missing; 3 (*in questions*) any; **tengo demasiadas plantas,**

¿quieres alguna? I've got too many plants, do you want any? *adjective* (*'alguno' becomes 'algún' before a masculine singular noun*) **1** some; **compré algunos libros** I bought some books; **algún día iré** I'll go some day; **2** (*in questions*) any; **¿tienes alguna razón para no ir?** do you have any reason for not going?; **¿tienes algún problema?** do you have any problems?; **3 en algún lugar** somewhere; **en algún momento** sometime; **4 alguna vez lo he pensado** I've thought about it sometimes; **¿has estado alguna vez en España?** have you ever been to Spain?

aliado/aliada *noun* M/F ally. *adjective* allied.

alianza *noun* F alliance.

aliarse *reflexive verb* [32] **aliarse con alguien** to form an alliance with somebody.

alicates *plural noun* M **1** pliers; **tengo varios alicates** I've got several pairs of pliers; **2** nail clippers.

aliento *noun* M breath; **mal aliento** bad breath; **estar sin aliento** to be breathless; **recuperar el aliento** to get your breath back.

alimentar *verb* [17] **1** to feed; **2** to be nutritious; **las lentejas alimentan mucho** lentils are very nutritious.
alimentarse *reflexive verb* [17] to feed; **se alimentan de insectos** they feed on insects.

alimenticio/alimenticia *adjective* **productos alimenticios** foodstuffs; **valor alimenticio** nutritional value.

alimento *noun* M **1** food; **el arroz es su alimento básico** rice is their staple food; **buenos alimentos** good food; **2 tiene mucho alimento** it's very nutritious.

aliñar *verb* [17] **1** to dress (*salad*); **2** to season.

aliño *noun* M **1** salad dressing; **2** seasoning.

alioli *noun* M garlic mayonnaise.

alistarse *reflexive verb* [17] to join up; **alistarse en el ejército** to join the army.

aliviar *verb* [17] to relieve (*pain*).

allá *adverb* **1** there; **allá abajo** down there; **¡allá voy!** here I come/go!; **ahora vamos para allá** we're on our way; **2 más allá** further away; **no lo pongas muy allá** don't put it too far away; **3 allá tú** that's your lookout.

allí *adverb* there; **allí arriba** up there; **lo puso por allí** she put it somewhere around there; **se fueron por allí** they went that way.

alma *noun* F (*even though 'alma' is a feminine noun, it is used with 'el' and 'un'*) soul.

almacén *noun* M warehouse.

almacenes *plural noun* M **unos (grandes) almacenes** a department store.

almacenar *verb* [17] to store (*goods*).

almeja *noun* F clam (*shellfish*).

almendra *noun* F almond.

almíbar *noun* M syrup; **peras en almíbar** pears in syrup.

almidón *noun* M starch.

almohada *noun* F pillow; **una almohada de plumas** a feather pillow; **una funda de almohada** a pillowcase; ★ **consultarlo con la almohada** to sleep on it (*a decision*).

almohadón *noun* M cushion.

almorzar *verb* [26] **1** to have a mid-morning snack; **2** to have lunch (*in some areas of Spain*).

almuerzo *noun* M **1** mid-morning snack; **2** lunch (*in some areas of Spain*).

alojamiento *noun* M accommodation.

alojarse *reflexive verb* [17] to stay; **se alojaron en un hotel** they stayed in a hotel.

alondra *noun* F lark (*bird*).

Alpes *plural noun* M **los Alpes** the Alps.

alpinismo *noun* M mountaineering.

alpinista *noun* M/F mountaineer.

alquilar *verb* [17] **1** to rent; **hemos alquilado un apartamento en la playa** we've rented an appartment at the seaside; **2** to hire (*a car or equipment, for example*); **alquilar una bicicleta** to hire a bike; **3** to let (*a house, flat, or room*); **se aquila esa casa** that house is to let; **4** to hire out (*equipment*); **allí alquilan botas de esquiar** they hire out ski boots over there.

alquilarse *reflexive verb* [17] **se alquila local** premises to let; **se alquilan coches** cars for hire.

alquiler *noun* M **1** rent (*for a flat or premises*); **2** hire charge (*for cars or equipment*); **3 una casa de alquiler** a rented house; **una casa en alquiler** a house to let; **coches de alquiler** hire cars.

alrededor *adverb* **1** around; **a nuestro alrededor** around us; **mirar alrededor** to look around; **2 alrededor de algo** around something; **se sentaron alrededor de la mesa** they sat around the table; **3 de alrededor** surrounding; **los campos de alrededor** the surrounding fields.

alrededores *plural noun* M **1** outskirts (*of a town or city*); **2** surrounding area (*of an airport or building*).

altavoz *noun* M **1** loudspeaker; **2** megaphone.

alternar *verb* [17] to alternate.

alternarse *reflexive verb* [17] to take turns; **nos alternábamos para hacer la comida** we took turns to cook.

alternativa[1] *noun* F alternative; **no tenemos otra alternativa** we have no alternative.

alternativo/alternativa[2]
adjective alternative.

altitud *noun* F altitude.

altivo/altiva *adjective* arrogant.

alto/alta *adjective* 1 high; **la montaña más alta de España** the highest mountain in Spain; **habitaciones de techo alto** rooms with high ceilings; **los precios están muy altos** prices are very high; **en lo alto de la torre** on the top of the tower; **tiene la tensión alta** he has high blood pressure; 2 tall; **todos sus hijos son muy altos** all their children are very tall; **¡qué alta está!** hasn't she grown!; 3 loud; **en voz alta** in a loud voice; **no pongas la radio tan alta** don't play the radio so loud.

alto *noun* M **de alto** high; **un muro de dos metros de alto** a two-metre high wall.
adverb 1 loud; **habla un poco más alto, por favor** speak a little louder, please; 2 high; **volar alto** to fly high.

altura *noun* F 1 height; **a la misma altura** at the same height; **¿qué altura tiene?** how high is it?; 2 altitude; **volar a una altura de 10.000m** to fly at an altitude of 10,000 metres; 3 **a estas alturas** at this stage; **a estas alturas no importa** it doesn't matter at this stage.

alubia *noun* F haricot bean.

alucinación *noun* F hallucination.

alucinado/alucinada *adjective* (*informal*) **estar alucinado/ alucinada** to be stunned; **nos quedamos alucinados** we were stunned.

alucinante *adjective* (*informal*) amazing; **es un espectáculo alucinante** it's an amazing spectacle.

alucinar *verb* [17] (*informal*) 1 to amaze; **me alucina** it amazes me; 2 to be amazed; **con este disco es que alucinas** this record's amazing.

alud *noun* M 1 avalanche; 2 landslide.

aluminio *noun* M aluminium.

alumno/alumna *noun* M/F pupil, student.

alusión *noun* F allusion.

amabilidad *noun* F kindness; **tuvieron la amabilidad de ayudarme** they were kind enough to help me.

amable *adjective* kind; **¿sería tan amable de sujetar esto?** would you be so kind as to hold this?

ama de casa *noun* F (*even though 'ama de casa' is a feminine noun, it is used with 'el' and 'un'*) housewife; **un ama de casa** a housewife.

amado/amada *adjective* beloved; **mi amado** my beloved.

amaestrar *verb* [17] to train (*an animal*).

amanecer *noun* M dawn; **al amanecer** at dawn.
verb [35] to get light; **¿a qué hora amanece?** what time does it get light?

amante *noun* M/F lover.
adjective **ser amante de algo** to be fond of something; **son grandes amantes del cine** they're great film-lovers.

amapola *noun* F poppy.

amar *verb* [17] to love.

amargo/amarga *adjective* bitter.

amarillo[1] *noun* M yellow.

amarillo[2]**/amarilla** *adjective* yellow.

amasar *verb* [17] to knead (*dough*).

Amazonas *noun* M **el Amazonas** the Amazon.

ambición *noun* F ambition.

ambicioso/ambiciosa *adjective* ambitious.

ambientador *noun* M air freshener.

ambiental *adjective* environmental.

ambiente *noun* M **1** environment; **la contaminación del ambiente** the pollution of the environment; **2** atmosphere (*at a party, for example*); **había muy buen ambiente** there was a good atmosphere.

ambiguo/ambigua *adjective* ambiguous.

ambos/ambas *plural pronoun*, *plural adjective* both; **se lo dije a ambos** I told both of them; **ambas ciudades** both cities.

ambulancia *noun* F ambulance.

ambulante *adjective* travelling; **un grupo de teatro ambulante** a travelling theatre group; **una biblioteca ambulante** a mobile library.

ambulatorio *noun* M outpatients' department.

amén *noun* M amen.

amenaza *noun* F threat.

amenazador/amenazadora *adjective* threatening.

amenazar *verb* [22] to threaten; **amenazó con despedirme** he threatened to fire me; **amenazar de muerte a alguien** to threaten to kill somebody.

América *noun* F America; **América del Sur** South America; **América Latina** Latin America.

americana[1] *noun* F jacket.

americano/americana[2] *noun* M/F *adjective* American.

ametralladora *noun* F machine gun.

amigo/amiga *noun* M/F friend; **un amigo nuestro** a friend of ours; **un amigo de Carmen** a friend of Carmen's; **son amigos íntimos** they are very close friends; **mi amigo del alma** my best friend.
adjective **son muy amigos** they are very good friends; **hacerse amigos** to become friends.

amistad *noun* F friendship.

amistades *plural noun* F friends; **mis amistades** my friends.

amistoso/amistosa *adjective* friendly.

amo/ama *noun* M/F (*even though 'ama' is a feminine noun, it is used with 'el' and 'un'*) owner (*of an animal*); **el ama del perro** the owner of the dog.

amontonar *verb* [17] to pile up. **amontonarse** *reflexive verb* [17] to pile up.

amor *noun* M **1** love; **amor mío** my love; **amor a primera vista** love at first sight; **2 amor propio** self esteem; ★ **por amor al arte** for the sake of it.

amoroso/amorosa *adjective* **relaciones amorosas** relationships.

ampliar *verb* [32] **1** to enlarge (*a photograph*); **2** to extend (*a road or building*); **3** to increase (*vocabulary or knowledge*).

amplificador *noun* M amplifier.

amplio/amplia *adjective* **1** wide (*a road*); **2** spacious (*a room*); **3** loose-fitting (*a garment*).

amplitud *noun* F **1** width (*of a road*); **2** spaciousness (*of a room*).

ampolla *noun* F blister; **me han salido ampollas en las manos** I've got blisters in my hands.

amueblar *verb* [17] to furnish (*a house or room*).

analfabeto/analfabeta *adjective* illiterate.

análisis *noun* M analysis.

analizar *verb* [22] to analyse.

anatomía *noun* F anatomy.

ancho[1] *noun* M width; **¿cuánto tiene de ancho?/¿qué ancho tiene?** how wide is it?; **mide/tiene dos metros de ancho** it's two metres wide.

ancho[2]**/ancha** *adjective* **1** wide; **una carretera muy ancha** a very wide road; **2** broad; **ser ancho de espaldas** to have broad shoulders; **3** loose-fitting (*a garment*); **te está muy ancho** it's too loose for you.

anchura *noun* F width; **tiene una anchura de cinco metros** it's five metres wide; **¿qué anchura tiene?** how wide is it?

anciano/anciana *noun* M/F old man/old woman. *adjective* elderly; **un hombre muy anciano** a very elderly man.

ancla *noun* F (*even though 'ancla' is a feminine noun, it is used with 'el' and 'un'*) anchor; **el ancla** the anchor; **echar (las) anclas** to drop anchor.

Andalucía *noun* F Andalusia.

andamio *noun* M scaffolding.

andar *verb* [21] **1** to walk; **¿has venido andando?** did you walk here?; **casi no podía andar** I could hardly walk; **2 ¿cómo andas?** how are you?; **¿cómo andas de dinero?** how are you doing for money?; **3** to work; **mi coche no anda** my car's not working; **4** (*expressing surprise*) **¡anda! si es Pedro** well, if it isn't Pedro!; **5** (*urging somebody to do something*) **anda, date prisa** come on, hurry up.

andén *noun* M platform.

Andes *plural noun* M **los Andes** the Andes.

Andorra *noun* F Andorra.

andrajo *noun* M rag; **estaba vestido de andrajos** he was dressed in rags.

anécdota *noun* F anecdote.

anestesia *noun* F **1** anaesthesia; **2** anaesthetic.

anfitrión *noun* M host.

anfitriona *noun* F hostess.

ángel *noun* M angel; **no es ningún angelito** he's no angel; ★ **que sueñes con los angelitos** sweet dreams (*literally: dream with the angels*).

angelical *adjective* angelic.

anginas *plural noun* F throat infection; **tener anginas** to have a throat infection.

anglicano/anglicana *noun* M/F Anglican.

anguila *noun* F eel.

angustiado/angustiada *adjective* worried; **sus padres están angustiados porque no saben nada de él** his parents are really worried because they haven't heard from him.

angustiarse *reflexive verb* [17] to get worried; **no hay por qué angustiarse** there's no reason to get worried.

angustioso/angustiosa *adjective* worrying.

anillo *noun* M ring; **anillo de boda** wedding ring.

animado/animada *adjective* **1** lively (*a bar or party, for example*); **2** in good spirits; **muy animada** she was in high spirits.

animal¹ *noun* M animal; **animal doméstico** pet, domestic animal.

animal² *noun* M/F brute; **es un animal** he's a brute.
adjective stupid; **¡qué animal eres!** you are so stupid!

animar *verb* [17] **1** to liven up (*a party, for example*); **2** to cheer up (*a person*).
animarse *reflexive verb* [17] to cheer up; **¡anímate!** cheer up!

ánimo *noun* M **1** **no tengo ánimo para nada** I don't feel in the mood for anything; **se la ve con mucho ánimo** she's in high spirits; **con el ánimo por los suelos** feeling really low; **2** **¡ánimo!** cheer up!

anís *noun* M anisette.

aniversario *noun* M anniversary.

anoche *adverb* last night; **anoche no dormí bien** I didn't sleep well last night; **antes de anoche** the night before last.

anochecer *noun* M nightfall; **al anochecer** at nightfall.

verb [35] to get dark; **está anocheciendo** it's getting dark.

anónimo¹ *noun* M anonymous letter.

anónimo²/anónima *adjective* anonymous.

anormal *adjective* abnormal.

anotar *verb* [17] to write down.

ansiedad *noun* F anxiety.

ante¹ *noun* M suede.

ante² *preposition* before; **ante el juez** before the judge.

anteanoche *adverb* the night before last.

anteayer *adverb* the day before yesterday.

antemano *in phrase* **de antemano** in advance.

antena *noun* F 1 aerial; 2 antenna.

antepasados *plural noun* M ancestors.

anterior *adjective* previous; **la noche anterior** the previous night; **anterior a algo** prior to something.

antes *adverb* 1 before; **la noche antes** the night before; **haberlo dicho antes** you should have said it before; 2 **antes de** before; **antes del viernes** before Friday; **piénsalo antes de comprarlo** think about it before you buy it; 3 earlier; **este año la primavera ha llegado antes** this year spring has come earlier; **a las cinco está bien, no hace falta que vengas antes** five is fine, you don't

need to come any earlier; 4 first; **ésta va antes** this goes first; 5 **lo antes posible** as soon as possible.

antibiótico *noun* M antibiotic.

anticipación *noun* F **con mucha anticipación** well in advance; **con dos dias de anticipación** two days in advance.

anticipo *noun* M advance.

anticonceptivo *noun* M contraceptive.

anticuado/anticuada *adjective* old-fashioned.

antídoto *noun* M antidote.

antiguamente *adverb* in the old days.

antigüedad *noun* F 1 antique; **tienda de antigüedades** antique shop; 2 seniority (*at work*); 3 **en la antigüedad** in the old days.

antiguo/antigua *adjective* 1 old; **una costumbre muy antigua** a very old tradition; 2 former; **el antiguo presidente** the former president; 3 ancient; **una civilización antigua** an ancient civilization.

Antillas *plural noun* F **las Antillas** the West Indies.

antipático/antipática *adjective* unpleasant; **es muy antipático** he's very unpleasant; **¡qué mujer más antipática!** what a horrible woman!

antojarse *reflexive verb* [17] **se le antojó un helado** he fancied an ice cream; **se me antojó comprar el jarrón** I felt like buying the vase.

antropología *noun* F
anthropology.

anual *adjective* annual.

anunciar *verb* [17] **1** to announce
(*news or a decision*); **2** to advertise
(*a product, for example*).

anuncio *noun* M **1** announcement;
2 advertisement.

anzuelo *noun* M hook.

añadidura *in phrase* **por añadidura**
in addition.

añadir *verb* [19] to add.

año *noun* M **1** year; **el año pasado**
last year; **los años cincuenta** the
50s; **el Año Nuevo** the New Year; **año
bisiesto** leap year; **2** (*talking about
age*) **mi madre tiene cincuenta años**
my mother is fifty; **¿cuántos años
tienes?** how old are you?

apagado/apagada *adjective*
1 off; **con la luz apagada** with the
light off; **¿está la televisión
apagada?** is the television off?;
2 out; **el fuego estaba casi apagado**
the fire was almost out.

apagar *verb* [28] **1** to switch off (*the
television or a light*); **2** to put out (*a
fire or cigarette*).

aparato *noun* M **1** appliance;
aparatos eléctricos electrical
appliances; **2 los aparatos de
laboratorio** the laboratory
equipment; **3** piece of apparatus (*in
the gym*).

aparcamiento *noun* M car park.

aparcar *verb* [31] to park.

aparecer *verb* [35] **1** to appear (*a
person or symptom*); **2** to turn up (*a
lost object*).

aparente *adjective* apparent.

apariencia *noun* F **1** appearance; **a
juzgar por las apariencias** judging
by appearances; **en apariencia no
estaba roto** it appeared not to be
broken; **2 un niño de apariencia
delicada** a delicate-looking child.

apartado/apartada *adjective*
isolated.

apartamento *noun* M flat.

apartar *verb* [17] **1** to move away;
aparta la manta del fuego move the
blanket away from the fire; **2** to move
out of the way; **aparta la planta para
que pueda ver** move the plant out of
the way so that I can see.

apartarse *reflexive verb* [17] to move
away; **se apartó de la ventana** she
moved away from the window.

aparte *adverb* **1** aside; **poner algo
aparte** to put something aside;
llamar a alguien aparte to call
somebody aside; **2** separately; **esto
lo pago aparte** I'll pay for this
separately; **3 aparte de eso** apart
from that.

apasionado/apasionada
adjective passionate.

apasionar *verb* [17] **el deporte me
apasiona** I have a passion for sports;
la ópera no me apasiona I'm not
wild about opera.

apearse *reflexive verb* [17] **apearse de** to get off (*a bus or train*); to get out of (*a car*); to dismount from (*a horse*).

apellidarse *reflexive verb* [17] **me apellido Alejos** my surname is Alejos.

apellido *noun* M surname; **¿qué apellido tienes?/¿cuál es tu apellido?** what's your surname?; **apellido de soltera** maiden name.

apenas *adverb* 1 hardly; **apenas hay suficiente** there's hardly enough; 2 hardly ever; **ahora apenas nos vemos** we hardly ever see each other now; 3 scarcely; **hace apenas tres horas que se fueron** it's scarcely three hours since they went; 4 **apenas me había sentado, cuando sonó el teléfono** no sooner had I sat down than the telephone rang.

apéndice *noun* M appendix.

apendicitis *noun* F appendicitis.

aperitivo *noun* M 1 drink (*usually alcoholic, before a meal*); 2 nibbles (*food*).

apetecer *verb* [35] **no me apetece** I don't feel like it; **¿te apetece ir a cenar fuera?** do you fancy going out for dinner?; **haz lo que te apetezca** do whatever you like.

apetito *noun* M appetite; **no tengo apetito** I don't feel hungry; **para abrirte el apetito** to give you an appetite.

apio *noun* M celery.

aplastar *verb* [17] to squash.

aplaudir *verb* [19] to applaud.

aplauso *noun* M round of applause; **los aplausos del público** the applause of the audience.

aplazamiento *noun* M postponement.

aplazar *verb* [22] to postpone.

aplicado/aplicada *adjective* hard-working.

aplicar *verb* [31] to apply.

apodo *noun* M nickname.

apostar *verb* [24] to bet; **te apuesto mil pesetas** I bet you a thousand pesetas; **te apuesto a que no viene** I bet she won't come; **apostar a las carreras** to bet on horses; **apostaron por el favorito** they bet on the favourite.

apóstrofo *noun* M apostrophe.

apoyar *verb* [17] 1 to support; (*a candidate or plan, for instance*) 2 to lean; **apoyé la bicicleta en la pared** I leaned the bicycle against the wall; 3 to rest; **apoya la cabeza en este cojín** rest your head on this cushion. **apoyarse** *reflexive verb* [17] **apoyarse en** to lean on; **me apoyé en la puerta** I leaned against the door.

apoyo *noun* M support.

apreciar *verb* [17] 1 to appreciate; 2 **apreciar a alguien** to be fond of somebody; **la aprecio mucho** I'm very fond of her.

aprecio *noun* M **sentir aprecio por alguien** to be fond of somebody.

aprender *verb* [18] to learn; **aprender español** to learn Spanish; **aprender a conducir** to learn to drive; **aprender algo de memoria** to learn something by heart.

aprendiz/aprendiza *noun* M/F apprentice.

aprendizaje *noun* M apprenticeship.

apretado/apretada *adjective* tight.

apretar *verb* [29] **1** to press (*a button*); **2** to tighten (*a bolt or knot*); **3 apretar el acelerador** to put your foot on the accelerator; **4** to be too tight (*shoes*); **5** to squeeze; **me apretó el brazo** she squeezed my arm.

apretón *noun* M **un apretón de manos** a handshake.

aprieto *noun* M predicament; **meterse en un aprieto** to get into a predicament; **poner a alguien en un aprieto** to put somebody in an awkward situation.

aprisa *adverb* quickly.

aprobar *verb* [24] **1** to approve (*a plan or decision, for example*); **2** to approve of (*behaviour or an idea*); **3** to pass; **aprobar un examen** to pass an exam.

aprovechado/aprovechada *adjective* **es un aprovechado** he takes advantage of people.

aprovechar *verb* [17] **1** to use; **podemos aprovechar estos trozos de madera** we can use these pieces of wood; **2** to make the most of (*time or resources*); **3** to take advantage of (*an opportunity or offer*); **4 aproveché para decírselo** I took the chance to tell him; **quiero aprovechar esta oportunidad para** … I want to take this opportunity to …; **5 ¡que aproveche!** enjoy your meal!

aproximado/aproximada *adjective* approximate, rough.

aproximadamente *adverb* approximately, roughly.

aproximar *verb* [17] to bring nearer.
aproximarse *reflexive verb* [17] **1** to go/come up to; **se aproximó a la ventana** she went/came up to the window; **2** to approach; **se aproximaba el momento** the moment was approaching; **se me aproximó un hombre** a man approached me.

apto/apta *adjective* **apto para algo** suitable for something.

apuesta *noun* F bet; **hacerle una apuesta a alguien** to make a bet with somebody; **me hicieron una apuesta** they made a bet with me.

apuntar *verb* [17] **1** to write down (*telephone number or address, for example*); **2** to point out; **apuntó con el dedo hacia la torre** she pointed out the tower; **3** to aim; **me apuntó con la pistola** he aimed the gun at me; **4 me apuntaron las**

respuestas they whispered the answers to me.

apuntarse *reflexive verb* [17] **apuntarse a algo** to enrol on something; to put your name down for something.

apuntes *plural noun* M notes; **tomar apuntes** to take notes.

apuro *noun* M **estar en un apuro** to be in a tight spot; **pasar apuros** to go through a lot.

aquel/aquella *adjective* 1 that; **en aquel momento** at that moment; 2 **aquellos/aquellas** those.

aquél/aquélla *pronoun* 1 that one; **quiero aquél** I want that one; 2 **aquéllos/aquéllas** those; **éstas no, dame aquéllas** not these, give me those.

aquello *pronoun* that; **¿qué es aquello?** what's that?; **aquello que vimos** what we saw.

aquí *adverb* here; **lo puse aquí abajo** I put it down here; **aquí llegan** here they are; **debe estar por aquí** it must be around here; **el vino es de aquí** the wine is from here.

árabe[1] *noun* M Arabic (*the language*).

árabe[2] *noun* M/F *adjective* Arab.

Aragón *noun* M Aragon.

aragonés/aragonesa *noun* M/F *adjective* Aragonese.

araña *noun* F spider.

arañar *verb* [17] to scratch.

arañazo *noun* M scratch.

árbitro/árbitra *noun* M/F 1 referee; 2 umpire.

árbol *noun* M tree; **un árbol de Navidad** a Christmas tree.

arbusto *noun* M shrub.

arcén *noun* M hard shoulder (*on the motorway*).

archivador *noun* M 1 filing cabinet; 2 ring binder.

archivar *verb* [17] to file.

archivo *noun* M 1 archive; 2 file (*on a computer*).

arcilla *noun* F clay.

arco *noun* M 1 arch; 2 bow (*for firing arrows or playing the violin or cello*); 3 **arco iris** rainbow.

arder *verb* [18] to burn; **el bosque estaba ardiendo** the forest was burning.

ardiente *adjective* burning.

ardilla *noun* F squirrel.

área *noun* F area; (*even though 'área' is a feminine noun, it is used with 'el' and 'un'*) **el área de penalty** the penalty area; **las áreas más peligrosas** the most dangerous areas.

arena *noun* F sand.

Argentina *noun* F Argentina.

argentino/argentina *noun* M/F *adjective* Argentinian.

argot *noun* M slang; **el argot juvenil** youth slang.

argumento *noun* M **1** argument; **2** plot (*of a film, for example*).

aries *noun* M/F Aries; **soy aries** I'm Aries.

Aries *noun* M Aries.

aritmética *noun* F arithmetic.

arma *noun* F weapon; (*even though 'arma' is a feminine noun, it is used with 'el' and 'un'*) **un arma de fuego** a fire arm; **armas nucleares** nuclear weapons; **un arma blanca** a knife (*as a weapon*).

armado/armada *adjective* armed.

armar *verb* [17] **1** to arm; **2** to assemble (*a piece of furniture*); **3** to pitch (*a tent*); **4** (*informal*) **armar ruido** to make a noise; **armar jaleo** to make a racket; **armar un escándalo** to cause a scene.
armarse *reflexive verb* [17] **1 armarse un lío** to get confused; **me armé un lío con las fechas** I got confused with the dates; **2 armarse de paciencia** to be patient.

armario *noun* M wardrobe.

armonía *noun* F harmony.

armónica *noun* F harmonica.

armonioso/armoniosa *adjective* harmonious.

aro *noun* M **1** hoop; **2** hoop earring.

aroma *noun* M **1** scent; **2** aroma.

aromático/aromática *adjective* aromatic.

arpa *noun* F harp (*even though 'arpa' is a feminine noun, it is used with 'el' and 'un'*).

arqueología *noun* F archaeology.

arqueólogo/arqueóloga *noun* M/F archaeologist.

arquitecto/arquitecta *noun* M/F architect; **mi madre es arquitecta** my mum's an architect.

arquitectura *noun* F architecture.

arrancar *verb* [31] **1** to tear out; **arrancar una hoja del cuaderno** to tear out a sheet from the notebook; **2** to tear off; **arrancar una etiqueta** to tear off a label; **3** to pull up (*a plant*); **4** to pull off (*a button*); **5** to snatch; **me arrancó el libro de las manos** she snached the book from my hands; **6** to start (*a car or engine*).

arrastrar *verb* [17] to drag (*an object*).
arrastrarse *reflexive verb* [17] to crawl.

arrebatar *verb* [17] to snatch.

arreglado/arreglada *adjective* **1** tidy; **deja tu habitación arreglada** leave your room tidy; **2** well dressed; **siempre va muy arreglado** he's always very well dressed.

arreglar *verb* [17] **1** to fix; **2** to mend; **3** to tidy (*a room or house*); **4** to sort out (*a problem, for* *example*); **no te preocupes, yo lo arreglaré** don't worry, I'll sort it out.

arreglarse *reflexive verb* [17] **1** to get ready; **me arreglo enseguida y salimos** I'll get ready straight away and we can go out; **2** to dress up; **mi hermana siempre se arregla mucho** my sister always dresses up a lot; **3 arreglárselas** to manage; **se las arregla muy bien sola** she manages very well on her own.

arrepentirse *reflexive verb* [14] **arrepentirse de algo** to regret something; **no me arrepiento** I don't regret it.

arrestar *verb* [17] to arrest; **queda usted arrestado** you're under arrest.

arresto *noun* M arrest.

arriba *adverb* **1** up; **aquí arriba** up here; **lo puse más arriba** I put it a bit higher up; **2 de arriba** (*next up*) above; (*highest*) top; **el cajón de arriba** (*the next up*) the drawer above; (*highest*) the top drawer; **3** upstairs; **ha ido arriba** he's gone upstairs; **viven en el piso de arriba** they live upstairs; **4 arriba de(l) todo** at the very top; **de arriba a abajo** from top to bottom.

arriesgado/arriesgada *adjective* risky.

arriesgar *verb* [28] to risk.
arriesgarse *reflexive verb* [28] to take a risk.

arrodillarse *reflexive verb* [17] to kneel down; **estaba arrodillado** he was on his knees.

arrogante *adjective* arrogant.

arrojar *verb* [17] to throw.

arropar *verb* [17] **1** to wrap up (*a child or sick person*); **2** to tuck in (*in bed*).
arroparse *reflexive verb* [17] to wrap up; **arrópate bien** wrap up well.

arroyo *noun* M stream.

arroz *noun* M rice.

arruga *noun* F wrinkle.

arrugar *verb* [28] **1** to wrinkle; **2** to crease; **3** to crumple up.

arruinar *verb* [17] to ruin.
arruinarse *reflexive verb* [17] to go bankrupt.

arte *noun* M art; (*'arte' is a masculine noun in the singular and a feminine noun in the plural*) **el arte moderno** modern art; **las artes gráficas** graphic arts; ★ **por arte de magia** as if by magic.

artesanía *noun* F crafts; **objetos de artesanía** handicrafts.

artesano/artesana *noun* M/F craftsman/craftswoman.

ártico/ártica *adjective* Arctic.

Ártico *noun* M **el Ártico** the Arctic.

articulación *noun* F joint (*in arm, etc.*).

artículo *noun* M article.

artificial *adjective* artificial.

artista *noun* M/F artist.

artístico/artística *adjective* artistic.

arzobispo *noun* M archbishop.

asa *noun* F handle; (*even though 'asa' is a feminine noun, it is used with 'el' and 'un'*) **cógelo por el asa** take it by the handle.

asado *noun* M roast.

asamblea *noun* F meeting.

asar *verb* [17] **1** to roast (*meat*); **2** to bake (*vegetables*).

ascender *verb* [36] **1** to be promoted; **ha ascendido** he's been promoted; **2** to promote; **3** to rise (*temperature, prices or a balloon*).

ascenso *noun* M promotion.

ascensor *noun* M lift.

asco *noun* M **le dio asco** it made him feel sick; **¡qué asco!** how disgusting!

asegurar *verb* [17] **1** to insure; **2** to secure; **3** to assure; **te aseguro que** … I can assure you that …
asegurarse *reflexive verb* [17] to make sure; **asegúrate de que cierras el grifo** make sure you turn the tap off.

asentir *verb* [14] **asentir con la cabeza** to nod (*in agreement*).

aseo *noun* M toilet; **los aseos de señoras** the Ladies.

asesinar *verb* [17] to murder.

asesinato *noun* M murder.

asesino/asesina *noun* M/F murderer.

asfixia *noun* F **1** asphyxia; **2** suffocation; **tenía sensación de asfixia** I felt I was suffocating.

asfixiante *adjective* **1** asphyxiating (*air or fumes*); **2** suffocating (*heat*).

asfixiarse *reflexive verb* [17] **1** to suffocate; **2** to choke to death.

así *adverb* **1** like this; **hazlo así** do it like this; **2** like that; **el pueblo se llama Robellón, o algo así** the village is called Robellón, or something like that; **3** that way; **me llevaré el coche, así podremos volver pronto** I'll take the car, that way we can come back early; **4** **así que** so; **así que te vas de vacaciones** so you're going on holiday; **5** **así es** that's right; **6** **así, así** so, so; **'¿te gusta?'** – **'así, así'** 'do you like it?' – 'so, so'; **7** **¡así me gusta!** that's what I like to see!; **¡así se hace!** well done!

Asia *noun* F Asia.

asiático/asiática *noun* M/F *adjective* Asian.

asiento *noun* M seat; **asiento delantero** front seat; **asiento trasero** back seat.

asignatura *noun* F subject.

asilo político *noun* M political asylum.

asistente *noun* M/F assistant.

asistente social *noun* M/F social worker.

asma *noun* F asthma (*even though 'asma' is a feminine noun, it is used with 'el' and 'un'*).

asmático/asmática *adjective* asthmatic.

asociación *noun* F association.

asociar *verb* [17] to associate (*two ideas or words, for example*).
asociarse *reflexive verb* [17] to go into partnership (*in business*).

asomar *verb* [17] **asomar la cabeza** to stick your head out/in; **'no asomar la cabeza por la ventana'** 'do not lean out of the window'.
asomarse *reflexive verb* [17] **se asomó a la ventana** he had a look out of the window; **'prohibido asomarse por la ventana'** 'do not lean out of the window'.

asombrar *verb* [17] to amaze; **me asombra su actitud** I'm amazed by her attitude.
asombrarse *reflexive verb* [17] to be amazed; **ya no me asombro con/de nada** nothing amazes me anymore.

asombro *noun* M surprise; **con cara de asombro** with a look of surprise on her face.

asombroso/asombrosa *adjective* amazing.

aspecto *noun* M look; **tiene aspecto de aristócrata** he looks like an aristocrat; **una mujer de aspecto elegante** an elegant-looking woman; **¿qué aspecto tenían?** what did they look like?; **tienes muy buen aspecto** you look very well.

áspero/áspera *adjective* rough.

aspirador *noun* M SEE **aspiradora**.

aspiradora *noun* F vacuum cleaner; **pasar la aspiradora por el salón** to vacuum the living room.

aspirina *noun* F aspirin.

astilla *noun* F splinter.

astrología *noun* F astrology.

astronauta *noun* M/F astronaut.

astronomía *noun* F astronomy.

astuto/astuta *adjective* **1** shrewd; **2** cunning.

asunto *noun* M **1** matter; **asuntos de negocios** business matters; **un asunto complicado** a complicated matter; **2** business; **no quiero saber nada de este asunto** I don't want to know anything about this business; **no es asunto tuyo** mind your own business.

asustar *verb* [17] to frighten.
asustarse *reflexive verb* [17] to get frightened; **me asusté al oir un ruido** I got frightened when I heard a noise.

atacar *verb* [31] to attack.

atajo *noun* M shortcut.

ataque *noun* M **1** attack; **un ataque cardíaco/un ataque al corazón** a heart attack; **2** fit; **un ataque de celos** a fit of jealousy; **me dio un ataque de risa** I got a fit of the giggles.

atar *verb* [17] to tie (up).

atardecer *noun* M dusk; **al atardecer** at dusk.
verb [35] to get dark; **estaba atardeciendo** it was getting dark.

atascar *verb* [31] to block (*a pipe*).
atascarse *reflexive verb* [31] to get blocked.

atasco *noun* M **1** traffic jam;
2 blockage.

ataúd *noun* M coffin.

atención *noun* F attention; **presta
atención** pay attention; **no pones
atención en lo que haces** you don't
concentrate on what you are doing;
¡atención, por favor! your attention,
please!

atender *verb* [36] **1** to pay attention;
atiende a la profesora pay attention
to your teacher; **2** **¿la atiende
alguien?** are you being served?

atentado *noun* M **un atentado
terrorista** a terrorist attack.

atentamente *adverb*
1 attentively; **2** **le saluda
atentamente** yours faithfully, yours
sincerely.

atento/atenta *adjective* attentive.

ateo/atea *noun* M/F atheist.

aterrizaje *noun* M landing (*of a
plane*).

aterrizar *verb* [22] to land (*a plane*).

ático *noun* M **1** top-floor
apartment; **2** loft.

atlántico/atlántica *adjective*
Atlantic.

Atlántico *noun* M **el Atlántico** the
Atlantic.

atlas *noun* M atlas.

atleta *noun* M/F athlete.

atlético/atlética *adjective*
1 athletic (*person*); **2** **competición
atlética** athletics competition.

atletismo *noun* M athletics.

atómico/atómica *adjective*
atomic.

átomo *noun* M atom.

atracador/atracadora *noun* M/
F **1** robber; **2** mugger.

atracar *verb* [31] **1** to hold up (*a
bank or shop*); **2** to mug (*a person*).

atracción *noun* F attraction.

atraco *noun* M **1** hold-up (*of a bank
or shop*); **2** mugging.

atractivo/atractiva *adjective*
attractive.

atraer *verb* [42] to attract.

atragantarse *reflexive verb* [17]
atragantarse con algo to choke on
something.

atrapar *verb* [17] to catch.

atrás *adverb* **1** back; **nos sentamos
demasiado atrás** we sat too far back;
hacia atrás backwards; **la parte de
atrás** the back; **2** at the back; **esto
va atrás** this goes at the back;
3 **quedarse atrás** to be left behind.

atrasado/atrasada *adjective*
1 slow (*a watch or clock*); **llevo el
reloj atrasado** my watch is slow;
2 backward (*a country*); **3** old-
fashioned (*ideas or a person*);
4 behind; **voy atrasado en los
estudios** I'm behind at school; **van
muy atrasados con los ensayos**
they're very behind with the
rehearsals; **5** **pagos atrasados**
outstanding payments.

atrasar *verb* [17] **1** to put back (*a watch or clock*); **hay que atrasar los relojes una hora** we have to put the clocks back an hour; **2** to lose time (*a watch or clock*); **este reloj atrasa** this watch loses time; **3** to postpone.

atrasarse *reflexive verb* [17] to lose time (*a watch or clock*).

atravesar *verb* [29] to cross

atrayente *adjective* appealing.

atreverse *reflexive verb* [18] to dare; **no me atrevo a preguntarle** I don't dare ask him.

atrevido/atrevida *adjective* **1** daring; **2** cheeky; **¡qué niño más atrevido!** what a cheeky child!

atropellar *verb* [17] to run over, to knock down; **lo atropelló un coche** he was run over by a car.

atún *noun* M tuna.

aula *noun* F (*even though 'aula' is a feminine noun, it is used with 'el' and 'un'*) **1** classroom; **2** lecture theatre.

aullido *noun* M howl.

aumentar *verb* [17] **1** to increase; **aumentar el sueldo** to give a rise; **2** to rise (*temperature or pressure*).

aumento *noun* M **1** increase; **2** rise.

aun *adverb* even; **aun así** even so; **ni aun con tu ayuda** not even with your help.

aún *adverb* **1** still; **aún estoy esperando** I'm still waiting; **2** yet; **aún no se lo he dicho a ellos** I haven't told them yet; **3** even; **éste es aún mejor** this one is even better.

aunque *conjunction* **1** although; **aunque estaba cansada, la ayudé** although I was tired, I helped her; **2** even though; **3** even if; **aunque llegues tarde, llámame** even if you arrive late, give me a ring; **aunque no lo parezca** even if it doesn't look like it.

au pair (*plural* **au pairs**) *noun* M/F au pair.

auricular *noun* M **1** receiver (*of a phone*); **2 auriculares** headphones.

ausente *adjective* **estar ausente** to be absent, to be away.

Australia *noun* F Australia.

australiano/australiana *noun* M/F *adjective* Australian.

Austria *noun* F Austria.

austriaco/austriaca *noun* M/F *adjective* Austrian.

auténtico/auténtica *adjective* authentic.

auto *noun* M car.

autoadhesivo *adjective* self-adhesive.

autobiografía *noun* F autobiography.

autobús *noun* M bus.

autocar *noun* M coach.

autoescuela *noun* F driving school.

autógrafo *noun* M autograph.

automático/automática *adjective* automatic.

automóvil *noun* M car.

automovilismo *noun* M motor racing.

automovilista *noun* M/F motorist.

autonomía *noun* F **1** autonomy; **2** autonomous region (*of Spain*).

autonómico/autonómica *adjective* regional (*elections or a candidate*).

autopista *noun* F motorway.

autor/autora *noun* M/F author.

autoridad *noun* F authority.

autoritario/autoritaria *adjective* authoritarian.

autorización *noun* F authorization.

autorizar *verb* [22] to authorize.

autoservicio *noun* M **1** self-service restaurant; **2** supermarket.

autostop *noun* M hitch-hiking; **hacer autostop** to hitch-hike.

autostopista *noun* M/F hitch-hiker.

autovía *noun* F dual carriageway.

auxilio *noun* M aid; **acudir en auxilio de alguien** to go to the aid of somebody; **primeros auxilios** first aid.

avanzar *verb* [22] **1** to move forward (*traffic or a person*); **2** to make

progress (*a student or researcher*); **3** to wind on (*a tape*).

avaricia *noun* F greed.

avaricioso/avariciosa *adjective* greedy.

Avda. *abbreviation* (*short for: avenida*) Ave., Avenue.

ave *noun* F bird; (*even though 'ave' is a feminine noun, it is used with 'el' and 'un'*) **un ave** a bird; **las aves** the birds.

avellana *noun* F hazelnut.

avenida *noun* F avenue.

aventura *noun* F adventure.

aventurero/aventurera *adjective* adventurous.

avergonzado/avergonzada *adjective* **1** ashamed; **2** embarrassed.

avería *noun* F breakdown (*of a car, for example*); **sufrir una avería** to break down.

averiado/averiada *adjective* **1** broken down; **2** out of order.

avestruz *noun* M ostrich.

avión *noun* M aeroplane; **avión a reacción** jet (*plane*).

avisar *verb* [17] **1 avisar a alguien de algo** to let somebody know about something; **le avisé del problema** I let him know about the problem; **me avisaron que llegarían tarde** they told me they would be late; **2** to warn; **avisar a alguien del peligro** to warn somebody about the danger;

3 avisar al médico to call the doctor.

aviso *noun* M **1** warning; **el profesor ya le ha dado tres avisos** the teacher has already given him three warnings; **sin previo aviso** without prior warning; **2** notice; **hasta nuevo aviso** until further notice; **3 último aviso para los pasajeros del vuelo** ... last call for passengers on flight ...

avispa *noun* F wasp.

ayer *adverb* yesterday; **antes de ayer** the day before yesterday.

ayuda *noun* F **1** help; **ir en ayuda de alguien** to go to somebody's assistance; **2** aid.

ayudante *noun* M/F assistant.

ayudar *verb* [17] to help; **¿en qué puedo ayudarle?** how can I help you?

ayuntamiento *noun* M **1** town council, city council; **2** town hall.

azar *noun* M **1** chance; **por azar** by chance; **2 al azar** at random.

azote *noun* M smack.

azúcar *noun* M or F sugar; (*'azúcar' always takes 'el', but it can take an adjective in the feminine form*) **el azúcar blanca/blanco** white sugar; **el azúcar morena/moreno** brown sugar; **un terrón de azúcar** a sugar lump.

azucarero *noun* M sugar bowl.

azul *noun* M blue; **azul claro** light blue; **azul marino** navy blue; **azul celeste** sky blue.

adjective blue; **ojos azules** blue eyes.

azulejo *noun* M tile.

B b

baca *noun* F luggage-rack.

bacalao *noun* M cod.

bachillerato *noun* M secondary education.

bahía *noun* F bay.

bailar *verb* [17] to dance.

bailarín/bailarina *noun* M/F dancer.

baile *noun* M **1** dance; **2** dancing; **una clase de baile** a dancing class.

bajar *verb* [17] **1** to bring down; **¿puedes bajarme el abrigo?** could you bring down my coat?; **2** to take down; **baja las maletas a recepción** take the suitcases down to reception; **3** to go down; **el ascensor está bajando** the lift's going down; **bajamos por las escaleras** we went down the stairs; **bajar la calle** to go down the street; **4** to come down; **¡ya bajo!** I'm coming down!; **creo que ya bajan** I think they're coming down now; **5** to fall (*the temperature or prices*); **6** to turn down (*volume*); **baja un poco la tele** turn the television down a bit; **7** to lower (*blind or prices*).

bajarse *reflexive verb* [17] **bajarse de un coche** to get out of a car; **se bajó de la bicicleta** he got off the bike.

bajo¹ *noun* M ground floor.
preposition **1** under; **bajo los árboles** under the trees; **2 bajo cero** below zero.
adverb **1** low; **volar bajo** to fly low; **2** quietly; **hablar bajo** to speak quietly.

bajo²/baja *adjective* **1** short (*a person*); **soy bastante baja** I'm quite short; **2** low; **pon la música baja** put the music on low; **los precios están bajos** prices are low.

bala *noun* F bullet.

balanza *noun* F scales.

balbucear, balbucir *verb* [17] to stammer.

balcón *noun* M balcony.

baldosa *noun* F tile.

Baleares *plural noun* F Balearic Islands.

ballena *noun* F whale.

ballet *noun* M ballet.

balón *noun* M ball; **un balón de fútbol** a football.

baloncesto *noun* M basketball.

balonmano *noun* M handball.

balonvolea *noun* M volleyball.

banco *noun* M **1** bench (*in a park*); **2** pew (*in church*); **3** bank; **trabaja en un banco** she works in a bank.

banda *noun* F **1** band (*of musicians*); **2** gang (*of criminals*); **3 banda sonora** soundtrack.

bandeja *noun* F tray.

bandera *noun* F flag.

banderilla *noun* F banderilla (*a decorated dart used in bullfighting*).

bandido/bandida *noun* M/F bandit.

banqueta *noun* F stool.

banquete *noun* M banquet; **un banquete de bodas** a wedding banquet.

bañador *noun* M **1** swimming trunks; **2** swimming costume.

bañar *verb* [17] **bañar a** to bath (*a baby*).
bañarse *reflexive verb* [17] **1** to have a bath; **esta noche voy a bañarme** I'm going to have a bath tonight; **2** to have a swim; **¿te apetece bañarte?** do you fancy going for a swim?

bañera *noun* F bath (*bathtub*).

baño *noun* M **1** bath; **darse un baño** to have a bath; **voy a darme un baño** I'm going to have a bath; **2** swim; **darse un baño** to go for a swim; **¿te apetece darte un baño?** do you fancy going for a swim?; **3** bathroom; **¿dónde está el baño?** where's the bathroom?

bar *noun* M bar.

baraja *noun* F pack of cards.

barajar *verb* [17] to shuffle (*cards*).

barandilla *noun* F rail.

baratija *noun* F knick-knack.

barato/barata *adjective* cheap.

barba *noun* F beard; **afeitarse la barba** to shave off your beard; **dejarse barba** to grow a beard; **voy a dejarme barba** I'm going to grow a beard.

barbacoa *noun* F barbecue.

barbaridad *noun* F 1 fortune; **nos cobraron una barbaridad** they charged us a fortune; 2 **eso es una barbaridad** that's far too much; 3 **deja de decir barbaridades** stop saying crazy things; 4 **¡qué barbaridad!** my God!

barbero *noun* M barber.

barbilla *noun* F chin.

barca *noun* F boat; **una barca de pesca** a fishing boat; **una barca de remos** a rowing boat.

Barcelona *noun* F Barcelona.

barco *noun* M 1 boat; **viajar en barco** to travel by boat; **un barco de pesca** a fishing boat; 2 ship; **un barco de guerra** a warship.

barniz *noun* M 1 varnish; 2 **barniz de uñas** nail varnish.

barra *noun* F 1 rail (*for clothes*); 2 bar; **una barra de jabón** a bar of soap; **nos sirvieron en la barra** they served us at the bar; 3 **una barra de** pan a baguette; 4 **una barra de labios** a lipstick.

barrer *verb* [18] to sweep.

barrera *noun* F barrier.

barriga *noun* F belly; **tener dolor de barriga** to have a bellyache.

barril *noun* M barrel.

barrio *noun* M area (*of a town*).

barro *noun* M 1 mud; **lleno de barro** covered in mud; 2 clay (*for making pots*).

bártulos *plural noun* M (*informal*) stuff, things; **coge todos tus bártulos** take all your stuff.

basar *verb* [17] to base; **basar algo en algo** to base something on something.
basarse *reflexive verb* [17] **¿en qué te basas para decir eso?** what basis do you have for saying that?

base *noun* F 1 base; 2 **base de datos** database; 3 **base de maquillaje** foundation (*make-up*); 4 **a base de** by; **lo aprendió a base de repetirlo** he learnt it by repeating it; ★ **a base de bien** (*informal*) a lot; **nos divertimos a base de bien** we enjoyed ourselves a lot.

básico/básica *adjective* basic.

bastante *adjective* 1 enough; **no tenemos bastante pan** we don't have enough bread; **ya tenemos bastantes sillas** we've got enough chairs now; 2 quite a lot of; **bastante gente** quite a lot of people; **bebimos bastante café** we drank quite a lot of coffee.

pronoun enough; **con esto ya hay bastante** there's enough with this. *adverb* **1** enough; **¿has comido bastante?** have you eaten enough?; **2** (*before an adjective or adverb*) quite; **se puso bastante contenta** she was quite happy; **3** quite a lot; **ha mejorado bastante** he's improved quite a lot.

bastar *verb* [17] **1** to be enough; **con esto basta** this is enough; **¡ya basta!** that's enough!; **2 basta con preguntarle** you just need to ask him.

bastón *noun* M walking stick.

bastoncillo *noun* M cotton bud.

basura *noun* F **1** rubbish; **hay que sacar la basura** we have to put the rubbish out; **2** dustbin, bin; **tirar algo a la basura** to throw something in the bin.

basurero¹ *noun* M rubbish tip.

basurero²/basurera *noun* M/F refuse collector.

bata *noun* F **1** dressing gown; **2 una bata de médico** a white coat (*doctor's*).

batalla *noun* F battle.

bate *noun* M bat.

batería² *noun* F **1** battery (*for a car*); **2** drum kit; **tocar la batería** to play the drums.

batería² *noun* M/F drummer.

batido *noun* M milkshake; **un batido de fresa** a strawberry milkshake.

batir *verb* [19] **1** to beat; **batir las claras a punto de nieve** beat the egg whites until stiff; **2** to whip (*cream*); **3 batir un récord** to break a record.

baúl *noun* M trunk (*for clothes*).

bautismo *noun* M christening.

bautizar *verb* [22] to christen.

baya *noun* F berry.

bayeta *noun* F cloth (*for wiping*).

bebé *noun* M baby.

beber *verb* [18] to drink; **¿quieres beber algo?** do you want something to drink?

bebida *noun* F drink; **una bebida caliente** a hot drink.

beca *noun* F **1** grant; **2** scholarship.

béisbol *noun* M baseball.

belén *noun* M nativity scene, crib.

belga *noun* M/F *adjective* Belgian.

Bélgica *noun* F Belgium.

belleza *noun* F beauty.

bendito/bendita *adjective* **1** blessed; **2** holy (*water or bread*).

beneficiar *verb* [17] to benefit.

beneficio *noun* M benefit.

benéfico/benéfica *adjective* charity; **una organización benéfica** a charity.

berenjena *noun* F aubergine.

berro *noun* M watercress.

besamel *noun* F white sauce.

besar *verb* [17] to kiss.

beso *noun* M kiss; **dame un beso** give me a kiss; **me dio un beso en la mejilla** he gave me a kiss on the cheek.

bestia *noun* F 1 beast (*animal*); 2 ignorant person; **es un bestia, no sabe nada** he's so ignorant, he doesn't know a thing; 3 brute. *adjective* 1 ignorant; 2 **no seas bestia y habla bien** don't be so crude, mind your language.

betún *noun* M shoe polish.

Biblia *noun* F Bible.

biblioteca *noun* F library.

bibliotecario/bibliotecaria *noun* M/F librarian.

bicho *noun* M creepy-crawly.

bici *noun* F (*informal*) bike; **montar en bici** to ride a bike.

bicicleta *noun* F bicycle; **montar en bicicleta** to ride a bicycle; **¿sabes montar en bicicleta?** can you ride a bicycle?

bien *noun* M good; **la diferencia entre el bien y el mal** the difference between good and evil. *adverb*, *adjective* 1 well; **lo has hecho muy bien** you've done it really well; **no me siento bien** I don't feel well; **'¿cómo están tus padres?'** – **'muy bien, gracias'** 'how are your parents?' – 'very well, thank you';

¡bien hecho! well done!; **¡muy bien!** (*expressing approval*) well done!; 2 all right; **¿estás bien en esa silla?** are you all right on that chair?; **así está bien** it's all right like this; **¡está bien!** (*expressing agreement*) all right!, okay!; 3 **huele bien** it smells nice; **sabe bien** it tastes nice; 4 **hablas muy bien español** you speak very good Spanish; 5 properly; **no funciona bien** it doesn't work properly; 6 **¡bien!** hurray!

bienestar *noun* M welfare.

bienvenida[1] *noun* F welcome; **dar la bienvenida a alguien** to welcome somebody.

bienvenido/bienvenida[2] *adjective* welcome; **¡bienvenido!** welcome!; **aquí siempre sois bienvenidos** you're always welcome here.

bigote *noun* M moustache.

bikini *noun* M bikini.

bilingüe *adjective* bilingual.

billar *noun* M 1 billiards; 2 pool; 3 snooker.

billares *plural noun* M amusement arcade.

billete *noun* M 1 note (*money*); **un billete de cinco mil pesetas** a five thousand pesetas note; 2 ticket; **un billete de tren** a train ticket; **un billete sencillo/un billete de ida** a single ticket; **un billete de ida y vuelta** a return ticket.

billetera *noun* F wallet.

billetero *noun* M wallet.

biografía *noun* F biography.

biología *noun* F biology.

biólogo/bióloga *noun* M/F biologist.

biquini *noun* M bikini.

bisabuela *noun* F great-grandmother.

bisabuelo *noun* M 1 great-grandfather; 2 **mis bisabuelos** my great-grandparents.

bisnieta *noun* F great-granddaughter.

bisnieto *noun* M 1 great-grandson; 2 **mis bisnietos** my great-grandchildren.

bistec *noun* M steak.

bizcocho *noun* M sponge cake.

blanco¹ *noun* M 1 white; 2 target; **dar en el blanco** to hit the target.

blanco²/blanca *adjective* white.

blando/blanda *adjective* 1 soft; **un colchón blando** a soft mattress; **la mantequilla se ha puesto blanda** the butter's gone soft; 2 tender (*meat*); 3 soft (*person*).

bloc *noun* M writing pad.

bloque *noun* M block; **un bloque de pisos** a block of flats.

bloquear *verb* [17] to block; **una muchedumbre nos bloqueaba el camino** a crowd was blocking our way.

blusa *noun* F blouse.

bobo/boba *adjective* (*informal*) silly; **eres bobo** you are silly.

boca *noun* F 1 mouth; **no abrió la boca en toda la tarde** he didn't open his mouth all afternoon; 2 **una boca de metro** an entrance to the underground; 3 **boca arriba** face up (*card or photograph*); **pon el vaso boca arriba** put the glass the right way up; **túmbate boca arriba** lie on your back; 4 **boca abajo** (*card or photograph*) face down; upside down; **estaba tumbado boca abajo** he was lying face down; ★ **quedarse con la boca abierta** to be flabbergasted.

bocacalle *noun* F side street; **es la segunda bocacalle a la derecha** it's the second turning on the right.

bocadillo *noun* M baguette sandwich; **un bocadillo de queso** a cheese baguette.

bochorno *noun* M 1 **hoy hace bochorno** it's really muggy today; 2 embarrassment; **¡qué bochorno pasamos!** we were so embarrassed!; **fue un bochorno** it was really embarrassing.

bocina *noun* F horn (*of a car*).

boda *noun* F wedding; **bodas de plata** silver wedding; **bodas de oro** golden wedding.

bodega *noun* F 1 wine merchant's; 2 cellar; 3 bar; **fuimos a la bodega a tomar unos vinos** we went to the bar to have a few glasses of wine.

borde

bofetada *noun* F slap.

bofetón *noun* M slap.

boina *noun* F beret.

bola *noun* F **1** ball; **una bola de nieve** a snowball; **una bola de billar** a billiards ball; **2** scoop (*of ice cream*); **3** (*informal*) fib; **contar bolas** to tell fibs.

bolera *noun* F bowling alley.

boletín *noun* M bulletin; **boletín informativo** news bulletin; **boletín meteorológico** weather report.

boleto *noun* M **1** ticket (*raffle or lottery*); **2** coupon (*football pools*).

boli (*informal*) *noun* M (ballpoint) pen.

bolígrafo *noun* M ballpoint pen.

bollo *noun* M bun.

bolsa *noun* F bag; **una bolsa de palomitas** a bag of popcorn; **una bolsa de plástico** a plastic bag; **una bolsa de viaje** a travel bag; **una bolsa de la basura** a bin liner; **mi bolsa de la compra** my shopping bag.

bolsillo *noun* M pocket; **un diccionario de bolsillo** a pocket dictionary; **libro de bolsillo** paperback book.

bolso *noun* M handbag; **me robaron el bolso** they stole my handbag; **bolso de mano/bolso de viaje** overnight bag.

bomba *noun* F **1** bomb; **pusieron una bomba en un restaurante** they planted a bomb in a restaurant;

lanzar una bomba to drop a bomb; **la bomba atómica** the atomic bomb; **2** pump; **una bomba de bicicleta** a bicycle pump; **una bomba de agua** a water pump.

bombero/bombera *noun* M/F firefighter.

bombilla *noun* F light bulb; **se ha fundido la bombilla** the bulb's gone.

bombón *noun* M chocolate; **una caja de bombones** a box of chocolates.

bonachón/bonachona *adjective* (*informal*) kind.

bondad *noun* F kindness.

bonito/bonita *adjective* **1** pretty; **es una chica muy bonita** she's a very pretty girl; **un pueblo muy bonito** a very pretty village; **2** nice; **ropa bonita** nice clothes.

bono *noun* M voucher.

boquiabierto/boquiabierta *adjective* astonished; **me quedé boquiabierto** I was astonished.

bordado *noun* M embroidery.

bordar *verb* [17] to embroider.

borde *noun* M **1** edge; **me di con el borde de la mesa** I bumped myself on the edge of the table; **se acercó al borde del andén** he went to the edge of the platform; **2** rim (*of a glass or cup*); **3** **llenar algo hasta el borde** to fill something to the brim; **4** **el borde del río** the river bank; **5** **al borde de la guerra** on the brink of war; **al borde de las lágrimas** on the verge of tears.

bordear

bordear *verb* [17] to go round (*the edge of something*); **bordeamos el lago** we went round the lake.

bordillo *noun* M kerb.

bordo *noun* M **a bordo** on board; **subimos a bordo** we went on board.

borrachera *noun* F **cogerse una borrachera** to get drunk.

borracho/borracha *noun* M/F drunk.
adjective drunk; **estaban borrachos** they were drunk.

borrador *noun* M **1** rough draft; **hacedlo primero a borrador** do it in rough first; **papel de borrador** rough paper; **2** board rubber (*eraser*).

borrar *verb* [17] **1** to rub out (*a pencil mark or word*); **2** to erase (*a track or tape*); **3** to clean (*the blackboard*).
borrarse *reflexive verb* [17] to fade; **se ha borrado el nombre** the name has faded.

borrasca *noun* F **1** area of low pressure; **2** storm.

borroso/borrosa *adjective* **1** blurred (*image or photograph*); **2** vague (*memory*).

bosque *noun* M **1** wood; **2** forest; **el bosque ecuatorial** the rainforest.

bostezar *verb* [22] to yawn.

bota *noun* F boot; **botas de esquiar** ski boots; **botas de agua** wellingtons.

botánica[1] *noun* F botany.

botánico/botánica[2] *adjective* botanical.

bote *noun* M **1** boat; **un bote de pesca** a fishing boat; **un bote de remos** a rowing boat; **un bote salvavidas** a lifeboat; **2** jar; **un bote de aceitunas** a jar of olives; **3** can; **un bote de barniz** a can of varnish; **4** jump; **pegar un bote** to jump; **pegué un bote de alegría** I jumped for joy.

botella *noun* F bottle.

botijo *noun* M drinking jug (*with a long spout: the art is to be able to drink the content as it spurts out in an arc*).

botón *noun* M button (*on a garment or a machine*); **se me ha caído un botón** I've lost a button; **coser un botón** to sew on a button; **para encender la tele tienes que apretar este botón** to switch on the television you have to press this button.

boxeador/boxeadora *noun* M/F boxer.

boxear *verb* [17] to box.

boxeo *noun* M boxing; **un combate de boxeo** a boxing match.

bragas *plural noun* F knickers; **un par de bragas** a pair of knickers.

bragueta *noun* F flies (*in trousers*).

brasileño/brasileña *noun* M/F *adjective* Brazilian.

bravo/brava *adjective* fierce (*animal*).

exclamation **¡bravo!** well done!, bravo!

brazo *noun* M arm; **me cogió del brazo** he took me by the arm; **iban del brazo** they were arm in arm; **cruzar los brazos** to cross your arms; **cogió al niño en brazos** he picked the child up in his arms; **yo llevaba al bebé en brazos** I was carrying the baby in my arms; **el brazo del sofá** the arm of the sofa; ★ **con los brazos abiertos** with open arms; ★ **ser el brazo derecho de alguien** to be somebody's right-hand man/woman.

brécol *noun* M broccoli.

breve *adjective* short; **una pausa breve** a short pause.

brevemente *adective* briefly.

brezo *noun* M heather.

bribón/bribona *noun* M/F rascal.

bricolaje *noun* M DIY.

brillante *noun* M diamond. *adjective* **1** shiny; **2** bright (*light or colour*).

brillar *verb* [17] **1** to shine; **2** to sparkle.

brindar *verb* [17] to toast.

brindis *noun* M toast; **hacer un brindis por alguien** to drink a toast to somebody.

brisa *noun* F breeze.

británico/británica *noun* M/F British man/woman; **los británicos** the British.

adjective British.

brocha *noun* F **1** paintbrush; **2 brocha de afeitar** shaving brush.

broche *noun* M brooch.

broma *noun* F joke; **hacerle/gastarle una broma a alguien** to play a joke on somebody; **lo he dicho en broma** I was joking; **bromas aparte** joking apart; **¡ni en broma!** no way!

bromear *verb* [17] to joke.

bromista *noun* M/F *adjective* **es un bromista/es muy bromista** he's always joking.

bronca *noun* F (*informal*) **1 armar una bronca** to kick up a fuss; **si no me devuelven el dinero, voy a armar una bronca** if they don't give me the money back I'm going to kick up a fuss; **2** telling-off; **echar una bronca a alguien** to tell somebody off; **tu madre te va a echar una buena bronca** your mum's going to give you a good telling-off.

bronceado/bronceada *adjective* suntanned.

bronceador *noun* M suntan lotion.

broncearse *reflexive verb* [17] to get a suntan.

bronquitis *noun* F bronchitis.

bruja *noun* F witch.

brujo *noun* M wizard.

brújula *noun* F compass.

bruma *noun* F mist.

bruto/bruta *adjective* **1** ignorant; **2** rude; **es muy bruto, ¡dice unas**

cosas! he's very rude, he says such things!; **3 ¡qué bruto! ¡cómo trata a su hijo!** what a brute! what a way to treat his child!

buceador/buceadora *noun* M/F diver.

bucear *verb* [17] to dive.

buen *adjective* SEE **bueno²/buena**.

bueno¹ *adverb* **1** okay; **'¿quieres venir?' – 'bueno'** 'do you want to come?' – 'okay'; **2 bueno, no importa** well, it doesn't matter; **bueno, no estoy segura** well, I'm not sure; **bueno, ya basta** right, that's enough.

bueno²/buena *adjective* (*'bueno' becomes 'buen' before a masculine singular noun*) **1** good; **es muy buena persona** she's a very good person; **de buena calidad** good quality; **ser bueno para algo** to be good at something; **es muy buena para las matemáticas** she's very good at maths; **es muy buen amigo mío** he's a very good friend of mine; **¡buen viaje!** have a good journey!; **2 buenos días** good morning; **buenas tardes** good afternoon, good evening; **buenas noches** good evening, goodnight; **3** nice; **hace buen tiempo** the weather is nice; **el pastel estaba muy bueno** the cake was very nice; **¡está buenísimo!** it's delicious!

bufanda *noun* F scarf.

bufar *verb* [17] to snort.

bufet *noun* M buffet.

bufón *noun* M clown (*silly person*).

buhardilla *noun* F attic.

búho *noun* M owl.

bujía *noun* F spark plug.

bulto *noun* M **1** shape; **vi un bulto en la oscuridad** I saw a shape in the darkness; **2** piece of luggage; **¿cuántos bultos llevas?** how many pieces of luggage do you have?; **3** bag; **yo te llevos los bultos** I'll carry your bags; **iba cargada de bultos** she was carrying loads of bags.

bungalow *noun* M cabin, chalet (*in holiday resorts*).

buñuelo *noun* M fritter.

buque *noun* M ship; **buque de guerra** warship.

burbuja *noun* F **1** bubble; **2 una bebida sin burbujas** a still drink; **una bebida con burbujas** a fizzy drink.

burdo/burda *adjective* coarse.

burlarse *reflexive verb* [17] **burlarse de alguien** to make fun of somebody; **¡deja de burlarte de mí!** stop making fun of me!

burocracia *noun* F bureaucracy.

burrada *noun* F **¡vaya burrada has dicho!** what a stupid thing to say!; **¡no hagas esa burrada!** don't do such a stupid thing!; **sólo dijo burradas** he just talked rubbish.

burro¹ *noun* M donkey.

burro²/burra *noun* M/F **es un burro** he's really stupid. *adjective* stupid.

bus *noun* M (*informal*) bus.

busca *noun* F search; **ir en busca de algo** to go in search of something.

buscar *verb* [31] **1** to look for; **¿qué buscas?** what are you looking for?; **mi hermana está buscando trabajo** my sister's looking for a job; **estoy buscando un ayudante** I'm looking for an assistant; **2** to look; **si no lo encuentras aquí busca en la oficina** if you don't find it here look in the office; **3 ir a buscar algo** to go to pick up something; **mañana iré a buscar mis cosas** I'll go and pick up my things tomorrow; **4 ir a buscar a alguien** to pick somebody up; **yo te iré a buscar al aeropuerto** I'll pick you up at the airport; **5 ir a buscar a alguien** to go to get someone (*the police or a doctor, for example*); **fueron a buscar a un médico enseguida** they went to get a doctor straightaway.

búsqueda *noun* F search.

butaca *noun* F **1** armchair; **2** seat (*in a cinema or theatre*); **una butaca de patio** a seat in the stalls.

butano *noun* M butane gas; **una bombona del butano** a bottle of butane gas.

buzo *noun* M diver.

buzón *noun* M **1** letterbox; **2** postbox.

C c

caballa *noun* F mackerel.

caballero *noun* M **1** gentleman; **es un verdadero caballero** he's a real gentleman; **2** sir; **caballero, ¿me deja pasar?** could you let me through, sir?; **3 caballeros** Gents (*toilets*); men's department (*in a store*).

caballo *noun* M **1** horse; **montar a caballo** to ride a horse; **un caballo de carreras** a racehorse; **2** knight (*in chess*); **3** horse (*in Spanish cards: equivalent to the queen*).

cabaña *noun* F cabin.

cabecear *verb* [17] to head (*a ball*).

cabecera *noun* F **1** headboard; **2** head (*of table*); **se sentó a la cabecera de la mesa** he sat at the head of the table.

cabello *noun* M hair; **tener el cabello rubio** to have blond hair; **cabello rizado** curly hair; **cabello liso** straight hair.

caber *verb* [33] **1 caber en** to fit into; **es demasiado grande, no cabe en la caja** it's too big, it doesn't fit into the box; **no vamos a caber en el coche** we won't all fit in the car; **2 aquí ya no cabe nada más** there's no room for anything else in here; **¿caben estos libros en la maleta?** is there room for these books in the suitcase?; **3 caber por algo** to fit through something; **no cabía por la puerta** it wouldn't fit through the door.

cabeza *noun* F **1** head; **me duele la cabeza** I've got a headache; **asentir con la cabeza** to nod; **2 lavarse la cabeza** to wash your hair; **tengo que lavarme la cabeza** I've got to wash my hair; **3 una cabeza de ajos** a head of garlic; **4 tirarse al agua de cabeza** to dive; **5 cabeza abajo** upside down; **el cuadro está cabeza abajo** the picture's upside down; **6 a la cabeza de** at the head of; **iban a la cabeza de la manifestación** they were at the head of the demonstration; ★ **está mal de la cabeza** he's not right in the head.

cabeza rapada *noun* M/F skinhead.

cabina *noun* F **1** cab (*of a lorry*); **2** cockpit (*of a plane*); **3** cabin (*on a plane or boat*); **4** booth (*in a language lab*); **5 cabina de teléfonos** telephone box.

cabo *noun* M **1** corporal; **2** cape; **cabo de Buena Esperanza** Cape of Good Hope; **3 al cabo de** after; **al cabo de tres semanas** after three weeks; **4** end (*of a length of rope or piece of string*); ★ **atar cabos** to put two and two together.

cabra *noun* F goat.

cabré, cabría, etc. *verb* SEE **caber**.

cacahuete *noun* M peanut.

cacao *noun* M **1** cocoa (*drink*); **2** lipsalve.

cacerola *noun* F saucepan.

cachete *noun* M slap.

cachorro/cachorra *noun* M/F puppy.

cada *adjective* **1** each; **un alumno de cada clase** a pupil from each class; **hay diez para cada uno** there are ten each; **2** every; **me llaman cada día** they phone me every day; **cada tres días** every three days; **3 cada vez más** more and more; **se parecen cada vez más** they look more and more alike; **cada vez menos** less and less; **cada vez mejor** better and better; **lo hace cada vez mejor** she's getting better and better all the time; **cada vez peor** worse and worse.

cadena *noun* F **1** chain; **una cadena de hierro** an iron chain; **una cadena antirrobo** a bicycle lock; **una cadena de supermercados** a supermarket chain; **2** channel (*on the TV*); **lo ponen en la segunda cadena** they're showing it on Channel Two; **3** station (*on the radio*); **4 cadenas** snow chains; **5 tirar de la cadena** to flush the toilet; **6 condenar a alguien a cadena perpetua** to sentence somebody to life imprisonment.

cadera *noun* F hip.

caer *verb* [34] **1** to fall; **el jarrón cayó al suelo** the vase fell to the ground; **2 dejar caer** algo to drop something (*on purpose*); **dejé caer la bandeja** I dropped the tray; **3 se dejó caer en el sofá** he flopped into the sofa; **4** (*informal*) **tu hermano me cae bien** I like your brother; **Ana me cae fatal** I can't stand Ana.

caerse *reflexive verb* [34] **1** to fall over; **tropecé y me caí** I tripped and fell over; **2** to fall; **casi se cayó del tejado** he almost fell off the roof; **me caí por las escaleras** I fell down the stairs; **se cayó de la bici** he fell off his bike; **3 se me cayó el plato** I dropped the plate (*accidentally*); **4 se le ha caído un diente** he's lost a tooth; **se me está cayendo el pelo** I'm losing my hair.

café *noun* M coffee; **¿quieres un café?** do you want a cup of coffee?; **un café solo** an expresso; **un café con leche** a white coffee; **un café cortado** a coffee with a dash of milk; **café descafeinado** decaffeinated coffee.

cafetera *noun* F coffee maker.

cafetería *noun* F café.

caído/caída *adjective* fallen.

caiga, caigo, etc. *verb* SEE **caer**.

caja *noun* F **1** box; **una caja de cartón** a cardboard box; **caja de las herramientas** toolbox; **caja de cambios** gearbox; **2** crate; **una caja de naranjas** a crate of oranges; **3** checkout (*in a supermarket*); **pague en caja** pay at the checkout; **4** till (*in a shop*); **5 una caja fuerte** a safe; **6 caja de ahorros** savings bank, building society.

cajero/cajera *noun* M/F **1** cashier; **2** checkout operator; **3 cajero automático** cash dispenser.

cajón *noun* M drawer.

calabacín *noun* M courgette.

calamar *noun* M squid; **calamares a la romana** squid rings in batter.

calambre *noun* M **1** cramp; **me dio un calambre** I got cramp; **2** electric shock; **la lámpara me ha dado** calambre the lamp gave me an electric shock.

calamidad *noun* F disaster.

calcetín *noun* M sock; **unos calcetines** a pair of socks.

calculadora *noun* F calculator.

calcular *verb* [17] to calculate, to work out.

caldo *noun* M **1** stock; **caldo de verdura** vegetable stock; **2** broth.

calefacción *noun* F heating; **calefacción central** central heating; **calefacción de gas** gas heating.

calendario *noun* M calendar.

calentador *noun* M **1** boiler; **2** water heater.

calentar *verb* [29] **1** to heat (up); **voy a calentar la sopa** I'm going to heat up the soup; **2** to give off heat; **esta estufa calienta mucho** this heater gives off a lot of heat; **3 calentar los músculos** to warm up (*before sport or dancing*).
calentarse *reflexive verb* [29] to heat up.

calidad *noun* F quality; **materiales de calidad** high quality materials; **productos de mala calidad** poor quality products.

calienta, caliento, etc. *verb* SEE **calentar**.

caliente *adjective* **1** hot; **los platos están muy calientes** the plates are very hot; **2** warm; **un baño caliente** a hot bath; **en el salón se está más**

caliente it's warmer in the living-room.

calificación *noun* F mark; **obtuvo buenas calificaciones** he got good marks.

callado/callada *adjective* quiet; **¡estáte callado!** be quiet!

callar *verb* [17] to be quiet; **calla, no oigo** be quiet, I can't hear; **¡calla ya!** shut up!
callarse *reflexive verb* [17] to go quiet; **al verla todos se callaron** everybody went quiet when they saw her; **¡cállate!** shut up!

calle *noun* F street; **una calle cortada** a cul-de-sac; **una calle de sentido único** a one way street; (*when writing an address, the word 'calle' is abbreviated to 'C/'*).

callejón *noun* M alley; **un callejón sin salida** a blind alley.

calma *noun* F calm; **hazlo con calma** do it calmly; **mantener la calma** to keep calm; **la ciudad está en calma** the city is calm.

calmar *verb* [17] to calm down.
calmarse *reflexive verb* [17] to calm down; **después de un rato me calmé** I calmed down after a while.

calor *noun* M 1 heat; **el calor de la estufa** the heat of the stove; **2 hoy hace mucho calor** it's very hot today; **¡qué calor hace!** it's so hot!; **3 tener calor** to be hot; **tengo mucho calor** I'm very hot.

caluroso/calurosa *adjective* hot (*a day or place*).

calvo/calva *adjective* bald; **quedarse calvo** to go bald.

calzado *noun* M footwear.

calzar *verb* [22] **¿qué número calzas?** what size do you take?

calzoncillos *plural noun* M underpants; **unos calzoncillos** a pair of underpants.

cama *noun* F bed; **una cama individual** a single bed; **una cama doble/una cama de matrimonio** a double bed; **camas gemelas** twin beds; **hacer la cama** to make the bed; **¡a la cama!** off to bed!

cámara *noun* F camera; **una cámara de fotos** a camera; **una cámara de vídeo** a video camera.

camarera *noun* F 1 waitress; **2 camarera de habitación** chambermaid.

camarero *noun* M waiter.

camarón *noun* M shrimp.

cambiar *verb* [17] **1** to change; **no has cambiado** you haven't changed; **cambiar libras a pesetas** to change pounds into pesetas; **2 cambiar de** to change; **ha cambiado de trabajo** he's changed his job; **cambiar de idea** to change your mind; **cambiar de canal** to change channels; **3** to exchange; **quiero cambiar estos zapatos** I want to exchange these shoes; **4 cambiar de casa** to move house; **5** to swap; **te cambio mi pluma por esa cinta** I'll swap my pen for that tape.
cambiarse *reflexive verb* [17] **1** to get changed; **voy a cambiarme y ahora**

vuelvo I'm going to get changed, I'll be back in a minute; **voy a cambiarme de ropa** I'm going to change my clothes; **2 cambiarse de sitio** to change places.

cambio *noun* M **1** change; **un cambio a mejor** a change for the better; **ha habido un cambio de planes** there's been a change of plan; **2** exchange; **no se admiten cambios** goods will not be exchanged; **3** change; **¿tienes cambio?** do you have any change?; **me dieron mal el cambio** they gave me the wrong change; **'cambio'** 'bureau de change'; **4 a cambio de** in return for; **a cambio de información** in return for information.

caminar *verb* [17] to walk; **me gusta caminar** I like walking.

caminata *noun* F long walk.

camino *noun* M **1** road; **todos los caminos están cortados** all the roads are closed; **el camino al éxito** the road to success; **2** path; **un camino por el bosque** a path through the forest; **3** way; **¿puede indicarme el camino a la estación?** could you tell me the way to the station?; **yo sé el camino** I know the way.

camión *noun* M lorry; **el camión de la mudanza** the removal van.

camionero/camionera *noun* M/F lorry driver.

camioneta *noun* F van.

camisa *noun* F shirt.

camiseta *noun* F **1** T-shirt; **2** vest.

camisón *noun* M nightdress.

campamento *noun* M camp; **se han ido de campamento** they've gone camping.

campana *noun* F bell; **tocar la campana** to ring the bell.

campaña *noun* F campaign; **campaña electoral** electoral campaign.

campeón/campeona *noun* M/F champion.

campeonato *noun* M championship.

campesino/campesina *noun* M/F **1** country person; **2** peasant.

camping *noun* M campsite; **ir de camping** to go camping.

campista *noun* M/F camper.

campo *noun* M **1** country; **una casa en el campo** a house in the country; **2** countryside; **el campo está muy bonito** the countryside looks very beautiful; **3** field; **un campo de trigo** a field of wheat; **4 un campo de fútbol** a football pitch.

cana *noun* F white hair; **me están saliendo canas** I'm going grey.

Canadá *noun* M Canada.

canadiense *noun* M/F *adjective* Canadian.

canal *noun* M **1** channel (*on the TV*); **no cambies de canal** don't change channels; **2** channel (*water*); **el canal de la Mancha** the English Channel; **3** canal; **el canal de Panamá** the Panama Canal.

canario *noun* M canary.

canasta *noun* F basket.

canasto *noun* M basket (*usually with a lid*).

cancelar *verb* [17] to cancel.

cáncer[1] *noun* M cancer; **tiene cáncer** he's got cancer; **cáncer de mama** breast cancer; **cáncer de piel** skin cancer.

cáncer[2] *noun* M/F Cancer; **soy cáncer** I'm Cancer.

Cáncer *noun* M Cancer.

cancha *noun* F court; **una cancha de baloncesto** a basketball court.

canción *noun* F song; **canción de cuna** lullaby.

candidato/candidata *noun* M/F candidate.

canela *noun* F cinnamon; **canela en rama** stick cinnamon; **canela en polvo** ground cinnamon.

cangrejo *noun* M **1** crab; **2** crayfish.

canguro[1] *noun* M kangaroo.

canguro[2] *noun* M/F babysitter.

canica *noun* F marble; **jugar a las canicas** to play marbles.

canoa *noun* F canoe.

cansado/cansada *adjective* **1** tired; **estoy muy cansado** I'm very tired; **2** tiring; **esperar es muy cansado** waiting's very tiring.

cansar *verb* [17] **1** to make tired; **le cansa andar** walking makes him tired; **2** to be tiring; **es un trabajo que cansa mucho** it's a very tiring job; **3** to be boring; **esta música cansa un poco** this music's a bit boring.

cansarse *reflexive verb* [17] **1** to get tired; **se cansa muy fácilmente** he gets tired very easily; **se me cansa la vista** my eyes get tired; **2** to get bored; **me canso de repetir siempre lo mismo** I get bored always repeating the same thing.

Cantábrico *noun* M **el mar Cantábrico** the Bay of Biscay.

cantante *noun* M/F singer.

cantar *verb* [17] to sing.

cantera *noun* F quarry.

cantidad *noun* F **1** amount; **una enorme cantidad de nieve** a huge amount of snow; **2** ¿**qué cantidad de vasos necesitamos?** how many glasses do we need?; **es increíble cuanta cantidad de aceite gastas** it's incredible how much oil you use; **3 tanta cantidad** so much; **no pongas tanta cantidad de leche** don't put so much milk in; **4 cantidad de/cantidades de** lots of; **había cantidad de gente** there were lots of people; **con grandes cantidades de flores** with lots of flowers; **5** sum; **una cantidad importante de dinero** a considerable sum of money.

cantina *noun* F **1** cafeteria; **2** canteen.

caña *noun* F **1** cane; **caña de azúcar** sugar cane; **2 caña de pescar** fishing rod.

cañería *noun* F pipe.

capa *noun* F **1** layer; **la capa de ozono** the ozone layer; **2** cape, cloak.

capacidad *noun* F capacity.

capaz *adjective* **1** capable; **es capaz de cualquier cosa** he's capable of anything; **soy capaz de no ir** I'm quite capable of not going; **2** able; **no fueron capaces de darme una respuesta** they weren't able to give me an answer.

capital *noun* F **1** capital; **la capital de España** the capital of Spain; **2 Bilbao capital** the city of Bilbao.

capitán/capitana *noun* M/F captain (*in sports*).

capítulo *noun* M **1** chapter; **2** episode (*of a TV series*).

capó *noun* M bonnet (*of a car*).

capricornio *noun* M/F Capricorn; **es capricornio** he's Capricorn.

Capricornio *noun* M Capricorn.

cara[1] *noun* F **1** face; **tiene una cara bonita** she has a pretty face; **tienes cara de cansada** you look tired; **al oírlo puso cara de sorpresa** he looked surprised when he heard it; **tu hermana tenía mala cara** your sister looked ill; ★ **¡qué cara más dura tienes!** (*informal*) you've got some nerve!** (*literally: what a hard face you have!*); **2** side; **la otra cara del disco** the other side of the record; **3 ¿cara o cruz?** heads or tails.

caracol *noun* M **1** snail; **2** winkle.

carácter *noun* M **1** character; **el carácter Latino** the Latin character; **2 tiene muy mal carácter** he's got a very bad temper; **es una persona de buen carácter** she's a good-natured person; **3 no tiene mucho carácter** he doesn't have much personality.

caramba *exclamation* **1** good heavens!; **2** damn it!

caramelo *noun* M **1** sweet; **un caramelo de menta** a mint; **2** caramel.

caravana *noun* F **1** tailback; **hay caravana para entrar en Sevilla** there's a tailback into Seville; **una caravana de diez kilómetros** a ten-kilometre tailback; **2** caravan.

carbón *noun* M coal; **carbón vegetal** charcoal.

cárcel *noun* F jail; **meter a alguien en la cárcel** to put somebody in jail.

cardíaco/cardíaca *adjective* heart; **un ataque cardíaco** a heart attack.

careta *noun* F mask.

carga *noun* F **1** burden; **no quiero ser una carga para nadie** I don't want to be a burden on anybody; **2** freight, cargo; **3** load; **carga máxima** maximum load; **4** refill (*for a pen*); **5 ¡a la carga!** charge!

cargado/cargada *adjective*
1 loaded; **la pistola estaba cargada** the gun was loaded; **vas muy cargada** you're loaded down; **iba cargado de paquetes** he was loaded down with parcels; 2 **un café cargado** a strong coffee.

cargar *verb* [28] 1 to load (*a lorry or weapon*); 2 to fill (*a pen*).

cargo *noun* M 1 position; **un cargo de responsabilidad** a position of responsibility; 2 **a cargo de** in charge of; **estoy a cargo del departamento** I'm in charge of the department; **dejó los niños a mi cargo** she left the children in my care.

cariño *noun* M 1 affection; **tenerle cariño a** to be fond of; **les tengo cariño** I'm fond of them; **tomarle cariño a** to become fond of; **les tomó cariño** he became fond of them; 2 **con cariño, Maya** love, Maya (*in letters*); 3 dear; **ven, cariño** come here, dear.

cariñoso/cariñosa *adjective*
1 affectionate, loving (*a person*);
2 warm; **un cariñoso saludo** warm regards (*in a letter*).

carmín *noun* M lipstick.

carnaval *noun* M carnival.

carne *noun* F 1 meat; **carne de vaca** beef; **carne de cerdo** pork; **carne de cordero** lamb; **carne de ternera** veal; 2 flesh.

carné, carnet *noun* M card; **carné de identidad** identity card; **carné de** estudiante student card; **carné de conducir** driver's licence.

carnicería *noun* F butcher's.

carnicero/carnicera *noun* M/F butcher.

carnívoro/carnívora *adjective* carnivorous.

caro/cara² *adjective* expensive; **cuesta muy caro** it's very expensive; **eso lo vas a pagar caro** you're going to pay dearly for this.

carpeta *noun* F folder; **carpeta de anillas** ring binder.

carpintero/carpintera *noun* M/F carpenter.

carrera *noun* F 1 race; **una carrera automovilística** a car race; **las carreras de caballos** the races; **una carrera de obstáculos** a steeplechase; **una carrera de relevos** a relay race; 2 **echar una carrera** to have a race (*against somebody*); **¿echamos una carrera?** shall we have a race?; **te echo una carrera** I'll race you; 3 **echar una carrera** to run; **eché una carrera y alcancé el autobús** I ran and got the bus; 4 degree course; **hacer una carrera** to study on a degree course; **no quiero hacer una carrera** I don't want to go to university; **está haciendo la carrera de medicina** she's studying medicine.

carretera *noun* F road; **carretera nacional** A-road; **carretera comarcal** B-road; **carretera de circunvalación** ringroad.

carretilla *noun* F wheelbarrow.

carril *noun* M lane; **carril bus** bus lane.

carrito *noun* M trolley.

carro *noun* M cart.

carta *noun* F 1 letter; **mandar una carta** to send a letter; **echar una carta al correo** to post a letter; **una carta certificada** a registered letter; 2 menu; **¿nos puede traer la carta, por favor?** could you bring us the menu, please?; 3 card (*in a pack*); **jugar a las cartas** to play cards.

cartel *noun* M 1 poster (*for publicity*); 2 sign; **¿qué dice el cartel?** what does the sign say?

cartelera *noun* F **la cartelera de cine** 'what's on' at the cinema; **la obra lleva tres años en cartelera** the play has been running for three years; **la película sigue en cartelera** the film is still showing.

cartera *noun* F 1 wallet; 2 briefcase; 3 satchel.

carterista *noun* M/F pickpocket.

cartero/cartera *noun* M/F postman/postwoman.

cartón *noun* M cardboard.

casa *noun* F 1 house; **una casa adosada** a semi-detached house; **una casa de campo** a country house; 2 flat; **su casa está en la quinta planta** her flat's on the fifth floor; 3 home; **no están en casa** they're not at home; **estoy pasando unos días en casa de Juan** I'm staying at Juan's for a few days.

casado/casada *adjective* married; **estar casado/ser casado** to be married.

casarse *reflexive verb* [17] to get married; **se casó con mi primo** she married my cousin.

cascar *verb* [31] to crack.

cáscara *noun* F 1 peel; 2 shell.

casco *noun* M 1 helmet; **un casco protector** a safety helmet, crash helmet; 2 hoof (*of a horse*); 3 empty bottle; **guardo los cascos para reciclarlos** I keep the empty bottles for recycling; 4 **cascos** headphones.

casero/casera *noun* M/F landlord/landlady. *adjective* homemade.

caseta *noun* F 1 hut (*for a watchman or guard*); 2 stand (*in an exhibition*); 3 kennel.

casete[1] *noun* M cassette recorder.

casete[2] *noun* M or F cassette.

casi *adverb* 1 almost; **casi me pierdo** I almost got lost; **¡casi, casi!** almost!; 2 hardly; **casi no había gente** there was hardly anybody there; **casi nunca** hardly ever.

casilla *noun* F 1 square (*in a crossword*); 2 box (*on a form*).

cassette *noun* M or F cassette.

caso *noun* M 1 case; **en ese caso** in that case; **en caso de accidente** in case of accident; **en todo caso/en cualquier caso** in any case; **en el peor de los casos** if the worst comes to the worst; **2 el caso es que** ... the thing is ...; **3 hacer caso de** to pay attention to; **haz caso de las señales** pay attention to the signs; **no me hace caso** he pays no attention to me.

castaña[1] *noun* F chestnut.

castaño/castaña[2] *adjective* chestnut brown.

castañuelas *plural noun* F castanets.

castellano[1] *noun* M **1** Castilian; **2** Castilian Spanish (*as opposed to different varieties of Spanish, particularly those used in Spanish-speaking countries within the continent of America; Castilian Spanish is generally used to mean the Spanish spoken in Spain*).

castellano[2]**/castellana** *noun* M/F *adjective* Castilian.

castigar *verb* [28] **1** to punish; **2 castigar a alguien sin salir** to ground somebody; **3** to give a detention (*at school*); **la profesora me dejó castigado** the teacher gave me a detention.

castigo *noun* M punishment.

Castilla *noun* F Castile.

castillo *noun* M castle; **castillo de/por arena** sandcastle.

casualidad *noun* F **1** chance; **de casualidad** by chance; **lo vi de casualidad** I saw it by chance; **2 da la casualidad de que** ... it so happens that ...; **dio la casualidad**

de que llevaba las señas en mi bolso it so happened that I had the address in my bag; **3 ¡qué casualidad!** what a coincidence!

catalán[1] *noun* M Catalan (*the language*).

catalán[2]**/catalana** *noun* M/F *adjective* Catalan.

Cataluña *noun* F Catalonia.

catarata *noun* F **1** waterfall; **2** cataract (*of the eye*).

catarro *noun* M cold; **coger un catarro** to catch a cold.

catear *verb* [17] (*informal*) to fail; **he cateado las mates** I've failed maths; **me han cateado en inglés** I've failed English.

catedral *noun* F cathedral.

categoría *noun* F **1** category; **2 de primera categoría** first class; **un hotel de mucha categoría** a top-quality hotel; **un restaurante de poca categoría** a second-rate restaurant.

católico/católica *noun* M/F *adjective* Catholic.

catorce *number* **1** fourteen; **tiene catorce años** he's fourteen (years old); **2** fourteenth (*in dates*); **el catorce de mayo** the fourteenth of May.

caucho *noun* M rubber.

causa *noun* F **1** cause; **sin causa** without cause; **2 a causa de** because of; **a causa de esto lo despidieron** they sacked him because of this.

causar *verb* [17] to cause.

cava *noun* M cava (*sparkling wine*).

cavar *verb* [17] to dig.

caverna *noun* F cave.

cayendo SEE **caer**.

caza *noun* F hunting; **ir de caza** to go hunting.

cazar *verb* [22] to hunt.

cazuela *noun* F casserole.

cebolla *noun* F onion.

cebollino *noun* M chives.

cebolleta *noun* F spring onion.

ceder *verb* [18] **1** to give in; **finalmente cedí** I finally gave in; **2 ceder el paso** to give way; **3 le cedí mi asiento a un anciano** I gave my seat to an elderly man.

ceja *noun* F eyebrow.

celda *noun* F cell (*in a prison*).

celebración *noun* F celebration.

celebrar *verb* [17] **1** to celebrate; **2** to hold (*a meeting*).
celebrarse *reflexive verb* [17] to take place; **la boda se celebró el sábado pasado** the wedding took place last Saturday.

célebre *adjective* famous.

celo *noun* M Sellotape™.

celos *plural noun* M **1** jealousy; **2 tener celos de alguien** to be jealous of somebody; **tiene celos de su hermana pequeña** she's jealous of her little sister; **3 darle celos a alguien** to make somebody feel

jealous; **lo hace para darte celos** he does it to make you feel jealous.

celoso/celosa *adjective* jealous.

cementerio *noun* M cemetery.

cemento *noun* M cement.

cena *noun* F dinner; **¿qué hay de cena?** what's for dinner?

cenar *verb* [17] to have dinner; **normalmente cenamos a las nueve** we normally have dinner at nine; **salimos a cenar fuera** we went out for dinner.

cenicero *noun* M ashtray.

ceniza *noun* F ash.

centenar *noun* M hundred; **un centenar de libros** (about) a hundred books; **centenares de cartas** hundreds of letters.

centenario *noun* M centenary.

centeno *noun* M rye.

centésima¹ *noun* F hundredth; **una centésima de segundo** a hundredth of a second.

centésimo/centésima² *adjective* hundredth.

centígrado *adjective* centigrade.

centímetro *noun* M centimetre.

céntimo *noun* M **no tengo ni un céntimo** I am penniless.

central *noun* F **1** head office; **2 central telefónica** telephone exchange; **central de correos** general post office; **3** power station; **central nuclear** nuclear power station.
adjective central.

céntrico/céntrica *adjective* central; **un barrio céntrico** an area in the centre of town.

centrifugar *verb* [28] to spin-dry.

centro *noun* M 1 centre; **el centro de la ciudad** the centre of the town; **un centro cultural** a cultural centre; **estaba justo en el centro** it was right in the middle; 2 **un centro comercial** a shopping mall.

ceñido/ceñida *adjective* tight; **una camiseta muy ceñida** a very tight T-shirt.

ceño *noun* M **fruncir el ceño** to frown.

cepillar *verb* [17] to brush.
cepillarse *reflexive verb* [17] to brush; **cepillarse los dientes** to brush your teeth; **cepillarse el pelo** to brush your hair.

cepillo *noun* M brush; **un cepillo de dientes** a toothbrush; **un cepillo del pelo** a hairbrush.

cera *noun* F wax.

cerámica *noun* F pottery.

cerca *adverb* 1 near, close; **viven aquí cerca** they live near here; **ponlos cerca el uno del otro** put them close to each other; 2 nearby; **mi casa está cerca** my house is nearby; 3 **cerca de** near; **se sentó cerca de mí** he sat near me; **está cerca de la estación** it's near the station; **vive muy cerca de mí** she lives very near me; 4 **cerca de** almost; **cerca de diez mil personas** almost ten thousand people.

cercanía *noun* F proximity.

cercano/cercana *adjective* 1 nearby; **las casas cercanas** the nearby houses; 2 **cercano a algo** near something; **los pueblos cercanos al aeropuerto** the villages near the airport; 3 near; **en un futuro cercano** in the near future.

cercanías *plural noun* F 1 surrounding area; **Barcelona y sus cercanías** Barcelona and the surrounding area; **en las cercanías del aeropuerto** in the area around the airport; 2 vicinity; **en las cercanías del bar** in the vicinity of the bar.

cerdo[1] *noun* M pork; **no como cerdo** I don't eat pork.

cerdo[2]**/cerda** *noun* M/F pig.

cereales *plural noun* M cereals.

ceremonia *noun* F ceremony.

cereza *noun* F cherry.

cerilla *noun* F match.

cero *noun* M 1 zero; **tres grados bajo cero** three degrees below zero; 2 0; **mi prefijo en Londres es cero, uno, ocho, uno** my dialling code in London is 0181; 3 love (*in tennis*); 4 nil (*in football*).

cerrado/cerrada *adjective* 1 closed; **la ventana está cerrada** the window's closed; 2 **cerrado con llave** locked; **cerrado con cerrojo** bolted; 3 **el grifo está cerrado** the tap's turned off.

cerradura *noun* F 1 lock; 2 **el ojo de la cerradura** the keyhole.

cerrar *verb* [29] **1** to close; **cierrra la puerta** close the door; **cerramos a las ocho** we close at eight; **han cerrado la fábrica** they've closed the factory; **2 cerrar algo de un portazo** to slam something; **cerró la puerta de un portazo** he slammed the door shut; **3 cerrar con llave** to lock; **no te olvides de cerrar con llave** don't forget to lock up; **4 cerrar con cerrojo** to bolt; **5 cerrar el grifo** to turn off the tap; **6 cierra la botella** put the top on the bottle; **¿has cerrado el frasco?** have you put the lid on the jar?; **7 cerrar una carta** to seal a letter.

cerrarse *reflexive verb* [29] to close; **la puerta se cerró** the door closed; **cerrarse de un portazo** to slam shut.

certificado[1] *noun* M certificate.

certificado[2]**/certificada** *adjective* registered (*a letter or parcel*).

certificar *verb* [31] to certify.

cervecería *noun* F bar (*selling lots of different beers*).

cerveza *noun* F beer; **¿quieres una cerveza?** do you want a beer?; **cerveza de barril** draught beer; **cerveza negra** stout; **cerveza rubia** lager.

césped *noun* M lawn; **'prohibido pisar el césped'** 'keep off the grass'.

cesta *noun* F **1** basket; **una cesta de mimbre** a wicker basket; **2 una cesta de Navidad** a Christmas hamper.

cesto *noun* M basket.

chalado/chalada (*informal*) *adjective* crazy.

chalé, chalet *noun* M villa.

chaleco *noun* M waistcoast; **un chaleco de punto** a sleeveless sweater.

champán *noun* M champagne.

champaña *noun* M or F champagne.

champiñón *noun* M mushroom.

champú *noun* M shampoo.

chándal *noun* M tracksuit.

chapa *noun* F **1** top (*of a bottle*); **2** badge; **una chapa de policía** a police badge.

chaparrón *noun* M downpour.

chaqueta *noun* F jacket; **chaqueta de punto** cardigan.

charca *noun* F pond.

charco *noun* M puddle; **no pises los charcos** don't walk in the puddles.

charcutería *noun* F delicatessen (*specializing in pork products*).

chasco *noun* M disappointment; **me llevé un chasco** I felt really disappointed.

cheque *noun* M cheque; **extender un cheque** to write out a cheque; **me puedes extender un cheque a mi nombre** you can make out a cheque to me; **un cheque a nombre de Alberto López** a cheque payable to Alberto López; **cobrar un cheque** to cash a cheque; **un cheque de viaje/**

un cheque de viajero a traveller's cheque.

chequeo *noun* M checkup; **hacerse un chequeo** to have a checkup.

chica *noun* F girl.

chichón *noun* M bump; **me di un golpe en la frente y me ha salido un chichón** I banged my forehead and I've got a bump now.

chicle *noun* M chewing gum; **¿quieres un chicle?** do you want some chewing gum?

chico *noun* M **1** boy; **2 unos chicos** some children; **había unos chicos jugando en la calle** there were some children playing in the street; **3** guy; **sale con un chico** she's going out with a guy.

chiflado/chiflada *adjective* (*informal*) crazy.

chile *noun* M chilli.

Chile *noun* M Chile.

chileno/chilena *noun* M/F *adjective* Chilean.

chillar *verb* [17] to shout.

chimenea *noun* F **1** chimney; **2** fireplace.

China *noun* F **(la) China** China.

chincheta *noun* F drawing pin.

chino[1] *noun* M Chinese (*the language*).

chino[2]/**china** *noun* M/F Chinese man/Chinese woman. *adjective* Chinese.

Chipre *noun* F Cyprus.

chirriar *verb* [32] to squeak (*a door*).

chis *exclamation* **1** shush!; **2 ¡chis, chis !** hey! (*calling somebody in the street, for example*).

chisme *noun* M **1** piece of gossip; **siempre está contando chismes** he's always gossiping; **2** thing; **¿para qué sirve este chisme?** what's this thing for?; **3 tiene un montón de chismes que no sirven para nada** he's got all sorts of useless stuff.

chispa *noun* F **1** spark; **saltaron chispas del fuego** sparks flew out of the fire; **2 una chispa de** (*informal*) a drop of; **una chispa de ginebra** a drop of gin; **pon una chispa de sal** add a tiny bit of salt. *adjective* (*informal*) tipsy; **estaba un poco chispa** she was a bit tipsy.

chiste *noun* M joke; **contar un chiste** to tell a joke; **un chiste verde** a dirty joke.

chocar *verb* [31] **1** to crash; **dos coches chocaron en la autopista** two cars crashed on the motorway; **2 chocar con** to run into; **chocaron con una farola** they ran into a lamp-post; **me choqué con ella** I bumped into her.

chocolate *noun* M chocolate; **chocolate con leche** milk chocolate; **chocolate negro** dark chocolate; **una barra de chocolate** a bar of chocolate.

chocolatina *noun* F chocolate bar.

chollo *noun* M (*informal*) **1** cushy job; **2 este chico es un chollo, sabe**

hacer de todo this guy's a real find, he can do anything.

choque *noun* M **1** crash; **un choque frontal** a head-on collision; **2** clash; **choques entre los manifestantes y la policía** clashes between demonstrators and police.

chorizo *noun* M chorizo (*spicy sausage*).

chorrada *noun* F (*informal*) **eso es una chorrada** that's nonsense; **decir chorradas** to talk nonsense; **se enfada por cualquier chorrada** he gets upset over the smallest thing.

chuchería *noun* F trinket.

chuleta *noun* F chop; **una chuleta de cerdo** a pork chop.

chupar *verb* [17] **1** to suck; **2** to absorb; **este papel chupa la tinta** this paper absorbs ink.
chuparse *reflexive verb* [17] to suck; **chuparse el dedo** to suck your thumb.

churro *noun* M **1** fritter; **2** (*informal*) botched job; **¡vaya churro ha salido!** it's turned out a real mess!

chutar *verb* [17] to shoot (*at goal*).

cicatriz *noun* F scar.

ciclismo *noun* M cycling.

ciclista *noun* M/F cyclist.

ciego/ciega *noun* M/F blind person; **los ciegos** the blind.
adjective blind; **quedarse ciego** to go blind.

cielo *noun* M **1** sky; **2** heaven; **ir al cielo** to go to heaven; **¡cielos!** good heavens!

cien *number* hundred (*see also 'ciento'*); **cien personas** a hundred people; **el cien por cien** a hundred per cent; **cien mil pesetas** a hundred thousand pesetas.

ciencia *noun* F **1** science; **ciencia ficción** science fiction; **2 ciencias** science (*subject at school*); **ciencias naturales** natural science; **Ciencias Económicas** Economic Sciences; **Ciencias Empresariales** Business Studies; **Ciencias de la Información** Media Studies.

cieno *noun* M silt.

científico/científica *noun* M/F scientist.
adjective scientific.

ciento *number* **1** hundred; **ciento cinco** one hundred and five; **dos cientos diez** two hundred and ten; **cientos de cartas** hundreds of letters; **2 por ciento** per cent; **cinco por ciento** five per cent; **tanto por ciento** percentage.

cierra, cierro, etc. *verb* SEE **cerrar**.

cierto/cierta *adjective* **1** true; **eso no es cierto** that's not true; **2** certain; **cierta clase de negocios** certain types of business; **en cierta ocasión** on a certain occasion; **3 en cierto modo** in a way; **en cierto modo, lo entiendo** in a way, I understand; **4 hasta cierto punto** up to a point; **5 por cierto** by the way;

por cierto, ¿se lo has preguntado? by the way, did you ask him?

ciervo *noun* M **1** deer; **2** stag.

cifra *noun* F figure; **una cifra muy alta** a very high figure.

cigarrillo *noun* M cigarrette.

cima *noun* F top (*of a mountain*).

cinco *number* **1** five; **Julia tiene cinco años** Julia's five (years old); **2** fifth (*in dates*); **hoy es día cinco** today is the fifth; **3** five (*in clock time*); **son las cinco** it's five o'clock; **a las dos y cinco** at five past two.

cincuenta *number* fifty; **mi madre tiene cincuenta años** my mum's fifty (years old); **cincuenta y ocho** fifty-eight; **los años cincuenta** the fifties.

cine *noun* M cinema; **ir al cine** to go to the cinema; **¿qué ponen en el cine?** what's on at the cinema?; **cine de barrio** local cinema; **la cartelera de cine** 'what's on' at the cinemas.

cineasta *noun* M/F film-maker.

cinta *noun* F **1** ribbon; **una cinta para el pelo** a hair ribbon; **2** tape; **una cinta de vídeo** a video tape; **grabar una cinta** to record a tape; **una cinta virgen** a blank tape; **cinta magnetofónica** magnetic tape; **cinta adhesiva** adhesive tape; **cinta métrica** tape measure.

cintura *noun* F waist; **¿cuánto tienes de cintura?** what's your waist measurement?

cinturón *noun* M belt; **cinturón de seguridad** seatbelt; **es cinturón negro de karate** he's a karate black

belt; ★ **apretarse el cinturón** to tighten one's belt.

circo *noun* M circus.

circulación *noun* F **1** circulation; **2** traffic.

circular *noun* F *adjective* circular. *verb* [17] **1** to flow (*blood or water*); **2** to drive; **circulen por la derecha** drive on the right; **el coche circulaba a mucha velocidad** the car was travelling very fast.

círculo *noun* M circle.

circunstancia *noun* F **1** reason; **por alguna circunstancia no pudo hacerlo** he couldn't do it for some reason; **2** circumstances; **bajo ninguna circunstancia** under no circumstances; **en estas circunstancias** in these circumstances; **dadas las circunstancias** given the circumstances.

cirio *noun* M candle.

ciruela *noun* F plum; **ciruela pasa** prune.

cirujano/cirujana *noun* M/F surgeon.

cisne *noun* M swan.

cita *noun* F **1** appointment; **tengo cita con el médico** I've got an appointment with the doctor; **el dentista me ha dado cita para el jueves** the dentist has given me an appointment for Thursday; **pedir cita** to make an appointment; **llamé al abogado para pedir cita** I phoned

the lawyer to make an appointment;
2 date; **esta noche tengo una cita**
I've got a date tonight, I'm meeting
somebody tonight; **3** quotation.

citar *verb* [17] **1** to quote (*a writer or
book*); **2** to mention; **citó algunos
casos** he mentioned a few cases;
3 to give an appointment; **el médico
me ha citado para esta tarde** the
doctor's given me an appointment
for this afternoon.

citarse *reflexive verb* [17] to arrange
to meet; **se citaron para las cinco**
they arranged to meet at five.

ciudad *noun* F **1** town; **ciudad
dormitorio** dormitory town; **2** city;
3 ciudad universitaria university
campus.

ciudadano/ciudadana *noun* M/
F citizen.

civil *adjective* **1** civil; **un matrimonio
civil** a civil marriage; **2** civilian; **la
población civil** the civilian
population.

clarinete *noun* M clarinet.

claro *adjective* **1** light; **un verde
claro** a light green; **un chico de ojos
claros** a guy with light-coloured eyes
(*blue, green, or grey: opposite of 'dark
eyes'*); **2** bright; **un día claro** a bright,
sunny day; **3** clear; **está muy claro**
it's very clear; **no lo tengo muy claro**
I'm not very clear about it.
adverb **1** clearly; **no habla claro** he
doesn't speak clearly; **lo veo claro** I
can see it clearly; **2 ¡claro!** of
course!; **claro que sí** of course; **claro
que no** of course not.

clase *noun* F **1** kind, type; **¿qué
clase de material?** what kind of
material?; **2 de primera clase** top-
quality; **3** class; **la clase de
matemáticas** the maths class; **entro
en clase a las nueve** I start my
classes at nine; **toda la clase ha ido
al museo** the whole class has gone
to the museum; **4 dar clase de algo**
to teach something; **da clase de
física en un colegio** he teaches
physics in a school; **dar clase a
alguien** to give somebody lessons;
me da clases de inglés he gives me
English lessons; **5 dar clase de algo**
to have lessons in something; **da
clases de música por las tardes** she
goes to music lessons in the
evenings; **6** classroom; **¿en qué
clase están?** what classroom are
they in?; **7 clase social** social class;
un familia de clase media a middle-
class family; **8** class (*of travel*); **viajar
en primera clase** to travel first class;
clase turista economy class; **clase
ejecutiva/clase preferente**
business class; **9** class (*elegance*);
tener clase to have class.

clásico/clásica *adjective*
1 classical (*decoration*);
2 traditional (*method*); **3** classic; **la
clásica broma** the classic joke.

clasificación *noun* F
1 classification; **2** qualifying (*in
sports*); **sin posibilidades de
clasificación** with no chance of
qualifying; **3** placings (*in sports*); **la
clasificación es la siguiente** ... the
placings are as follows ...

clasificar *verb* [31] to sort into order
(*papers, for example*).

clasificarse *reflexive verb* [17] to qualify; **clasificarse para la final** to qualify for the final.

clavar *verb* [17] to hammer; **clavar un clavo en la pared** to hammer a nail into the wall.

clave *noun* F 1 key (*to a mystery or problem*); **la clave es …** the key to it is …; 2 code; **mensaje en clave** coded message; 3 clef (*in music*); **clave de sol** treble clef.
adjective key; **un factor clave** a key factor.

clavija *noun* F 1 peg; 2 plug (*for an electrical appliance*).

clavo *noun* M 1 nail; 2 clove (*spice*).

claxon *noun* M horn.

cliente/clienta *noun* M/F 1 customer; 2 client (*of a company or a lawyer*); 3 guest (*in a hotel*).

clima *noun* M climate.

climatizado/climatizada *adjective* air-conditioned.

clínica *noun* F private hospital.

clip *noun* M 1 paper clip; 2 **un clip para el pelo** a hairgrip; 3 **de clip** clip-on.

club *noun* M club; **club de jóvenes** youth club.

cobarde *noun* M/F coward.
adjective cowardly.

cobrador/cobradora *noun* M/F conductor.

cobrar *verb* [17] 1 to get paid; **cobro doscientas mil pesetas al mes** I get paid two hundred thousand pesetas a month; **cobramos a fin de mes** we get paid at the end of the month; **cobra el paro** he's on unemployment benefit; **cobra bastante de pensión** he gets a good pension; 2 to charge; **me cobraron diez mil pesetas por todo** they charged me ten thousand pesetas for everything; **cobrar de más** to overcharge; **cobrar de menos** to undercharge; 3 to collect; **han venido a cobrar la deuda** they've come to collect the money owing; 4 to draw; **cobrar un cheque** to draw a cheque; **cuando vengas a cobrar tu pensión** when you come to draw your pension.

cobre *noun* M copper.

cocer *verb* [41] 1 to boil (*in water*); **cocer algo a fuego lento** to simmer something over a low heat; 2 to bake.

coche *noun* M 1 car; **he venido en coche** I drove here; **coche de carreras** racing car; 2 carriage, coach (*on a train*); **¿qué número de coche es?** what coach number is it?; **coche cama** sleeping car; **coche restaurante** restaurant car; 3 **coche de bomberos** fire engine.

cochecito de bebé *noun* M pram.

cochera *noun* F bus depot.

cocido *noun* M stew (*made with chickpeas*).

cocina *noun* F **1** kitchen; **¿dónde está la cocina?** where's the kitchen?; **2** cooker; **cocina de gas** gas cooker; **cocina eléctrica** electric cooker; **3** cooking; **la cocina española** Spanish cooking; **un libro de cocina** a cookery book.

cocinar *verb* [17] to cook; **cocinar algo a fuego lento** to cook something on a low heat.

cocinero/cocinera *noun* M/F cook.

coco *noun* M **1** coconut; **2** (*informal*) head; **me duele el coco** I've got a headache; ★ **darle al coco** (*informal*) to think; ★ **comerse el coco** (*informal*) to worry your head off; **no te comas el coco** don't worry your head about it; ★ **comerle el coco a alguien** (*informal*) to try to convince somebody.

cocodrilo *noun* M crocodile.

cóctel *noun* M **1** cocktail; **2** cocktail party.

código *noun* M code; **código de barras** bar code; **código postal** postcode.

codo *noun* M elbow.

coger *verb* [3] **1** to take; **voy a coger el autobús** I'm going to take the bus; **¿has cogido los paquetes que había aquí?** have you taken the parcels that were here?; **la cogí del brazo** I took her by the arm; **2** to get; **cogió un resfriado** he got a cold; **coger una insolación** to get sunstroke; **voy a coger entradas para el teatro** I'll get tickets for the theatre; **3** **coger el teléfono** to answer the phone; **4** to catch; **no pudo coger la pelota** he couldn't catch the ball; **¡a que no me coges!** I bet you can't catch me!; **cogieron al asesino** they caught the murderer; **no me dio tiempo a coger el tren** I didn't have time to catch the train; **5** to pick; **coger fresas** to pick strawberries; **coger algo del suelo** to pick something up off the floor.

cogerse *reflexive verb* [3] **1** **cogerse de algo** to hold on to something; **cógete de la barra** hold on to the rail; **2** **se cogieron de la mano** they held hands.

cogido/cogida *adjective* **1** taken; **esta silla ya está cogida** this chair is already taken; **2** **ir cogidos de la mano** to walk hand in hand; **Ir cogidos del brazo** to walk arm in arm.

coincidencia *noun* F coincidence; **¡qué coincidencia!** what a coincidence!; **dio la coincidencia de que …** it so happened that …

coincidir *verb* [19] to coincide.

coja, cojo, etc. *verb* SEE **coger**.

cojín *noun* M cushion.

cojo/coja *adjective* **1** lame; **es cojo** he's lame; **2** **está cojo** he has a limp; **3** **andar a la pata coja** to hop.

col *noun* F cabbage; **coles de Bruselas** Brussels sprouts.

cola *noun* F **1** tail; **2** queue; **hacer cola** to queue up; **saltarse la cola** to jump the queue; **me puse a la cola** I joined the queue; **3** glue; **cola de**

carpintero wood glue; **lo pegué con cola** I glued it.

colada *noun* F laundry; **hacer la colada** to do the washing.

colador *noun* M strainer.

colar *verb* [24] to strain (*vegetables*).

colarse *reflexive verb* [24] **1** to jump the queue; **esa señora se ha colado** that lady has jumped the queue; **2 colarse en un sitio** to get in somewhere without paying; **se coló en el cine** he got into the cinema without paying.

colcha *noun* F bedspread.

colchón *noun* M mattress.

colección *noun* F collection.

coleccionar *verb* [17] to collect.

colega *noun* M/F colleague.

colegial/colegiala *noun* M/F schoolboy/schoolgirl.

colegio *noun* M school; **colegio público** state school; **colegio privado** private school; **un colegio de curas** a catholic boys' school.

coleta *noun* F ponytail.

colgado/colgada *adjective* **1 colgado de algo** hanging from something; **2 el teléfono está mal colgado** the phone's off the hook; **¿tienes el teléfono bien colgado?** have you put the phone down properly?

colgar *verb* [23] **1** to hang; **2 colgar la ropa** to hang out the washing; **3 colgar un cuadro** to put up a picture; **4** to put down (*telephone*);

cuelga el teléfono put the phone down; **me ha colgado** she's hung up on me; **no cuelgue, por favor** hold the line, please.

colgarse *reflexive verb* [23] **colgarse de algo** to hang from something.

coliflor *noun* F cauliflower.

colilla *noun* F cigarette end.

colina *noun* F hill.

collar *noun* M **1** necklace; **un collar de perlas** a string of pearls; **2** collar; **el collar del perro** the dog's collar.

colmo *noun* M **1 el colmo de la incompetencia** the height of incompetence; **2 ¡esto es el colmo!** this is the limit!; **¡y para colmo … !** and to cap it all … !; **sería el colmo que no viniesen** it would be the limit if they didn't come.

colocación *noun* F job; **está buscando colocación** he's looking for a job.

colocar *verb* [31] **1** to put; **colócalo ahí** put it there; **¿dónde coloco esta silla?** where should I put this chair?; **2 aún tenemos que colocar los muebles** we still have to arrange the furniture; **3 colocar a alguien** to get somebody a job; **su tío lo ha colocado** his uncle's got him a job.

colocarse *reflexive verb* [31] to find a job; **se ha colocado muy bien** she's found a very good job.

Colombia *noun* F Colombia.

colombiano/colombiana *noun* M/F *adjective* Colombian.

colonia *noun* F **1** cologne;
2 colony; **3** **una colonia de
vacaciones** a summer camp.

coloquial *adjective* colloquial.

coloquio *noun* M discussion.

color *noun* M colour; **¿de qué color
es?** what colour is it?; **colores claros**
light colours; **es de color azul** it's
blue; **telas de colores** coloured
materials; **televisión en color** colour
television.

colorado/colorada *adjective* red;
ponerse colorado to go red; **¡te has
puesto colorado!** you've gone red!

colorante *noun* M colouring.

colorear *verb* [17] to colour;
colorear algo de rojo to colour
something red.

colorete *noun* M blusher.

columna *noun* F **1** column;
2 spine; **la columna vertebral** the
spine.

columpiar *verb* [17] to push (*on a
swing*).
columpiarse *reflexive verb* [17] to
swing.

columpio *noun* M swing.

coma *noun* F **1** comma; **2** decimal
point; **dos coma cinco** two point
five.
noun M coma; **entrar en coma** to go
into a coma.

comba *noun* F skipping rope; **saltar
a la comba** to skip; **jugar a la comba**
to skip.

combinar *verb* [17] to combine.

comedia *noun* F comedy; **una
comedia musical** a musical.

comedor *noun* M **1** dining-room;
2 dining hall; **3** canteen.

comentar *verb* [17] **1** to talk about;
comentamos un poco la noticia we
talked a bit about the news; **2** to
mention; **me lo comentó de pasada**
he mentioned it to me in passing;
3 to remark; **comentó que** … he
remarked that …

comentario *noun* M comment; **sin
comentarios** no comment.

comenzar *verb* [25] to begin.

comer *verb* [18] **1** to eat; **2** to have
lunch; **normalmente comemos a
las dos** we normally have lunch at
two; **¿qué había de comer?** what
was for lunch?; **3** to take (*a piece in
chess or draughts*); **te como el
caballo** I take your knight.

comercial *adjective* commercial.

comerciante *noun* M/F
1 shopkeeper; **2** trader.

comercio *noun* M **1** trade; **el
comercio de animales exóticos** the
trade in exotic animals; **2** shop; **un
comercio pequeño** a small shop.

comestibles *plural noun* M
foodstuffs.

cometa *noun* F **1** kite; **hacer volar
una cometa** to fly a kite; **2** comet.

cometer *verb* [18] **1** to commit (*a
crime*); **2** **he cometido un error** I've
made a mistake.

cómic *noun* M comic.

cómico/cómica *adjective* **1** funny (*a situation or face*); **2** comedy (*actor*).
noun M/F **1** comedian; **2** comedy actor/comedy actress.

comida *noun* F **1** food; **tenemos suficiente comida** we have enough food; **2** lunch; **a la hora de la comida** at lunch time; **3** meal; **cuatro comidas al día** four meals a day; **mi comida fuerte es a mediodía** my main meal is at midday.

comienza, comienzo¹, etc. *verb* SEE **comenzar**.

comienzo² *noun* M beginning; **al comienzo** in the beginning.

comillas *plural noun* F inverted commas; **poner algo entre comillas** to put something in inverted commas.

comino *noun* M cumin; ★ **me importa un comino** (*informal*) I couldn't care less.

comisaría *noun* F police station.

comisión *noun* F commission.

como *adverb* **1** like; **uno como éste** one like this; **ser como** to be like; **eres como tu padre** you're like your father; **pienso como tú** I agree with you; **2** as; **negro como el carbón** as black as coal; **3** such as; **metales como el hierro** metals such as iron; **4** around; **eran como cincuenta personas** there were around fifty people; **como a las dos y media** around half past two; **5** **como mucho** at the most; **como poco** at least; **serán como poco quince niños** there will be at least fifteen children.
conjunction **1** since; **como estaba cerca de su casa, me pasé a verla** since I was near her house, I went to see her; **2** if; **como no tengas cuidado te vas a caer** if you're not careful you'll fall; **3** **como si** as if; **como si no me importase** as if I didn't care; **4** the way; **así es como lo hizo** that's the way he did it; **5** **como quieras** whatever you want; however you want; **hazlo como quieras** do it however you want.

cómo *adverb* **1** how; **¿cómo estás?** how are you?; **¿cómo se dice 'mesa' en francés?** how do you say 'table' in French?; **¿cómo se escribe tu nombre?** how do you write your name?; **no sé cómo se enteraron** I don't know how they found out; **2** **¿cómo es?** what's it like?; **¿cómo es tu casa?** what's your house like?; **3** **¿cómo?** pardon? (*when you haven't heard properly*); **4** (*in exclamations*) **¡cómo quema!** it's so hot!; **¡cómo se parecen!** they really look like each other!; **¡cómo no!** of course!; **¡cómo! ¿no la has visto aún?** what! you haven't seen her yet?

cómoda¹ *noun* F chest of drawers.

comodín *noun* M joker (*in cards*).

cómodo/cómoda² *adjective* comfortable; **¿estás cómodo?** are you comfortable?; **un sillón muy cómodo** a very comfortable armchair; **ponerse cómodo** to make yourself comfortable.

compact disc *noun* M **1** CD; **2** CD player.

compañero/compañera *noun* M/F **1** colleague; **mis compañeros de trabajo** my colleagues at work; **2** **un compañero de clase** a school mate; **su compañera de piso** her flatmate; **3** partner (*in a relationship*).

compañía *noun* F company; **hacerle compañía a alguien** to keep somebody company; **el director de la compañía** the company director.

comparación *noun* F comparison; **hacer una comparación** to make a comparison; **en comparación con** in comparison with.

comparar *verb* [17] to compare.

compartir *verb* [19] to share; **compartir algo con alguien** to share something with somebody; **compartieron su comida conmigo** they shared their food with me.

compás *noun* M **1** time, rhythm; **llevar el compás** to keep time; **2** pair of compasses.

compensar *verb* [29] to compensate.

competencia *noun* F competition; **nos hacen la competencia** they're in competition with us.

competición *noun* F competition (*in a magazine, for example*).

competir *verb* [57] to compete.

compita, compito, etc. *verb* SEE **competir**.

completar *verb* [17] to complete.

completo/completa *adjective* **1** complete; **2** full; **el hotel está completo** the hotel is full; **'completo'** 'no vacancies'.

complicado/complicada *adjective* complicated.

complicar *verb* [31] to complicate.

complicarse *reflexive verb* [31] to become complicated; **la situación se ha complicado** the situation has become complicated.

componer *verb* [11] **1** to make up; **el equipo está compuesto de once jugadores** the team is made up of eleven players; **2** to compose (*music or a poem*).

componerse *reflexive verb* [11] **componerse de** to be made up of.

comportamiento *noun* M behaviour; **mal comportamiento** bad behaviour.

comportarse *reflexive verb* [17] to behave; **comportarse mal** to misbehave.

composición *noun* F composition.

compositor/compositora *noun* M/F composer.

compra *noun* F purchase; **fue una buena compra** it was a good buy; **ir de compras** to go shopping; **hacer la compra** to do the shopping.

comprar *verb* [17] **1** to buy; **2** **comprar algo a alguien** to buy something for somebody (*as a* *present*); **le he comprado un jersey por su cumpleaños** I've bought him a jumper for his birthday; **3 comprar algo a alguien** to buy something from somebody; **voy a comprarle su bicicleta** I'm going to buy his bike from him.

comprender *verb* [18] to understand; **no me comprenden** they don't understand me; **no comprendo su actitud** I don't understand his attitude.

compresa *noun* F sanitary towel.

comprimido *noun* M pill.

comprobar *verb* [24] to check; **creo que sí, pero voy a comprobarlo** I think so, but I'm going to check it.

compromiso *noun* M
1 commitment; **compromiso político** political commitment;
2 obligation; **sin compromiso** without obligation; **3 poner a alguien en un compromiso** to put somebody in an awkward situation; **ahora me has puesto en un compromiso** now you've put me in an awkward situation.

computador/computadora *noun* M/F computer (*large, mainframe machine*).

común *adjective* common; **en común** in common; **no tenemos nada en común** we have nothing in common; **trabajar en común** to work together.

comunicación *noun* F
1 communication; **2 ponerse en comunicación con alguien** to get in touch with someone; **3 cortarse la comunicación** to be cut off (*on the phone*); **se ha cortado la comunicación** I've been cut off; **4 un barrio con buena comunicación** an area with good public transport services.

comunicar *verb* [31] **1** to inform; **debo comunicarles que …** I must inform you that …; **2** to be engaged (*a telephone*); **estaba comunicando** it was engaged.

comunicarse *reflexive verb* [31] **1** to communicate; **comunicarse por carta** to communicate by letter; **2** to be connected.

comunidad *noun* F community; **la Comunidad Europea** the European Community.

comunión *noun* F communion; **hacer la primera comunión** to take communion for the first time.

con *preposition* **1** with; **lo hice con un cuchillo** I did it with a knife; **2** to; **hablar con alguien** to speak to somebody; **estar casado con alguien** to be married to somebody; **3 bistec con patatas** steak and chips; **pan con mantequilla** bread and butter; **4 con tal de que** as long as; **te lo dejo, con tal de que lo cuides** I'll lend it to you as long as you look after it.

concentración *noun* F concentration.

concentrar *verb* [17] to concentrate.

concentrarse *reflexive verb* [17] to concentrate; **me concentré en mi trabajo** I concentrated on my work.

concha *noun* F shell.

concierto *noun* M concert.

conclusión *noun* F conclusion; **llegar a una conclusión** to reach a conclusion.

concurrido/concurrida *adjective* **1** busy (*bar or street*); **2** well-attended (*concert or exhibition*).

concurso *noun* M competition; **concurso hípico** show-jumping competition; **programa concurso** quiz show.

conde *noun* M count.

condesa *noun* F countess.

condición *noun* F condition; **a condición de que/con la condición de que** on condition that.

condón *noun* M condom.

conducir *verb* [60] **1** to drive; **yo conduzco** I'll drive; **2** to lead; **el camino que conduce al pueblo** the road that leads to the village.

conductor/conductora *noun* M/F driver.

conduje, condujo *verb* SEE **conducir**.

conduzca, conduzco, etc. *verb* SEE **conducir**.

conectar *verb* [17] to connect; **el teléfono aún no está conectado** the telephone's not connected yet.

conejillo de Indias *noun* M guinea pig.

conejo/coneja *noun* M/F rabbit.

conexión *noun* F connection.

conferencia *noun* F **1** lecture; **una conferencia de prensa** a press conference; **2** long-distance call; **poner una conferencia a alguien** to make a long distance call to somebody.

confesar *verb* [29] to confess.

confianza *noun* F **1** trust; **una persona de confianza** a trustworthy person; **2 tener confianza en alguien** to have confidence in somebody; **tiene mucha confianza en sí mismo** he's very self-confident; **3 tener confianza con alguien** to know somebody very well; **tenemos mucha confianza** we know each other very well.

confiar *verb* [32] to trust; **confío en ti** I trust you.

confidencia *noun* F confidence; **hacerle una confidencia a alguien** to tell somebody something in confidence.

confirmar *verb* [17] to confirm.

confitería *noun* F patisserie.

confitura *noun* F fruit preserve.

conforme *adjective* **1 estar conforme** to agree; **no estoy conforme** I don't agree; **¿conforme?** do you agree?; **¡conforme!** ok!; **2 estar conforme con algo** to be happy with something.

confortable *adjective*
comfortable.

confortar *verb* [17] to comfort.

confundir *verb* [19] **1** to confuse;
no me confundas don't confuse me;
2 to get mixed up; **he confundido las
fechas** I've got the dates mixed up;
3 confundir a alguien con alguien
to mistake somebody for somebody;
la confundí con Cristina I mistook
her for Cristina.
confundirse *reflexive verb* [19] **1** to
make a mistake; **creo que te has
confundido con la cuenta** I think
you've made a mistake with the bill;
2 se confundió de carpeta he got
the wrong folder.

confusión *noun* F confusion.

confuso/confusa *adjective*
1 confused; **estaba confuso** he was
confused; **2** confusing; **esto es muy
confuso** this is very confusing.

congelado/congelada *adjective*
1 frozen; **¡estoy congelada!** I'm
freezing!; **alimentos congelados**
frozen food; **2 murió congelado** he
died from exposure; **3 tenía un dedo
congelado** he had frostbite in one
finger.

congelador *noun* M **1** freezer
compartment; **2** deep freezer.

congelar *verb* [17] to freeze.
congelarse *reflexive verb* [17] to
freeze; **¡me estoy congelando!** I'm
freezing!

conjugar *verb* [28] to conjugate.

conjunto¹/conjunta *adjective*
joint; **un esfuerzo conjunto** a joint
effort.

conjunto² *noun* M **1** group; **un
conjunto de personas** a group of
people; **un conjunto de música** a
pop group; **2** collection; **un
conjunto de cosas** a collection of
things; **3** outfit; **¡qué conjunto más
bonito!** what a nice outfit!; **un
conjunto de falda y chaleco** a
matching skirt and waistcoat; **hacer
conjunto con algo** to match
something; **4 en conjunto** as a
whole.

conmigo *pronoun* **1** with me; **ven
conmigo** come with me; **2** to me; **no
habló conmigo** he didn't talk to me;
3 conmigo mismo/misma with
myself; **no estoy contento conmigo
mismo** I'm not happy with myself.

conocer *verb* [35] **1** to know;
conozco la historia I know that
story; **los conozco de vista** I know
them by sight; **se conocen bien** they
know each other well; **2** to meet;
¿conoces a su hermana? have you
met her sister?; **aún no conozco al
nuevo profesor** I haven't met the
new teacher yet; **3 ¿conoces
España?** have you been to Spain?;
4 to recognize; **te conocí por la
forma de andar** I recognized you by
the way you walk.

conocido/conocida *noun* M/F
acquaintance.
adjective **1** well-known (*actor or*

song); **2** familiar; **una cara conocida** a familiar face.

conocimiento *noun* M knowledge.

conozca, conozco, etc. *verb* SEE **conocer**.

conque *conjunction* so; **conque ésta es tu novia** so, this is your girlfriend.

conseguir *verb* [64] **1** to achieve; **han conseguido su objetivo** they've achieved their objective; **2** to get; **he conseguido un trabajo** I've got a job.

consejero/consejera *noun* M/F **1** adviser; **2** minister (*in certain autonomous Spanish regions*).

consejo *noun* M **1** piece of advice; **te voy a dar un consejo** I'm going to give you a piece of advice; **2** advice; **no hacen caso de mis consejos** they aren't following my advice; **3** board; **el consejo de administración** the board of directors; **consejo escolar** board of governors (*of a school*); **4 un consejo de ministros** a cabinet meeting; **5 el Consejo de Europa** the Council of Europe.

conserje *noun* M/F **1** caretaker (*in a school or a public building*); **2** receptionist (*in a hotel*).

conservador/conservadora *noun* M/F *adjective* conservative.

conservar *verb* [17] **1** to preserve (*food*); **2** to keep up (*traditions*); **3** to keep; **conservo todas tus cartas** I keep all your letters; **intenta**

conservar la calma try to keep calm.
conservarse *reflexive verb* [17] to keep (*food*); **las manzanas se conservan bien** apples keep well.

conservas *plural noun* F tinned food.

considerar *verb* [17] to consider.

consiga, consigo¹, consiguiendo, etc. *verb* SEE **conseguir**.

consigna *noun* F left-luggage office.

consigo² *pronoun* **1** with him/her; **lo trae consigo** he's bringing it with him/she's bringing it with her; **2 consigo mismo** with himself; **consigo misma** with herself; **no está contento consigo mismo** he is not happy with himself; **3 consigo mismo** to himself; **consigo misma** to herself; **estaba hablando consigo misma** she was talking to herself; **4** with them; **el dinero que tenían consigo** the money they had with them; **5** with you (*talking politely to somebody*); **si usted quiere lo puede traer consigo** if you wish, you can bring it with you.

consistir *verb* [19] **consistir en algo** to consist of something; **consiste en tres piezas de madera** it consists of three pieces of wood; **el trabajo consiste en …** the job involves …

consonante *noun* F consonant.

constipado¹/constipada *adjective* **estar constipado** to have a cold.

constipado² *noun* M cold; **coger un constipado** to catch a cold.

constructor/constructora *noun* M/F builder.

construir *verb* [54] to build.

construya, construyendo, construyo, etc. *verb* SEE **construir**.

consulado *noun* M consulate.

consulta *noun* F 1 **hacer una consulta** to ask something; 2 **de consulta** reference; **libro de consulta** reference book; 3 surgery; **tiene su consulta en esta calle** his surgery is in this street; **horas de consulta** surgery hours.

consultar *verb* [17] 1 to consult; **consultarle algo a alguien** to consult somebody about something; 2 **tengo que consultarlo en diccionario** I have to look it up in the dictionary.

consultorio *noun* M surgery.

contable *noun* M/F accountant.

contacto *noun* M 1 contact; **estar en contacto** to be in contact; 2 ignition (*in a car*).

contado *noun* M **al contado** cash; **pagar al contado** to pay cash; **lo compré al contado** I paid for it in cash.

contador *noun* M meter.

contagiar *verb* [17] to pass on (*an illness*); **no me beses, no quiero contagiarte el resfriado** don't kiss me, I don't want to give you my cold.

contagiarse *reflexive verb* [17] to become infected; **se ha contagiado de su hermana** she's got it from her sister.

contaminación *noun* F 1 pollution; 2 contamination (*by radioactivity*).

contaminar *verb* [17] 1 to pollute (*air or water, for example*); 2 to contaminate (*with radioactivity*).

contar *verb* [24] 1 to count; **cuenta el dinero** count the money; 2 **contar con alguien** to count on somebody; **nunca puedo contar contigo** I can never count on you; 3 to tell; **cuéntamelo** tell me about it; **le conté el secreto** I told him the secret.

contenedor *noun* M 1 container; 2 skip; 3 **un contenedor de vidrio** a bottle bank.

contener *verb* [9] 1 to contain; **no contiene conservantes** it does not contain preservatives; 2 **contener las lágrimas** to hold back the tears; **contener la risa** to stop yourself laughing; **contener la respiración** to hold your breath.

contenido *noun* M 1 contents; **el contenido de la botella** the contents of the bottle; 2 content; **el contenido del libro** the content of the book.

contento/contenta *adjective* 1 happy; **los niños estaban muy contentos** the children were very happy; 2 pleased; **estoy contento de verte** I'm pleased to see you.

contestación *noun* F **1** answer; **no nos dio una contestación** he didn't give us an answer; **2** reply; **quedo a la espera de su contestación** looking forward to your reply.

contestador (automático) *noun* M answering machine.

contestar *verb* [17] **1** answer; **contestar el teléfono** to answer the phone; **no contestó** he didn't answer; **2** reply; **no ha contestado a mi carta** he hasn't replied to my letter.

contigo *pronoun* **1** with you; **yo voy contigo** I'll go with you; **2** to you; **no estoy hablando contigo** I'm not talking to you; **3 contigo mismo/misma** with yourself; **¿estás contento contigo mismo?** are you pleased with yourself?

continente *noun* M continent.

continuación *noun* F continuation; **a continuación** … next …

continuar *verb* [20] to continue; **continuaron hablando** they went on talking; **continuará** to be continued.

continuo/continua *adjective* constant.

contra *preposition* **1** against; **se apoyó contra la pared** he leant against the wall; **son dos contra uno** it's two against one; **estar en contra de algo** to be against something; **2 chocar contra algo** to run into something.

contrabandista *noun* M/F smuggler.

contrabando *noun* M **1** smuggling; **pasar algo de contrabando** to smuggle something; **2** smuggled goods.

contrario/contraria *adjective* **1** opposite; **la dirección contraria** the opposite direction; **todo lo contrario** quite the opposite; **soy contrario a las reformas** I'm opposed to the reforms; **2 pasarse al bando contrario** to change sides; **3 al contrario** on the contrary; **al contrario, me gusta mucho** on the contrary, I like it a lot; **4 por el contrario** on the other hand; **5 de lo contrario** otherwise.

contrato *noun* M contract.

contribución *noun* F **1** contribution; **2** tax.

control *noun* M **1** control; **bajo control** under control; **control de pasaportes** passport control; **control remoto** remote control; **2 llevar el control de algo** to keep a check on something; **3** test.

controlar *verb* [17] **1** to control; **2** to keep a check on; **3 controlar la línea** to watch you weight.

convencer *verb* [44] **1** to convince; **2** to persuade; **le convencimos para que fuera** we persuaded him to go; **3 no me convence mucho la idea** I'm not sure about the idea.

conveniente *adjective* **1** convenient; **2** advisable.

convenir *verb* [15] **1 te conviene preguntar** you should ask; **te conviene descansar** you should

rest; **conviene informarse antes** it's
advisable to find out in advance;
2 (*in negative sentences*) **no te
conviene cansarte** you should avoid
tiring yourself out; **por ese sueldo
no te conviene** for that salary it's not
worth your while; **3 convenir en
algo** to agree on something;
4 sueldo a convenir salary
negotiable.

convenza, convenzo, etc. *verb*
SEE **convencer**.

conversación *noun* F
conversation.

convertir *verb* [14] **1 convertir algo
en algo** to turn something into
something; **convertir agua en vino**
to turn water into wine; **convertir
libras en pesetas** to convert pounds
into pesetas; **2** to convert (*to a
religion*).
convertirse *reflexive verb* [14]
1 convertirse en algo to turn into
something; **2** to convert;
convertirse al budismo to convert to
Buddhism.

convierta, convierto, etc. *verb*
SEE **convertir**.

coñac *noun* M brandy.

copa *noun* F **1** wine glass; **una copa
de vino** a glass of wine; **2** drink; **te
invito a una copa** I'll buy you a drink;
tomar una copa to have a drink.

copia *noun* F copy; **copia de
seguridad** back-up copy.

copiar *verb* [17] **1** to copy; **2** to make
a copy of; **3** to copy down.

coraje *noun* M courage.

corazón *noun* M heart; **un ataque
al corazón** a heart attack; **una
persona de buen corazón** a kind-
hearted person; ★ **partirle el
corazón a alguien** to break
someone's heart.

corbata *noun* F tie.

corcho *noun* M cork.

cordero *noun* M lamb; **una pierna
de cordero** a leg of lamb; **una
chuleta de cordero** a lamb chop.

cordón *noun* M string; **un cordón
de zapato** a shoelace.

coro *noun* M choir; **a coro** in chorus.

corona *noun* F **1** crown; **2** wreath;
una corona de flores a wreath of
flowers.

corral *noun* M farmyard.

correa *noun* F **1** strap; **correa de
reloj** watchstrap; **2** lead (*for a dog*).

correcto/correcta *adjective*
1 correct; **la respuesta correcta** the
correct answer; **2** polite; **siempre es
muy correcto** he's always very
polite.

corredor/corredora *noun* M/F
1 runner; **corredor de fondo** long-
distance runner; **2 corredor de
coches** racing driver.

corregir *verb* [48] to correct.

correo *noun* M post; **mandar algo
por correo** to send something by
post; **echar algo al correo** to post
something; **correo aéreo** airmail; (**la

oficina de) correos the post office; **correo urgente** special delivery.

correr *verb* [18] **1** to run; **crucé la calle corriendo** I ran across the street; **salió corriendo de la habitación** she ran out of the room; **bajar las escaleras corriendo** to run down the stairs; **echar a correr** to start running; **correr mucho** to run very fast (*a person*); to drive very fast (*a driver*); to go very fast (*a car or bike*); **2 ¡corre, vístete!** hurry up and get dressed!; **hice la comida corriendo** I made dinner quickly; **vino corriendo a verme** she rushed to see me; **se tiene que marchar corriendo** he has to rush off; **3 correr las cortinas** to draw the curtains; **4 no debemos correr riesgos** we shouldn't take any risks; **5 correr peligro** to be in danger.

correspondiente *adjective* corresponding.

corresponsal *noun* M/F correspondent.

corrida *noun* F bullfight.

corriente *noun* F **1** current (*water or electricity*); **me ha dado la corriente** I got an electric shock; **no hay corriente** there's no electricity; **2** draught; **hace corriente** there's a draught.
adjective **1** common; **un error muy corriente** a very common mistake; **una chica normal y corriente** an ordinary kind of girl; **lo más corriente es …** the most usual thing is …; **2 agua corriente** running water; **3 estar al corriente de algo** to be aware of something; **mantener a alguien al corriente de algo** to keep somebody up to date about something.

corrija, corrijo, etc. *verb* SEE **corregir**.

corrompido/corrompida *adjective* corrupt.

corrupto/corrupta *adjective* corrupt.

cortacésped *noun* M lawnmower.

cortado¹ *noun* M small coffee (*with a dash of milk*).

cortado²/cortada *adjective* **1** closed (*a road or street*); **2 la leche está cortada** the milk is sour; **la mayonesa está cortada** the mayonnaise has separated; **3 ser muy cortado** (*informal*) to be very shy; **ser un poco cortado** (*informal*) to be a bit shy; **4 estar cortado** (*informal*) to be embarrassed.

cortar *verb* [17] **1** to cut; **cortar un pastel** to cut a cake; **cortar algo por la mitad** to cut something in two; **cortar algo a rodajas** to slice something; **2 cortar el césped** to mow the lawn; **3** to chop; **cortar leña** to chop wood; **cortar un árbol** to chop down a tree; **4** to cut off; **nos han cortado la luz** our electricity has been cut off; **corta esa punta** cut this end off.

cortarse *reflexive verb* [17] **1** to cut oneself; **me he cortado la mano** I've cut my hand; **2 cortarse el pelo** to have your hair cut; **mañana me voy a cortar el pelo** I'm going to have my

hair cut tomorrow; **3 se ha cortado
el agua** the water's been cut off; **4** to
curdle; **5** (*informal*) to get
embarrassed **¡no te cortes!** don't get
embarrassed!

cortaúñas *noun* M nail clippers.

corte[1] *noun* M **1** cut; **hacerse un
corte** to cut yourself; **se hizo un
corte en el dedo** he cut his finger; **un
corte de pelo** a haircut; **ha habido
un corte de agua** the water's been
cut off; **2 corte y confección**
dressmaking; **3** (*informal*)
embarrassment; **me da corte
preguntar** I'm embarrassed to ask;
¡qué corte! how embarrassing!

corte[2] *noun* F **1** court; **2 las Cortes**
the Spanish Parliament.

cortés *adjective* polite.

corteza *noun* F **1** bark (*of a tree*);
2 rind (*of cheese*); **3** crust (*of bread*);
4 peel (*of an orange or a lemon*).

cortina *noun* F curtain.

corto/corta *adjective* short.

cosa *noun* F **1** thing; **te he
comprado una cosa** I've bought
something for you; **¿qué tal van las
cosas?** how are things going?; **se
llevó todas sus cosas** he took all his
things; **¡qué cosa más rara!** how
strange!; **2 cualquier cosa**
anything; **3 alguna cosa**
something; **por si pasa alguna cosa**
in case something happens;
4 alguna cosa anything (*in
questions*); **¿buscas alguna cosa en
especial?** are you looking for
anything in particular?; **¿quiere**

alguna otra cosa? do you want
anything else?

cosecha *noun* F **1** harvest; **2** crop;
3 vintage.

cosechar *verb* [17] to harvest.

coser *verb* [18] to sew.

cosmético[1] *noun* M cosmetic.

cosmético[2]**/cosmética**
adjective cosmetic.

cosquillas *plural noun* F **hacerle
cosquillas a alguien** to tickle
somebody; **tener cosquillas** to be
ticklish.

costa *noun* F coast.

costado *noun* M side.

costar *verb* [24] **1** to cost; **¿cuánto
cuesta?** how much is it?; **cuesta
muy caro** it's very expensive; **la
comida cuesta poco** food is cheap;
me costó barato it didn't cost me
very much; **2** to be hard; **cuesta
mucho entenderlo** it's very hard to
understand; **cuesta un poco
acostumbrarse** it takes a bit of
getting used to; **me costó hacerlo** I
found it difficult to do.

Costa Rica *noun* F Costa Rica.

coste *noun* M cost.

costilla *noun* F rib.

costoso/costosa *adjective*
expensive.

costra *noun* F scab.

costumbre *noun* F **1** habit; **coger
la costumbre de hacer algo** to get
into the habit of doing something;

tengo la costumbre de leer un poco antes de dormir I normally read for a bit before I go to sleep; **por costumbre** out of habit; **2 de costumbre** usual; **el lugar de costumbre** the usual place; **3** custom (*in a country or place*).

costura *noun* F **1** needlework; **2** seam.

cotilla *noun* M/F
adjective gossip; **es muy cotilla** he's such a gossip.

cotillear *verb* [17] to gossip.

COU *abbreviation* M (*short for: Curso de Orientación Universitaria*) preparation course for university entrance.

creación *noun* F creation.

creador/creadora *noun* M/F creator.
adjective creative.

crear *verb* [17] to create.

crecer *verb* [35] **1** to grow; **¡cuánto has crecido!** you've really grown!; **2** to grow up; **creció en Escocia** she grew up in Scotalnd.

crédito *noun* M **1** credit (*in a shop, for example*); **tengo crédito aquí** they give me credit here; **2** loan; **me han concedido el crédito** they've granted me the loan; **crédito hipotecario** mortgage.

creer *verb* [37] **1** to think; **creo que se llama Nekane** I think she's called Nekane; **¿crees que me llamará?** do you think he'll phone me?; **creo que sí** I think so; **no creo** I don't think so;

2 to believe; **no creo en el destino** I don't believe in fate; **¡no lo puedo creer!** I don't believe it!

creíble *adjective* believable.

crema *noun* F cream; **crema hidratante** moisturizer; **crema bronceadora** suntan lotion.

cremallera *noun* F zip; **subirse la cremallera** to do up your zip.

crepúsculo *noun* M twilight.

creyendo, creyó, etc. *verb* SEE **creer**.

crezca, crezco, etc. *verb* SEE **crecer**.

cría *noun* F baby animal; **una cría de leopardo** a baby leopard.

criada *noun* F maid.

criado *noun* M servant.

criar *verb* [17] **1** to bring up; **lo crió su tía** he was brought up by his aunt; **2** to raise; **criar ganado** to raise cattle.

criarse *reflexive verb* [17] to grow up; **se crió en un pueblo** he grew up in a village.

crimen *noun* M **1** crime; **cometer un crimen** to commit a crime; **2** murder.

criminal *noun* M/F criminal.

crisis *noun* F crisis; **estar en crisis** to be in crisis; **sufrir una crisis nerviosa** to have a nervous breakdown.

cristal *noun* M **1** glass; **viene en botella de cristal** it comes in a glass bottle; **2** cristal; **cristal tallado** cut glass; **3** window pane; **tengo que limpiar los cristales del salón** I've got to clean the sitting-room windows; **la pelota rompió un cristal** the ball broke a window; **4** piece of broken glass; **el suelo estaba lleno de cristales** the floor was covered with broken glass.

cristiano/cristiana *noun* M/F *adjective* Christian.

Cristo *noun* M Christ.

crítica *noun* F **1** criticism; **recibió duras críticas** he's come in for a lot of harsh criticism; **2** review; **la película ha recibido muy buenas críticas** the film has got very good reviews.

criticar *verb* [31] **1** to criticize; **2** to review.

cromo *noun* M sticker.

cruce (*plural* **cruces**) *noun* M **1** crossroads; **2** 'cruce peligroso' 'dangerous junction'; **3** crossing; **cruce de peatones** pedestrian crossing.

crucero *noun* M cruise.

crucigrama *noun* M crossword.

crudo/cruda *adjective* **1** raw; **una zanahoria cruda** a raw carrot; **2 la verdura aún está cruda** the vegetables aren't cooked yet; **3** harsh; **la cruda realidad** the harsh reality.

cruel *adjective* cruel.

cruz (*plural* **cruces**) *noun* F **1** cross; **2 ¿cara o cruz?** heads or tails?

cruzar *verb* [22] to cross; **ten cuidado al cruzar** be careful when you cross the road; **crucé la calle corriendo** I ran across the road; **cruzar los brazos** to cross your arms.

cruzarse *reflexive verb* [22] **1** to intersect (*roads, for example*); **2** to pass each other; **los dos coches se cruzaron** the two cars passed each other; **3 me crucé con ella en la calle** I met her in the street.

Cruz Roja *noun* F Red Cross.

cuaderno *noun* M **1** exercise book; **2** notebook.

cuadra *noun* F stable.

cuadrado¹/cuadrada *adjective* square; **de forma cuadrada** square-shaped.

cuadrado² *noun* M square.

cuadro *noun* M **1** painting; **2** picture; **3 a cuadros/de cuadros** checked; **una tela a cuadros** a piece of checked material.

cual *pronoun* **1** el cual/la cual/los cuales/las cuales who; **pregunté a mi hermano, el cual me dio las señas** I asked my brother, who gave me the address; **2 el cual/la cual/los cuales/las cuales** whom; **los familiares a los cuales invitó** the relatives whom he invited; **3 el cual/ la cual/los cuales/las cuales** which; **los instrumentos con los cuales se hace la operación** the instruments with which the operation is carried out; **4 lo cual** which; **no ha llamado, lo cual es extraño** he hasn't rung, which is strange; **5 cada cual** everybody; **6 por lo cual** therefore.

cuál *pronoun* 1 which; **¿cuál te gusta?** which do you like?; 2 what; **¿cuál es el problema?** what's the problem?

cualesquiera *adjective, pronoun* SEE **cualquiera**.

cualidad *noun* F quality.

cualquier *adjective* SEE **cualquiera**.

cualquiera (*plural* **cualesquiera**) *adjective* ('*cualquiera*' *becomes* '*cualquier*' *if you put it before a singular noun*) any; **en un país cualquiera** in any country; **cualquier cosa** anything; **cualquier persona** anybody; **si por cualquier motivo** if for any reason.
pronoun 1 anybody, anyone; **cualquiera sabe algo así** anybody knows that sort of thing; 2 either; **'¿cuál de los dos quieres?'** – **'cualquiera'** 'which of the two do you want?' – 'either'; 3 whichever (*when referring to more than two people or things*); **coge cualquiera de los que hay ahí** pick whichever you want from the ones that are there.

cuando *conjunction* when?; **cuando estuve en Barcelona** when I was in Barcelona; **cuando la vea la próxima semana** when I see her next week.

cuándo *adverb* when; **¿cuándo la conociste?** when did you meet her?; **¿desde cuándo?** since when?

cuanto¹/cuanta *adjective* 1 as much as; **cuanta tela necesites** as much fabric as you need; 2 **cuantos/**
cuantas as many as; **compra cuantos libros necesites** buy as many books as you need; 3 **unos cuantos** a few; **unos cuantos empleados** a few employees.
pronoun 1 **tengo cuanto necesito** I've got everything I need; 2 **cuantos/cuantas** as many as; **coge cuantas quieras** take as many as you want; 3 **unos cuantos** a few.

cuanto² *adverb* 1 as much as; **llama cuanto quieras** phone as much as you want; 2 **cuanto más** the more; **cuanto más insiste, menos quiero ayudarlo** the more he insists, the less I want to help him; **cuanto menos ruido hagas mejor** the less noise you make, the better; 3 **cuanto antes** as soon as possible; 4 **en cuanto pueda** as soon as I can.

cuánto¹/cuánta *adjective* 1 **cuánto/cuánta** how much; **¿cuánto café quieres?** how much coffee do you want?; 2 **cuántos/cuántas** how many; **¿cuántas tazas saco?** how many cups should I put out?; 3 (*in exclamations*) **¡cuántas personas hay!** there are so many people!; **¡cuánta comida has hecho!** you've made so much food!; 4 (*in time*) **¿cuánto tiempo has tardado en hacerlo?** how long did you take to do it?; **¿cada cuánto tiempo la ves?** how often do you see her?
pronoun 1 **cuánto/cuánta** how much; **'pon agua'** – **'¿cuánta?'** 'add some water'- 'how much?'; 2 **cuántos/cuántas** how many; **dime cuántos necesitas** tell me how many you need; 3 how long (*in*

time); **¿cuánto se tarda en llegar?**
how long does it take to get there?;
¿cada cuánto la llamas? how often
do you call her?; **4** (*in exclamations*)
¡cuántas hay! there are so many!;
¡cuánto ha quedado! there's so
much left!; **¡cuánto has tardado!**
you've taken so long!

cuánto² *adverb* **1** how much;
¿cuánto cuesta? how much is it?; **no
sabes cuánto te he echado de
menos** you don't know how much
I've missed you; **2** **¿cuánto mide la
mesa?** what's the size of the table?;
¿cuánto mide de ancho? how wide
is it?; **3** (*in exclamations*) **¡cuánto te
quiero!** I love you so much!

cuarenta *number* forty; **mi madre
tiene cuarenta años** my mum's forty;
cuarenta y siete forty-seven.

cuaresma *noun* F Lent.

cuarta¹ *noun* F fourth gear; **meter la
cuarta** to change into fourth.

cuarto¹ *noun* M **1** room; **el cuarto
de estar** the living room; **el cuarto
de baño** the bathroom; **el cuarto de
los niños** the children's bedroom;
2 quarter (*in clock time*); **son las
dos y cuarto** it's quarter past two; **a
las doce menos cuarto** at quarter to
twelve; **3** quarter; **corté la tarta en
cuatro cuartos** I cut the cake into
four quarters; **un cuarto de kilo** a
quarter of a kilo.

cuarto²/cuarta² *adjective* fourth;
en el cuarto piso on the fourth floor;
llegar en cuarto lugar to finish in
fourth position.

cuatro *number* **1** four; **Juan tiene
cuatro años** Juan's four (years old);
2 fourth (*in dates*); **el cuatro de
mayo** the fourth of May; **3** four (*in
clock time*); **son las cuatro** it's four
o'clock.

cuatrocientos/cuatrocientas
number four hundred;
cuatrocientos quince four hundred
and fifteen.

Cuba *noun* F Cuba.

cubierto¹/cubierta *adjective*
covered.

cubierto² *noun* M **1** **los cubiertos**
the cutlery; **pon los cubiertos en la
mesa** put the knives and forks on the
table; **cubiertos de plata** silver
cutlery; **2** **poner otro cubierto en la
mesa** to lay another place at the
table.

cubo *noun* M **1** cube; **2** bucket; **un
cubo de agua** a bucket of water; **3** **el
cubo de la basura** the bin.

cubrecama *noun* M bedspread.

cubrir *verb* [46] to cover.
cubrirse *reflexive verb* [46] **1** to cover
yourself; **me cubrí las rodillas** I
covered my legs; **2** to cloud over;
**esta mañana hacía sol, pero ahora
se ha cubierto** this morning it was
sunny, but now it's clouded over.

cucaracha *noun* F cockroach.

cuchara *noun* F spoon; **cuchara de
postre** dessert spoon; **cuchara
sopera** soup spoon.

cucharada *noun* F spoonful.

cucharadita *noun* F teaspoonful.

cucharilla, cucharita *noun* F teaspoon; **una cucharilla de café/ una cucharita de café** a coffee spoon.

cuchichear *verb* [17] to whisper.

cuchilla *noun* F blade; **una cuchilla de afeitar** a razor blade.

cuchillo *noun* M knife.

cuelga, cuelgo, etc. *verb* SEE **colgar**.

cuello *noun* M 1 neck; 2 collar; **el cuello de la camisa** the shirt collar; **un jersey de cuello redondo** a round-neck jumper; **un jersey de cuello alto** a polo-neck jumper.

cuenco *noun* M bowl.

cuenta¹, cuento¹, etc. *verb* SEE **contar**.

cuenta² *noun* F 1 bill; **¿nos puede traer la cuenta, por favor?** could you bring us the bill, please?; 2 sum; **hacer una cuenta** to do a sum; **hacer cuentas** to work something out; **haz las cuentas de lo que te debo** work out how much I owe you; 3 **llevar la cuenta de algo** to keep count of something; **perder la cuenta de algo** to lose count of something; 4 account; **cuenta corriente** current account; **cuenta de ahorros** savings account; **abrir una cuenta** to open an account; 5 **tener algo en cuenta** to bear something in mind; 6 **darse cuenta de algo** to realize something; **me di cuenta de que había perdido la cartera** I realized I'd lost my wallet; 7 **trabajar por su cuenta** to be self-employed; **trabajo por mi cuenta** I'm self-employed; **montar una tienda por su cuenta** to set up your own shop; 8 **más de la cuenta** too much; **bebieron más de la cuenta** they drank too much; 9 **cuenta atrás** countdown; 10 bead (*of necklace*).

cuento² *noun* M 1 short story; 2 tale; **un cuento de hadas** a fairy tale; 3 **eso no viene a cuento** that has nothing to do with it; ★ **¡eso es un cuento chino!** (*informal*) that's a load of rubbish!

cuerda *noun* F 1 rope; 2 **saltar a la cuerda** to skip; 3 **dar cuerda a un juguete** to wind up a toy; **dar cuerda a un reloj** to wind a watch.

cuerno *noun* M 1 horn; 2 antler.

cuero *noun* M leather; **un bolso de cuero** a leather bag.

cuerpo *noun* M body.

cuervo *noun* M crow.

cuesta¹, cueste, etc. *verb* SEE **costar**.

cuesta² *noun* F 1 slope; **subir una cuesta** to go up a slope; **ir cuesta arriba** to go uphill; **ir cuesta abajo** to go downhill; 2 **llevar algo a cuestas** to carry something on your back.

cuestión *noun* F 1 matter; **en la reunión se hablará de esta cuestión** this matter will be discussed in the meeting; 2 **la cuestión es …** the thing is …

cueva *noun* F cave.

cueza, cuezo, etc. *verb* SEE **cocer**.

cuidado *noun* M **1 tener cuidado con** to be careful with; **ten cuidado con los vasos** be careful with the glasses; **¡cuidado con el escalón!** mind the step!; **2 hacer algo con cuidado** to do something carefully; **lo cogí con cuidado** I took it carefully; **3 cuidados intensivos** intensive care.
exclamation **¡cuidado!** watch out!

cuidadoso/cuidadosa *adjective* careful.

cuidar *verb* [17] **1** to look after; **yo me quedo cuidando a los niños** I'll stay and look after the children; **cuidan de su padre enfermo** they look after their sick father; **2** to take care of; **sé cuidar de mí misma** I can take care of myself.

culebra *noun* F snake.

culebrón *noun* M (*informal*) soap (opera).

culo *noun* M (*informal*) **1** bum; **2 el culo del vaso** the bottom of the glass.

culpa *noun* F **1** fault; **no es mi culpa** it's not my fault; **es su culpa si se queda sin ir** it's his fault if he ends up not going; **no lo terminamos a tiempo por tu culpa** it's your fault we didn't finish it on time; **¿y qué culpa tengo yo?** and why is it my fault?; **2 echarle la culpa a alguien** to blame someone; **me echan la culpa de lo sucedido** they blame me for

what happened; **3** guilt; **sentimiento de culpa** guilty feelings.

culpable *noun* M/F **él es el único culpable de todo esto** he's the only one to blame for all this.
adjective **1** guilty; **sentirse culpable de algo** to feel guilty about something; **2 ser culpable de algo** to be to blame for something; **yo no soy culpable de la situación** I'm not to blame for the situation; **3 ser culpable de algo** to be guilty of something (*a crime*).

culpar *verb* [17] to blame; **culpar a alguien de algo** to blame somebody for something.

cultivar *verb* [17] **1** to grow (*fruit or vegetables*); **2** to cultivate (*land*).

cultura *noun* F **1** culture; **2** knowledge; **preguntas de cultura general** general knowledge questions.

culturismo *noun* M bodybuilding.

cumpleaños *noun* M birthday; **fiesta de cumpleaños** birthday party; **¿cuándo es tu cumpleaños?** when's your birthday?; **¡feliz cumpleaños!** Happy Birthday!

cumplir *verb* [19] **1 ¿cuándo cumples años?** when's your birthday?; **mañana cumplo quince años** I'll be fifteen tomorrow; **¡que cumplas muchos más!** many happy returns!; **2 cumplir una promesa** to keep a promise; **no has cumplido con tu palabra** you haven't kept your word; **3** to fulfill (*conditions*); **4** to

carry out (*a task or an order*);
5 cumplir con una condena to serve
a sentence.

cuna *noun* F **1** cradle; **2** cot.

cuñada *noun* F sister-in-law.

cuñado *noun* M brother-in-law.

cupe, cupiera, cupo, etc. *verb*
SEE **caber**.

cura[1] *noun* M priest.

cura[2] *noun* F cure.

curar *verb* [17] **1** to cure (*an illness
or sick person*); **2** to dress (*a
wound*).
curarse *reflexive verb* [17] to get
better.

curioso/curiosa *noun* M/F
busybody.
adjective **1** nosy; **¡qué curiosa eres!**
you're so nosy; **2 lo curioso es que ...**
the funny thing is ...; **es curioso
que ...** it's strange that ...

cursiva *noun* F italics; **en cursiva** in
italics.

curso *noun* M **1** year; **¿en qué curso
estás?** what year are you in?; **mi
hermana está en el primer curso**
my sister's in first year; **el curso
escolar** the academic year; **2** course;
un curso intensivo an intensive
course.

cursor *noun* M cursor.

curva[1] *noun* F bend; **curva
peligrosa** sharp bend; **tomar una
curva** to take a bend.

curvo/curva[2] *adjective* curved.

cuyo/cuya *adjective* whose; **el
amigo cuyo ordenador utilicé** the
friend whose computer I used.

D d

dado *noun* M dice; **tirar los dados**
to throw the dice.

dama *noun* F lady; **damas y
caballeros** ladies and gentlemen;
una dama de honor a bridesmaid.

danés[1] *noun* M Danish (*the
language*).

danés[2]**/danesa** *noun* M/F Dane.
adjective Danish.

dañar *verb* [17] to damage.

dañino/dañina *adjective* harmful.

daño *noun* M **1 hacerse daño** to
hurt yourself; **te vas a hacer daño**
you are going to hurt yourself; **¿se
hizo daño al caer?** did she hurt
herself when she fell?; **me hice daño
en la pierna** I hurt my leg; **2 hacerle
daño a alguien** to hurt someone; **no
quiero hacerte daño** I don't want to
hurt you; **3 daños y perjuicios**
damages.

dar *verb* [4] **1** to give; **me dio su
número de teléfono** he gave me his
telephone number; **dale esta carta
a María** give this letter to María; **dale
recuerdos** give him my regards;
dame un beso give me a kiss; **2 ¿me
da un kilo de tomates?** can I have a

kilo of tomatoes?; **3 me dieron un premio** I got a prize; **4** to turn on; **dar la luz** to turn on the light; **5 darle a un botón** to press a button; **darle a un interruptor** to flick a switch; **6 el reloj dio las doce** the clock struck twelve; **7 dar una fiesta** to have a party; **8** to say; **dar las gracias** to say thank you; **dar los buenos días** to say good morning; **darle la bienvenida a alguien** to welcome someone; **9 dar un grito** to shout; **10 darle la mano a alguien** to shake somebody's hand; **11 dar un paseo** to go for a walk; **fuimos a dar una vuelta** we went for a walk; **12 dar de comer a alguien** to feed somebody; **dar de beber a alguien** to give somebody something to drink; **13 me dio miedo** it scared me; **las patatas fritas le dieron sed** the crisps made him feel thirsty; **este jersey da mucho calor** this jumper is very warm; **14 da lo mismo** it doesn't matter; **da lo mismo si lo hacemos luego** it doesn't matter if we do it later; **15 me da lo mismo** I don't mind; **si te da lo mismo, te hago un cheque** if you don't mind, I'll write you a cheque; **16 el hotel da al mar** the hotel faces the sea; **la puerta da al salón** the door opens onto the living room.

darse *reflexive verb* [4] **1** to have; **darse un baño** to have a bath; **darse una ducha** to have a shower; **2 darse un golpe** to bump yourself; **me di con el pie en el bordillo** I hit my foot on the kerb; **3 darse prisa** to hurry up; **4 darse cuenta de algo** to realize something; **me di cuenta de que se me habían olvidado las** llaves I realized I'd forgotten my keys; **5 se le dan bien las matemáticas** she's good at maths; **no se me da bien pintar** I'm not good at painting.

dardo *noun* M dart.

dC *abbreviation* (*short for: después de Cristo*) AD.

d. de J.C. *abbreviation* (*short for: después de Jesucristo*) AD.

de *preposition* **1 el coche de mis padres** my parent's car; **esto es de Juan** this is Juan's; **fuimos a casa de Isa** we went to Isa's; **2** of; **el nombre del libro** the name of the book; **el respaldo del asiento** the back of the chair; **3** from; **soy de Sevilla** I'm from Sevilla; **de Madrid a Bilbao** from Madrid to Bilbao; **de la cabeza a los pies** from head to toe; **no hemos tenido noticias de María** we haven't had any news from María; **4 una silla de madera** a wooden chair; **flores de plástico** plastic flowers; **5** of (*in quantities*); **un vaso de leche** a glass of milk; **una caja de naranjas** a box of oranges; **6 una clase de conducir** a driving lesson; **las copas de vino** the wine glasses; **una moneda de cien pesetas** a hundred peseta coin; **el cubo de la basura** the rubbish bin; **una película de miedo** a scary film; **7 la estación de Victoria** Victoria Station; **la ciudad de Barcelona** Barcelona; **el mes de marzo** the month of March; **8** (*describing people*) **un hombre de cincuenta años** a fifty-year-old man; **una niña de pelo corto** a girl with short hair; **es la chica del**

jersey a rayas it's the girl with a striped jumper; **yo iba vestida de rojo** I was dressed in red; **9 el mejor de todos** the best of all; **el más bonito de los tres** the nicest of the three; **más de quince** more than fifteen; **el más inteligente de la clase** the cleverest in the class; **10 un tercio del total** a third of the total; **el doble de lo que yo gano** twice what I earn; **poco a poco** little by little; **de tres en tres** three at a time; **11 a las dos de la tarde** at two in the afternoon; **de noche** by night; **trabajan de noche** they work at night; **viajaron de día** they travelled by day; **12 trabajar de algo** to work as something; **trabajo de enfermera** I work as a nurse.

dé *verb* SEE **dar**.

debajo *adjective* **1** underneath; **pon un plato debajo** put a plate underneath; **2 el que está debajo** the one underneath; **el de debajo del todo** the one right at the bottom; **3 debajo de** under; **está debajo de la caja** it's under the box; **4 por debajo de** under; **pasé por debajo de la valla** I went under the fence; **por debajo de los diez grados** below ten degrees.

deber¹ *noun* M **1** duty; **cumplir con tu deber** to do your duty; **2 deberes** homework; **hacer los deberes** to do your homework; **aún no he hecho los deberes** I haven't done my homework yet.

deber² *verb* [18] **1** to owe; **te debo mil pesetas** I owe you a thousand pesetas; **2** must; **debes intentarlo**

you must try; **deberás estudiar mucho** you will have to study hard; **3 deberías descansar** you should have a rest; **deberías haber seguido mis consejos** you should have followed my advice.

debido/debida *adjective* **1** due; **a su debido tiempo** in due course; **con el debido respeto** with due respect; **con el debido cuidado** with the necessary care; **2 como es debido** properly; **pórtate como es debido** behave properly; **3 debido a** due to; **debido al accidente** due to the accident.

débil *adjective* weak.

década *noun* F decade; **la década de los sesenta** the sixties.

decena *noun* F **una decena de libros** about ten books; **divídelos por decenas** divide them into tens.

decente *adjective* decent.

decepción *noun* F disappointment.

decepcionar *verb* [17] to disappoint; **la película nos decepcionó** the film disappointed us.

decidir *verb* [19] to decide; **decidí quedarme** I decided to stay.
decidirse *reflexive verb* [19] to make up your mind; **aún no se ha decidido del todo** she hasn't completely made up her mind.

décimo/décima *adjective* tenth; **el décimo piso** the tenth floor.

decir *verb* [5] **1** to say; **¿qué has dicho?** what did you say?; **aquí dice que ...** here it says that ...; **2** to tell; **me ha dicho que no viene** he's told me he's not coming; **dime lo que quieres** tell me what you want; **3** to mean; **¿qué quieres decir?** what do you mean?; **¿qué quiere decir 'paloma'?** what does 'paloma' mean?; **4 no digas tonterías** don't talk nonsense; **5 ¿diga?** hello? (*on the phone*); **6 dime** yes? (*when somebody says your name*); **'¡mamá!' – '¿dime?'** 'Mum!' – 'yes?'.

decisión *noun* F decision; **tomar una decisión** to make a decision.

declarar *verb* [17] **1** to declare; **declarar la guerra** to declare war; **¿algo que declarar?** anything to declare? (*at the customs*); **2** to give evidence; **se ha negado a declarar** he's refused to give evidence.
declararse *reflexive verb* [17] **declararse culpable** to plead guilty; **declararse inocente** to plead not guilty.

decorar *verb* [17] to decorate.

dedo *noun* M **1** finger; **dedo índice** index finger; **dedo anular** ring finger; **dedo meñique** little finger; **dedo pulgar** thumb; **2 dedo del pie** toe; **el dedo gordo del pie** the big toe; **3 hacer dedo** to hitchhike.

defecto *noun* M flaw, defect.

defectuoso/defectuosa *adjective* faulty.

defender *verb* [36] to defend.
defenderse *reflexive verb* [36] **1** to defend yourself; **2 me defiendo en inglés** I get by in English.

defensa *noun* F **1** defence; **defensa personal** self-defence; **2** defender (*in sport*).

definición *noun* F definition.

definitivo/definitiva *adjective* definitive.

dejar *verb* [17] **1** to leave; **quiere dejar el colegio** she wants to leave school; **ha dejado a su novia** he's left his girlfriend; **¡déjala en paz!** leave her alone!; **2** to let; **no la dejan salir los domingos** they don't let her go out on Sundays; **¡déjame entrar!** let me in!; **3** to lend; **le he dejado mis apuntes** I've lent him my notes; **¿me dejas un boli?** can you lend me a pen?; **4 dejar caer algo** to drop something; **5 dejar paso** to give way; **6 dejar de hacer algo** to stop doing something; **¡deja de molestar!** stop being a nuisance!; **dejar de fumar** to give up smoking; **7 no dejes de llamarme cuando llegues** make sure you phone me when you get there.
dejarse *reflexive verb* [17] **1** to leave; **me he dejado las gafas en el coche** I left my glasses in the car; **2 dejarse el pelo largo** to grow your hair long; **dejarse barba** to grow a beard.

del (*'del' is what 'de + el' becomes; look under 'de' for more examples*) **el dedo gordo del pie** the big toe.

delantal *noun* M apron.

delante *adverb* **1 delante de** in front of; **delante de la iglesia** in front of the church; **delante de mí** in front of me; **2 el asiento de delante** the front seat; **la parte de delante** the front; **3 ir delante** to go ahead; **4 lleva un bolsillo por delante** it has a pocket at the front; **entraron por delante** they came in through the front.

delantero/delantera *noun* M/F forward (*in sport*).
adjective front; **la rueda delantera** the front wheel.

deletrear *verb* [17] to spell.

delfín *noun* M dolphin.

delgado/delgada *adjective* thin.

delicado/delicada *adjective* **1** delicate; **una situación delicada** a delicate situation; **2** fragile (*a piece of china, etc.*); **3** sensitive (*skin*).

delicioso/deliciosa *adjective* delicious.

delincuente *noun* M/F criminal.

delito *noun* M crime; **cometer un delito** to commit a crime.

demás *adjective* **los demás alumnos** the rest of the pupils; **las demás cartas** the rest of the letters.
pronoun **1 lo demás** the rest; **lo demás lo traigo mañana** I'll bring the rest tomorrow; **aquí está todo lo demás** here's everything else; **2 los/las demás** the rest, the others; **los demás pueden venir conmigo** the rest can come with me; **los**

problemas de los demás other people's problems.

demasiado¹/demasiada *adjective, pronoun* **1** too much; **gasta demasiado dinero** he spends too much money; **2** too many; **hay demasiadas personas aquí** there are too many people here; **3 demasiadas veces** too often; **4 hacía demasiado calor** it was too hot.

demasiado² *adverb* **1** too much; **gasta demasiado** he spends too much; **no trabajes demasiado** don't work too hard; **2** too; **era demasiado caro** it was too expensive.

democracia *noun* F democracy.

demoler *verb* [38] to demolish.

demolición *noun* F demolition.

demonio *noun* M devil.

demora *noun* F delay; **sin demora** without delay.

demos, dan, den, etc. *verb* SEE **dar**.

densidad *noun* F **1** density; **2** denseness.

dentífrico *noun* M toothpaste.

dentista *noun* M/F dentist.

dentro *adverb* **1** inside; **pasar dentro** to go inside; **desde dentro** from inside; **2 aquí dentro** in here; **allí dentro** in there; **ponlo aquí dentro** put it in here; **3 dentro de** inside, in; **dentro del edificio** inside the building; **dentro de la caja** in the box; **4 por dentro** on the inside; **por dentro es verde** it's green on the inside; **lo limpié por dentro** I cleaned the inside.

denunciar *verb* [17] to report (*a person or crime*).

departamento *noun* M department.

depender *verb* [18] to depend; **depender de algo** to depend on something; **depende del resultado** it depends on the result; **'¿se lo vas a decir?'** – **'depende'** 'are you going to tell him?' – 'it depends'.

dependiente/dependienta *noun* M/F shop assistant.

deporte *noun* M sport; **hacer deporte** to play sports; **me gusta hacer deporte** I like playing sports; **los deportes acuáticos** water sports; **los deportes de invierno** winter sports.

deportista *noun* M/F sportsman/ sportswoman.
adjective sporty; **soy muy deportista** I do a lot of sport.

deportivo¹ *noun* M sports car.

deportivo²/deportiva *adjective* sports; **club deportivo** sports club; **ropa deportiva** sports clothes; casual clothes.

depositar *verb* [17] **1** to place; **deposite su solicitud en esta caja** place your application in this box; **2** to deposit (*money in an account*).

depósito *noun* M deposit.

deprimido/deprimida *adjective* depressed.

deprimirse *reflexive verb* [19] to get depressed.

deprisa *adverb* fast, quickly; **no lo hagas tan deprisa** don't do it so quickly; **andaba muy deprisa** he was walking very fast; **¡deprisa, vístete!** hurry up and get dressed!

derecha¹ *noun* F **1** right; **gira a la derecha** turn right; **conducir por la derecha** to drive on the right; **la segunda calle a la derecha** the second road on the right; **2** right hand; **escribo con la derecha** I write with my right hand; **3 la derecha** the right (*in politics*); **ser de derechas** to be right-wing.

derecho¹ *noun* M **1** right; **tener derecho a** to have a right to; **tienes derecho a reclamar** you've got the right to claim; **los derechos humanos** human rights; **2** law; **estudiar derecho** to study law; **derecho penal** criminal law; **3 derechos de autor** royalties.
adverb straight; **ponlo derecho** put it straight; **siga todo derecho** go straight on; **siéntate derecho** sit up.

derecho²/derecha² *adjective* **1** right; **el guante derecho** the right glove; **en la esquina superior derecha** in the top right-hand corner; **2** straight; **no está derecho** it's not straight.

derribar *verb* [17] **1** to demolish (*a building or wall, for example*); **2** to break down (*a door*); **3** to shoot down (*a plane*).

derrotar *verb* [17] to defeat.

des *verb* SEE **dar**.

desabrochar *verb* [17] to undo (*a jacket or shirt*).
desabrocharse *reflexive verb* [17] to undo; **se desabrochó la chaqueta** he undid his jacket.

desafilado/desafilada *adjective* blunt.

desafortunadamente *adverb* unfortunately.

desafortunado/desafortunada *adjective* **1** unlucky (*a person*); **2** unfortunate (*an event*).

desagradable *adjective* unpleasant.

desanimado/desanimada *adjective* discouraged.

desaparecer *verb* [35] **1** to disappear; **2** to go missing.

desaparición *noun* F disappearance.

desaprovechar *verb* [17] to waste; **han desaprovechado mucho papel** they've wasted a lot of paper.

desarrollo *noun* M development.

desastre *noun* M disaster.

desatar *verb* [17] untie.
desatarse *reflexive verb* [17] to come undone.

desatornillar *verb* [17] to unscrew.

desayunar *verb* [17] **1** to have breakfast; **desayuné muy temprano** I had breakfast very early; **2** to have for breakfast; **desayuno café y tostadas** I have coffee and toast for breakfast.

desayuno *noun* M breakfast; **tomar el desayuno** to have breakfast.

desbordar *verb* [17] to exceed.
desbordarse *reflexive verb* [17] to overflow.

descafeinado/descafeinada *adjective* decaffeinated.

descalificar *verb* [31] to disqualify.

descalzarse *reflexive verb* [22] to take your shoes off.

descalzo/descalza *adjective* barefoot.

descansado/descansada *adjective* rested.

descansar *verb* [17] **1** to rest; **necesitas descansar** you need to rest; **descansar la vista** to give your eyes a rest; **2 que descanses** sleep well; **3 ¡descansen!** at ease! (*in the army*).

descansillo *noun* M landing (*on stairs*).

descanso *noun* M **1** rest; **2** half-time.

descapotable *noun* M *adjective* convertible.

descargar *verb* [28] to unload.

descender *verb* [36] **1** to go down (*a mountaineer*); **2** to descend (*a plane*); **3** to fall (*prices or temperature, for example*).

descolgar *verb* [23] **1** to pick up (*the phone*); **2 han dejado el teléfono descolgado** they've left the phone off the hook; **3** to take down (*a picture, for example*).

desconfiar *verb* [32] to mistrust; **desconfiar de alguien** to mistrust someone.

descongelar *verb* [17] to defrost (*the fridge or food*).

decongelarse *reflexive verb* [17] to defrost (*the fridge or food*).

desconocido/desconocida *noun* M/F stranger. *adjective* unknown.

descontento[1] *noun* M dissatisfaction.

descontento[2]**/descontenta** *adjective* dissatisfied; **quedar descontento con algo** to be dissatisfied with something.

describir *verb* [52] to describe.

descripción *noun* F description.

descrito *verb* SEE **describir**.

descubrir *verb* [53] **1** to discover; **2** to unveil (*a statue*).

descuento *noun* M discount.

descuidado/descuidada *adjective* **1** careless (*a person*); **2** neglected; **el jardín está muy descuidado** the garden is very neglected.

desde *preposition* **1** since; **desde la semana pasada** since last week; **desde que nos conocimos** since we met; **2** from; **mídelo desde este** extremo hasta el otro measure it from this end to the other; **puedo mandarlo desde Madrid** I can send it from Madrid; **desde el principio** from the beginning; **desde el primer momento** right from the start; **3 desde hace** for; **no les veo desde hace años** I haven't seen them for years; **trabajo allí desde hace tres meses** I've been working there for three months; **4 desde luego** of course.

desear *verb* [17] **1** to wish; **te deseo lo mejor** I wish you all the best; **te deseo un feliz cumpleaños** wishing you a happy birthday (*in a card*); **2 ¿qué desea?** can I help you? (*in a shop, for example*); **3 estoy deseando verte** I'm looking forward to seeing you; **están deseando que llegue el verano** they can't wait for the summer to come.

desembarcar *verb* [31] **1** to unload; **2** to disembark.

desempleado/desempleada *noun* M/F unemployed person. *adjective* unemployed.

desempleo *noun* M unemployment; **cobrar subsidio de desempleo** to get unemployment benefit.

desenchufar *verb* [17] to unplug.

deseo *noun* M **1** wish; **pedir un deseo** to make a wish; **se cumplió mi deseo** my wish came true; **2 con mis mejores deseos** best wishes; **3** desire.

desfavorable *adjective* unfavourable.

desfile *noun* M **1** parade; **2 un desfile de modelos** a fashion show.

desgracia *noun* F misfortune; **por desgracia** unfortunately; ★ **las desgracias nunca vienen solas** it never rains but it pours.

desgraciado/desgraciada *adjective* **1** unhappy; **soy muy desgraciado** I'm very unhappy; **2** ill-fated; **aquel desgraciado día** that ill-fated day.

deshacer *verb* [7] **1** to undo (*a knot*); **2** to unwrap (*a parcel*); **3** to take apart (*a mechanism*); **4** to crumble (*a biscuit or stock cube, for example*); **5 deshacer las maletas** to unpack.

deshacerse *reflexive verb* [7] **1** to come undone (*a knot or seam*); **2** to melt (*ice*); **3 deshacerse de algo** to get rid of something; **voy a deshacerme de este sofá** I'm going to get rid of this sofa.

desierto[1] *noun* M desert.

desierto[2]/**desierta** *adjective* deserted.

designar *verb* [17] to appoint.

desigual *adjective* **1** uneven (*a surface or road*); **2** unequal (*a fight*).

desmaquillarse *reflexive verb* [17] to remove your make-up.

desmayarse *reflexive verb* [17] to faint.

desmontar *verb* [17] **1** to take apart; **2** to take down (*a tent*).

desnudar *verb* [17] to undress.
desnudarse *reflexive verb* [17] to take your clothes off, to undress.

desnudo/desnuda *adjective* **1** naked; **2** bare; **con los hombros desnudos** with bare shoulders.

desobedecer *verb* [35] to disobey.

desobedezca, desobedezco, etc. *verb* SEE **desobedecer**.

desobediente *noun* M/F **eres un desobediente** you are very disobedient.
adjective disobedient.

desodorante *noun* M deodorant; **desodorante en barra** stick deodorant.

desorden *noun* M mess.

desorganizado/desorganizada *adjective* disorganized.

despacho *noun* M **1** office; **2** study (*at home*); **3 despacho de billetes** ticket office; **despacho de lotería** lottery agency.

despacio *adverb* slowly; **hazlo despacio** do it slowly; **¡más despacio!** slower!

despedida *noun* F farewell; **una cena de despedida** a farewell dinner.

despedir *verb* [57] **1** to dismiss; **lo han despedido del trabajo** they've sacked him; **2** to lay off; **han tenido que despedir a algunos empleados** they've had to lay off some employees; **3** to say goodbye; **fuimos todos a despedirla** we all went to say goodbye to her;

¿**vendrás a despedirme a la estación?** will you come to see me off at the station?

despedirse *reflexive verb* [57] to say goodbye; **despedirse de alguien** to say goodbye to someone.

despegar *verb* [28] **1** to take off (*a plane*); **2** to peel off (*a label or a sticker*).

despegarse *reflexive verb* [28] to come unstuck.

despegue *noun* M takeoff (*of a plane*).

despejado/despejada *adjective* clear (*sky or a day, for example*).

despejar *verb* [17] to clear.

desperdiciar *verb* [17] to waste.

desperdicio *noun* M **1** waste; **no tiene desperdicio** it's excellent; **2 desperdicios** scraps.

despertador *noun* M alarm (clock); **poner el despertador** to set the alarm.

despertar *verb* [29] to wake up; ¿**puedes despertarme a las siete?** can you wake me up at seven?

despertarse *reflexive verb* [29] to wake up; **me desperté a las diez** I woke up at ten.

despida, despido, etc. *verb* SEE **despedir**.

despierta¹, despierto¹, etc. *verb* SEE **despertar**.

despierto²/despierta² *adjective* awake.

despistado/despistada *noun* M/F scatterbrain. *adjective* absent-minded.

desplegar *verb* [30] to unfold.

despliega, despliego, etc. *verb* SEE **desplegar**.

después *adverb* **1** afterwards; **después me arrepentí** I regretted it afterwards; **poco después** shortly afterwards; **2** later; **lo haré después** I'll do it later; **se vieron mucho después** they saw each other much later; **3 después de** after; **después de las clases** after school; **4 después de todo** after all.

destino *noun* M **1** destination; ¿**qué destino tiene?** what's its destination?; **el vuelo con destino a Milán** the plane to Milan; **2** fate.

destornillador *noun* M screwdriver.

destrucción *noun* F destruction.

destruir *verb* [54] to destroy.

desván *noun* M attic.

desventaja *noun* F disadvantage; **estar en desventaja** to be at a disadvantage.

desvestirse *reflexive verb* [57] to undress.

desviar *verb* [32] to divert (*a plane or traffic*).

desvío *noun* M diversion; **tomar un desvío** to make a detour.

detalle *noun* M detail; **describir algo con todo detalle** to describe something in great detail.

detective *noun* M/F detective; **detective privado** private detective.

detener *verb* [9] **1** to stop (*traffic*); **2** to arrest; **¡queda detenido!** you're under arrest!

detenerse *reflexive verb* [9] to stop; **detenerse a hacer** to stop to do; **me detuve a descansar** I stopped to rest.

detergente *noun* M **1** washing powder; **2** washing-up liquid.

detestar *verb* [17] to detest.

detrás *adverb* **1** behind; **creo que están detrás** I think they're behind; **2 detrás de** behind; **ponte detrás de mí** go behind me; **detrás de la estación** behind the station; **3 se abrocha por detrás** it buttons up at the back; **entraron por detrás** they got in through the back.

deuda *noun* F debt; **tiene muchas deudas** he has a lot of debts.

devolver *verb* [45] **1** to bring back; **te devolveré el libro mañana** I'll bring you the book back tomorrow; **2** to take back; **he devuelto la camisa** I've taken the shirt back; **3** to return; **lo devolví a su dueño** I returned it to its owner; **4** to refund (*money*); **5** to be sick (*vomit*); **creo que voy a devolver** I think I'm going to be sick.

devuelto, devuelvo, etc. *verb* SEE **devolver**.

di *verb* SEE **dar**.

día *noun* M **1** day; **el día siguiente** the following day; **el día anterior** the previous day; **el día tres de mayo** the third of May; **¿qué día es hoy?** what day is it today?; **todos los días** every day; **cada día** every day; **un día festivo** a public holiday; **se ha tomado el día libre** she's taken the day off; **día de Reyes** Twelfth Night (*the 6th of January, which is when people get Christmas presents in Spain*); **el día de los Inocentes** the 28th of December (*equivalent to April's fool day in Spain*); **el día de los enamorados** St Valentine's Day; **2 buenos días** good morning; **3 hacerse de día** to get light (*in the morning*); **aún no se ha hecho de día** it's not light yet; **en pleno día** in broad daylight; **4 estar al día** to be up to date; **poner a alguien al día** to keep someone up to date.

diabético/diabética *noun* M/F *adjective* diabetic.

diablo *noun* M devil.

diagonal *noun* F *adjective* diagonal.

diagrama *noun* M diagram.

dial *noun* M dial.

diálogo *noun* M **1** conversation; **2** dialogue.

diamante *noun* M diamond.

diámetro *noun* M diameter.

diapositiva *noun* F slide.

diario¹ *noun* M **1** diary; **llevar un diario** to keep a diary; **2** newspaper.

diario²/diaria *adjective* **1** daily; **la rutina diaria** the daily routine; **a diario** every day; **se escriben a diario** they write to each other every day; **2** a day; **ensayan dos horas diarias** they practise two hours a day; **3 de diario** everyday; **ropa de diario** everyday clothes.

diarrea *noun* F diarrhoea.

dibujar *verb* [17] to draw.

dibujo *noun* M **1** drawing; **hacer un dibujo** to do a drawing; **dibujo técnico** technical drawing; **2 dibujos animados** cartoons; **una película de dibujos animados** an animated cartoon film.

diccionario *noun* M dictionary.

dice, dicho, etc. *verb* SEE **decir**.

diciembre *noun* M December.

dictado *noun* M dictation.

diecinueve *number* **1** nineteen; **tiene diecinueve años** she's nineteen (years old); **2** nineteenth (*in dates*); **el diecinueve de agosto** the nineteenth of August.

dieciocho *number* **1** eighteen; **tiene dieciocho años** she's eighteen (years old); **2** eighteenth (*in dates*); **el dieciocho de agosto** the eighteenth of August.

dieciséis *number* **1** sixteen; **tiene dieciséis años** she's sixteen (years old); **2** sixteenth (*in dates*); **el dieciséis de agosto** the sixteenth of August.

diecisiete *number* **1** seventeen; **tiene diecisiete años** she's seventeen (years old); **2** seventeenth (*in dates*); **el diecisiete de agosto** the seventeenth of August.

diente *noun* M **1** tooth; **se le ha caído un diente** she's lost a tooth; **ya le están saliendo los dientes** he's already teething; **2 un diente de ajo** a clove of garlic.

diera, dieras, etc. *verb* SEE **dar**.

diesel *noun* M *adjective* diesel.

dieta *noun* F diet; **estar a dieta** to be on a diet; **ponerse a dieta** to go on a diet.

diez *number* **1** ten; **tiene diez años** she's ten (years old); **2** tenth (*in dates*); **el diez de agosto** the tenth of August; **3** ten (*in clock time*); **son las diez** it's ten o'clock; **a las diez y cinco** at five past ten.

diferencia *noun* F **1** difference; **hay poca diferencia de precio** there's not much difference in price; **2 a diferencia de** unlike; **a diferencia de su padre** unlike his father.

diferente *adjective* different; **ser diferente a/de** to be different from.

difícil *adjective* difficult.

dificultad *noun* F difficulty; **con muchas dificultades** with great difficulty.

diga, digo, etc. *verb* SEE **decir**.

diluir *verb* [54] **1** to dilute; **2** to thin down (*paint*).

dimensión *noun* F dimension.

dimisión *noun* F resignation; **presentar la dimisión** to hand in your resignation.

dimitir *verb* [19] to resign.

dimos *verb* SEE **dar**.

Dinamarca *noun* F Denmark.

dinero *noun* M money; **dinero de bolsillo** pocket money; **dinero en efectivo** cash; **dinero suelto** change; **no tengo dinero suelto** I haven't got any change.

dinosaurio *noun* M dinosaur.

dio *verb* SEE **dar**.

dios *noun* M god.

Dios *noun* M God; **gracias a Dios** thank heavens; **¡por Dios!** for heaven's sake!; **¡Dios mío!** oh, my God!; **¡sabe Dios!** God knows!

diploma *noun* M diploma.

diplomático/diplomática *noun* M/F diplomat. *adjective* diplomatic.

diputado/diputada *noun* M/F member of parliament.

dirá, diré, etc. *verb* SEE **decir**.

dirección *noun* F 1 address; **mi dirección es …** my address is …; 2 direction; **¿en qué dirección se fueron?** what direction did they go in?; **venían en dirección contraria** they were coming the other way; 3 'dirección prohibida' 'no entry'; 'dirección obligatoria' 'one way'; 4 management (*of a company*).

directo/directa *adjective* 1 direct; **¿hay un vuelo directo a Santiago?** is there a direct flight to Santiago?; 2 **un tren directo** a through train;

3 **en directo** live; **retransmisión en directo** live broadcast.

director/directora *noun* M/F 1 headmaster/headmistress; 2 manager (*of a company*); 3 director (*of a film or play*); 4 conductor (*of an orchestra*); 5 editor (*of a newspaper*).

dirigir *verb* [49] 1 to manage (*a company*); 2 to direct (*a film or play*); 3 to conduct (*an orchestra*); 4 **no me dirigió la palabra en toda la tarde** he didn't say a word to me all afternoon.

dirigirse *reflexive verb* [49] **dirigirse hacia algo** to head towards something; **se dirigió hacia la puerta** he headed towards the door.

disciplina *noun* F discipline.

disco *noun* M 1 record; **grabar un disco** to make a record; **disco sencillo** single; **disco compacto** compact disk; 2 disk; **disco duro** hard disk; **disco flexible** floppy disk; 3 traffic light; **el disco se ha puesto rojo** the lights are red.

discoteca *noun* F disco.

disculpa *noun* F apology; **pedir disculpas a alguien por algo** to apologize to someone for something.

disculparse *reflexive verb* [17] to apologize.

discusión *noun* F 1 argument; 2 discussion.

discutir *verb* [19] 1 to argue; **ha discutido con su novio** she's had an argument with her boyfriend; **2** to discuss.

diseñar *verb* [17] to design.

diseño *noun* M design.

disfraz *noun* M **1** disguise;
2 costume, fancy dress outfit; **un disfraz de pirata** a pirate outfit; **una fiesta de disfraces** a fancy dress party.

disfrazarse *reflexive verb* [22] to dress up; **me disfracé de bruja** I dressed up as a witch.

disfrutar *verb* [17] to enjoy yourself; **disfrutar de algo** to enjoy something; **he disfrutado mucho de las vacaciones** I really enjoyed my holiday.

disgustar *verb* [17] to upset.
disgustarse *reflexive verb* [17] to get upset.

disgusto *noun* M **tengo un disgusto enorme** I'm very upset.

disolvente *noun* M solvent.

disolver *verb* [45] to dissolve.
disolverse *reflexive verb* [45] to dissolve.

disparar *verb* [17] **1** to fire; **2** to shoot.

disparo *noun* M shot.

disposición *noun* F
1 arrangement; **2** aptitude; **3** **estoy a tu disposición** I'm at your disposal.

dispuesto/dispuesta *adjective*
1 arranged; **2** ready; **ya está todo dispuesto** everything's ready;

3 **estar dispuesto a hacer** to be prepared to do; **no estoy dispuesto a esperar** I'm not prepared to wait.

disquete *noun* M diskette, floppy disk.

disquetera *noun* F disk drive.

distancia *noun* F distance; **¿a qué distancia está el colegio de tu casa?** how far is the school from your house?; **los dos postes están a una distancia de dos metros** the two posts are two metres apart; **está a poca distancia** it's quite near.

diste *verb* SEE **dar**.

distinguir *verb* [50] to distinguish.
distinguirse *reflexive verb* [50]
1 **distinguirse por algo** to distinguish yourself by something;
2 **distinguirse de algo** to be different from something.

distintivo/distintiva *adjective* distinctive.

distinto *adjective* different; **ser distinto a** to be different from; **es distinto al resto** it's different from the rest.

distracción *noun* F
1 entertainment; **es su distracción favorita** it's his favourite entertainment; **la tele le sirve de distracción** television is a way of passing the time for him; **2** **se lo quitaron en un momento de distracción** they stole it from her when she wasn't paying attention.

distraer *verb* [42] **1** to distract; **distraer a alguien de algo** to distract somebody from something;

2 la costura me distrae sewing keeps me occupied.

distraerse *reflexive verb* [42] **1** to get distracted; **2 se distrae con la jardinería** gardening gives him something to do.

distribuidor/distribuidora *noun* M/F distributor.

distribuir *verb* [54] to distribute.

distrito *noun* M district; **distrito postal** postal area.

diversión *noun* F **1** fun; **por diversión** for fun; **2 un lugar lleno de diversiones** a place with plenty of things to do.

divertido/divertida *adjective* **1** funny; **es un chico muy divertido** he's really funny; **2 la fiesta fue muy divertida** the party was real fun.

divertir *verb* [14] to amuse.

divertirse *reflexive verb* [14] **1** to amuse yourself; **2** to have fun; **¡que te diviertas!** have fun!

dividir *verb* [19] to divide.

divisa *noun* F currency; **divisas extranjeras** foreign currency.

división *noun* F division.

divorciado/divorciada *noun* M/F divorcee.
adjective divorced.

divorciarse *reflexive verb* [17] to get divorced.

divorcio *noun* M divorce.

DNI *abbreviation* (*short for: Documento Nacional de Identidad*) identity card.

doblar *verb* [17] **1** to fold (*a piece of paper or clothes*); **2** to bend (*a piece of metal or your leg*); **3** to double (*an offer or amount*); **4 doblar la esquina** to turn the corner.

doble *noun* M **1 el doble de personas** twice as many people; **el doble de harina que de azúcar** twice as much flour as sugar; **el doble de peso** twice the weight; **el doble de largo** twice the length; **2 dobles** doubles (*in tennis*).
adjective double.

doce *number* **1** twelve; **tiene doce años** she's twelve (years old); **2** twelfth (*in dates*); **el doce de enero** the twelfth of January; **3** twelve (*in clock time*); **a las doce** at twelve o'clock; **son las doce del mediodía** it's twelve noon; **a las doce de la noche** at midnight.

doceavo/doceava *adjective* twelfth.

docena *noun* F dozen; **una docena de huevos** a dozen eggs.

doctor/doctora *noun* M/F doctor.

documentación *noun* F **1** papers; **no llevaba mi documentación** I didn't have my papers on me; **2** documents (*for a car*).

documental *noun* M documentary.
adjective **un programa documental** a documentary.

documento *noun* M document; **mi documento de identidad** my identity card.

dólar *noun* M dollar.

doler *verb* [38] **1** to hurt; **2 me duele el tobillo** my ankle hurts; **¿te duele mucho?** does it hurt a lot?; **me duele la cabeza** I've got a headache; **le dolía el estómago** he had stomachache.

dolor *noun* M pain; **tengo dolor de garganta** I have a sore throat; **tengo dolor de muelas** I have toothache; **con dolor de estómago** with a stomachache.

doméstico/doméstica *adjective* domestic.

domicilio *noun* M **¿cuál es su domicilio?** what's your address?; **en su domicilio particular** in his own home.

domingo *noun* M Sunday; **domingo de Resurrección** Easter Sunday; **vienen el domingo** they're coming on Sunday; **el domingo pasado** last Sunday; **el domingo por la mañana** on Sunday morning; **un domingo sí y otro no** every other Sunday; **cierran los domingos** they close on Sundays.

dominó *noun* M dominoes; **jugar al dominó** to play dominoes.

don *noun* M Mr; **Don Juan Pozo** Mr Juan Pozo.

donde *adverb* where; **el sitio donde nací** the place where I was born; **el lugar a donde nos dirigimos** the place we're going to; **iré a donde quiera** I'll go wherever I want; **ponlo donde sea** put it down anywhere.

dónde *adverb* where; **¿dónde está mi abrigo?** where's my coat?; **¿de dónde eres?** where are you from?; **no sé dónde lo guarda** I don't know where he keeps it; **¿por dónde se va a la oficina de correos?** what's the way to the post office?

donut *noun* M doughnut.

doña *noun* F Mrs, Ms; **Doña María del Valle** Mrs María del Valle.

dorado/dorada *adjective* gold, golden.

dormido/dormida *adjective* asleep; **estar dormido** to be asleep; **quedarse dormido** to fall asleep.

dormir *verb* [51] **1** to sleep; **¿has dormido bien?** did you sleep well?; **no he dormido nada** I couldn't sleep at all; **2 ¡a dormir!** time for bed!; **ya es hora de irse a dormir** it's time to go to bed; **3** to get to sleep; **no puedo dormir** I can't get to sleep; **4 estar durmiendo** to be asleep; **Juan está todavía durmiendo** Juan is still asleep; **5 dormir la siesta** to have a nap.

dormirse *reflexive verb* [51] **1** to fall asleep; **no puedo dormirme** I can't get to sleep; **2** to oversleep; **me dormí y llegué tarde al trabajo** I overslept and was late for work.

dormitorio *noun* M **1** bedroom; **2** dormitory.

dorso *noun* M back; **el dorso de la mano** the back of the hand.

dos *number* **1** two; **tiene dos años** she's two (years old); **2** second (*in dates*); **el dos de enero** the second of January; **3** two (*in clock time*); **son las dos** it's two o'clock.

doscientos/doscientas *number* two hundred; **doscientos veinte** two hundred and twenty.

doy *verb* SEE **dar**.

dragón *noun* M dragon.

drama *noun* M drama.

dramático/dramática *adjective* dramatic.

droga *noun* F drug.

drogadicto/drogadicta *noun* M/F drug addict.

droguería *noun* F hardware shop.

ducha *noun* F shower; **pegarse una ducha** to have a shower.

ducharse *reflexive verb* [17] to have a shower.

duda *noun* F **1** doubt; **sin duda es el mejor** it's undoubtedly the best; **no me queda la menor duda** I have no doubts whatsoever; **2** query; **¿tienes alguna duda?** do you have any queries?; **tengo algunas dudas** I have a few queries.

dudar *verb* [17] to doubt; **no lo dudo** I don't doubt it; **dudo que sepa hacerlo** I doubt he knows how to do it.

duela, duelo, etc. *verb* SEE **doler**.

dueño/dueña *noun* F **1** owner; **¿quién es el dueño de este coche?** who's the owner of this car?; **se lo devolví a la dueña** I returned it to its owner; **2** landlord/landlady (*of a pub or a guesthouse*).

duerma, duermo, etc. *verb* SEE **dormir**.

dulce *noun* M **no me gustan los dulces** I don't like sweet things. *adjective* sweet.

duodécimo/duodécima *adjective* twelfth.

duque *noun* M duke.

duquesa *noun* F duchess.

duración *noun* F **1** length; **la duración de la película** the length of the film; **2** **disco de larga duración** LP.

durante *preposition* **1** during; **durante aquel tiempo** during that time; **lo haré durante las vacaciones** I'll do it during the holidays; **2** for; **no se vieron durante tres semanas** they didn't see each other for three weeks.

durar *verb* [17] to last; **la guerra duró tres años** the war lasted three years; **¿cuánto dura?** how long is it?; **no dura mucho** it's not very long.

dureza *noun* F hardness.

duro¹ *noun* M five-peseta coin. *adverb* hard; **estudiar duro** to study hard.

duro²/dura *adjective* **1** hard; **al secarse se pone duro** it goes hard when it dries; **fue un golpe muy duro para todos** it was a hard blow for all of us; **un profesor muy duro** a very strict teacher; **2** tough (*meat*); **3** stale (*bread*); **4** **un huevo duro** a hard-boiled egg; **5** **ser duro de oído** to be hard of hearing.

E e

e *conjunction* and ('*e*' is used instead of '*y*' before words beginning with '*i-*' or '*hi-*'); **padres e hijos** parents and children.

echar *verb* [17] **1** to put; **echa más sal a la sopa** put more salt in the soup; **eché el monedero en la bolsa** I put my purse in my bag; **tengo que echar gasolina al coche** I have to put some petrol in the car; **2** to give; **¿te echo un poco de salsa?** shall I give you some sauce?; **3** to throw; **eché agua al fuego** I threw water on the fire; **4** **echar a alguien** to throw someone out; **los eché de mi casa** I threw them out of my house; **5** **echar a alguien del trabajo** to sack someone; **lo han echado del trabajo** he's been sacked; **6** to show; **echan una película en la tele** they're showing a film on the television; **¿qué echan en el cine Rex?** what's on at the Rex cinema?; **7** **echar una carta (al correo)** to post a letter; **8** **echar de menos a alguien** to miss somebody; **echo de menos a mi hermana** I miss my sister; **te echo mucho de menos** I miss you a lot.

echarse *reflexive verb* [17] **1** **echarse al suelo** to throw yourself on the ground; **2** **echarse a la derecha** to move to the right; **echarse para atrás** to move backwards; **me eché a un lado** I moved to one side; **3** **echarse una siesta** to have a nap.

eco *noun* M echo.

ecológico/ecológica *adjective* ecological.

economía *noun* F economics.

económico/económica *adjective* **1** economic; **una crisis económica** an economic crisis; **2** financial; **los problemas económicos** financial problems; **3** cheap; **un hotel muy económico** a very cheap hotel; **4** thrifty (*person*).

ecuación *noun* F equation.

ecuador *noun* M equator.

edad *noun* F age; **¿qué edad tienes?** how old are you?; **Carmen y yo tenemos la misma edad** Carmen and I are the same age; **tendrá tu edad más o menos** he must be around the same age as you; **una mujer de unos treinta años de edad** a woman of about thirty; **la edad de piedra** the Stone Age; **la edad media** the Middle Ages; **está en la edad del pavo** he's at that awkward age.

edición *noun* F **1** publication; **2** edition; **edición de bolsillo** pocket edition.

edificio *noun* M building.

editar *verb* [17] **1** to publish; **2** to edit (*a text*).

edredón *noun* M quilt; **un edredón nórdico** a duvet.

educación *noun* F 1 education; **educación física** physical education; **educación secundaria** secondary education; **educación a distancia** distance learning; 2 upbringing; 3 manners; **tiene mucha educación** she's very polite; **eso es de mala educación** that's bad manners.

educado/educada *adjective* polite; **una persona mal educada** a rude person.

educar *verb* [31] 1 to educate; 2 to bring up.

EE.UU. *abbreviation* (*short for: Estados Unidos*) USA.

efectivo¹ *noun* M cash; **un millón de pesetas en efectivo** a million pesetas in cash; **pagar en efectivo** to pay cash.

efectivo²/efectiva *adjective* effective (*remedy or method*).

efecto *noun* M effect; **la pastilla no me hizo efecto** the pill didn't have any effect on me; **efectos secundarios** side effects; **efectos especiales** special effects; **el efecto invernadero** the greenhouse effect.

efectuar *verb* [20] 1 to carry out; **efectuar un registro** to carry out a search; 2 **efectuar un viaje** to go on a trip; 3 **el tren efectuará su salida a las nueve treinta** the train will depart at 9:30; 4 **efectuar un disparo** to fire a shot.

eficaz *adjective* effective.

egoísta *noun* M/F **eres un egoísta** you're really selfish.
adjective selfish.

ejecutivo/ejecutiva *noun* M/F *adjective* executive.

ejemplar *noun* M 1 copy (*of a book*); 2 issue (*of a magazine*); 3 specimen (*of an animal or a plant*).

ejemplo *noun* M example; **por ejemplo** for example; **no puedes poner ese caso como ejemplo** you can't take that case as an example; **dar buen ejemplo** to set a good example.

ejercicio *noun* M exercise; **hacer ejercicio** to do exercise.

ejército *noun* M army; **el ejército de tierra** the army; **el ejército de aire** the air force; **alistarse en el ejército** to join the army.

el *definite article* ('*el*' *is used before masculine singular nouns; see also* '*la*', '*los*' *and* '*las*') 1 the; **el libro blanco** the white book; **el sol** the sun; 2 ('*el*' *is also used before feminine nouns that start with stressed* '*a*' *or* '*ha*') **el águila** the eagle; **el hada** the fairy; 3 (*sometimes* '*el*' *is not translated*) **el caviar es muy caro** caviar is very dear; (*a* '*a*' *followed by* '*el*' *becomes* '*al*') **le llevaron al hospital** they took him to hospital; **éste es el señor Martínez** this is Mr Martínez; **el coche de Juan** Juan's car; 4 (*with parts of the body or personal belongings*) **se rompió el brazo** she broke her arm; **se afeitó el**

bigote he shaved off his moustache; **me quité el abrigo** I took my coat off; **5** (*talking about dates and days of the week*) **el dos de mayo** the second of May; **iré el próximo lunes** I'll go next Monday; **el miércoles abren a las diez** they open at ten on Wednesdays; **6 me gustó el rojo** I liked the red one; **7 el mío es mejor** mine is better; **el suyo es más caro** his is more expensive; **8 el mío y el de usted** mine and yours; **éste es el de María** this one is María's; **me gusta más el de Toni** I like Toni's better; **9 el que** the one; **el que yo compré** the one I bought; **el que quieras** whichever you want.

él *pronoun* **1** he; **él no lo sabe** he doesn't know; **2** him; **estaba hablando con él** I was talking to him; **pregúntale a él** ask him; **iba detrás de él** I was behind him; **3 es de él** it's his; **4 él mismo** himself.

elástico/elástica *adjective* elastic.

elección *noun* F **1** choice; **no tener elección** to have no choice; **2 las elecciones** the election; **convocar elecciones** to call an election.

electorado *noun* M electorate.

electoral *adjective* **campaña electoral** election campaign.

electricidad *noun* F electricity.

electricista *noun* M/F electrician.

eléctrico/eléctrica *adjective* **1** electric; **2** electrical.

electrocutar *verb* [17] to electrocute.

electrodoméstico *noun* M electrical appliance.

electrónico/electrónica *adjective* electronic.

elefante *noun* M elephant.

elegante *adjective* **1** elegant; **2** smart; **siempre va muy elegante** he's always very smartly dressed.

elegir *verb* [48] to choose.

elepé *noun* M LP.

elija, elijo *verb* SEE **elegir**.

eliminar *verb* [17] **1** to eliminate; **2** to remove.

eliminatorio/eliminatoria *adjective* qualifying (*round or match*).

ella *pronoun* **1** she; **ella no lo sabe** she doesn't know; **2** her; **estaba hablando con ella** I was talking to her; **pregúntale a ella** ask her; **yo iba detrás de ella** I was behind her; **3 es de ella** it's hers; **4 ella misma** herself.

ellas *pronoun* (*'ellas' is the feminine plural form of the pronoun; it is used to refer to two or more females*) **1** they; **ellas no lo saben** they don't know; **2** them; **estaba hablando con ellas** I was talking to them; **pregúntale a ellas** ask them; **iba detrás de ellas** I was behind them; **3 es de ellas** it's theirs; **4 ellas mismas** themselves.

ello *pronoun* **1** it; **se beneficiaron de ello** they benefited from it; **2** this; **para ello es necesario** ... for this, it is necessary ...

ellos *pronoun* ('*ellos*' *is the masculine plural form of the pronoun; is used to refer to two or more males or a group of mixed sex*) **1** they; **ellos no lo saben** they don't know; **2** them; **estaba hablando con ellos** I was talking to them; **pregúntale a ellos** ask them; **iba detrás de ellos** I was behind them; **3 es de ellos** it's theirs; **4 ellos mismos** themselves.

embajada *noun* F embassy.

embajador/embajadora *noun* M/F ambassador.

embalse *noun* M reservoir.

embarazada *noun* F pregnant woman.
adjective pregnant; **quedarse embarazada** to get pregnant; **estoy embarazada de tres meses** I'm three months pregnant.

embarcación *noun* F vessel (*boat*).

embarcadero *noun* M wharf.

embarcar *verb* [31] **1** to board (*a plane*); **2** to embark (*on a boat*); **3** to load (*goods or luggage*).
embarcarse *reflexive verb* [31] **1** to board (*a plane*); **2** to embark (*on a boat*); **3 embarcarse en algo** to get involved in something.

emboscada *noun* F ambush.

embotellamiento *noun* M traffic jam.

embrague *noun* M clutch.

embrujado/embrujada *adjective* **1** haunted; **2** bewitched.

emergencia *noun* F emergency.

emigrar *verb* [17] to emigrate.

emisión *noun* F emission.

emisora *noun* F radio station.

emoción *noun* F **1** emotion; **2** excitement; **¡qué emoción!** how exciting!; **un espectáculo lleno de emoción** a really exciting show.

emocionado/emocionada *adjective* **1** moved; **2** excited.

emocional *adjective* emotional.

emocionante *adjective* **1** moving; **2** exciting; **¡qué emocionante!** how exciting!

empacho *noun* M (*informal*) **tener empacho** to have a stomach ache (*from eating too much*); **se cogió un empacho de pasteles** he ate so many cakes he had a stomach ache.

empanada *noun* F pie; **empanada de atún** tuna pie.

empapado/empapada *adjective* soaking wet; **venían empapados** they were soaking wet.

empaparse *verb* [17] to get soaking wet.

empastar *verb* [17] to fill (*a tooth*).

empaste *noun* M filling (*in a tooth*).

empatar *verb* [17] to draw; **empataron a dos** they drew two all.

empate *noun* M draw (*in sports*).

empecé *verb* SEE **empezar**.

empeorar *verb* [17] **1** to get worse; **la situación ha empeorado** things have got worse; **2** to make worse; **va a empeorar las cosas** it's going to make things worse.

empezar *verb* [25] **1** to begin; **el colegio empieza el quince de septiembre** school begins on the fifteenth of September; **2** to start; **tendré que empezar otra vez** I'll have to start again; **empezó a llover** it started raining.

empiece, empieza, empiezo, etc. *verb* SEE **empezar**.

empinado/empinada *adjective* steep (*a road or street*).

empleado/empleada *noun* M/F **1** employee; **2** clerk (*in a bank or office*); **3** shop assistant; **4 los empleados** the staff (*in a company*); **todos los empleados se beneficiarán** all the staff will benefit.

emplear *verb* [17] **1** to employ; **2** to use; **emplearon materiales viejos** they used old materials.

empleo *noun* M **1** employment; **2** job; **buscar empleo** to look for a job; **3 estar sin empleo** to be unemployed.

emprendedor/emprendedora *adjective* enterprising.

empresa *noun* F company.

empujar *verb* [17] to push.

en *preposition* **1** in; **ponlo en el cajón** put it in the drawer; **vivo en Londres** I live in London; **en español** in Spanish; **en invierno** in winter; **2** into; **entró en la casa** he went into the house; **3** on; **está en la mesa** it's

on the table; **en el segundo piso** on the second floor; **4** at; **estaré en casa toda la tarde** I'll be at home all afternoon; **es muy buena en inglés** she's very good at English; **5 nunca he estado en París** I've never been to Paris; **6** by; **ir en coche** to go by car.

enamorado/enamorada *adjective* in love; **estar enamorado de alguien** to be in love with someone.

enamorarse *reflexive verb* [17] to fall in love; **enamorarse de alguien** to fall in love with someone.

enano/enana *noun* M/F dwarf.

encantado/encantada *adjective* **1** delighted; **están encantados con la casa** they're delighted with the house; **2 ¡encantado de conocerte!** pleased to meet you!; **3** enchanted.

encantador/encantadora *noun* M/F magician; **encantador de serpientes** snake-charmer. *adjective* lovely.

encantar *verb* [17] **me encantó el libro** I loved the book; **nos encantó el hotel** we loved the hotel; **le encantaría venir a verte** he'd love to come and see you.

encargado/encargada *noun* M/F manager. *adjective* **encargado de algo** responsible for something; **la persona encargada del reparto** the person responsible for the delivery.

encendedor *noun* M lighter.

encender *verb* [36] **1** to light; **2** to turn on.

encendido/encendida *adjective* **1** on; **2** alight.

encerado *noun* M blackboard.

enchufar *verb* [17] **1** to plug in; **2** to turn on.

enchufe *noun* M plug.

enciclopedia *noun* F encyclopedia.

encienda, enciendo, etc. *verb* SEE **encender**.

encima *adverb* **1** on; **pon un plástico encima** put a piece of plastic on it; **ponlo ahí encima** put it on there; **el piso de encima** the flat above; **no llevaba el carnet de identidad encima** he didn't have his identity card on him; **2 encima de** on, on top of; **está encima de la cama** it's on the bed; **encima del armario** on top of the wardrobe; **llevaba una gabardina encima de la chaqueta** I was wearing a raincoat over my jacket; **el niño estaba sentado encima de su madre** the baby was sitting on his mother's lap; **3 el/la de encima** the top one; **4 por encima de** over; **5 encima de llegar tarde se queja** he arrives late and on top of that he complains; **¡y encima no me lo devolvió!** and on top of that he didn't give it back to me!

encontrar *verb* [24] to find; **no he encontrado cerillas en ninguna parte** I couldn't find any matches anywhere.

encontrarse *reflexive verb* [24] **1** to meet; **me encontré con Carmen en la calle** I met Carmen in the street; **2** to find; **me encontré un billete de mil pesetas** I found a thousand-peseta note; **3** to be; **el pueblo se encuentra situado en la montaña** the village is situated in the mountains.

encuentra, encuentro, etc. *verb* SEE **encontrar**.

encuesta *noun* F survey; **encuesta de opinión** opinion poll.

enemigo/enemiga *noun* M/F enemy.

energía *noun* F energy.

enérgico/enérgica *adjective* energetic.

enero *noun* M January.

enfadado/enfadada *adjective* **1** angry; **2** annoyed.

enfadar *verb* [17] **1** to make angry; **2** to annoy.
enfadarse *reflexive verb* [17] **1** to get angry; **se enfadó muchísimo** he got really angry; **2** to get annoyed; **se enfadó conmigo** he got annoyed with me; **3** to get cross; **mamá se va a enfadar** Mum's going to get cross.

enfermar *verb* [17] to get ill.

enfermedad *noun* F illness.

enfermero/enfermera *noun* M/F nurse.

enfermo/enferma *noun* M/F sick person; **los enfermos** sick people. *adjective* ill; **está gravemente**

enferma she's seriously ill; **caer enfermo** to fall ill.

enfrente *adverb* opposite; **la tienda está justo enfrente de la casa** the shop is just opposite the house.

engañar *verb* [17] **1** to deceive; **2** to cheat, swindle; **3** to be unfaithful to. **engañarse** *reflexive verb* [17] to fool yourself.

engaño *noun* M **1** deception; **2** swindle.

engordar *verb* [17] **1** to put on weight; **2** to be fattening.

enhorabuena *noun* F ¡**enhorabuena por tu trabajo nuevo!** congratulations on your new job!; **darle la enhorabuena a alguien** to congratulate someone.

enjuagar *verb* [28] to rinse. **enjuagarse** *reflexive verb* [28] **enjuagarse el pelo** to rinse your hair.

enmohecerse *reflexive verb* [35] to go mouldy.

enojado/enojada *adjective* **1** angry; **2** annoyed.

enorme *adjective* huge.

enormemente *adverb* extremely, a lot; **enormemente preocupado** extremely worried.

ensalada *noun* F salad; **ensalada mixta** mixed salad; **ensalada de frutas** fruit salad.

ensaladera *noun* F salad bowl.

ensaladilla, ensaladilla rusa *noun* F potato salad.

ensayo *noun* M rehearsal; **ensayo general** dress rehearsal.

enseguida *adverb* right away; **enseguida lo hago** I'll do it right away.

enseñanza *noun* F **1** teaching; **me gusta la enseñanza** I like teaching; **2** education; **enseñanza primaria** primary education; **enseñanza secundaria** secondary education; **enseñanza superior** higher education.

enseñar *verb* [17] **1** to teach; **le enseñé a montar en bicicleta** I taught him to ride a bike; **2** to show; **nos enseñó la casa** he showed us the house.

ensuciar *verb* [17] to dirty; **no ensucies la mesa** don't get the table dirty; **ensucié el mantel de salsa de tomate** I got tomato sauce on the tablecloth. **ensuciarse** *reflexive verb* [17] to get dirty; **te vas a ensuciar las manos** you'll get your hands dirty; **me he ensuciado las botas de barro** I got mud on my boots.

entender *verb* [36] **1** to understand; **entiendo un poco de español** I can understand a little bit of Spanish; **entiendo lo que dices** I understand what you are saying; **no te entiendo** I can't understand you; **2 entender algo mal** to misunderstand something; **la entendí mal** I misunderstood her; **3 dar a entender algo** to imply something; **4 entender de algo** to know about something; **entiendo un poco de**

fontanería I know a bit about plumbing.

entenderse *reflexive verb* [36]
1 entenderse con alguien to communicate with someone; **nos entendimos por señas** we communicated with each other by signs; **2 entenderse con alguien** to get along with someone; **se entiende muy bien con su hermana** she gets along very well with her sister.

entendido/entendida *adjective*
1 understood; **queda bien entendido** it's perfectly understood; **¿entendido?** is that clear?; **2 ser entendido en algo** to know about something.

entero/entera *adjective* **1** whole; **un día entero** a whole day; **2 leche entera** full-cream milk.

enterrar *verb* [29] to bury.

entienda, entiendo, etc. *verb* SEE **entender**.

entonces *adverb* **1** then; **desde entonces** since then; **entonces llegó Carlos** then Carlos arrived; **2** so; **entonces nos vemos mañana** so we'll see each other tomorrow.

entrada *noun* F **1** entrance; **¿dónde está la entrada?** where is the entrance?; **2** ticket (*for the cinema or theatre*); **ya he comprado las entradas para el teatro** I've already bought the tickets for the theatre; **¿cuánto cuesta la entrada?** how much is a ticket?; **los niños pagan media entrada** it's half-price for children; **3 'entrada libre'** 'admission free'; **4** deposit; **pagué la**

entrada para el coche I put down a deposit on the car.

entrar *verb* [17] **1** to get in; **no puedo entrar** I can't get in; **entraron por una ventana** they got in through a window; **2** to go in; **han entrado en esa tienda** they've gone into that shop; **entraron en la clase corriendo** they ran into the classroom; **3** to come in; **¡entra!** come in!; **4 dejar entrar a alguien** to let someone in; **5 hacer entrar a alguien** to show someone in; **6** to fit; **no entra por la puerta** it doesn't fit through the door; **7** to join; **entrar en la ONU** to join the UN; **8 me entró hambre** I got hungry; **te va a entrar frío si te sientas ahí** you'll get cold if you sit there; **9** to be included; **el desayuno no entra en el precio** breakfast is not included in the price; **10 no me entra** (*informal*) I don't get it; **no le entran las matemáticas** (*informal*) he just can't get to grips with maths.

entre *preposition* **1** between; **estaba sentado entre Jaime y Margarita** I was sitting between Jaime and Margarita; **2** among; **lo encontré entre mis papeles** I found it among my papers; **3 lo hicimos entre todos** we did it all together; **4** by; **nueve dividido entre tres** nine divided by three; **5 entre paréntesis** in brackets; **6 cerrado entre semana** closed during the week.

entreabierto/entreabierta *adjective* half-open.

entreacto *noun* M interval.

entrega *noun* F **1** delivery (*of goods*); **2** presentation (*of a prize or award*); **3 la fecha límite para la entrega de formularios** the deadline for handing in the forms.

entregar *verb* [28] **1** to deliver; **vino a entregar una carta** he came to deliver a letter; **2** to give, to hand; **me entregó los documentos** he handed me the documents; **tenemos que entregar el trabajo el próximo lunes** we have to hand in the essay next Monday; **3** to present (*a prize or award*); **4** to surrender (*a town or weapons*); **5** to turn in (*a criminal*).
entregarse *reflexive verb* [28] to give yourself up; **se entregó a la policía** he gave himself up to the police.

entremés *noun* M starter (*in a meal*).

entrenador/entrenadora *noun* M/F trainer.

entrenamiento *noun* M training.

entrenar *verb* [17] to train.
entrenarse *reflexive verb* [17] to train.

entretanto *adverb* in the meantime.

entretenido/entretenida *adjective* entertaining.

entrevista *noun* F interview; **una entrevista de trabajo** a job interview.

entrevistar *verb* [17] to interview.

entusiasmar *verb* [17] **me entusiasmó la idea** I loved the idea; **le entusiasma el deporte** she's really keen on sports; **no me entusiasma viajar** I'm not very keen on travelling.
entusiasmarse *reflexive verb* [17] **entusiasmarse con algo/por algo** to get excited about something.

entusiasmo *noun* M enthusiasm.

enviar *verb* [32] to send.

envidia *noun* F **1** envy; **se muere de envidia** he's green with envy; **2** jealousy; **tenerle envidia a alguien** to be jealous of someone; **me tienen envidia** they're jealous of me; **le da envidia que yo tenga una bici mejor** she's jealous because I've got a better bike.

envolver *verb* [45] to wrap up.

envuelto¹/envuelta *adjective* **1** wrapped; **envuelto para regalo** gift-wrapped; **2 envuelto en algo** involved in something.

envuelto² *verb* SEE **envolver**.

epidemia *noun* F epidemic.

episodio *noun* M episode.

época *noun* F **1** age; **era otra época** it was a different age; **2** time; **en aquella época** at that time; **3** times; **en la época de los romanos** in Roman times.

equilibrio *noun* M balance; **estar en equilibrio** to be balanced; **perder el equilibrio** to lose your balance.

equipaje *noun* M luggage; **equipaje de mano** hand luggage.

equipo *noun* M **1** team; **formar un buen equipo** to make a good team;

el equipo visitante the away team; **el equipo visitante** the away team; **trabajo en equipo** team work; **2** equipment; **3 equipo de música** sound system; **equipo de alta fidelidad** hi-fi system.

equis *noun* F the Spanish name for the letter 'x'.

equitación *noun* F horse riding.

equivaler *verb* [43] **equivaler a algo** to be equivalent to something.

equivocado/equivocada *adjective* wrong.

equivocarse *reflexive verb* [31] **1** to make a mistake; **creo que me he equivocado** I think I've made a mistake; **2** to be wrong; **te equivocas si piensas eso** you're wrong if you think like that; **3 me equivoqué de carpeta** I picked up the wrong folder; **se equivocó de calle** he took the wrong street.

era, érais, eras, eres, etc. *verb* SEE **ser**.

error *noun* M mistake; **cometer un error** to make a mistake; **un error tipográfico** a typing error; **un error de cálculo** a miscalculation.

eructar *verb* [17] to burp.

eructo *noun* M burp.

es *verb* SEE **ser**.

esa *adjective* that (*see 'ese/esa' for examples*).

ésa *pronoun* that one (*see 'ése/ésa' for examples*).

esas *adjective* those (*see 'esos/esas' for examples*).

ésas *pronoun* those ones (*see 'ésos/ésas' for examples*).

escala *noun* F **1** stopover; **hacer escala en París** to stop over in Paris; **2** scale (*of a map or measurements*); **hacer algo a escala** to do something to scale; **a gran escala** on a large scale; **3** scale (*in music*).

escalador/escaladora *noun* M/F climber.

escalar *verb* [17] to climb.

escalera *noun* F staircase; **subir las escaleras** to go up the stairs; **una escalera de caracol** a spiral staircase; **una escalera mecánica** an escalator; **una escalera de incendios** a fire escape; **una escalera de mano** a ladder.

escalofrío *noun* M shiver; **tener escalofríos** to be shivering.

escalope *noun* M escalope.

escalón *noun* M step.

escándalo *noun* M **1** scandal; **un escándalo político** a political scandal; **¡su comportamiento fue un escándalo!** his behaviour was really outrageous!; **2** racket; **armar un escándalo** to make a racket; **¡qué escándalo están armando!** what a racket they are making!

escandaloso/escandalosa *adjective* **1** shocking (*behaviour or clothes*); **2** noisy (*people*).

Escandinavia *noun* F Scandinavia.

escandinavo/escandinava
noun M/F Scandinavian; **los escandinavos** Scandinavians.
adjective Scandinavian.

escapar *verb* [17] to escape;
escapar de algo to escape from something.
escaparse *reflexive verb* [17] **1** to escape; **se ha escapado de la cárcel** he's escaped from prison; **2** to run away; **escaparse de casa** to run away from home; **3** to leak (*gas or water*).

escaparate *noun* M shop window.

escarabajo *noun* M beetle.

escarcha *noun* F frost.

escasez *noun* F shortage; **hay escasez de agua** there's a water shortage.

escena *noun* F scene.

escenario *noun* M stage.

esclusa *noun* F lock (*on a canal*).

escoba *noun* F broom.

escocés/escocesa *noun* M/F Scot.
adjective Scottish.

Escocia *noun* F Scotland.

escoger *verb* [3] to choose.

escoja, escojo, etc. *verb* SEE **escoger**.

escolar *noun* M/F schoolboy/schoolgirl.
adjective school; **la vida escolar** school life.

esconder *verb* [18] to hide.
esconderse *reflexive verb* [18] to hide; **esconderse de algo** to hide from something.

escondido/escondida *adjective* hidden.

Escorpión, Escorpio *noun* M Scorpio.

escorpión¹, escorpio *noun* M/F Scorpio; **soy escorpión** I'm Scorpio.

escorpión² *noun* M scorpion.

escribir *verb* [52] **1** to write;
escribir una novela to write a novel; **le escribí una carta** I wrote a letter to him; **2 escribir a máquina** to type; **3** to spell; **¿cómo se escribe tu nombre?** how do you spell your name?

escrito *verb* SEE **escribir**.

escritor/escritora *noun* M/F writer.

escritorio *noun* M desk.

escuchar *verb* [17] **1** to listen;
escuchamos atentamente we listen carefully; **2** to listen to; **escucha bien lo que digo** listen carefully to what I say; **escúchame** listen to me.

escuela *noun* F school; **escuela primaria** primary school; **escuela nocturna** night school.

escultor/escultora *noun* M/F sculptor.

escultura *noun* F sculpture.

escupir *verb* [19] **1** to spit; **escupir a alguien** to spit at someone; **2** to spit out; **escupió la comida** he spat out the food.

ese/esa *adjective* that; **ese libro** that book; **esa chica** that girl.

ése/ésa *pronoun* that one; **ése es más bonito** that one is nicer; **ésa es tu bolsa** that one is your bag.

esfuerzo *noun* M effort; **hacer un esfuerzo** to make an effort.

eslogan *noun* M slogan.

eslovaco/eslovaca *noun* M/F Slovak.
adjective Slovak.

Eslovaquia *noun* F Slovakia.

Eslovenia *noun* F Slovenia.

esloveno/eslovena *noun* M/F Slovene.
adjective Slovene.

eso *pronoun* that; **eso no importa** that doesn't matter; **por eso** that's why.

esos/esas *adjective* those; **esos libros** those books; **esas chicas** those girls.

ésos/ésas *pronoun* those ones; **ésos son más bonitos** those ones are nicer.

espacio *noun* M 1 space; **la conquista del espacio** the conquest of space; **dejar un espacio** leave a space; 2 room; **no tengo mucho espacio para ponerlo** I haven't got much room for it.

espaguetis *plural noun* M spaghetti.

espalda *noun* F back; **ser ancho de espaldas** to be broad-shouldered; **darle la espalda a alguien** to have your back to somebody; to turn your back on somebody; **nos daba la espalda** he had his back to us; **nadar de espaldas** to swim backstroke; **tumbarse de espaldas** to lie on your back.

espantapájaros *noun* M scarecrow.

espantoso/espantosa *adjective* 1 horrific (*crime*); 2 horrible; **un vestido espantoso** a horrible dress; **tiene un gusto espantoso** he has a horrible sense of taste; 3 **hacía un frío espantoso** it was terribly cold; **tengo un sueño espantoso** I'm terribly sleepy.

España *noun* F Spain.

español[1] *noun* M Spanish (*the language*).

español[2]**/española** *noun* M/F Spaniard; **los españoles** the Spanish.
adjective Spanish.

esparadrapo *noun* M sticking plaster.

espárrago *noun* M asparagus.

especia *noun* F spice.

especial *adjective* special.

especialidad *noun* F speciality.

espectáculo *noun* M 1 sight; **era un espectáculo espantoso** it was a terrible sight; 2 show; **el mundo del espectáculo** show business.

espectador/espectadora
noun M/F spectator.

espejo *noun* M mirror; **espejo retrovisor** rear-view mirror.

espera *noun* F wait; **una corta espera** a short wait; **estar a la espera de algo** to be waiting for something.

esperanza *noun* F hope; **darle esperanzas a alguien** to build up somebody's hopes; **hay pocas esperanzas de encontrarlos** there's little hope of finding them.

esperar *verb* [17] **1** to wait; **espera aquí** wait here; **2** to wait for; **te he estado esperando más de una hora** I've been waiting for you for more than an hour; **3** to hope; **espero que vengas** I hope you'll come; **espero que sí/eso espero** I hope so; **4** to expect; **no esperaba esa respuesta** I didn't expect that answer.

espeso/espesa *adjective* thick.

espía *noun* M/F spy.

espiar *verb* [32] to spy on.

espinaca *noun* F spinach.

espionaje *noun* M spying, espionage.

espléndido/espléndida *adjective* **1** splendid (*a party, day, or house*); **2** generous (*a person*).

espliego *noun* M lavender.

esponja *noun* F sponge.

esposa *noun* F **1** wife; **la esposa de Juan** Juan's wife; **2** **esposas** handcuffs.

esposo *noun* M husband; **el esposo de mi hermana** my sister's husband.

espuma *noun* F **1** foam; **espuma de afeitar** shaving foam; **2** lather (*of soap*); **3** froth (*of beer*); **4** **espuma para el pelo** styling mousse.

espumoso/espumosa *adjective* **1** foaming; **2** frothy (*beer*); **3** **vino espumoso** sparkling wine.

esqueleto *noun* M skeleton; ★ **estar hecho un esqueleto** to be all skin and bones.

esquí *noun* M ski; **esquí acuático** waterskiing; **esquí nórdico/esquí de fondo** cross-country skiing.

esquiador/esquiadora *noun* M/F skier.

esquiar *verb* [32] to ski.

esquimal *noun* M/F *adjective* Eskimo.

esquina *noun* F corner; **doblar la esquina** to turn the corner; **vivo en la esquina de la calle León con la calle Viriato** I live on the corner of Leon Street and Viriato Street.

esta *adjective* this (*see 'este/esta' for examples*)

ésta *pronoun* this one (*see 'éste/ésta' for examples*).

está *verb* SEE **estar**.

estación *noun* F **1** station; **la estación de autobuses** the bus station; **una estación de servicio** a service station; **2** season; **el otoño es mi estación preferida** autumn is my favourite season; **la estación de**

las lluvias the rainy season; **3 una estación de esquí** a ski resort.

estacionar *verb* [17] to park; **estacionar en doble fila** to double park.

estadio *noun* M stadium; **el estadio de fútbol** the football stadium.

estado *noun* M **1** state; **estado de guerra** state of war; **2 en buen estado** in good condition (*a picture, table, etc.*); **3 estado civil** marital status; **4 estar en estado** to be pregnant; **5 un estado de cuenta** a bank statement.

Estados Unidos *plural noun* M United States.

estáis *verb* SEE **estar**.

estallar *verb* [17] **1** to explode (*a bomb*); **2** to burst (*a balloon*); **3** to blow out (*a tyre*).

estancia *noun* F stay; **su estancia en Madrid durará tres días** his stay in Madrid will last three days.

estanco *noun* M tobacconist's.

estanque *noun* M pond.

estante *noun* M shelf.

estar *verb* [2] **1** (*location*) to be; **¿dónde está mi abrigo?** where's my coat?; **¿has estado en Buenos Aires?** have you been to Buenos Aires?; **estaré en Leeds un mes** I'll be in Leeds for a month; **2** (*state*) to be; **estoy contento** I'm happy; **está casado** he's married; **¿cómo estás?** how are you?; **desde que hablé con él está más simpático** he's nicer since I had a chat with him;

3 (*appearance, taste*) **esta paella está muy buena** this paella is very nice; **con ese vestido estás muy guapa** you look very nice in that dress; **4** (*with dates*) **estamos a tres de julio** it's the third of July today; **5 estar de** to be; **estar de viaje** to be away on a trip; **están de vacaciones** they're on holiday; **6** (*with a gerund or past participle*) to be; **están trabajando en Soria** they're working in Soria; **está nevando** it's snowing; **estaban sentados allí** they were sitting over there; **aún no está terminado** it's not finished yet; **7** (*talking about how clothes fit*) **la chaqueta no me está bien** the jacket doesn't fit me; **esa falda te está corta** this skirt is too short for you; **me está grande** it's too big for me; **8 lo firmas y ya está** you sign it and that's that; **¿están ya las fotocopias?** are the photocopies ready?; **las patatas ya están** the potatoes are done.

estarse *reflexive verb* [2] **1** to be; **se estuvo sentado toda la tarde** he was sitting down all afternoon; **2** to stay; **se está horas mirando la tele** he stays in front of the TV for hours; **¡estáte quieto!** keep still!

estatua *noun* F statue.

este¹ *noun* M east.

este²/esta *adjective* this; **este libro** this book; **esta chica** this girl.

éste/ésta *pronoun* this one; **éste es más bonito** this one is nicer; **ésta es tu bolsa** this one is your bag.

esté, estén *verb* SEE **estar**.

estéreo *noun* M stereo.

estés *verb* SEE **estar**.

estilo *noun* M 1 style; 2 **ni nada por el estilo** or anything like that; **o algo por el estilo** or something of the kind.

estilográfica *noun* F fountain pen.

estirar *verb* [17] to stretch.

esto *pronoun* this; **¿qué es esto?** what is this?; **esto es lo más importante** this is the most important thing.

estofado *noun* M stew.

estómago *noun* M stomach; **me duele el estómago** I've got stomachache.

Estonia *noun* F Estonia.

estornudar *verb* [17] to sneeze.

estos/estas *adjective* these; **estos libros** these books.

éstos/éstas *pronoun* these ones.

estoy *verb* SEE **estar**.

estrecho/estrecha *adjective* 1 narrow; **una calle estrecha** a narrow street; 2 tight; **me queda muy estrecho** it's too tight for me.

estrella *noun* F star; **estrella fugaz** shooting star; **estrella de cine** film star.

estrellarse *reflexive verb* [17] to crash; **estrellarse contra algo** to crash into something.

estrenar *verb* [17] 1 **la película se estrena el próximo lunes** the film comes out next Monday; 2 **el domingo estrenaré los zapatos** I'll wear my new shoes on Sunday; **aún no he estrenado la bici** I haven't used the new bike yet.

estricto/estricta *adjective* strict.

estropear *verb* [17] 1 to break; **vas a estropear la tele si sigues haciendo eso** you'll wreck the TV if you carry on doing that; 2 to spoil; **el tiempo nos estropeó las vacaciones** the weather spoiled our holidays; 3 to damage; **me estropeó el coche** he damaged my car; 4 to ruin (*a carpet or dress, for example*).
estropearse *reflexive verb* [17] 1 to break down; **se ha estropeado el coche otra vez** the car's broken down again; 2 to go off (*fruit*); 3 to go bad (*milk or fish*); 4 to get ruined (*a carpet or dress, for example*).

estudiante *noun* M/F student.

estudiar *verb* [17] 1 to study; **estudiar medicina** to study medicine; 2 to learn; **tenemos que estudiar dos temas para mañana** we have to study two topics for tomorrow.

estudio *noun* M 1 study (*in a house*); 2 studio flat; 3 study; **el estudio de la naturaleza** the study of nature.

estudios *plural noun* M studies; **estudios de medicina** medical studies; **estudios de mercado** market research.

estufa *noun* F heater, fire.

estupendo/estupenda *adjective* great; ¿ganaste? ¡estupendo! did you win? great!

estúpido/estúpida *noun* M/F stupid person; es un estúpido he's really stupid.
adjective stupid.

estuve, estuvo, etc. *verb* SEE **estar**.

etapa *noun* F stage; por etapas in stages.

etcétera *noun* M etcetera.

eternidad *noun* F eternity.

ética *noun* F ethics.

etiqueta *noun* M 1 label; 2 price tag.

euro *noun* M euro.

Europa *noun* F Europe.

europeo/europea *noun* M/F *adjective* European.

Euskadi *noun* F the Basque Country.

euskera *adjective* Basque.

Euskera *noun* M Basque (*the language*).

evidencia *noun* F evidence.

evidente *adjective* obvious.

evidentemente *adverb* obviously.

evitar *verb* [17] 1 to avoid; evitan tomar la responsabilidad they avoid taking responsibility; 2 to prevent; evitar un accidente to prevent an accident.

evolución *noun* F evolution.

exactamente *adverb* exactly.

exacto/exacta *adjective* 1 exact; 2 accurate.

exagerar *verb* [17] to exaggerate.

examen *noun* M exam; hacer un examen to take an exam; presentarse a un examen to sit an exam; aprobar un examen to pass an exam; un examen oral an oral exam.

examinar *verb* [17] to examine.
examinarse *reflexive verb* [17] to take an exam.

excelente *adjective* excellent.

excepción *noun* F exception; hacer una excepción to make an exception; a excepción de with the exception of.

excepcional *adjective* exceptional.

excepcionalmente *adverb* exceptionally.

excepto *preposition* except for.

excursión *noun* F trip; ir de excursión al campo to go on a trip to the countryside.

excusa *noun* F excuse; poner excusas to make excuses.

exigente *adjective* demanding.

exigir *verb* [49] to demand.

existir *verb* [19] 1 to exist; 2 existen motivos para pensarlo there are reasons to think that.

éxito *noun* M success; tener éxito to be successful.

experiencia *noun* F experience.

experimentado/experimentada *adjective* experienced.

experimento *noun* M experiment.

experto/experta *noun* M/F expert.

explicación *noun* F explanation.

explicar *verb* [31] to explain.

explotar *verb* [17] to explode.

exportar *verb* [17] to export.

exposición *noun* F exhibition.

expresar *verb* [17] to express.

expresión *noun* F expression.

expreso¹ *noun* M **1** express train; **2** espresso (*coffee*).

expreso²/expresa *adjective* express; **correo expreso** express mail.

exterior *noun* M **1** exterior, outside; **el exterior de la casa** the outside of the house; **2** outward appearance; **en su exterior estaba tranquilo** his outward appearance was calm. *adjective* **1** outer (*layer*); **2** outside (*temperature*); **3** **la parte exterior de la casa** the outside of the house; **4** foreign; **política exterior** foreign policy.

externo/externa *adjective* **1** outward (*appearance or signs*); **2** external.

extintor *noun* M **extintor (de incendios)** fire extinguisher.

extranjero¹ *noun* M **vivir en el extranjero** to live abroad; **viaja**

mucho al extranjero he travels abroad a lot.

extranjero²/extranjera *noun* M/F foreigner. *adjective* foreign.

extrañar *verb* [17] **me extraña que no hayan llamado** I'm surprised they haven't phoned; **le extrañó verla allí** he was surprised to see her there.

extraño/extraña *noun* M/F stranger. *adjective* strange.

extraordinario/extraordinaria *adjective* extraordinary.

extremo¹ *noun* M **1** extreme; **2** end.

extremo²/extrema *noun* M/F winger (*in sports*). *adjective* extreme.

F f

fábrica *noun* F factory.

fabricar *verb* [31] to manufacture.

fácil *adjective* easy; **es un trabajo fácil** it's an easy job; **fácil de hacer** easy to do; **es fácil de entender** it's easy to understand.

facilidad *noun* F **1** ease; **lo hice con facilidad** I did it with ease; **2** **tener facilidad de palabra** to have a way with words.

fácilmente *adverb* easily.

factura *noun* F 1 invoice; 2 bill.

facultad *noun* F 1 faculty; **perder facultades** to lose your faculties; 2 **ir a la facultad** to go to college; **la Facultad de Medicina** the Faculty of Medicine.

faena *noun* F task; **las faenas de la casa/domésticas** the housework.

faisán *noun* M pheasant.

falda *noun* F skirt; **una falda escocesa** a tartan skirt; a kilt; **una falda de tubo** a straight skirt.

falla *noun* F flaw.

fallar *verb* [17] 1 to fail (*equipment or brakes, for example*); 2 to go wrong (*a plan*); **algo ha fallado** something's gone wrong; 3 **me falló la puntería** I missed (*the target*).

fallo *noun* M 1 fault; **el motor tiene un fallo** there's something wrong with the engine; 2 failure; **un fallo en el sistema** a failure in the system; 3 **fallo humano** human error; 4 verdict (*in court or competition*).

falso/falsa *adjective* 1 false; 2 fake (*a diamond or picture, for example*).

falta *noun* F 1 **falta de algo** lack of something; **por falta de dinero** due to lack of money; **falta de personal** staff shortage; 2 **falta de educación** bad manners; **eso es una falta de educación** that's bad manners; **fue una falta de educación por su parte** it was really rude of him; 3 **una falta grave** a serious misdemeanour; 4 **falta de asistencia** absence (*from school*); **poner una falta a alguien** to mark someone absent; **ya tiene tres faltas** he's been absent three times already; 5 **una falta de ortografía** a spelling mistake; 6 **hace falta lavarlo** it needs to be washed; **hace falta comprar pan** we need to buy bread; **no hace falta cambiarlo** it doesn't need to be changed; **no hace falta que me esperes** you don't need to wait for me; 7 **me hace falta un bolígrafo** I need a pen; **no me hace falta nada más, gracias** I don't need anymore, thank you.

faltar *verb* [17] 1 to be missing; **¿quién falta?** who's missing?; 2 **faltar al colegio** to be absent from school; 3 **nos falta práctica** we need practice; **nos faltan mil pesetas para poder comprarlo** we need another thousand pesetas to buy it; **le falta interés** he lacks interest; 4 **sólo faltan tres días** there are only three more days to go; **faltan diez días para mi cumpleaños** it's ten days to my birthday; **falta poco para el verano** it's almost summertime; **aún falta mucho para las doce** there's still a long way to go till twelve o'clock; **¿te falta mucho?** are you going to be long?; **no les falta mucho para terminar** they've almost finished; **nos faltó tiempo** we didn't have enough time.

fama *noun* F 1 fame; 2 reputation; **tener buena fama** to have a good reputation; **tener fama de mentiroso** to have a reputation for being a liar.

familia *noun* F family; **ser de familia numerosa** to be from a large family.

familiar *noun* M/F relative.
adjective **1** family; **tuve problemas familiares** I had family problems;
2 familiar.

famoso/famosa *adjective* famous.

fantasía *noun* F **1** fantasy; **un mundo de fantasía** a fantasy world;
2 imagination; **tener mucha fantasía** to have a lot of imagination;
3 joyas de fantasía costume jewellery.

fantasma *noun* M ghost.

fantástico/fantástica *adjective* fantastic.

farmacéutico/farmacéutica *noun* M/F chemist.
adjective pharmaceutical.

farmacia *noun* F chemist's;
farmacia de guardia/de turno duty chemist.

faro *noun* M **1** lighthouse;
2 headlamp.

farola *noun* F **1** streetlight; **2** lamp post.

fascinar *verb* [17] to fascinate.

fastidiar *verb* [17] to annoy; **¡deja de fastidiar!** stop being a pain!
fastidiarse *reflexive verb* [17] **¡que se fastidie!** he'll have to put up with it!;
¡te fastidias! tough!

fastidio *noun* M annoyance; **¡qué fastidio!** how annoying!

fatal *adjective* **1** (*informal*) awful;
sentirse fatal to feel awful; **estar fatal** to be really ill; to be really badly

done; **2** fatal (*an accident or illness*).
adverb **canto fatal** I am hopeless at singing.

favor *noun* M **1** favour; **hacerle un favor a alguien** to do someone a favour; **pedir un favor** to ask for a favour; **estar a favor de algo** to be in favour of something; **2 por favor** please.

favorito/favorita *adjective* favourite.

fe *noun* F faith.

febrero *noun* M February.

fecha *noun* F date; **fecha de nacimiento** date of birth; **¿a qué fecha estamos hoy?** what is the date today?; **fecha de caducidad** expiry date (*for medicines*); use-by date (*for food*).

felicidad *noun* F **1** happiness;
2 ¡felicidades! happy birthday!;
congratulations!

felicitar *verb* [17] **felicitar a alguien** to wish someone happy birthday; to congratulate someone.

feliz (*plural* **felices**) *adjective* happy; **¡feliz Año Nuevo!** Happy New Year!; **¡feliz Navidad!** Merry Christmas!; **feliz cumpleaños** happy birthday; **felices Pascuas** Merry Christmas.

felpudo *noun* M doormat.

femenino¹ *noun* M feminine.

femenino²/femenina *adjective*
1 woman's; **el equipo femenino** the women's team; **2** feminine (*style,*

manners, or noun); **3** female; **el sexo femenino** the female sex.

fenomenal *adjective* (*informal*) great.
adverb great; **pasarlo fenomenal** to have a great time.

feo/fea *adjective* ugly.

feria *noun* F fair.

feroz *adjective* fierce.

ferretería *noun* F ironmonger's.

ferrocarril *noun* M railway.

ferry *noun* M ferry.

festivo/festiva *adjective* **1** festive (*atmosphere*); **2** **un día festivo** a public holiday.

fiable *adjective* reliable.

fiambre *noun* M cold meats.

fiarse *reflexive verb* [32] **1** to believe; **no te fíes de los periódicos** don't believe what the newspapers say; **2 fiarse de alguien** to trust someone.

fibra *noun* F fibre.

ficción *noun* F fiction.

ficha *noun* F **1** card; **2 ficha médica** medical card; **ficha policial** police records; **3** token (*for the telephone*); **4** counter (*in games*).

fideo *noun* M noodle.

fiebre *noun* F **1** temperature; **tener fiebre** to have a temperature; **le ha subido la fiebre** his temperature has gone up; **2** fever; **fiebre del heno** hay fever.

fiel *adjective* **1** faithful; **no le es fiel a su mujer** he's not faithful to his wife; **2** loyal; **3** accurate (*a translation or copy, for example*).

fiesta *noun* F **1** party; **2** public holiday; **mañana es fiesta** tomorrow's a holiday.

figura *noun* F figure.

figurar *verb* [17] to appear.
figurarse *reflexive verb* [17] to imagine; **me figuro que sí** I imagine so.

fijar *verb* [17] to fix; **fijar una fecha** to fix a date.
fijarse *reflexive verb* [17] **1 fijarse en algo** to look at something; **2** to notice; **se fija en todo** she notices everything.

fijo/fija *adjective* **1** fixed; **precios fijos** fixed prices; **está fijo a la pared** it's fixed to the wall; **2** permanent (*a job*); **3 ¿está la escalera bien fija?** is the ladder steady?

fila *noun* F **1** line; **hacer fila** to form a line; **en fila india** in single file; **2** row (*of seats in the theatre or cinema*).

filete *noun* M **1** steak; **2** fillet (*of fish*).

filmar *verb* [17] **1** to shoot (*a film*); **2** to film.

filosofía *noun* F philosophy.

fin *noun* M **1** end; **llegar al fin** to get to the end; **el fin de semana** the weekend; **a fin de mes** at the end of the month; **fin de año** New Year's Eve; **2 al fin/por fin** at last; **3 en fin,**

ya te llamaré anyway, I'll give you a ring.

final *noun* M **1** end; **el final de las vacaciones** the end of the holidays; **2** ending; **una película con final feliz** a film with a happy ending; **3** **al final** at the end; **al final del libro** at the end of the book; **4** **al final** in the end; **al final lo conseguí hacer** I managed to do it in the end.
noun F final.
adjective final.

finca *noun* F **1** plot of land; **2** farm.

finlandés[1] *noun* M Finnish (*the language*).

finlandés[2]/**finlandesa** *noun* M/F Finn.
adjective Finnish.

Finlandia *noun* F Finland.

fino[1] *noun* M dry sherry.

fino[2]/**fina** *adjective* **1** fine (*a line, for example*); **2** thin (*a layer or slice*); **3** slender (*a waist or finger*); **4** refined (*a person*); **5** subtle (*sense of humour*); **6** **tener el oído muy fino** to have a very acute sense of hearing; **tener el olfato muy fino** to have a very acute sense of smell.

firma *noun* F **1** signature; **2** company.

firmar *verb* [17] to sign.

firme *adjective* **1** steady (*a ladder or chair, for example*); **con pulso firme** with a steady hand; **2** firm; **3** **estudiar de firme** to study hard.

física[1] *noun* F physics.

físico[1] *noun* M **1** physique; **2** appearance.

físico[2]/**física**[2] *noun* M/F physicist.
adjective physical.

fisioterapia *noun* F physiotherapy.

flaco/flaca *adjective* thin.

flamenco[1] *noun* M flamenco.

flamenco[2]/**flamenca** *adjective* flamenco; **baile flamenco** flamenco dancing.

flan *noun* M caramel custard.

flauta *noun* F flute; **flauta dulce** recorder.

flecha *noun* F arrow.

flequillo *noun* M fringe.

flexible *adjective* flexible.

flojo/floja *adjective* **1** loose (*a knot or screw*); **2** slack (*rope*); **3** weak (*coffee or tea*); **4** poor (*piece of work*).

flor *noun* F flower; **de flores** flower-patterned; **una falda de flores** a flower-patterned skirt.

florero *noun* M flowerpot.

florista *noun* M/F florist.

floristería *noun* F florist's.

flotar *verb* [17] to float.

fluir *verb* [54] to flow.

flujo *noun* M flow.

foca *noun* F seal (*animal*).

foco *noun* M **1** focus; **el foco de atención** the focus of attention; **2** spotlight.

folclórico/folclórica *adjective* folk; **musica folclórica** folk music.

folleto *noun* M **1** leaflet; **2** brochure.

fondo *noun* M **1** bottom; **el fondo del lago** the bottom of the lake; **al fondo del baúl** at the bottom of the trunk; **llegar al fondo de la cuestión** to get to the bottom of the matter; **sin fondo** bottomless; **2** back; **está al fondo de la sala** it's at the back of the room; **3** end; **al fondo del pasillo** at the end of the corridor; **4** kitty; **hacer un fondo común** to make a kitty; **5 fondos** funds (*money*); **6 estudiar algo a fondo** to study something in depth; **prepararse a fondo** to prepare thoroughly; **7 ruido de fondo** background noise; **música de fondo** background music.

fontanero/fontanera *noun* M/F plumber.

footing *noun* M jogging; **hacer footing** to go jogging.

forastero/forastera *noun* M/F stranger.

forma *noun* F **1** shape; **con la forma de una hoja** leaf-shaped; **tiene forma cuadrada** it's square; **2** way; **es mi forma de ser** it's the way I am; **3 en forma** fit; **mantenerse en forma** to keep fit; **4 de todas formas** anyway.

formación *noun* F **1** education; **un chico con una buena formación** a well educated boy; **2** training; **formación profesional** vocational training.

formal *adjective* **1** reliable (*person*); **2** formal (*dinner or invitation*); **3** firm (*offer*).

formar *verb* [17] **1** to form; **formar un grupo de música** to form a band; **2** to make up; **el equipo está formado por doce miembros** the team's made up of twelve members; **3 formar parejas** to get into pairs (*in class or games*); **4** to educate (*a person*).

formarse *reflexive verb* [17] **1** to be educated; **2** to form; **formarse una opinión** to form an opinion; **se formó un atasco** a traffic jam formed.

formidable *adjective* formidable.

formulario *noun* M form.

fortuna *noun* F **1** fortune; **ganar una fortuna** to earn a fortune; **2 por fortuna** fortunately; **3 tener la buena fortuna de hacer** to have the good fortune of doing; **tuve la buena fortuna de conocerlos** I had the good fortune of meeting them; **4 probar fortuna** to try your luck.

forzar *verb* [26] **1** to force; **me forzaron a aceptar** they forced me to accept; **2 forzar la vista** to strain your eyes.

forzarse *reflexive verb* [26] **forzarse a hacer** to force yourself to do.

fósforo *noun* M match (*that you strike*).

foto *noun* F photo; **sacar/hacer una foto** to take a photo.

fotocopia *noun* F photocopy.

fotocopiadora *noun* F photocopier.

fotocopiar *verb* [17] to photocopy.

fotografía *noun* F 1 photography; 2 photograph; **sacer una fotografía** to take a photograph.

fotógrafo/fotógrafa *noun* M/F photographer.

fracasar *verb* [17] to fail.

fracaso *noun* M failure.

frágil *adjective* fragile.

frambuesa *noun* F raspberry; **mermelada de frambuesas** raspberry jam.

francés¹ *noun* M French (*the language*).

francés²/francesa *noun* M/F Frenchman/Frenchwoman. *adjective* French.

Francia *noun* F France.

frasco *noun* M 1 bottle; 2 jar; **un frasco de mermelada** a jar of jam.

frase *noun* F 1 sentence; 2 phrase; **frase hecha** set phrase.

fraude *noun* M fraud.

frecuencia *noun* F frequency; **con frecuencia** often.

frecuente *adjective* frequent.

frecuentemente *adverb* often.

fregadero *noun* M sink.

fregar *verb* [30] 1 to wash; **fregar los platos** to wash the dishes;

2 **fregar el suelo** to mop the floor; 3 to scrub.

freír *verb* [53] to fry.

frenar *verb* [17] 1 to brake; 2 to slow down (*a process*); 3 to curb (*inflation*).

freno *noun* M brake.

frente *noun* M 1 front; 2 **al frente de la manifestación** at the head of the demostration; **al frente de la patrulla** leading the patrol; 3 **al frente del equipo** in charge of the team; 4 **dar un paso al frente** to step forward; 5 **hacer frente a** to face (*a problem or attacker*). *noun* F forehead.

fresa *noun* F strawberry; **mermelada de fresas** strawberry jam.

fresco¹ *noun* M 1 fresh air; **tomar el fresco** to get some fresh air; **estar al fresco** to be out in the fresh air; 2 **hace fresco** it's chilly; 3 fresco (*painting*).

fresco²/fresca *adjective* 1 cool; **una bebida fresca** a cool drink; **una brisa fresca** a cool breeze; 2 **hoy hace fresco** it's chilly today; 3 fresh; **pescado fresco** fresh fish; 4 **pintura fresca** wet paint; 5 **¡qué fresco!** what a nerve!; **ser muy fresco** to have a nerve.

fría, frío, etc. *verb* SEE **freír**.

friega, friego, friegue, etc. *verb* SEE **fregar**.

frigorífico *noun* M fridge.

frío[1] *noun* M cold; **hace frío** it's cold; **tengo frío** I'm cold; **una ola frió** a cold spell.

frío[2]**/fría** *adjective* cold.

frito/frita *adjective* 1 fried; 2 **quedarse frito** (*informal*) to fall asleep.

frontera *noun* F border.

frotar *verb* [17] to rub.
frotarse *reflexive verb* [17] to rub.

fruncir *verb* [66] **fruncir el ceño** to frown.

frustrar *verb* [17] 1 to frustrate (*person*); **me frustra que ...** I find it frustrating that ...; 2 to thwart (*plans*).

fruta *noun* F fruit.

frutería *noun* F fruit shop.

frutero *noun* M fruit bowl.

fruto *noun* M fruit; **frutos secos** nuts and dried fruits.

fue *verb* SEE ser, ir.

fuego *noun* M 1 fire; **encender el fuego** to light the fire; **prender fuego a algo** to set fire to something; 2 **¿tienes fuego?** have you got a light?; 3 **a fuego lento** on a low heat.

fuente *noun* F 1 spring; 2 fountain; 3 large dish; **una fuente de servir** a serving dish; **una fuente de horno** an ovenproof dish.

fuera, fuéramos, etc. *verb* SEE ser, ir.

fuera *adverb* 1 out; **¡sal fuera!** go out!; **ahí fuera** out there; **salimos a cenar fuera** we went out for dinner; 2 outside; **están esperando fuera** they're waiting outside; **la parte de fuera de la maleta** the outside of the suitcase; **deja las cajas fuera** leave the boxes outside; **por fuera es plateado** it's silver on the outside; 3 away; **el jefe está fuera** the boss is away; 4 abroad; **están fuera del país** they're abroad; 5 **fuera de peligro** out of danger; **fuera de lugar** out of place; **fuera de serie** exceptional; 6 **fuera de juego** offside.

fueron *verb* SEE ser, ir.

fuerte *adjective* 1 strong; **ser fuerte** to be strong; **un olor fuerte** a strong smell; 2 loud; **no pongas la música tan fuerte** don't play the music so loud; 3 hard (*blow*); 4 big; **un beso fuerte** a big kiss; 5 substantial; **tomamos una comida fuerte al mediodía** we have a big meal at lunchtime; 6 **un dolor fuerte** an intense pain.
adverb 1 hard; **pega fuerte** hit it hard; 2 tight; **agárralo fuerte** hold on tight (to it).

fuerza *noun* F 1 strength; **tener fuerza** to be strong; **no tuvo fuerza para levantarlo** he wasn't strong enough to lift it; 2 **hice fuerza y conseguí abrirlo** I used all my strength and I managed to open it; 3 **empujar con fuerza** to push hard; 4 **por la fuerza** by force; **lo obligaron a entrar en el coche por la fuerza** they forced him to get into the car;

5 a fuerza de by; **a fuerza de empujar** by pushing; **6** force; **fuerza aérea** air force; **fuerzas armadas** armed forces; **7 fuerza de voluntad** willpower.

fuga *noun* F **1** leak; **una fuga de gas** a gas leak; **2 una fuga de prisioneros** a jailbreak; **3 darse a la fuga** to flee.

fui, fuimos, fuiste, etc. *verb* SEE **ser, ir**.

fumador/fumadora *noun* M/F smoker.

fumar *verb* [17] to smoke.

función *noun* F **1** function; **2** performance; **función de noche** late-night performance; **función benéfica** charity performance.

funcionar *verb* [17] **1** to work; **¿cómo funciona?** how does it work?; **'no funciona'** 'out of order'; **2** to run; **funciona con electricidad** it runs on electricity.

funcionario/funcionaria *noun* M/F government employee.

funda *noun* F **1** cover (*for a cushion, pillow, etc.*); **2** sleeve (*of a record*).

fundamental *adjective* fundamental.

fundir *verb* [19] to melt.
fundirse *reflexive verb* [19] to melt.

funeral *noun* M funeral.

funeraria *noun* F funeral director's.

furgoneta *noun* F van.

furia *noun* F fury; **estar hecho una furia** (*informal*) to be furious.

furioso/furiosa *adjective* furious; **ponerse furioso** to get furious.

fusible *noun* M fuse; **saltaron los fusibles** the fuses blew.

fusil *noun* M rifle.

futbito *noun* M five-a-side football.

fútbol *noun* M football; **jugar al fútbol** to play football; **fútbol sala** five-a-side football.

futbolín *noun* M **1** table football; **2 los futbolines** the amusement arcade.

futbolista *noun* M/F footballer.

futuro[1] *noun* M future.

futuro[2]**/futura** *adjective* future.

G g

gafas *plural noun* F glasses; **gafas de sol** sunglasses; **llevar gafas** to wear glasses.

galápago *noun* M **1** giant turtle; **2** terrapin.

galería *noun* F **1** gallery; **galería de arte** art gallery; **2 galería comercial** shopping arcade.

Gales *noun* M **el país de Gales** Wales.

galés[1] *noun* M Welsh (*the language*).

galés[2]/**galesa** *noun* M/F Welshman/Welshwoman. *adjective* Welsh.

gallego[1] *noun* M Galician (*the language*).

gallego[2]/**gallega** *noun* M/F Galician. *adjective* Galician.

galleta *noun* F biscuit.

gallina *noun* F hen.

gallo *noun* M cockerel.

galopar *verb* [17] to gallop.

gamba *noun* F prawn.

gamberro/**gamberra** *noun* M/F **1** lout; **2** hooligan. *adjective* **es muy gamberro** he's a real lout; he's a real hooligan.

gana *noun* F **1** **tener ganas de hacer algo** to feel like doing something; **no tengo ganas de ir al cine** I don't feel like going to the cinema; **2** **tengo ganas de verlos** I'm looking forward to seeing them; **3** (*informal*) **no lo hace porque no le da la gana hacerlo** he doesn't do it because he doesn't want to; **voy porque me da la gana** I'm going because I feel like it; **hace siempre lo que le da la gana** she always does as she pleases; **4** **hacer algo sin ganas** to do something half-heartedly; **hacer algo de buena gana** to do something willingly;

hacer algo de mala gana to do something reluctantly.

ganancia *noun* F profit.

ganador/**ganadora** *noun* M/F winner. *adjective* winning (*number*).

ganar *verb* [17] **1** to win; **ganar una carrera** to win a race; **ganaron el primer premio** they won first prize; **2** to earn; **gano un buen sueldo** I earn a good salary.

ganarse *reflexive verb* [17] **1** to earn; **ganarse la vida** to earn your living; **se gana la vida pintando** he earns his living painting; **2** to win; **ganarse la confianza de alguien** to win someone's trust.

gancho *noun* M hook.

ganso/**gansa** *noun* M/F **1** goose; **2** (*informal*) **ser un ganso** to be a clown; **hacer el ganso** to clown around.

garaje *noun* M garage.

garantía *noun* F guarantee; **bajo garantía** under guarantee.

garantizar *verb* [22] to guarantee.

garbanzo *noun* M chickpea.

garganta *noun* F throat; **me duele la garganta** I have a sore throat.

gas *noun* M **1** gas; **una cocina a gas** a gas cooker; **2** **gases tóxicos** toxic fumes.

gaseosa *noun* F lemonade.

gasoil, gasóleo *noun* M **1** heating oil; **2** diesel.

gasolina *noun* F petrol; **voy a echar gasolina al coche** I'm going to put some petrol in the car; **gasolina sin plomo** unleaded petrol.

gasolinera *noun* F petrol station.

gastar *verb* [17] **1** to spend; **gastan mucho en comida** they spend a lot of money on food; **2** to use; **mi coche gasta mucha gasolina** my car uses a lot of petrol; **me gastó todo el champú** she used up all my shampoo; **3 ¿qué número de pie gastas?** what shoe size do you take?

gastarse *reflexive verb* [17] to run out; **se han gastado las pilas** the batteries have run out.

gasto *noun* M expense; **tenemos muchos gastos** we have a lot of expenses; **gastos de desplazamiento** travel expenses; **gastos de envío** postage and packing.

gatear *verb* [17] to crawl.

gato/gata *noun* M/F cat.

gaviota *noun* F seagull.

gazpacho *noun* M gazpacho (*a chilled soup made with tomatoes, cucumber, and other vegetables*).

gel *noun* M gel.

gelatina *noun* F jelly.

gemelo/gemela *noun* M/F *adjective* twin.

gemelos *plural noun* M binoculars.

Géminis *noun* M Gemini

géminis *noun* M/F Gemini; **soy géminis** I'm Gemini.

gemir *verb* [57] to groan; **gemir de dolor** to groan with pain.

generación *noun* F generation.

general *noun* M/F general (*in the army*).
adjective general; **en general** in general; **por lo general** generally; **en líneas generales** broadly speaking.

generalmente *adverb* generally.

generoso/generosa *adjective* generous.

genética *noun* F genetics.

genial *adjective* **1** brilliant; **una idea genial** a brilliant idea; **2** (*informal*) great, brilliant; **¡es genial!** it's great!

genio *noun* M **1** genius; **Ana es un genio** Ana is a genius; **2** temper; **tener mal genio** to be bad-tempered; **¡vaya genio!** what a temper!

gente *noun* F people; **vino mucha gente** a lot of people came; **la gente dice que** … people say that …

geografía *noun* F geography.

gerente *noun* M/F manager.

gestión *noun* F **1** management; **la gestión de la empresa** the management of the company; **2 tengo que hacer una gestión en el consulado** I have to sort things out at the consulate.

gesto *noun* M gesture; **me hizo un gesto para que me acercara** he gestured to me to come over; **hice un gesto de asentimiento** I nodded.

Gibraltar *noun* M Gibraltar.

gigante/giganta *noun* M/F giant.

gimnasia *noun* F **1** gymnastics; **2** exercise; **es bueno hacer gimnasia** it's good to exercise; **gimnasia de mantenimiento** keep-fit; **clase de gimnasia** PE class.

gimnasio *noun* M gym.

ginebra *noun* F gin.

gin tonic *noun* M gin and tonic.

girar *verb* [17] **1** to turn; **gira a la derecha en el semáforo** turn right at the traffic lights; **girar la cabeza** to turn your head; **2** to go round; **la tierra gira alrededor del sol** the earth goes round the sun; **3** to spin; **4 girar un cheque** to draw a cheque; **5 girar dinero** to send money.

girasol *noun* M sunflower.

gitano/gitana *noun* M/F gypsy.

glaciar *noun* M glacial.

globo *noun* M balloon.

glorieta *noun* F **1** square (*in a town*); **2** roundabout (*on the road*).

glotón/glotona *adjective* greedy.

gobernar *verb* [17] **1** to rule; **2** to govern.

gobierno *noun* M government.

gol *noun* M goal; **marcar/meter un gol** to score a goal.

golf *noun* M golf; **jugar al golf** to play golf.

golfo *noun* M **1** gulf (*in geography*); **2** scoundrel; **eres un golfo** you're a

scoundrel; **3** little rascal (*to a child*).

golondrina *noun* F swallow.

golpe *noun* M **1** knock; **darse un golpe** to knock yourself; **se dio un golpe en la pierna** he knocked his leg; **2** blow; **fue un duro golpe** it was a hard blow; **3 darle un golpe a alguien** to hit someone; **4** tap; **dar unos golpes en la mesa** to tap the table; **5 la ventana se cerró de golpe** the window slammed shut; **cerré el baúl de golpe** I slammed the trunk shut.

golpear *verb* [17] **1** to hit; **le golpeé el brazo con una revista** I hit him on the arm with a magazine; **2** to bang; **la ventana golpeaba por el viento** the window was banging in the wind; **3** to beat; **golpear un tambor** to beat a drum; **4** to tap.
golpearse *reflexive verb* [17] to bang; **se golpeó el brazo con la mesa** he banged his arm on the table.

goma *noun* F **1** rubber; **botas de goma** rubber boots; **goma espuma** foam rubber; **2 una goma (de borrar)** a rubber; **3 una goma (elástica)** a rubber band.

gordo[1] *noun* M **1** fat man; **2** jackpot (*in the state lottery*).

gorda[1] *noun* F fat woman.

gordo[2]**/gorda**[2] *adjective* **1** fat; **ponerse gordo** to get fat; **2** thick (*book or jumper*); **3** serious (*problem or mistake*); ★ **me cae gordo** (*informal*) I can't stand him.

gorila *noun* M gorilla.

gorra *noun* F cap.

gorro *noun* M cap.

gota *noun* F drop.

gotear *verb* [17] **1** to drip; **2 una gota de** (*informal*) a drop of; **tomaré una gota de café** I'll have a drop of coffee; **no tiene ni una gota de paciencia** he hasn't got the slightest bit of patience.

gozar *verb* [22] to enjoy; **todos gozamos del espectáculo** we all enjoyed the show; **gozo mucho oyendo música** I enjoy listening to music a lot.

grabación *noun* F recording.

grabador *noun* M tape recorder.

grabadora *noun* F tape recorder.

grabar *verb* [17] to record.

gracia *noun* F **1** joke; **hacer una gracia** to make a joke; **2 tener gracia** to be funny; **esa broma no tiene gracia** that joke isn't funny; **tiene mucha gracia contando cosas** she's very funny telling stories; **3 me hace gracia verlo** seeing it makes me laugh; **4 no me hace ninguna gracia ir** I don't like the idea of going at all.

gracias *plural noun* F thank you; **muchas gracias** thank you very much; **darle las gracias a alguien** to thank someone; **gracias a ellos** thanks to them.

gracioso/graciosa *adjective* funny.

grado *noun* M degree; **veinte grados centígrados** twenty degrees centigrade; **cinco grados bajo cero** five degrees below zero.

gradual *adjective* gradual.

graduarse *reflexive verb* [20] to graduate.

gramática *noun* F grammar.

gramo *noun* M gram.

gran *adjective* SEE **grande**.

Gran Bretaña *noun* F Great Britain.

grande, gran *adjective* (*'grande' becomes 'gran' before a singular noun*) **1** big; **tienen una casa muy grande** they have a very big house; **la chaqueta me queda grande** the jacket's too big for me; **un gran número de personas** a great number of people; **2** great; **soy un gran admirador suyo** I'm a great admirer of hers; **es un gran actor** he's a great actor; **una gran oportunidad** a great opportunity; **3** grown-up; **cuando sea grande** when I grow up; **ya eres muy grande para hacer eso** you're too grown-up to do that; **4 grandes almacenes** department store.

granizado *noun* M crushed ice drink; **granizado de limón** iced lemon drink.

granizar *verb* [22] to hail.

granizo *noun* M hail.

granja *noun* F farm.

granjero/granjera *noun* M/F farmer; **es granjero** he's a farmer.

grano *noun* M 1 grain; **un grano de arena** a grain of sand; 2 (coffee) bean; 3 spot, pimple; **me ha salido un grano** I've got a spot.

grapa *noun* F staple.

grapadora *noun* F stapler.

grapar *verb* [17] to staple.

grasa *noun* F 1 fat; **el contenido de grasa** the fat content; 2 grease; **el horno estaba llena de grasa** the oven was covered in grease.

grasiento/grasienta *adjective* greasy.

gratis *adjective* free; **entrada gratis** free entry.
adverb free; **los niños viajan gratis** children travel free.

gratuito/gratuita *adjective* free; **entrada gratuita** free entry.

grava *noun* F gravel.

grave *adjective* serious; **está muy grave** he's seriously ill.

Grecia *noun* F Greece.

griego¹ *noun* M Greek (*the language*).

griego²/griega *noun* M/F *adjective* Greek.

grifo *noun* M tap; **abrir el grifo** to turn the tap on; **cerrar el grifo** to turn the tap off.

grillo *noun* M cricket.

gripe *noun* F flu; **tener (la) gripe/ estar con gripe** to have flu.

gris *noun* M *adjective* grey.

gritar *verb* [17] to shout; **gritar de alegría** to shout for joy; **gritar de dolor** to scream with pain.

grito *noun* M 1 shout; **dar un grito** to shout; 2 cry; **un grito de protesta** a cry of protest; 3 **un grito de dolor** a cry of pain; **un grito de horror** a scream of horror.

grosella *noun* F redcurrant.

grosería *noun* F **no digas groserías** don't say rude things; **¡qué grosería!** how rude!

grosero/grosera *adjective* rude.

grúa *noun* F crane.

grueso/gruesa *adjective* 1 thick; 2 fat (*person*).

gruñón/gruñona *adjective* grumpy.

grupo *noun* M group; **salir en grupo** to go out in a group; **un grupo musical** a group (*playing music*).

guante *noun* M glove.

guapo/guapa *adjective* good-looking.

guarda *noun* M/F 1 guard; 2 keeper (*in museum*).

guardabarros *noun* M mudguard.

guardaespaldas *noun* M/F bodyguard.

guardar *verb* [17] 1 to keep; **guardo todas sus cartas** I keep all his letters; 2 to put away; **guarda tus juguetes** put your toys away; 3 **guardar cama** to stay in bed.

guardería infantil *noun* F
nursery.

guardia *noun* M/F **1** policeman/
policewoman; **2 Guardia Civil** Civil
Guard.

guardián/guardiana *noun* M/F
guard.

guarro/guarra *adjective*
(*informal*) **1** filthy; **2** disgusting (*a
person*).
noun M/F (*informal*) filthy pig.

guau *exclamation* wow!

guerra *noun* F war.

guerrilla *noun* F guerrilla.

guía *noun* F **1** guide; **guía de
restaurantes** restaurant guide;
2 map (*of a city or town*); **3 guía
telefónica** telephone directory.
noun M/F guide (*person*); **es guía
turístico** he's a tourist guide.

guiar *verb* [32] to guide.
guiarse *reflexive verb* [32] **guiarse por
un mapa** to follow a map.

guijarro *noun* M pebble.

guiñar *verb* [17] to wink.

guiño *noun* M wink.

guión *noun* M **1** dash; **2** hyphen;
una palabra con guión a
hyphenated word; **3** script (*of a
film*).

guisante *noun* M pea.

guisar *verb* [17] to cook; **guisa muy
bien** he's a very good cook.

guitarra¹ *noun* F guitar; **guitarra
española** Spanish guitar.

guitarra² *noun* M/F guitarist.

gusano *noun* M worm.

gustar *verb* [17] **me gusta mucho** I
like it a lot; **me gustan los animales**
I like animals; **no le gustó el libro** he
didn't like the book; **a mi padre le
gustan las fresas** my dad likes
strawberries; **el que más me gusta**
the one I like the most; **les gusta
mirar la tele** they like watching telly;
¡así me gusta! that's what I like to
hear/see!

gusto *noun* M **1** taste; **tiene gusto
a menta** it tastes of mint; **tiene buen
gusto** it tastes nice; **tengo mal gusto
en la boca** I have a nasty taste in my
mouth; **2 tiene muy buen gusto** she
has very good taste; **3 mucho gusto
en conocerle** pleased to meet you.

H h

ha *verb* SEE **haber**.

haba *noun* F **1** bean; **2** broad bean.

habéis *verb* SEE **haber**.

haber *verb* [6] **1** (*used with another
verb in the same way as 'have' in
English to form past tenses*); **he
escrito a mi hermano** I have written
to my brother; **él no lo ha cogido** he
hasn't taken it; **aún no había comido**
I hadn't eaten yet; **después de
haberlo pensado bien** after having
thought about it properly; **2** there is;
aquí no hay suficiente there's not
enough here; **había un paquete en**

recepción there was a parcel in reception; **3** there are; **hay varios errores** there are various mistakes; **había más de treinta personas en la sala** there were more than thirty people in the room; **4 ¿qué hay que hacer?** what needs to be done?; **hay que limpiar la cocina** the kitchen needs to be cleaned; **hay que sacar dinero** we need to take some money out; **ahora hay que pintarlo** it needs painting now; **5 hola, ¿qué hay?** hi, how are things?; **6 'muchas gracias' – 'no hay de qué'** 'thank you very much' – 'don't mention it'.

hábil adjective **1** skilful; **un jugador hábil** a skilful player; **2** clever; **es muy hábil para conseguir lo que quiere** he's very clever when it comes to getting what he wants.

habitación noun F room; **una habitación sencilla/individual** a single room; **una habitación doble** a double room.

habitante noun M/F inhabitant.

habla noun F **1** speech; **se quedó sin habla** he was speechless; **2 un país de habla hispana** a Spanish-speaking country; **3 al habla** speaking (on the phone); **'¿el Señor López?' – 'al habla'** 'Mr López?' – 'speaking'.

hablador/habladora noun M/F **1** chatterbox; **2** gossip. adjective **1** talkative; **2** gossipy.

hablar verb [17] **1** to speak; **sabe hablar inglés** he speaks English; **¿hablas algún idioma?** do you speak any foreign languages?; **2** to talk; **no**

habla mucho she doesn't talk very much; **hablar de** to talk about; **siempre habla mucho de ti** she's always talking about you; **me habló de sus proyectos** he talked to me about his plans.

habrán, habré, etc. verb SEE haber.

hacer verb [7] **1** to make; **hacer un pastel** to make a cake; **hacer la cama** to make the bed; **2** to do; **no sé qué hacer** I don't know what to do; **hacer los deberes** to do your homework; **¿qué haces?** what are you doing?; **estoy haciendo derecho** I'm doing law; **3 hacer la comida** to cook lunch; **hacer la cena** to cook dinner; **4** to build (a house or road, for example); **5 hacer una visita** to pay a visit; **6 hacer un regalo a alguien** to give somebody a present; **7 hace (el papel) de Otelo** he plays Othello; **8** (talking about the weather) **hace frío** it's cold; **hacía mucho viento** it was very windy; **este verano ha hecho muy mal tiempo** the weather's been very bad this summer; **9** (talking about time) **hace tres días** three days ago; **hace tres días que se fueron** they left three days ago; **eso pasó hace mucho tiempo** that happened a long time ago; **¿cuánto tiempo hace que vives aquí?** how long have you been living here?; **hacía dos meses que no iba a verlos** I hadn't been to see them for two months; **trabaja aquí desde hace tres meses** she's been working here for three months now; **10 hacer a alguien hacer algo** to make someone do something; **le hice**

repetirlo I made him do it again; **eso me hizo pensar** that made me think.

hacerse *reflexive verb* [7] **1** to become; **hacerse famoso** to become famous; **se hicieron amigos** they became friends; **2 se están haciendo viejos** they're getting old; **3 hacerse daño** to hurt yourself; **me he hecho un corte en el dedo** I've cut my finger; **4 me he hecho un vestido** I've made myself a dress; **se ha hecho una mesa para la cocina** she's made a table for her kitchen; **5 ¿cómo se hace?** how do you do it?

hacha *noun* F axe (*even though 'hacha' is a feminine noun, it is used with 'el' and 'un'*).

hacia *preposition* **1** towards; **vinieron hacia mí** they came towards me; **hacia el norte** northwards; **muévelo hacia abajo** move it down; **2** (*with time*) about; **llamaré hacia las dos de la tarde** I'll call at about two o'clock; **te pagaré hacia final de mes** I'll pay you towards the end of the month.

hacienda *noun* F estate, ranch.

hada *noun* F fairy (*even though 'hada' is a feminine noun, it is used with 'el' and 'un'*).

haga, hago, etc. *verb* SEE **hacer**.

halagar *verb* [28] to flatter.

halcón *noun* M falcon.

hallar *verb* [17] to find; **no pudieron hallar una solución** they couldn't find a solution.

hallarse *reflexive verb* [17] **1** to be; **el pueblo se halla (situado) cerca del mar** the village is situated near the sea; **2** to feel; **me hallaba tranquilo** I was feeling calm.

hamaca *noun* F hammock.

hambre *noun* F hunger; **tener hambre** to be hungry; **me muero de hambre** (*informal*) I'm starving; **el aire del mar me da hambre** the sea air makes me feel hungry.

hamburguesa *noun* F hamburger.

hamburguesería *noun* F hamburger bar.

hámster *noun* M hamster.

han *verb* SEE **haber**.

harán, haré, etc. *verb* SEE **hacer**.

harina *noun* F flour; **harina integral** wholemeal flour.

hartarse *reflexive verb* [17] to get fed up; **me estoy hartando de este color** I'm getting fed up with this colour; **se hartó de esperar** he got fed up of waiting.

harto/harta *adjective* **estar harto de** to be fed up of/with; **están hartos de comer siempre lo mismo** they're fed up of always eating the same thing; **estoy harta de tus excusas** I'm fed up with your excuses.

has *verb* SEE **haber**.

hasta *preposition* **1** until; **me quedaré hasta la semana que viene** I'll stay until next week; **hasta que** until; **no lo mandes hasta que yo lo diga** don't send it until I tell you;

2 ¡hasta mañana! see you tomorrow!; ¡hasta luego! see you later!; ¡hasta pronto! see you soon!; **3** up to; hasta ahora up to now; hasta hace tres meses up to three months ago; **4** la falda me llega hasta los tobillos the skirt goes down to my ankles; **5** as far as; llegamos hasta Bilbao we went as far as Bilbao.

hay *verb* SEE **haber**.

haz *verb* SEE **hacer**.

he *verb* SEE **haber**.

hechizo *noun* M spell.

hecho[1] *noun* M **1** fact; el hecho es que ... the fact is ...; ¿cuáles son los hechos? what are the facts?; **2** tenemos que pasar de las palabras a los hechos we must stop talking and do something; **3** de hecho in fact.

hecho[2]/**hecha** *adjective* **1** made; hecho a mano hand-made; un trabajo bien hecho a job well done; **2** ¡bien hecho! well done!

helada[1] *noun* F frost.

helado[1] *noun* M ice cream; un helado de fresa a strawberry ice cream.

helado[2]/**helada**[2] *adjective* **1** frozen; el río estaba helado the river was frozen; la pobre chica estaba helada the poor girl was frozen; **2** freezing; tienes las manos heladas your hands are freezing; estoy helado I'm freezing; la casa está helada the house is freezing.

helar *verb* [29] esta noche va a helar there's going to be a frost tonight.

helarse *reflexive verb* [29] to freeze; el río se ha helado the river has frozen over.

hélice *noun* F propeller.

helicóptero *noun* M helicopter.

hemos *verb* SEE **haber**.

heno *noun* M hay; fiebre del heno hay fever.

heredar *verb* [17] **1** to inherit; **2** heredar el trono to succeed to the throne.

heredero/heredera *noun* M/F heir.

herida[1] *noun* F injury.

herido/herida[2] *adjective* **1** injured; estar seriamente herido to be seriously injured; **2** wounded; resultó herido en la pelea he was wounded in the fight.

herir *verb* [14] **1** to wound; **2** to hurt; hirieron mis sentimientos they hurt my feelings.

hermana *noun* F sister; hermana gemela twin sister; hermana política sister-in-law.

hermanastro/hermanastra *noun* M/F **1** stepbrother/ stepsister; **2** half-brother/half-sister.

hermano *noun* M **1** brother; hermano gemelo twin brother; hermano político brother-in-law; **2** hermanos brothers; brothers and sisters; **¿tienes hermanos?** do you have any brothers and sisters?

hermoso/hermosa *adjective* beautiful.

héroe *noun* M hero.

heroína *noun* F 1 heroine; 2 heroin.

herramienta *noun* F tool.

hervir *verb* [14] to boil; **hervir unas patatas** to boil some potatoes.

hice *verb* SEE **hacer**.

hidratante *adjective* moisturizing.

hiedra *noun* F ivy.

hielo *noun* M ice; **cubito de hielo** ice cube.

hierba *noun* F 1 grass; **'no pisar la hierba'** 'do not walk on the grass'; 2 herb; **hierbas de cocina** (cooking) herbs; 3 **una mala hierba** a weed.

hierro *noun* M iron.

hígado *noun* M liver.

higiénico/higiénica *adjective* hygienic.

higo *noun* M fig.

hija *noun* F daughter; **hija política** daughter-in-law.

hijo *noun* M 1 son; **su hijo se llama Carlos** his son is called Carlos; **hijo político** son-in-law; 2 **hijos** children; **tienen tres hijos** they've got three children.

hilo *noun* M thread.

himno *noun* M hymn.

hincha *noun* M/F supporter; **es hincha del Sevilla** he's a Seville supporter.

hinchado/hinchada *adjective* swollen.

hinchar *verb* [17] 1 to blow up (*a balloon*); 2 to pump up (*a tyre*).

hincharse *reflexive verb* [17] to swell up; **se me ha hinchado el tobillo** my ankle has swollen up.

hipermercado *noun* M hypermarket.

hipo *noun* M hiccups; **tener hipo** to have hiccups.

hipoteca *noun* F mortgage.

hispano/hispana *noun* M/F *adjective* 1 Hispanic; 2 Spanish American; **países de habla hispana** Spanish-speaking countries.

Hispanoamérica *noun* F Spanish America.

hispanoamericano/ hispanoamericana *noun* M/F Spanish American. *adjective* Spanish American.

hispanohablante *noun* M/F Spanish-speaker. *adjective* Spanish-speaking.

historia *noun* F 1 history; **la historia de Chile** the history of Chile; 2 story; **una historia de miedo** a horror story.

histórico/histórica *adjective* 1 historical; 2 historic.

hizo *verb* SEE **hacer**.

hogar *noun* M home; **éste es mi hogar** this is my home; **labores del hogar** housework.

hoguera *noun* F bonfire.

hoja *noun* F **1** leaf (*of a tree or plant*); **2** sheet (*of paper or metal*); **3** page (*of a book*).

hola *exclamation* hello.

Holanda *noun* F Holland.

holandés[1] *noun* M Dutch (*the language*).

holandés[2]**/holandesa** *noun* M/F Dutchman/Dutchwoman. *adjective* Dutch.

holgado/holgada *adjective* loose-fitting.

hombre *noun* M **1** man; **un hombre de negocios** a businessman; **el hombre del tiempo** the weatherman; **un hombre rana** a frogman; **2 ¡hombre! ¡tú por aquí!** hey! look who's here!; **¡no, hombre!** of course not!

hombro *noun* M shoulder.

homosexual *noun* M/F *adjective* homosexual.

hondo[1] *adverb* **respirar hondo** to breathe deeply.

hondo[2]**/honda** *adjective* **1** deep; **un pozo hondo** a deep well; **2 en lo más hondo de mi corazón** deep in my heart.

honesto/honesta *adjective* honest.

hongo *noun* M **1** fungus; **2 tener hongos** to have athlete's foot.

honor *noun* M honour; **tener el honor de** to have the honour of; **en honor de** in honour of.

honra *noun* F honour.

honradez *noun* F honesty.

honrado/honrada *adjective* honest.

hora *noun* F **1** hour; **la película dura dos horas** the film lasts two hours; **media hora** half an hour; **hora y media** an hour and a half; **a las quince horas** at fifteen hours; **la hora punta** the rush hour; **durante las horas de trabajo** during working hours; **horas de visita** visiting hours (*at the hospital*); **2** time; **¿qué hora es?** what's the time?; **¿a qué hora empieza?** what time does it start?; **¿tiene hora?** have you got the time?; **¿me puede dar la hora?** could you tell me what time is it?; **a la hora de comer** at lunchtime; **es hora de ir a la cama** it's bedtime; **ya es hora de entrar** it's time to go in; **en mis horas libres** in my free time; **hacer horas extra** to do overtime; **llegar a la hora** to arrive on time; **3 pedir hora** to make an appointment; **he pedido hora con el dentista** I made an appointment with the dentist; **4 a primera hora de la mañana** first thing in the morning.

horario *noun* M **1** timetable; **el horario de clase** the school timetable; **2 horario de visitas** visiting hours (*at the hospital*).

horchata *noun* F a cold drink made from tiger nuts.

horizonte *noun* M horizon.

hormiga *noun* F ant.

hormigón *noun* M concrete.

horno *noun* M 1 oven; **verduras al horno** roast vegetables; 2 kiln.

horóscopo *noun* M horoscope.

horquilla *noun* F hairpin.

horrible *adjective* horrible.

horror *noun* M 1 horror; 2 (*informal*) **¡qué horror!** how awful!

horrorizar *verb* [22] to horrify.

horroroso/horrorosa *adjective* 1 horrific (*crime*); 2 (*informal*) awful (*a dress, book or picture, for example*).

hospedarse *reflexive verb* [17] to stay; **nos hospedamos en una pensión** we stayed in a guesthouse.

hospital *noun* M hospital.

hospitalidad *noun* F hospitality.

hostal *noun* M hotel (*small and not expensive*).

hotel *noun* M hotel.

hotelero/hotelera *noun* M/F hotel manager.
adjective hotel.

hoy *adverb* 1 today; **hoy es mi cumpleaños** it's my birthday today; **¿a qué estamos hoy?** what day is it today?; 2 **hoy en día** nowadays.

hoyo *noun* M hole.

hube, hubo, etc. *verb* SEE **haber**.

hucha *noun* F moneybox.

hueco¹ *noun* M 1 hollow; **suena a hueco** it sounds hollow; 2 space; **hazme un hueco** make a bit of room for me; **un hueco para aparcar** a parking space; 3 **el hueco de la escalera** the stairwell; **el hueco del ascensor** the lift shaft.

hueco²/hueca *adjective* hollow.

huela, huelo, etc. *verb* SEE **oler**.

huelga *noun* F strike; **hacer huelga** to strike; **estar en huelga** to be on strike; **huelga de celo** work-to-rule.

huella *noun* F 1 footprint; 2 track (*of an animal or tyre, for example*); 3 **huellas dactilares** fingerprints.

huérfano/huérfana *noun* M/F orphan.

huerto/huerta *noun* M/F 1 vegetable garden; 2 orchard.

hueso *noun* M 1 bone; **romperse un hueso** to break a bone; 2 stone (*in fruit*).

huésped *noun* M/F guest.

huevo *noun* M egg; **huevo duro** hard-boiled egg; **huevo pasado por agua** soft-boiled egg; **huevos revueltos** scrambled eggs.

huir *verb* [54] to flee; **huir de la cárcel** to escape from prison.

humano/humana *noun* M/F human being.

adjective 1 human; **la naturaleza humana** human nature; 2 humane.

humedad *noun* F 1 dampness; **la casa tiene humedad** the house is damp; 2 humidity.

húmedo/húmeda *adjective* 1 damp; 2 wet; 3 moist.

humillar *verb* [17] to humiliate.

humo *noun* M smoke.

humor *noun* M 1 humour; **tener sentido del humor** to have a sense of humour; 2 mood; **estar de buen humor** to be in a good mood; **estar de mal humor** to be in a bad mood; **no estoy de humor para verlos** I'm not in the mood to see them.

hundir *verb* [19] to sink.
hundirse *reflexive verb* [19] to sink.

húngaro[1] *noun* M Hungarian (*the language*).

húngaro[2]**/húngara** *noun* M/F *adjective* Hungarian.

Hungría *noun* F Hungary.

huracán *noun* M hurricane.

hurra *exclamation* hurrah!

huyas, huyo, etc. *verb* SEE **huir**.

I i

iba, iban, etc. *verb* SEE **ir**.

ida[1] *noun* F departure; **un billete de ida** a single ticket; **un billete de ida y vuelta** a return ticket.

ida[2] *verb* SEE **ir**.

idea *noun* F idea; **'¿a qué hora llegan?' – 'no tengo ni idea'** 'what time will they arrive?' – ' I haven't a clue'; **no tienen ni idea de cómo ir** they have no idea how to get there; **tengo una idea** I've got an idea.

ideal *adjective* ideal.

idéntico/idéntica *adjective* identical.

identidad *noun* F identity; **un carné de identidad** an identity card.

identificación *noun* F identification.

identificar *verb* [31] to identify.
identificarse *reflexive verb* [31] 1 to identify yourself; 2 **identificarse con** to identify with; **me identifico mucho con la protagonista del libro** I identify a lot with the heroine of the book.

idioma *noun* M language; **hablar varios idiomas** to speak several languages.

idiota *noun* M/F idiot.
adjective stupid.

ido *verb* SEE **ir**.

iglesia *noun* F church.

ignorante *adjective* ignorant.

ignorar *verb* [17] 1 to ignore; **no me gusta que me ignoren** I don't like being ignored; 2 not to know; **ignoro las razones** I don't know the reasons.

igual *adjective* **1** same; **uno de igual tamaño** one of the same size; **parecen todos iguales** they all look the same; **2 igual a/igual que** the same as; **era igual a éste** it was the same as this one; **no es igual que los demás** it's not the same as the others; **3 todo le da igual** he doesn't care about anything; **'¿quieres ir al cine o al teatro?' – 'me da igual'** 'do you want to go to the cinema or to the theatre?' – 'I don't mind'; **les da igual lo uno que lo otro** either way it makes no difference to them.
adverb **1** the same; **suenan igual** they sound the same; **2** equally; **los quiero a todos igual** I love them all equally; **los dos sistemas son igual de eficientes** both systems are equally efficient; **3** (*in comparisons*) **es igual de alto que su padre** he's as tall as his father; **es igual de ancho que la mesa** it's as wide as the table; **es Géminis, igual que yo** she's a Gemini, just like me; **4** maybe; **igual la vemos en la fiesta** maybe we'll see her at the party; **5 al igual que** just like.

igualdad *noun* F equality; **igualdad de oportunidades** equal opportunities; **en igualdad de condiciones** on equal terms.

igualmente *adverb* **1** equally; **igualmente aburrido** equally boring; **2 'que pases una feliz Navidad' – 'igualmente'** 'have a nice Christmas' – 'you too'.

ilegal *adjective* illegal.

ilegalmente *adverb* illegally.

ilimitado/ilimitada *adjective* unlimited.

iluminación *noun* F **1** lighting (*in a room or theatre*); **2** illumination (*of a building or statue*).

iluminar *verb* [17] **1** to light (*a room or theatre*); **2** to illuminate (*a building or statue*).

ilusión *noun* F **1** hope; **2 me hace ilusión ir** I'm excited about going; **3** illusion.

ilustración *noun* F illustration.

ilustrar *verb* [17] to illustrate.

imagen *noun* F **1** image; **es la viva imagen de su madre** she's the spitting image of her mother; **2** picture (*on a TV screen*); **3** reflection (*in a mirror*).

imaginación *noun* F imagination; **son imaginaciones suyas** he's just imagining things.

imaginar *verb* [17] to imagine.
imaginarse *reflexive verb* [17] **1** to imagine; **me imaginaba que sería más grande** I imagined it would be bigger; **2 me imagino que no** I suppose not; **me imagino que sí** I imagine so.

imán *noun* M magnet.

imbécil *noun* M/F idiot.
adjective stupid.

impacientar *verb* [17] to make impatient.
impacientarse *reflexive verb* [17] to get impatient.

impaciente *adjective* impatient.

impar *adjective* odd.

impecable *adjective* impeccable.

impedir *verb* [57] **1** to prevent; **impedirle a alguien hacer algo** to prevent someone from doing something; **2 impedir el paso** to block the way.

imperativo *noun* M imperative.

imperdible *noun* M safety pin.

imperfecto[1] *noun* M imperfect.

imperfecto[2]**/imperfecta** *adjective* imperfect.

impermeable *noun* M raincoat.

impersonal *adjective* impersonal.

implicar *verb* [31] to involve.

imponer *verb* [11] to impose (*a condition or punishment*).

importación *noun* F import; **artículos de importación** imports.

importado/importada *adjective* imported.

importancia *noun* F importance; **darle importancia a algo** to attach importance to something.

importante *adjective* **1** important; **lo importante es …** the important thing is …; **2** considerable; **una importante suma de dinero** a considerable sum of money.

importar *verb* [17] **1** to matter; **no importa, déjalo así** it doesn't matter, leave it like this; **no importa mucho el color** the colour doesn't matter very much; **2 no me importa**

ayudarles I don't mind helping them; **¿te importa que use el teléfono?** do you mind if I use your phone?; **¿le importaría comprobarlo?** would you mind checking it?; **3 ¿y a ti que te importa?** it's none of your business; **no me importa lo que diga** I don't care what he says; **4** to import (*goods*); ★ **me importa un comino/un rábano** (*informal*) I couldn't care less.

imposible *adjective* impossible.

impresión *noun* F impression; **1 causar una buena impresión** to make a good impression; **2 me da la impresión de que …** I've got the feeling that…

impresionante *adjective* impressive.

impresionar *verb* [17] **1** to impress; **quiere impresionarte** she wants to impress you; **2** to affect; **me impresionó mucho verlos discutir** seeing them argue really affected me; **la violencia de la escena me impresionó mucho** the violence of the scene shocked me.

impreso[1] *noun* M form; **impreso de solicitud** application form.

impreso[2]**/impresa** *adjective* printed.

impresora *noun* F printer.

imprevisible *adjective* **1** unpredictable; **2** unforeseeable.

imprevisto[1] *noun* M unforeseen event.

imprevisto²/imprevista
adjective unforeseen, unexpected.

improvisado/improvisada
adjective improvised.

improvisar *verb* [17] to improvise.

improviso *in phrase* de improviso
unexpectedly, out of the blue.

imprudente *noun* M/F 1 careless
person; 2 reckless person; es un
imprudente conduciendo he's a
reckless driver.
adjective 1 careless; 2 reckless.

impuesto *noun* M tax.

impulsivo/impulsiva *adjective*
impulsive.

inaccesible *adjective* inaccessible.

inaceptable *adjective*
unacceptable.

inadecuado/inadecuada
adjective 1 inappropriate;
2 inadequate.

inadmisible *adjective*
unacceptable.

inadvertido/inadvertida
adjective pasar inadvertido to go
unnoticed.

incapaz *adjective* es incapaz de
hacer daño a nadie he's incapable
of harming anyone; fui incapaz de
entenderlo I was unable to
understand it.

incendio *noun* M fire.

incertidumbre *noun* F
uncertainty.

incierto/incierta *adjective*
uncertain.

incitar *verb* [17] incitar a alguien a
hacer to incite someone to do.

incluido/incluida *adjective*
included; diez mil pesetas, todo
incluido ten thousand pesetas,
everything included; seremos diez
personas, nosotros incluidos there
will be ten people including us.

incluir *verb* [54] to include.

inclusive *adjective* inclusive; los
viernes inclusive including Fridays.

incluso *adverb* even; es incluso
mejor it's even better.

incluya, incluyo, etc. *verb* SEE
incluir.

incoloro/incolora *adjective*
colourless.

incómodo/incómoda *adjective*
uncomfortable.

incompetente *adjective*
incompetent.

incompleto/incompleta
adjective incomplete.

incomprensible *adjective*
incomprehensible.

incondicional *adjective*
unconditional.

inconsciente *adjective*
unconscious.

inconveniente *noun* M drawback,
disadvantage.
adjective inconvenient.

incorporar *verb* [17] to incorporate.
incorporarse *reflexive verb* [17] to sit up.

incorrecto/incorrecta *adjective* incorrect.

increíble *adjective* unbelievable, incredible.

indecente *adjective* indecent.

indeciso/indecisa *adjective*
1 indecisive; 2 undecided; **están indecisos sobre la cantidad** they're undecided about the quantity.

indefenso/indefensa *adjective* defenceless.

indefinidamente *adverb* indefinitely, for good.

indefinido/indefinida *adjective*
1 indefinite; 2 vague (*outline, for example*).

indemnizar *verb* [22] to compensate; **los indemnizaron con dos millones de pesetas** they received two million pesetas in compensation.

independencia *noun* F independence.

independiente *adjective* independent.

India *noun* F (la) **India** India.

indicación *noun* F 1 indication; 2 sign; **me hizo una indicación para que lo siguiese** he signalled to me to follow him; **hay una indicación en el camino** there's a sign on the road.

indicar *verb* [31] 1 to indicate; 2 to point to.

índice *noun* M index.

indiferente *adjective*
1 indifferent; 2 **me es indiferente** it makes no difference to me.

indigestión *noun* F indigestion.

indigesto/indigesta *adjective* indigestible.

indignación *noun* F 1 indignation; 2 outrage.

indignar *verb* [17] 1 to make angry; 2 to outrage.
indignarse *reflexive verb* [17] 1 to get angry; 2 to be outraged.

indio/india *noun* M/F*adjective* Indian.

indirecta¹ *noun* F hint.

indirecto/indirecta² *adjective* indirect.

indiscreto/indiscreta *adjective* indiscreet.

indispensable *adjective* essential.

indispuesto/indispuesta *adjective* **estar indispuesto** to be unwell.

individual *adjective* individual.

individuo *noun* M 1 man; **un individuo con pelo largo** a man with long hair; 2 (*pejorative*) character; **un individuo con muy mal aspecto** a nasty looking character.

industria *noun* F industry.

industrial *adjective* industrial.

ineficaz *adjective* 1 ineffective (*remedy, measure*); 2 inefficient (*person*).

inepto/inepta *noun* M/F *adjective*
incompetent.

inesperado/inesperada
adjective unexpected.

inevitable *adjective* unavoidable;
era inevitable que pasase it was
bound to happen.

inexperto/inexperta *adjective*
inexperienced.

infancia *noun* F childhood.

infantil *adjective* 1 childish; **eres
muy infantil** you're so childish;
2 childlike; 3 **literatura infantil**
children's books.

infarto *noun* M heart attack; **le dio
un infarto** he had a heart attack.

infección *noun* F infection.

infectar *verb* [17] to infect.
infectarse *reflexive verb* [17] to
become infected.

infeliz *adjective* unhappy.

infiel *adjective* unfaithful; **serle
infiel a alguien** to be unfaithful to
someone.

infierno *noun* M hell.

infinitivo *noun* M infinitive.

infinito[1] *noun* M infinite.

infinito[2]**/infinita** *adjective*
infinite.

inflable *adjective* inflatable.

inflación *noun* F inflation.

inflamable *adjective* flammable.

inflar *verb* [17] 1 to inflate (*a tyre, for
example*); 2 to blow up (*a balloon,
for example*).

influencia *noun* F influence.

influir *verb* [54] to influence.

información *noun* F
1 information; **'Información'**
'Information Desk' (*on a sign*);
2 news (*in newspaper or TV news*);
la información internacional the
foreign news; 3 directory enquiries
(*on the telephone*); **llamar a
información** to phone directory
enquiries.

informal *adjective* 1 informal (*a
chat or meal, for example*); 2 casual
(*clothes*); 3 unreliable (*person*).

informar *verb* [17] to inform; **me
informaron mal** I was misinformed;
¿podría informarme sobre ... ?
could you give me information
about ... ?
informarse *reflexive verb* [17] to find
out information; **me informaré
sobre el horario** I'll find out about
the timetable.

informática *noun* F computer
science, IT.

informe *noun* M report.

infracción *noun* F offence; **cometer
una infracción** to commit an
offence; **una infracción de tráfico** a
traffic offence.

infusión *noun* F herbal tea; **una infusión de menta** a peppermint tea.

ingeniero/ingeniera *noun* M/F engineer.

ingenuo/ingenua *noun* M/F **eres un ingenuo** you're so naive.
adjective naive.

Inglaterra *noun* F England.

inglés[1] *noun* M English (*the language*).

inglés[2]**/inglesa** *noun* M/F Englishman/Englishwoman; **los ingleses** the English, English people.
adjective English.

ingrato/ingrata *adjective* ungrateful.

ingrediente *noun* M ingredient.

inicial *noun* F initial.
adjective initial.

iniciativa *noun* F initiative; **por iniciativa propia** on her own initiative.

injusto/injusta *adjective* unfair.

inmediatamente *adverb* immediately.

inmediato/inmediata *adjective* immediate; **de inmediato** immediately.

inmenso/inmensa *adjective* 1 immense; 2 huge; **un salón inmenso** a huge living room.

inmigración *noun* F immigration.

inmigrante *noun* M/F immigrant.

inmobiliaria *noun* F estate agent's.

inmoral *adjective* immoral.

inmueble *noun* M property.

inmunizar *verb* [22] to immunize.

innecesario/innecesaria *adjective* unnecessary.

innovación *noun* F innovation.

innovar *verb* [17] to innovate.

innumerable *adjective* innumerable.

inocentada *noun* F practical joke; (*this is also used for a joke played on someone on the 28th of December, which is the Spanish equivalent of April Fool's Day*) **gastarle una inocentada a alguien** to play a practical joke on someone.

inocente *adjective* 1 innocent; 2 naive.

inofensivo/inofensiva *adjective* harmless.

inolvidable *adjective* unforgettable.

inoxidable *adjective* **acero inoxidable** stainless steel.

inquieto/inquieta *adjective* 1 worried; 2 restless.

inquilino/inquilina *noun* M/F tenant.

inscribir *verb* [52] 1 to register (*on a course, for example*); 2 to engrave.

inscribirse *reflexive verb* [52] to register.

inscripción *noun* F **1** registration (*on a course, for example*); **2** inscription.

insecto *noun* M insect.

insignificante *adjective* insignificant.

insistir *verb* [19] to insist; **insistir en algo** to insist on something.

insolación *noun* F sunstroke; **coger una insolación** to get sunstroke.

insolente *adjective* rude.

insoportable *adjective* unbearable.

inspección *noun* F inspection.

inspeccionar *verb* [17] to inspect.

inspector/inspectora *noun* M/F inspector.

inspiración *noun* F inspiration.

inspirar *verb* [17] to inspire.
inspirarse *reflexive verb* [17] **inspirarse en algo** to be inspired by something.

instalación *noun* F installation.

instalar *verb* [17] to install (*a washing machine or a computer, for example*).
instalarse *reflexive verb* [17] to install yourself.

instantáneo/instantánea *adjective* **1** instant; **2** immediate.

instante *noun* M moment; **un instante, por favor** one moment, please.

instinto *noun* M instinct; **instinto de conservación** survival instinct; **por instinto** instinctively.

instituto *noun* M institute; **instituto de bachillerato** secondary school.

instrucción *noun* F **1** education; **2** training; **instrucción militar** military training; **3 instrucciones** instructions (*for a computer, for example*).

instructor/instructora *noun* M/F instructor; **instructor de autoescuela** driving instructor; **instructor de esquí** ski instructor.

instruir *verb* [54] **1** to instruct; **2** to educate.

instrumento *noun* M instrument; **tocar un instrumento** to play an instrument.

insuficiente *noun* M fail (*at school*).
adjective inadequate.

insultar *verb* [17] to insult.

insulto *noun* M insult.

intacto/intacta *adjective* intact.

integral *adjective* **1** comprehensive; **2 pan integral** wholemeal bread.

íntegro/íntegra *adjective* **la versión íntegra de la película** the full-length version of the film; **el texto íntegro** the unabridged text.

intelectual *noun* M/F *adjective* intellectual.

inteligencia *noun* F intelligence.

inteligente *adjective* intelligent.

intención *noun* F intention; **no fue mi intención** it wasn't my intention; **no era mi intención ofenderla** I didn't mean to offend her; **tiene buenas intenciones** she means well; **lo preguntó con mala intención** he asked the question deliberately.

intensivo/intensiva *adjective* intensive.

intenso/intensa *adjective* 1 intense; 2 deep (*feeling*).

intentar *verb* [17] to try; **¡inténtalo otra vez!** try again!; **intentar hacer** to try to do; **intenté cerrarlo** I tried to shut it; **intenta llegar temprano** try to arrive early.

intercambiar *verb* [17] 1 to exchange; 2 to swap.

intercambiarse *reflexive verb* [17] to swap; **se intercambiaron las revistas** they swapped their magazines.

intercambio *noun* M 1 exchange; 2 swap.

interés *noun* M interest.

interesante *adjective* interesting; **un película interesante** an interesting film; **resulta interesante que …** it's interesting that …

interesar *verb* [17] **no me interesa el deporte** I'm not interested in sport; **¿te interesa la historia?** are you interested in history?

interesarse *reflexive verb* [17] **interesarse en algo/interesarse**

por algo to take an interest in something.

interfono *noun* M 1 entryphone; 2 intercom.

interior *noun* M 1 inside; **el interior de la caja** the inside of the box; 2 **en mi interior, tenía miedo** deep down inside, I was afraid.
adjective 1 interior; **escalera interior** interior staircase; 2 **un piso interior** a flat with windows facing into an inner courtyard; 3 inside; **en la parte interior** on the inside.

intermediario/intermediaria *noun* M/F intermediary.

intermedio¹ *noun* M interval.

intermedio²/intermedia *adjective* 1 intermediate (*level or stage, for example*); 2 medium; **de tamaño intermedio** medium-sized.

intermitente *adjective* 1 flashing (*a light*); 2 intermittent.

internacional *adjective* international.

internado¹ *noun* M boarding school.

internado²/internada *adjective* **está internado** he's been taken into hospital.

Internet *noun* F Internet; **en la Internet** on the Internet.

interno/interna *noun* M/F boarder (*in a school*).
adjective internal.

interpretar *verb* [17] 1 to interpret; 2 **interpretar un papel** to play a part (*in a play or film*); **interpretar una pieza de música** to play a piece of music; **interpretar una canción** to sing a song.

intérprete *noun* M/F
1 interpreter; 2 performer (*of a piece of music*); 3 singer (*of a song*).

interrogación *noun* F interrogation.

interrogante *noun* M or F
1 question; **quedan muchos interrogantes sin responder** there are many questions left unanswered; 2 question mark; **pon un interrogante** put a question mark.

interrogar *verb* [28] to question (*a suspect*).

interrumpir *verb* [19] to interrupt.

interrupción *noun* F interruption.

interruptor *noun* M switch.

interurbano/interurbana *adjective* 1 long-distance; **una llamada interurbana** a long-distance call; 2 **un tren interurbano** an intercity train.

intervalo *noun* M interval.

intervención *noun* F intervention.

intervenir *verb* [15] 1 to take part; **intervenir en las negociaciones** to take part in the negociations; 2 to intervene; **no quiero intervenir** I don't want to intervene; 3 **intervenir a alguien** to operate on somebody.

interviú *noun* F interview.

intimidar *verb* [17] to intimidate.

íntimo/íntima *adjective* 1 private; **mi vida íntima** my private life; 2 intimate; **un ambiente íntimo** an intimate atmosphere; 3 **mis amigos íntimos** my close friends; 4 **una cena íntima** a candlelit dinner.

intolerante *adjective* intolerant.

intoxicación *noun* F poisoning; **intoxicación alimenticia** food poisoning.

intransitivo/intransitiva *adjective* intransitive.

intriga *noun* F intrigue.

introducir *verb* [60] 1 to introduce; **introducir cambios** to introduce changes; 2 to insert; **introducir la moneda en la ranura** insert the coin in the slot.
introducirse *reflexive verb* [60] 1 to be introduced; 2 to get in; **el ladrón se introdujo por la ventana** the burglar got in through the window.

intruso/intrusa *noun* M/F intruder.

intuitivo/intuitiva *adjective* intuitive.

inundación *noun* F flooding; **ha habido inundaciones en Cataluña** there's been flooding in Cataluña.

inútil *noun* M/F **es una inútil** she's useless.
adjective 1 useless; 2 **es inútil intentarlo** it's useless trying.

invadir *verb* [19] to invade.

inválido/inválida *noun* M/F disabled person.

invasión *noun* F invasion.

inventar *verb* [17] **1** to invent; **2** to make up (*a story or game*).

inventarse *reflexive verb* [17] to invent, to make up; **se inventó una excusa** he made up an excuse.

invento *noun* M invention.

invernadero *noun* M greenhouse.

inversión *noun* F investment.

inverso/inversa *adjective* reverse.

investigación *noun* F
1 investigation (*of a crime or accident, for example*); **2** research; **investigación de mercado** market research.

invierno *noun* M winter; **en invierno** in winter; **el invierno pasado** last winter.

invisible *adjective* invisible.

invitación *noun* F invitation.

invitado/invitada *noun* M/F guest.

invitar *verb* [17] **1** to invite; **invitar a alguien a una fiesta** to invite someone to a party; **me han invitado a su casa** they've invited me to their house; **2 te invito a cenar** I'll take you out for dinner; **nos invitó a una copa** he bought us a drink; **¡yo invito!** it's on me!

involuntario/involuntaria *adjective* involuntary.

inyección *noun* F injection.

ir *verb* [8] **1** to go; **van a casa de Alicia** they're going to Alicia's; **iremos al museo** we'll go to the museum; **¿adónde vas?** where are you going?; **¿dónde van los platos?** where do the plates go?; **aún no va al colegio** she doesn't go to school yet; **2** to come; **¡ya voy!** I'm coming!; **3** (*talking about how things are progressing*); **¿cómo van las cosas?** how are things?; **¿cómo te va?** how are you doing?; **¿cómo va el enfermo?** how is the patient doing?; **le va muy bien en el trabajo** he's doing very well at work; **me fue muy mal en la entrevista** I did very badly at the interview; **el proyecto va bien** the project is going well; **4** (*talking about how something works*) **la lavadora no va bien** the washing machine is not working properly; **5** to be; **iba solo** he was alone; **ellos iban en la parte de delante** they were at the front; **yo iba de pie** I was standing up; **6** (*referring to the way you dress*) **iba con un abrigo marrón** he was wearing a brown coat; **iban bien vestidos** they were well dressed; **7** (*talking about whether something suits you*) **el negro te va bien** black suits you; **8** (*talking about an activity*) **ir de vacaciones** to go on holiday; **voy a ir a España de vacaciones** I'm going to Spain for my holidays; **ir de compras** to go shopping; **ir a la compra** to do the shopping; **siempre tengo yo que ir a la compra** I'm always the one who does the shopping; **9** (*talking about* *transport*) **ir en coche** to go by car; **fueron en coche** they drove there; **ir en avión** to go by plane; **ir en bicicleta** to go by bike; **va en bicicleta a todas partes** she goes everywhere by bike; **ir a pie** to go on foot; **ir a caballo** to go on horseback; **10 ir a por algo/alguien** to go to get something/someone; **voy a por pan** I'm going to buy some bread; **fuimos a por ella** we went to fetch her; **vete a por el médico** go and get the doctor; **11 ir a hacer** to go to do; **fuimos a ver su casa nueva** we went to see their new house; **ve a recoger tu habitación** go and tidy up your room; **12** (*expressing the future*) **voy a comprar leche** I'm going to buy some milk; **voy a ser médico** I'm going to be a doctor; **iré a recogerla** I'll go to pick her up; **iba a mandártelo hoy** I was going to send it to you today; **13 su salud va mejorando** her health is getting better; **iban acercándose** they were getting closer; **14 ¡vamos!** come on!; **15** (*expressing surprise or annoyance*) **¡vaya hombre, un billete de mil pesetas!** hey look, a thousand peseta note!; **¡vaya, si es Carlos!** what a surprise, it's Carlos!; **¡vaya, se ha fundido la luz!** oh dear, the light has gone!; **¡vaya, no lo encuentro!** bother, I can't find it!; **16 ¿lo ha hecho él solo?' – '¡qué va!'** 'did he do it on his own?' – 'not likely!'; **'¿te molesta?' – '¡qué va!'** 'do you mind?' – 'not at all!'.

irse *reflexive verb* [8] **1** to leave; **nos fuimos pronto** we left early; **bueno, me voy** well, I'm off; **2** to go; **se fueron a casa** they went home;

3 ¿cómo se va a la estación? which is the way to the station.

ira *noun* F rage; **en un arrebato de ira** in a fit of rage; ★ **ciego de ira** in a blind rage.

Irlanda *noun* F Ireland.

irlandés¹ *noun* M Irish (*the language*).

irlandés²/irlandesa *noun* M/F Irishman/Irishwoman. *adjective* Irish.

ironía *noun* F irony.

irónico/irónica *adjective* ironic.

irreal *adjective* unreal.

irresponsable *adjective* irresponsible.

irritación *noun* F irritation.

irritar *verb* [17] to irritate.
irritarse *reflexive verb* [17] **1** to get irritated (*a person*); **2** to become irritated.

isla *noun* F island.

islámico/islámica *adjective* Islamic.

Islandia *noun* F Iceland.

islandés/islandesa *noun* M/F Icelander.

Israel *noun* M Israel.

israelí *noun* M/F Israeli.

Italia *noun* F Italy.

italiano¹ *noun* M Italian (*the language*).

italiano²/italiana *noun* M/F *adjective* Italian.

IVA *abbreviation* M (*short for: Impuesto al Valor Agregado*) VAT.

izquierda¹ *noun* F **1** left; **tuerce a la izquierda** turn left; **se sentaron a mi izquierda** they sat on my left; **2 está a la izquierda** it's on the left-hand side; **3 ser de izquierdas** to be left-wing (*in politics*).

izquierdo/izquierda² *adjective* left.

J j

jabalí *noun* M wild boar.

jabón *noun* M soap; **una pastilla de jabón** a cake of soap.

jabonera *noun* F soapdish.

jamás *adverb* never; **no lo he visto jamás** I've never seen it; **nunca jamás volveré** I'll never ever go back again.

jamón *noun* M ham; **jamón de York** cooked ham; **jamón serrano** cured raw ham.

Japón *noun* M (**el**) **Japón** Japan.

jarabe *noun* M syrup; **jarabe para la tos** cough mixture.

jardín *noun* M **1** garden; **está en el jardín** she's in the garden; **2 jardín de infancia** nursery (school).

jardinero/jardinera *noun* M/F gardener.

jarra *noun* F jug.

jarro *noun* M jug.

jarrón *noun* M vase.

jaula *noun* F cage.

jefe/jefa *noun* M/F **1** boss (*at work*); **2** manager (*of a company*); **3** chief; **el jefe de bomberos** the chief fire officer; **4** leader (*of a group*).

jengibre *noun* M ginger.

jerez *noun* M sherry.

jersey *noun* M sweater.

Jesucristo *noun* M Jesus Christ.

JJ.OO. *abbreviation* (*short for: Juegos Olímpicos*) Olympic Games.

jornada *noun* F day; **una jornada de trabajo** a working day; **trabajar media jornada** to work part time; **trabajar la jornada completa** to work full time.

joven *noun* M/F **un joven** a young man; **una joven** a young woman. *adjective* young; **moda joven** young fashion.

jovencito/jovencita *noun* M/F young man/young woman.

joya *noun* F **1** piece of jewellery; **no me gustan las joyas** I don't like jewellery; **2 esa chica es una joya** that girl's a real gem.

joyería *noun* F jeweller's.

jubilación *noun* F retirement.

jubilado/jubilada *noun* M/F pensioner; **los jubilados** retired people. *adjective* retired.

jubilarse *reflexive verb* [17] to retire.

judía¹ *noun* F bean; **judías verdes** green beans.

judío/judía² *noun* M/F Jew. *adjective* Jewish.

judo *noun* M judo.

juega, juego¹**, etc.** *verb* SEE **jugar**.

juego² *noun* M **1** game; **juegos de mesa** board games; **un juego de azar** a game of chance; **los Juegos Olímpicos** the Olympic Games; **a los diez minutos de juego** ten minutes into the game; **2 un juego de manos** a conjuring trick; **3** gambling; **es aficionado al juego** he likes gambling; **4** play; **un juego de palabras** a play on words; **juego limpio** fair play; **5** set; **un juego de cacerolas** a set of pans; **un juego de llaves** a set of keys; **6 hacer juego con algo** to match something; **no hace juego con los pantalones** it doesn't match the trousers; **7 fuera de juego** offside; ★ **es un juego de niños** it's child's play.

juegue *verb* SEE **jugar**.

juerga *noun* F **ir de juerga** (*informal*) to go out on the town.

juerguista *noun* M/F (*informal*) raver.

jueves *noun* M Thursday; **el jueves** on Thursday; **el jueves por la mañana** on Thursday morning; **los jueves** on Thursdays.

juez *noun* M/F **1** judge; **2** referee.

jugador/jugadora *noun* M/F **1** player; **2** gambler.

jugar *verb* [27] **1** to play; **jugar al fútbol** to play football; **jugar a la pelota** to play ball; **¿a qué quieres jugar?** what do you want to play?; **2** to gamble; **3** to move (*in board games*); **te toca jugar a ti** it's your turn (to move).

jugo *noun* M juice.

jugoso/jugosa *adjective* juicy.

juguete *noun* M toy; **un coche de juguete** a toy car.

juguetería *noun* F toyshop.

juicio *noun* M **1** trial; **llevar a alguien a juicio** to take someone to court; **2** sense; **no tiene ningún juicio** he's not very sensible; **3 no estar en su sano juicio** to be out of one's mind; **perder el juicio** to lose one's mind.

julio *noun* M July; **en julio/en el mes de julio** in July.

jungla *noun* F jungle.

junio *noun* M June; **en junio/en el mes de junio** in June.

júnior *adjective* junior.

junta¹ *noun* F **1** board, committee; **2** meeting.

juntar *verb* [17] **1** to put together; **2** to join.

juntarse *reflexive verb* [17] **1** to join; **2** to meet; **me junté con unos amigos** I met some friends; **3** to get closer; **juntaos más** come closer.

junto/junta [2] *adjective* **1** together; **ahora todos juntos** all together now; **no los pongas tan juntos** don't put them so close together; **2 junto a** next to; **junto a la ventana** next to the window; **3 junto con** with, together with.

jurado *noun* M jury.

jurar *verb* [17] to swear; **te lo juro** I swear.

jurídico/jurídica *adjective* legal.

justamente *adverb* **1** fairly; **tratar a alguien justamente** to treat someone fairly; **2** exactly; **justamente eso es lo que yo quería decir** that's exactly what I meant; **¡justamente!** exactly!

justicia *noun* F justice.

justificar *verb* [31] to justify.

justo[1]**/justa** *adjective* **1** fair; **no has sido justo con él** you haven't been fair with him; **una sociedad justa** a fair society; **2** exact; **la cantidad justa** the exact amount; **son ciento cincuenta pesetas justas** it's exactly one hundred and fifty pesetas; **3** just enough; **tengo lo justo para el autobús** I have just enough for my bus fare; **viven con lo justo** they have just enough to live on; **4** tight; **te está un poco justo** it's a bit tight on you; **los zapatos me quedan muy justos** the shoes are too tight on me.

justo[2] *adverb* **1** just; **justo a tiempo** just in time; **2 justo en el centro** right in the middle.

juvenil *adjective* **1** youthful (*appearance*); **2** young (*fashion*); **3** junior (*team or competition*).

juventud *noun* F youth.

juzgado *noun* M court.

juzgar *verb* [28] **1** to judge (*people or behaviour*); **te he juzgado mal** I've misjudged you; **2** to try (*a case or person*).

K k

kaki *adjective* khaki.

kárate *noun* M karate.

karting *noun* M go-karting.

Kg. *abbreviation* (*short for: kilogramo*) kg.

kilo *noun* M kilo.

kilogramo *noun* M kilogram.

kilómetro *noun* M kilometre.

Km. *abbreviation* (*short for: kilómetro*) km.

kiosco *noun* M **1** kiosk (*selling sweets, cigarrettes, etc*); **2** newspaper kiosk; **3** stand; **un kiosko de helados** an ice cream stand; **4 el kiosko de la orquesta** the bandstand.

kiwi *noun* M **1** kiwifruit; **2** kiwi.

L l

la *definite article* (*'la' is used before feminine singular nouns; see also 'el', 'los' and 'las'*) **1** the; **la casa es grande** the house is big; **2** (*sometimes 'la' is not translated*) **no me gusta la sandía** I don't like watermelon; **irse a la cama** to go to bed; **la maleta de Isabel** Isabel's suitcase; **ésta es la señora Martínez** this is Mrs Martínez; **3** (*with parts of the body or personal belongings*) **se rompió la pierna** she broke her leg; **se afeitó la barba** he shaved his beard off; **me quité la chaqueta** I took my jacket off; **4** (*talking about time*) **iré la próxima semana** I'll go next week; **5** **me gustó la verde** I liked the green one; **la mía es roja** mine is red; **ésa es la tuya** that one is yours; **6** **ésta es la de Ana** this one is Ana's; **la mía y la de usted** mine and yours; **me gusta más la de Toni** I like Toni's better; **7** **la que yo compré** the one I bought; **la que quieras** whichever you want.
pronoun **1** her; **la acompañé a casa** I took her home; **2** it (*referring to a noun which is feminine in Spanish*); **compré una camiseta, pero la voy a cambiar** I bought a T-shirt, but I'm going to change it.

labio *noun* M lip.

laborable *adjective* **día laborable** working day.

laboratorio *noun* M laboratory.

laca *noun* F **1** lacquer; **2** hairspray; **3 laca de uñas** nail varnish.

ladera *noun* F slope.

lado *noun* M **1** side; **el otro lado** the other side; **hacerse a un lado** to move to the side; **al otro lado de la carretera** on the other side of the road; **2** **al lado de** next to; **al lado de Miguel** next to Miguel; **se sentó a mi lado** he sat next to me; **viven en la casa de al lado** they live next door; **3** **de lado** sideways; **ponlo de lado** put it sideways; **tumbarse de lado** to lie on your side; **4** **en todos lados/por todos lados** everywhere; **he buscado por todos lados** I've looked everywhere; **5** **en otro lado** somewhere else; **deben estar en otro lado** they must be somewhere else; **6** **en cualquier lado** anywhere; **deja siempre sus cosas en cualquier lado** he always leaves his things all over the place; **7** **en algún lado** somewhere; **debe estar en algún lado** it must be somewhere; **8** **en ningún lado/por ningún lado** nowhere, not anywhere; **no está por ningún lado** it's nowhere; **no lo encuentro en ningún lado** I can't find it anywhere; **9** **por un lado … por otro …** on the one hand … on the other hand …

ladrar *verb* [17] to bark.

ladrillo *noun* M brick.

ladrón/ladrona *noun* M/F **1** thief, burglar; **2** robber.

lagarto *noun* M lizard.

lago *noun* M lake.

lágrima *noun* F tear.

laguna *noun* F **1** lake; **2** lagoon.

lamentar *verb* [17] **1** to regret; **lamento tener que informarle de …** I regret to have to inform you that …; **2 lo lamento mucho** I'm very sorry; **lamento no poder ayudarle** I'm sorry I can't help you.

lamer *verb* [18] to lick.

lámpara *noun* F lamp; **lámpara de pie** standard lamp.

lana *noun* F wool; **una chaqueta de lana** a wool jacket.

langosta *noun* F lobster.

langostino *noun* M king prawn.

lanzar *verb* [22] **1** to throw (*a ball or stone*); **2** to launch (*a product or an attack*).

lanzarse *reflexive verb* [22] **1** to throw yourself; **se lanzó al agua** he leapt into the water; **lanzarse en paracaídas** to parachute; **2 lanzarse sobre alguien** to pounce on someone.

lápiz *noun* M **1** pencil; **2 un lápiz de color** a crayon; **3 lápiz de ojos** eyeliner; **lápiz de labios** lipstick.

largo[1] *noun* M length; **¿cuánto mide de largo?** how long is it?; **cinco metros de largo** five metres long.

largo[2]**/larga** *adjective* **1** long; **una falda larga** a long skirt; **te está muy largo** it's too long for you; **2 a lo largo de** along; **a lo largo de la costa** along the coast; **3 a lo largo de** throughout; **a lo largo del día** throughout the day.

las *definite article* ('*las*' *is used before feminine plural nouns; see also 'el', 'la' and 'los'*) **1** the; **deja las cajas ahí** leave the boxes there; **2** (*sometimes 'las' is not translated*) **no me gustan las naranjas** I don't like oranges; **las maletas de Isabel** Isabel's suitcases; **3** (*with parts of the body or personal belongings*) **se lavó las manos** she washed her hands; **me quité las botas** I took my boots off; **4 las mías son rojas** mine are red; **ésas son las tuyas** those are yours; **me gustaron las verdes** I liked the green ones; **5 éstas son las de Ana** these ones are Ana's; **las mías y las de usted** mine and yours; **me gustan más las de Toni** I like Toni's better; **6 las que yo compré** the ones I bought; **las que quieras** whichever you want.
pronoun them (*referring to a plural noun which is feminine in Spanish*); **las vi ayer** I saw them yesterday; **te las puedes llevar** you can take them with you.

láser *noun* M laser.

lástima *noun* F **1** shame; **es una lástima que no puedas venir** it's a shame you can't come; **¡qué lástima!** what a shame!; **2 sentir lástima de alguien** to feel sorry for someone; **su madre me da lástima** I feel sorry for her mother; **3 estar hecho una lástima** to be in a pitiful state.

lata *noun* F **1** tin; **una lata de tomates** a tin of tomatoes; **en lata**

tinned; **sardinas en lata** tinned sardines; **2** (*informal*) nuisance; **¡qué lata!** what a nuisance!; **es una lata tener que esperar** it's a nuisance having to wait; **3 dar la lata** (*informal*) to be a nuisance; **¡deja de dar la lata!** stop being a nuisance!; **siempre están dando la lata** they're always such a nuisance.

latín *noun* M Latin.

Latinoamérica *noun* F Latin America.

latinoamericano/ latinoamericana *noun* M/F *adjective* Latin American.

latón *noun* M brass.

laurel *noun* M. **1** laurel; **2 una hoja de laurel** a bayleaf.

lavabo *noun* M **1** washbasin; **2** toilet; **¿dónde están los lavabos?** where are the toilets?

lavado *noun* M wash; **lavado en seco** dry cleaning; **lavado a mano** handwashing.

lavadora *noun* F washing machine.

lavanda *noun* F lavender.

lavandería *noun* F laundrette.

lavaplatos *noun* M (*does not change in the plural*) dishwasher.

lavar *verb* [17] **1** to wash; **lavar la ropa** to wash the clothes; **lavar los platos** to wash the dishes; **2 lavar algo en seco** to dry-clean something; **3 lavar y marcar** wash and blowdry.

lavarse *reflexive verb* [17] to wash; **lavarse las manos** to wash your hands; **lavarse la cabeza** to wash your hair; **me lavo la cabeza todos los días** I wash my hair everyday; **lavarse los dientes** to clean your teeth.

lavavajillas *noun* M (*does not change in the plural*) dishwasher.

lazo *noun* M ribbon.

le *pronoun* **1** him (*as indirect object*); **quedé con Carlos y le di las llaves** I met Carlos and gave him the keys; **le mandé el paquete el lunes** I sent him the parcel on Monday; **¿qué le quitaron?** what did they take from him?; **2** her (*as indirect object*); **quedé con Inés y le di las llaves** I met Inés and gave her the keys; **le mandé el paquete el lunes** I sent her the parcel on Monday; **¿qué le quitaron?** what did they take from her?; **3** you (*polite form: as indirect object*); **¿le llevo las maletas a su habitación?** shall I carry your suitcases to your room?; **le mandaré el paquete el lunes** I'll send you the parcel on Monday; **4** it (*as indirect object*); **le puse la tapa** I put the lid on it; **le puse otra estantería** I added another shelf to it.

lección *noun* F lesson.

leche *noun* F milk; **leche desnatada/leche descremada** skimmed milk; **leche en polvo** powdered milk.

lechuga *noun* F lettuce.

lectura *noun* F reading.

leer *verb* [37] to read; **estoy leyendo una novela** I'm reading a novel; **¿has leído a Lorca?** have you read Lorca?

legal *adjective* legal.

lejía *noun* F bleach.

lejos *adverb* **1** far; **no está muy lejos** it's not very far; **está demasiado lejos para ir andando** it's too far to walk; **2** a long way; **está lejos del centro** it's a long way from the centre; **viven lejos de aquí** they live a long way from here; **está muy lejos** it's a long way (away); **3 desde lejos** from a distance.

lengua *noun* F **1** tongue; **morderse la lengua** to bite your tongue; **mi lengua materna** my mother tongue; **2** language; **una lengua muy difícil** a very difficult language.

lenguado *noun* M sole.

lenguaje *noun* M language; **lenguaje corporal** body language.

lente *noun* F lens; **lentes de contacto** contact lenses.

lenteja *noun* F lentil.

lentilla *noun* F contact lens.

lento¹ *adverb* slowly; **caminan muy lento** they're walking very slowly.

lento²/lenta *adjective* slow; **son muy lentos** they're very slow; **cocinar algo a fuego lento** to cook something over a low heat.

leña *noun* F firewood.

leño *noun* M log.

Leo *noun* M Leo.

leo *noun* M/F Leo; **es leo** she's Leo.

león *noun* M lion.

leopardo *noun* M leopard.

leotardos *plural noun* M woollen tights.

les *pronoun* **1** them (*as indirect object*); **les di las llaves** I gave them the keys; **les mandé el paquete el lunes** I sent them the parcel on Monday; **¿qué les quitaron?** what did they take from them? **les puse la tapa** I put the lids on them; **2** you (*polite form, talking to more than one person: as indirect object*); **les mandé el paquete el lunes** I sent you the parcel on Monday.

lesión *noun* F injury.

letón/letona *noun* M/F *adjective* Latvian.

Letonia *noun* F Latvia.

letra *noun* F **1** letter; **letras mayúsculas** capital letters; **letras minúsculas** lower case letters; **2** handwriting; **tiene muy buena letra** she has very nice handwriting; **casi no se le entiende la letra** you can hardly read his handwriting; **3** lyrics (*of a song*); **4** instalment; **me quedan dos letras por pagar** I still have two instalments to pay.

letrero *noun* M notice, sign.

levadura *noun* F yeast.

levantar *verb* [17] **1** to lift; **levantar un peso** to lift a weight; **levantar la tapadera** to lift the lid; **2** to raise; **levantar la mano** to raise your hand; **3** to pick up; **levantamos a la niña del suelo** we picked the girl up from the floor; **4** ¡**levanta ese ánimo**! cheer up!

levantarse *reflexive verb* [17] **1** to get up; **levantarse de la cama** to get out of bed; **2** **levántate del suelo** get up off the floor; **3** **levantarse de la mesa** to leave the table.

ley *noun* F law.

leyenda *noun* F legend.

leyó *verb* SEE **leer**.

libanés/libanesa *noun* M/F Lebanese.

Líbano *noun* M (el) **Líbano** Lebanon.

liberar *verb* [17] **1** to free; **2** to liberate.

libertad *noun* F freedom; **libertad de expresión** freedom of speech; **libertad condicional** parole.

libra¹ *noun* F pound; **diez libras esterlinas** ten pounds sterling.

libra² *noun* M/F Libra; **Susana es libra** Susana's Libra.

Libra *noun* M Libra.

librar *verb* [17] **librar a alguien de un castigo** to save someone from being punished.

librarse *reflexive verb* [17] **1** **librarse de morir ahogado** to escape from drowning; **me libré del castigo** I escaped punishment; **2** **librarse de una obligación** to get out of an obligation; **se libró de lavar los platos** he got out of doing the dishes.

libre *adjective* **1** free; **dejar libre a alguien** to set someone free; ¿**está libre este asiento?** is this seat free?; **quinientos metros libres** five hundred metres freestyle; **2** **trabajar por libre** to work freelance; **3** **al aire libre** in the open air.

librería *noun* F **1** bookshop; **2** bookcase.

libreta *noun* F notebook.

libro *noun* M book; **libro de texto** textbook; **libro de bolsillo** paperback; **libro de consulta** reference book.

licencia *noun* F licence, permit.

licenciado/licenciada *noun* M/F graduate.

licor *noun* M liqueur.

licuadora *noun* F liquidizer.

líder *noun* M/F leader.

liebre *noun* F hare.

liga *noun* F league; **la liga de fútbol** the football league.

ligeramente *adverb* slightly.

ligero/ligera *adjective* **1** light; **un paquete ligero** a light parcel; **tener el sueño ligero** to be a light sleeper; **2** slight; **hay un ligero problema** there's a slight problem; **un ligero**

sabor a almendras a slight taste of almonds; **3** thin (*fabric*); **4** fast; **un caballo muy ligero** a very fast horse; **5** agile.

lima *noun* F **1** file; **una lima de uñas** a nailfile; **2** lime.

limitar *verb* [17] **1** to limit; **2 limitar con algo** to border on something; **España limita con Francia** Spain has a border with France.

limitarse *reflexive verb* [17] **1 el problema no se limita a eso** the problem is not just that; **2 me limité a ayudarlos con el ordenador** I just helped them with the computer.

límite *noun* M **1** limit; **el límite de velocidad** the speed limit; **hay un tiempo límite** there's a time limit; **2 la fecha límite** the deadline; **3 ¡todo tiene un límite!** enough is enough!; **4** border (*of a country*).

limón *noun* M lemon.

limonada *noun* F lemonade.

limonero *noun* M lemon tree.

limosna *noun* F **pedir limosna** to beg; **dar limosna** to give money to beggars.

limpiaparabrisas *noun* M (*does not change in the plural*) windscreen wiper.

limpiar *verb* [17] **1** to clean; **limpiar la casa** to clean the house; **2** to clean off; **limpiar una mancha de la mesa** to clean a dirty mark off the table; **3 limpiar algo con un trapo** to wipe something; **4 limpiar los zapatos** to polish the shoes;

5 limpiar algo en seco to dry-clean something.

limpieza *noun* F **1 hacer la limpieza** to do the cleaning; **hacer una limpieza general** to do a spring-clean; **2 limpieza en seco** dry-cleaning; **3 una limpieza de cutis** a facial.

limpio/limpia *adjective* **1** clean (*clothes, a house, or person, for example*); **2** fair (*a game or business deal, for example*).

lindo/linda *adjective* lovely.

línea *noun* F **1** line; **línea de llegada** finishing line; **línea de meta** goal line; **2 línea aérea** airline; **línea regular** airline operating scheduled flights; **3 línea telefónica** telephone line; **no me da línea** the line is dead; **4 escribirle unas líneas a alguien** to drop someone a line; **leer entre líneas** to read between the lines; **5 un jugador de primera línea** a top player; **productos de primera línea** top-quality products; **6** figure; **mantener la línea** to watch your figure.

lino *noun* M linen.

linterna *noun* F torch.

lío *noun* M (*informal*) **1** mess; **¡vaya lío!** what a mess!; **2 hacerse un lío** to get muddled up; **me hice un lío con las fechas** I got the dates all muddled up; **3 armar un lío** to kick up a fuss; **4** trouble; **¡no te metas en líos!** don't get into any trouble!

liquidación *noun* F **1** sale; **liquidación por cierre** closing-down sale; **liquidación total** clearance sale; **2** liquidation (*of a business*); **3** settlement (*of a debt or an account*).

líquido[1] *noun* M liquid.

líquido[2]/**líquida** *adjective* liquid.

liso/lisa *adjective* **1** smooth; **piel lisa** smooth skin; **2** straight; **tiene el pelo liso** she's got straight hair; **3** flat (*ground*).

lista[1] *noun* F **1** list; **una lista de espera** a waiting list; **una lista de bodas** a wedding list; **una lista de precios** a price list; **la lista de vinos** the wine list; **2** (*at school*) register; **pasar lista** to take the register.

listín *noun* M **listín telefónico/listín de teléfonos** telephone directory.

listo/lista[2] *adjective* **1** clever; **2 estar listo** to be ready; **ya estamos listos para salir** we're ready to go now.

litera *noun* F **1** bunk bed; **2** berth.

literatura *noun* F literature.

litro *noun* M litre.

Lituania *noun* F Lithuania.

lituano/lituana *noun* M/F *adjective* Lithuanian.

llama *noun* F **1** flame; **2** llama.

llamada *noun* F call; **una llamada telefónica** a telephone call; **una llamada interurbana** a long-distance call; **una llamada urbana** a local call; **una llamada a cobro revertido** a reverse-charge call.

llamar *verb* [17] **1** to call; **te llama tu madre** your mother is calling you; **llamar al médico** to call the doctor; **llamamos a un taxi** we called a taxi; **la llamamos Tintina** we call her Tintina; **2** to phone; **¿cuándo llamarás?** when will you phone?; **le llamé por teléfono** I phoned him.

llamarse *reflexive verb* [17] to be called; **se llama Ángeles** she's called Ángeles; **¿cómo te llamas?** what's your name?

llano/llana *adjective* flat, level (*ground*).

llave *noun* F **1** key; **una llave maestra** a master key; **la llave de contacto** the ignition key; **cerrar algo con llave** to lock something; **2 la llave del gas** the gas tap; **la llave del agua** the mains water tap; **3** switch (*for a light*); **4** spanner; **una llave inglesa** an adjustable spanner; **5** hold; **una llave de judo** a judo hold.

llavero *noun* M keyring.

llegada *noun* F arrival; **a su llegada al hotel** when he arrived at the hotel.

llegar *verb* [28] **1** to arrive; **llegan a las siete** they arrive at seven; **cuando lleguemos a casa** when we get home; **2** to come; **ya llega el invierno** winter is coming; **3 llegar pronto a un sitio** to get somewhere early; **siempre llegas tarde** you're always late; **llegó justo a tiempo** he was just in time; **4** to reach; **no llego a la lámpara** I can't reach the lamp; **5 la hierba me llega hasta las rodillas** the grass comes up to my knees; **las cortinas llegan hasta el suelo** the curtains go down to the floor; **mi parte del jardín llega hasta la valla** my part of the garden goes up to the fence; **6** to be enough; **con tres litros de leche llega para todos** three litres of milk will be enough for everybody; **7 llegar a hacer** to get to do; **llegué a conocerlo** I got to meet him; **no llegué a verlo** I didn't get to see it; **8 llegar a ser** to become; **llegó a ser famoso** he became famous.

llenar *verb* [17] **1** to fill; **llenar la bañera** to fill the bath; **2** to fill up; **llene el depósito, por favor** fill up the tank, please; **3** fill in (*a form, for example*).

lleno/llena *adjective* **1** full; **la botella está llena de agua** the bottle is full of water; **2** covered; **el suelo estaba lleno de papeles** the floor was covered with papers.

llevar *verb* [17] **1** to take; **te lo puedes llevar** you can take it with you; **llevaré una botella de vino a la fiesta** I'll take a bottle of wine to the party; **yo te puedo llevar a la estación** I can take you to the station; **la llevé a comer a un restaurante** I took her for lunch to a restaurant; **2** to carry; **yo llevaba al niño en brazos** I was carrying the baby in my arms; **3 la llevé en coche a su casa** I drove her home; **4** to have; **¿qué llevas en el bolso?** what have you got in your bag?; **no llevo las llaves encima** I don't have the keys on me; **5** to wear; **llevaba un vestido verde** she was wearing a green dress;

6 lleva tiempo it takes time; **me llevó dos semanas terminarlo** it took me two weeks to finish it; **le llevó mucho hacerlo** it took her a lot of time to do it; **lleva media hora hablando por teléfono** he's been on the phone for half an hour; **¿cuánto tiempo llevas trabajando aquí?** how long have you been working here?; **llevamos dos semanas en Londres** we've been in London for two weeks; **7 le llevo cuatro años** I'm four years older than him; **8** to lead; **el camino que lleva al río** the road that leads to the river.

llevarse *reflexive verb* [17] **1** to take (away); **se llevó los discos** he took the records; **ya puedes llevarte esto** you can take this away now; **2 llevarse bien con alguien** to get on with someone; **no se llevan bien** they don't get on.

llorar *verb* [17] to cry.

llover *verb* [38] to rain; **está lloviendo** it's raining; ★ **está lloviendo a cántaros** it's pouring down (*literally: it's raining in jugfuls*).

llovizna *noun* F drizzle.

llueva, llueve, etc. *verb* SEE **llover**.

lluvia *noun* F rain.

lluvioso/lluviosa *adjective* rainy.

lo *definite article* **1** the; **lo mejor es ...** the best thing is ...; **lo curioso es ...** the funny thing is ...; **prefiero lo salado a lo dulce** I prefer savoury things to sweet things; **2 lo mío**

mine; **esto es lo tuyo** that's yours; **lo vuestro está en la habitación** your things are in the bedroom; **3 esto es lo de mi madre** this is my mother's; **lo de Marta lo he puesto en la mesa** I've put Marta's things on the table; **4 ¿sabes lo de Eva?** have you heard about Eva?; **lo de Pablo es muy raro** it's really strange this thing with Pablo; **lo del accidente fue horrible** that thing about the accident was horrible; **le conté lo tuyo** I told her about you; **5 lo que** what; **eso es lo que yo compré** that's what I bought; **coge lo que quieras** take whatever you want; **dime todo lo que sepas** tell me everything you know.

pronoun **1** him; **lo vi ayer** I saw him yesterday; **2** it; **lo metí en tu bolso** I put it in your bag; **3 ya lo sé** I know.

lobo *noun* M wolf.

local *noun* M premises.

localidad *noun* F **1** town; **una pequeña localidad** a small town; **2** ticket; **'no hay localidades'** 'sold out'.

loción *noun* F lotion; **loción para después del afeitado** aftershave lotion; **loción bronceadora** suntan lotion.

loco/loca *noun* M/F madman, madwoman.
adjective **1** mad; **¡tú estás loco!** you're mad!; **2 estar loco por alguien** to be crazy about somebody; **3 ¡este niño me va a volver loco!** that child's going to drive me mad!; **las fresas la vuelven loca** she loves

strawberries; ★ **estar loco de remate** (*informal*) to be completely bonkers; ★ **hacer algo a lo loco** to do something any old how.

locomotora *noun* F engine (*of a train*).

locura *noun* F **1** madness; **2 eso es una locura** that's crazy; **otra de sus locuras** another one of his crazy ideas.

locutor/locutora *noun* M/F **1** announcer; **2** newsreader; **3 locutor deportivo** sports commentator.

lógico/lógica *adjective* logical.

lograr *verb* [17] **1** to achieve; **lograr la victoria** to achieve victory; **2 lograr hacer** to manage to do; **lograr que alguien haga** to get someone to do.

lombriz *noun* F worm.

lomo *noun* M **1** back (*of an animal*); **2** spine (*of a book*); **3 lomo de cerdo** loin of pork; **4 filete de lomo** sirloin steak.

loncha *noun* F slice; **una loncha de jamón** a slice of ham; **una loncha de bacon** a rasher of bacon.

londinense *noun* M/F Londoner.
adjective London.

Londres *noun* M London.

longaniza *noun* F spicy pork sausage.

longitud *noun* F **1** length; **tiene doce metros de longitud** it's twelve metres long; **2** longitude; **3 longitud de onda** wavelength.

loro *noun* M parrot; ★ **hablar como un loro** (*informal*) to be a chatterbox; ★ **repetir algo como un loro** to repeat something parrot-fashion.

los *definite article* ('*los*' *is used before masculine plural nouns; see also* '*el*', '*la*' *and* '*las*') **1** the; **deja los libros ahí** leave the books there; **2** (*sometimes* '*los*' *is not translated*) **no me gustan los tomates** I don't like tomatoes; **los discos de Isabel** Isabel's records; **3** (*with parts of the body or personal belongings*) **se frotó los ojos** she rubbed her eyes; **me quité los zapatos** I took my shoes off; **4 los míos son rojos** mine are red; **ésos son los tuyos** those are yours; **me gustaron los verdes** I liked the green ones; **5 éstos son los de Ana** these ones are Ana's; **los míos y los de usted** mine and yours; **me gustan más los de Toni** I like Toni's better; **6 los que yo compré** the ones I bought; **los que quieras** whichever you want.
pronoun them; **los vi ayer** I saw them yesterday; **te los puedes llevar** you can take them with you.

lotería *noun* F lottery; **tocarle a alguien la lotería** to win the lottery.

luces *plural noun* SEE **luz**.

lucha *noun* F fight.

luchar *verb* [17] **1** to fight; **luchar cuerpo a cuerpo** to fight hand to hand; **2** to struggle.

luego *adverb* **1** then; **luego vino su madre** then her mother came; **2** later; **luego te veo** I'll see you later; **¡hasta luego!** see you later!; **3** afterwards; **luego te arrepentirás** you'll be sorry afterwards; **luego podemos cenar** we can have dinner afterwards; **4** then; **primero está su casa y luego la mía** first comes her house and then mine; **primero iré al banco y luego a tu casa** I'll go to the bank first and then to your house; **5 desde luego** of course.

lugar *noun* M **1** place; **un lugar precioso** a beautiful place; **lugar de nacimiento** place of birth; **me siento fuera de lugar** I feel out of place; **2 en cualquier lugar** anywhere; **por cualquier otro lugar** anywhere else; **3 en otro lugar** somewhere else; **4 yo en su lugar** ... if I were him ...; **5** position (*in a race or competition*); **en primer lugar** in first position; **llegó en último lugar** he finished in last place; **6 en primer lugar** first of all; **en segundo lugar** ... second ...; **en último lugar** last of all; **7 en lugar de** instead of.

lujo *noun* M luxury; **apartamentos de lujo** luxury apartments.

lujoso/lujosa *adjective* luxurious.

luminoso/luminosa *adjective* **1** bright; **2** luminous.

luna *noun* F **1** moon; **esta noche hay luna** the moon is out tonight; **luna llena** full moon; **luna creciente** waxing moon; **luna menguante** waning moon; **la luna de miel** the honeymoon; **2 una luna de espejo**

a mirror; **la luna del escaparate** the shopwindow.

lunar *noun* M **1** mole (*on your skin*); **2** polka-dot; **una camisa de lunares** a polka-dot shirt.

lunes *noun* M Monday (*see 'domingo' for examples*).

lupa *noun* F magnifying glass.

luto *noun* M mourning; **ir de luto** to be in mourning; **ponerse de luto** to go into mourning.

Luxemburgo *noun* M Luxembourg.

luz (*plural* **luces**) *noun* F **1** light; **dar la luz** to switch on the light; **apagar la luz** to switch off the light; **la luz del sol** the sunlight; **2** electricity; **se ha ido la luz** the electricity's gone off; **3** **luces de cruce/luces cortas** dipped headlights; **luces largas** full beam; **luces de freno** brake lights; **4** **dar a luz** to give birth; ★ **tener pocas luces** to be a bit stupid.

M m

macarrones *plural noun* M macaroni.

macedonia *noun* F fruit salad.

maceta *noun* F flowerpot.

machista *noun* M/F male chauvinist.
adjective sexist.

macho *adjective* male.

madera *noun* F **1** wood; **2** timber.

madrastra *noun* F stepmother.

madre *noun* F **1** mother; **ser madre soltera** to be a single mother; **madre política** mother-in-law; **2** **¡madre mía!** my goodness!

Madrid *noun* M Madrid.

madrileño/madrileña *noun* M/F person from Madrid.
adjective of/from Madrid; **las iglesias madrileñas** the churches of Madrid.

madrina *noun* F **1** godmother; **2** in Spanish weddings, the woman who accompanies the groom, usually his mother.

madrugada *noun* F dawn; **de madrugada** at dawn; **nos levantamos de madrugada** we got up at dawn; **llegamos de madrugada** we arrived in the early hours of the morning; **a las cuatro de la madrugada** at four in the morning.

madurar *verb* [17] **1** to ripen; **2** to mature.

maduro/madura *adjective* **1** ripe; **2** mature; **es muy poco maduro** he's quite immature.

maestro/maestra *noun* M/F **1** teacher (*primary school*); **2** master (*of a trade*).

magdalena *noun* F fairycake.

magia *noun* F magic.

mágico/mágica *adjective* magical.

magnético/magnética *adjective* magnetic.

magnetofón, magnetófono *noun* M tape recorder.

magnífico/magnífica *adjective* 1 wonderful; 2 magnificent.

mago/maga *noun* M/F 1 magician; 2 wizard.

mahonesa *noun* F mayonnaise.

maíz *noun* M 1 sweetcorn; **una mazorca de maíz** a corn on the cob; 2 maize.

mal *noun* M evil; **el bien y el mal** good and evil.
adjective 1 bad; **es un mal amigo** he's a bad friend; **vinieron en mal momento** they came at a bad time; 2 wrong; **la respuesta está mal** the answer's wrong; **está mal criticar** it's wrong to criticize; 3 ill; **¿te sientes mal?** do you feel ill?; **su padre está muy mal** his father's very ill.
adverb 1 badly; **está muy mal pintado** it's really badly painted; **lo leyó muy mal** she read it really badly; **le va muy mal en el trabajo** he's doing very badly at work; **el país marcha mal** the country's not doing well; 2 wrong; **lo hizo mal** he did it wrong; **hace mal en no pedir perdón** he's wrong not to apologize; 3 **contestar mal a alguien** to answer someone back; 4 **te oigo mal** I can't hear you very well; 5 **la comida**

sabe mal the food tastes horrible; **olía muy mal** there was a nasty smell; 6 **portarse mal** to misbehave; **entender mal algo** to misunderstand something; 7 **¡menos mal!** thank goodness!

malabarista *noun* M/F juggler.

malcriado/malcriada *noun* M/F **es un malcriado** he's really spoiled. *adjective* spoiled.

maldición *noun* F 1 curse; 2 **soltar una maldición** to swear; 3 **¡maldición!** damn!

maleducado/maleducada *noun* M/F **es una maleducada** she's really rude. *adjective* rude.

malentendido *noun* M misunderstanding.

maleta *noun* F suitcase.

maletero *noun* M boot (*of a car*).

maletín *noun* M 1 briefcase; 2 overnight case; 3 **el maletín del médico** the doctor's bag.

malhumor *noun* M bad temper.

malla *noun* F 1 mesh; **malla de alambre** wire mesh; 2 leotard; 3 **mallas** leggings.

Mallorca *noun* F Majorca.

mallorquín/mallorquina *noun* M/F *adjective* Majorcan.

malo/mala *adjective* 1 bad; **una mala costumbre** a bad habit; **es malo para la salud** it's bad for your health; 2 naughty; **¡qué niño más**

malo! what a naughty child!;
3 nasty; **no seas mala y
devuélveselo** don't be nasty and give
it back to her; **4** poor; **de mala
calidad** poor quality; **5 ayer hizo
malo** the weather wasn't very nice
yesterday; **nos hizo muy malo
durante las vacaciones** we had
horrible weather during the
holidays; **6 estar malo** to be ill; **no
puede venir porque está mala** she
can't come because she's ill; **el pobre
está muy malo** the poor thing is in a
really bad way; **7 estar malo** to be
off (*food*); **la leche está mala** the
milk's gone off; **8 estar malo** to taste
horrible; **la sopa estaba muy mala**
the soup was horrible; **9 ser malo
para** (*a person*) to be bad at; **soy muy
malo para las matemáticas** I'm very
bad at maths.

mamá *noun* F (*informal*) Mum.

mancha *noun* F **1** stain; **una
mancha de chocolate** a chocolate
stain; **quitar una mancha** to remove
a stain; **2** mark.

manchar *verb* [17] **1** to get
(something) dirty; **mancharon la
alfombra de barro** they got mud all
over the carpet; **2** to stain.

mancharse *reflexive verb* [17] to get
yourself dirty; **cuidado, no te
manches** careful, don't get yourself
dirty; **se manchó los pantalones de
barro** he got mud all over his
trousers.

mandar *verb* [17] **1** to order; **2 le
gusta mandar** she likes to order
people around; **3 mandar a alguien
hacer** to tell somebody to do; **me**

mandó recoger la habitación she
told me to tidy my bedroom; **haz lo
que te mandan** do as you're told; **4** to
send; **mandar una carta a alguien**
to send somebody a letter; **los
mandé a comprar fruta** I sent them
to buy some fruit; **5 mandar llamar
a alguien** to send for someone.

mandarina *noun* F mandarine,
tangerine.

mando *noun* M **1** command; **estar
al mando de** to be in charge of;
2 control (*of a machine or a
television, for example*); **mando a
distancia** remote control.

manejar *verb* [17] **1** to use (*a
machine, for example*); **2** to manage
(*a business*).

manera *noun* F **1** way; **lo hice a mi
manera** I did it my way; **no hubo
manera de arreglarlo** there was no
way of fixing it; **es su manera de ser**
it's the way he is; **2 de alguna
manera** somehow; **me las arreglaré
de alguna manera** I'll do it
somehow; **3 de cualquier manera**
any old how; **puedes decorarlo de
cualquier manera** you can decorate
it any way you want; **4 de una
manera u otra** one way or another;
5 ¡de ninguna manera! no way!;
'¿me dejas el coche?' – **'¡de
ninguna manera!'** 'can I borrow your
car?' – 'no way'; **6 de todas maneras**
anyway; **de todas maneras no
pensaba comprarlo** I wasn't thinking
of buying it anyway; **7 de manera
que** so; **de manera que al final no la
vi** so I didn't see her in the end.

manga *noun* F **1** sleeve; **camisa de manga corta** a short-sleeved shirt; **sin mangas** sleeveless; **2** hose (*for watering*).

mango *noun* M **1** handle (*of a knife or tool*); **2** mango.

manguera *noun* F hosepipe.

manía *noun* F **1 tiene la manía del orden** he's obsessed with tidiness; **es maja pero tiene sus manías** she's nice but she has her funny little ways; **2 tenerle manía a alguien** to have it in for somebody.

maniático/maniática *noun* M/F **es una maniática de la limpieza** she's obsessed with cleanliness. *adjective* fussy.

manifestación *noun* F **1** demonstration; **2** sign (*of disapproval, for instance*); **3 manifestaciones** statements.

manifestar *verb* [29] **1** to express (*disapproval or an opinion*); **2** to show (*emotions*).
manifestarse *reflexive verb* [29] **1** to demonstrate; **2** to become evident; **3 manifestarse en contra de algo** to come out against something.

manillar *noun* M handlebars.

manipular *verb* [17] **1** to operate (*a machine*); **2** to manipulate (*data or information*).

maniquí *noun* M mannequin.

manivela *noun* F handle.

mano *noun* F **1** hand; **levantar la mano** to raise your hand; **ir de la mano** to go hand in hand; **coger a alguien de la mano** to take somebody's hand; **2 darle la mano a alguien** to give somebody your hand; to shake somebody's hand; **3 decir adiós con la mano** to wave goodbye; **4** coat; **una mano de pintura** a coat of paint.

manso/mansa *adjective* **1** tame (*an animal*); **2** gentle (*a person*).

manta *noun* F blanket.

manteca *noun* F lard.

mantel *noun* M tablecloth.

mantendrá, mantendría, etc. *verb* SEE **mantener**.

mantener *verb* [9] **1** to keep; **mantener la calma** to keep calm; **mantener el equilibrio** to keep your balance; **2** to support (*a family, for example*).
mantenerse *reflexive verb* [9] to keep; **mantenerse en equilibrio** to keep your balance; **mantenerse en contacto con alguien** to keep in touch with somebody.

mantengo, mantenga, etc. *verb* SEE **mantener**.

mantenimiento *noun* M **1** maintenance; **2 ejercicios de mantenimiento** keep-fit exercises.

mantequilla *noun* F butter.

mantilla *noun* F mantilla (*a lace scarf*).

mantuve, mantuvo, etc. *verb* SEE **mantener**.

manual *adjective* manual.

manzana *noun* F **1** apple; **2** block (*in a town*); **dar una vuelta a la manzana** to go round the block.

manzanilla *noun* F **1** camomile tea; **2** dry sherry.

manzano *noun* M apple tree.

mañana *noun* F morning; **a la mañana siguiente** the next morning; **por la mañana** in the morning; **a las once de la mañana** at eleven o'clock in the morning.
adverb tomorrow; **pasado mañana** the day after tomorrow; **hasta mañana** see you tomorrow; **mañana por la tarde** tomorrow afternoon.

mapa *noun* M map; **un mapa de carreteras** a road map.

maquillaje *noun* M make-up.

maquillar *verb* [17] to make up.
maquillarse *reflexive verb* [17] to put your make-up on; **apenas se maquilla** she hardly wears any make-up.

máquina *noun* F **1** machine; **una máquina de escribir** a typewriter; **escribir a máquina** to type; **una máquina de coser** a sewing machine; **2** **una máquina de fotos** a camera; **3** **una máquina de afeitar** an electric shaver.

maquinilla *noun* F safety razor.

mar *noun* M sea; **viajar por mar** to travel by sea; **el mar Cantábrico** the Bay of Biscay.

maratón *noun* M or F marathon.

maravilla *noun* F wonder; **es una maravilla de casa** it's a wonderful house; ★ **a las mil maravillas** (*informal*) wonderfully.

maravilloso/maravillosa *adjective* wonderful.

marca *noun* F **1** mark; **el cuadro ha dejado una marca en la pared** the picture has left a mark on the wall; **2** brand; **artículos de marca** brand products; **ropa de marca** designer clothes; **3** **marca registrada** registered trademark; **4** record (*in sports*); **establecer una nueva marca** to establish a new record; **batir una marca** to break a record.

marcar *verb* [31] **1** to mark; **la experiencia me marcó mucho** the experience really marked me; **2** **mi reloj marca las nueve** my watch says nine o'clock; **el termómetro marcaba cinco grados** the thermometer was registering five degrees; **3** **marcar un número** to dial a number; **4** **marcar un gol** to score a goal; **5** **marcar el ritmo/marcar el compás** to beat time.

marcha *noun* F **1** hike; **ir de marcha** to go hiking; **fuimos de marcha a la montaña** we went hiking in the mountains; **2** march (*a demonstration*); **3** gear (*in a car*); **marcha atrás** reverse; **meter la marcha atrás** to put the car into reverse; **4** speed; **disminuir la marcha** to reduce speed; **5** **estar en marcha** to be running (*a car engine,* *for example*); **6 poner en marcha** to start (*a car, for example*); **7 ¡en marcha!** let's go!; **8** (*informal*) **una discoteca con mucha marcha** a really fun disco; **¡qué marcha tiene ese grupo!** this group's really wild! **9** (*informal*) **ir de marcha** to go out partying.

marchar *verb* [17] **1** to work (*a machine or a company*); **esto no marcha** this isn't working; **2** to march; **3 ¡marchando dos cafés!** two coffees coming up!
marcharse *reflexive verb* [17] to leave; **nos marchamos mañana** we're leaving tomorrow.

marco *noun* M **1** (picture) frame; **2** framework; **3** mark (*German currency*).

marea *noun* F tide; **está subiendo la marea** the tide's coming in; **cuando baje la marea** when the tide goes out.

mareado/mareada *adjective* **1 estar mareado** to feel dizzy, to feel queasy; **2 estar mareado** (*informal*) to be muddled up; **estoy mareado con tantos números** I'm all muddled up with all these numbers.

marear *verb* [17] **1** to make (somebody) feel dizzy, to make (somebody) feel queasy; **2** (*informal*) to confuse; **me marearon a preguntas** they asked me so many questions my head was spinning.

mareo *noun* M **1** sick feeling; **me mareo si viajo en coche** I get carsick; **2** seasickness; **3** dizziness.

margarina *noun* F margarine.

margarita *noun* F **1** daisy; **2** marguerite.

margen *noun* M margin; **escribir algo al margen** to write something in the margin.

marido *noun* M husband.

marina *noun* F navy.

marinero *noun* M sailor.

marioneta *noun* F puppet.

mariposa *noun* F butterfly.

mariquita *noun* F ladybird.

marisco *noun* M shellfish; **me gusta el marisco** I like shellfish.

mármol *noun* M marble.

marrón *noun* M brown.
adjective brown; **zapatos marrones** brown shoes; **unos pantalones marrón claro** a pair of light brown trousers (*note that 'marrón' does not change in the plural when it is used with another word such as 'claro'*).

martes *noun* M Tuesday (*see 'domingo' for examples*).

martillo *noun* M hammer.

marzo *noun* M March; **en marzo/en el mes de marzo** in March.

más *adverb, adjective, pronoun* **1** more; **éste me gusta más** I like this one more; **pon más azúcar** add more sugar; **tres más** three more; **más o menos** more or less; **¿necesitas más?** do you need any more?; **no comas más** don't eat any more; **no**

lo hagas más don't do it again; **2 es un poco más grande** it's a bit bigger; **tenemos que hacerlo más rápido** we have to do it faster; **3 es más interesante que su primer libro** it's more interesting than his first book; **más que nunca** more than ever; **me gusta más el de cuero que el de tela** I prefer the leather one to the cloth one; **más blanco que la nieve** as white as snow; **4 el de más peso** the heaviest one; **los de más prestigio** the most prestigious ones; **el libro con más páginas** the book with the most pages; **5 el que más me gusta** the one I like the most; **los que son más altos** the tallest ones; **6 más de** more than; **más de veinte kilos** more than twenty kilos; **vinieron más de veinte personas** more than twenty people came; **7 hay tres sillas de más** there are three chairs too many; **hay tres pasteles de más** there are three cakes left over; **si quieres venir, tengo un billete de más** I've got a spare ticket if you want to come; ★ **estar de más** to feel out of place; **8** (*referring to time*) **no les he visto más** I've never seen them again; **no me quedo más** I won't stay any longer; **9** else; **¿esperas a alguien más?** are you expecting anybody else?; **nadie más** nobody else; **no quiero nada más** I don't want anything else; **¿querías algo más?** did you want anything else?; **10 no … más** only; **no tardo más de diez minutos** I'll only take ten minutes; **no es más que un resfriado** it's only a cold; **11** (*in exclamations*) **¡es más bonito!** it's so beautiful!; **¡había más gente!** there were so many people!; **¡le gustó más!** he liked it a lot!
preposition plus; **cinco más siete** five plus seven.

masa *noun* F **1** dough; **masa de pan** bread dough; **2** pastry; **masa de hojaldre** puff pastry.

masaje *noun* M massage.

máscara *noun* F mask.

mascarilla *noun* F mask.

masculino[1] *noun* M masculine (*in grammar*).

masculino[2]**/masculina** *adjective* masculine.

masticar *verb* [31] to chew.

mástil *noun* M **1** mast; **2** flagpole.

matador *noun* M matador.

matar *verb* [17] to kill.
matarse *reflexive verb* [17] **1** to kill yourself; **2** to get killed; **si sigues conduciendo así, te vas a matar** if you carry on driving like that you're going to get killed.

mate *noun* M **jaque mate** checkmate.
adjective matt.

matemáticas *plural noun* F maths.

materia *noun* F **1** material; **materia prima** raw material; **2** **materia grasa** fat; **3** subject (*of study or of a book*).

material *noun* M *adjective* material.

maternal *adjective* maternal.

materno/materna *adjective*
1 motherly; 2 mother; **lengua
materna** mother tongue; 3 **abuelos
maternos** grandparents on the
mother's side.

matiz *noun* M shade (*of a colour*).

matrícula *noun* F 1 registration;
hacer la matrícula to register;
2 registration number (*of a car*); **un
coche con matrícula de Sevilla** a car
with a Seville number plate;
3 **matrícula de honor** distinction;
sacar matrícula en física to get a
distinction in physics.

matrimonio *noun* M 1 marriage;
matrimonio civil civil wedding;
2 married couple; **son un
matrimonio muy unido** they're a
very close couple.

máximo/máxima *adjective*
1 maximum; 2 top (*speed*);
3 highest; **el punto máximo** the
highest point.

mayo *noun* M May; **en mayo/en el
mes de mayo** in May.

mayonesa *noun* F mayonnaise.

mayor *noun* M/F adult.
adjective 1 greater; 2 greatest;
3 higher; **un número mayor que
cien** a number higher than one
hundred; **a la mayor altura** at the
maximum height; 4 bigger; **¿tienes
una talla mayor?** do you have a
bigger size?; 5 biggest; **el de mayor
tamaño** the biggest one; 6 older; **es
cinco años mayor que su mujer** he's
five years older than his wife;

7 oldest; **mi hermana mayor** my
oldest sister; **soy el mayor de todos
mis hermanos** I'm the oldest of my
brothers and sisters; 8 **cuando seas
mayor** when you grow up; **las
personas mayores** the grown-ups;
ya son muy mayores they're quite
old now; 9 **la mayor parte de** most
of; **la mayor parte de los
estudiantes** most of the students;
10 **ser mayor de edad** to be of age.

mayores *plural noun* M **los
mayores** the grown-ups; the elderly.

mayoría *noun* F majority; **la
mayoría de** most of.

mayúscula[1] *noun* F capital letter.

mayúsculo/mayúscula[2]
adjective 1 capital (*letter*); 2
(*informal*) terrible (*mistake or
fright*).

mazapán *noun* M marzipan.

me *pronoun* 1 me; **me invitaron a
su fiesta** they invited me to their
party; **no me han visto** they haven't
seen me; 2 to me; **me lo dieron ellos**
they gave it to me; **me mintió** he lied
to me; **me lo ha comprado mi madre**
my mother bought it for me;
3 myself; **me corté** I cut myself;
4 (*with reflexive verbs*) **me reí mucho**
I laughed a lot; **voy a bañarme** I'm
going for a swim; **me senté a la mesa**
I sat at the table; 5 (*with parts of the
body or clothes*) **me quité el abrigo** I
took my coat off; **me limpié los pies
al entrar** I wiped my feet at the door;
6 (*having things done*) **el sábado iré
a cortarme el pelo** I'll go and have
my hair cut on Saturday.

mecánico/mecánica² *noun* M/F
mechanic.
adjective mechanical.

mecedora *noun* F rocking chair.

mechero *noun* M lighter.

medalla *noun* F medal.

media¹ *adjective* F average; **la altura media** the average height.

media² *noun* F **1** stocking;
2 medias tights; **3** average; **la media europea** the European average; **4** (*telling the time*) **la dos y media** half past two; **dos horas y media** two and a half hours; **5 hacer algo a medias** to half-do something; **lo dejó a medias** he didn't finish it; **6 lo hicimos a medias** we did it between the two of us; **pagar a medias** to pay half each.

mediados *plural noun* M **a mediados de semana** midweek; **a mediados de año** halfway through the year.

mediano/mediana *adjective*
1 medium; **de peso mediano** medium weight; **2** average; **3 de mediana calidad** mediocre.

medianoche *noun* F midnight; **a media noche** at midnight.

medicamento *noun* M medicine.

medicina *noun* F medicine;
estudiar medicina to study medicine; **tomarse la medicina** to take your medicine.

médico/médica *noun* M/F doctor;
médico de cabecera family doctor.

medida *noun* F **1** measure; **tomar medidas a algo** to measure something; **2** measurement; **¿qué medidas tiene la mesa?** what are the measurements of the table?;
3 traje a medida a made-to-measure suit; **4 a medida que** as; **a medida que pase el tiempo** as time goes by; **5 en gran medida** to a large extent; **en cierta medida** to a certain extent; **en la medida de lo posible** as far as possible.

medio¹ *noun* M **1** middle; **ponlo en el medio** put it in the middle; **la casa de en medio** the house in the middle; **2 quitarse de en medio** to get out of the way; **3** way; **es el mejor medio** it's the best way; **no hubo medio de localizarlo** there was no way of finding him; **lo intenté por todos los medios** I tried every possible way; **4** means; **por cualquier medio** by any means; **por todos los medios** by any possible means; **medios de transporte** means of transport; **5 por medio de** through; **por medio de un amigo** through a friend; **6 en medio de todo aquel jaleo** amidst all that racket; **7 los medios de comunicación** the media.
adverb half; **ya está medio convencido** he's half convinced now.

medio²/media *adjective* **1** half;
medio kilo half a kilo; **media docena** half a dozen; **media pensión** half board; **2** average; **de estatura media** of average height; **3** (*in time expressions*) half; **media hora** half

an hour; **a las dos y media** at half past two.

medio ambiente *noun* M environment.

mediodía *noun* M midday; **al mediodía** at midday.

medir *verb* [57] **1** to measure; **¿cuánto mide de ancho?** how wide is it?; **mide sesenta centímetros de largo** it's sixty centimetres long; **2 ¿cuánto mides?** how tall are you?

Mediterráneo *noun* M Mediterranean.

mediterráneo/mediterránea *adjective* Mediterranean.

mejicano/mejicana *noun* M/F *adjective* Mexican.

Méjico *noun* M SEE **México**.

mejilla *noun* F cheek.

mejillón *noun* M mussel.

mejor *noun* M/F **el/la mejor** the best one.
adjective **1** better; **éste es de mejor calidad** this one is better quality; **cuanto antes mejor** the earlier the better; **es mejor que no vayamos** it's better if we don't go; **2** best; **la mejor forma es …** the best way is …
adverb **1** better; **Isabel toca la guitarra mejor** Isabel plays the guitar better; **mejor que** better than; **mejor que el otro** better than the other one; **cada vez mejor** better and better; **2** best; **es la que mejor dibuja** she's the one that draws the best; **hazlo lo mejor que puedas** do your best; **3 a lo mejor** maybe; **a lo**

mejor es de Sara maybe it's Sara's; **a lo mejor no voy** I might not go; **4 mejor no preguntes** it's better if you don't ask; **mejor déjalo así** it's better if you leave it like this; **mejor venid en tren** you'd be better come by train.

mejora *noun* F improvement.

mejorar *verb* [17] **1** to improve; **2** to get better; **ha mejorado del estómago** he's got over his stomach problems.

mejorarse *reflexive verb* [17] to get better; **¡que te mejores!** get well soon!

mellizo/melliza *noun* M/F *adjective* twin.

melocotón *noun* M peach.

melodía *noun* F melody.

melón *noun* M melon.

memoria *noun* F **1** memory; **aprenderse algo de memoria** to learn something by heart; **2 memorias** memoirs.

mencionar *verb* [17] to mention.

mendigar *verb* [17] to beg.

mendigo/mendiga *noun* M/F beggar.

menestra *noun* F **menestra de verduras** vegetable stew.

menor *noun* M/F **1 el/la menor** the younger; **2 un/una menor** a minor.
adjective **1** younger; **mi hermana menor** my younger sister; **soy menor que tú** I'm younger than you; **2** youngest; **el menor de la familia**

the youngest of the family; **3** little;
con el menor esfuerzo posible with
as little effort as possible; **4** less; **su
importancia es cada vez menor** it
gets less and less important all the
time; **en menor grado** to a lesser
extent; **5** minor; **de menor
importancia** of minor importance;
6 smaller; **un número menor de
alumnos** a smaller number of
pupils; **7** smallest; **hasta el menor
detalle** even the smallest detail; **8 no
tengo la menor idea** I haven't got the
slightest idea.

menos *adjective* (*does not change in
the plural*) **1** less; **de menos peso**
of less weight; **2** few; **había menos
de cien personas** there were fewer
than a hundred people.
adverb **1** less; **ahora sale menos** he
goes out less now; **cada vez menos**
less and less every time; **2** least; **los
menos informados** those least
informed; **es lo menos que
esperaba** it's the least I expected;
3 el menos alto the shortest one; **el
que corre menos** the slowest of all;
4 menos que less than; fewer than;
habla menos que yo he speaks less
than I do; **cuesta menos que el otro**
it costs less than the other one; **había
menos que ayer** there were fewer
than yesterday; **5 menos de** less
than; **cuesta menos de cien libras**
it costs less than a hundred pounds;
adultos de menos de treinta años
adults under thirty; **6 ahora los veo
menos** I don't see them as often now;
7 ahora sale menos she doesn't go
out as much now.
pronoun **1 ahora compramos**
menos now we don't buy as much;
2 cobrar de menos to undercharge;
hay diez tarjetas de menos there
are ten cards too few; **3 al
menos/por lo menos** at least;
4 ¡menos mal! thank goodness!
preposition except; **todos menos su
madre** everybody except her
mother.

mensaje *noun* M message.

mensajero/mensajera *noun* M/
F **1** messenger; **2** courier; **servicio
de mensajeros** courier service.

mensual *adjective* monthly;
quinientas pesetas mensuales five
hundred pesetas a month.

menta *noun* F mint; **un caramelo de
menta** a mint.

mental *adjective* mental.

mente *noun* F mind; **se me quedó
la mente en blanco** my mind went
blank.

mentir *verb* [14] to lie.

mentira *noun* F lie.

mentiroso/mentirosa *noun* M/F
liar.

mentón *noun* M chin.

menú *noun* M menu; **menú del día**
set menu.

menudo/menuda *adjective*
1 small; **es muy menuda** she's quite
small; **2 a menudo** often; **nos
vemos a menudo** we see each other
often; **3 ¡menudo problema!** what a
problem!; **¡menuda moto!** what an
incredible motorbike!

meñique *noun* M little finger.

mercado *noun* M market; **ir al mercado** to go to the market; **el Mercado Común** the Common Market.

mercancías *plural noun* F goods.

mercería *noun* F haberdashery.

merecer *verb* [35] **1** to deserve; **mereces un castigo** you deserve to be punished; **2 merecer la pena** to be worthwhile; **la película merece la pena** the film is worth seeing.
merecerse *reflexive verb* [35] to deserve; **no me merezco que me traten así** I don't deserve to be treated like this.

merendar *verb* [29] to have a teatime snack; **siempre merienda pan y chocolate** he always has bread and chocolate in the afternoon; **¿quieres merendar algo?** do you want something to eat?; **¡a merendar!** teatime!

merezca, merezco, etc. *verb* SEE **merecer**.

meridional *adjective* southern.

merienda¹ *noun* F **1** afternoon snack; **2 merienda campestre** picnic; **ir de merienda** to go for a picnic.

merienda², **meriendo, etc.** *verb* SEE **merendar**.

mérito *noun* M merit.

mermelada *noun* F jam.

mes *noun* M month; **el mes que viene** next month; **diez mil pesetas al mes** ten thousand pesetas a month; **un bebé de siete meses** a seven-month-old baby.

mesa *noun* F table; **sentarse a la mesa** to sit at the table; **poner la mesa** to set the table; **quitar la mesa/recoger la mesa** to clear the table; **¡a la mesa!** food's ready!

mesita *noun* F **mesita de noche** bedside table.

meta *noun* F **1** finishing line; **2** aim; **tiene como meta ser actriz** her aim is to become an actress.

metal *noun* M metal.

metálico/metálica *adjective* metallic.

meteorológico/meteorológica *adjective* meteorological; **parte meteorológico** weather forecast.

meter *verb* [18] **1** to put (something) in; **metió la mano** he put his hand in; **mét[e]lo en la carpeta** put it in the folder; **2** to fit; **¿puedes meter algo más en la maleta?** can you fit anything else in the suitcase?; **3 meter la primera** to put the car in first gear; **meter la marcha atrás** to put the car into reverse; **4 meter un gol** to score a goal.
meterse *reflexive verb* [18] **1 meterse en** to get in(to); **meterse en la cama** to get into bed; **2 meterse en algo** to get involved in something; **no te metas en mis asuntos** mind your own business.

método *noun* M method.

métrico *adjective* metric.

metro *noun* M **1** underground;
2 metre; **los cien metros libres** the
hundred metres freestyle.

mexicano/mexicana *noun* M/F
adjective Mexican.

México *noun* M Mexico.

mezcla *noun* F **1** mixture; **2** mix;
una mezcla de culturas a mix of
cultures.

mezclar *verb* [17] **1** to mix; **2** to mix
up; **has mezclado todos los
papeles** you've mixed up all the
papers.
mezclarse *reflexive verb* [17]
mezclarse en algo to get mixed up
in something.

mezquita *noun* F mosque.

mi *adjective* my; **mis amigos** my
friends.

mí *pronoun* **1** me; **detrás de mí**
behind me; **se olvidaron de mí** they
forgot about me; **2** (*as indirect
object*) **me lo dio a mí** he gave it to
me; **3 a mí me gusta** I like it; **a mí
me parece que** … I think that …;
4 mí mismo/misma myself; **sé
cuidar de mí misma** I can look after
myself; **5 por mí** … as far as I'm
concerned.

micrófono *noun* M microphone.

microondas *noun* M (*does not
change in the plural*) microwave
(oven).

microscopio *noun* M microscope.

**mida, midiendo, midió, mido,
etc.** *verb* SEE **medir**.

miedo *noun* M **1** fear; **tener miedo**
to be scared; **tengo mucho miedo**
I'm really scared; **tengo miedo de
intentarlo** I'm afraid of trying; **¡qué
miedo!** how frightening!; **miedo a
algo** fear of something; **2 me da
miedo la altura** I'm afraid of heights;
les da miedo ir solos they are afraid
of going on their own; **3 pasamos
un rato de miedo** (*informal*) we had
a great time.

miedoso/miedosa *adjective* **es
muy miedoso** he's afraid of
everything.

miel *noun* F honey.

miembro *noun* M **1** member;
2 limb.

mienta, miento, etc. *verb* SEE
mentir.

mientras *adverb* meanwhile;
mientras tanto in the meantime.
conjunction **1** while; **pon la mesa
mientras yo hago la comida** lay the
table while I cook the meal; **2** as long
as.

miércoles *noun* M Wednesday; **el
miércoles** on Wednesday; **el
miércoles por la mañana** on
Wednesday morning; **los miércoles**
on Wednesdays.

miga *noun* F crumb.

mil *number* thousand; **mil
doscientos** one thousand two
hundred.

milagro *noun* M miracle.

milésimo/milésima *adjective* thousandth.

mili *noun* F (*informal*) military service.

milímetro *noun* M milimetre.

militar *noun* M/F soldier. *adjective* military.

millón *number* million; **un millón de gracias** thank you ever so much.

millonario/millonaria *noun* M/F millionaire.

mina *noun* F mine; **una mina de carbón** a coalmine.

mineral *noun* M *adjective* mineral.

minero/minera *noun* M/F miner. *adjective* mining.

mini *noun* F (*informal*) mini.

minifalda *noun* F miniskirt.

mínimo¹ *noun* M minimum.

mínimo²/mínima *adjective* minimum; **no me importa lo más mínimo** I couldn't care less.

ministerio *noun* M ministry.

ministro/ministra *noun* M/F minister.

minoría *noun* F minority.

mintamos, mintió, etc. *verb* SEE **mentir**.

minúscula¹ *noun* F small letter (*not capital*).

minúsculo/minúscula² *adjective* tiny.

minusválido/minusválida *noun* M/F disabled person. *adjective* disabled.

minuto *noun* M minute.

mío/mía *adjective* mine; **un amigo mío** a friend of mine. *pronoun* mine; **el mío es verde** mine is green.

miope *adjective* shortsighted.

mirada *noun* F look; **una mirada alegre** a happy look; **dirigir una mirada a** to look at; **me dirigió una mirada** she looked at me; **bajar la mirada** to look down.

mirar *verb* [17] **1** to look; **miré afuera** I looked outside; **mira en el cajón** look in the drawer; **2 mirar algo** to look at something; **miró el cuardro con interés** he looked at the picture with interest; **me miró** he looked at me; **3** to watch; **mirar la tele** to watch TV; **4 mirar fijamente** to stare. **mirarse** *reflexive verb* [17] **mirarse en el espejo** to look at yourself in the mirror; **mirarse las manos** to look at your hands.

mirlo *noun* M blackbird.

misa *noun* F mass; **ir a misa** to go to mass.

miserable *adjective* **1** miserable; **2** stingy.

miseria *noun* F misery.

mismo¹ *adverb* **1** right; **ahora mismo** right now; **en ese mismo momento** right at that moment; **está**

ahí mismo it's right there; **al lado mismo de casa** right next to the house; **2** just; **lo mismo que yo** just like me; **eso mismo dije yo** that's just what I said.

mismo²/misma *adjective* **1** same; **al mismo tiempo** at the same time; **llevan los mismos zapatos** they have the same shoes; **lo mismo** the same; **2** very; **en este mismo lugar** in this very spot; **3** **yo mismo** myself; **lo vi yo mismo** I saw it myself; **lo dijo ella misma** she said it herself. *pronoun* **1** **el mismo** the same; **he usado la misma** I've used the same; **Sara tiene los mismos** Sara has the same ones; **2** **da lo mismo** it doesn't matter; **me da lo mismo el color** I don't mind the colour.

misterio *noun* M mystery.

misterioso/misteriosa *adjective* mysterious.

mitad *noun* F **1** half; **la mitad del pastel** half the cake; **a mitad de precio** half-price; **2** halfway; **a mitad de camino paramos a comer** we stopped halfway to eat; **llenar algo hasta la mitad** to half fill something; **he leído hasta la mitad** I'm halfway through reading it; **3** **cortar algo por la mitad** to cut something in two.

mito *noun* M myth.

mixto/mixta *adjective* mixed.

mobiliario *noun* M furniture; **mobiliario de cocina** kitchen fittings.

mochila *noun* F backpack.

mocos *plural noun* M **tener mocos** to have a runny nose.

moda *noun* F fashion; **la moda juvenil** young fashion; **estar de moda** to be in fashion; **pasarse de moda** to go out of fashion; **siempre va a la última moda** he's always wearing the latest fashion.

modales *plural noun* M manners; **tener buenos modales** to have good manners.

modelo¹ *noun* M model; **utilizar algo como modelo** to use something as a model.

modelo² *noun* M/F model (*fashion*).

moderno/moderna *adjective* **1** modern; **2** trendy.

modesto/modesta *adjective* **1** modest; **2** humble.

modificar *verb* [31] to change.

modisto/modista *noun* M/F **1** dressmaker; **2** (fashion) designer.

modo *noun* M **1** way; **lo haré a mi modo** I'll do it my way; **a mi modo de ver** to my way of thinking; **no hubo modo** there was no way (of doing it); **2** **lo hizo de cualquier modo** he did it any old way; **3** **de cualquier modo te llamaré antes** in any case, I'll phone you first; **4** **¡de ningún modo!** no way!; **5** **de todos modos** anyway; **de todos modos no iba a comprarlo** I wasn't going to buy it anyway; **6** **de modo que** so; **7** **en**

cierto modo somehow; **8 modo de empleo** instructions for use.

mohoso/mohosa *adjective* mouldy.

mojado/mojada *adjective* wet.

mojar *verb* [17] to wet.
mojarse *reflexive verb* [17] to get wet; **se me mojó el pelo** my hair got wet.

moler *verb* [38] to grind.

molestar *verb* [17] **1** to disturb; **'no molestar'** 'do not disturb'; **no molestes a tu madre, que está trabajando** don't disturb your mother, she's working; **2** to bother; **perdona que te moleste** sorry to bother you; **3** ¿**te molesta que ponga la tele?** do you mind if I put the TV on?; **4** to annoy; **me molesta que no me hayan invitado** I'm annoyed that they haven't invited me.
molestarse *reflexive verb* [17] **1** to get upset; **se molestó porque fuimos sin ella** she got upset because we went without her; **2 molestarse en hacer algo** to bother to do something; **no se molestó en preguntar** she didn't bother to find out.

molestia *noun* F **1** trouble; **no es ninguna molestia** it's no trouble at all; **causar molestias a alguien** to inconvenience someone; **2 tomarse la molestia de hacer algo** to take the trouble to do something; **3 perdone la molestia** sorry to bother you; **4 si no es molestia** … if you don't mind …

molesto/molesta *adjective* **1** annoying; **2** uncomfortable; **3 estar molesto** to be upset; **sé que está molesto conmigo** I know he's upset with me.

momento *noun* M moment; **justo en ese momento** right at that moment; **dentro de un momento** in a moment; **¡un momento!** just a moment!; **de momento** at the moment; **en cualquier momento** any moment now; **en este momento** right now.

monarquía *noun* F monarchy.

monasterio *noun* M monastery.

moneda *noun* F **1** coin; **2** currency.

monedero *noun* M purse.

monja *noun* F nun.

monje *noun* M monk.

mono/mona *noun* M/F monkey.
adjective **1** cute (*a puppy or baby, for example*); **2** pretty (*person, garment*).

monopatín *noun* M skateboard.

monstruo *noun* M monster.

montaña *noun* F **1** mountain; **en la montaña** in the mountains; **2 la montaña rusa** the roller coaster.

montar *verb* [17] **1** to get on; **montar en el avión** to get on the plane; **2** to get in; **montar en el coche** to get in the car; **3** to ride; **montar a caballo** to ride a horse; **montar en la moto** get on the motorbike; **montar en bicicleta** to ride a bike; **4** to mount (*a horse*); **5** to set up (*a business or*

an exhibition); **6** to put up (*a tent*);
7 montar claras a punto de nieve
to whisk the egg whites until stiff;
8 montar un escándalo (*informal*)
to cause a scene.
montarse *reflexive verb* [17] **1** to get
on; **se montó en el tren** he got on
the train; **2** to get in; **montarse en
un coche** to get in a car.

montón *noun* M **1** pile; **puse todas
las revistas en un montón** I put all
the magazines in a pile; **2 un montón
de** (*informal*) loads of; **había un
montón de niños** there were loads of
children; **montones de** (*informal*)
loads of; **montones de dinero** loads
of money; **3 me gusta un montón**
(*informal*) I like it a lot.

monumento *noun* M monument.

moqueta *noun* F fitted carpet.

mora *noun* F blackberry.

morado[1] *noun* M purple.

morado[2]**/morada** *adjective*
purple.

moral *noun* F **1** morals; **no tienen
ninguna moral** they have no morals;
2 morale; **estar bajo de moral** to feel
low.
adjective moral.

morder *verb* [38] to bite.

mordisco *noun* M bite; **darle un
mordisco a algo** to bite (on)
something.

moreno/morena *adjective* **1** dark
(*hair*); **2 es morena** she's dark-
haired; **3 estar moreno** to be

tanned; **ponerse moreno** to get
tanned.

morir *verb* [55] to die; **morir ahogado**
to drown; **morir en un accidente** to
be killed in an accident.
morirse *reflexive verb* [55] to die.

moro/mora *noun* M/F **1** Moor;
2 North African.
adjective Moorish.

mortal *adjective* **1** deadly; **2** fatal.

mosca *noun* F fly; ★ **por si las
moscas** (*informal*) just in
case; ★ **¿qué mosca le ha picado?**
(*informal*) what's got into him?
(*literally:* '*what fly has bitten him?*').

mosquito *noun* M mosquito.

mostaza *noun* F mustard.

mostrador *noun* M **1** counter (*in a
shop*); **2** bar (*in a pub*); **3** check-in
desk.

mostrar *verb* [24] to show.
mostrarse *reflexive verb* [24]
mostrarse interesado to show
interest; **mostrarse amable** to be
kind; **mostrarse contento** to be
happy.

motivo *noun* M **1** cause; **el motivo
del accidente** the cause of the
accident; **2** reason; **por motivos
personales** for personal reasons.

moto *noun* F motorbike; **montar en
moto** to ride a motorbike; **montar en
la moto** to get on the motorbike;
moto acuática ski jet.

motocicleta *noun* F motorbike.

motociclista *noun* M/F motorcyclist.

motor *noun* M engine; **motor a reacción** jet engine.

mover *verb* [38] to move.
moverse *reflexive verb* [38] to move; **no te muevas** don't move.

movimiento *noun* M movement.

moza *noun* F young girl.

mozo *noun* M 1 young boy; 2 **mozo de estación** porter.

muchacha *noun* F girl.

muchacho *noun* M boy.

muchedumbre *noun* F crowd.

mucho[1] *adverb* 1 a lot; **lo usan mucho** they use it a lot; **eso es mucho mejor** that's a lot better; **salen mucho** they go out a lot; 2 very; **lo siento mucho** I'm very sorry; **'¿te interesa?' – 'mucho'** 'are you interested?' – 'very'; **trabajar mucho** to work very hard; **voy a estudiar mucho** I'm going to study very hard; 3 **mucho antes** long before; **mucho después** long after; 4 **como mucho** at the most; 5 **ni mucho menos** far from it.

mucho[2]**/mucha** *adjective* 1 a lot of; **mucho tiempo** a lot of time; 2 much; **no tienen mucho interés** they haven't got much interest; 3 many; **¿había muchos niños?** were there many children?; **muchas veces** many times; 4 **hacía mucho frío** it was very cold; **tengo mucho sueño** I'm very sleepy; 5 **tengo**

mucha prisa I'm in a real hurry; 6 **nos vimos hace mucho tiempo** we saw each other a long time ago; 7 **muchas gracias** thanks a lot; **mucho gusto** nice to meet you; **lo haré con mucho gusto** I'd be very pleased to do it.
pronoun 1 a lot; **tienes mucho que aprender** you have a lot to learn; 2 much; **no tengo mucho** I haven't got much; 3 many; **no quedan muchas** there aren't many left; **muchos se sorprendieron** many were surprised; 4 (*talking about time*) **tardan mucho** they are taking a long time; **¿hace mucho que ha llamado?** did she call a long time ago?; **hace mucho que no sé nada de ella** it's a long time since I last heard from her; **ya no falta mucho para mi cumpleaños** it's not long to my birthday now.

mudanza *noun* F removal; **camión de mudanzas** removal van; **estar de mudanza** to be in the process of moving.

mudar *verb* [17] move (*from one house to another*).
mudarse *reflexive verb* [17] to move; **mudarse de casa** to move house.

mueble *noun* M piece of furniture; **muebles** furniture.

muela *noun* F back tooth; **tener dolor de muelas** to have toothache.

muera, muero, etc. *verb* SEE **morir**.

muerda, muerdo, etc. *verb* SEE **morder**.

muerte *noun* F death; **muerte repentina** sudden death; **estar condenado a muerte** to be sentenced to death.

muerto/muerta *noun* M/F dead person; **no ha habido muertos** there were no casualties; **hubo un muerto** one person died.
adjective dead; **muerto de sed** dying of thirst; **estoy muerto de frío** I'm freezing to death; **estoy muerto de hambre** I'm starving; **estábamos muertos de cansancio** we were dead tired.

muestra, muestro, etc. *verb* SEE **mostrar**.

mueva, muevo, etc. *verb* SEE **mover**.

mujer *noun* F 1 woman; 2 wife; **mi mujer** my wife.

muleta *noun* F crutch.

mulo/mula *noun* M/F mule.

multa *noun* F fine; **me pusieron una multa** I was fined.

multiplicación *noun* F multiplication.

multiplicar *verb* [31] to multiply.

mundial *noun* M **el mundial de fútbol** the World Cup.
adjective world; **un récord mundial** a world record; **la economía mundial** the world economy; **de fama mundial** world-famous.

mundo *noun* M world.

municipal *adjective* 1 local; 2 municipal.

muñeca *noun* F 1 doll; **jugar a las muñecas** to play dolls; **muñeca de trapo** rag doll; 2 wrist.

muñeco *noun* M 1 toy; **muñeco de peluche** soft toy; 2 puppet.

muralla *noun* F wall.

murciélago *noun* M bat.

muriendo, murió, etc. *verb* SEE **morir**.

murmullo *noun* M 1 whispering; **hablar en un murmullo** to whisper; 2 murmur.

murmurar *verb* [17] 1 to whisper; 2 to murmur; 3 **murmurar sobre alguien** to gossip about someone; **se murmura que ...** the rumour is ...

muro *noun* M wall.

músculo *noun* M muscle.

museo *noun* M museum; **un museo de pintura** a gallery; **un museo de arte moderno** a modern art museum.

música[1] *noun* F music; **música en directo/música en vivo** live music; **música pop** pop music.

musical *adjective* musical.

músico/música[2] *noun* M/F 1 musician; 2 composer.

muslo *noun* M 1 thigh; 2 leg (*of a chicken*).

musulmán/musulmana *noun* M/F *adjective* Muslim.

mutuo/mutua *adjective* mutual.

muy *adverb* **1** very; **es muy difícil** it's very difficult; **está muy bien** it's very good; **muy bien, sigamos** very good, let's continue; **2** too; **era muy pequeño para entenderlo** he was too small to understand it; **3 muy señor mío** Dear sir (*in a letter*).

N n

nabo *noun* M turnip.

nácar *noun* M mother-of-pearl.

nacer *verb* [35] to be born; **nací en Valencia** I was born in Valencia; **¿dónde has nacido?** where were you born.

nacido/nacida *adjective* born; **nacido en Sevilla** born in Seville; **un niño recién nacido** a new-born baby.

nacimiento *noun* M **1** birth; **es ciego de nacimiento** he was born blind; **2** crib (*nativity scene*).

nación *noun* F nation.

nacional *adjective* national.

nacionalidad *noun* F nationality; **¿de qué nacionalidad eres?** what nationality are you?

nada *pronoun* **1** nothing; **no hay nada nuevo** there's nothing new; **no hay nada como …** there's nothing like …; **2** anything; **no me queda nada** I haven't got anything left; **yo**

no sé nada de eso I don't know anything about that; **no me dijeron nada** they didn't say anything to me; **3 no tengo nada de dinero** I have no money at all; **4 nada más** nothing else; **sólo quiero hablar con ella, nada más** I only want to speak to her, nothing else; **nada más, gracias** that's all thank you; **5 nada más** anything else; **no quiero nada más** I don't want anything else; **6 nada más** only; **no quiero nada más que un kilo** I only want one kilo; **7 de nada** not at all (*to someone who has said thank you*); **8** love (*in tennis*); **treinta nada** thirty love.
adverb at all; **no me gusta nada** I don't like it at all; **no me ayudan nada** they don't help me at all.

nadar *verb* [17] to swim.

nadie *pronoun* **1** nobody; **al final nadie llamó** nobody phoned in the end; **2 no se lo dije a nadie** I didn't tell anybody.

nailon *noun* M nylon.

naipe *noun* M card.

nana *noun* F lullaby.

naranja *noun* F orange; **zumo de naranja** orange juice.
noun M orange (*the colour*).
adjective orange (*never changes*); **unos pantalones naranja** orange trousers.

naranjada *noun* F orangeade.

naranjo *noun* M orange tree.

nariz *noun* F nose; **sonarse la nariz** to blow your nose; ★ **darse de narices con alguien** (*informal*) to bump into someone; ★ **en mis propias narices** (*informal*) right under my nose.

nata *noun* F cream; **nata líquida** single cream; **nata para montar** double cream; **nata montada** whipped cream.

natación *noun* F swimming.

natillas *plural noun* F custard.

natural *adjective* natural.

naturaleza *noun* F **1** nature; **respetar la naturaleza** to respect nature; **la naturaleza humana** human nature; **2 naturaleza muerta** still life.

naturalmente *adverb* naturally.

náusea *noun* F nausea; **tener náuseas** to feel sick; **el olor me daba náuseas** the smell was making me feel sick.

navaja *noun* F **1** penknife; **2 navaja de afeitar** razor.

nave *noun* F **1** ship; **nave espacial** spaceship; **2** premises; **nave industrial** industrial premises.

navegar *verb* [28] to sail.

Navidad *noun* F **1** Christmas; **el día de Navidad** Christmas Day; **feliz Navidad** Merry Christmas; **2 Navidades** Christmas time; **pasaré las Navidades con mi hermana** I'll spend Christmas with my sister.

nazca, nazco, etc. *verb* SEE **nacer**.

neblina *noun* F mist.

necesario/necesaria *adjective* necessary.

necesidad *noun* F need; **no hay necesidad de llamarlos** there's no need to call them; **en caso de necesidad** … if necessary ….

necesitar *verb* [17] **1** to need; **no necesitas llevar el pasaporte** you don't need to take your passport; **2 'se necesitan camareros'** (*on sign*) 'waiters wanted'.

nectarina *noun* F nectarine.

neerlandés[1] *noun* M Dutch (*the language*).

neerlandés[2]**/neerlandesa** *noun* M/F Dutchman/ Dutchwoman. *adjective* Dutch.

nefasto/nefasta *adjective* **1** disastrous (*consequences*); **2** awful (*weather or taste in clothes*).

negar *verb* [30] **1** to deny; **lo niega todo** he denies everything; **2** to refuse; **nos negaron su ayuda** they refused to help us.

negarse *reflexive verb* [30] to refuse; **se niega a colaborar** he refuses to colaborate.

negativo/negativa *adjective* negative.

negociación *noun* F negotiation.

negociar *verb* [17] to negotiate.

negocio *noun* M **1** business; **montar un negocio** to set up a business; **un viaje de negocios** a business trip; **2 negocios** business; **dedicarse a los negocios** to be in business; **3** deal; **hacer un buen negocio** to make a good deal.

negro/negra *noun* M/F black man/ black woman.
adjective black.

nervio *noun* M nerve; **tengo muchos nervios** I'm very nervous; ★ **tener los nervios de punta** to be on edge.

nervioso/nerviosa *adjective* nervous; **ponerse nervioso** to get nervous.

neumático *noun* M tyre.

neutro/neutra *adjective* **1** neutral; **2** neuter (*in grammar*).

nevar *verb* [29] to snow; **está nevando** it's snowing.

nevera *noun* F fridge.

ni *conjunction* **1** not … even; **ni lo he abierto** I haven't even opened it; **ni uno de ellos llamó** not even one of them called; **2** no … ni … neither … nor; **no vino él ni su hermana** neither he nor his sister came; **no es mío ni suyo** it's not mine and it's not hers either; **una casa sin luz ni agua corriente** a house with neither water nor electricity; **ni uno ni otro** neither one nor the other; **3 no es ni grande ni pequeño** it's neither big nor small; **4 ¡ni hablar!** no way!

nido *noun* M nest.

niebla *noun* F fog; **había mucha niebla** it was very foggy.

nieta *noun* F granddaughter.

nieto *noun* M **1** grandson; **2 mis nietos** my grandchildren.

nieva, nieve¹, etc. *verb* SEE **nevar**.

nieve² *noun* F **1** snow; **2 batir claras a punto de nieve** to beat eggwhites until stiff; ★ **blanco como la nieve** as white as snow.

ningún *adjective* SEE **ninguno**.

ninguno/ninguna *adjective* (*'ninguno' becomes 'ningún' in front of a masculine singular noun*) **1** any; **no trajeron ninguna caja** they didn't bring any boxes; **no he comprado ningún libro** I didn't buy any books; **no hay ninguna necesidad** there's no need; **2 en ningún momento** never; **en ningún lugar** nowhere; **no lo veo por ningún lado** I can't see it anywhere; **3 de ninguna manera** no way.
pronoun **1** neither; **ninguno de los dos vale** neither of them is suitable; **ninguno de los dos me gusta** I don't like either of them; **2** none; **ninguno de los que estaban allí** none of those who were there; **no compró ninguno** he didn't buy any of them; **3** nobody; **ninguno lo vio** nobody saw him.

niña *noun* F girl.

niño *noun* M **1** boy; **2** child; **van a tener un niño** they're going to have a baby; **3 niños** children; **ropa de niños** children's clothes.

nivel *noun* M **1** level; **el nivel del agua** the level of the water; **2** standard; **el nivel de vida** the standard of living.

no *adverb* **1** no; **'¿es tuyo?' – 'no'** 'is it yours?' – 'no'; **2** not; **no es mi amigo** he's not my friend; **no sabe nadar** he can't swim; **no se sabe** it's not known; **no mucho** not much; **ahí no** not there; **3 no comió nada** he didn't eat anything; **no voy nunca al cine** I never go to the cinema; **no se parecen en nada** they are not similar at all; **4 somos siete ¿no?** there are seven of us, aren't there?; **tú hablaste con ella, ¿no?** you spoke to her, didn't you?; **5 la no violencia** non-violence; **los no fumadores** non smokers; **6 ¡cómo no!** of course!

noche *noun* F **1** evening; night; **a las ocho de la noche** at eight o'clock in the evening; **a las once de la noche** at eleven o'clock at night; **esta noche** this evening, tonight; **por la noche** in the evening, at night; **la noche anterior** the previous evening, the night before; **el lunes por la noche** Monday evening, Monday night; **de noche** in the evening, at night; **buenas noches** good evening; goodnight; **2 hacerse de noche** to get dark.

Nochebuena *noun* F Christmas Eve.

Nochevieja *noun* F New Year's Eve.

nocturno/nocturna *adjective* **1** nocturnal; **2** evening; **clases nocturnas** evening lessons.

nombrar *verb* [17] **1** to mention; **2** to appoint.

nombre *noun* M **1** name; **¿qué nombre tiene el grupo?** what's the name of the group?; **¿qué nombre le** van a poner al niño? what are they going to call the baby?; **nombre de pila** first name; **2** (*on forms*) **'nombre'** first name; **'nombre y apellidos'** 'full name'; **3** noun (*in grammar*).

nordeste, noreste *noun* M northeast.

norma *noun* F rule.

normal *adjective* **1** normal; **eso es normal** that's normal; **2 normal y corriente** ordinary.

normalmente *adverb* normally.

noroeste *noun* M northwest.

norte *noun* M north; **hacia el norte** northwards; **al norte de Madrid** to the north of Madrid.

Noruega *noun* F Norway.

noruego[1] *noun* M Norwegian (*the language*).

noruego[2]/**noruega** *noun* M/F *adjective* Norwegian.

nos *pronoun* **1** us; **nos invitaron a la fiesta** they invited us to the party; **2** to us; **nos mintió** he lied to us; **3** ourselves; **nos portamos bien** we behaved ourselves; **4** each other; **siempre nos ayudamos** we always help each other; **5** (*with reflexive verbs*) **nos reímos mucho** we laughed a lot; **vamos a bañarnos** let's go for a swim; **nos sentamos a la mesa** we sat at the table; **6** (*with parts of the body or clothes*) **nos quitamos los abrigos** we took our coats off; **nos limpiamos los pies al entrar** we wiped our feet at the door; **7** (*having* *something done*) **el sábado iremos a cortarnos el pelo** we'll go and get our hair cut on Saturday.

nosotros/nosotras *pronoun*
1 we; **lo hicimos nosotras** we did it; **2** us; **detrás de nosotros** behind us; **3 nosostros mismos** ourselves.

nota *noun* F **1** note; **tomar nota de algo** to write something down; **tomar notas** to take notes; **2** mark; **¿qué nota has sacado en física?** what did you get in physics?; **sacar buenas notas** to get good marks; **3 nota musical** note.

notar *verb* [17] to notice; **te noto preocupado** you look worried; **se nota que ...** you can tell that ...

notario/notaria *noun* M/F notary public.

noticia *noun* F **una noticia interesante** an interesting piece of news; **la noticia me sorprendió** the news surprised me; **dar la noticia a alguien** to break the news to someone; **tengo buenas noticias** I've got good news; **las noticias de las nueve** the nine o'clock news.

novecientos/novecientas *number* nine hundred; **novecientos veinte** nine hundred and twenty.

novela *noun* F novel.

noveno/novena *adjective* ninth; **el noveno piso** the ninth floor.

noventa *number* ninety; **tiene noventa años** she's ninety (years old); **noventa y siete** ninety-seven; **los años noventa** the nineties.

novia *noun* F **1** bride; **2** fiancée; **3** girlfriend.

noviembre *noun* M November; **en noviembre/en el mes de noviembre** in November.

novio *noun* M **1** groom; **2** fiancé; **3** boyfriend.

nube *noun* F cloud; **un cielo cubierto de nubes** a cloudy sky.

nublado/nublada *adjective* cloudy.

nuclear *noun* F nuclear power station.
adjective nuclear.

nudo *noun* M knot.

nuera *noun* F daughter-in-law.

nuestro/nuestra *adjective* our; **nuestra casa** our house; **un familiar nuestro** a relative of ours.
pronoun ours; **la nuestra es verde** ours is green; **los nuestros están en el salón** ours are in the living room; **aquél es el nuestro** that one is ours.

nueve *number* **1** nine; **Jaime tiene nueve años** Jaime's nine (years old); **2** ninth (*in dates*); **hoy estamos a nueve** it's the ninth today; **3** nine (*in clock time*); **son las nueve** it's nine o'clock.

nuevo/nueva *adjective* **1** new; **mis zapatos nuevos** my new shoes; **2 de nuevo** once more; **3 ¿qué hay de nuevo?** (*informal*) what's new?

nuez *noun* F **1** walnut; **2** Adam's apple; **3 nuez moscada** nutmeg.

número *noun* M 1 number; **mi número de teléfono** my telephone number; 2 issue (*of a magazine, for example*); 3 size; **¿qué número de zapatos calzas?** what size shoes do you take?

nunca *adverb* never; **nunca he estado en ese bar** I've never been to that bar; **nunca más** never again; **más que nunca** more than ever; **casi nunca** hardly ever.

nutritivo/nutritiva *adjective* nourishing.

Ñ ñ

ñoño/ñona *adjective* **no seas ñoño** don't be so wet.

O o

o *conjunction* 1 or; **antes o después** sooner or later; (*note that when 'o' appears between numbers, it has an accent; before a word starting with 'o' it becomes 'u'*) **11 ó 12** 11 or 12; 2 **o sea** so; **¿o sea que no te importa?** so you don't mind?

obedecer *verb* [35] to obey; **tienes que obedecerme** you must do as I say.

obedezca, obedezco, etc. *verb* SEE **obedecer**.

obediencia *noun* F obedience.

obediente *adjective* obedient.

obispo *noun* M bishop.

objetivo[1] *noun* M objective.

objetivo[2]**/objetiva** *adjective* objective.

objeto *noun* M object; **objetos de valor** valuables.

obligar *verb* [28] **obligar a alguien a hacer algo** to make somebody do something.
obligarse *reflexive verb* [28] **obligarse a hacer** to force yourself to do.

obligatorio/obligatoria *adjective* compulsory.

obra *noun* F 1 deed; **una buena obra** a good deed; 2 play; **una obra de Shakespeare** a Shakespeare play; 3 work; **una obra de arte** a work of art; 4 **una obra maestra** a masterpiece; 5 building site; **estar en obras** to be having some building work done.

obrero/obrera *noun* M/F 1 worker; 2 labourer.

obsceno/obscena *adjective* obscene.

obscuridad *noun* F darkness.

obscuro/obscura *adjective* dark; **a obscuras** in the dark.

observación *noun* F 1 observation; 2 remark.

observador/observadora *noun* M/F observer.
adjective observant.

observar *verb* [17] **1** to observe; **2** to remark.

observatorio *noun* M observatory.

obsesión *noun* F obsession; **tiene la obsesión de que la siguen** she's obsessed with the idea that she's being followed.

obstáculo *noun* M obstacle; **superar un obstáculo** to overcome an obstacle.

obstante *in phrase* **no obstante** neverthless.

obstinado/obstinada *adjective* obstinate.

obstinarse *reflexive verb* [17] **obstinarse en hacer** to insist on doing.

obtendré, obtendría, etc. *verb* SEE **obtener**.

obtener *verb* [9] **1** to obtain; **2 obtener un premio** to win a prize.

obtenga, obtengo, obtuve, etc. *verb* SEE **obtener**.

obvio/obvia *adjective* obvious.

oca *noun* F goose.

ocasión *noun* F **1** occasion; **2** opportunity; **si hay ocasión** if there's an opportunity; **3 precios de ocasión** bargain prices; **coches de ocasión** second-hand cars.

ocasionar *verb* [17] to cause.

Occidente *noun* M the West.

occidental *adjective* Western.

océano *noun* M ocean.

ochenta *number* eighty; **tiene ochenta años** she's eighty (years old); **ochenta y cinco** eighty-five; **los años ochenta** the eighties.

ocho *number* **1** eight; **tiene ocho años** she's eight (years old); **2** eighth (*in dates*); **estamos a ocho** it's the eighth today; **3** eight (*in clock time*); **son las ocho** it's eight o'clock.

ochocientos/ochocientas *number* eight hundred; **ochocientos siete** eight hundred and seven.

ocio *noun* M spare time.

octavo/octava *adjective* eighth; **el octavo piso** the eighth floor.

octubre *noun* M October; **en octubre/en el mes de octubre** in October.

ocupación *noun* F occupation.

ocupado/ocupada *adjective* **1** busy; **está muy ocupado** he's very busy; **2** engaged; **la línea está ocupada** the line is engaged; **3** taken; **¿está ocupado este asiento?** is this seat taken?

ocupar *verb* [17] **1 ocupar un asiento** to have a seat; **ocupa el asiento 11b** he's in seat 11b; **¿quién ocupa esa habitación?** who's in that room?; **2** to occupy (*land or a building*); **3** (*talking about time*)

ocupo mi tiempo libre leyendo I spend my free time reading.

ocuparse *reflexive verb* [17] **ocuparse de algo** to take care of something.

ocurrir *verb* [19] to happen; **me ocurrió una cosa muy graciosa** something really funny happened to me; **¿qué le ocurre?** what's the matter with him?

ocurrirse *reflexive verb* [19] **¿se te ocurre alguna idea?** can you think of anything?; **se me ocurrió que podríamos** … I thought we could …

odiar *verb* [17] to hate.

odio *noun* M hate, hatred.

oeste *noun* M west; **hacia el oeste** westwards; **al oeste de Madrid** to the west of Madrid.

ofender *verb* [18] to offend.

ofenderse *reflexive verb* [18] to take offence.

oferta *noun* F offer; **estar de/en oferta** to be on offer.

oficial *adjective* official.

oficina *noun* F office; **oficina de cambio** bureau de change; **oficina de objetos perdidos** lost property (office); **oficina de (información y) turismo** tourist (information) office.

oficinista *noun* M/F office worker.

oficio *noun* M 1 trade; 2 service (*in a church*).

ofrecer *verb* [35] to offer.

ofrezca, ofrezco, etc. *verb* SEE **ofrecer**.

oído *noun* M 1 ear; **tener dolor de oídos** to have earache; 2 **tener buen oído** to have a good ear.

oiga, oigo, etc. *verb* SEE **oír**.

oír *verb* [56] 1 to hear; **no oigo nada** I can't hear anything; 2 listen to; **oír las noticias** to listen to the news; **oír música** to listen to music; 3 **¡oye!** listen!

ojalá *exclamation* **¡ojalá me llame!** I hope he rings me!; **¡ojalá pudiera!** I wish I could!

ojo *noun* M 1 eye; **tiene los ojos verdes** he's got green eyes; **ojos claros** light-coloured eyes (*blue, green, or grey as opposed to brown*); **con los ojos cerrados** with your eyes closed; 2 **el ojo de la cerradura** the keyhole; ★ **no pegué ojo en toda la noche** I didn't sleep a wink; ★ **salir por un ojo de la cara** (*informal*) to cost an arm and a leg.
exclamation **¡ojo!** watch out!

ola *noun* F wave; **una ola de calor** a heatwave; **una ola de frío** a cold spell.

ole, olé *exclamation* olé.

oler *verb* [39] to smell; **oler una flor** to smell a flower; **oler a algo** to smell of something; **huele a lavanda** it smells of lavender.

olimpiadas *plural noun* F Olympic Games.

olímpico/olímpica *adjective* Olympic.

oliva *noun* F olive; **aceite de oliva** olive oil.

olivo *noun* M olive tree.

olla *noun* F pan; **olla a presión** pressure cooker.

olor *noun* M smell; **tiene un olor raro** it has a funny smell; **tiene olor a almendras** it smells of almonds.

olvidar *verb* [17] to forget; **olvídalo** forget it.
olvidarse *reflexive verb* [17] to forget; **se me olvidó llamarte** I forgot to ring you; **se me olvidó la cartera** I forgot my wallet.

once *number* **1** eleven; **tiene once años** she's eleven (years old); **2** eleventh (*in dates*); **hoy estamos a once** it's the eleventh today; **3** eleven (*in clock time*); **son las once** it's eleven o'clock.

onceavo/onceava *adjective* eleventh.

onda *noun* F wave; **onda larga** long wave; ★ **estar en la onda** (*informal*) to be trendy.

ondulado/ondulada *adjective* wavy.

ONU *abbreviation* F (*short for: Organización de las Naciones Unidas*) UN.

opcional *adjective* optional.

ópera *noun* F opera.

operación *noun* F operation; **ha sufrido una operación** he's had an operation.

operador/operadora *noun* M/F operator.

operar *verb* [17] **1** to operate on (*a person*); **2** to produce (*a change*).
operarse *reflexive verb* [17] to have an operation; **se va a operar del corazón** she's going to have a heart operation.

opinar *verb* [17] **1** to think; **opino que …** I think that …; **¿qué opinas del diseño?** what do you think of the design?; **prefiero no opinar** I prefer not to say what I think; **2** to express an opinion.

opinión *noun* F opinion; **¿cuál es vuestra opinión?** what do you think?; **cambiar de opinión** to change your mind.

oponer *verb* [11] **1** to raise (*an objection*); **2 oponer resistencia** to put up a fight.
oponerse *reflexive verb* [11] **oponerse a algo** to oppose something.

oporto *noun* M port.

oportunidad *noun* F opportunity; **aprovechar una oportunidad** to make the most of an opportunity.

oposición *noun* F **1** opposition; **2** competitive exam for a job.

optativo/optativa *adjective* optional.

óptico/óptica *noun* M/F optician.

optimismo *noun* M optimism.

optimista *noun* M/F optimist. *adjective* optimistic.

opuesto/opuesta *adjective* **1** conflicting (*views or opinions*); **2** opposite; **venían en dirección**

opuesta they were coming from the opposite direction.

oral *noun* M *adjective* oral.

orden *noun* M order; **en orden alfabético** in alphabetical order; **en orden de importancia** in order of importance; **puestos en orden de tamaño** arranged according to size; **ponlos en orden** put them in order; **mantener el orden** to keep order; **poner la habitación en orden** to tidy up the room; **¡orden!** order!
noun F order; **dar una orden** to give an order.

ordenado/ordenada *adjective* tidy; **es muy ordenado** he's very tidy.

ordenador *noun* M computer.

ordenar *verb* [17] **1** to tidy up (*a room or house*); **2** to put in order; **ordenar algo alfabéticamente** to put something in alphabetical order; **3** to order; **nos ordenó seguir** he ordered us to carry on.

ordinario/ordinaria *adjective* **1** vulgar; **2** rude (*a person*); **3** ordinary, normal (*a method or system*).

oreja *noun* F ear.

orgánico/orgánica *adjective* organic.

organización *noun* F organization.

organizar *verb* [22] to organize.

órgano *noun* M organ.

orgullo *noun* M pride; **tiene mucho orgullo** he's very proud.

orgulloso/orgullosa *adjective* proud; **estar orgulloso de algo** to be proud of something.

orientación *noun* F **1** **¿qué orientación tiene la casa?** which way does the house face?; **2** orientation; **3** bearings; **4** **orientación profesional** careers guidance.

oriental *noun* M/F Oriental.
adjective **1** Eastern; **2** Oriental.

orientar *verb* [17] **1** to guide; **2** to give guidance to (*a young person or student*).
orientarse *reflexive verb* [17] to get your bearings.

Oriente *noun* M East; **el Lejano Oriente** the Far East.

original *noun* M *adjective* original.

orilla *noun* F **1** bank; **sentados a la orilla del río** sitting on the river bank; **2** shore; **una casa a orillas del mar** a house by the sea.

ornamental *adjective* ornamental.

oro *noun* M gold; **un reloj de oro** a gold watch.

orquesta *noun* F orchestra; **una orquesta de jazz** a jazz band.

ortiga *noun* F nettle.

ortografía *noun* F spelling.

oruga *noun* F caterpillar.

os *pronoun* 1 you (*talking to more than one person*); **os vimos desde la ventana** we saw you from the window; **¿os dieron suficiente información?** did they give you enough information?; 2 to you; **os mintió** he lied to you; 3 yourselves; **os tenéis que portar bien** you must behave yourselves; 4 each other; **¿os conocéis?** do you know each other?; 5 (*with a reflexive verb*) **¿os divertisteis?** did you have a good time?; **iros a bañar** go for a swim; 6 (*with parts of the body or clothes*) **os podéis quitar los abrigos** you can take your coats off; **¿os habéis lavado las manos?** have you washed your hands?; 7 (*having something done*) **os tenéis que cortar el pelo** you have to have your hair cut.

osado/osada *adjective* bold.

oscuridad *noun* F darkness.

oscuro/oscura *adjective* dark; **a oscuras** in the dark.

osito *noun* M **un osito de peluche** a teddy bear.

oso/osa *noun* M/F bear.

ostra *noun* F oyster.

OTAN *abbreviation* (*short for: Organización del Tratado del Atlántico Norte*) NATO.

otoño *noun* M autumn.

otro/otra *adjective* 1 another; **¿te has comprado otro casete?** did you buy another cassette?; **añade otros dos** add another two; 2 other; **en otros colores** in other colours; **la otra tarde le vi** I saw him the other evening; **¿no tienes ningún otro color?** don't you have any other colours?; 3 **otra cosa** something else; **me gustaría comprarle otra cosa** I would like to buy her something else; **eso es otra cosa diferente** that's something different; **¿quieres alguna otra cosa?** do you want something else?; **no me gusta ninguna otra cosa** I don't like anything else; 4 **otra vez** again; **hazlo otra vez** do it again.
pronoun 1 another one; **éste no, dame otro** not this one, give me another one; 2 other one; **el otro te queda mejor** the other one suits you better; **las otras están en el cajón** the other ones are in the drawer; 3 (*talking about people*) **los otros vendrán en coche** the others will come by car; **a otros les gustaría** other people would like it; 4 (*talking about time*) **un mes sí y otro no** every other month; **de un día para otro** from one day to the next.

oveja *noun* F sheep.

OVNI *abbreviation* (*short for: objeto volante no identificado*) UFO.

oxidado/oxidada *adjective* rusty.

oxígeno *noun* M oxygen.

oyendo, oyó *verb* SEE **oír**.

ozono *noun* M ozone; **la capa de ozono** the ozone layer.

P p

pabellón *noun* M pavilion.

paciencia *noun* F patience; **tener paciencia** to be patient.

paciente *noun* M/F *adjective* patient.

padecer *verb* [35] to suffer; **padecer de algo** to suffer from something.

padrastro *noun* M stepfather.

padre *noun* M 1 father; 2 **mis padres** my parents.

padrino *noun* M 1 godfather; 2 **mis padrinos** my godparents.

paella *noun* F paella.

pagar *verb* [28] 1 to pay; 2 to pay off (*a debt*); 3 to pay for (*tickets, for example*); 4 to repay (*a favour*).

página *noun* F page.

pago *noun* M payment; **pago anticipado** payment in advance; **pago inicial** down payment; **pago al contado** payment in cash; **efectuar un pago** to make a payment.

país *noun* M country.

paisaje *noun* M landscape.

País de Gales *noun* M **el País de Gales** Wales.

Países Bajos *plural noun* M **los Países Bajos** the Netherlands.

País Vasco *noun* M **el País Vasco** the Basque Country.

paja *noun* F 1 straw; 2 **pajita** drinking straw.

pajarita *noun* F bow tie.

pájaro *noun* M bird; ★ **matar dos pájaros de un tiro** to kill two birds with one stone.

pala *noun* F 1 spade; 2 shovel; 3 bat (*for table tennis*); 4 slice (*in cooking*).

palabra *noun* F 1 word; **palabra compuesta** compound word; **no cumplió con su palabra** he didn't keep his word; 2 speech; **el don de la palabra** the gift of speech; 3 **pedir la palabra** to ask permission to speak.

palabrota *noun* F swearword; **decir palabrotas** to swear.

palacio *noun* M palace.

palanca *noun* F 1 lever; **abrir algo haciendo palanca** to lever something open; 2 crowbar; 3 **palanca de cambios** gearstick; **palanca de mando** joystick.

paleta *noun* F 1 palette; 2 spatula (*for cooking*); 3 trowel; 4 bat (*in table tennis*).

palidecer *verb* [35] to go pale.

pálido/pálida *adjective* pale.

palillo *noun* M 1 chopstick; 2 drumstick; 3 **palillo de dientes** toothpick.

palma *noun* F palm (*of hand*); **dar palmas** to clap your hands.

palmera *noun* F palm tree.

palo *noun* M **1** stick; **2** pole (*for a tent*); **3 palo de escoba** broomstick.

paloma *noun* F **1** dove; **la paloma de la paz** the dove of peace; **2** pigeon.

palomitas *plural noun* F popcorn.

pan *noun* M bread; **un pan de molde** a loaf of bread; **una barra de pan** a baguette; **pan integral** wholewheat bread; **pan tostado** toast; **pan rallado** breadcrumbs.

pana *noun* F corduroy.

panadería *noun* F bakery.

panadero/panadera *noun* M/F baker.

Panamá *noun* M Panama; **el Canal de Panamá** the Panama Canal.

panameño/panameña *noun* M/F *adjective* Panamanian.

pancarta *noun* F banner.

panceta *noun* F belly pork.

panecillo *noun* M bread roll.

pánico *noun* M panic.

panorama *noun* M **1** panorama; **2** view.

pantalla *noun* F **1** screen; **la pantalla grande** the big screen; **2** monitor (*of a computer*); **3** shade (*of a lamp*).

pantalón *noun* M trousers; **un pantalón** a pair of trousers.

pantalones *plural noun* M trousers; **un par de pantalones/unos pantalones** a pair of trousers; **pantalones vaqueros** jeans; **pantalones cortos** shorts; **pantalones de peto** dungarees.

pantano *noun* M **1** swamp; **2** reservoir.

pantorrilla *noun* F calf.

panty, panti *noun* M tights.

pañal *noun* M nappy.

paño *noun* M cloth; **un paño** a piece of cloth; **un paño de cocina** a dishcloth; ★ **estar en paños menores** (*informal*) to be in your undies.

pañuelo *noun* M **1** handkerchief; **2** headscarf; **3** scarf.

papá *noun* M daddy; **mis papás** my mum and dad.

papagayo *noun* M parrot.

papel *noun* M paper; **un trozo de papel** a piece of paper; **se encontró un papel en la mesa** he found a piece of paper on the table; **papel higiénico** toilet paper; **papel pintado** wallpaper; **papel de envolver** wrapping paper; **papel de lija** sandpaper.

papelera *noun* F **1** paperbasket; **2** litter bin (*in the street*).

papelería *noun* F stationer's.

paperas *plural noun* F mumps.

paquete *noun* M **1** parcel; **mandar un paquete** to send a parcel;

2 packet; **un paquete de cigarrillos** a packet of cigarettes.

par noun M **1** pair; **un par de zapatos** a pair of shoes; **2** couple; **un par de veces** a couple of times; ★ **de par en par** wide open. adjective even; **un número par** an even number.

para preposition **1** for; **es para ti** it's for you; **sirve para limpiar** it's for cleaning; **¿para qué quieres la carpeta?** what do you want the folder for?; **hay suficiente para todos** there's enough for everybody; **estará terminado para el doce** it'll be finished for the twelfth; **2** to; **se dijo para sí** he said to himself; **es demasiado difícil para hacerlo** it's too difficult to do; **3** (direction) **me voy para casa** I'm going home; **iban para la estación** they were going to the station; **4 para que** so that.

parabrisas noun M (does not change in the plural) windscreen.

paracaídas noun M (does not change in the plural) parachute.

parachoques noun M (does not change in the plural) bumper.

parada[1] noun F stop; **la parada del autobús** the bus stop; **parada de taxis** taxi rank.

parado/parada[2] noun M/F unemployed person. adjective unemployed.

parador noun M state-owned hotel.

paraguas noun M (does not change in the plural) umbrella.

Paraguay noun M Paraguay.

paraguayo/paraguaya noun M/F adjective Paraguayan.

paraíso noun M paradise.

paralelo[1] noun M parallel.

paralelo[2]**/paralela** adjective parallel; **paralelo a algo** parallel to something.

parar verb [17] **1** to stop; **parar de hablar** to stop talking; **bailamos sin parar toda la noche** we didn't stop dancing all night; **paré el coche** I stopped the car; **2 para un momento** hang on a minute; **3** to save; **parar un gol** to make a save (in football, hockey); **4 ir a parar** to end up; **fueron a parar al hospital** they ended up in hospital; **¡no sé a dónde vamos a ir a parar!** I don't know what the world is coming to!

pararse reflexive verb [17] to stop; **no te pares en medio de la calle** don't stop in the middle of the road; **se paró a pensar** he stopped to think; **se me ha parado el reloj** my watch has stopped.

pararrayos noun M lightning conductor.

parasol noun M parasol.

parcela noun F plot of land.

parche noun M patch.

parchís noun M ludo.

parecer verb [35] **1** to seem; **no parece demasiado complicado** it doesn't seem too complicated; **parece que ya no vienen** it seems they're not coming any more; **2** to seem like, to look like; **parece de madera** it looks as if it's made of wood; **esa nube parece un pájaro** that cloud looks like a bird; **parece que está roto** it looks like it's broken; **3 ¿qué te pareció la película?** what did you think of the film?; **me parece que llegan hoy** I think they arrive today; **me parece que no** I don't think so; **le pareció muy mal que no llamasen** he thought it was really bad of them not to call; **4 según parece/al parecer** apparently.

parecerse *reflexive verb* [35] **1** to look like; **se parece mucho a su padre** she looks very like her father; **nos parecemos mucho** we look a lot like each other; **2** to be like (*in character*); **se parece mucho a su madre** she's just like her mother.

parecido[1] *noun* M **1** similarity; **el parecido era increíble** the similarity was incredible; **2 ser bien parecido** to be good-looking.

parecido[2]/**parecida** *adjective* similar.

pared *noun* F wall.

pareja *noun* F **1** pair; **trabajar en pareja** to work in pairs **2** couple; **3 mi pareja** my partner.

paréntesis *noun* M (*does not change in the plural*) brackets.

parezca, parezco, etc. *verb* SEE **parecer**.

pariente *noun* M/F relative.

parking *noun* M car park.

parlamento *noun* M parliament.

paro *noun* M **1** unemployment; **estar en paro** to be unemployed; **cobrar el paro** to receive unemployment benefit; **2** strike; **hicieron un paro de 24 horas** they went on a 24-hour strike; **3 un paro cardíaco** heart failure.

parpadear *verb* [17] to blink.

párpado *noun* M eyelid.

parque *noun* M **1** park; **parque nacional** national park; **parque infantil** play park; **2 parque de atracciones** amusement park; **parque zoológico** zoo.

parquímetro *noun* M parking meter.

párrafo *noun* M paragraph.

parrilla *noun* F grill; **chuletas a la parrilla** barbecued chops.

parte *noun* F **1** part; **es parte de Asia** it's part of Asia; **una tercera parte de la herencia** a third of the inheritance; **la parte antigua de la ciudad** the old part of town; **2** share; **mi parte del trabajo** my share of the work; **3 la mayor parte de** most of; **la mayor parte de los alumnos** most of the students; **4 en/por alguna parte** somewhere; **en/por cualquier parte** anywhere; **en/por todas partes** everywhere; **5 en parte** partly; **en parte tienen razón** they're partly right; **6 en gran parte** largely; **7 de un tiempo a esta parte** for some time now; **8 ¿de parte de quién?** who shall I say is calling? (*on the phone*); **saludos de parte de Juan** Juan says hello; **felicítalos de mi parte** give them my congratulations; **9 yo por mi parte** ... as far as I'm concerned ...

participación *noun* F
1 participation; 2 share in lottery ticket.

participar *verb* [17] to participate.

participio *noun* M participle; **participio pasado** past participle.

particular *adjective* 1 private (*lesson or teacher*); 2 particular (*feature, for example*); 3 **un colegio particular** a fee-paying school; 4 **mi teléfono particular** my home telephone number; **nuestro domicilio particular** our home address; 5 **es muy particular** (*informal*) he's very peculiar.

partida *noun* F game; **una partida de ajedrez** a game of chess.

partido *noun* M 1 party; 2 game.

partir *verb* [19] 1 to cut; **partir algo por la mitad** to cut something in two; 2 to break (*a branch, for example*); 3 to crack (*a nut*); 4 to leave (*a train or person*); 5 **a partir de ese momento** from that moment on; **a partir de ahora** from now on.
partirse *reflexive verb* [19] to break (*a branch, for example*); **la rama se partió** the branch broke; **me partí un diente** I broke a tooth.

partitura *noun* F score (*music*).

parto *noun* M labour; **estar de parto** to be in labour.

pasa *noun* F raisin.

pasado[1] *noun* M past.

pasado[2]**/pasada** *adjective* 1 last; **el verano pasado** last summer; 2 **pasados dos días, le llamé** after two days, I phoned him; 3 **son las diez pasadas** it's past ten o'clock; **pasado mañana** the day after tomorrow; 4 off; **la leche está pasada** the milk is off; 5 **quiero el filete muy pasado** I want my steak well done.

pasaje *noun* M ticket.

pasajero/pasajera *noun* M/F passenger.

pasamanos *noun* M (*does not change in the plural*) 1 banister; 2 handrail.

pasaporte *noun* M passport.

pasar *verb* [17] 1 to go past; **pasaron por enfrente de mi casa** they went past my house; **pasar de largo** to go straight past; **me vió y pasó de largo** he saw me and walked straight past me; 2 to come past; **pasaron por aquí** they came past here; 3 to get past; **no podíamos pasar** we couldn't get past; 4 **pásate por mi casa por la tarde** call round at my house in the evening; **el cartero pasa a las diez** the postman comes at ten; **pasaré por el banco para recoger los impresos** I'll pop into the bank to collect the forms; 5 to go in;

pasaron todos al salón they all went into the living room; **6** to come in; **pase, por favor** please come in; **7 pasar de un lado a otro** to go from one side to the other; **8 pasar por** to go through; **pasar por la aduana** to go through customs; **el tren no pasa por Talavera** the train does not go through Talavera; **9 pasar algo por algo** to put something through something; **10** to go by; **pasaron tres meses** three months went by; **11** to pass; **¿me pasas las tijeras?** could you pass me the scissors?; **me pasó el balón** he passed the ball to me; **12** to happen; **¿qué ha pasado?** what's happened?; **no le ha pasado nada** nothing has happened to him; **¿qué te ha pasado en la mano?** what's happened to your hand?; **¿qué te pasa?** what's the matter?; **13** to spend; **pasaremos las vacaciones en España** we'll spend our holidays in Spain; **pasé la noche en casa de un amigo** I spent the night at a friend's house; **14 pasarlo bien** to have a good time; **no me lo pasé muy bien en las vacaciones** I didn't enjoy myself at all during the holidays.

pasarse *reflexive verb* [17] **1** to go off (*milk or fish*); **2** to go bad (*vegetables or fruit*); **3 pasarse de un lado a otro** to go from one side to the other; **4** to come (by); **pásate por la oficina cuando quieras** come by my office whenever you want; **me pasaré por correos antes de ir a trabajar** I'll stop by the post office before going to work; **5** to go past; **nos pasamos de parada** we missed our stop.

pasatiempo *noun* M pastime.

Pascua *noun* F **1** Easter; **2** Christmas; **¡felices Pascuas!** Merry Christmas!

pasear *verb* [17] **1** to go for a walk; **me gusta pasear por la playa** I like walking on the beach; **sacar al perro a pasear** to take the dog for a walk; **2 pasear en coche** to go for a drive; **fuimos a pasear en bicicleta** we went for a bike ride.

pasearse *reflexive verb* [17] to go for a walk.

paseo *noun* M **1** walk; **fuimos a dar un paseo** we went for a walk; **2 ir a dar un paseo en coche** to go for a drive; **ir a dar un paseo en bicicleta** to go for a bike ride.

pasillo *noun* M corridor.

pasión *noun* F passion.

pasivo/pasiva *adjective* passive; **un fumador pasivo** a passive smoker.

paso *noun* M **1** step; **dar un paso adelante** to take a step forward; **paso a paso** step by step; **2 oír pasos** to hear footsteps; **3 un paso a nivel** a level crossing; **un paso elevado** a flyover; **un paso subterráneo** a subway; **un paso de peatones** a pedestrian crossing; **un paso de cebra** a zebra crossing; **4 'ceda el paso'** 'give way'; **5 'prohibido el paso'** 'no entry'; **6 te viene de paso/te pilla de paso** it's on your way.

pasta *noun* F **1** pasta; **prefiero el arroz a la pasta** I prefer rice to pasta; **2** paste; **3 pastas** biscuits; **4 pasta de dientes** toothpaste.

pastel *noun* M cake.

pastelería *noun* F cake shop.

pastilla *noun* F 1 pill; 2 **una pastilla de jabón** a bar of soap.

pastor/pastora *noun* M/F shepherd/shepherdess.

pata¹ *noun* F 1 leg; 2 paw; ★ **meter la pata** (*informal*) to put your foot in it.

patada *noun* F kick; **dar una patada a alguien** to kick someone.

patata *noun* F potato; **patatas fritas** chips; (potato) crisps.

paternal *adjective* paternal.

patín *noun* M 1 roller skate; 2 ice skate; 3 skateboard; 4 pedalo.

patinaje *noun* M 1 roller skating; 2 ice skating; **patinaje artístico** figure skating.

patinar *noun* 17 1 to roller skate; 2 to ice skate; 3 to slip; **patiné en una mancha de aceite** I slipped on a patch of oil; 4 to skid (*a car*).

patio *noun* M 1 patio; 2 playground.

pato/pata² *noun* M/F duck; ★ **ser un pato** (*informal*) to be very clumsy.

patria *noun* F homeland.

patrocinar *verb* [17] to sponsor.

patrón *noun* M 1 boss; 2 landlord.

patrona *noun* F landlady.

pausa *noun* F pause; **hacer una pausa** to have a break.

pavo/pava *noun* M/F 1 turkey; 2 **pavo real** peacock.

payaso/payasa *noun* M/F clown.

paz (*plural* **paces**) *noun* F 1 peace; 2 **hacer las paces** to make up; **nos peleamos pero al final hicimos las paces** we had a fight, but we made up in the end; 3 **dejar en paz** to leave alone; **¡deja mi calculadora en paz!** leave my calculator alone!; **¡deja a tu hermano en paz!** leave your brother alone!; **¡estos niños nunca me dejan en paz!** these children never give me a moment's peace!; 4 **en paz descanse** rest in peace.

peaje *noun* F toll; **carretera de peaje** toll road.

peatón *noun* M pedestrian.

peca *noun* F freckle.

pecado *noun* M sin.

pecho *noun* M 1 breast; **dar el pecho a un bebé** to breastfeed a baby; 2 chest.

pechuga *noun* F breast; **pechuga de pollo** chicken breast.

pedal *noun* M pedal; **pedal de arranque** kickstart.

pedazo *noun* M piece; **un pedazo de queso** a piece of cheese; **hacer pedazos** to smash to pieces; **hizo pedazos el cristal** he smashed the glass to pieces; **el jarrón se cayó y se hizo pedazos** the vase fell and smashed to pieces.

pedir *verb* [57] 1 to ask for; **pedir un favor** to ask for a favour; **pedir ayuda** to ask for help; **pedir consejo** to ask for advice; **2 pedir perdón** to apologize; **3 piden medio millón por el cuadro** they're asking half a million for the picture; **me pidió que le comprase un libro** he asked me to buy a book for him; **4 pedir hora** to ask for an appointment; **5 pedir prestado** to ask to borrow; **me pidió prestada la moto** he asked to borrow my motorbike; **pedir dinero prestado** to ask to borrow some money, to ask for a loan; **6** to order (*in a restaurant*); **¿qué vas a pedir?** what are you going to order?

pegajoso/pegajosa *adjective* sticky.

pegamento *noun* M glue.

pegar *verb* [28] **1** to hit; **me pegó** he hit me; **pegar una torta a alguien** to slap somebody; **pegar una patada a alguien** to kick somebody; **pegar una paliza a alguien** to give somebody a beating; **2 pegar un grito** to let out a yell; **3 pegar un salto** to jump; **pegar saltos de alegría** to jump for joy; **4 pegarle un susto a alguien** to give somebody a fright; **5** to stick; **he pegado una foto suya en la pared** I've stuck a picture of him on the wall; **6** to glue; **7** (*informal*) **me vas a pegar el resfriado** you're going to give me your cold.

pegarse *reflexive verb* [28] **1** to hit each other; **empezaron a pegarse** they started hitting each other; **2** to stick; **este sello no se pega** this stamp won't stick.

pegatina *noun* F sticker.

peinado *noun* M hairstyle.

peinar *verb* [17] **1** to comb; **2** to brush.

peinarse *reflexive verb* [17] **1** to comb your hair; **2** to brush your hair.

pela *noun* F (*informal*) peseta; **no me quedan pelas** I've got no money left.

peine *noun* M comb.

pelar *verb* [17] **1** to peel (*a potato, for example*); **2 pelar a alguien al cero** to cut somebody's hair very short.

pelarse *reflexive verb* [17] **1** to peel (*from sunburn*); **se me está pelando la nariz** my nose is peeling; **2** (*informal*) to have your hair cut.

peldaño *noun* M **1** step; **2** rung.

pelea *noun* F **1** fight; **2** row; **tuvo una pelea con su novio** she had a row with her boyfriend.

pelear *verb* [17] **1** to fight; **2** to quarrel.

pelearse *reflexive verb* [17] **1** to fight; **había dos hombres peleándose** two men were fighting; **2** to quarrel; **se pelearon por dinero** they quarrelled over money; **siempre se está peleando con sus padres** she's always quarrelling with her parents.

película *noun* F **1** film; **¿qué película ponen hoy?** what film are they showing today?; **una película de terror** a horror film; **una película de risa** a comedy film; **una película de suspense** a thriller; **2** film (*for a camera*).

peligro *noun* M danger; **estar en peligro/correr peligro** to be in danger; **poner a alguien en peligro** to put somebody at risk; **fuera de peligro** out of danger; **un peligro para la salud** a health risk; **peligro de incendio** fire hazard.

peligroso/peligrosa *adjective* dangerous.

pelirrojo/pelirroja *adjective* 1 red-haired; 2 **pelo pelirrojo** red hair.

pellizcar *verb* [31] to pinch.

pellizco *noun* M pinch; **le di un pellizco en el brazo** I pinched her arm.

pelo *noun* M 1 hair; **pelo liso/lacio** straight hair; **pelo rizado** curly hair; **tengo el pelo negro** I've got black hair; 2 **un pelo de la barba** a whisker; 3 fur (*of an animal*); ★ **salvarse por los pelos** (*informal*) to escape by the skin of your teeth; **no se cayó por los pelos** he very nearly fell; ★ **ponerle a alguien los pelos de punta** (*informal*) to make somebody's hair stand on end; ★ **tomarle el pelo a alguien** (*informal*) to pull somebody's leg (*literally: to take somebody's hair*).

pelota *noun* F ball; **una pelota de fútbol** a football.

peluca *noun* F wig.

peluche *noun* M **un juguete de peluche** a cuddly toy; **un osito de peluche** a teddy bear.

peludo/peluda *adjective* hairy.

peluquería *noun* F hairdresser's.

peluquero/peluquera *noun* M/F hairdresser.

pena *noun* F 1 shame; **¡qué pena!** what a shame; **es una pena que no puedas venir** it's a shame you can't come; 2 sadness; **me da pena verte llorar** it makes me sad to see you cry; 3 **Sara me da mucha pena** I feel really sorry for Sara; 4 sentence; **pena de muerte** death penalty; 5 **valer la pena** to be worth it; **no vale la pena** it's not worth it; **vale la pena ver la película** the film's worth seeing; 6 **penas** problems; **cuéntame tus penas** tell me all your problems; ★ **a duras penas** with difficulty.

penalti *noun* M penalty.

pendiente *noun* M earring. *noun* F slope. *adjective* unresolved.

pene *noun* M penis.

penetrar *verb* [17] to penetrate.

península *noun* F peninsula.

penique *noun* M penny.

pensamiento *noun* M thought.

pensar *verb* [29] to think; **piénsalo bien antes de decidir** think about it carefully before deciding anything; **pensándolo bien ...** on second thoughts ...; **pensar en** to think about; **estaba pensando en ti** I was thinking about you; **¿piensas llamarlo?** are you thinking of calling him?; **pensar mal de alguien** to think badly of someone; **¿qué piensas del nuevo entrenador?** what do you think of the new coach?

pensión *noun* F **1** pension; **cobrar la pensión** to draw your pension; **pensión de viudedad** widow's pension; **2** guesthouse; **3 pensión completa** full board; **media pensión** half board.

pensionista *noun* M/F pensioner.

peor *noun* M/F **el/la peor** the worst one; **los/las peores** the worst ones. *adjective* **1** worse; **éstas son peores que las de la otra tienda** these are worse than the ones in the other shop; **mucho peor** much worse; **2** worst; **mi peor enemigo** my worst enemy; **en el peor de los casos** in the worst scenario; **3 peor para ti** it's your loss. *adverb* worse; **es aún peor** it's even worse; **cada vez peor** worse and worse; **de mal en peor** from bad to worse; **yo bailo peor que tú** I'm a worse dancer than you.

pepinillo *noun* M gherkin.

pepino *noun* M cucumber.

pequeño/pequeña *noun* M/F small boy/small girl. *adjective* **1** small; **una casa pequeña** a small house; **la chaqueta me está pequeña** the jacket's too small for me; **2** slight; **un pequeño esfuerzo** a slight effort; **3** young; **mi hermana pequeña** my little sister.

pera *noun* F pear.

peral *noun* M pear tree.

percha *noun* F **1** hanger; **2** coat hook.

perder *verb* [36] **1** to lose; **he perdido la cartera** I've lost my wallet; **perder la paciencia** to lose patience; **perder el conocimiento** to lose consciousness; **2** to miss; **perder el tren** to miss the train; **has perdido una gran oportunidad** you've missed a great opportunity; **3 perder la costumbre** to get out of the habit; **4 perder el tiempo** to waste time. **perderse** *reflexive verb* [36] to get lost.

pérdida *noun* F **1** loss; **2 es una pérdida de tiempo** it's a waste of time.

perdón *noun* M pardon. *exclamation* excuse me.

perdonar *verb* [17] **1** to forgive; **no la he perdonado** I haven't forgiven her; **2 te perdono el castigo** I'll let you off (*without a punishment*); **3 ¡perdona !/¡perdone !** sorry !; (*more formal*) excuse me !

perejil *noun* M parsley.

perezoso/perezosa *adjective* lazy.

perfeccionar *verb* [17] **1** to improve; **2** to perfect.

perfectamente *adverb* perfectly.

perfecto/perfecta *adjective* perfect.

perfil *noun* M profile; **visto de perfil** from the side.

perfume *noun* M perfume.

perfumería *noun* F perfume shop.

periódico *noun* M newspaper.

periodista *noun* M/F journalist.

período, periodo *noun* M period (*of time*).

periquito *noun* M budgie.

perla *noun* F pearl.

permanecer *verb* [35] **1** to stay (*in a place*); **2** to remain; **permanecer callado** to remain silent.

permanente *noun* F perm; **hacerse la permanente** to have your hair permed.
adjective permanent.

permanezca, permanezco, etc. *verb* SEE **permanecer**.

permiso *noun* M **1** permission; **darle permiso a alguien para hacer** to give someone permission to do; **2 con permiso** may I come in?; excuse me (*to get past someone*); **3** permit; **permiso de trabajo** work permit; **4** leave; **estar de permiso** to be on leave; **un permiso de una semana** a week's leave; **5 permiso de conducir** driving licence.

permitir *verb* [19] **1** to allow; **no nos permitieron pasar** they didn't allow us in; **2 no te permito que me contestes** I won't have you answering me back; **3** (*when asking permission*) **¿me permite?** may I?; **¿me permite una sugerencia?** may

I suggest something?; **4** to make possible; **este proceso permite ...** this process makes it possible to ...

pero *conjunction* but.

perrito *noun* M **1** puppy; **2 perrito caliente** hot dog.

perro/perra *noun* M/F dog; **perro callejero** stray dog; ★ **estar de un humor de perros** (*informal*) to be in a foul mood.

persecución *noun* F **1** pursuit; **salir en persecución de alguien** to set off in pursuit of someone; **2** persecution.

perseguir *verb* [64] to pursue.

persiana *noun* F blind.

persistir *verb* [19] to persist.

persona *noun* F **1** person; **una persona importante** an important person; **2 personas** people; **en la sala había diez personas** there were ten people in the room.

personaje *noun* M **1** character (*in a book, for example*); **2** important figure; **un personaje del mundo de la música** an important figure in the music world.

personal *noun* M staff.
adjective personal.

personalidad *noun* F personality.

perspectiva *noun* F **1** perspective; **2** prospect; **hay buenas perspectivas** there are good prospects.

persuadir *verb* [19] to persuade.

pertenecer *verb* [35] to belong.

pertenezca, pertenezco, etc. *verb* SEE **pertenecer**.

Perú *noun* M Peru.

peruano/peruana *noun* M/F *adjective* Peruvian.

pesa *noun* F weight; **hacer pesas** to do weightlifting.

pesadilla *noun* F nightmare.

pesado/pesada *noun* M/F **¡eres un pesado!** (*informal*) you're such a pain!
adjective 1 heavy (*a box or piece of furniture, for example*); 2 **ser muy pesado** (*informal*) to be a pain (*a person*); 3 **ser muy pesado** to be boring (*a job or book, for example*).

pesar *verb* [17] 1 to weigh; **peso sesenta kilos** I weigh sixty kilos; 2 **pesar mucho** to be very heavy; **puedo llevarlo, pesa poco** I can carry it, it's not very heavy; **¿te pesan mucho las bolsas?** are the bags too heavy for you?

pesca *noun* F fishing; **ir de pesca** to go fishing.

pescadería *noun* F fishmonger's.

pescado *noun* M fish.

pescador/pescadora *noun* M/F fisherman/fisherwoman.

pescar *verb* [31] 1 to fish; **ir a pescar** to go fishing; 2 to catch; **no pescamos nada** we didn't catch anything.

peseta *noun* F peseta.

pesimista *noun* M/F pessimist. *adjective* pessimistic.

peso *noun* M weight; **perder peso** to lose weight; **ganar peso** to put on weight; **peso bruto** gross weight; **vender al peso** to sell by weight.

pestaña *noun* F eyelash.

pétalo *noun* M petal.

petardo *noun* M banger.

petróleo *noun* M oil.

pez *noun* M fish.

piano *noun* M piano; **tocar el piano** to play the piano.

picado/picada *adjective* 1 decayed (*tooth*); **tengo una muela picada** I have a cavity in one of my back teeth; 2 **carne picada** mince; 3 **el mar estaba picado** the sea was choppy; 4 (*informal*) **estar picado** to be miffed (*a person*); **está picada porque no la llamaste** she's a bit miffed that you didn't call her.

picadura *noun* F bite, sting.

picante *adjective* hot (*spicy*).

picaporte *noun* M door handle.

picar *verb* [31] 1 to bite, to sting; 2 to mince (*meat*); 3 to chop (*vegetables*); 4 to rot (*teeth*); 5 to be hot (*spicy*); **esta salsa pica mucho** this sauce is too hot; 6 to itch; **me pica la nariz** my nose is itching; 7 **me pican los ojos** my eyes are stinging.

pico *noun* M **1** beak; **2** pick; **3** peak (*of a mountain*); **4** corner (*of a table, for example*); **5 un cuello de pico** a V-neck; **6** ... **y pico** ... and something; **fueron tres mil y pico** it was three thousand and something; **llegaron a las cinco y pico** they arrived just after five.

pida, pido, pidió, etc. *verb* SEE **pedir**.

pie *noun* M **1** foot; **ir a pie** to go on foot; **2 de pie** standing; **estaban de pie** they were standing; **ponerse de pie** to stand up; **3** base (*of a lamp or glass*).

piedra *noun* F **1** stone; **una mesa de piedra** a stone table; **piedra preciosa** precious stone; **tener piedras en el riñón** to have kidney stones; **2** flint (*of a lighter*).

piel *noun* F **1** skin; **tener la piel seca** to have dry skin; **2** peel; **3** fur; **un abrigo de pieles** a fur coat; **4** leather; **bolsos de piel** leather bags.

piensa, pienso, etc. *verb* SEE **pensar**.

pierna *noun* F leg.

pieza *noun* F **1** piece; **2 pieza de recambio** spare part.

pijama *noun* M pyjamas.

pila *noun* F **1** pile; **una pila de libros** a pile of books; **2** battery; **3** (kitchen) sink.

píldora *noun* F pill.

piloto *noun* M/F pilot.

pimentón *noun* M **1** paprika; **2** cayenne pepper.

pimienta *noun* F pepper.

pimiento *noun* M pepper; **un pimiento rojo** a red pepper.

pimpón *noun* M table tennis.

pincel *noun* M **1** paintbrush; **2** make-up brush.

pinchadiscos *noun* M/F (*informal*) disc jockey.

pinchar *verb* [17] **1** to prick; **2** to be prickly; **3** to burst; **4** to puncture; **creo que hemos pinchado** I think we've got a flat tyre; **5** (*informal*) to give an injection to.
pincharse *reflexive verb* [17] **1** to burst; **2** to puncture; **se me ha pinchado una rueda** I've got a flat tyre; **3** to get miffed.

pinchazo *noun* M puncture; **tuvimos un pinchazo** we got a flat tyre.

pingüino *noun* M penguin.

pino *noun* M pine tree; **muebles de pino** pine furniture.

pinta *noun* F **1 tiene pinta de oficinista** he looks like an office worker; **¡qué pinta más rara!** that looks very strange!; **la comida tiene muy buena pinta** the food looks delicious; **2** pint.

pintadas *plural noun* F graffiti.

pintado/pintada *adjective* painted.

pintar *verb* [17] to paint.

pintor/pintora *noun* M/F painter.

pintura *noun* F 1 painting; **pintura al óleo** oil painting; 2 **pinturas** crayons.

pinza *noun* F 1 clothes peg; 2 hairgrip; 3 pincer; 4 dart; **pantalón con pinzas** trousers with pleats.

pinzas *plural noun* F tweezers.

piña *noun* F 1 pineapple; 2 pine cone.

pipa *noun* F pipe; **fumar en pipa** to smoke a pipe.

piragua *noun* F canoe.

pirámide *noun* F pyramid.

Pirineos *plural noun* M **los Pirineos** the Pyrenees.

pisar *verb* [17] 1 to step; **pisar a alguien** to step on somebody's foot; 2 'prohibido pisar el césped' 'keep off the grass'.

piscina *noun* F swimming pool.

Piscis *noun* M Pisces.

piscis *noun* M/F Pisces; **soy piscis** I'm Pisces.

piso *noun* M 1 floor; **vivo en el tercer piso** I live on the third floor; 2 storey; **un edificio de cinco pisos** a five-storey building; 3 **un autobús de dos pisos** a double-decker bus;

4 flat; **se han comprado un piso** they've bought a flat.

pista *noun* F 1 track; **seguirle la pista a alguien** to be on somebody's trail; 2 racecourse; 3 (tennis) court; 4 **pista de hielo** ice rink; **pista de patinaje** skating rink; 5 **pista de esquí** sky slope; 6 **pista de despegue** runway.

pistacho *noun* M pistachio.

pistola *noun* F gun.

pitar *verb* [17] 1 to blow a whistle; 2 to sound the horn, to hoot (*in a car*).

pito *noun* M 1 whistle; **tocar el pito** to blow the whistle; 2 horn; **tocar el pito** to sound the horn.

pizarra *noun* F 1 blackboard; 2 slate.

placa *noun* F 1 plate, sheet (*of metal, for example*); 2 **placa de matrícula** number plate; 3 badge.

placer *noun* M pleasure.

plan *noun* M 1 plan; **hacer planes** to make plans; **¿qué planes tienes para las vacaciones?** what are your plans for the holidays?; 2 (*informal*) **está en plan tirano** he's behaving like a tyrant; 3 (*informal*) **viajar en plan económico** to travel on the cheap.

plancha *noun* F 1 iron; 2 **a la plancha** grilled; 3 sheet; **una plancha de plástico** a sheet of plastic.

planchar *verb* [17] to iron.

planear *verb* [17] **1** to plan; **2** to glide.

planeta *noun* M planet.

plano[1] *noun* M **1** street map; **un plano de Madrid** a street map of Madrid; **2** plan (*of a building*).

plano[2]**/plana** *adjective* flat.

planta *noun* F **1** plant; **2** floor; **la planta baja** the ground floor; **la sexta planta** the sixth floor.

plantar *verb* [17] to plant.

plástico *noun* M plastic.

plata *noun* F silver; **cubiertos de plata** silver cutlery.

plataforma *noun* F **1** platform; **2** plataforma de lanzamiento launching pad.

plátano *noun* M banana.

platillo *noun* M saucer.

plato *noun* M **1** plate; **plato llano** dinner plate; **plato de postre** dessert plate; **2** dish; **plato del día** dish of the day; **lavar los platos** to wash the dishes; **plato combinado** complete meal served on a plate; **3** course; **tomé pescado de segundo plato** I had fish for the second course.

playa *noun* F **1** beach; **2** seaside; **veranear en la playa** to spend your summer holidays at the seaside.

playera *noun* F canvas shoe.

plaza *noun* F **1** square; **plaza mayor** main square; **2** market; **los martes hay plaza** there's a market on Tuesdays; **3** seat (*in a bus or train*); **4** position (*at work*); **hay plazas vacantes** there are vacancies; **5 plaza de toros** bullring.

plazo *noun* M **1** period; **el plazo de entrega acaba el once** the deadline is on the eleventh; **2 plazo de vencimiento** expiry date (*of a passport, for example*); **3 a corto plazo** in the short term; **a largo plazo** in the long term; **4 pagar algo a plazos** to pay something in instalments.

plegar *verb* [30] to fold.

pleno/plena *adjective* **1** full; **2 en pleno verano** in the middle of summer; **en pleno centro** right in the centre.

pliega, pliego, pliegue, etc. *verb* SEE **plegar**.

plomo *noun* M **1** lead; **2** (*informal*) **ser un plomo** to be really boring; **3** fuse; **se han fundido los plomos** the fuses have blown.

pluma *noun* F **1** pen; **2** feather.

plumier *noun* M pencil case.

plural *noun* M plural; **en plural** in the plural.
adjective plural.

población *noun* F population.

pobre *noun* M/F poor person; **los pobres** the poor; **¡la pobre!** poor thing!
adjective poor; **¡pobre Jaime!** poor Jaime!

pobreza *noun* F poverty.

poco[1] *adverb* not very much; **habla poco** he doesn't talk very much; **soy muy poco paciente** I'm very impatient; **estaban poco interesados** they weren't very interested.

poco[2]**/poca** *adjective* **1** little; **con poco esfuerzo** with little effort; **hay poco pan** there's not much bread; **es poca cosa** it's not much; **2** few; **había pocas personas** there were only a few people; **pocos días más tarde** a few days later.
pronoun **1** little; **basta con poco** a little is enough; **queda poco** there's not much left; **2** few; **vinieron pocos** only a few came; **pon unos pocos aquí** put a few here; **3** **un poco** a bit; **espera un poco** wait a bit; **me molesta un poco** it's a bit uncomfortable; **un poco de sal** a bit of salt; **4** (*referring to time*) **hace poco** not long ago; **hace poco que me escribió** he wrote to me not long ago; **aún voy a tardar un poco** it's going to take me a little while yet; **falta poco para las cinco** it's not long till five now; **dentro de poco** soon; **poco antes de comer** shortly before eating; **5** **poco a poco** little by little.

poder *noun* M power.
verb [10] **1** to be able to (*but often translated as 'can' in sentences*); **no puedo levantarlo** I can't lift it; **no pude ir** I couldn't go; **pueden hacerlo solos** they can do it on their own; **lo mejor que puedas** the best you can; **¿podrás ayudarme?** will

you be able to help me?; **¿pudiste encontrarlo?** were you able to find it?; **2** may (*asking permission*); **¿puedo abrir la ventana?** may I open the window?; **¿se puede?** may I come in?; **¿podría usar tu ordenador?** may I use your computer?; **3** (*possibility*) **puede que lleguen más tarde** they might come later; **puede que se haya roto** it might have got broken; **podía suceder** it could happen; **has podido romperlo** you could have broken it; **'¿crees que se habrán olvidado?' – 'puede ser'** 'do you think they might have forgotten?' – 'they might have'; **puede ser que no lo sepan** it might be that they don't know; **puede ser que se hayan perdido** they might have got lost; **4** (*suggesting*) **podrías preguntar** you could ask; **podríamos comer fuera** we could eat out; **5** (*reproaching*) **¡podrías haberlo dicho!** you could have said!; **6** **no puedo con tanto trabajo** I can't cope with so much work; **7** **¡ya no puedo más!** I can't carry on!; **8** **si puede ser** if possible.

poderoso/poderosa *adjective* powerful.

podrá, podré, podría, etc. *verb* SEE **poder**.

podrido/podrida *adjective* rotten.

poema *noun* M poem.

poesía *noun* F poetry.

poeta *noun* M/F poet.

polaco[1] *noun* M Polish (*the language*).

polaco²/polaca *noun* M/F Pole.
adjective Polish.

policía *noun* M/F police officer.
noun F police.

policíaco/policíaca *adjective*
novela policíaca detective novel.

polideportivo *noun* M sports
centre.

polilla *noun* F moth.

política *noun* F politics.

político/política *noun* M/F
politician.
adjective political.

pollito/pollita *noun* M/F chick.

pollo *noun* M chicken; **pollo asado**
roast chicken.

polo *noun* M **1** pole; **el Polo Norte**
the North Pole; **2** ice-lolly.

Polonia *noun* F Poland.

polución *noun* F pollution.

polvo *noun* M **1** dust; **quitar el polvo
a los muebles** to dust the furniture;
2 polvos face powder; **polvos de
talco** talcum powder; **3 estar hecho
polvo** (*informal*) to be all in;
**después de la excursión nos
quedamos hechos polvo** we were
worn out after the trip; **este sofá
está hecho polvo** this sofa's a wreck.

pomada *noun* F ointment.

pomelo *noun* M grapefruit.

pondría, pondrías, etc. *verb* SEE
poner.

poner *verb* [11] **1** to put; **ponlo
encima de la mesa** put it on the
table; **lo puse en el armario** I put it
in the wardrobe; **pusimos mil
pesetas cada uno** we put in a
thousand pesetas each; **2** (*with
food*) **¿te pongo más sopa?** shall I
serve you more soup?; **3** (*in a
restaurant*) **¿me pones un café?** can
I have a coffee please?; **¿qué les
pongo?** what can I get you?; **4** to put
on; **le puso la silla al caballo** she
put the saddle on the horse; **no le he
puesto camiseta al niño** I haven't
put a vest on the baby; **5** to put on
(*radio, hi-fi, etc.*); **poner la tele** to
put on the telly; **poner música** to put
on some music; **pon el volumen más
alto** turn the volume up; **6 poner el
despertador** to set the alarm clock;
puse el despertador a las ocho I set
the alarm clock for eight; **7 poner la
mesa** to lay the table; **8** to install;
9 to fit (*a carpet*); **10** (*with names*)
**¿qué nombre le vais a poner al
niño?** what are you going to call the
baby?; **le pusieron el apodo de 'el
Rubio'** they nicknamed him
'Blondy'; **11 poner una película** to
show a film; **¿qué ponen en el
'Maxin'?** what are they showing at
the 'Maxin'?; **poner una obra de
teatro** to put on a play; **12 poner una
tienda** to open a shop; **poner un
negocio** to set up a business; **13 ¿me
pone con el señor Sanz?** could you
put me through to Mr Sanz? (*on the
telephone*); **14 poner a alguien
nervioso** to make somebody
nervous; **poner a alguien triste** to
make somebody sad; **poner a
alguien de mal humor** to put
somebody in a bad mood; **15 poner
atención** to pay attention.

ponerse *reflexive verb* [11] **1** to put on; **ponerse la chaqueta** to put your jacket on; **me puse los zapatos** I put my shoes on; **2 ponerse enfermo** to get ill; **ponerse triste** to get sad; **se puso nervioso** he got nervous; **me puse muy contento al oír la noticia** the news made me very happy; **3 ponerse moreno** to get a tan; **4 ponerse a hacer** to start doing; **me puse a trabajar** I started working; **se puso a chillar** he started shouting; **5 ponerse al lado de alguien** to stand next to someone; **6 ponerse de pie** to stand up; **ponerse de rodillas** to kneel down; **7** (*on the telephone*) **'¿el señor Ferranz?' – 'ahora se pone'** 'Mr Ferranz?' – 'I'll just get him for you'; **dile a Ana que se ponga** tell Ana I want to speak to her.

ponga, pongo, etc. *verb* SEE **poner**.

poni *noun* M pony.

popular *adjective* popular.

por *preposition* **1** for; **por esa razón** for that reason; **por ejemplo** for example; **me ofrecieron cuatrocientas mil pesetas por el coche viejo** they offered me four hundred thousand pesetas for my old car; **lo hago por tu bien** I'm doing it for your own good; **2** through; **no entra por la ventana** it won't go in through the window; **me enteré por mi hermana** I heard through my sister; **pasamos por Toledo** we went through Toledo; **3** by; **mandar algo por correo** to send something by post; **viajar por carretera** to travel

by road; **4 mide tres metros por cuatro** it measures three metres by four; **cinco por tres son quince** five times three is fifteen; **5 por la mañana** in the morning; **6** (*place*) **lo dejé por aquí** I left it around here somewhere; **viven por la Avenida Mayor** they live somewhere around Mayor Avenue; **¿por dónde queda la estación?** whereabouts is the station?; **por todos lados** everywhere; **7** per; **cinco mil pesetas por persona** five thousand pesetas per person; **a cien kilómetros por hora** at a hundred kilometres an hour; **8** in; **por escrito** in writing; **por adelantado** in advance; **9 preguntó por ti** he asked after you; **10 lo dijeron por la tele** they said it on the TV; **11 andar por la calle** to walk along the road; **caerse por la escalera** to fall down the stairs; **12 ¿por qué?** why?; **13 por supuesto** of course; **14 por eso no lo hice** that's why I didn't do it; **15 por cierto** by the way.

porcentaje *noun* M percentage.

porche *noun* M porch.

porción *noun* F **1** portion; **2** share.

porque *conjunction* because.

porrón *noun* M wine bottle (*with a long spout from which you drink, holding it as far away from your mouth as possible*).

portada *noun* F **1** title page (*of a book*); **2** cover (*of a magazine*); **3** front page (*of a newspaper*).

portaequipajes *noun* M (*does not change in the plural*) **1** roof rack; **2** luggage rack (*on a train*).

portarse *reflexive verb* [17] to behave; **portarse mal** to misbehave; **¡pórtate bien!** behave yourself!

portazo *noun* M **dar un portazo** to slam the door.

portería *noun* F goal.

portero/portera *noun* M/F **1** goalkeeper; **2** caretaker; **3** porter; **4 portero automático** entry-phone.

portorriqueño/portorriqueña *noun* M/F *adjective* Puerto Rican.

Portugal *noun* M Portugal.

portugués¹ *noun* M Portuguese (*the language*).

portugués²/portuguesa *noun* M/F Portuguese man/woman. *adjective* Portuguese.

porvenir *noun* M future.

posar *verb* [17] **1** to pose; **2** to lay (*hand or object*). **posarse** *reflexive verb* [17] to land.

poseer *verb* [37] **1** to own; **2** to hold (*a title or record*).

posibilidad *noun* F **1** possibility; **es una posibilidad** it's a possibility; **2 tener posibilidades de hacer** to have a good chance of doing; **no tienen muchas posibilidades de ganar** they don't have much chance of winning; **¿qué posibilidades tienen?** what are their chances?

posible *adjective* possible; **a ser posible** if possible; **no fue posible impedirlo** it was impossible to avoid it.
adverb **lo más tarde posible** as late as possible; **hazlo lo mejor posible** do the best you can.

posición *noun* F **1** position; **en quinta posición** in fifth place; **2 posición social** social status.

positivo/positiva *adjective* positive.

postal *noun* F postcard. *adjective* postal.

póster *noun* M poster.

posterior *adjective* **1** back; **el asiento posterior** the back seat; **la parte posterior de la casa** the back of the house; **2** subsequent, later.

postizo/postiza *adjective* false; **dentadura postiza** false teeth.

postre *noun* M pudding, dessert; **¿qué hay de postre?** what's for pudding?

potable *adjective* **agua potable** drinking water.

potencial *adjective* potential.

práctica *noun* F practice; **lo aprenderás con la práctica** you'll learn with practice; **tener mucha práctica** to have a lot of practice; **he perdido la práctica** I'm out of practice; **en la práctica** in practice.

practicar *verb* [31] **1** to practise; **practicar el violín** to practise the violin; **2 practicar deportes** to do sports.

práctico/práctica *adjective* practical.

prado *noun* M meadow.

precaución *noun* F **1** precaution; **tomar precauciones** to take precautions; **2** caution; **actuar con precaución** to act with caution.

precedente *adjective* previous.

precio *noun* M price; **¿qué precio tiene?** how much is it?; **precio fijo** fixed price; **precios de saldo** bargain prices; **los precios han subido mucho** prices have gone up a lot.

precioso/preciosa *adjective* **1** beautiful; **2** precious; **piedras preciosas** precious stones.

precipicio *noun* M precipice.

precipitación *noun* F **1** rush; **hacer algo con mucha precipitación** to do something in a rush; **salió con mucha precipitación** he rushed out; **2** habrá alguna precipitación there will be showers.

precipitarse *reflexive verb* [17] **1** to rush; **no te precipites** don't rush into anything; **2** precipitarse hacia algo to rush towards something.

precisamente *adverb* precisely.

precisión *noun* F precision.

preciso/precisa *adjective* **1** precise; **2** llegaron en el momento preciso they arrived just in time; **en este preciso momento no puedo** I can't right now; **3** necessary; **si es preciso** if necessary; **no es preciso pagar por adelantado** you don't have to pay in advance; **es preciso que nos aseguremos** we must make sure.

predilecto/predilecta *adjective* favourite.

preescolar *adjective* preschool.

preferencia *noun* F **1** preference; **2** right of way; **yo tenía preferencia** I had right of way; **3** priority; **tener preferencia** to have priority.

preferible *adjective* preferable; **ser preferible a algo** to be preferable to something.

preferido/preferida *adjective* favourite.

preferir *verb* [14] to prefer; **preferir algo a algo** to prefer something to something; **preferiría no tener que ir** I'd rather not go.

prefiera, prefiero, etc. *verb* SEE **preferir**.

prefijo *noun* M **1** prefix; **2** dialling code; **el prefijo de España** the dialling code for Spain.

pregunta *noun* F question; **hacer una pregunta** to ask a question.

preguntar *verb* [17] to ask; **preguntar acerca de/sobre algo** to ask about something; **preguntar por alguien** to ask about someone; **me preguntó por tus padres** he asked me about your parents.
preguntarse *reflexive verb* [17] to wonder; **me pregunto si dice la verdad** I wonder if he's telling the truth.

prejuicio *noun* M prejudice; **tener prejuicios contra** to be prejudiced against.

prematuro/prematura *adjective* premature.

premiar *verb* [17] **premiar a alguien** to give somebody a prize.

premio *noun* M prize; **dar un premio a alguien** to give someone a prize; **ganar un premio** to win a prize; **me tocó un premio en la rifa** I won a prize in the raffle; **¿qué dan de premio?** what's the prize?; **premio gordo** jackpot (*in the lottery*).

prender *verb* [18] **1** to catch (*a criminal*); **2** to light (*a cigarette or match*); **3 prenderle fuego a algo** to set something on fire.

prensa *noun* F **la prensa** the press; **leer la prensa** to read the newspapers.

preocupado/preocupada *adjective* worried; **estar preocupado por algo** to be worried about something.

preocupar *verb* [17] to worry; **me preocupan los exámenes** I'm worried about the exams.
preocuparse *reflexive verb* [17] to get worried; **se preocupó porque no la llamé** she got worried because I didn't phone her.

preparación *noun* F
1 preparation; **2** training (*in sport*); **3 un trabajador con muy buena preparación** a highly trained worker.

preparar *verb* [17] **1** to prepare; **preparar la cena** to prepare dinner; **preparar un examen** to prepare for an exam; **2** to train (*a player or athlete*); **3** to coach (*a student*); **4 preparar la cuenta** to draw up the bill.
prepararse *reflexive verb* [17] to get ready.

preparativos *plural noun* M preparations.

preposición *noun* F preposition.

presa *noun* F **1** dam; **2** reservoir; **3** prey; **4 ser presa del terror** to be seized with panic.

presencia *noun* F presence; **en presencia de sus padres** in front of his parents.

presentación *noun* F
1 introduction; **hacer las presentaciones** to do the introductions; **2** presentation.

presentador/presentadora *noun* M/F presenter.

presentar *verb* [17] **1** to introduce; **te presento a mi novio** I'd like you to meet my boyfriend; **les presentó a su jefe** he introduced them to his boss; **2** to present (*a programme, for example*); **3** to submit (*an application*).
presentarse *reflexive verb* [17] **1** to introduce yourself; **2** to turn up; **se presentaron sin avisar a nadie** they turned up without letting anybody know; **3 presentarse voluntario** to volunteer; **4 presentarse a un examen** to sit an exam;

5 presentarse a un concurso to enter a competition; **6 presentarse para un cargo** to apply for a post; **7 presentarse a la presidencia** to run for the presidency.

presente *noun* M present.

preservativo *noun* M condom.

presidencia *noun* F presidency.

presidente/presidenta *noun* M/F president.

presión *noun* F **1** pressure; **2 cerveza a presión** draught beer.

preso/presa *noun* M/F prisoner.
adjective **estar preso** to be in prison; **meter preso a alguien** to send somebody to prison.

préstamo *noun* M loan; **préstamo hipotecario** mortgage.

prestar *verb* [17] **1** to lend; **le presté dinero para el coche** I lent him money for the car; **2 ¿me prestas tu abrigo?** can I borrow your coat?; **3 prestar atención** to pay attention.

prestidigitador/prestidigitadora *noun* M/F conjurer.

presumido/presumida *noun* M/F **es un presumido** he's so conceited.
adjective conceited.

presumir *verb* [19] to show off; **presumen de casa grande** they like to boast about how big their house is; **presume de guapa** she thinks she's very good-looking.

pretender *verb* [18] **1** to try; **¿qué pretendes conseguir?** what are you trying to achieve?; **pretendía que pagase yo** he was trying to make me pay for it; **2 pretender que alguien haga** to expect somebody to do; **pretende que yo le ayude** he expects me to help him.

pretexto *noun* M pretext, excuse; **siempre tiene algún pretexto para no hacerlo** he always has some excuse or other not to do it.

prevenir *verb* [15] **1** to prevent; **2** to warn.

prever *verb* [16] to forsee.

previsto/prevista *adjective* **está previsto que vengan mañana** they're due to come tomorrow; **a la hora prevista** at the scheduled time.

primavera *noun* F spring.

primer *adjective* first SEE **primero/ primera**.

primero¹/primera *adjective*, *pronoun* first; **primera clase** first class; **el primero de mayo** the first of May; (*note that 'primero' becomes 'primer' before a masculine singular noun*) **primer piso** first floor; **llegar en primer lugar** to finish in first position; **en primer lugar, no me interesa** first of all, I'm not interested.

primero² *adverb* first; **yo estaba primero** I was here first; **primero vamos a informarnos** first of all, let's find out.

primo/prima *noun* M/F cousin.

princesa *noun* F princess.

principal *adjective* main.

príncipe *noun* M prince.

principiante/principianta
noun M/F beginner.

principio *noun* M beginning; **a principios de mes** at the beginning of the month; **al principio de la temporada** at the beginning of the season; **un buen principio** a good start.

prisa *noun* F 1 hurry; **tener prisa** to be in a hurry; **date prisa, que llegamos tarde** hurry up or we'll be late; **2 de prisa** fast; **hacer algo de prisa** to do something fast; **a toda prisa** in a hurry; **3 correr prisa** to be urgent; **este trabajo corre prisa** this job is urgent.

prisión *noun* F prison.

prisionero/prisionera *noun* M/F prisoner.

prismáticos *plural noun* M binoculars.

privado/privada *adjective* private.

privar *verb* [17] **privar a alguien de algo** to deprive somebody of something.
privarse *reflexive verb* [17] **privarse de algo** to deprive yourself of something.

privilegiado/privilegiada
adjective privileged.

privilegio *noun* M privilege.

probable *adjective* probable.

probador *noun* M changing room.

probar *verb* [24] **1** to try; **prueba a abrirlo con esta llave** try opening it with this key; **es la primera vez que pruebo la comida tailandesa** it's the first time I've tried Thai food; **probar no cuesta nada** there's no harm in trying; **2** to taste; **¿has probado la sopa?** have you tasted the soup?; **3** to test (*brakes, for example*); **4** to prove; **no pudo probar su inocencia** he could not prove his innocence.
probarse *reflexive verb* [24] to try on; **¿quiere probárselo?** would you like to try it on?

probeta *noun* F test tube; **niño probeta** test-tube baby.

problema *noun* M problem.

procedente *adjective* from; **el vuelo procedente de Londres** the flight from London.

proceder *verb* [18] **1 proceder de algo** to come from something; **2** to proceed; **procedieron con cautela** they proceeded with caution.

procesador *noun* M **procesador de textos** word processor.

procesión *noun* F procession.

proceso *noun* M process.

procurar *verb* [17] **procurar hacer** to try to do; **procura terminarlo para el viernes** try to finish it by Friday.

producción *noun* F production.

producir *verb* [60] **1** to produce; **producir coches** to produce cars; **2** to cause; **la tormenta produjo daños** the storm caused damage.

producto *noun* M **1** product; **2** production.

productor/productora *noun* M/F producer.
adjective producing; **países productores de petróleo** oil-producing countries.

produje, produzca, etc. *verb* SEE **producir**.

profe *noun* M/F (*informal*) **1** teacher; **2** Sir/Miss (*when talking directly to a teacher*).

profesión *noun* F profession.

profesional *adjective* professional.

profesor/profesora *noun* M/F **1** professor; lecturer; **2** teacher (*in a secondary school*).

profundidad *noun* F depth.

profundo/profunda *adjective* deep.

programa *noun* M **1** programme; **2** program.

programar *verb* [17] to program (*a computer*).

progresar *verb* [17] to progress.

progreso *noun* M progress; **hacer progresos** to make progress.

prohibido/prohibida *adjective* forbidden; **está terminantemente prohibido** it's strictly forbidden;

'prohibido fumar' 'no smoking'; **'prohibido el paso'/'prohibida la entrada'** 'no entry'; **'prohibido pisar el césped'** 'keep off the grass'.

prohibir *verb* [58] to prohibit; **se prohíbe la entrada a menores de dieciséis años** no admission to persons under 16.

prolongar *verb* [28] to prolong. **prolongarse** *reflexive verb* [28] to go on (*a meeting or party, for example*).

promedio *noun* M average; **un promedio de quince libras por semana** an average of fifteen pounds a week.

promesa *noun* F promise; **no cumplió con su promesa** he didn't keep his promise.

prometer *verb* [18] to promise; **te lo prometo** I promise.

promoción *noun* F promotion.

pronombre *noun* M pronoun.

pronóstico *noun* M **1** forecast; **pronóstico del tiempo** weather forecast; **2** prognosis.

pronto *adverb* **1** soon; **tan pronto como sea posible** as soon as possible; **2** quickly; **respondieron muy pronto** they answered very quickly; **3** early; **se marcharon pronto** they left early; **4 de pronto** all of a sudden.

pronunciación *noun* F pronunciation.

pronunciar *verb* [17] to pronounce.

propaganda *noun* F **1** advertising; **hacer propaganda de un producto** to advertise a product; **2** propaganda.

propiedad *noun* F **1** property; **propiedad privada** private property; **2 ser propiedad de alguien** to belong to somebody.

propietario/propietaria *noun* M/F owner.

propina *noun* F tip.

propio/propia *adjective* **1** own; **mi propio hermano** my own brother; **2 la propia Elena lo admitió** Elena herself admitted it.

proponer *verb* [11] **1** to suggest; **nos propuso ir a cenar fuera** he suggested we went out for dinner; **2** to propose; **proponer una idea** to propose an idea; **proponer un trato** to make a proposition; **3** to put forward (*a candidate*).
proponerse *reflexive verb* [11] **1** to set yourself a goal; **me propuse encontrar un trabajo** I set myself the goal of finding a job; **siempre consigue lo que se propone** he always achieves what he sets out to do; **2** to decide; **me propuse ir a verlos** I decided to go and see them.

proporción *noun* F **1** proportion; **en proporción** in proportion; **2 proporciones** dimensions.

proposición *noun* F proposal.

propósito *noun* M intention.

prórroga *noun* F **1** extension; **2** extra time (*in sports*).

prospecto *noun* M **1** patient information leaflet (*supplied with medicine*); **2** advertising leaflet.

próspero/próspera *adjective* **1** prosperous; **2 ¡Próspero Año Nuevo!** Happy New Year!

protección *noun* F protection.

protector/protectora *noun* M/F protector.
adjective **1** protective; **2 Sociedad Protectora de Animales** Society for the Prevention of Cruelty to Animals.

proteger *verb* [3] to protect.
protegerse *reflexive verb* [3] to protect yourself.

protesta *noun* F protest; **en señal de protesta** in protest.

protestante *noun* M/F *adjective* protestant.

protestar *verb* [17] to protest.

provecho *noun* M **1** benefit; **sacar provecho de algo** to benefit from something; **2 siempre piensa primero en su propio provecho** he always thinks of himself first; **3 ¡buen provecho!** enjoy your meal!

proveniente *adjective* **personas provenientes de otros países** people from other countries.

proverbio *noun* M proverb.

provincia *noun* F province.

provisional *adjective* provisional.

provocador/provocadora
noun M/F political agitator.
adjective provocative.

provocar *verb* [31] **1** to provoke (*a person*); **2** to cause (*an explosion or fire*).

proximidad *noun* F proximity.

próximo/próxima *adjective*
1 next; **la próxima semana** next
week; **2 en fecha próxima** in the
near future.

proyecto *noun* M **1** project; **2** plan;
**¿qué proyectos tienes para el
verano?** what are your plans for the
summer?; **3 tengo varios trabajos
en proyecto** I've got a few jobs lined
up.

proyector *noun* M projector.

prudente *adjective* sensible; **sé
prudente conduciendo** drive
carefully.

prueba¹ *noun* F **1** proof; **no tienen
pruebas** they have no proof; **2** test;
3 hacer la prueba to try; **hice la
prueba y funcionó** I tried and it
worked; **haz la prueba de limpiarlo
con lejía** try cleaning it with bleach;
4 a prueba on trial; **trabajadores a
prueba** people working on a trial
basis; **5 a prueba de balas** bullet-
proof; **a prueba de agua**
waterproof.

prueba², pruebo, etc. *verb* SEE
probar.

psicólogo/psicóloga *noun* M/F
psychologist.

psiquiatra *noun* M/F psychiatrist.

pts *abbreviation* (*short for: pesetas*)
pts.

publicar *verb* [31] to publish.

publicidad *noun* F **1** publicity;
2 advertising.

público¹ *noun* M **1** public;
2 audience.

público²/pública *adjective*
public.

pude, pudo, etc. *verb* SEE **poder**.

pudrir *verb* [59] to rot.
pudrirse *reflexive verb* [59] to rot.

pueblo *noun* M **1** village; **2** small
town; **3** people; **el pueblo español**
the Spanish people.

puente *noun* M **1** bridge; **2 puente
aéreo** shuttle service; **3 hacer
puente** take a long weekend (*usually
when the Thursday before or the
Tuesday after is a public holiday*).

puerco/puerca *noun* M/F pig.

puerro *noun* M leek.

puerta *noun* F **1** door; **puerta
principal** main door; **puerta
giratoria** revolving door; **puerta
trasera** back door; **quedamos en la
puerta del cine** we arranged to meet
outside the cinema; **2 puerta de
embarque** gate (*in an airport*); **3 la
puerta del jardín** the garden gate.

puerto *noun* M **1** port; **un puerto pesquero** a fishing port; **2** harbour; **un puerto deportivo** a marina.

Puerto Rico *noun* M Puerto Rico.

puertorriqueño/puertorriqueña *noun* M/F *adjective* Puerto Rican.

pues *conjunction* **1 pues bien, como te iba diciendo** … well, as I was telling you …; **pues no estoy seguro** I'm not sure now; **pues mira, ahora no me acuerdo** well, look, I can't remember now; **2 ¡pues no vayas!** don't go then!; **pues si no te interesa el libro, no lo leas** if you don't like the book, don't read it then; **3 ¡pues claro!** of course!; **¡pues claro que no!** of course not!; **'¿lo querías tú?'** – **'¡pues sí!'** 'did you want it?' – 'yes, I did!'

puesto¹ *noun* M **1** position; **llegar en primer puesto** to finish in first position; **sacar el primer puesto en un examen** to come top in an exam; **2** job; **puestos de trabajo** jobs; **perdió su puesto de trabajo** he lost his job; **puestos vacantes** vacancies; **un puesto fijo** a permanent job; **3** post; **un puesto de socorro** a first-aid post; **4** stall (*in a market*). *conjunction* **puesto que** since.

puesto²/puesta *adjective* **1 la mesa estaba puesta** the table was laid; **2 llevaba el abrigo puesto** I had my coat on.

pulga *noun* F flea.

pulgada *noun* F inch.

pulgar *noun* M thumb.

pulir *verb* [19] to polish.

pulmón *noun* M lung.

pulpo *noun* M octopus.

pulsar *verb* [17] **1** to press (*a key or button*); **2** to pluck (*a string*).

pulsera *noun* F bracelet.

pulso *noun* M **1** pulse; **le tomó el pulso** he took his pulse; **2 tener buen pulso** to have a steady hand; **me temblaba el pulso** my hand was shaking; **3 levantar algo a pulso** to lift something with your bare hands; **dibujar algo a pulso** to draw something freehand.

punta *noun* F **1** point (*of a knife or needle, for example*); **acaba en punta** it's pointed; **2** tip (*of pencil, tongue, finger, etc.*); ★ **tener algo en la punta de la lengua** (*informal*) to have something on the tip of your tongue; **3** end; **a la otra punta del pasillo** at the other end of the corridor; **4 cortarse las puntas** to have your hair trimmed; **tener las puntas abiertas** to have split ends; **5 sacar punta a un lápiz** to sharpen a pencil; **6 hora punta** rush hour.

puntada *noun* F stitch.

puntapié *noun* M kick; **darle un puntapié a algo** to kick something.

puntilla *noun* F **1** lace edging; **2 ponerse de puntillas** to stand on tiptoe; **andar de puntillas** to walk on tiptoe.

punto *noun* M **1** point; **un punto de vista** a point of view; **es mi punto débil** it's my weak point; **llevan tres puntos de ventaja** they're three points ahead; **hasta cierto punto** up to a point; **punto por punto** point by point; **2** dot; **el punto sobre la 'i'** the dot on the 'i'; **3** (*in punctuation*) **punto final** full stop; **punto y coma** semicolon; **4** stitch; **hacer punto** to knit; **de punto** knitted; **una falda de punto** a knitted skirt; **5 estar a punto de hacer** to be about to do; **6 estar algo en su punto** to be just right; **la carne está en su punto** the meat is just right; **7 batir las claras a punto de nieve** beat the egg whites until stiff; **8 punto muerto** neutral (*gear*); **9 las cinco en punto** five o'clock sharp; **a las dos en punto** at two on the dot; **llegar en punto** to arrive exactly on time.

puntuación *noun* F
1 punctuation; **2** score (*in sports*); **3** marks (*in an exam*).

puntual *adjective* punctual; **ser puntual** to be always on time; **llegaron puntuales** they arrived on time.

puñetazo *noun* M punch; **me dio un puñetazo** he punched me; **di un puñetazo en la mesa** I slammed my fist on the table.

puño *noun* M **1** fist; **2** cuff; **3** handle (*of a tool*).

pupila *noun* F pupil.

pupitre *noun* M desk.

puré *noun* M **1** purée; **2** thick soup; **puré de guisantes** pea soup; **3** **puré de patatas** mashed potatoes.

puro[1] *noun* M cigar.

puro[2]**/pura** *adjective* **1** pure; **2** **la pura verdad** the simple truth; **3** **de**

puro aburrimiento out of sheer boredom.

púrpura *adjective* purple.

puse, puso, etc. *verb* SEE **poner**.

puzzle *noun* M jigsaw puzzle.

Q q

que *pronoun* **1** who; **el hombre que me lo dijo** the man who told me; **los que están interesados** those who are interested; **2** which, that; **el libro que recomendé** the book which I recommended; **la marca que me gusta** the brand (that) I like; **3 el que prefiero** the one (that) I prefer. *conjunction* **1** that; **dijo que no lo necesitaba** she said (that) she didn't need it; **sé que le gusta** I know (that) he likes it; **nos pidió que le ayudásemos** he asked us to help him (*'que' is followed by the subjunctive in certain constructions*); **2** (*in comparisons*) than; **es más alto que yo** he's taller than me; **3** (*for emphasis*) **¡que te he dicho que sí me gusta!** I've already told you that I like it!; **¡que es mío!** I'm telling you it's mine!; **'¿te importa?'** – **'¡que no!'** 'do you mind?' – 'I've already told you that I don't!'; **4** (*expressing surprise*) **¿que tiene veinte años?** she's twenty?; **5** (*expressing a wish*) **que te mejores pronto** get well soon; **que pases unas buenas vacaciones** have a nice holiday; **6** (*giving an order*) **¡que te calles!** shut up!; **que**

pasen show them in; **7 yo que tú** if I were you.

qué *pronoun* **1** what; **¿qué es eso?** what's that?; **¿a qué te refieres?** what are you referring to?; **2 ¿qué?** what?; **3 ¿qué tal?** how are you doing?; **¿qué tal va?** how's it going?; **¿qué hay de nuevo?** what's new?; **4 ¡qué va!** no way!
adjective **1** which; **¿qué abrigo es el tuyo?** which coat is yours?; **2** what (*in exclamations*); **¡qué casa tan grande!** what a big house!
adverb **¡qué bonito!** how nice!; **¡qué egoísta eres!** you're so selfish!

quebrado *noun* M fraction.

quebrar *verb* [29] to break.

quedar *verb* [17] **1** to be left; **quedan tres paquetes** there are three packets left; **¿te queda dinero?** do you have any money left?; **no queda leche** there's no milk; **2** (*in time expressions*) **aún quedan dos días** there are still two days to go; **quedaban quince minutos para el final de la clase** it was still fifteen minutes till the end of the class; **¿cuánto tiempo me queda?** how much time do I have left?; **aún queda tiempo** there's still time; **3** (*with distances*) **quedaban quince kilómetros** there were still fiteen kilometres to go; **4** (*expressing a person's situation*) **quedó viudo** he was widowed; **quedó ciego tras el accidente** he was left blind after the accident; **quedaron solos** they were left alone; **quedar en último lugar** to end up last; **5** (*talking about the appearance of something*) **así queda mejor** it's better like this; **queda muy feo con esa tela** it's horrible with that material; **6** (*arranging meetings*) **quedamos en la plaza** we arranged to meet in the square; **¿te apetece quedar?** would you like to meet?; **¿quedamos para el sábado?** shall we meet on Saturday?; **7** (*when talking about clothes, hairstyles, etc.*) **me queda apretado** it's too tight on me; **¿te queda bien?** does it fit you?; **esos pantalones te quedan fenomenal** those trousers look great on you; **ese color te queda muy bien** that colour really suits you; **8** (*impressions*) **quiere quedar bien con mi familia** she wants to make a good impression on my family; **9 va a quedar mal si no lo hacemos** it will look bad if we don't do it; **quedamos muy mal con sus padres** we made a bad impression on her parents; **10 quedar en algo** to agree on something; **quedamos en vernos hoy** we agreed to see each other today; **11** (*talking about location*) to be; **queda cerca de mi casa** it's near my house; **queda bastante lejos** it's quite a long way away; **¿dónde queda la estación?** where is the station?

quedarse *reflexive verb* [17] **1** to stay; **prefiero quedarme en casa** I'd rather stay at home; **se quedó en la cama** he stayed in bed; **2** (*expressing somebody's situation or state*) **quedarse ciego** to go blind; **quedarse calvo** to lose your hair; **quedarse sin trabajo** to lose your job; **quedarse viudo** to be widowed;

quedarse soltero to stay single;
quedarse dormido to fall asleep;
quedarse callado to remain silent;
3 quedarse con algo to keep
something.

queja *noun* F complaint.

quejarse *reflexive verb* [17] to
complain; **se quejan de la comida**
they complain about the food; **se
quejan de que tardamos mucho**
they complain about how long we
take.

quemado/quemada *adjective*
burnt.

quemadura *noun* F burn.

quemar *verb* [17] **1** to burn; **2** to
scald; **3** to be very hot; **la sopa
quema mucho** the soup's really hot;
4 quemar un motor to burn out an
engine; **5 quemar calorías** to burn
up calories; **6 ¡cómo quema el sol!**
the sun's scorching!

quemarse *reflexive verb* [17] **1** to burn
yourself; **me quemé la mano** I burnt
my hand; **2** to scald; **3** to get burned;
el mantel se quemó un poco the
tablecloth got slightly burnt; **¡cómo
te has quemado!** you've got really
burnt! (*in the sun*); **4** to burn down;
la casa se quemó toda the house
burned down.

querer *verb* [12] **1** to want; **¿qué
quieres para tu cumpleaños?** what
do you want for your birthday?; **no
quiero ir al cine** I don't want to go to
the cinema; **2** to love; **te quiero** I love
you; **3** (*making an offer*) **¿quieres
beber algo?** would you like
something to drink?; **si quieres voy**

más tarde if you like I'll go later;
4 (*asking for something in a shop,
café, etc.*) **quisiera ver plumas** I
would like to see some pens; **yo
quiero un café** I'll have a coffee;
**quisiera reservar una mesa para
cuatro** I'd like to book a table for
four; **5** (*asking somebody to do
something*) **¿quieres apagar la tele,
por favor?** would you mind
switching off the television, please?;
6 querer decir to mean; **¿qué
quieres decir?** what do you mean?

quererse *reflexive verb* [17] to love
each other.

querido/querida *adjective* dear;
Querido Pablo Dear Pablo (*starting a
letter*).

querrá, querré, querría, etc.
verb SEE **querer**.

queso *noun* M cheese; **queso
rallado** grated cheese.

quiebra *noun* F bankruptcy.

quien *pronoun* **1** who; **no fui yo
quien lo dijo** it wasn't me who said
it; **ellos son quienes no quisieron**
they're the ones who didn't want to;
(*sometimes not translated*) **la
persona con quien hablé** the person
I spoke to; **2** whom; **Isabel, a quien
vi ayer** Isabel, whom I saw yesterday.

quién *pronoun* **1** who; **¿quién es?**
who is it?; **¡quién lo hubiese dicho!**
who would have said!; **2** which;
¿quién de vosotros es Carlos?
which of you is Carlos?; **3 ¿de quién?**
whose?; **¿de quién es esta cartera?**
whose is this wallet?

quienquiera *pronoun* whoever.

quiera, quiere, etc. *verb* SEE **querer**.

quieto/quieta *adjective* still; ¡estáte quieto! keep still!

química[1] *noun* F chemistry.

químico/química[2] *noun* M/F chemist.
adjective chemical.

quince *number* 1 fifteen; **tiene quince años** he's fifteen (years old); 2 **quince días** a fortnight; 3 fifteenth (*in dates*); **hoy estamos a quince** it's the fifteenth today.

quinceañero/quinceañera *noun* M/F teenager.

quincena *noun* F **una quincena** a fortnight; **la primera quincena de mayo** the first two weeks in May.

quiniela *noun* F pools coupon; **rellenar una quiniela** to fill in a pools coupon; **jugar a las quinielas** to do the pools.

quinientos/quinientas *number* five hundred; **quinientos cinco** five hundred and five.

quinto/quinta *adjective* fifth; **el quinto piso** the fifth floor; **llegar en quinto lugar** to finish in fifth position.

quiosco *noun* M 1 news-stand; 2 **el quiosco de los helados** the ice cream stand; **el quiosco de bebidas** the drinks stand; 3 kiosk.

quiosquero/quiosquera *noun* M/F 1 newspaper vendor; 2 kiosk vendor.

quirúrgico/quirúrgica *adjective* surgical.

quise, quisiera, quiso, etc. *verb* SEE **querer**.

quitaesmalte *noun* M nail varnish remover.

quitanieves *noun* M snowplough.

quitar *verb* [17] 1 to take off; **quita los pies de la mesa** take your feet off the table; **no puedo quitar la tapa** I can't get the lid off; 2 **le quité los zapatos al niño** I took the child's shoes off; 3 **quitarle algo a alguien** to take something from someone; **le quitaron la cartera** they took his wallet; 4 to take away; **le han quitado el carnet de conducir** they've taken his driving licence away; **quita esa silla de ahí** take that chair away from there; 5 to remove; **quitar la suciedad** to remove the dirt; **quitar el polvo** to dust.

quitarse *reflexive verb* [17] 1 to come out (*a stain, for example*); 2 to go away (*a pain*); 3 **quitarse algo** to take something off; **se quitó el abrigo** he took his coat off.

quizá, quizás *adverb* perhaps.

R r

rábano *noun* M radish; ★ **me importa un rábano** (*informal*) I couldn't care less (*literally: it matters a radish to me*).

rabia *noun* F **1** rabies; **2 me da mucha rabia** it really annoys me; **me da mucha rabia llegar tarde** I get very annoyed when I'm late; **le dio mucha rabia que no se lo dijeran** it really annoyed him that they didn't tell him; **3 tenerle rabia a alguien** to have it in for someone; **4 con rabia** angrily.

rabo *noun* M tail.

racha *noun* F **1 una racha de mala suerte** a spell of bad luck; **pasar una mala racha** to go through a bad patch; **tener una buena racha** to be on a winning streak; **2** gust (*of wind*).

racimo *noun* M bunch; **un racimo de uvas** a bunch of grapes.

ración *noun* F portion; **una ración de gambas** a portion of prawns (*in a tapas bar*).

racionar *verb* [17] to ration.

racismo *noun* M racism.

racista *noun* M/F *adjective* racist.

radiación *noun* F radiation.

radiactivo/radiactiva *adjective* radioactive.

radiador *noun* M radiator.

radio *noun* F radio; **escuchar la radio** to listen to the radio; **poner la radio** to put on the radio.

radiocassette *noun* M radio cassette player.

radiografía *noun* F X-ray; **hacerse una radiografía** to have an X-ray taken.

ráfaga *noun* F **1** gust; **una ráfaga de viento** a gust of wind; **2 una ráfaga de ametralladora** a burst of machine-gun fire.

raíz *noun* F **1** root; **echar raíces** to take root; **2 raíz cuadrada** square root; **3 a raíz de** as a result of.

rallado/rallada *adjective* **1** grated; **2 pan rallado** breadcrumbs.

rallador *noun* M grater.

rallar *verb* [17] to grate.

rama *noun* F branch; ★ **irse por las ramas** to beat about the bush.

ramo *noun* M **1** bunch (*of flowers*); **2** bouquet.

rampa *noun* F ramp; **rampa de lanzamiento** launch pad.

rana *noun* F frog.

ranura *noun* F coin slot.

rape *noun* M **1** monkfish; **2 llevar el pelo cortado al rape** to have your hair closely cropped.

rápidamente *adverb* quickly.

rápido[1] *noun* M express train. *adverb* fast, quickly; **todo lo rápido**

que podía as fast as I possibly could.

rápido²/rápida *adjective* 1 quick, fast; **comida rápida** fast food; 2 rapid.

raqueta *noun* F 1 racket; 2 snowshoe.

raro/rara *adjective* 1 strange; ¡qué raro que no hayan llamado! how strange they haven't called!; 2 rare; **es raro que llueva en esa zona** it's rare for it to rain in that area.

rascacielos *noun* M (*does not change in the plural*) skyscraper.

rascar *verb* [31] to scratch.
rascarse *reflexive verb* [31] to scratch yourself; **se rascó la nariz** he scratched his nose.

rasgar *verb* [28] to tear.

rasguño *noun* M scratch.

rastrillo *noun* M rake.

rastro *noun* M 1 trail; **sin dejar rastro** without a trace; 2 flea market.

rata *noun* F rat.

ratero/ratera *noun* M/F 1 pickpocket; 2 petty thief.

rato *noun* M 1 while; **tardaré un rato en hacerlo** it will take me a while to do it; **después de un rato** after a while; **dentro de un rato** in a while; **ya hace rato que se han ido** they went a while ago; **al rato** after a while; **al poco rato** soon afterwards; 2 **pasar el rato** to kill time; 3 **pasar un buen rato** to have a good time; 4 **ratos libres** spare time.

ratón *noun* M mouse.

raya *noun* F 1 line; 2 dash (*in punctuation*); 3 parting (*in your hair*); **hacerse la raya** to part your hair; 4 **a rayas** striped, stripy (*a dress or material, for example*); **una falda a rayas** a stripy skirt; 5 skate (*fish*).

rayar *verb* [17] 1 to scratch; 2 **rayar en** to border on; **raya en lo ridículo** it's bordering on the ridiculous.

rayo *noun* M 1 ray; **un rayo de luz** a ray of light; 2 flash of lightning; 3 **un rayo láser** a laser beam; 4 **rayos X** X-rays.

raza *noun* F 1 race; 2 breed; **un perro de raza** a pedigree dog.

razón *noun* F 1 reason; **por alguna razón** for some reason; ¿por qué razón se enfadó? why did he get cross?; **con razón** with good reason; 2 **tener razón** to be right; **no tienes razón en eso** you're wrong about that; **darle la razón a alguien** to agree that somebody is right; 3 **perder la razón** to lose your mind; 4 **razón: 279452** call 279452 for information.

razonable *adjective* reasonable.

reacción *noun* F reaction.

reactor *noun* M 1 jet; 2 reactor.

real *adjective* 1 real; 2 true; **una historia real** a true story; 3 royal.

realidad *noun* F 1 reality; **hacerse realidad** to come true; 2 **en realidad** actually.

realizador/realizadora *noun* M/F producer.

realizar *verb* [22] **1** to carry out (*a task*); **2** to make (*a visit or trip*); **3** to fulfil (*a dream*).
realizarse *reflexive verb* [22] **1** to come true (*a dream*); **2** to fulfil yourself.

rebaja *noun* F **1** reduction; **hacer una rebaja** to give a reduction; **me hizo una rebaja de mil pesetas** he gave me a thousand peseta reduction; **lo rebajó a cinco mil pesetas** he reduced it to five thousand pesetas; **2 rebajas** sales; **esa tienda está de rebajas** this shop has a sale on.

rebajar *verb* [17] **1** to bring down (*prices*); **2** to reduce (*an article*); **todas las faldas están rebajadas** all the skirts are reduced; **3 rebajar peso** to lose weight.

rebanada *noun* F slice.

rebaño *noun* M **1** flock (*of sheep*); **2** herd (*of goats*).

rebeca *noun* F cardigan.

rebelde *noun* M/F rebel.
adjective **1** rebel; **2** unruly; **3 una tos rebelde** a persistent cough.

rebobinar *verb* [17] rewind.

rebotar *verb* [17] **1** to bounce; **la pelota rebotó en el poste** the ball bounced off the post; **2** to ricochet.

recado *noun* M **1** message; **no han dejado recado** they didn't leave a message; **2** errand; **hacer un recado** to run an errand.

recalentar *verb* [29] reheat.

recambio *noun* M **1** spare part; **2** refill (*for a pen*).

recepción *noun* F reception.

recepcionista *noun* M/F receptionist.

receta *noun* F **1** recipe; **2** prescription.

recibidor *noun* M entrance hall.

recibir *verb* [19] **1** to receive; **he recibido una carta de Lola** I've received a letter from Lola; **2** to get; **recibí una llamada del editor** I got a phone call from the editor; **3 recibir a alguien con los brazos abiertos** to welcome somebody with open arms; **4 ir a recibir a alguien** to go to meet somebody; **fuimos a recibirlos a la estación** we went to meet them at the station; **5** (*ending a letter*) **recibe un fuerte abrazo** best wishes; **reciba un cordial saludo** yours sincerely.

recibo *noun* M receipt.

reciclar *verb* [17] recycle.

recién *adverb* **1 pasteles recién hechos** freshly baked cakes; **recién pintado** wet paint; **2 un recién nacido** a newborn baby; **los recién casados** the newly-weds; **los recién llegados** the newcomers.

reciente *adjective* recent.

recientemente *adverb* recently.

recipiente *noun* M container.

recitar *verb* [17] to recite.

reclamación *noun* F complaint;
hacer una reclamación to make a
complaint.

reclamar *verb* [17] **1** to complain;
2 to demand (*rights, money*).

recoger *verb* [3] **1** to pick up;
recoge ese papel del suelo pick up
that piece of paper off the floor; **fui a
recogerlos a la estación** I went to
pick them up from the station; **2** to
tidy up; **tienes que recoger tu
habitación** you have to tidy up your
room; **3 recoger la mesa** to clear
the table; **4** to collect (*money or
signatures*); **5** to pick (*fruit or
flowers*).

recogerse *reflexive verb* [3]
recogerse el pelo to tie your hair
back.

recogida *noun* F collection.

recomendar *verb* [29] to
recommend.

recomendación *noun* F
1 recommendation; **2** reference (*for
a job*).

recompensa *noun* F reward.

recompensar *verb* [17] to reward.

reconciliarse *reflexive verb* [17]
reconciliarse con alguien to make
it up with somebody.

reconocer *verb* [35] **1** to recognize;
al principio no la reconocí I didn't

recognize her to start with; **2** to
admit (*a mistake*); **3** to examine (*a
patient*).

reconocimiento *noun* M
1 reconocimiento médico medical
examination; **2** reconnaissance.

reconozca, etc. *verb* SEE
reconocer.

récord *noun* M record.

recordar *verb* [24] **1** to remember;
si mal no recuerdo if I remember
rightly; **recuerdo que terminamos a
las tres** I remember that we finished
at three; **2** to remind; **me recuerda
mucho a ella** he reminds me of her
a lot; **3 recordarle a alguien que** to
remind somebody to; **recuérdale
que traiga los papeles** remind him
to bring the papers.

recreo *noun* M break (*at school*).

recta¹ *noun* F straight line.

rectángulo *noun* M rectangle.

recto/recta² *adjective* **1** straight;
2 honest.
adverb **seguir todo recto** to carry
straight on.

recuerda, recuerdo¹, etc. *verb*
SEE **recordar**.

recuerdo² *noun* M **1** memory;
tengo buenos recuerdos I've got
happy memories; **2** souvenir;
'recuerdo de España' 'souvenir
from Spain'; **3 recuerdos** regards;
**dale recuerdos a tu hermana de mi
parte** say hello to your sister from
me.

recuperar *verb* [17] **1** to recover (*money, strength*); **2 recuperar tiempo** to make up for lost time.

recuperarse *reflexive verb* [17] **recuperarse de una enfermedad** to recover from an illness.

red *noun* F **1** net; **2** network; **3 la Red** the Net (*Internet*); ★ **caer en las redes de alguien** to fall into somebody's clutches.

redacción *noun* F **1** essay; **2** editorial team.

redactor/redactora *noun* M/F editor.

redondo/redonda *adjective* round; **en números redondos** in round figures.

reducción *noun* F reduction.

reducir *verb* [60] to reduce.

reduje, reduzca, reduzco, etc. *verb* SEE **reducir**.

reembolsar *verb* [17] to refund.

reembolso *noun* M refund.

reemplazar *verb* [22] **reemplazar a alguien** to stand in for somebody.

referencia *noun* F reference; **hacer referencia a** to refer to.

referirse *reflexive verb* [14] **referirise a** to refer to.

refiera, refiero, refiramos, refirió, etc. *verb* SEE **referirse**.

reflejar *verb* [17] to reflect.
reflejarse *reflexive verb* [17] to be reflected.

reflejo *noun* M **1** reflection; **2 reflejos** highlights; **3 reflejos** reflexes.

reflexión *noun* F reflection.

reflexionar *verb* [17] to reflect on; **después de reflexionarlo bien** after thinking it over.

refrán *noun* M saying.

refrescante *adjective* reflreshing.

refresco *noun* M soft drink.

refugiado/refugiada *noun* M/F refugee.

refugio *noun* M shelter; **dar refugio a alguien** to give somebody shelter.

regadera *noun* F watering can; ★ **estar como una regadera** (*informal*) to be raving mad (*literally: to be like a watering can*).

regalar *verb* [17] **1** to give (*as a present*); **mis padrinos me han regalado un reloj** my godparents have bought me a watch; **¿qué vas a regalarle por Navidad?** what are you going to get her for Christmas?; **2** to give away; **me ha regalado su abrigo** he's given his coat to me; **¿te gusta? te lo regalo** do you like it? you can have it.

regalo *noun* M **1** present; **regalo de cumpleaños** birthday present; **2 compre dos y llévese uno de regalo** buy two and get one free.

regañar *verb* [17] **1** to tell off; **mi madre me regañó por llegar tarde** my mother told me off because I got home late; **2 regañar con alguien** to quarrel with somebody; **ha**

regañado con su hermano he's had an argument with his brother.

regar *verb* [30] to water.

régimen *noun* M diet; **ponerse a régimen** to go on a diet.

región *noun* F region.

regional *adjective* regional.

registrar *verb* [17] **1** to search; **nos registraron** we were searched; **2** to go through; **me registró todos los papeles** he went through all my papers; **3** to register (*a birth, for example*); **4** to record (*temperature*).
registrarse *reflexive verb* [17] to register.

registro *noun* M **1** register; **2 el registro civil** the registry office; **3** search.

regla *noun* F **1** ruler (*for measuring*); **2** rule; **por regla general** as a general rule; **3 estar con la regla** to have your period.

reglamento *noun* M regulations.

regresar *verb* [17] to return.

regreso *noun* M return.

regular *adjective* **1** regular; **2** poor (*mark*); **3 de tamaño regular** medium-sized; **4 por lo regular** as a general rule.
adverb **'¿qué tal está tu padre?'** – **'regular'** 'how's your father?' – 'so-so'.

regularidad *noun* F regularity; **con regularidad** regularly.

rehacer *verb* [7] **1 rehacer algo** to do something again; **2 rehízo su vida** she rebuilt her life.

reina *noun* F queen.

reinar *verb* [17] to reign.

reino *noun* M kingdom.

Reino Unido *noun* M United Kingdom.

reír *verb* [61] to laugh; **echarse a reír** to start laughing.
reírse *reflexive verb* [61] **reírse de** to laugh about; **siempre se están riendo de mí** they're always laughing at me; **reírse a carcajadas** to roar with laughter.

reja *noun* F **1** railing; **2** grating.

relación *noun* F **1** relationship; **2 relaciones públicas** public relations; **3** connection; **en relación con** mix with (*people*).

relacionado/relacionada *adjective* related.

relacionar *verb* [17] to relate; **relacionar algo con algo** to relate something to something.
relacionarse *reflexive verb* [17] to be related (*facts, for example*); **relacionarse con** to mix with (*a person*).

relajar *verb* [17] to relax.
relajarse *reflexive verb* [17] to relax.

relámpago *noun* M flash of lightning; ★ **como un relámpago** like greased lightning.

religión *noun* F religion.

religioso/religiosa *adjective* religious.

rellenar *verb* [17] **1 rellenar un impreso** to fill in a form; **2** to fill up; **3** to stuff (*a chicken, for example*).

relleno¹ *noun* M **1** filling; **2** stuffing.

relleno²/rellena *adjective* **1** filled; **2** stuffed (*peppers, for example*).

reloj *noun* M **1** clock; **un reloj despertador** an alarm clock; **2** watch; **un reloj de pulsera** a wristwatch; **mi reloj va atrasado** my watch is slow.

relojería *noun* F watchmaker's.

remar *verb* [17] to row.

remate *noun* M **1** smash (*in tennis*); **2** finish (*in football*); **un remate de cabeza** a header; **3** end (*of a pole, for example*); **4** top (*of a tower, for example*); **5 y para remate** and to cap it all; ★ **loco de remate** (*informal*) completely nuts.

remediar *verb* [17] **1** to remedy; **2 no lo puede remediar** he can't help it; **no pudimos remediarlo** we couldn't do anything about it.

remedio *noun* M **1** remedy; **remedios naturales** natural remedies; **2 si no queda más remedio** if there's no other alternative; **no quedó más remedio que aguantarse** we had to put up with it, there was nothing else we could do; **no tuvimos más remedio**

que ir we had no other option but to go; **¡qué remedio me queda!** what else can I do!; **eso ya no tiene remedio** there's nothing we can do about it now.

remendar *verb* [29] to mend.

remite *noun* M return address.

remitente *noun* M/F sender (*of a letter*).

remo *noun* M oar.

remojar *verb* [17] to soak.

remojo *noun* M **poner algo en remojo** to soak something.

remolacha *noun* F beetroot.

remolcar *verb* [31] to tow.

remolque *noun* M **1** trailer; **2 llevar algo a remolque** to tow something.

remorder *verb* [38] **aún me remuerde la conciencia** I still feel guilty about it.

remoto/remota *adjective* remote.

remover *verb* [38] **1** to stir (*a sauce, for example*); **2** to toss (*a salad*); **3** to turn over (*soil*).

remueva, remuevo, etc. *verb* SEE **remover**.

renacuajo *noun* M tadpole.

rencor *noun* M **guardarle rencor a alguien** to bear someone a grudge.

rendir *verb* [57] **1 rendirle homenaje a alguien** to pay tribute to someone; **2 ayer me rindió mucho en el trabajo** I managed to get a lot done yesterday at work.

rendirse *reflexive verb* [57] to surrender.

RENFE *abbreviation* F (*short for: Red Nacional de Ferrocarriles Españoles*) Spanish Rail (*the Spanish national rail network*).

renglón *noun* M line.

renta *noun* F **1** rent; **2** income.

rentable *adjective* profitable.

renunciar *verb* [17] **renunciar a** to renounce, to give up; **renunciar a un puesto** to resign from a job.

reparación *noun* F repair; **taller de reparaciones** repair shop.

reparar *verb* [17] **1** to repair; **2** to mend.

repartir *verb* [19] **1** to deliver; **2** to hand out (*leaflets, for example*); **3** to distribute; **lo repartiremos entre todos nosotros** we'll share it between us.

reparto *noun* M **1** delivery; **reparto a domicilio** home delivery service; **2** distribution; **hacer el reparto del dinero** to share out the money.

repasar *verb* [17] **1** to revise; **repasar los apuntes** to revise your notes; **2** to check through (*a list*).

repaso *noun* M **1** revision; **dar un repaso a los apuntes** to revise your notes; **2** check (*for mistakes*).

repente *in phrase* **de repente** all of a sudden.

repentino/repentina *adjective* sudden.

repetición *noun* F repetition.

repetir *verb* [57] to repeat.

repita, repitió, repito, etc. *verb* SEE **repetir**.

repleto/repleta *adjective* full up; **estar repleto de algo** to be packed with something; **una sala repleta de gente** a room packed with people.

repollo *noun* M cabbage.

reponer *verb* [11] **1** to replace; **2** to repay; **3 reponer fuerzas** to get your strength back.
reponerse *reflexive verb* [11] to recover; **cuando me repuse del susto** when I recovered from the shock.

reportaje *noun* M **1** article (*in a newspaper*); **2** report (*on TV*).

reportero/reportera *noun* M/F reporter.

reposar *verb* [17] **1** to rest; **2 dejar reposar** to leave to stand.

reposo *noun* M rest.

repostería *noun* F confectionery.

representante *noun* M/F representative.

representar *verb* [17] **1** to represent; **2 representar una obra** to perform a play; **representar un papel** to play a part.

reproducción *noun* F reproduction.

reproducir *verb* [60] to reproduce.
reproducirse *reflexive verb* [60] to reproduce.

reptil *noun* M reptile.

república *noun* F republic.

República Checa *noun* F **la República Checa** the Czech Republic.

repugnante *adjective* disgusting.

repulsivo/repulsiva *adjective* repulsive.

reputación *noun* F reputation.

requisito *noun* M requirement.

resaca *noun* F hangover.

resbaladizo/resbaladiza *adjective* slippery.

resbalar *verb* [17] to slip.
resbalarse *reflexive verb* [17] to slip.

rescatar *verb* [17] to rescue.

rescate *noun* M rescue; **una operación de rescate** a rescue operation.

reserva *noun* F 1 reservation; **hacer una reserva** to make a reservation; 2 reserve; **jugadores de reserva** reserve players; **una reserva natural** a nature reserve; 3 **tengo otro de reserva** I have a spare one; 4 **tengo mis reservas** I have my reservations.

reservado/reservada *adjective* reserved.

reservar *verb* [17] 1 to reserve; 2 to book.

resfriado *noun* M cold; **tener un resfriado** to have a cold.

resfriarse *reflexive verb* [32] to catch a cold.

residencia *noun* F 1 residence; **permiso de residencia** residence permit; 2 hall of residence; 3 **residencia de ancianos** old people's home.

residir *verb* [19] **residir en** to live in.

resistencia *noun* F 1 resistance; 2 element (*electrical*); 3 **tener mucha resistencia** to have a lot of stamina.

resistir *verb* [19] 1 to resist; 2 to stand (*pain or cold*); **¡no puedo resistirlo!** I can't stand it!
resistirse *reflexive verb* [19] to resist.

resolver *verb* [45] 1 to solve; 2 to resolve.

resorte *noun* M spring.

respaldo *noun* M 1 back; 2 backing.

respecto *noun* M **respecto a ...** regarding ...

respetable *adjective* respectable.

respetar *verb* [17] to respect.

respeto *noun* M respect.

respiración *noun* F breathing; **contener la respiración** to hold your breath.

respirar *verb* [17] to breathe.

responder *verb* [18] 1 to answer; **responder a algo** to answer something; 2 to respond; 3 to answer back; **¡a mí no me respondas!** don't answer back!

responsabilidad *noun* F responsibility.

responsable *noun* M/F **1** person
in charge; **el responsable de ventas**
the person in charge of sales;
2 person responsible.
adjective responsible.

respuesta *noun* F **1** answer;
2 response.

restante *adjective* remaining; **lo
restante** the remainder.

restar *verb* [17] to subtract, to take
away.

restaurante *noun* M restaurant.

restaurar *verb* [17] to restore.

resto *noun* M **1** rest; **el resto de los
libros** the rest of the books; **2 restos**
remains; **los restos del castillo** the
remains of the castle; **3 restos**
leftovers (*from a meal*).

restricción *noun* F restriction.

restringir *verb* [49] to restrict.
restringirse *reflexive verb* [49] to
restrict yourself.

resultado *noun* M **1** result;
2 outcome; **3 dar resultado** to work
(*a plan or an idea*).

resultar *verb* [17] **1** to work (*a plan
or an idea*); **2 así resulta más fácil**
it's easy this way; **resultó imposible
convencerlo** it was impossible to
convince him.

resumen *noun* M summary.

resumir *verb* [19] **1** to summarize;
2 to sum up.

retener *verb* [9] **1** to retain; **2** to
keep back.

retirar *verb* [17] **1** to withdraw; **2** to
move back; **retira esa silla** move that
chair back.

retirarse *reflexive verb* [17] **1** to
withdraw; **2** to move back.

retrasado/retrasada *noun* M/F
mentally handicapped.
adjective **1** mentally handicapped;
**2 vamos muy retrasados con el
trabajo** we're very late with the job;
3 me reloj va retrasado my watch is
slow.

retrasar *verb* [17] **1** to delay
(*departure*); **2** to postpone;
3 retrasar un reloj to put a clock
back.

retrasarse *reflexive verb* [17] **1** to be
late; **me retrasé diez minutos** I was
ten minutes late; **2** to fall behind;
voy retrasado con mi trabajo I'm
behind with my work.

retraso *noun* M **1** delay; **una media
hora de retraso** a half-hour delay;
llevan retraso they're late; **2 con
retraso** late; **llegaron con retraso**
they arrived late.

retrato *noun* M portrait; ★ **ser el
vivo retrato de alguien** to be the
spitting image of somebody.

retrovisor *noun* M **1** rear-view
mirror; **2** wing mirror.

reuma, reúma, reumatismo
noun M rheumatism.

reunión *noun* F **1** meeting;
2 gathering.

reunir *verb* [62] **1** to gather
(*information, for example*); **2** to
have; **reúne los elementos que**

busco it has all the elements I'm looking for; **no reúne los requisitos necesarios** it doesn't satisfy the necessary requirements; **3 reunir dinero** to raise money.

reunirse *reflexive verb* [62] to meet.

revancha *noun* F **1** return game; **jugar la revancha** to play a rematch; **2 tomarse la revancha** to get your own back.

revelar *verb* [17] **1** to reveal; **2** to develop (*a film*).

reverencia *noun* F bow; curtsey; **hacer una reverencla** to bow; to curtsey.

reverso *noun* M back.

revés *noun* M **1** back; **el revés de la página** the back of the page; **2** inside; **el revés del abrlgo** the inside of the coat; **3 se puso el jersey al revés** he had his jumper on inside out, he had his jumper on back-to-front; **ese cuadro está al revés** that picture's upside down; **4 del revés** inside out.

revisar *verb* [17] **1** to check; **2** to revise; **3** to service.

revisión *noun* F **1** (medical) checkup; **2** revision; **3** service (*for a car or a machine*).

revisor/revisora *noun* M/F ticket inspector.

revista *noun* F magazine.

revolución *noun* F revolution.

revolver *verb* [45] **1** to stir (*soup or sauce*); **2 me revolvieron todos los cajones** they went through all my

drawers; **le habían revuelto todos sus papeles** they'd left all his papers in a mess.

revólver *noun* M gun.

revuelto/revuelta *adjective* **1** in a mess; **los papeles estaban todos revueltos** all the papers were in a mess; **2** rough (*sea*); **3** unsettled (*weather*).

rey *noun* M **1** king; **2 los reyes** the king and queen.

rezar *verb* [22] to pray.

ría, rían, etc. *verb* SEE **reir**.

riada *noun* F flood.

ribera *noun* F riverbank.

rico/rica *noun* M/F rich person; **los ricos** the rich.
adjective rich.

ridículo[1] *noun* M **hacer el ridículo** to make a fool of yourself; **dejar a alguien en ridículo** to make a fool of somebody.

ridículo[2]**/ridícula** *adjective* ridiculous.

ríe, ríen, etc. *verb* SEE **reír**.

riega, riego, riegue, etc. *verb* SEE **regar**.

rienda *noun* F rein.

riesgo *noun* M risk; **correr un riesgo** to run a risk; **voy a correr el riesgo** I'll take the risk; **un riesgo para la salud** a health hazard.

rifa *noun* F raffle.

rímel *noun* M mascara.

rincón *noun* M **1** corner (*of a room*); **2 estará en algún rincón** it must be somewhere; **3 un rincón pintoresco** a lovely spot (*in the country*).

rinoceronte *noun* M rhinoceros.

riña *noun* F **1** fight; **una riña callejera** a street fight; **2** quarrel; **tuvo una riña con su novio** she quarrelled with her boyfriend.

riñón *noun* M **1** kidney; **2 tener dolor de riñones** to have backache.

río *noun* M river; **ir río abajo** to go downstream.

rió *verb* SEE **reír**.

riqueza *noun* F wealth.

risa *noun* F **1** laugh; **una risa histérica** an hysterical laugh; **2 risas** laughter; **las risas del público** the laughter of the audience; **3 me dio risa verlo** seeing him made me laugh; **de repente le dio la risa** suddenly he got the giggles; **4 ¡qué risa!** how funny!; **5 morirse de risa** (*informal*) to die laughing.

ritmo *noun* M rhythm; **llevar el ritmo** to keep time; **marcar el ritmo** to beat time.

rizado/rizada *adjective* curly.

rizo *noun* M curl.

robar *verb* [17] **1** to steal; **robarle algo a alguien** to steal something from somebody; **2** to rob; **robar un banco** to rob a bank; **3 robar en una** casa to burgle a house; **les robaron mientras estaban de vacaciones** they were burgled while they were away; **4** to rip (somebody) off.

roble *noun* M oak.

robo *noun* M **1** theft; **2** robbery; **3** burglary; **4** break in; **5 ¡esto es un robo!** this is a rip-off!

roca *noun* F rock; ★ **firme como una roca** solid as a rock.

rocío *noun* M dew.

rodaja *noun* F slice; **cortar en rodajas** to slice.

rodar *verb* (24) **1** to roll (*a ball, for example*); **2** to turn (*a wheel*); **3** to shoot (*a film*).

rodeado/rodeada *adjective* surrounded; **rodeado de** surrounded by.

rodear *verb* [17] to surround.

rodilla *noun* F knee; **ponerse de rodillas** to kneel down.

rogar *verb* (24) **1** to beg; **te ruego que me perdones** I beg you to forgive me; **2 'se ruega no fumar'** 'you are kindly requested not to smoke'.

rojo¹ *noun* M red.

rojo²/roja *adjective* red; **ponerse rojo** to turn red.

rollo *noun* M **1** roll (*of material or film*); **2** coil (*of rope*); **3** (*informal*) bore; **¡vaya rollo de película!** what a boring film!

romántico/romántica *adjective* romantic.

rompecabezas *noun* M (*does not change in the plural*) puzzle.

romper *verb* [40] **1** to break; **vas a romper la silla** you're going to break the chair; **2** to tear; **rompió la carta en pedazos** he tore up the letter; **3 romper algo en mil pedazos** to smash something to pieces.
romperse *reflexive verb* [40] to break; **la lámpara se ha roto** the lamp has broken; **romperse una pierna** to break your leg.

ron *noun* M rum.

roncar *verb* [31] to snore.

ronco/ronca *adjective* hoarse; **quedarse ronco** to go hoarse.

ronda *noun* F **1** round; **esta ronda la pago yo** it's my round; **2** patrol.

ronronear *verb* [31] to purr.

ropa *noun* F **1** clothes; **tengo mucha ropa** I have a lot of clothes; **2 cambiarse de ropa** to get changed; **3 la ropa sucia** the dirty laundry; **4 ropa interior** underwear.

ropero *noun* M wardrobe.

rosa *noun* M *adjective* pink.
noun F rose.

rosado[1] *noun* M **1** rosé (*wine*); **2** pink.

rosado[2]**/rosada** *adjective* pink.

rosario *noun* M rosary.

rosbif *noun* M roast beef.

rostro *noun* M **1** face; **2** nerve; **¡vaya rostro que tiene!** (*informal*) he's got a nerve!

roto/rota *adjective* **1** broken; **2** torn; **3** worn out (*shoes*).

rotulador *noun* M felt-tip pen.

rubio/rubia *adjective* blonde.

ruborizarse *reflexive verb* [22] to blush.

rueda *noun* F **1** wheel; **la rueda de repuesto** the spare wheel; **la rueda delantera** the front wheel; **2 una rueda de prensa** a press conference.

rugir *verb* [49] to roar.

ruido *noun* M noise; **hacer ruido** to make a noise.

ruidoso/ruidosa *adjective* noisy.

ruina *noun* F **1** ruin; **dejar a alguien en la ruina** to ruin somebody; **la empresa está en la ruina** the company is ruined; **2 ruinas** ruins; **las ruinas del castillo** the ruins of the castle; **estar en ruinas** to be in ruins; ★ **estar hecho una ruina** (*informal*) to be a wreck.

ruiseñor *noun* M nightingale.

rulo *noun* M roller (*curler*).

Rumania, Rumanía *noun* F Romania.

rumano/rumana *noun* M/F *adjective* Romanian.

rumbo *noun* M 1 course; **poner rumbo a** to set a course for; **el rumbo que tomaron los acontecimientos** the course of events; 2 direction; 3 **ir con rumbo a** to be heading for; 4 **sin rumbo fijo** aimlessly.

rumor *noun* M 1 rumour; 2 murmur.

Rusia *noun* F Russia.

ruso¹ *noun* M Russian (*the language*).

ruso²/rusa *noun* M/F *adjective* Russian.

ruta *noun* F route.

rutina *noun* F routine; **por rutina** out of habit.

S s

sábado *noun* M Saturday (*see 'domingo' for examples*).

sábana *noun* F sheet (*for a bed*).

saber *noun* M knowledge.
verb [13] 1 to know; **ya lo sé** I know; **no sabe** he doesn't know; **sabía que no iba a querer hacerlo** I knew he wouldn't want to do it; 2 **saber algo de memoria** to know something by heart; 3 **¿sabes montar en bicicleta?** can you ride a bike?; **sabe hablar inglés muy bien** she can speak English very well; **no sé alemán** I can't speak German; 4 to find out; **lo supe por su hermana** I found out through her sister; 5 to

taste; **la comida sabía muy rica** the food tasted very nice; **¡qué mal sabe!** it tastes disgusting!; 6 **saber a** to taste of; **sabe a fresa** it tastes of strawberry.

sabiduría *noun* F wisdom.

sabio/sabia *adjective* wise.

sabor *noun* M taste; **sabor a fresa** strawberry-flavoured.

sabrá, sabré, sabría, etc. *verb* SEE **saber**.

sabroso/sabrosa *adjective* tasty.

sacacorchos *noun* M (*does not change in the plural*) corkscrew.

sacapuntas *noun* M (*does not change in the plural*) pencil sharpener.

sacar *verb* [31] 1 to take out; **sacó su monedero del bolso** she took her purse out of her bag; **lo saqué de la caja** I took it out of the box; **sacar la basura** to take the rubbish out; **sacar al perro a pasear** to take the dog for a walk; 2 **sacar la pistola** to draw a gun; 3 to get; **sacar entradas** to get tickets; **aún no he sacado los billetes** I haven't got the tickets yet; 4 **sacar buenas notas** to get good marks; **he sacado un siete en matemáticas** I got seven (out of ten) in maths; 5 **sacar una foto** to take a picture; 6 **sacar una fotocopia** to make a photocopy; 7 **sacar un libro** to publish a book; **sacar un disco** to release a record; 8 **sacar la lengua** to stick your tongue out; 9 to serve (*in tennis*).

sacarse *reflexive verb* [31] **1 sacarse una muela** to have a tooth out; **2 sacarse una foto** to have a photograph taken; **me saqué una foto frente al palacio** I had a photograph taken of me in front of the palace.

sacerdote *noun* M priest.

saco *noun* M sack; **un saco de dormir** a sleeping bag.

sacrificar *verb* [31] to sacrifice.

sacrificio *noun* M sacrifice.

sacudida *noun* F **1** shake; **le di una sacudida** I gave it a shake; **2 el coche iba dando sacudidas** the car was jerking along.

sacudir *verb* [19] **1** to shake; **2** to shake off; **sacudió las migas del mantel** she shook the crumbs off the tablecloth.

sacudirse *reflexive verb* [19] to shake off; **se sacudió el polvo de la chaqueta** he shook off the dust from his jacket.

sagaz *adjective* shrewd.

Sagitario *noun* M Sagittarius.

sagitario *noun* M/F Sagittarius; **es sagitario** she's Sagittarius.

sagrado/sagrada *adjective* **1** sacred; **2** holy.

sal *noun* F salt; **sales de baño** bath salts.

sala *noun* F **1** room; **una sala de estar** a living room; **una sala de espera** a waiting room; **2** hall; **una sala de exposiciones** an exhibition

hall; **3** ward (*in a hospital*); **4 una sala de fiestas** a night club.

salado/salada *adjective* salted; **está muy salado** it's too salty; **agua salada** salt water.

salario *noun* M salary.

salchicha *noun* F sausage.

salchichón *noun* M spicy sausage.

saldar *verb* [17] **1** to settle (*a debt*); **2** to sell off.

saldo *noun* M **1** balance; **saldo positivo** credit balance; **saldo negativo** debit balance; **2** settlement; **3 saldos** sales; **precios de saldo** sale prices.

saldrá, saldré, saldría, salga, salgo, etc. *verb* SEE **salir**.

salero *noun* M **1** salt cellar; **2 tener mucho salero** (*informal*) to be very funny.

salida *noun* F exit.

salir *verb* [63] **1** to go out; **salen mucho por la noche** they go out a lot in the evenings; **2** to come out; **salieron uno a uno** they came out one by one; **3** to get out; **no pude salir** I couldn't get out; **4** to leave; **el vuelo sale a las cinco** the flight leaves at five; **5 salgo de casa a las ocho** I leave home at eight; **no sale nunca de su habitación** he never leaves his room; **salió de la casa corriendo** he ran out of the house; **sal de debajo de la cama** come out from under the bed; **6 salir con alguien** to go out with someone; **sale con mi hermano** she's going out with my brother; **7 salir en la televisión** to appear on television; **la noticia salió en el periódico** the news was in the paper; **8** to turn out; **las cosas salieron mal** things turned out badly; **todo salió como esperábamos** everything turned out as we expected; **9 las vacaciones nos salieron muy caras** the holidays were very expensive in the end; **si compras tres, sale más barato** it's cheaper if you buy three; **10 ¿cómo te salieron las cosas en Inglaterra?** how did things turn out for you in England?; **le sale muy bien la tortilla de patatas** he can cook a really good Spanish omelette; **el retrato te ha salido perfecto** you've done a perfect portrait; **el examen me salió fatal** I did terribly in the exam; **11 me ha salido un grano** I've got a spot; **me están saliendo canas** my hair's starting to go grey; **le salía sangre de la nariz** his nose was bleeding.

salirse *reflexive verb* [63] **1** to leave; **el cantante se ha salido del grupo** the singer has left the group; **salirse del colegio** to leave school; **2** to leak; **3 el agua se salió del fregadero** the sink overflowed; **se ha salido la leche** the milk has boiled over; **4 el coche se salió de la carretera** the car went off the road.

salmón *noun* M salmon. *adjective* salmon-pink.

salón *noun* M **1** living room; **2** function room; **3 salón de belleza** beauty salon; **4 salón de actos** assembly hall; **5 salón de fiestas** reception room.

salpicar *verb* [31] to splash.

salsa *noun* F **1** sauce; **salsa besamel** white sauce; **2** gravy; **3** salsa (*music*).

saltamontes *noun* M grasshopper.

saltar *verb* [17] to jump; **saltar por encima de la verja** to jump over the fence; **saltar un muro** to jump over a wall; **saltar al suelo** to jump to the ground; **saltar de la cama** to jump out of bed.

saltarse *reflexive verb* [17] **1** to skip (*a page or an appointment*); **2 se saltaron un semáforo en rojo** they drove through a red light.

salto *noun* M jump; **dar un salto** to jump; **ponerse de pie de un salto** to jump to your feet; **levantarse de un salto de la cama** to leap out of bed; **salto de altura** high jump.

salud *noun* F health; **estar bien de salud** to be in good health. *exclamation* cheers!; **¡a tu salud!** cheers!

saludable *adjective* healthy.

saludar *verb* [17] **1** to say hello; **nos saludó con la mano** she waved hello to us; **2 'le saluda atentamente'** 'Yours sincerely', 'Yours faithfully' (*ending a letter*).

saludo *noun* M **1** greeting; **te envían sus saludos** they send their regards; **dale saludos de mi parte** give him my regards; **2 Un afectuoso saludo** Best wishes.

salvadoreño *noun* M/F *adjective* Salvadorean.

salvamento *noun* M rescue; **bote de salvamento** lifeboat; **operación de salvamento** rescue operation.

salvar *verb* [17] to save.
salvarse *reflexive verb* [17] to survive.

salvavidas *noun* M (*does not change in the plural*) life jacket.

salvo¹/salva *adjective* safe.

salvo² *preposition, conjunction* except; **salvo que** unless.
in phrase **estar a salvo** to be out of danger; **ponerse a salvo** to reach safety.

San *adjective* St (*Saint*).

sanar *verb* [17] **1** to recover (*patient*); **2** to heal (*injury*).

sandalia *noun* F sandal.

sandía *noun* F watermelon.

sándwich *noun* M sandwich.

sangrar *verb* [17] to bleed.

sangre *noun* F blood; **te sale sangre** you're bleeding.

sangría *noun* F sangria (*a fruit punch made with red wine and lemonade*).

sano/sana *adjective* **1** healthy; **2** **sano y salvo** safe and sound.

San Salvador *noun* M San Salvador.

santo¹ *noun* M name day (*in Spain each day of the year is associated with the name of a saint and many people celebrate the day of the saint they are named after*).

santo²/santa *noun* M/F saint; **tener la paciencia de un santo** to have the patience of a saint.
adjective holy.

sapo *noun* M toad.

saque *noun* M **1** serve (*in tennis*); **2** kick-off (*in football*); **saque de banda** throw in; **saque de esquina** corner kick.

sarampión *noun* M measles.

sardina *noun* F sardine.

sargento *noun* M/F sergeant.

sarpullido *noun* M rash; **me ha salido un sarpullido** I've come out in a rash.

sartén *noun* F frying pan.

sastre *noun* M/F tailor.

satélite *noun* M satellite.

satén *noun* M satin.

satisfacción *noun* F satisfaction.

satisfacer *verb* [7] to satisfy; **la calidad del producto no nos satisface** we are not satisfied with the quality of the product; **para satisfacer mi curiosidad** to satisfy my curiosity.
satisfacerse *reflexive verb* [7] to be satisfied.

satisfecho/satisfecha *adjective* satisfied; **estamos muy satisfechos con los resultados** we are very happy with the results.

sauce *noun* M willow.

saxofón *noun* M saxophone.

sazonado/sazonada *adjective*
seasoned.

sazonar *verb* [17] to season.

se *pronoun* 1 himself/herself; **se
cortó** he cut himself/she cut herself;
2 itself; **se desconecta solo** it
disconnects itself; 3 themselves;
¿se han portado bien? did they
behave themselves?; 4 yourself
(*polite form*); **espero que no se
haya hecho daño** I hope you haven't
hurt yourself; 5 yourselves (*polite
form*); **¿se han divertido ustedes?**
did you enjoy yourselves?; 6 him/
her; **no se lo pregunté** I didn't ask
him/I didn't ask her; 7 to him/to her;
se lo mandaré I'll send it to him/I'll
send it to her; 8 them; **cuando les
vea se lo preguntaré** I'll ask them
when I see them; 9 to them; **cuando
les vea se lo daré** I'll give it to them
when I see them; 10 you (*polite
form*); **se lo dije a usted ayer** I told
you yesterday; 11 to you (*polite
form*); **se lo di a usted ayer** I gave it
to you yesterday; 12 each other; **se
quieren** they love each other; **se
miraron** they looked at each other;
13 (*with parts of your body and
personal belongings*); **se lavó las
manos** he washed his hands/she
washed her hands; **¿se ha cortado
usted el dedo?** have you cut your
finger?; **se pusieron la ropa** they put
their clothes on; 14 (*the infinitives
of many verbs in Spanish end in '-se'
but are not reflexive in English*) **me
reí mucho** I laughed a lot; **se cayó** he
fell down/she fell down; **se han
peleado** they've had a fight; **se
levantaron** they stood up; 15 (*used
in rather official or impersonal
phrases*) **'se vende piso'** 'flat for
sale'; **'se habla inglés'** 'English
spoken here'; **se hace así** it is done
like this; **se corta la hoja en dos** cut
the sheet in two.

sé *verb* SEE **saber**.

secador *noun* M **secador de pelo**
hairdryer.

secadora *noun* F dryer.

secar *verb* [31] to dry.
secarse *reflexive verb* [31] 1 to dry;
**¿cuánto tarda en secarse la
pintura?** how long does the paint
take to dry?; **la camisa ya se ha
secado** the shirt's dry already; 2 to
dry yourself; **secarse el pelo** to dry
your hair; **secarse las lágrimas** to
dry your tears; **sécate las manos
con este trapo** dry your hands with
this cloth; 3 to dry up.

sección *noun* F 1 section;
2 department.

seco/seca *adjective* 1 dry;
limpieza en seco dry-cleaning;
2 dried (*flowers, for example*).

secretaría *noun* F secretary's
office.

secretario/secretaria *noun* M/F
secretary.

secreto[1] *noun* M secret.

secreto[2]**/secreta** *adjective*
secret.

secuestrar *verb* [17] **1** to kidnap;
2 to hijack.

secuestro *noun* M **1** kidnapping;
2 hijacking.

secundario/secundaria
adjective secondary.

sed *noun* F thirst; **tenían sed** they
were thirsty; **las patatas fritas me
dan sed** crisps make me thirsty.

seda *noun* F silk.

sedal *noun* M fishing line.

sede *noun* F **la sede de las
Olimpiadas** the venue for the
Olympics; **la sede de la compañía**
the company's head office; **la sede
del gobierno** the seat of
government.

seguida¹ *in phrase* **en seguida**
straight away; **voy en seguida** I'll be
right there.

seguido¹/**seguida**² *adjective*
1 tres días seguidos three days in a
row; **dan las dos películas seguidas**
they show both films one after the
other; **los tres autobuses vinieron
seguidos** the three buses came one
after the other; **2 seguido de**
followed by.

seguido² *adverb* straight on; **vaya
todo seguido** go straight on.

seguir *verb* [64] **1** to follow; **seguir
a alguien** to follow somebody; **seguir
una pista** to follow a trail; **seguir un
consejo** to follow a piece of advice;
2 to carry on, to continue; **sigamos**
let's carry on; **3 seguir haciendo** to
carry on doing; **colgué el teléfono y**

seguí leyendo I put down the
telephone and carried on reading;
4 seguir haciendo to be still doing;
siguen viviendo en Sevilla they're
still living in Seville; **5** to go on; **siga
todo recto** go straight on; **siga por
esta calle** go on down this street.

según *preposition* **1** according to;
según la ley according to the law;
2 según parece apparently;
3 según dijo él from what he said.
adverb '**¿te interesa apuntarte?**' –
'**según**' 'would you be interested in
enrolling?' – 'it depends'.
conjunction as; **según los vayas
terminando** as you finish them.

segunda¹ *noun* F **la segunda**
second gear.

segundo¹ *noun* M **1** second;
espera un segundo wait a moment;
no tardé ni un segundo en hacerlo
it didn't take me a minute to do it;
2 el segundo the main course.

segundo²/**segunda**² *adjective*
1 second; **segunda clase** second
class; **viven en el segundo piso** they
live on the second floor; **llegar en
segundo lugar** to finish in second
position; **2 en segundo plano** in the
background.

seguridad *noun* F **1** security;
seguridad nacional national
security; **2** safety; **por razones de
seguridad** for safety reasons;
3 certainty; **no lo sé con seguridad**
I don't know for certain; **4 seguridad
social** social security.

seguro¹ *noun* M **1** insurance;
hacerse un seguro to take out

insurance; **seguro a todo riesgo** comprehensive insurance; **seguro contra incendios** fire insurance; **2** clasp (*of a bracelet*); **3** safety catch (*on a weapon*); **4 el Seguro** the Social Security.
adverb definitely; **irán seguro** they'll definitely go; **seguro que no están** I bet they're not there.

seguro²/segura *adjective* **1** safe; **la escalera no es muy segura** the ladder isn't very safe; **aquí me siento seguro** I feel safe here; **2** sure; **¿estás seguro de que se pone así?** are you sure this is the way to put it?; **estoy completamente seguro** I'm absolutely certain; **3** definite; **no es seguro todavía** it's not definite yet; **4** reliable; **un método muy seguro** a very reliable method.

seis *number* **1** six; **tiene seis años** he's six (years old); **2** sixth (*in dates*); **el seis de junio** the sixth of June; **3** six (*in clock time*); **son las seis** it's six o'clock.

seiscientos/seiscientas *number* six hundred; **seiscientos dos** six hundred and two.

selección *noun* F **1** selection; **2 la selección nacional** the national team.

seleccionar *verb* [17] to select.

self-service *noun* M self-service restaurant.

sello *noun* M **1** stamp; **2 sello discográfico** record label.

selva *noun* F **1** jungle; **2** forest; **la selva tropical** the tropical rainforest.

semáforo *noun* M traffic lights; **saltarse un semáforo en rojo** to go through a red light; **cuando llegue al semáforo, tuerza a la derecha** turn right at the traffic lights.

semana *noun* F week; **la próxima semana** next week; **entre semana** during the week; **Semana Santa** Easter; **en Semana Santa** at Easter.

semanal *adjective* weekly.

sembrar *verb* [29] **1** to sow; **2** to plant.

semejante *adjective* similar; **semejante a** similar to.

semifinal *noun* F semifinal.

semilla *noun* F seed.

sémola *noun* F semolina.

sencillo¹ *noun* M **1** single (*record*); **2** single ticket.

sencillo²/sencilla *adjective* **1** simple; **2** modest.

senda *noun* F path.

senderismo *noun* M trekking.

seno *noun* M **1** breast; **2** bosom.

sensación *noun* F **1** feeling; **tengo la sensación de que ...** I have the feeling that ...; **una sensación de tristeza** a feeling of sadness; **2** sense; **una sensación de pérdida** a sense of loss; **3** sensation; **causar sensación** to cause a sensation.

sensacional *adjective* sensational.

sensatez *noun* F sense; **tener sensatez** to be sensible; **actuar con sensatez** to act sensibly.

sensato/sensata *adjective* sensible.

sensibilidad *noun* F sensitivity.

sensible *adjective* 1 sensitive; 2 noticeable (*difference or change*).

sensiblemente *adverb* considerably.

sentado/sentada *adjective* **estar sentado** to be sitting; **estaban sentados cerca de la puerta** they were sitting near the door; **estábamos sentados a la mesa** we were sitting at the table; **permanezcan sentados, por favor** please remain seated.

sentar *verb* [29] 1 to sit; **senté al niño en su silla** I sat the baby on his chair; 2 to suit; **ese vestido te sienta muy bien** that dress really suits you; **el rojo me sienta fatal** red doesn't suit me at all; 3 **los pimientos me sientan mal** peppers don't agree with me.

sentarse *reflexive verb* [29] to sit down.

sentido *noun* M 1 sense; **sentido del deber** sense of duty; **sentido común** common sense; 2 **no tiene sentido** it doesn't make sense; **en sentido literal** in the literal sense; 3 consciousness; **perder el sentido** to lose consciousness; 4 direction; **venían en sentido contrario** they were coming from the opposite

direction; **en el sentido de las agujas del reloj** clockwise; **en el sentido contrario al de las agujas del reloj** anticlockwise; 5 **calle de sentido único** one-way street.

sentimental *adjective* 1 sentimental; 2 **¿qué tal tu vida sentimental?** how's your love life?

sentimiento *noun* M 1 feeling; 2 **te acompaño en el sentimiento** my condolences.

sentir *verb* [14] 1 to feel; **sentir dolor** to feel pain; **sentir sed** to feel thirsty; **sentir alegría** to feel happy; 2 **sentir un ruido** to hear a noise; 3 (*used to express apology*) **lo siento mucho** I'm very sorry; **siento llegar tarde** sorry I'm late; **sentimos tener que comunicarle que ...** we regret to inform you that ...

sentirse *reflexive verb* [14] to feel; **¿cómo te sientes?** how do you feel?; **no se sentía bien y se fue a casa** he wasn't feeling well and he went home; **me siento un poco cansado** I feel a bit tired.

seña *noun* F 1 sign; **hacer una seña** to make a sign; **me hizo señas para que entrase** he beckoned to me to come in; 2 **señas** address; **¿quieres darme tus señas?** would you like to give me your address?

señal *noun* F 1 sign; **señal de tráfico** traffic sign; 2 **en señal de amistad** as a token of friendship; 3 sign; **hacer una señal** to make a sign; **nos estaba haciendo señales** she was signalling to us; 4 deposit; **dar una señal** to pay a deposit.

señalar *verb* [17] **1** to point; **señaló hacia la casa** he pointed to the house; **no es de buena educación señalar con el dedo** it's bad manners to point at people; **2** to point out; **señaló que …** she pointed out that …; **3** to fix (*a date or time*).
señalarse *reflexive verb* [17] **se señaló la pierna** he pointed at his leg.

señor *noun* M **1** gentleman; **había un señor esperando** there was a gentleman waiting; **2** sir; **perdone señor, ¿me deja pasar?** excuse me sir, could you let me through?; **3** Mr; **el señor Puyol** Mr Puyol; **los señores López** Mr and Mrs López; (*note that sometimes 'señor' is used in Spanish before somebody's first name as a sign of respect, for example 'el señor Mateo' and also in front of titles*) **el señor presidente** the President; **4 Muy señor mío** Dear Sir; **5** (*for emphasis*) **no señor, eso no se hace** you mustn't do that; **si señor, es verdad** it is indeed true.

señora *noun* F **1** lady; **una señora se me acercó** a lady came up to me; **2** madam; **perdone señora, ¿me deja pasar?** excuse me madam, could you let me through?; **3** Mrs; Ms; **la señora Frutos** Ms Frutos; (*in Spain, women continue using their maiden name after they get married rather than using their husband's surname*) **Doña Ana Villa, señora de García** Mrs Ana García (*literally, Ms Ana Villa, marrried to Mr García*); (*note that sometimes 'señora' is used in Spanish before somebody's first name as a sign of respect, for example*

'la señora Juana'); **4** wife; **fui de vacaciones con mi señora** I went on holiday with my wife; **5** (*for emphasis*) **no señora, no fui yo** it was not me; **sí señora, es mío** it is mine.

señorita *noun* F **1** young lady; **le ha llamado una señorita** a young lady has called you; **2** Miss; Ms; **la señorita García** Miss García; Ms García; (*'señorita' is also used to address a teacher*) **aquí están mis deberes, señorita** here's my homework, Miss; **3** (*for emphasis*) **no señorita, no te lo dejo** I am certainly not lending it to you.

sepa, sepan, etc. *verb* SEE **saber**.

separación *noun* F **1** gap; **2** separation.

separado/separada *adjective* **1** separated; **2** por separado separately.

separar *verb* [17] **1** to separate; **2** to move (something) away; **separa la silla de la chimenea** move the chair away from the fire.
separarse *reflexive verb* [17] **1** to separate (*a couple*); **2** nunca nos hemos separado antes we've never been apart before.

septiembre *noun* M September; **en septiembre/en el mes de septiembre** in September.

séptimo/séptima *adjective* seventh; **el séptimo piso** the seventh floor.

sequía *noun* F draught.

ser *noun* M **ser humano** human
being.
verb [1] **1** to be; **es muy bonito** it's
very beautiful; **es soltero** he's single;
es muy simpática she's very friendly;
soy bastante alta I'm quite tall;
'**¿quién es?**' – '**soy yo**' 'who's that?' –
'it's me'; **mi madre es médico** my
mother's a doctor; **estas naranjas
son buenísimas** these oranges are
really nice; **¿cuánto es?** how much
is it?; **hoy es once** it's the eleventh
today; **eran las seis y media** it was
half past six; **2 ser** to be to be from; **mi
amiga es de Argentina** my friend is
from Agentina; **3 el coche es de
Juan** the car is Juan's; **era de mi
hermano** it was my brother's; **4 ser
de** to be made of; **es de madera** it's
made of wood; **es de metal** it's made
of metal; **5** (*pasive use*) to be; **la
propuesta ha sido rechazada** the
proposal has been rejected;
6 cuando sea whenever; **como sea**
however; **donde sea** wherever; **7 lo
que sea** whatever; **8 ya sea ... o ...**
either ... or ...; **ya sea por carta o
por teléfono** either by post or by
telephone; **9 o sea, que no lo has
terminado** so, you haven't finished;
**dentro de una semana, o sea el
próximo jueves** in a week, that is,
next Thursday; **10 a no ser** unless; **a
no ser que no le interese** unless he's
not interested.

será, seré, sería, *etc.* *verb* SEE
ser.

serie *noun* F **1** series; **fabricación
en serie** mass production; **2 fuera
de serie** out of this world.

serio/seria *adjective* **1** serious;
ponerse serio to have a serious
expression; **un problema serio** a
serious problem; **2** reliable (*a
person*); **3** reputable (*a company*);
4 lo digo en serio I mean it.

serpiente *noun* F snake.

servicio *noun* M **1** service;
servicios públicos public services;
servicio incluido service included;
2 estar de servicio to be on duty;
3 'servicios' 'toilets'; **4 servicio
militar** military service.

servilleta *noun* F serviette.

servir *verb* [57] **1** to serve; **servir la
sopa** to serve the soup; **¿te sirvo más
vino?** shall I pour you some more
wine?; **2** to be of use; **estas
herramientas ya no sirven** these
tools are no good any more; **3 servir
para algo** to be used for; **¿para qué
sirve este interruptor?** what's this
switch for?; **esto no nos sirve para
abrirlo** this is no use for opening it;
4 no sirves para nada you're useless;
yo no sirvo para camarera I'm no
good as a waitress.

servirse *reflexive verb* [57] to help
yourself to; **se sirvió ensalada** she
helped herself to some salad; **sírvete
más** help yourself to some more.

sesenta *number* sixty; **tiene
sesenta años** he's sixty (years old);
sesenta y dos sixty-two; **los años
sesenta** the sixties.

sesión *noun* F **1** session;
2 performance; **la sesión de noche**
the evening performance; **sesión
continua** continuous performance.

seta *noun* F **1** mushroom;
2 toadstool.

setecientos/setecientas
number seven hundred;
setecientos ochenta seven hundred
and eighty.

setenta *number* seventy; **tiene
setenta años** he's seventy (years
old); **setenta y dos** seventy-two; **los
años setenta** the seventies.

seto *noun* M hedge.

severo/severa *adjective* severe.

sexo *noun* M sex.

sexto/sexta *adjective* sixth; **el
sexto piso** the sixth floor.

sexual *adjective* sexual.

si *conjunction* **1** if; **si yo estuviera
en tu lugar** if I were you; **si lo
hubiese sabido** … if I had known …;
si tuviese dinero, lo compraría if I
had the money I would buy it;
2 whether; **no sé si podré** I don't
know whether I'll be able to; **tanto si
quiere como si no** whether he wants
to or not.

sí *adverb* yes; **sí, es cierto** yes, it's
true; **'¿lo vas a comprar?' – 'sí'** 'are
you going to buy it?' ' – 'yes I am'; **'¿es
suyo?' – 'creo que sí'** 'is it hers? ' –
'I think so'; **ellos no lo saben, pero
yo sí** they don't know, but I do.
pronoun **1** himself/herself; **pensó
para sí** he thought to himself/she
thought to herself; **2** (*polite form*)
yourself; (*polite form*) yourselves;
3 itself; **este problema es, en sí
mismo** … this problem is, in
itself …; **4** themselves; **los dos**
hermanos lo quieren todo para sí
both brothers want everything for
themselves; **5 sí mismo** himself; **sí
misma** herself; **quiere hacerlo por sí
mismo** he wants to do it by himself;
quiere hacerlo por sí misma she
wants to do it by herself; **6 sí mismo/
sí misma** yourself (*polite form*); **sí
mismos/sí mismas** yourselves
(*polite form*); **7 sí mismo** oneself;
reírse de sí mismo to laugh at
oneself; **8 entre sí** between
themselves.

Sicilia *noun* F Sicily.

sida *noun* M Aids.

sidra *noun* F cider.

siempre *adverb* **1** always; **casi
siempre** almost always; **desde
siempre** always; **2 para siempre** for
good; **¿te vas a quedar allí para
siempre?** are you going to stay there
for good?; **3 como siempre** as usual;
la historia de siempre the usual
story; **4 siempre que** whenever;
siempre que puedo whenever I can.

sienta, siento, etc. *verb* SEE
sentar, sentir.

sierra *noun* F **1** saw; **2** range of
mountains; **veranean en la sierra**
they spend their summer holidays in
the mountains.

siesta *noun* F nap; **echarse una
siesta** (*informal*) to have a nap; **está
durmiendo la siesta** he's having a
nap.

siete *number* **1** seven; **tiene siete
años** she's seven (years old);
2 seventh (*in dates*); **hoy es siete de**

abril it's the seventh of April today; **3** seven (*in clock time*); **son las siete** it's seven o'clock.

siga, sigan, etc. *verb* SEE **seguir**.

siglo *noun* M century; **el siglo XIII** the 13th century (*centuries are always indicated in roman numbers in Spanish*); **hace un siglo que no nos vemos** (*informal*) we haven't seen each other for ages.

significado *noun* M meaning.

significar *verb* [31] to mean; **¿qué significa esta palabra?** what does this word mean?; **eso no significa nada para él** that doesn't mean anything to him.

signo *noun* M **1** sign; **signo del zodiaco** star sign; **¿de qué signo eres?** what sign are you?; **2** mark; **signo de exclamación** exclamation mark; **signo de interrogación** question mark.

sigo, sigue, etc. *verb* SEE **seguir**.

siguiente *noun* M/F **el siguiente, por favor** next, please. *adjective* next, following; **al día siguiente ...** the next day ...

siguió *verb* SEE **seguir**.

sílaba *noun* F syllable.

silbar *verb* [17] to whistle.

silbato *noun* M whistle; **tocar el silbato** to blow the whistle.

silbido *noun* M whistle; **dar un silbido** to whistle.

silencio *noun* M silence.

silenciosamente *adverb* quietly.

silencioso/silenciosa *adjective* quiet.

silla *noun* F chair; **silla de montar** saddle (*for a horse*); **una silla de ruedas** a wheelchair.

sillín *noun* M saddle (*on a bicycle*).

sillón *noun* M armchair.

símbolo *noun* M symbol.

similar *adjective* similar; **similar a** similar to.

similitud *noun* F similarity.

simpático/simpática *adjective* nice; **me cae simpático** I think he's really nice.

simple *adjective* **1** simple; **2** mere; **una simple formalidad** a mere formality.

simplemente *adverb* simply.

simular *verb* [17] **1** to feign; **2** to fake.

simultáneo/simultánea *adjective* simultaneous.

sin *preposition* **1** without; **sin esfuerzo** without effort; **lo hice sin pensar** I did it without thinking; **2 agua mineral sin gas** still mineral water; **cerveza sin alcohol** non-alcoholic beer; **3 está sin revisar** it hasn't been checked yet; **terminó sin amigos** he ended up with no friends; **nos quedamos sin dinero** we've run out of money; **estamos sin azúcar** we're out of sugar; **4 sin querer**

unintentionally; **5 sin embargo** nevertheless.

sinagoga *noun* F synagogue.

sinceridad *noun* F sincerity.

sincero/sincera *adjective* sincere.

sindicalista *noun* M/F trade unionist.

sindicato *noun* M trade union.

singular *noun* M singular; **en singular** in the singular.

siniestro[1] *noun* M **1** accident; **2** disaster.

siniestro[2]**/siniestra** *adjective* sinister.

sino *conjunction* but; **no verde, sino amarillo** not green but yellow.

sinónimo *noun* M synonym. *adjective* synonymous.

sintético/sintética *adjective* synthetic.

sintieron, sintió, etc. *verb* SEE **sentir**.

síntoma *noun* M symptom.

sintonizar *verb* [22] to tune in.

sinvergüenza *noun* M/F **1** swine; **2** crook; **3** rascal.

siquiera *adverb* **1** at least; **dales siquiera un poco de dinero** give them at least a bit of money; **2 ni siquiera** not even; **ni siquiera me di cuenta** I didn't even realise.

sirena *noun* F **1** mermaid; **2** siren.

sistema *noun* M system.

sitio *noun* M **1** place; **ponlo otra vez en su sitio** put it back in its place; **2** room; **no tengo sitio en la maleta** I haven't got any room in my suitcase; **hay sitio para uno más en el coche** there's room for one more in the car; **hacer sitio** to make room; **3** seat; **hay un sitio al lado de la ventana** there's a seat by the window; **4 en cualquier sitio** anywhere; **en algún sitio** somewhere; **en ningún sitio** nowhere; **en otro sitio** somewhere else.

situación *noun* F **1** situation; **2** position; **la situación de la casa es buena** the house is in a good position.

situado/situada *adjective* situated.

situar *verb* [20] **1** to site (*a building*); **2** to set (*a plot in a novel*).
situarse *reflexive verb* [20] **1** to be situated; **2 situarse en primer puesto** to reach the first position; **3 situarse bien en la vida** to do very well for yourself.

smoking *noun* M dinner jacket.

sobra *in phrase* **1 de sobra** to spare; **tenemos pan de sobra** we have plenty of bread; **hay una silla de sobra** there's a spare chair; **2 saber algo de sobra** to know something full well; **3 aquí estás de sobra** you're not wanted here; **como estaba de sobra me fui** I wasn't needed, so I left.

sobrar *verb* [17] **1 nos ha sobrado vino** we had a lot of wine left over; **¿te sobró algo de papel?** did you have any paper left over?; **va a sobrar dinero** there will be money left over; **2 le sobraba una entrada** he had a spare ticket; **3 aquí sobra dinero** there is too much money here; **sobran tres sillas** there are three chairs too many; **4 nos sobraba un sitio** we'd got an extra place; **5 nos sobra tiempo** we have plenty of time.

sobras *plural noun* F leftovers.

sobre *noun* M envelope.
preposition **1** on; **lo dejó sobre la cama** he left it on the bed; **2** above; **la lámpara que está sobre el sofá** the lamp above the sofa; **sobre el nivel del mar** above sea level; **3** over; **el puente sobre el río** the bridge over the river; **4** about; **una conferencia sobre literatura** a lecture about literature; **5 sobre todo** especially.

sobrenatural *adjective* supernatural.

sobrepasar *verb* [17] to exceed.

sobresaliente *noun* M mark between 8.5 and 10 (out of 10).

sobresalir *verb* [63] **1 sobresalir en algo** to excel in something; **2** to overhang; **3** to protrude.

sobresalto *noun* M fright; **llevarse un sobresalto** to get a fright.

sobreviviente *noun* M/F survivor.

sobrevivir *verb* [19] to survive; **sobrevivir a algo** to survive something.

sobrina *noun* F niece.

sobrino *noun* M nephew; **sobrinos** nephews; nephews and nieces.

sociable *adjective* sociable.

social *adjective* social.

socialista *noun* M/F *adjective* socialist.

sociedad *noun* F **1** society; **la sociedad de consumo** the consumer society; **2 sociedad anónima** public limited company.

socio/socia *noun* M/F member; **hacerse socio de algo** to join something.

socorrer *verb* [18] to help.

socorro *noun* M help; **pedir socorro** to ask for help.
exclamation **¡socorro!** help!

sofá *noun* M sofa.

sofocar *verb* [31] to put out (*a fire*).
sofocarse *reflexive verb* [31] to get worked up.

sois *verb* SEE **ser**.

soja *noun* F soya.

sol *noun* M sun; **hacía sol** it was sunny; **un día de sol** a sunny day; **al ponerse el sol** at sunset; **el sol estaba saliendo** the sun was rising; **sentarse al sol** to lie in the sun.

solamente *adverb* only.

soldado *noun* M/F soldier.

soleado/soleada *adjective* sunny.

soler *verb* [38] **1** **suele salir por las noches** he usually goes out in the evenings; **suelen verse** they usually see each other; **no suele importarle** he usually doesn't mind; **2** **solía escribirme de vez en cuando** she used to write to me from time to time.

sólido/sólida *adjective* **1** solid; **2** sound.

solitario/solitaria *adjective* lonely.

solo/sola *adjective* **1** alone; **vive solo** he lives alone; **cuando me quedé solo** when I was left alone; **2** lonely; **está muy sola** she's very lonely; **sentirse solo** to feel lonely; **3** on your own; **desde que murió su madre está sola** she's on her own since her mother died; **4** by yourself; **lo hice sola** I did it by myself; **5** **con una sola mano** with one hand; **sin una sola queja** without a single complaint; **6** **un café solo** a black coffee; **una ginebra sola** a straight gin.

sólo *adverb* only.

solomillo *noun* M fillet steak.

soltar *verb* [24] **1** to let go of; **le solté la mano** I let go of his hand; **¡suéltame!** let go of me!; **2** to release (*a prisoner*); **3** to untie; **soltar un nudo** to untie a knot; **4** **soltar al perro** to let the dog off the lead; **5** **soltar un grito** to let out a cry;

soltar una carcajada to let out a laugh; **soltar una palabrota** to come out with a swearword.

soltarse *reflexive verb* [24] **1** **no te sueltes de la barandilla** don't let go of the banister; **se soltó de mi mano** he let go of my hand; **2** **soltarse el pelo** to let your hair down; **3** to come undone (*a knot*).

soltero/soltera *noun* M/F single person.
adjective single.

soltura *noun* F **hablar español con soltura** to speak Spanish fluently; **moverse con soltura** to move with ease.

soluble *adjective* soluble.

solución *noun* F solution.

solucionar *verb* [17] **1** to solve; **2** to settle (*a conflict*).

sombra *noun* F **1** shadow; **2** shade; **sentarse en la sombra** to sit in the shade; **dar sombra** to give shade; **3** **sombra de ojos** eye shadow.

sombrero *noun* M hat.

sombrilla *noun* F **1** parasol; **2** sunshade.

sombrío/sombría *adjective* **1** dark (*street or room*); **2** gloomy (*face or look*).

somos, son *verb* SEE **ser**.

sonar *verb* [24] **1** to sound; **suena a hueco** it sounds hollow; **sonó un ruido** there was a noise; **2** to ring (*a doorbell or telephone*); **3** **el despertador no ha sonado** the alarm clock hasn't gone off; **4** **me**

suena mucho su cara her face is very familiar to me; **¿Carlos Ramírez? no me suena** Carlos Ramírez? it doesn't ring any bells.

sonarse *reflexive verb* [24] **sonarse la nariz** to blow one's nose.

sondeo *noun* M survey.

sonido *noun* M sound.

sonreír *verb* [61] to smile; **me sonrió** he smiled at me.

sonreírse *reflexive verb* [61] to smile.

sonría, sonríe, sonrío, etc. *verb* SEE **sonreír**.

sonrisa *noun* F smile.

sonrojarse *verb* [17] to blush.

soñar *verb* [24] to dream.

sopa *noun* F soup.

soplar *verb* [17] **1** to blow; **2** to blow off; **soplar el polvo de la mesa** to blow the dust off the table; **3 soplarle la respuesta a alguien** (*informal*) to whisper the answer to someone (*in an exam*).

soportar *verb* [17] **1** to put up with (*situation*); **2** to bear (*pain or heat*); **3 no puedo soportar a Rafael** I can't stand Rafael; **4** withstand.

soporte *noun* M support.

sorbete *noun* M sorbet.

sorbo *noun* M **1** sip; **beber a sorbos** to sip; **2** gulp; **beberse algo de un sorbo** to drink something in one gulp.

sordo/sorda *noun* M/F deaf person.
adjective deaf.

sordomudo/sordomuda *noun* M/F deaf mute.
adjective deaf and dumb.

sorprendente *adjective* surprising.

sorprender *verb* [18] to surprise; **me sorprende que se retrase** I'm surprised he's late.

sorprenderse *reflexive verb* [18] to be surprised.

sorprendido/sorprendida *adjective* surprised.

sorpresa *noun* F surprise.

sospecha *noun* F suspicion; **tengo la sospecha de que …** I have a feeling that …

sospechar *verb* [17] to suspect.

sospechoso/sospechosa *adjective* suspicious; **me parece sospechoso** I find it suspicious.

sostén *noun* M **1** support; **2** bra.

sostener *verb* [9] **1** to support (*arch, ceiling, or family*); **2** to bear (*a weight or load*).

sótano *noun* M **1** basement; **2** cellar.

soy *verb* SEE **ser**.

Sr. *abbreviation* (*short for: Señor*) Mr.

Sra. *abbreviation* (*short for: Señora*) Mrs; Ms.

Sres. *abbreviation* (*short for: Señores*) Messrs.

Srta. *abbreviation* (*short for: Señorita*) Miss; Ms.

su *adjective* **1** his/her; **¿es su falda como ésta?** is her skirt like this one?; **ahí está Carlos con sus padres** there's Carlos with his parents; **2** its; **el perro duerme en su caseta** the dog sleeps in its kennel; **3** their; **mis padres viven allí y éste es su coche** my parents live there and that's their car; **4** your (*polite form*); **¿son éstos sus zapatos?** are these your shoes?

suave *adjective* **1** soft; **2** smooth; **3** gentle (*voice*); **4** mild (*weather*).

suavizante *noun* M **1** fabric softener; **2** hair conditioner.

subestimar *verb* [17] understimate.

subida *noun* F **1** rise (*in temperature or price, for example*); **2** climb.

subir *verb* [19] **1** to go up; **el ascensor está subiendo** the lift is going up; **subir al tercer piso** to go up to the third floor; **la temperatura ha subido tres grados** the temperature has gone up three degrees; **2** to come up; **¡sube!** come up!; **3** to bring up; **sube estas cajas al segundo piso** bring these boxes up to the third floor; **súbeme un vaso de agua** bring a glass of water up for me; **4** to take up; **¿le subo las maletas a su habitación?** shall I take the luggage up to your room?; **5** to put up; **han vuelto a subir el precio de la gasolina** they've put up the price of petrol again; **6** subir al tren to get on the train; **subir a un coche** to get into a car; **subir a bordo** to board; **7** to turn up (*volume*); **subió un poco la música** he turned up the music a bit; **8** to raise; **el nivel del agua ha subido** the level of water has risen; **subir una persiana** to raise a blind; **9** to come in (*the tide*).

subirse *reflexive verb* [19] **1** subirse **al tren** to get on the train; **subirse a un coche** to get into a car; **subirse a bordo** to board; **2** subirse a un **árbol** to climb up a tree; **3** subirse **los calcetines** to pull up your socks.

súbitamente *adverb* suddenly.

súbito/súbita *adjective* sudden.

subjuntivo *noun* M subjunctive.

submarino *noun* M submarine.

subrayar *verb* [17] to underline.

subsidio *noun* M **1** subsidy; **2** subsidio de desempleo unemployment benefit; **subsidio de invalidez** disability allowance.

subterráneo[1] *noun* M subway.

subterráneo[2]/**subterránea** *adjective* underground.

suburbio *noun* M **1** slum area (*on the outskirts of a town*); **2** suburb.

subvención *noun* F subsidy.

subvencionar *verb* [17] to subsidize.

suceder *verb* [18] **1** to happen; **¿qué le ha sucedido?** what's happened to him?; **sucedió todo muy rápido** it all happened very quickly; **2** to succeed (*to the throne*).

suceso *noun* M **1** event; **2** incident; **'página de sucesos'** 'accidents and crimes report' (*in a newspaper*).

suciedad *noun* F **1** dirt;
2 dirtiness.

sucio/sucia *adjective* **1** dirty;
tienes la cara sucia your face is
dirty; **2 primero hice el trabajo en
sucio** I did the essay in rough first.

sucursal *noun* F **1** branch (*of a
bank*); **2** office (*of a company*).

sudadera *noun* F sweatshirt.

Sudamérica *noun* F South
America.

sudamericano/sudamericana
noun M/F *adjective* South
American.

sudar *verb* [17] to sweat.

sudeste *noun* M southeast.

sudoeste *noun* M southwest.

sudor *noun* M sweat.

Suecia *noun* F Sweden.

sueco¹ *noun* M Swedish (*the
language*).

sueco²/sueca *noun* M/F Swede.
adjective Swedish.

suegra *noun* F mother-in-law.

suegro *noun* M **1** father-in-law;
2 mis suegros my parents in law.

suela¹, suelas, etc. *verb* SEE
soler.

suela² *noun* F sole.

sueldo *noun* M **1** salary; **2** wage;
3 aumento de sueldo pay rise.

suelo¹ *noun* M **1** floor; **2** ground;
tirarse al suelo to throw yourself to
the ground.

suelo² *verb* SEE **soler**.

suelta¹, suelte, suelto¹, etc.
verb SEE **soltar**.

suelto² *noun* M small change;
¿tienes suelto? do you have any
small change?

suelto³/suelta² *adjective* **1** loose;
el tornillo está suelto the screw is
loose; **2 dinero suelto** small change.

suena, suene, sueno, etc. *verb*
SEE **sonar**.

sueña, sueñe, sueño¹, etc. *verb*
SEE **soñar**.

sueño² *noun* M **1** dream; **2 tener
sueño** to be sleepy; **tener el sueño
ligero** to be a light sleeper.

suerte *noun* F luck; **tener suerte** to
be lucky; **traer mala suerte** to bring
bad luck; **¡qué mala suerte !** how
unlucky!

suéter *noun* M sweater.

suficiente *noun* M pass (*equivalent
to 5 out of 10*).
adjective enough.

sufrir *verb* [19] **1** to suffer; **sufre
mucho** he's suffering a lot; **2** to have;
sufrir un accidente to have an
accident; **sufre una grave
enfermedad** he has a serious illness.

sugerencia *noun* F suggestion.

sugerir *verb* [14] to suggest.

sugestión *noun* F suggestion.

**sugiera, sugiero, sugirieron,
etc.** *verb* SEE **sugerir**.

suicidarse *reflexive verb* [17] to commit suicide.

suicidio *noun* M suicide.

Suiza *noun* F Switzerland.

suizo/suiza *noun* M/F *adjective* Swiss.

sujetador *noun* M bra.

sujeto/sujeta *adjective* 1 secure; **está bien sujeto** it's really secure; 2 **tener sujeto a** to have hold of; 3 **estar sujeto a algo** to be subject to something.

suma *noun* F 1 addition; 2 **en suma** in short.

sumar *verb* [17] to add.

supe, supiste, etc. *verb* SEE **saber**.

super, súper *adjective* (*informal*) super.
adverb (*informal*) really; **cantan super bien** they sing really well; **me lo pasé super bien** I had a great time.

superar *verb* [17] 1 to overcome (*fear or a problem*); 2 to get over (*a shock*); 3 to exceed.

superficie *noun* F surface.

superior *adjective* 1 superior; **es superior a los demás en calidad** it's better quality than all the others; 2 top (*floor or layer*); 3 upper (*lip*); 4 higher (*level or class*).

supermercado *noun* M supermarket.

superstición *noun* F superstition.

supersticioso/supersticiosa *adjective* superstitious.

supervisar *verb* [17] supervise.

superviviente *noun* M/F survivor.

suplementario/suplementaria *adjective* additional.

suplemento *noun* M supplement.

supondrá, supondré, supondría, etc. *verb* SEE **suponer**.

suponer *verb* [11] to suppose; **supongo que sí** I suppose so.

suponga, supongo, etc. *verb* SEE **suponer**.

supositorio *noun* M suppository.

suprimir *verb* [19] 1 to suppress (*news*); 2 to abolish; 3 to delete.

supuesto *in phrase* **por supuesto** of course.

supuse, supuso *verb* SEE **suponer**.

sur *noun* M south.

Suramérica *noun* F South America.

suramericano/suramericana *noun* M/F *adjective* South American.

sureste *noun* M southest.

suroeste *noun* M southwest.

surtido[1] *noun* M 1 assortment; 2 selection.

surtido²/surtida *adjective*
1 assorted; 2 **una tienda bien
surtida** a well-stocked shop.

surtidor *noun* M petrol pump.

suspender *verb* [18] 1 to fail; **he
suspendido la física** I've failed
physics; 2 to suspend (*a payment or
service*); 3 **suspender un viaje** to call
off a trip.

suspense *noun* M suspense;
película de suspense thriller
(*film*).

suspenso *noun* M fail; **sacar un
suspenso en un examen** to fail an
exam.

suspirar *verb* [17] to sigh.

suspiro *noun* M sigh.

sustancia *noun* F substance.

sustantivo *noun* M noun.

sustituir *verb* [54] 1 to replace;
sustituir algo por algo to replace
something with something;
2 **sustituir a alguien** to stand in for
someone (*at work*); to come on as a
substitute for someone (*in football,
for example*).

sustituto/sustituta *noun* M/F
1 replacement; 2 substitute;
3 locum.

susto *noun* M fright; **darle un susto
a alguien** to give someone a fright;
¡qué susto me llevé! I got such a
fright!

sustraer *verb* [42] to subtract.

susurrar *verb* [17] to whisper.

sutil *adjective* subtle.

suyo/suya *adjective* 1 his/hers
(*goes after the noun*); **un conocido
suyo** a friend of his/hers; 2 theirs;
venían con un amigo suyo they
came with a friend of theirs; 3 yours
(*polite form*).
pronoun 1 his/hers; **el suyo es gris**
his/hers is grey; **las suyas son
mejores** his/hers are better; 2 yours
(*polite form*); 3 theirs; **no es el de
mis hijos, el suyo es más grande** it's
not my children's, theirs is bigger.

T t

tabaco *noun* M 1 tobacco;
2 cigarettes; **tengo que comprar
tabaco** I've got to buy some
cigarettes.

taberna *noun* F bar (*selling wine*).

tabla *noun* F 1 plank; 2 board; **una
tabla de planchar** an ironing board;
una tabla de picar a chopping
board; 3 **tabla de multiplicar**
multiplication table; 4 **tabla de
gimnasia** circuit training; 5 pleat.

tablao *noun* M **un tablao flamenco**
a flamenco bar.

tablero *noun* M 1 board (*for a
game*); **un tablero de damas** a
draughtboard; 2 noticeboard.

tablón *noun* M **1** plank; **2 tablón de anuncios** noticeboard.

taburete *noun* M stool.

tacaño/tacaña *noun* M/F miser. *adjective* stingy.

tachar *verb* [17] to cross out.

taco *noun* M **1** cue (*in billards*); **2** stud (*on a sports boot*); **3** (*informal*) swearword.

tacón *noun* M heel; **zapatos de tacón alto** high-heeled shoes; **tacón de aguja** stiletto heel.

tacto *noun* M **1** sense of touch; **2** feel; **3** tact; **fue una falta de tacto** it was really tactless.

tal *adjective* **1** such; **tal cosa es imposible** such a thing is impossible; **2 tenía tal preocupación que ...** I was so worried that ...; **había tal cantidad de cajas que ...** there were so many boxes that ...; **3 en tal caso** in that case.
adverb **1 ¿qué tal estás?** (*informal*) how are you doing?; **¿qué tal van las cosas?** (*informal*) how are things?; **2 tal vez** maybe; **3 con tal de que** as long as; ★ **son tal para cual** one is as bad as the other.

talco *noun* M talc; **polvos de talco** talcum powder.

talento *noun* M talent.

TALGO *abbreviation* M (*short for: Tren Articulado Ligero Goicoechea Oriol*) express train.

talla *noun* F size; **¿qué talla de pantalones tienes?** what size of trousers are you?

taller *noun* M **1** workshop; **2** garage; **llevar el coche al taller** to take the car to the garage.

talón *noun* M heel.

talonario *noun* M chequebook.

tamaño *noun* M size; **hay de todos los tamaños** they come in all sizes.

también *adverb* too; **ella también vive allí** she lives there too; **'tengo quince años' – 'yo también'** I'm fifteen' – 'so am I'; **'yo quiero tarta' – 'yo también'** 'I want some cake' - 'so do I'.

tambor *noun* M drum.

tampoco *adverb* **él tampoco irá** he won't go either; **'a mí no me gusta' – 'a mí tampoco'** 'I don't like it' – 'neither do I'.

tampón *noun* M tampon.

tan *adverb* **1** so; **no es tan fácil** it's not so easy; **2** such; **es una persona tan egoísta** he's such a selfish person; **3** (*in comparisons*) **es tan alto como su padre** he's as tall as his father; **no era tan caro como el otro** it wasn't as expensive as the other one; **4 ¡qué casa tan grande!** what a big house!

tanque *noun* M tank.

tanto¹ *noun* M **1 tanto por ciento** percentage; **gano un tanto por ciento de las ventas** I get a percentage on the sales; **2** point;

goal; **marcar un tanto** to score a point; to score a goal.

tanto² *adverb* **1** so; **tanto mejor** so much the better; **no corras tanto** don't go so fast; **se enfadó tanto** he got so upset; **2** so much; **no deberías gastar tanto** you shouldn't spend so much; **3** so often; **yo no les visito tanto** I don't visit them all that often; **4** so long; **lleva tanto hacerlo** it takes so long to do; **5 pesa tanto como éste** it's as heavy as this one.

tanto³/tanta *adjective* **1** so much; **tanto dinero** so much money; **tanta sal** so much salt; **2** so many; **tantos libros** so many books; **tantas cajas** so many boxes; **había tanta gente que no cabíamos** there were so many people that there wasn't room for us; **3 tanto/tanta … como …** as much … as …; **no gasta tanta gasolina como el coche viejo** it doesn't use as much petrol as the old car; **4 tantos/tantas … como …** as many … as …; **no hay tantos alumnos como antes** there aren't as many students as before.
pronoun **1** tanto/tanta so much; **no hace falta tanto/tanta** we don't need so much; **2 tantos/tantas** so many; **vinieron tantos que no había sillas libres** so many came that there weren't any chairs left; **3 tanto** (*referring to time*) so long; **no tardes tanto como ayer** don't take as long as yesterday; **'me llevará dos días hacerlo' – '¿tanto?'** 'it'll take me two days to do it' – 'as long as that?'; **4 por lo tanto** therefore; **5 mientras tanto** in the meantime; **entre tanto** in the meantime.

tapa *noun* F **1** lid; **2** top; **tapa de rosca** screw top; **3** tapa (*a small snack chosen from a selection in a tapas bar*); **un bar de tapas** a tapas bar; **comer de tapas** to eat tapas for lunch.

tapar *verb* [17] **1** to cover; **2** to put the top on; **3 tapar un agujero** to fill a hole; **4** to block (*a road or door*).

tapón *noun* M **1** cork; **2** top (*of a bottle*); **3** plug (*of a sink or bath*).

taquilla *noun* F **1** box office; **éxito de taquilla** box office hit; **2** ticket office.

tardar *verb* [17] to take a long time; **tardó mucho en contestarme** she took a long time to answer; **¿cuánto se tarda de Sevilla a Córdoba?** how long does it take from Seville to Cordoba?; **¡no tardes!** don't be long!; **no tardes en volver** come back soon.

tarde *noun* F afternoon, evening; **buenas tardes** good afternoon; good evening; **por la tarde** in the afternoon, in the evening.
adverb late; **llegar tarde** to be late; **se hizo tarde** it got late; **tarde o temprano** sooner or later.

tarea *noun* F **1** task; **2 las tareas de la casa** the housework; **3** homework.

tarifa *noun* F **1** price list; **2 tarifa telefónica** telephone charges.

tarjeta *noun* F card; **una tarjeta (postal)** a postcard; **una tarjeta de crédito** a credit card; **una tarjeta telefónica** a telephone card; **una**

tarjeta de embarque a boarding card; **una tarjeta de cumpleaños** a birthday card; **una tarjeta de Navidad** a Christmas card.

tarta *noun* F cake; **una tarta de cumpleaños** a birthday cake.

tasa *noun* F 1 rate; **la tasa de interés** the interest rate; **la tasa de desempleo** the level of unemployment; 2 valuation; 3 tax.

tatuaje *noun* M tatoo.

Tauro *noun* M Taurus.

tauro *noun* M/F taurus; **es tauro** he's Taurus.

taxi *noun* M taxi.

taxista *noun* M/F taxi driver.

taza *noun* F 1 cup; **una taza de café** a coffee cup; a cup of coffee; 2 (toilet) bowl.

tazón *noun* M bowl.

te *pronoun* 1 you; **te quiero** I love you; **te vi ayer** I saw you yesterday; 2 to you; **te lo mandaré por correo** I'll post it to you; 3 (*with parts of the body and personal belongings*) **¿te has cortado el dedo?** have you cut your finger?; **¿quieres quitarte los zapatos?** do you want to take your shoes off?; 4 (*having things done*) **¿te has cortado el pelo?** have you had your hair cut?; 5 yourself; **cuídate mucho** look after yourself; 6 **siéntate** sit down.

té *noun* M tea; **voy a tomar un té** I'm going to have a cup of tea.

teatro *noun* M theatre.

tebeo *noun* M comic (*for children*).

techo *noun* M 1 ceiling; 2 **techo corredizo/solar** sunroof; 3 **sin techo** homeless.

tecla *noun* F key.

teclado *noun* M keyboard.

técnica[1] *noun* F technique.

técnico/técnica[2] *noun* M/F technician.
adjective technical.

tecnología *noun* F technology.

teja *noun* F tile.

tejado *noun* M roof.

tejanos *plural noun* M jeans.

tejer *verb* [18] 1 to weave; 2 to knit.

tela *noun* F 1 fabric; **tela de algodón** cotton fabric; 2 canvas (*for painting*).

telaraña *noun* F spider's web; cobweb.

tele *noun* F (*informal*) telly, TV; **ver la tele** to watch telly; **poner la tele** to switch on the telly.

telediario *noun* M television news.

telefonear *verb* [17] to telephone.

telefónico/telefónica *adjective* telephone; **conversación telefónica** telephone conversation; **listín telefónico** telephone book.

teléfono *noun* M telephone; **llamar por teléfono a alguien** to phone somebody; **no tengo teléfono** I'm not on the phone (*I don't have a* *phone*); **contestar el teléfono** to answer the phone; **colgar el teléfono** to put down the phone; **estaba hablando por teléfono** I was on the phone; **no has colgado bien el teléfono** you've left the phone off the hook; **teléfono celular/móvil** mobile phone.

telegrama *noun* M telegram.

telenovela *noun* F TV series.

telescopio *noun* M telescope.

televisión *noun* F television; **ver la televisión** to watch television; **poner la televisión** to switch on the television; **hoy ponen una película en la televisión** they're showing a film on television today.

televisor *noun* M television set.

tema *noun* M **1** subject; **2** topic.

temblar *verb* [29] **1** to shiver; **2** to shake; **le temblaban las manos** his hands were shaking.

temer *verb* [18] **1** to fear (*danger or punishment*); **2 temer a alguien** to be afraid of somebody.

temerse *reflexive verb* [18] **1** to fear; **2 me temo que no podré acudir** I'm afraid I won't be able to come.

temperatura *noun* F temperature; **ha bajado la temperatura** the temperature has dropped.

tempestad *noun* F storm.

templado/templada *adjective* **1** mild (*climate*); **2** warm; **3** lukewarm.

temporada *noun* F season; **fuera de temporada** out of season.

temprano¹ *adverb* early; **llegar temprano** to arrive early.

temprano²/temprana *adjective* early.

tendencia *noun* F tendency.

tender *verb* [36] **1 tender a** to tend to; **tienden a molestarse** they tend to get upset; **2 tender la ropa** to hang out the washing.

tenderse *reflexive verb* [36] to lie down; **tenderse al sol** to lie down in the sun.

tendero/tendera *noun* M/F shopkeeper.

tenedor *noun* M fork.

tendrá, tendré, tendría, etc. *verb* SEE **tener**.

tener *verb* [9] **1** to have; **tengo dos hermanas** I've got two sisters; **tiene los ojos marrones** he's got brown eyes; **tener dolor de cabeza** to have a headache; **no tengo tiempo** I haven't got the time; **¿tienes hora?** have you got the time?; **ha tenido un niño** she's had a baby; **2 tener sed** to be thirsty; **tener frío** to be cold; **¡qué calor tengo !** I'm really hot!; **ten cuidado** be careful; **3 tener sueño** to feel sleepy; **tener envidia de alguien** to feel jealous of somebody; **4 tener que hacer** to have to do; **no puedo, tengo que estudiar** I can't, I have to work; **tienes que obedecerme** you must do as I tell you; **tengo que irla a ver un día** I must go and see her one day;

tendrían que ayudarme they would have to help me; **tendría que ir al banco** I should go to the bank; **5 tiene que haberse perdido** he must have got lost; **6 lo tengo hecho** I've done it; **lo tienen solucionado** they've sorted it out; **tenía pensado invitarlos** I'd thought about inviting them.

tenga, tengo, etc. *verb* SEE **tener**.

tenis *noun* M tennis; **tenis de mesa** table tennis.

tenista *noun* M/F tennis player.

tensión *noun* F 1 tension; 2 stress; 3 blood pressure; **tomarse la tensión** to have your blood pressure taken.

tentación *noun* F temptation.

tentar *verb* [29] to tempt.

teñir *verb* [65] to dye.
teñirse *reflexive verb* [65] to dye; **teñirse el pelo** to have your hair dyed.

tercer *adjective* third (*see also* '*tercero/tercera*').

tercero/tercera *adjective* (*note that 'tercero' becomes 'tercer' before a masculine singular noun*) third; **la tercera puerta a la derecha** the third door on the right; **el tercer piso** the third floor; **llegar en tercer lugar** to finish in third position; **el Tercer Mundo** the Third World.

terminado/terminada *adjective* finished.

terminal *noun* F 1 terminal; 2 bus station.
adjective terminal.

terminar *verb* [17] 1 to finish; **¿cuándo termina el colegio?** when does school finish; **aún no he terminado** I haven't finished yet; **no he terminado de revisarlo** I haven't finished checking it; 2 **terminar con** to finish with; **¿has terminado con el libro?** have you finished with the book?; **ha terminado con su novio** she's broken up with her boyfriend; 3 to end up; **terminamos en una discoteca** we ended up in a disco; **terminó harta** she was fed up in the end; **terminaron por pelearse** they ended up having a fight; 4 to end in; **su nombre termina en 'l'** her name ends in 'l'; **termina en punta** it's pointed; **termina en una cruz** it's got a cross at the end.

terminarse *reflexive verb* [17] 1 to be over; **la clase se terminó a las cinco** the lesson was over at five; 2 **se ha terminado la leche** we've run out of milk; **se me terminó la tinta del boli** my pen ran out (of ink).

termo™ *noun* M Thermos™.

termómetro *noun* M thermometer.

ternera¹ *noun* F veal.

ternero/ternera² *noun* M/F calf.

terraza *noun* F 1 balcony; 2 terrace (*of a café or bar*).

terremoto *noun* M earthquake.

terreno *noun* M 1 plot of land; 2 field; 3 land; **la casa tiene mucho terreno** the house has a lot of land; 4 **terreno de juego** football pitch.

terrible *adjective* terrible.

territorio *noun* M territory.

terror *noun* M terror.

terrorismo *noun* M terrorism.

terrorista *noun* M/F *adjective* terrorist.

tesoro *noun* M treasure.

test *noun* M **1** test; **2 examen tipo test** multiple-choice exam.

testamento *noun* M will; **hacer testamento** to make your will.

testigo *noun* M/F witness.

tétano *noun* M tetanus.

tetera *noun* F teapot.

texto *noun* M text.

ti *pronoun* **1** you; **detrás de ti** behind you; **se olvidaron de ti** they forgot about you; **a mí no me dijo nada, ¿y a ti?** he hasn't told me anything – has he told you?; **2** to you; **te lo dio a ti** he gave it to you; **3 ¿a ti te gusta?** do you like it?; **¿a ti qué te parece?** what do you think?; **4 ti mismo/misma** yourself; **sabes cuidar de ti misma** you can look after yourself.

tía *noun* F aunt.

tibio/tibia *adjective* lukewarm.

tiburón *noun* M shark.

tiembla, tiemblo, etc. *verb* SEE **temblar**.

tiempo *noun* M **1** time; **llegar a tiempo** to be on time; **tiempo libre** spare time; **ha pasado mucho tiempo desde entonces** it's been a long time since then; **hace mucho tiempo que no la veo** I haven't seen her for a long time; **¿cuánto tiempo hace que se fueron?** how long ago did they go?; **al mismo tiempo** at the same time; **la mayor parte del tiempo** most of the time; **2 ¿cada cuánto tiempo?** how often?; **cada cierto tiempo** every so often; **3 por un tiempo** for a while; **4 a su debido tiempo** in due course; **5 trabajar a tiempo completo** to work full time; **trabajar a tiempo parcial** to work part time; **6 en aquellos tiempos** in those days; **corren otros tiempos** things are different now; **7** weather; **el pronóstico del tiempo** the weather forecast; **nos hizo buen tiempo** we had nice weather; **8 el primer tiempo** the first half (*of a match*); **9** tense (*in grammar*).

tienda[1] *noun* F **1** shop; **una tienda de discos** a record shop; **una tienda de recuerdos** a souvenir shop; **una tienda de comestibles** a grocer's; **2 una tienda de campaña** a tent.

tienda[2]**, tiendo, etc.** *verb* SEE **tender**.

tierno/tierna *adjective* **1** tender (*meat*); **2** affectionate.

tierra *noun* F **1** land; **tierra adentro** inland; **viajar por tierra** to travel overland; **2** earth; **3** ground; **tierra firme** solid ground; **4 tomar tierra** to land.

tiesto *noun* M flowerpot.

tigre *noun* M tiger.

tijeras *plural noun* F scissors; **un par de tijeras/unas tijeras** a pair of scissors.

timbre *noun* M bell, doorbell; **tocar el timbre** to ring the bell.

tímido/tímida *adjective* shy.

tinta *noun* F ink.

tinto *noun* M red wine. *adjective* red (*wine*).

tintorería *noun* F dry cleaner's.

tiña, tiñeron, tiño, tiñó, etc. *verb* SEE **teñir**.

tío *noun* M **1** uncle; **2 mis tíos** my uncles, my aunt and uncle; **3** (*informal*) guy.

tiovivo *noun* M merry-go-round.

típico/típica *adjective* typical.

tipo *noun* M **1** type; **2** figure; physique; **tiene buen tipo** she's got a good figure; **3 tipo de cambio** exchange rate; **tipo de interés** interest rate.

tirar *verb* [17] **1** to throw; **tirar algo al suelo** to throw something on the floor; **2 tirarle algo a alguien** to throw something at somebody; **tírame ese boli** throw me that pen; **3** to throw away; **no tires esos papeles** don't throw those papers away; **tirar algo a la basura** to throw something out (*that you no longer want*); **4** to pull; **tira un poco más** pull a bit more; **5 tirar de algo** to pull something; **tira de la cuerda cuando yo te diga** pull the rope when I tell you; **6 tirarle de las orejas a alguien** to tweak somebody's ear (*in Spain you do this when you wish somebody happy birthday*); **7** to shoot; **tirar una flecha** to shoot an arrow; **tirar una bomba** to drop a bomb; **8** to knock over; **tiré una silla sin querer** I accidentally knocked a chair over; **9** to knock down; **tiraron la puerta abajo** they knocked the door down.

tirarse *reflexive verb* [17] **tirarse al suelo** to throw oneself to the ground; **tirarse al agua** to dive into the water; **tirarse en paracaídas** to parachute, to bale out.

tirita *noun* F sticking plaster.

tiritar *verb* [17] to shiver; **tiritar de frío** to shiver with cold.

tiro *noun* M **1** shot; **disparar un tiro** to fire a shot; **matar a alguien de un tiro** to shoot somebody dead; **tiro al blanco** target shooting; **2** shot (*in sport*); **un tiro a portería** a shot at goal; **un tiro libre** a free kick.

tirón *noun* M pull; **dar un tirón a algo** to pull something; ★ **de un tirón** (*informal*) in one go.

títere *noun* M **1** puppet; **2 títeres** puppet show.

título *noun* M **1** title; **2** heading; **3** degree; **título universitario** university degree; **4** certificate; **5 título nobiliario** title (*such as 'duke' or 'duchess'*).

tiza *noun* F chalk; **una tiza** a piece of chalk.

toalla *noun* F towel.

tobillo *noun* M ankle.

tobogán *noun* M slide.

tocador *noun* M dressing table.

tocar *verb* [31] **1** to touch; **me tocó el hombro** he touched me on the shoulder; **toqué la escultura** I touched the sculpture; **tocar un tema** to touch on a subject; **2 tocar el timbre** to ring the bell; **3 tocar la bocina** to blow the horn; **4** to play (*an instrument*); **tocar el violín** to play the violin; **5 tocarle a alguien hacer** to be somebody's turn to do; **te toca jugar** it's your turn to play; **6 les ha tocado un viaje** they've won a trip; **nunca me ha tocado la lotería** I've never won the lottery.

tocarse *reflexive verb* [31] to touch; **se tocó la cabeza** he touched his head; **los dos cables se están tocando** the two cables are touching.

tocino *noun* M bacon.

todavía *adverb* **1** still; **todavía nos vemos** we still see each other; **2** yet; **todavía no han llegado** they haven't arrived yet; **3** even; **todavía más tarde** even later.

todo¹/toda *adjective* **1** all; **todos mis amigos** all my friends; **viajar por todo el mundo** to travel all over the world; **2** whole; **toda la semana** the whole week; **se comieron toda la caja de bombones** they ate the whole box of chocolates; **3 todos los días** every day; **hay que revisar todas las carpetas** we have to check every folder; **4 a toda velocidad** at top speed.
pronoun **1** everything; **se lo conté todo** I told him everything; **a pesar de todo** despite everything; **2** all; **todo o nada** all or nothing; **vinieron todos** they all came; **todos estábamos de acuerdo** we were all in agreement; **3 ante todo** above all;

4 con todo even so; **5 de todo** everything; **tienen de todo** they've got everything; **6 sobre todo no te olvides del billete** above all, don't forget the ticket; **se divirtieron mucho, sobre todo Ana** they enjoyed themselves a lot, specially Ana.
adverb **1** all; **estaba todo nervioso** he was all nervous; **2** completely; **está todo roto** it's completely had it; **3 seguir todo derecho** to carry straight on.

todo² *noun* M **el todo** the whole.

tomar *verb* [17] **1** to take; **tomar el autobús** to take the bus; **me tomó del brazo** she took me by the arm; **2** to have; **tomar el desayuno** to have breakfast; **¿quieres tomar un café?** would you like a coffee?; **3 toma, tu billete** here's your ticket; **4 tomar el sol** to sunbathe; **5 tomar el aire** to get some fresh air; **6 tomar algo en serio** to take something seriously; **tomar algo a mal** to take something the wrong way; **tomarse algo mal/bien** to take something badly/well.

tomarse *reflexive verb* [17] **1** to take; **tomarse unas vacaciones** to take some holiday; **tomarse la molestia de hacer** to take the trouble to do; **2** to have; **se tomó un helado** she had an ice cream; **3 tomarse la tensión** to have your blood pressure taken; ★ **tomarle el pelo a alguien** (*informal*) to pull somebody's leg (*literally: to take somebody's hair*).

tomate *noun* M tomato; **salsa de tomate** tomato sauce; ★ **ponerse**

(colorado) **como un tomate** to go as red as a beetroot.

tonelada *noun* F ton.

tónica *noun* F tonic water.

tono *noun* M **1** tone; **en tono serio** in a serious tone; **2** shade; **telas de tonos suaves** materials in soft shades; **3 tono de marcar** dial tone; **tono de ocupado** engaged tone; ★ **fuera de tono** inappropriate (*a comment*).

tontería *noun* F **vaya tontería** how silly; **no te enfades por esa tontería** don't get upset over such a silly thing; **decir tonterías** to talk nonsense.

tonto/tonta *noun* M/F idiot; ★ **hacerse el tonto** (*informal*) to play the fool; ★ **hacer el tonto** (*informal*) to act dumb. *adjective* silly.

topo *noun* M mole (*animal*).

torbellino *noun* M whirlwind.

torcer *verb* [41] **1** to turn; **tuerce a la derecha al final de la calle** turn right at the end of the road; **torcer la esquina** to turn the corner; **torcer la cabeza** to turn your head; **2** to twist. **torcerse** *reflexive verb* [41] **1** to twist; **torcerse el tobillo** to twist your ankle; **2** to warp.

torcido/torcida *adjective* **1** twisted; **tiene el tobillo torcido** he's twisted his ankle; **2** crooked; **3** bent.

torero/torera *noun* M/F bullfighter.

tormenta *noun* F storm; **tormenta de nieve** snowstorm.

torneo *noun* M tournament.

tornillo *noun* M screw; ★ **le falta un tornillo** (*informal*) he's got a screw loose.

toro *noun* M **1** bull; **2 los toros** bullfighting; **ir a los toros** to go to a bullfight.

torpe *adjective* **1** clumsy; **2** awkward.

torre *noun* F tower.

torta *noun* F **1** cake; **2 darle una torta a alguien** to slap somebody; **3 me pegué una torta con la farola** I banged into the streetlamp (*on foot*); I crashed into the streetlamp (*in a car*); ★ **no entiendo ni torta** (*informal*) I don't understand a thing.

tortilla *noun* F omelette; **tortilla francesa** French omelette; **tortilla española** Spanish omelette, tortilla.

tortuga *noun* F **1** tortoise; **2** turtle.

torturar *verb* [17] to torture.

tos *noun* F cough; **tener tos** to have a cough; **le dio la tos** he started coughing.

toser *verb* [18] to cough.

tostada *noun* F **una tostada** a piece of toast; **tomo tostadas para desayunar** I have toast for breakfast.

tostador *noun* M toaster.

tostadora *noun* F toaster.

tostar *verb* [24] **1** to toast (*bread*);
2 to roast (*coffee*).
tostarse *reflexive verb* [24] to tan, to
go brown.

total *noun* M total; **¿cuánto es el
total?** how much is the total?; **son
cinco mil quinientas en total** it's five
thousand five hundred in total.
adjective total.

totalidad *noun* F **la totalidad del
colegio** the whole school; **la
totalidad de los alumnos** all the
pupils.

trabajador/trabajadora
noun M/F worker.
adjective hard-working.

trabajar *verb* [17] to work; **trabaja
de camarera** she works as a waitress;
trabaja de canguro she's a
babysitter; **trabajar a tiempo
completo** to work full-time; **trabajar
a tiempo parcial** to work part time.

trabajo *noun* M **1** work; **estar sin
trabajo** to be out of work; **trabajo a
tiempo completo** full-time work;
trabajo a tiempo parcial part-time
work; **el trabajo de la casa** the
housework; **2** job; **buscar trabajo** to
look for a job; **quedarse sin trabajo**
to lose your job; **un trabajo fijo** a
steady job; **3 trabajos manuales**
handicrafts; **4** piece of work; **un
trabajo sobre la contaminación** a
paper on pollution.

tractor *noun* M tractor.

tradición *noun* F tradition.

tradicional *adjective* traditional.

traducción *noun* F translation.

traducir *verb* [60] to translate.

traductor/traductora *noun* M/F
translator.

**traduje, traduzca, traduzco,
etc.** *verb* SEE **traducir**.

traer *verb* [42] **1** to bring; **he traído
algo de comida** I've brought some
food; **¿me trae un café, por favor?**
would you bring me a coffee, please?;
la traerá en coche a la estación he'll
bring her to the station in his car;
traer buena suerte to bring good
luck, to be lucky; **2** to carry; **la traía
en brazos** he was carrying her in his
arms.

traficante *noun* M/F dealer;
traficante de armas arms dealer.

tráfico *noun* M **1** traffic; **2** trade;
tráfico de armas arms trade; **tráfico
de drogas** drug dealing.

tragaperras *noun* M/F (*does not
change in the plural*) (*informal*) slot
machine.

tragar *verb* [28] to swallow.
tragarse *reflexive verb* [28] to swallow;
se tragó un hueso de aceituna he
swallowed an olive stone.

tragedia *noun* F tragedy.

trágico/trágica *adjective* tragic.

traición *noun* F **1** treason; **2 una
traición** an act of treachery.

traidor/traidora *noun* M/F traitor.

traiga, traigo, traje¹, etc. *verb* SEE **traer**.

traje² *noun* M **1** suit; **2 traje de baño** swimsuit; swimming trunks; **3** costume; **un traje de luces** a bullfighter's costume; **4** dress; **en traje típico** in traditional dress.

trampa *noun* F trap; **tenderle una trampa a alguien** to set a trap for somebody.

trampilla *noun* F trapdoor.

trampolín *noun* M **1** springboard, diving board; **2** trampoline; **3** ski jump.

tranquilo/tranquila *adjective* **1** quiet; **una calle tranquila** a quiet road; **2** relaxed; **se le ve tranquilo** he looks relaxed; **¡tranquilo!** relax!; **3** calm; **un ambiente tranquilo** a calm environment; **4** **¡déjame tranquilo!** leave me alone!; **5** **tengo la conciencia tranquila** my conscience is clear.

transbordador *noun* M **1** ferry; **2 transbordador espacial** space shuttle.

transbordar *verb* [17] **1** to transfer (*luggage or goods*); **2** to change (*trains, for example*).

transbordo *noun* M change; **hacer transbordo** to change (*trains, buses*); **haz transbordo en Sol** change at Sol.

transeúnte *noun* M/F passer-by.

transferencia *noun* F transfer; **transferencia bancaria** bank transfer.

transformar *verb* [17] **1** to transform; **2** to convert; **tranformar algo en algo** to convert something into something.

transformarse *reflexive verb* [17] **1** to be transformed; **2** to be converted.

transfusión *noun* F transfusion.

transmisión *noun* F broadcast; **transmisión en directo** live broadcast; **transmisión en diferido** pre-recorded broadcast.

transparente *adjective* transparent.

transportar *verb* [17] to transport; to carry (*people*).

transporte *noun* M transport.

tranvía *noun* M tram.

trapo *noun* M cloth; **un trapo del polvo** a duster; **un trapo de cocina** a tea towel.

tras *preposition* **1** behind; **tras de mí** behind me; **2** after; **hora tras hora** hour after hour; **tras despedirme, subí al coche** after saying goodbye, I got in the car.

trasero/trasera *adjective* **1** back; **la puerta trasera** the back door; **2** rear; **la rueda trasera** the rear wheel.

trasnochar *verb* [17] to stay up late; **anoche trasnochamos** we had a late night last night.

tratamiento *noun* M treatment;
estar en tratamiento to be
undergoing medical treatment.

tratar *verb* [17] **1** to treat; **no me
trataron bien** they didn't treat me
very well; **2 no trata sus libros con
cuidado** she's not careful with her
books; **3 tratar a alguien de usted**
to address somebody using the
polite 'usted' form; **tratar a alguien
de tú** to address somebody using the
less formal and more usual 'tú'
form; **4 tratar de hacer** to try to do; **trató
de impedirlo** he tried to avoid it;
5 tratar de algo to be about
something; **¿de qué trata la
película?** what's the film about?

tratarse *reflexive verb* [17] **1 tratarse
de algo** to be about something;
2 tratarse de usted to address each
other using the polite 'usted' form;
tratarse de tú to address each
other using the less formal and more usual
'tú' form.

través *in phrase* **a través de algo**
through something (*from one side to
the other*); across something.

travieso/traviesa *adjective*
naughty; **no seas travieso** don't be
naughty.

trayecto *noun* M **1** journey; **cubrir
un trayecto** to make a journey;
2 road; **3 final de trayecto** end of
the line (*on public transport*).

trazar *verb* [22] **1** to trace; **2** to draw
(*a map*); **3** to draw up (*a plan*).

trece *number* **1** thirteen; **tiene
trece años** she's thirteen (years old);

2 thirteenth (*in dates*); **el trece de
mayo** the thirteenth of May.

treinta *number* **1** thirty; **tiene
treinta años** she's thirty (years old);
treinta y siente thirty-seven;
2 thirtieth (*in dates*); **el treinta de
mayo** the thirtieth of May.

tren *noun* M **1** train; **coger el tren**
to catch the train; **ir en tren** to go by
train; **un tren directo** a through train;
un tren de cercanías a local train;
un tren de largo recorrido a long-
distance train; **un tren de alta
velocidad** a high-speed train; **2 tren
de aterrizaje** landing gear; **3 tren
de montaje** assembly line.

trepar *verb* [17] to climb; **trepar a un
árbol** to climb a tree.

tres *number* **1** three; **tiene tres años**
she's three (years old); **2** third (*in
dates*); **el tres de mayo** the third of
May; **3** three (*in clock time*); **son las
tres** it's three o'clock.

trescientos/trescientas
number three hundred; **trescientos
veinte** three hundred and twenty.

triángulo *noun* M triangle.

tribu *noun* F tribe.

tribunal *noun* M **1** court;
2 tribunal.

trigo *noun* M wheat.

trillizos/trillizas *plural noun* M/F
triplets.

trimestre *noun* M **1** term (*in
school*); **2** quarter (*three months*).

trineo *noun* M sledge.

tripa *noun* F 1 (*informal*) belly;
2 gut; 3 **tripas** innards.

triple *noun* M **el triple del precio
original** three times the original
price; **es el triple de ancho** it's three
times as wide; **subió al triple** it
tripled.
adjective triple.

tripulación *noun* F crew.

triste *adjective* 1 sad; 2 gloomy.

tristeza *noun* F sadness.

triunfar *verb* [17] to triumph.

triunfo *noun* M 1 victory;
2 triumph.

trivial *adjective* trivial.

trofeo *noun* M trophy.

trombón *noun* M trombone.

trompeta *noun* F trumpet.

tronar *verb* [24] to thunder.

tronco *noun* M 1 trunk;
2 log; ★ **dormir como un tronco** to
sleep like a log.

trono *noun* M throne.

tropezar *verb* [25] to trip; **tropezar
con algo** to trip over something.
tropezarse *reflexive verb* [25] to trip;
tropezarse con algo to trip over
something; to come up against
something (*a problem*).

tropezón *noun* M stumble; **dar un
tropezón** to stumble.

trópico *noun* M tropic.

tropiece, tropiezo, etc. *verb* SEE
tropezar.

trotar *verb* [17] to trot.

trozo *noun* M piece; **un trozo de tela**
a piece of cloth.

trucha *noun* F trout.

truco *noun* M trick; **el truco está en
hacerlo despacio** the trick is to do it
slowly.

trueno *noun* M thunder.

tu *adjective* your; **tu casa** your house;
tus amigos your friends.

tú *pronoun* 1 you; **tú no lo sabes** you
don't know it; 2 **tú mismo/misma**
yourself; **hazlo tú mismo** do it
yourself; 3 **tratar a alguien de tú** to
address somebody using the 'tú'
form (*rather than the more formal
and less usual 'usted'*).

tubo *noun* M 1 tube; 2 **tubo de
escape** exhaust pipe.

tuerza, tuerzo, etc. *verb* SEE
torcer.

tuesta, tueste, tuesto, etc.
verb SEE **tostar**.

tuerca *noun* F nut.

tulipán *noun* M tulip.

tumba *noun* F 1 grave; 2 tomb.

tumbar *verb* [17] to knock down;
tumbar a alguien de un puñetazo
to floor somebody (*with a punch*).
tumbarse *reflexive verb* [17] to lie
down; **se tumbó en el sofá** he lay
down on the sofa.

tumbona *noun* F deckchair.

tunecino/tunecina *noun* M/F *adjective* Tunisian.

túnel *noun* M tunnel.

Túnez *noun* M Tunisia.

turco/turca *noun* M/F *adjective* Turkish.

turismo *noun* M tourism; **oficina de turismo** tourist office; **hacer turismo** to travel around, to go sightseeing.

turista *noun* M/F tourist.

turístico/turística *adjective* tourist.

turnarse *reflexive verb* [17] to take turns.

turno *noun* M **1** turn; **tocarle el turno a alguien** to be somebody's turn; **te toca el turno a ti** it's your turn; **2** shift; **turno de noche** night shift; **hacer turnos de trabajo** to work shifts.

Turquía *noun* F Turkey.

turrón *noun* M nougat (*a special sort traditionally eaten in Spain at Christmas*).

tutear *verb* [17] **tutear a alguien** to address somebody using the familiar 'tú' form (*rather than the more formal and less usual 'usted'*).

tutearse *reflexive verb* [17] to address each other using the familiar 'tú' form (*see note above*).

tutor/tutora *noun* M/F **1** tutor; **2** class teacher.

tuvo, tuvieron, tuviste, etc. *verb* SEE **tener**.

tuyo/tuya *adjective* yours (*goes after the noun*); **un amigo tuyo** a friend of yours; **una vecina tuya** a neighbour of yours.
pronoun yours; **el tuyo es verde** yours is green; **las tuyas son mejores** yours are better.

U u

u *conjunction* or ('u' *is used instead of* 'o' *before words starting with* 'o-' *or* 'ho-'); **uno u otro** one or the other.

Ucrania *noun* F Ukraine.

ucraniano/ucraniana *noun* M/F *adjective* Ukrainian.

Ud. *abbreviation* (*short for: usted*) you.

Uds. *abbreviation* (*short for: ustedes*) you.

UE *abbreviation* (*short for: Unión Europea*) EU.

último/última *noun* M/F **el último** the last one; **ésta es la última que queda** this is the last one left; **coge el último del montón** take the one at the bottom of the pile.
adjective **1** last; **el último día fuimos a la playa** on the last day we went to the beach; **2** latest; **su última película** her latest film; **3** top; **el último libro del montón** the book at the bottom of the pile.

últimamente *adverb* lately.

ultramarinos *noun* M (*does not change in the plural*) grocer's shop.

un/una[1] *indefinite article* **1** a; an; **un hombre** a man; **una manzana** an apple; (*'un' is also used before feminine nouns starting with a stressed 'a' or 'ha'*) **un ala** a wing; **2 unos/unas** some; **compré unos sobres** I bought some envelopes; **3** a few; **se quedarán unas horas** they will stay for a few hours; **4 unos/unas** about; **cuesta unas tres mil pesetas** it costs about three thousand pesetas; **llevará unos treinta minutos hacerlo** it'll take about thirty minutes to do.

único/única *noun* M/F **el único/la única** the only one; **el único que funciona** the only one that works. *adjective* **1** unique; **2** only; **su único hijo** her only child; **3 talla única** one size.

unidad *noun* F **1** unit; **2** unity.

unido/unida *adjective* **1** united; **2** joined; **3** close; **las dos hermanas están muy unidas** the two sisters are very close.

uniforme *noun* M uniform. *adjective* **1** uniform; **2** even.

Unión Europea *noun* F European Union.

unir *verb* [19] **1** to join; **2** to combine; **el diseño une la elegancia con la eficacia** the design combines elegance and efficiency; **3** to merge (*companies, for example*).

unirse *reflexive verb* [19] **1** to join together; **2** to combine; **3** to merge.

universidad *noun* F university; **universidad a distancia** open university.

universitario/universitaria *noun* M/F university student. *adjective* university; **profesores universitarios** university teachers.

universo *noun* M universe.

uno[1] *pronoun* **1** one; **compré sólo uno** I bought only one; **tiene un año** she's one (year old); **2** first (*in dates*); **el uno de enero** the first of January.

uno[2]**/una**[2] *number* **1** one; **hay una razón** there is one reason (*note that 'uno' becomes 'un' before a masculine singular noun*); **2** one (*in clock time*); **la una** one o'clock; **es la una** it's one o'clock; **llegaron a la una** they arrived at one o'clock. *pronoun* **1** one; **de uno en uno** one by one; **2 unos/unas** some; **unos saben y otros no** some know and some don't.

uña *noun* F nail.

urbano/urbana *adjective* urban.

urgencia *noun* F **1** urgency; **2** (*in hospital*) **'urgencias'** 'accident and emergency'; **'sala de urgencias'** 'casualty'.

urgente *adjective* **1** urgent; **2** express (*post*).

Uruguay *noun* M Uruguay.

uruguayo/uruguaya *noun* M/F *adjective* Uruguayan.

usado/usada *adjective* **1** used; **2** second-hand; **ropa usada** second-hand clothes.

usar *verb* [17] to use; **¿qué champú usas?** what shampoo do you use?

uso *noun* M use; **instrucciones de uso** instructions for use.

usted *pronoun* you (*the formal, polite form: talking to one person*); **usted mismo/misma** yourself.

ustedes *pronoun* you (*the formal, polite form: talking to more than one person*); **ustedes mismos/mismas** yourselves.

usual *adjective* usual.

utensilio *noun* M **1** tool; **2** utensil.

útil *adjective* useful.

utilizar *verb* [22] to use.

uva *noun* F grape; **las uvas de la suerte** the twelve grapes eaten traditionally in Spain at midnight on New Year's Eve; **tomar las uvas** to eat a grape with each stroke of the bell at midnight on New Year's Eve.

V v

vaca *noun* F cow.

vacaciones *plural noun* F holiday; holidays; **irse de vacaciones** to go on holiday; **tomarse unas vacaciones** to take a holiday; **las vacaciones de Navidad** the Christmas holidays; **estar de vacaciones** to be on holiday.

vaciar *verb* [32] to empty.

vacilar *verb* [17] **1** to hesitate; **sin vacilar** without hesitating; **vacilaba entre quedarse o no** she was hesitating whether to stay or not; **2** to falter; **3** (*informal*) to joke; **¡deja de vacilar!** stop joking!

vacío/vacía *adjective* empty.

vacuna *noun* F vaccine.

vacunar *verb* [17] to vaccinate.

vagabundo/vagabunda *noun* M/F vagrant. *adjective* **un perro vagabundo** a stray dog.

vago/vaga *noun* M/F layabout. *adjective* lazy.

vagón *noun* M **1** carriage; **2** wagon.

vainilla *noun* F vanilla.

valdrá, valdré, valdría, etc. *verb* SEE **valer**.

vale *noun* M **1** voucher; **2** credit slip. *exclamation* okay; **'¿vamos a cenar fuera?' – '¡vale!'** 'shall we go out for dinner?' – 'okay!'.

valer *verb* [43] **1** to cost; **¿cuánto vale?** how much is it?; **vale trescientas cincuenta pesetas** it's three hundred and fifty pesetas; **2** to be worth; **vale bastante dinero** it's worth quite a lot of money; **3** **valer la pena** to be worth it; **vale la pena** it's worth it; **no vale la pena** it's not worth it; **no vale la pena enfadarse por ello** it's not worth getting upset about; **vale la pena el esfuerzo** it's worth the effort; **4** to be valid (*a ticket or coupon*); **5** to be allowed; **no vale preguntar** you can't ask; **eso no vale, tú ya lo habías visto** that's not fair, you'd already seen it.

valga, valgo, etc. *verb* SEE **valer**.

válido/válida *adjective* valid.

valiente *adjective* brave.

valioso/valiosa *adjective* valuable.

valle *noun* M valley.

valor *noun* M courage.

valorar *verb* [17] to value.

vals *noun* M waltz.

vamos *verb* SEE **ir**.

vandalismo *noun* M hooliganism.

vanidoso/vanidosa *adjective* vain.

vano/vana *adjective* **1** futile; **2** pointless.

vapor *noun* M steam; **al vapor** steamed.

vaquero *noun* M jeans; **vaqueros** jeans.

variado/variada *adjective* varied.

variar *verb* [32] **1** to vary; **2** to change.

varicela *noun* F chicken pox.

variedad *noun* F variety.

varios/varias *pronoun*, *adjective* several; **varias veces** several times.

varón *noun* M
adjective male.

varonil *adjective* manly.

vasco[1] *noun* M Basque (*the language*).

vasco[2]/**vasca** *noun* M/F
adjective Basque.

vasija *noun* F vessel.

vaso *noun* M glass; **un vaso de agua** a glass of water; **un vaso de papel** a paper cup.

Vd. *abbreviation* (*short for: usted*) you.

Vds. *abbreviation* (*short for: ustedes*) you.

vecindad *noun* F neighbourhood.

vecino/vecina *noun* M/F
neighbour.
adjective neighbouring.

vegetariano/vegetariana
noun M/F *adjective* vegetarian.

vehículo *noun* M vehicle; **vehículo espacial** spacecraft.

veía, veían, etc. *verb* SEE **ver**.

veinte *number* **1** twenty; **tiene veinte años** she's twenty (years old); **veintidós** twenty-two; **2** twentieth (*in dates*); **el veinte de diciembre** the twentieth of December; **3** twenty (*in clock time*); **a las veinticinco** at twenty-five past.

vejez *noun* F old age.

vela *noun* F 1 candle; 2 sail; 3 **he pasado toda la noche en vela** I've been awake all night.

velero *noun* M sailing ship; sailing boat.

velocidad *noun* F 1 speed; **el coche iba a mucha velocidad** the car was going very fast; **disminuir la velocidad** to slow down; 2 gear (*in a car*); **la cuarta velocidad** fourth gear.

vena *noun* F vein.

vencedor/vencedora *adjective* winning.

vencer *verb* [44] 1 to defeat; **vencer a alguien** to defeat somebody; 2 to win; 3 to overcome; 4 to expire (*a passport, for example*).

vencido/vencida *adjective* defeated.

venda *noun* F bandage.

vendar *verb* [17] 1 to bandage; 2 **vendar los ojos a alguien** to blindfold somebody.

vendaval *noun* M gale.

vendedor/vendedora *noun* M/F 1 shop assistant; 2 salesman/saleswoman.

vender *verb* [18] to sell; **le he vendido mi coche** I've sold him my car; **lo venden a treinta mil pesetas** they're selling it for thirty thousand pesetas; **'se vende'** 'for sale'.

vendimia *noun* F wine harvest.

vendrá, vendré, vendría, etc. *verb* SEE **venir**.

veneno *noun* M poison; venom.

venenoso/venenosa *adjective* poisonous.

venezolano/venezolana *noun* M/F *adjective* Venezuelan.

Venezuela *noun* F Venezuela.

venga, vengo, etc. *verb* SEE **venir**.

venir *verb* [15] 1 to come; **sus padres no vinieron** her parents didn't come; **ven a las siete** come at seven; 2 **venir de** to come from; **viene de Italia** it comes from Italy; 3 **venir a hacer** to come to do; **yo vendré a buscarte** I'll come and collect you; 4 **venir a por algo** to come to fetch something; **vengo a por el paquete** I've come to fetch the parcel; **venir a por alguien** to come to collect somebody; **yo vendré a buscarte** I'll come and collect you; 5 to be; **la noticia viene en la primera página** the news is on the front page; 6 **mañana no les viene bien** tomorrow is no good for them; **¿te viene bien quedar en la entrada?** is it okay for you if we meet at the entrance?; **esta parada de metro me viene muy bien** this tube station's very convenient for me; 7 **que viene** next; **la semana que viene** next week; **el domingo que viene** next Sunday; 8 **¡venga!** come on!

venta *noun* F sale; **estar en venta** to be for sale; **'prohibida su venta'** 'not for sale'.

ventaja *noun* F advantage.

ventana *noun* F window.

ventanilla *noun* F **1** window (*in a train or car*); **2** box office; **3 horario de ventanilla** opening hours (*at a consulate, for example*).

ventilador *noun* M fan.

ver *verb* [16] **1** to see; **los vi ayer** I saw them yesterday; **la vi cogerlo** I saw her take it; **no veo nada desde aquí** I can't see anything from here; **no veo bien de lejos** I'm shortsighted; **ya veo cuál es el problema** I can see the problem; **ya veremos lo que hacemos** we'll see what we do; **2** to watch; **ver la tele** to watch TV; **anoche vimos una película muy buena** we watched a very good film last night; **3** to think; **lo que ha hecho no lo veo bien** I don't think what he's done is right; **4 tener que ver con algo** to have something to do with something; **eso no tiene nada que ver** that has nothing to do with it; **5 a ver, ¿qué te pasa?** okay, what's the matter with you?; **'mira lo que he encontrado'** – **'¿a ver?'** 'look what I've found' – 'let's see'.

verse *reflexive verb* [16] **1** to see yourself; **verse en el espejo** to see yourself in the mirror; **2** to see each other; **se ven todas las semanas** they see each other every week; **3** to meet; **¿nos vemos a la entrada del cine?** shall we meet outside of the cinema?; ★ **verse en un aprieto** to find yourself in a tight spot.

veraneante *noun* M/F holidaymaker.

veranear *verb* [17] **veranear en** to spend your summer holidays in; **veranean en la montaña** they spend their summer holidays in the mountains.

veras *in phrase* **¡de veras!** really!

verbena *noun* F festival (*held to celebrate the Saint's Day of a town or village*); dance (*in the open air*).

verbo *noun* M verb.

verdad *noun* F **1** truth; **dime la verdad** tell me the truth; **la pura verdad** the absolute truth; **la verdad, no me acuerdo** I don't remember, honestly; **la verdad es que** ... the truth is that ...; **2 a decir verdad** ... to tell the truth ...; **3 de verdad** really; **de verdad que no me importa** I don't mind, really; **4 de verdad** real; **un amigo de verdad** a real friend.

verdadero/verdadera *adjective* **1** real; **su verdadero nombre** his real name; **es un verdadero idiota** he's a real idiot; **2** true; **una historia verdadera** a true story.

verde *noun* M **1** green; **verde botella** bottle-green; **2 los Verdes** the Greens (*in politics*). *adjective* **1** green; **tiene los ojos verdes** she has green eyes; **una blusa verde oscuro** a dark green blouse; **2 un chiste verde** a dirty joke.

verdulería *noun* F greengrocer's.

verdura *noun* F vegetable; (*can be used in the singular to mean 'vegetables'*) **cómete la verdura** eat your vegetables; **un puesto de verduras** a vegetable stall.

vergonzoso/vergonzosa *adjective* 1 timid; 2 shameful.

vergüenza *noun* F 1 shame; **¡qué poca vergüenza tienes!** have you no shame at all?; 2 **me da vergüenza haberme portado de esa forma** I'm ashamed of behaving the way I did; 3 embarrassment; **pasar vergüenza** to feel embarrassed; 4 **me da vergüenza hablar en público** I feel embarrassed when I have to speak in public.

verruga *noun* F 1 wart; 2 verruca.

versión *noun* F version; **una película en versión original** a film which has not been dubbed (*a foreign film, usually with subtitles*).

verso *noun* M 1 verse; **en verso** in verse; 2 poem; 3 line of a poem; **el tercer verso** the third line of the poem.

vertical *adjective* 1 vertical; 2 down (*in crosswords*); **ocho vertical** eight down.

vertiente *noun* F slope.

vértigo *noun* M vertigo; **me da vértigo mirar abajo** looking down makes me dizzy.

vestíbulo *noun* M 1 hall; 2 foyer.

vestido¹ *noun* M dress; **un vestido de noche** an evening dress; **un vestido de novia** a wedding dress.

vestido²/vestida *adjective* dressed; **ir bien vestido** to be well dressed; **iba vestida con un traje azul** she was wearing a blue suit; **tenemos que ir al colegio vestidos de uniforme** we have to wear school uniform.

vestir *verb* [57] to dress; **vestir bien** to dress well.

vestirse *reflexive verb* [57] 1 to get dressed; **voy a vestirme** I'm going to get dressed; 2 to dress; **se viste a la última moda** she wears the latest fashions; **me gusta vestirme de azul** I like wearing blue.

vestuario *noun* M 1 wardrobe; 2 changing room.

veterinario/veterinaria *noun* M/F veterinary surgeon.

vez (*plural* **veces**) *noun* F 1 time; **la primera vez que fui a Inglaterra** the first time I went to England; **por última vez** for the last time; **algunas veces** sometimes; **¿has estado alguna vez en Italia?** have you ever been to Italy?; **a veces** sometimes; **de vez en cuando** from time to time; **a la vez** at the same time; **cada vez** each time; 2 **muchas veces** often; **pocas veces** not very often; **rara vez** seldom; 3 **una vez** once; **dos veces** twice; **tres veces al año** three times a year; 4 **otra vez** again; 5 **cada vez más** more and more; **cada vez menos** less and less; 6 **en vez de**

instead of; **7 érase una vez** ... once upon a time ...

vía *noun* F **1** track; **la vía férrea** the railway track; **2 por vía aérea** by air; **por vía marítima** by sea; **3 vía de acceso** slip road; **4 Vía Láctea** Milky Way.

viajar *verb* [17] to travel; **viajar en avión** to travel by plane.

viaje *noun* M journey trip; **estar de viaje** to be away; **hacer un viaje** to go on a journey; to go on a trip; **salir de viaje** to go on a journey; to go on a trip; **¡buen viaje!** have a good journey!; **viaje de negocios** business trip; **viaje organizado** package tour; **viaje de novios** honeymoon.

viajero/viajera *noun* M/F **1** traveller; **2** passenger.

víbora *noun* F viper.

vibrar *verb* [17] to vibrate.

vicio *noun* M **1** vice; **2** bad habit; **tengo el vicio de morderme las uñas** I have the bad habit of biting my nails.

víctima *noun* F victim.

victoria *noun* F victory.

vid *noun* F vine.

vida *noun* F life; **¡esto es vida!** this is the life!; **la vida está muy cara** the cost of living is very high; **una cuestión de vida o muerte** a matter of life or death; **llevar una vida muy ajetreada** to lead a very busy life; **ganarse la vida** to earn a living.

vídeo *noun* M video; **en vídeo** on video.

videocámara *noun* F video camera.

videoclub *noun* M video shop.

videojuego *noun* M video game.

vidrio *noun* M glass.

viejo/vieja *noun* M/F old man/old woman.
adjective old.

viento *noun* M wind; **hace viento** it's windy.

vientre *noun* M **1** belly; **2** womb.

viernes *noun* M Friday; **Viernes Santo** Good Friday (*see 'domingo' for more examples*).

vigésimo/vigésima *adjective* twentieth.

villancico *noun* M Christmas Carol.

vinagre *noun* M vinegar.

vine, viniste, vino, etc. *verb* SEE **venir**.

vino *noun* M wine; **vino tinto** red wine; **vino blanco** white wine; **vino de mesa** table wine.

viñedo *noun* M vineyard.

violar *verb* [17] to rape.

violencia *noun* F violence.

violento/violenta *adjective* **1** violent; **2** embarrassing (*situation*); **3** embarrassed.

violeta *noun* F
adjective violet.

violín *noun* M violin; **tocar el violín** to play the violin.

violoncelo, violonchelo *noun* M cello.

virgen *noun* F virgin.

Virgo *noun* M Virgo.

virgo *noun* M/F Virgo; **es virgo** he's Virgo.

virtud *noun* F virtue.

virus *noun* M virus.

visado *noun* M visa.

visibilidad *noun* F visibility.

visible *adjective* visible.

visión *noun* F 1 vision; 2 sight; **perder la visión** to lose your sight.

visita *noun* F 1 visit; **una visita al museo** a visit to the museum; **hacer una visita a alguien** to visit somebody; 2 visitor; **tienes una visita** you have a visitor.

visitar *verb* [17] to visit.

víspera *noun* F **la víspera** the day before; **la víspera del partido** the day before the match.

vista¹ *noun* F 1 eyesight; **tener buena vista** to have good eyesight; **perder la vista** to lose your sight; **el sol me hace daño a la vista** the sun's hurting my eyes; **conocer a alguien de vista** to know someone by sight; 2 **estar a la vista** to be within sight; **no estar a la vista** to be out of sight; 3 view; **el hotel tiene unas vistas preciosas** the hotel has beautiful

views; 4 **con vistas a** with a view to; 5 **¡hasta la vista!** see you!

vistieron, vistió, etc. *verb* SEE **vestir**.

visto¹ *verb* SEE **ver**.

visto²/vista² *adjective* 1 clear; **está visto que …** it's clear that …; 2 **por lo visto** apparently; 3 **estar bien visto** to be acceptable; **está mal visto** it's not the done thing; 4 **eso está muy visto** that's not very original.

vitamina *noun* F vitamin.

viudo/viuda *noun* F widow/ widower.

viva¹ *exclamation* ¡viva! hurray!; **¡viva los novios!** three cheers for the bride and groom!

vivienda *noun* F 1 housing; **el problema de la vivienda** the housing problem; 2 flat; house; **un bloque de viviendas** a block of flats.

vivir *verb* [19] to live; **vive en casa de su hermana** she lives with her sister; **vive de las traducciones** she makes her living from translation; **vive de su pension** she lives off her pension.

vivo/viva² *adjective* 1 alive; 2 **actuación en vivo** live performance.

vocabulario *noun* M vocabulary.

volante *noun* M steering wheel. *adjective* flying.

volar *verb* [24] 1 to fly; 2 to blow up; **volar un edificio** to blow up a building.

volcán *noun* M volcano.

volcar *verb* [24] **1** to turn over; **el camión volcó** the lorry turned over; **2 volcar el contenido de algo** to empty something; **3** to knock over.

volcarse *reflexive verb* [24] **1** to turn over (*a vehicle*); **2 volcarse en algo** to throw yourself into something.

vóleibol, voleibol *noun* M volleyball; **jugar al vóleibol** to play volleyball.

voltereta *noun* F somersault.

volumen *noun* M volume; **subir el volumen** to turn up the volume.

voluntad *noun* F **1** will; **fuerza de voluntad** will power; **lo hice por mi propia voluntad** I did it of my own free will; **2** wish; ★ **siempre hace su santa voluntad** she always does exactly as she pleases.

voluntario/voluntaria *noun* M/F volunteer.
adjective voluntary.

volver *verb* [45] **1** to turn; **volver la página** to turn the page; **volvió la cabeza** she turned her head; **al volver la esquina …** when I turned the corner …; **2** to come back; **aún no ha vuelto** he hasn't come back yet; **¿cuándo volverás?** when will you come back?; **3** to go back; **volver al colegio** to go back to school; **¿quieres que volvamos a casa?** do you want to go back home?; **ha vuelto con su novia** he's gone back to his girlfriend; **4** to be back; **volveré a eso de las siete** I'll be back by about seven; **no había vuelto a Sevilla**

desde el verano pasado I hadn't been back to Seville since last summer; **5** to get back; **¿cuándo volviste de tu viaje?** when did you get back from your trip?; **6 volver a hacer** to do again; **volví a revisarlo** I checked it again; **¡no lo vuelvas a hacer!** don't do it again!; **tenemos que volver a empezar** we have to start again; **7 volver loco a alguien** to drive someone mad; **me está volviendo loca con tantas preguntas** she's driving me mad with all her questions; **8 volver en sí** to come round (*recover consciousness*).

volverse *reflexive verb* [45] **1** to turn around; **me volví para mirar** I turned around to see; **2 volverse de espaldas** to turn your back; **¡no te vuelvas de espaldas cuando te estoy hablando!** don't turn your back on me when I'm talking to you!; **3 volverse boca abajo** to turn over onto your stomach; **volverse boca arriba** to turn over onto your back; **4** to turn; **se ha vuelto muy vanidosa** she's turned very vain; **5** to become; **la situación se ha vuelto insoportable** the situation has become unbearable; **volverse loco** to go mad.

vomitar *verb* [17] to be sick; **tener ganas de vomitar** to feel sick.

vosotros/vosotras *pronoun* you (*talking to more than one person*); **¿vosotras queréis ir?** do you want to go?; **vosotros mismos/vosotras mismas** yourselves.

votar *verb* [17] to vote; **votar por alguien** to vote for somebody.

voto *noun* M **1** vote; **un voto a favor** a vote for; **un voto en contra** a vote against; **un voto secreto** a secret ballot; **un voto en blanco** a blank ballot paper; **un voto de censura** a vote of no confidence; **2** vow.

voy *verb* SEE **ir**.

voz *noun* F voice; **oír voces** to hear voices; **tener la voz tomada** to be hoarse; **en voz baja** quietly; **hablar en voz alta** to speak loudly; **leer algo en voz alta** to read something out loud.

vuelo *noun* M flight; **un vuelo regular** a scheduled flight.

vuelta *noun* F **1** turn; **una vuelta a la derecha** a turn to the right; **2** return; **a la vuelta podemos visitar el museo** we can visit the museum on our way back; **'vuelta al colegio'** 'back to school' (*after the summer holidays*); **3 dar la vuelta a algo** to turn something; **dar la vuelta a la página** to turn the page; **dale la vuelta al cuadro** turn the picture round the other way; **dar la vuelta a un disco** to turn a record over; **4 dar la vuelta a la esquina** to turn the corner; **5 dar la vuelta al mundo** to go round the world; **dar una vuelta a la manzana** to go round the block; **6 dar una vuelta** to go for a walk; **¿te vienes a dar una vuelta?** are you coming for a walk?; **dar una vuelta en coche** to go for a drive; **7 dar una vuelta alrededor de algo** to go around something.

vuelva, vuelvo, etc. *verb* SEE **volver**.

vuestro/vuestra *adjective* your (*talking to more than one person*); **vuestra casa** your house; **un familiar vuestro** a relative of yours. *pronoun* yours; **la vuestra es verde** yours is green; **los vuestros están en el salón** yours are in the living room; **aquel es el vuestro** that one is yours.

vulgar *adjective* **1** vulgar; **2** common.

W w

wáter *noun* M toilet.

whisky *noun* M whisky.

windsurf *noun* M windsurfing.

X x

xilófono *noun* M xylophone.

Y y

y *conjunction* ('y' becomes 'e' before a word beginning with 'i' or 'hi') **1** and; **Amanda y yo** Amanda and I; **2** (*with numbers and times*) **treinta y siete** thirty-seven; **3** (*with clock time*) **las dos y media** half past two; **a las diez y cinco** at five past ten; **4 ¿y a mí qué?** so what's it to me?

ya *adverb* **1** already; **ya está hecho** it's already done; **¿has comido ya?**

have you already eaten?; **2** yet; **¿han llegado ya?** have they arrived yet?; **3** any more; **ya no importa** it doesn't matter any more; **4** now; **antes no quería, pero ya ha cambiado de idea** he didn't want to before but he's changed his mind now; **tenemos que decidirnos ya** we must decide now; **5** (*in the future*) **ya veremos** we'll see; **ya te contaré** I'll tell you about it; **6** (*not translated but used to stress what you are saying*) **ya lo sé** I know; **ya entiendo** I understand; **ya era hora** it's about time too; **¡ya está!** that's it!; **¡ya estoy!** I'm ready!; **¡ya voy!** I'm just coming!; **¡ya lo creo!** you bet!; **preparados, listos, ¡ya!** ready, steady, go!; **7** '**esto es de Juan' – 'ya'** 'this is Juan's' – 'I know'; **8** '**yo no he sido' – 'ya, ya'** 'it wasn't me' – 'yeah, yeah!'; **9 ya que** since; **ya que vas a estar aquí** since you're going to be here.

yate *noun* M yacht.

yedra *noun* F ivy.

yegua *noun* F mare.

yema *noun* F **1** yolk; **2 la yema del dedo** the fingertip.

yerno *noun* M son-in-law.

yo *pronoun* **1** I; **yo no lo sé** I don't know; **2** me; **soy yo** it's me; **3 yo mismo/misma** myself; **lo haré yo mismo** I'll do it myself.

yogur *noun* M yoghurt.

yudo *noun* M judo.

Yugoslavia *noun* F Yugoslavia.

yugoslavo/yugoslava *noun* M/F *adjective* Yugoslavian.

Z z

zanahoria *noun* F carrot.

zapatería *noun* F shoe shop.

zapatero/zapatera *noun* M/F **1** shoemaker; **2** shoe repairer.

zapatilla *noun* F **1** slipper; **2** canvas shoe; **3 zapatilla de deporte** trainer; **4 zapatilla de esparto** espadrille; **5 zapatilla de ballet** ballet shoe.

zapato *noun* M shoe; **zapato de tacón** high heeled shoe; **zapato bajo** flat shoe.

zarzamora *noun* F blackberry.

zodíaco, zodiaco *noun* M zodiac.

zona *noun* F area; **zona peatonal** pedestrian precinct; **zona comercial** commercial district.

zoo *noun* M zoo.

zoológico *noun* M zoo.

zorro *noun* M fox.

zumo *noun* M juice; **zumo de fruta** fruit juice; **zumo de naranja** orange juice.

zurdo/zurda *noun* M/F left handed person.

VERB TABLES
AND FORMS

ser
to be

Gerund	Past participle
siendo	sido

Present indicative

soy
eres
es
somos
sois
son

Imperfect indicative

era
eras
era
éramos
erais
eran

Past simple indicative

fui
fuiste
fue
fuimos
fuisteis
fueron

Future indicative

seré
serás
será
seremos
seréis
serán

Conditional (present)

sería
serías
sería
seríamos
seríais
serían

Present subjunctive

sea
seas
sea
seamos
seáis
sean

Imperfect subjunctive

fuera
fueras
fuera
fuéramos
fuerais
fueran

Imperative

sé (tú)
sea (usted)
seamos (nosotros)
sed (vosotros)
sean (ustedes)

2

Gerund	**Past participle**	**estar**
estando	estado	to be

Present indicative

estoy
estás
está
estamos
estáis
están

Imperfect indicative

estaba
estabas
estaba
estábamos
estabais
estaban

Past simple indicative

estuve
estuviste
estuvo
estuvimos
estuvisteis
estuvieron

Future indicative

estaré
estarás
estará
estaremos
estaréis
estarán

Conditional (present)

estaría
estarías
estaría
estaríamos
estaríais
estarían

Present subjunctive

esté
estés
esté
estemos
estéis
estén

Imperfect subjunctive

estuviera
estuvieras
estuviera
estuviéramos
estuvierais
estuvieran

Imperative

está (tú)
esté (usted)
estemos (nosotros)
estad (vosotros)
estén (ustedes)

coger
to take

Gerund	Past participle
cogiendo	cogido

Present indicative

cojo
coges
coge
cogemos
cogéis
cogen

Conditional (present)

cogería
cogerías
cogería
cogeríamos
cogeríais
cogerían

Imperfect indicative

cogía
cogías
cogía
cogíamos
cogíais
cogían

Present subjunctive

coja
cojas
coja
cojamos
cojáis
cojan

Past simple indicative

cogí
cogiste
cogió
cogimos
cogisteis
cogieron

Imperfect subjunctive

cogiera
cogieras
cogiera
cogiéramos
cogierais
cogieran

Future indicative

cogeré
cogerás
cogerá
cogeremos
cogeréis
cogerán

Imperative

coge (tú)
coja (usted)
cojamos (nosotros)
coged (vosotros)
cojan (ustedes)

Gerund	**Past participle**	**dar**
dando	dado	to give

Present indicative

doy
das
da
damos
dais
dan

Imperfect indicative

daba
dabas
daba
dábamos
dabais
daban

Past simple indicative

di
diste
dio
dimos
disteis
dieron

Future indicative

daré
darás
dará
daremos
daréis
darán

Conditional (present)

daría
darías
daría
daríamos
daríais
darían

Present subjunctive

dé
des
dé
demos
deis
den

Imperfect subjunctive

diera
dieras
diera
diéramos
dierais
dieran

Imperative

da (tú)
de (usted)
demos (nosotros)
dad (vosotros)
den (ustedes)

decir
to say, to tell

Gerund	**Past participle**
diciendo	dicho

Present indicative

digo
dices
dice
decimos
decís
dicen

Imperfect indicative

decía
decías
decía
decíamos
decíais
decían

Past simple indicative

dije
dijiste
dijo
dijimos
dijisteis
dijeron

Future indicative

diré
dirás
dirá
diremos
diréis
dirán

Conditional (present)

diría
dirías
diría
diríamos
diríais
dirían

Present subjunctive

diga
digas
diga
digamos
digáis
digan

Imperfect subjunctive

dijera
dijeras
dijera
dijéramos
dijerais
dijeran

Imperative

di (tú)
diga (usted)
digamos (nosotros)
decid (vosotros)
digan (ustedes)

Gerund	**Past participle**	**haber**
habiendo	habido	to have

Present indicative
he
has
ha
hemos
habéis
han

Conditional (present)
habría
habrías
habría
habríamos
habríais
habrían

Imperfect indicative
había
habías
había
habíamos
habíais
habían

Present subjunctive
haya
hayas
haya
hayamos
hayáis
hayan

Past simple indicative
hube
hubiste
hubo
hubimos
hubisteis
hubieron

Imperfect subjunctive
hubiera
hubieras
hubiera
hubiéramos
hubierais
hubieran

Future indicative
habré
habrás
habrá
habremos
habréis
habrán

Imperative
he (tú)
haya (usted)
hayamos (nosotros)
habed (vosotros)
hayan (ustedes)

hacer
to make, to do

Gerund
haciendo

Past participle
hecho

Present indicative
hago
haces
hace
hacemos
hacéis
hacen

Imperfect indicative
hacía
hacías
hacía
hacíamos
hacíais
hacían

Past simple indicative
hice
hiciste
hizo
hicimos
hicisteis
hicieron

Future indicative
haré
harás
hará
haremos
haréis
harán

Conditional (present)
haría
harías
haría
haríamos
haríais
harían

Present subjunctive
haga
hagas
haga
hagamos
hagáis
hagan

Imperfect subjunctive
hiciera
hicieras
hiciera
hiciéramos
hicierais
hicieran

Imperative
haz (tú)
haga (usted)
hagamos (nosotros)
haced (vosotros)
hagan (ustedes)

ir
to go

Gerund	**Past participle**
yendo	ido

Present indicative	**Conditional (present)**
voy	iría
vas	irías
va	iría
vamos	iríamos
vais	iríais
van	irían

Imperfect indicative	**Present subjunctive**
iba	vaya
ibas	vayas
iba	vaya
íbamos	vayamos
ibais	vayáis
iban	vayan

Past simple indicative	**Imperfect subjunctive**
fui	fuera
fuiste	fueras
fue	fuera
fuimos	fuéramos
fuisteis	fuerais
fueron	fueran

Future indicative	**Imperative**
iré	ve (tú)
irás	vaya (usted)
irá	vayamos (nosotros)
iremos	id (vosotros)
iréis	vayan (ustedes)
irán	

tener
to have

Gerund	Past participle
teniendo	tenido

Present indicative

tengo
tienes
tiene
tenemos
tenéis
tienen

Imperfect indicative

tenía
tenías
tenía
teníamos
teníais
tenían

Past simple indicative

tuve
tuviste
tuvo
tuvimos
tuvisteis
tuvieron

Future indicative

tendré
tendrás
tendrá
tendremos
tendréis
tendrán

Conditional (present)

tendría
tendrías
tendría
tendríamos
tendríais
tendrían

Present subjunctive

tenga
tengas
tenga
tengamos
tengáis
tengan

Imperfect subjunctive

tuviera
tuvieras
tuviera
tuviéramos
tuvierais
tuvieran

Imperative

ten (tú)
tenga (usted)
tengamos (nosotros)
tened (vosotros)
tengan (ustedes)

10

Gerund	Past participle	**poder**
pudiendo	podido	to be able

Present indicative

puedo
puedes
puede
podemos
podéis
pueden

Imperfect indicative

podía
podías
podía
podíamos
podíais
podían

Past simple indicative

pude
pudiste
pudo
pudimos
pudisteis
pudieron

Future indicative

podré
podrás
podrá
podremos
podréis
podrán

Conditional (present)

podría
podrías
podría
podríamos
podríais
podrían

Present subjunctive

pueda
puedas
pueda
podamos
podáis
puedan

Imperfect subjunctive

pudiera
pudieras
pudiera
pudiéramos
pudierais
pudieran

Imperative

puede (tú)
pueda (usted)
podamos (nosotros)
poded (vosotros)
puedan (ustedes)

poner
to put

Gerund	Past participle
poniendo	puesto

Present indicative

pongo
pones
pone
ponemos
ponéis
ponen

Imperfect indicative

ponía
ponías
ponía
poníamos
poníais
ponían

Past simple indicative

puse
pusiste
puso
pusimos
pusisteis
pusieron

Future indicative

pondré
pondrás
pondrá
pondremos
pondréis
pondrán

Conditional (present)

pondría
pondrías
pondría
pondríamos
pondríais
pondrían

Present subjunctive

ponga
pongas
ponga
pongamos
pongáis
pongan

Imperfect subjunctive

pusiera
pusieras
pusiera
pusiéramos
pusierais
pusieran

Imperative

pon (tú)
ponga (usted)
pongamos (nosotros)
poned (vosotros)
pongan (ustedes)

12

Gerund

queriendo

Past participle

querido

querer

to want, to love

Present indicative

quiero
quieres
quiere
queremos
queréis
quieren

Imperfect indicative

quería
querías
quería
queríamos
queríais
querían

Past simple indicative

quise
quisiste
quiso
quisimos
quisisteis
quisieron

Future indicative

querré
querrás
querrá
querremos
querréis
querrán

Conditional (present)

querría
querrías
querría
querríamos
querríais
querrían

Present subjunctive

quiera
quieras
quiera
queramos
queráis
quieran

Imperfect subjunctive

quisiera
quisieras
quisiera
quisiéramos
quisierais
quisieran

Imperative

quiere (tú)
quiera (usted)
queramos (nosotros)
quered (vosotros)
quieran (ustedes)

saber
to know

Gerund	Past participle
sabiendo	sabido

Present indicative

sé
sabes
sabe
sabemos
sabéis
saben

Imperfect indicative

sabía
sabías
sabía
sabíamos
sabíais
sabían

Past simple indicative

supe
supiste
supo
supimos
supisteis
supieron

Future indicative

sabré
sabrás
sabrá
sabremos
sabréis
sabrán

Conditional (present)

sabría
sabrías
sabría
sabríamos
sabríais
sabrían

Present subjunctive

sepa
sepas
sepa
sepamos
sepáis
sepan

Imperfect subjunctive

supiera
supieras
supiera
supiéramos
supierais
supieran

Imperative

sabe (tú)
sepa (usted)
sepamos (nosotros)
sabed (vosotros)
sepan (ustedes)

| **Gerund** | **Past participle** | **sentir** |
| sintiendo | sentido | to feel |

Present indicative

siento
sientes
siente
sentimos
sentís
sienten

Conditional (present)

sentiría
sentirías
sentiría
sentiríamos
sentiríais
sentirían

Imperfect indicative

sentía
sentías
sentía
sentíamos
sentíais
sentían

Present subjunctive

sienta
sientas
sienta
sintamos
sintáis
sientan

Past simple indicative

sentí
sentiste
sintió
sentimos
sentisteis
sintieron

Imperfect subjunctive

sintiera
sintieras
sintiera
sintiéramos
sintierais
sintieran

Future indicative

sentiré
sentirás
sentirá
sentiremos
sentiréis
sentirán

Imperative

siente (tú)
sienta (usted)
sintamos (nosotros)
sentid (vosotros)
sientan (ustedes)

venir
to come

Gerund	Past participle
viniendo	venido

Present indicative

vengo
vienes
viene
venimos
venís
vienen

Conditional (present)

vendría
vendrías
vendría
vendríamos
vendríais
vendrían

Imperfect indicative

venía
venías
venía
veníamos
veníais
venían

Present subjunctive

venga
vengas
venga
vengamos
vengáis
vengan

Past simple indicative

vine
viniste
vino
vinimos
vinisteis
vinieron

Imperfect subjunctive

viniera
vinieras
viniera
viniéramos
vinierais
vinieran

Future indicative

vendré
vendrás
vendrá
vendremos
vendréis
vendrán

Imperative

ven (tú)
venga (usted)
vengamos (nosotros)
venid (vosotros)
vengan (ustedes)

Gerund	**Past participle**	**ver**
viendo	visto	to see

Present indicative

veo
ves
ve
vemos
veis
ven

Imperfect indicative

veía
veías
veía
veíamos
veíais
veían

Past simple indicative

vi
viste
vio
vimos
visteis
vieron

Future indicative

veré
verás
verá
veremos
veréis
verán

Conditional (present)

vería
verías
vería
veríamos
veríais
verían

Present subjunctive

vea
veas
vea
veamos
veáis
vean

Imperfect subjunctive

viera
vieras
viera
viéramos
vlerais
vieran

Imperative

ve (tú)
vea (usted)
veamos (nosotros)
ved (vosotros)
vean (ustedes)

hablar
to talk, to speak

Gerund	Past participle
habl**ando**	habl**ado**

Present indicative	**Conditional (present)**
habl**o**	habl**aría**
habl**as**	habl**arías**
habl**a**	habl**aría**
habl**amos**	habl**aríamos**
habl**áis**	habl**aríais**
habl**an**	habl**arían**

Imperfect indicative	**Present subjunctive**
habl**aba**	habl**e**
habl**abas**	habl**es**
habl**aba**	habl**e**
habl**ábamos**	habl**emos**
habl**abais**	habl**éis**
habl**aban**	habl**en**

Past simple indicative	**Imperfect subjunctive**
habl**é**	habl**ara**
habl**aste**	habl**aras**
habl**ó**	habl**ara**
habl**amos**	habl**áramos**
habl**asteis**	habl**arais**
habl**aron**	habl**aran**

Future indicative	**Imperative**
habl**aré**	habl**a** (tú)
habl**arás**	habl**e** (usted)
habl**ará**	habl**emos** (nosotros)
habl**aremos**	habl**ad** (vosotros)
habl**aréis**	habl**en** (ustedes)
habl**arán**	

regular –er 18

comer
to eat

Gerund	**Past participle**
comiendo	comido

Present indicative

como
comes
come
comemos
coméis
comen

Imperfect indicative

comía
comías
comía
comíamos
comíais
comían

Past simple indicative

comí
comiste
comió
comimos
comisteis
comieron

Future indicative

comeré
comerás
comerá
comeremos
comeréis
comerán

Conditional (present)

comería
comerías
comería
comeríamos
comeríais
comerían

Present subjunctive

coma
comas
coma
comamos
comáis
coman

Imperfect subjunctive

comiera
comieras
comiera
comiéramos
comierais
comieran

Imperative

come (tú)
coma (usted)
comamos (nosotros)
comed (vosotros)
coman (ustedes)

vivir
to live

Gerund	Past participle
viviendo	vivido

Present indicative

vivo
vives
vive
vivimos
vivís
viven

Imperfect indicative

vivía
vivías
vivía
vivíamos
vivíais
vivían

Past simple indicative

viví
viviste
vivió
vivimos
vivisteis
vivieron

Future indicative

viviré
vivirás
vivirá
viviremos
viviréis
vivirán

Conditional (present)

viviría
vivirías
viviría
viviríamos
viviríais
vivirían

Present subjunctive

viva
vivas
viva
vivamos
viváis
vivan

Imperfect subjunctive

viviera
vivieras
viviera
viviéramos
vivierais
vivieran

Imperative

vive (tú)
viva (usted)
vivamos (nosotros)
vivid (vosotros)
vivan (ustedes)

20 actuar – like 17 hablar except:

Present indicative	Present subjunctive
actúo	actúe
actúas	actúes
actúa	actúe
actuamos	actuemos
actuáis	actuéis
actúan	actúen

	Imperative
	actúa (tú)
	actúe (usted)
	actuemos (nosotros)
	actuad (vosotros)
	actúen (ustedes)

21 andar – like 17 hablar except:

Past simple indicative	Imperfect subjunctive
anduve	anduviera
anduviste	anduvieras
anduvo	anduviera
anduvimos	anduviéramos
anduvisteis	anduvierais
anduvieron	anduvieran

22 cazar – like 17 hablar except:

Past simple indicative	Present subjunctive
cacé	cace
cazaste	caces
cazó	cace
cazamos	cacemos
cazasteis	cacéis
cazaron	cacen

	Imperative
	caza (tú)
	cace (usted)
	cacemos (nosotros)
	cazad (vosotros)
	cacen (ustedes)

23 colgar – like 17 hablar except:

Present indicative	Present subjunctive
cuelgo	cuelgue
cuelgas	cuelgues
cuelga	cuelgue
colgamos	colguemos
colgáis	colguéis
cuelgan	cuelguen

Past simple indicative	Imperative
colgué	cuelga (tú)
colgaste	cuelgue (usted)
colgó	colguemos (nosotros)
colgamos	colgad (vosotros)
colgasteis	cuelguen (ustedes)
colgaron	

24 contar – like 17 hablar except:

Present indicative	Present subjunctive
cuento	cuente
cuentas	cuentes
cuenta	cuente
contamos	contemos
contáis	contéis
cuentan	cuenten

	Imperative
	cuenta (tú)
	cuente (usted)
	contemos (nosotros)
	contad (vosotros)
	cuenten (ustedes)

25 empezar – like 17 hablar except:

Present indicative	Present subjunctive
empiezo	empiece
empiezas	empieces
empieza	empiece
empezamos	empecemos
empezáis	empecéis
empiezan	empiecen

Past simple indicative	Imperative
empecé	empieza (tú)
empezaste	empiece (usted)
empezó	empecemos (nosotros)
empezamos	empezad (vosotros)
empezasteis	empiecen (ustedes)
empezaron	

26 forzar – like 17 hablar except:

Present indicative	Present subjunctive
fuerzo	fuerce
fuerzas	fuerces
fuerza	fuerce
forzamos	forcemos
forzáis	forcéis
fuerzan	fuercen

Past simple indicative	Imperative
forcé	fuerza (tú)
forzaste	fuerce (usted)
forzó	forcemos (nosotros)
forzamos	forzad (vosotros)
forzasteis	fuercen (ustedes)
forzaron	

27 jugar – like 17 hablar except:

Present indicative	Present subjunctive
juego	juegue
juegas	juegues
juega	juegue
jugamos	juguemos
jugáis	juguéis
juegan	jueguen

Past simple indicative	Imperative
jugué	juega (tú)
jugaste	juegue (usted)
jugó	juguemos (nosotros)
jugamos	jugad (vosotros)
jugasteis	jueguen (ustedes)
jugaron	

28 pagar – like 17 hablar except:

Past simple indicative	Present subjunctive
pagué	pague
pagaste	pagues
pagó	pague
pagamos	paguemos
pagasteis	paguéis
pagaron	paguen

	Imperative
	paga (tú)
	pague (usted)
	paguemos (nosotros)
	pagad (vosotros)
	paguen (ustedes)

29 pensar – like 17 hablar except:

Present indicative	Present subjunctive
pienso	piense
piensas	pienses
piensa	piense
pensamos	pensemos
pensáis	penséis
piensan	piensen

	Imperative
	piensa (tú)
	piense (usted)
	pensemos (nosotros)
	pensad (vosotros)
	piensen (ustedes)

31 sacar – like 17 hablar except:

Past simple indicative	Present subjunctive
saqué	saque
sacaste	saques
sacó	saque
sacamos	saquemos
sacasteis	saquéis
sacaron	saquen

	Imperative
	saca (tú)
	saque (usted)
	saquemos (nosotros)
	sacad (vosotros)
	saquen (ustedes)

30 regar – like 17 hablar except:

Present indicative	Present subjunctive
riego	riegue
riegas	riegues
riega	riegue
regamos	reguemos
regáis	reguéis
riegan	rieguen

Past simple indicative	Imperative
regué	riega (tú)
regaste	riegue (usted)
regó	reguemos (nosotros)
regamos	
regasteis	regad (vosotros)
regaron	rieguen (ustedes)

32 vaciar – like 17 hablar except:

Present indicative	Present subjunctive
vacío	vacíe
vacías	vacíes
vacía	vacíe
vaciamos	vaciemos
vaciáis	vaciéis
vacían	vacíen

	Imperative
	vacía (tú)
	vacíe (usted)
	vaciemos (nosotros)
	vaciad (vosotros)
	vacíen (ustedes)

33 caber – like 18 comer except:

Present indicative	Conditional (present)
quepo	cabría
cabes	cabrías
cabe	cabría
cabemos	cabríamos
cabéis	cabríais
caben	cabrían

Past simple indicative	Present subjunctive
cupe	quepa
cupiste	quepas
cupo	quepa
cupimos	quepamos
cupisteis	quepáis
cupieron	quepan

Future indicative	Imperfect subjunctive
cabré	cupiera
cabrás	cupieras
cabrá	cupiera
cabremos	cupiéramos
cabréis	cupierais
cabrán	cupieran

Imperative
cabe (tú)
quepa (usted)
quepamos (nosotros)
cabed (vosotros)
quepan (ustedes)

34 caer – like 18 comer except:

Gerund cayendo
Past participle caído

Present indicative	Present subjunctive
caigo	caiga
caes	caigas
cae	caiga
caemos	caigamos
caéis	cagáis
caen	caigan

Past simple indicative	Imperfect subjunctive
caí	cayera
caíste	cayeras
cayó	cayera
caímos	cayéramos
caísteis	cayerais
cayeron	cayeran

Imperative
cae (tú)
caiga (usted)
caigamos (nosotros)
caed (vosotros)
caigan (ustedes)

35 conocer – like 18 comer except:

Present indicative	Present subjunctive
conozco	conozca
conoces	conozcas
conoce	conozca
conocemos	conozcamos
conocéis	conozcáis
conocen	conozcan

Imperative
conoce (tú)
conozca (usted)
conozcamos (nosotros)
conoced (vosotros)
conozcan (ustedes)

36 entender – like 18 comer except:

Present indicative	Present subjunctive
entiendo	entienda
entiendes	entiendas
entiende	entienda
entendemos	entendamos
entendéis	entendáis
entienden	entiendan

Imperative
entiende (tú)
entienda (usted)
entendamos
(nosotros)
entended (vosotros)
entiendan (ustedes)

37 leer – like 18 comer except:

Gerund leyendo
Past participle leído

Past simple indicative	Imperfect subjunctive
leí	leyera
leíste	leyeras
leyó	leyera
leímos	layéramos
leísteis	leyerais
leyeron	leyeran

38 mover – like 18 comer except:

Present indicative	Present subjunctive
muevo	mueva
mueves	muevas
mueve	mueva
movemos	movamos
movéis	mováis
mueven	muevan

Imperative
mueve (tú)
mueva (usted)
movamos
(nosotros)
moved (vosotros)
muevan (ustedes)

39 oler – like 18 comer except:

Present indicative	Present subjunctive
huelo	huela
hueles	huelas
huele	huela
olemos	olamos
oléis	oláis
huelen	huelan

Imperative
huele (tú)
huela (usted)
olamos (nosotros)
oled (vosotros)
huelan (ustedes)

40 romper – like 18 comer except:

Past participle roto

41 torcer – like 18 comer except:

Present indicative	Present subjunctive
tuerzo	tuerza
tuerces	tuerzas
tuerce	tuerza
torcemos	torzamos
torcéis	torzáis
tuercen	tuerzan

Imperative
tuerce (tú)
tuerza (usted)
torzamos (nosotros)
torced (vosotros)
tuerzan (ustedes)

42 **traer** − like **18 comer** except:

Gerund trayendo
Past participle traído

Present participle	Present simple indicative
traigo	traje
traes	trajiste
trae	trajo
traemos	trajimos
traéis	trajisteis
traen	trajeron

Present subjunctive	Imperative
traiga	trae (tú)
traigas	traiga (usted)
traiga	traigamos
traigamos	(nosotros)
traigáis	traed (vosotros)
traigan	traigan (ustedes)

Imperfect subjunctive

trajera	trajéramos
trajeras	trajerais
trajera	trajeran

43 **valer** − like **18 comer** except:

Present indicative	Present subjunctive
valgo	valga
vales	valgas
vale	valga
valemos	valgamos
valéis	valgáis
valen	valgan

Future indicative	Imperfect subjunctive
valdré	valiera
valdrás	valieras
valdrá	valiera
valdremos	valiéramos
valdréis	valierais
valdrán	valieran

Conditional (present)	Imperative
valdría	vale (tú)
valdrías	valga (usted)
valdría	valgamos (nosotros)
valdríamos	valed (vosotros)
valdríais	valgan (ustedes)
valdrían	

44 **vencer** − like **18 comer** except:

Present indicative	Present subjunctive
venzo	venza
vences	venzas
vence	venza
vencemos	venzamos
vencéis	venzáis
vencen	venzan

Imperative

vence (tú)
venza (usted)
venzamos (nosotros)
venced (vosotros)
venzan (ustedes)

45 **volver** − like **18 comer** except:

Past participle vuelto

Present indicative	Present subjunctive
vuelvo	vuelva
vuelves	vuelvas
vuelve	vuelva
volvemos	volvamos
volvéis	volváis
vuelven	vuelvan

Imperative

vuelve (tú)
vuelva (usted)
volvamos (nosotros)
volved (vosotros)
vuelvan (ustedes)

46 abrir – like 19 vivir except:

Past participle abierto

47 adquirir – like 19 vivir except:

Present indicative	Present subjunctive
adquiero	addquiera
adquieres	adquieras
adquiere	adquiera
adquirimos	adquiramos
adquirís	adquiráis
adquieren	adquieran

	Imperative
	adquiere (tú)
	adquiera (usted)
	adquiramos (nosotros)
	adquirid (vosotros)
	adquieran (ustedes)

48 corregir – like 19 vivir except:

Present indicative	Present subjunctive
corrijo	corrija
corriges	corrijas
corrige	corrija
corregimos	corrijamos
corregís	corrijáis
corrigen	corrijan

Past simple indicative	Imperative
corregí	corrige (tú)
corregiste	corrija (usted)
corrigió	corrijamos (nosotros)
corrigieron	corregid (vosotros)
corregisteis	corrijan (ustedes)
corrigieron	

49 dirigir – like 19 vivir except:

Present indicative	Present subjunctive
dirijo	dirija
diriges	dirijas
dirige	dirija
dirigimos	dirijamos
dirigís	dirijáis
dirigen	dirijan

	Imperative
	dirige (tú)
	dirija (usted)
	dirijamos (nosotros)
	dirigid (vosotros)
	dirijan (ustedes)

50 distinguir – like 19 vivir except:

Present indicative	Present subjunctive
distingo	distinga
distingues	distingas
distingue	distinga
distinguimos	distingamos
distinguís	distingáis
distinguen	distingan

	Imperative
	distingue (tú)
	distinga (usted)
	distingamos (nosotros)
	distinguid (vosotros)
	distingan (ustedes)

51 dormir – like 19 vivir except:

Gerund durmiendo
Past participle dormido

Present indicative	Past simple indicative
duermo	dormí
duermes	dormiste
duerme	durmió
dormimos	dormimos
dormís	dormisteis
duermen	durmieron

Imperfect subjunctive	Imperative
durmiera	duerme (tú)
dirmieras	duerma (usted)
durmiera	durmamos (nosotros)
durmiéramos	dormid (vosotros)
durmierais	duerman (ustedes)
durmieran	

Present subjunctive

duerma	durmamos
duermas	durmáis
duerma	duerman

52 escribir − like 19 vivir except:

Past participle escrito

53 freír − like 19 vivir except:

Gerund friendo
Past participle frito

Present indicative	Present subjunctive
frío	fría
fríes	frías
fríe	fría
freímos	friamos
freís	friáis
fríen	frían

Past simple indicative	Imperfect subjunctive
freí	friera
freíste	frieras
frió	friera
freímos	friéramos
freísteis	frierais
frieron	frieran

Imperative

fríe (tú)
fría (usted)
friamos (nosotros)
freíd (vosotros)
frían (ustedes)

54 huir − like 19 vivir except:

Gerund huyendo
Past participle huido

Present indicative	Present subjunctive
huyo	huya
huyes	huyas
huye	huya
huimos	huyamos
huís	huyáis
huyen	huyan

Past simple indicative	Imperfect subjunctive
huí	huyera
huiste	huyeras
huyó	huyera
huimos	huyéramos
huisteis	huyerais
huyeron	huyeran

Imperative

huye (tú)
huya (usted)
huyamos (nosotros)
huid (vosotros)
huyan (ustedes)

55 morir − like 19 vivir except:

Gerund muriendo
Past participle muerto

Present indicative	Past simple indicative
muero	morí
mueres	moriste
muere	murió
morimos	morimos
morís	moristeis
mueren	murieron

Present subjunctive	Imperfect subjunctive
muera	muriera
mueras	murieras
muera	muriera
muramos	muriéramos
muráis	murierais
mueran	murieran

56 oír – like 19 vivir except:

Gerund oyendo
Past participle oído

Present indicative	Imperfect indicative
oigo	oía
oyes	oías
oye	oía
oímos	oíamos
oís	oíais
oyen	oían

Past simple indicative	Present subjunctive
oí	oiga
oíste	oigas
oyó	oiga
oímos	oigamos
oísteis	oigáis
oyeron	oigan

Future indicative	Imperfect subjunctive
oiré	oyera
oirás	oyeras
oirá	oyera
oiremos	oyéramos
oiréis	oyerais
oirán	oyeran

Conditional (present)	Imperative
oiría	oye (tú)
oirías	oiga (usted)
oiría	oigamos (nosotros)
oiríamos	oíd (vosotros)
oiríais	oigan (ustedes)
oirían	

57 pedir – like 19 vivir except:

Gerund pidiendo

Present indicative	Present subjunctive
pido	pida
pides	pidas
pide	pida
pedimos	pidamos
pedís	pidáis
piden	pidan

Past simple indicative	Imperfect subjunctive
pedí	pidiera
pediste	pidieras
pidió	pidiera
pedimos	pidiéramos
pedisteis	pidierais
pidieron	pidieran

	Imperative
	pide (tú)
	pida (usted)
	pidamos (nostros)
	pedid (vosotros)
	pidan (ustedes)

58 prohibir – like 19 vivir except:

Present indicative	Present subjunctive
prohíbo	prohíba
prohíbes	prohíbas
prohíbe	prohíba
prohibimos	prohibamos
prohibís	prohibáis
prohíben	prohíban

	Imperative
	prohíbe (tú)
	prohíba (usted)
	prohibamos (nosotros)
	prohibid (vosotros)
	prohíban (ustedes)

59 pudrir – like 19 vivir except:

Past participle podrido

60 reducir – like 19 vivir except:

Present indicative	Present subjunctive
reduzco	reduzca
reduces	reduzcas
reduce	reduzca
reducimos	reduzcamos
reducís	reduzcáis
reducen	reduzcan

Past simple indicative	Imperfect subjunctive
reduje	redujera
redujiste	redujeras
redujo	redujera
redujimos	redujéramos
redujisteis	redujerais
redujeron	redujeran

Imperative
reduce (tú)
reduzca (usted)
reduzcamos (nosotros)
reducid (vosotros)
reduzcan (ustedes)

61 reír – like 19 vivir except:

Gerund riendo
Past participle reído

Present indicative	Conditional (present)
río	reiría
ríes	reirías
ríe	reiría
reímos	reiríamos
reís	reiríais
ríen	reirían

Imperfect indicative	Present subjunctive
reía	ría
reías	rías
reía	ría
reíamos	riamos
reíais	riáis
reían	rían

Past simple indicative	Imperfect subjunctive
reí	riera
reíste	rieras
rió	riera
reímos	riéramos
reísteis	rierais
rieron	rieran

Future indicative	Imperative
reiré	ríe (tú)
reirás	ría (usted)
reirá	riamos (nosotros)
reiremos	reíd (vosotros)
reiréis	rían (ustedes)
reirán	

62 reunir – like 19 vivir except:

Present indicative	Imperative
reúno	reúne (tú)
reúnes	reúna (usted)
reúne	reunamos (nosotros)
reunimos	reunid (vosotros)
reunís	reúnan (ustedes)
reúnen	

Present subjunctive
reúna
reúnas
reúna
reunamos
reunáis
reúnan

63 salir – like 19 vivir except:

Present indicative	Present subjunctive
salgo	salga
sales	salgas
sale	salga
salimos	salgamos
salís	salgáis
salen	salgan

Future indicative	Imperfect subjunctive
saldré	saliera
saldrás	salieras
saldrá	saliera
saldremos	saliéramos
saldréis	salierais
saldrán	salieran

Conditional (present)	Imperative
saldría	sal (tú)
saldrías	salga (usted)
saldría	salgamos (nosotros)
saldríamos	salid (vosotros)
saldríais	salgan (ustedes)
saldrían	

64 seguir – like 19 vivir except:

Gerund siguiendo

Present indicative	Past simple indicative
sigo	seguí
sigues	seguiste
sigue	siguió
seguimos	seguimos
seguís	seguisteis
siguen	siguieron

Imperfect subjunctive	Imperative
siguiera	sigue (tú)
siguieras	siga (usted)
siguiera	sigamos (nosotros)
siguiéramos	seguid (vosotros)
siguierais	sigan (ustedes)
siguieran	

Present subjunctive

siga
sigas
siga
sigamos
sigáis
sigan

65 teñir – like 19 vivir except:

Gerund tiñendo

Present indicative	Imperfect subjunctive
tiño	tiñera
tiñes	tiñeras
tiñe	tiñera
teñimos	tiñéramos
teñís	tiñerais
tiñen	tiñeran

Past simple indicative	Imperative
teñí	tiñe (tú)
teñiste	tiña (usted)
tiñó	tiñamos (nosotros)
teñimos	teñid (vosotros)
teñisteis	tiñan (ustedes)
tiñeron	

Present subjunctive

tiña
tiñas
tiña
tiñamos
tiñáis
tiñan

A a

a *indefinite article* 1 (*before a noun which is masculine in Spanish*) un; **a tree** un árbol; 2 (*before a noun which is feminine in Spanish*) una; **a table** una mesa; 3 (*before professions, occupations, etc. 'a' is not translated*) **I'm a doctor** soy médico; 4 **eighty pesetas a kilo** ochenta pesetas el kilo; 5 **fifty kilometres an hour** cincuenta kilómetros por hora; 6 **three times a day** tres veces al día.

abandon *verb* abandonar [17].

abbey *noun* abadía F; **Westminster Abbey** la abadía de Westminster.

abbreviation *noun* abreviatura F.

abide *verb* **I can't abide** … no puedo soportar …

ability *noun* 1 capacidad F; **the ability to do** la capacidad de hacer; 2 **do it to the best of your ability** hazlo lo mejor que puedas; **I did it to the best of my ability** lo hice lo mejor que pude.

able *adjective* **to be able to do** poder [10] hacer; **she wasn't able to come** no pudo venir.

abnormal *adjective* anormal.

about *preposition* 1 (*on the subject of*) sobre; **a film about Picasso** una película sobre Picasso; 2 **what's it about?** ¿de qué trata?; 3 (*concerning or in relation to*) acerca de; **he wants to talk to you about your exam** quiere hablarte acerca de tu examen; 4 **to talk about something** hablar de algo; **what is she talking about?** ¿de qué está hablando?; 5 **to think about something/somebody** pensar en algo/alguien; **I'm thinking about you** estoy pensando en ti. *adverb* 1 (*approximately*) **there are about sixty people** hay unas sesenta personas; 2 (*when talking about time*) **at about three o'clock** como a las tres; **about three weeks/a month ago** hace cosa de tres semanas/de un mes; 3 **to be about to do** estar a punto de hacer; **I'm (just) about to leave** estoy a punto de marcharme.

above *preposition* 1 encima de; **above the sink** encima del fregadero; 2 **above all** sobre todo. *adverb* de arriba; **the flat above** el piso de arriba.

abroad *adverb* **to go abroad** irse al extranjero; **to live abroad** vivir en el extranjero.

abscess *noun* flemón M.

abseiling *noun* rappel M.

absent *adjective* ausente; **to be absent from** faltar a; **he was absent from the lesson** faltó a clase; **she's often absent from meetings** falta a menudo a las reuniones; (*when referring to the present moment, 'to be absent' is translated by the present perfect*) **he's absent from school today** hoy ha faltado a clase.

absent-minded *adjective*
despistado/despistada.

absolute *adjective* absoluto/
absoluta; **an absolute disaster** un
desastre absoluto.

absolutely *adverb* 1 (*completely*)
totalmente; **I'm absolutely certain**
estoy totalmente segura;
2 (*extremely*) realmente; **it's
absolutely dreadful** es realmente
terrible; 3 **you're absolutely right**
tienes toda la razón; 4 **absolutely!**
¡por supuesto!

absorb *verb* absorber [18].

abuse *noun* 1 **alcohol abuse**
alcoholismo M; **drug abuse**
consumo M de drogas; 2 (*violent
treatment of a person*) malos
tratos M (*plural*); 3 (*insults*)
insultos M (*plural*).
verb **to abuse somebody** maltratar
[17] a alguien.

academic *adjective* académico/
académica; **the academic year** el
año académico.

accelerate *verb* acelerar [17].

accelerator *noun* acelerador M.

accent *noun* acento M; **she has a
Spanish accent** tiene acento
español.

accept *verb* aceptar [17].

acceptable *adjective* aceptable.

access *noun* acceso M.
verb **to access something** obtener
[9] acceso a algo.

accessory *noun* accesorio M.

accident *noun* 1 (*an unfortunate
happening*) accidente M; **to have an
accident** tener [9] un accidente; **a
road accident** un accidente de
carretera; **a car accident** un
accidente de coche; 2 (*chance*)
casualidad F; **it's no accident** no es
casualidad; 3 **by accident** (*by
chance*) por casualidad; (*without
meaning to*) sin querer; **I found it by
accident** lo encontré por casualidad;
she broke it by accident lo rompió
sin querer.

accidental *adjective* fortuito/
fortuita; **an accidental discovery** un
descubrimiento fortuito.

accidentally *adverb* 1 (*without
meaning to*) sin querer; **I
accidentally knocked over his
glass** le tiré el vaso sin querer; 2 (*by
chance*) por casualidad; **I
accidentally discovered that ...**
descubrí por casualidad que ...

accommodation *noun*
alojamiento M; **I'm looking for
accommodation** estoy buscando
alojamiento; **hostel
accommodation** alojamiento en
hostal.

accompany *verb* **to accompany
somebody** acompañar [17] a
alguien.

according *in phrase* **according to**
según; **according to Sophie** según
Sophie.

accordion *noun* acordeón M.

account *noun* 1 (*in a bank, shop, or post office*) cuenta F; **a bank account** una cuenta bancaria; **to open an account** abrir [46] una cuenta; **I have fifty pounds in my account** tengo cincuenta libras en mi cuenta; 2 (*a description of an experience or event*) relato M; 3 **on account of** debido a; **the station is closed on account of the strike** la estación está cerrada debido a la huelga; 4 **to take something into account** tener [9] algo en cuenta; **we will take his illness into account** tendremos en cuenta su enfermedad.

accountant *noun* contable M/F; **she's an accountant** es contable.

accuracy *noun* precisión F.

accurate *adjective* preciso/precisa.

accurately *adverb* con precisión.

accuse *verb* acusar [17]; **to accuse somebody of something** acusar a alguien de algo; **to accuse somebody of doing something** acusar a alguien de hacer algo; **she accused me of stealing her pen** me acusó de haber robado su pluma.

ace *noun* as M; **the ace of hearts** el as de corazones.
adjective de primera (*informal*); **he's an ace drummer** es un batería de primera.

ache *verb* **my arm aches** me duele el brazo; **my head aches** me duele la cabeza.

achieve *verb* 1 conseguir [64]; **she's achieved a great deal** consiguió mucho; 2 **to achieve an ambition** hacer [7] realidad una ambición; 3 **to achieve an aim** lograr [17] un objetivo; 4 **to achieve success** tener [9] éxito.

achievement *noun* 1 éxito M; **it's a great achievement** es un gran éxito; 2 **a sense of achievement** un sentimiento de satisfacción.

acid *noun* ácido M.

acid rain *noun* lluvia F ácida.

acne *noun* acné M.

acorn *noun* bellota F.

acrobat *noun* acróbata M/F.

across *preposition* 1 (*over to the other side of*) **to walk across something** cruzar [22] algo; **we walked across the park** cruzamos el parque; **to run across the road** cruzar la calle corriendo; 2 (*on the other side of*) al otro lado de; **the house across the street** la casa de enfrente; 3 **across from** en frente de; **she was sitting across from me** estaba sentada en frente de mí.

acrylic *noun* acrílica F.

act *noun* acto M.
verb actuar [20].

action *noun* acción F.

active *adjective* activo/activa.

activity *noun* actividad F.

activity holiday *noun* vacaciones F (*plural*) con actividades programadas.

actor *noun* actor M; **who's your favourite actor?** ¿quién es tu actor favorito?

actress *noun* actriz F (*plural* actrices); **who's your favourite actress?** ¿quién es tu actriz favorita?

actual *adjective* 1 **his actual words** sus palabras textuales; 2 **actual cases** casos reales; 3 **in actual fact** de hecho.

actually *adverb* 1 (*in fact, as it happens*) la verdad es que; **actually, I've changed my mind** la verdad es que he cambiado de idea; **he's not actually here at the moment** la verdad es que no está aquí en este momento; 2 (*really and truly*) de verdad; **did she actually say that?** ¿dijo eso de verdad?

acupuncture *noun* acupuntura F.

acute *adjective* 1 (*pain*) agudo/aguda; 2 **an acute accent** un acento agudo.

ad *noun* anuncio M; **to put an ad in the paper** poner un anuncio en el periódico; **the small ads** los anuncios por palabras.

AD d. de C. (*después de Cristo*); **in 400 AD** en el año 400 d. de C..

adapt *verb* 1 **to adapt something** adaptar [17] algo; 2 **to adapt to something** adaptarse [17] a algo; **she's adapted to the new system** se adaptó al nuevo sistema.

adaptor *noun* adaptador M.

add *verb* añadir [19]; **add three eggs** añadir tres huevos

● **to add something up** sumar [17] algo.

addict *noun* 1 (*drug addict*) drogadicto M, drogadicta F; 2 (*of television, chocolate, for example*) adicto M, adicta F; **she's a telly addict** es una adicta a la televisión; 3 (*of sport*) fanático M, fanática F; **he's a football addict** es un fanático del fútbol.

addicted *adjective* 1 (*to drugs, television, computer games, etc.*) adicto/adicta; **she's addicted to heroin** es adicta a la heroína; **he's addicted to the Net** es un adicto a la Internet; 2 (*to food*) **I'm addicted to tomatoes** los tomates son mi vicio (*informal*); 3 **to become addicted to something** (*to drugs*) hacerse adicto a algo; (*to television, chocolate*) enviciarse con algo.

addition *noun* 1 (*adding up*) suma F; 2 **in addition** además; 3 **in addition to** además de.

additional *adjective* adicional; **additional costs** costes M (*plural*) adicionales.

additive *noun* aditivo M.

address *noun* 1 (*of person, house, office*) señas F (*plural*); **what's your address?** ¿qué señas tienes?; 2 (*on a form*) domicilio M; 3 **to change address** cambiar [17] de domicilio.

address book *noun* libreta F de direcciones.

adequate *adjective* suficiente.

adhesive *noun* pegamento M.
adjective adhesivo/adhesiva;
adhesive tape cinta F adhesiva.

adjective *noun* adjetivo M.

adjust *verb* **1** regular [17] (*volume, temperature*); ajustar [17] (*height, width*); **2 to adjust to something** adaptarse [17] a algo.

adjustable *adjective* regulable.

administration *noun* administración F.

admiral *noun* almirante M/F.

admiration *noun* admiración F.

admire *verb* admirar [17].

admission *noun* entrada F; **'no admission'** prohibida la entrada; **'admission free'** entrada libre.

admit *verb* **1** (*confess*) admitir [19]; **she admits she lied** admite que mintió; **2** (*concede*) reconocer [35]; **I must admit that …** debo reconocer que …; **3** (*allow to enter*) dejar [17] entrar; **to admit somebody to a restaurant** dejar entrar a alguien en un restaurante.

adolescence *noun* adolescencia F.

adolescent *noun* adolescente M/F.

adopt *verb* adoptar [17].

adopted *adjective* adoptado/adoptada.

adoption *noun* adopción F.

adore *verb* adorar [17].

Adriatic Sea *noun* **the Adriatic Sea** el mar Adriático.

adult *noun* adulto M, adulta F.
adjective adulto/adulta; **the adult population** la población adulta.

Adult Education *noun* educación F para adultos.

advance *noun* avance M; **advances in technology** avances en tecnología.
verb avanzar [22].

advanced *adjective* avanzado/avanzada.

advantage *noun* **1** ventaja F; **there are several advantages** hay varias ventajas; **2 to take advantage of something** aprovechar [17] algo; **I took advantage of the sales to buy myself some shoes** aproveché las rebajas para comprarme unos zapatos; **3 to take advantage of somebody** (*unfairly*) aprovecharse [17] de alguien.

adventure *noun* aventura F.

adventurous *adjective* **1** (*person*) aventurero/aventurera; **2** (*design, designer, composer, etc.*) innovador/innovadora.

adverb *noun* adverbio M.

advert, advertisement *noun* **1** (*on television, in a news paper*) anuncio M; **2** (*small ad in a newspaper advertising a job, an article for sale, etc.*) anuncio M por palabras.

advertise *verb* **1 to advertise a product** hacer [7] publicidad de un producto; **2 to advertise something in the newspaper** anunciar [17] algo en el periódico; **I saw it advertised on telly** lo vi anunciado en la tele; **I saw a bike advertised in the paper** (*in the small ads*) vi un anuncio (por palabras) de una bicicleta en el periódico.

advertising *noun* publicidad F.

advice *noun* **1** consejos M (*plural*); **his advice is good** sus consejos son buenos; **2 a piece of advice** un consejo; **3 to give somebody advice** aconsejar [17] a alguien; **they gave me good advice** me aconsejaron bien; **4 to ask for advice about something** pedir [57] consejo sobre algo.

advise *verb* aconsejar [17]; **to advise somebody to …** aconsejar a alguien que … (*followed by the subjunctive*); **I advised him to study more** le aconsejé que estudiase más; **I advised her not to wait** le aconsejé que no esperase.

aerial *noun* antena F.

aerobics *noun* aerobic M; **to do aerobics** hacer [7] aerobic.

aeroplane *noun* avión M.

aerosol *noun* **an aerosol can** un aerosol.

affair *noun* **1** asunto M; **international affairs** asuntos internacionales; **2 a love affair** una aventura amorosa.

affect *verb* afectar [17].

affectionate *adjective* cariñoso/cariñosa.

afford *verb* **to be able to afford to do** tener [9] dinero para hacer; **I can't afford to go out much** no tengo dinero para salir mucho; **I can't afford a new bike** no tengo dinero para una bicicleta nueva.

afraid *adjective* **1 to be afraid** tener [9] miedo; **I'm afraid** tengo miedo; **2** (*with 'of'*) **I'm afraid of dogs** me dan miedo los perros; **Dan's afraid of spiders** a Dan le dan miedo las arañas; **he's afraid of flying** le da miedo volar; **she's afraid of failing the exam** le da miedo suspender el examen; **3 I'm afraid there's no milk left** me temo que no queda leche; **I'm afraid so** me temo que sí; **I'm afraid not** me temo que no.

Africa *noun* África F.

African *noun* africano M, africana F. *adjective* africano/africana.

after *preposition*, *adverb conjunction* **1** (*later in time*) después de; **after 10 o'clock** después de las diez en punto; **after lunch** después de comer; **after school** después del colegio; **after I've finished my homework** después de terminar mis deberes; **2 soon after** poco después; **3 the day after tomorrow** pasado mañana.
● **to run after somebody** correr [18] tras alguien.

after all *adverb* después de todo; **after all, she's only six** después de todo, sólo tiene seis años.

afternoon *noun* tarde F; **this afternoon** esta tarde; **tomorrow afternoon** mañana por la tarde; **yesterday afternoon** ayer por la tarde; **on Saturday afternoon** el sábado por la tarde; **on Saturday afternoons** los sábados por la tarde; **at four o' clock in the afternoon** a las cuatro de la tarde; **every afternoon** todas las tardes.

afters *noun* postre M.

after-shave *noun* loción F para después del afeitado.

afterwards *adverb* después; **shortly afterwards** poco después.

again *adverb* **1** (*one more time*) otra vez; **try again** inténtalo otra vez; **I've forgotten it again** se me ha olvidado otra vez; **you should ask again** deberías preguntar otra vez; **2** (*with a negative verb*) **I don't want to see her again** no quiero volver a verla; **don't do it again** no lo vuelvas a hacer; **3 never again!** ¡nunca más!

against *preposition* contra; **against the wall** contra la pared; **to lean against the wall** apoyarse contra la pared; **I'm against the idea** estoy en contra de la idea; **to fight against racism** luchar contra el racismo.

age *noun* **1** edad F; **at the age of fifteen** a la edad de quince años; **she's the same age as me** tiene mi misma edad; **to be under age** ser menor de edad; **2 I haven't seen**

Johnny for ages hace siglos que no he visto a Johnny (*informal*); **I haven't been to London for ages** hace un montón de tiempo que no voy a Londres (*informal*).

agenda *noun* agenda F.

aggressive *adjective* agresivo/agresiva.

ago *adverb* **an hour ago** hace una hora; **three days ago** hace tres días; **five years ago** hace cinco años; **a long time ago** hace mucho tiempo; **not long ago** no hace mucho (tiempo); **how long ago was it?** ¿cuánto tiempo hace de eso?

agree *verb* **1 to agree with somebody** estar [2] de acuerdo con alguien; **I agree with Laura** estoy de acuerdo con Laura; **I don't agree** no estoy de acuerdo; **2 I agree that …** estoy de acuerdo en que …; **I agree that it's too late now** estoy de acuerdo en que ya es muy tarde; **3 to agree to do** acceder [18] a hacer; **Steve's agreed to help me** Steve ha accedido a ayudarme; **4 coffee doesn't agree with me** el café no me sienta bien.

agreement *noun* acuerdo M.

agricultural *adjective* agrícola.

agriculture *noun* agricultura F.

ahead *adverb* **1 go ahead!** ¡adelante!; **2 straight ahead** todo recto; **go straight ahead until you get to the crossroads** sigue todo recto hasta que llegues al cruce; **3 our team was ten points ahead** nuestro equipo llevaba diez puntos de ventaja; **I'll go ahead** yo voy delante; **4 to be ahead of time** ir [8] adelantado.

aid *noun* **1** ayuda F; **aid to developing countries** ayuda a los países en vías de desarrollo; **2 in aid of** en beneficio de; **in aid of the homeless** en beneficio de la gente sin hogar.

Aids *noun* sida M (*síndrome de inmunodeficiencia adquirida*); **to have Aids** tener [9] el sida.

aim *noun* objetivo M; **their aim is to control pollution** su objetivo es controlar la contaminación.
verb **1 to aim to do** proponerse [11] hacer; **we're aiming to finish it today** nos proponemos terminarlo hoy; **2 a campaign aimed at young people** una campaña dirigida a los jóvenes; **3 to aim a gun at somebody** apuntar [17] una pistola a alguien.

air *noun* **1** aire M; **in the open air** al aire libre; **to go out for a breath of air** salir [63] a tomar el aire; **2 to travel by air** viajar [17] en avión.

airbag *noun* airbag M.

air-conditioned *adjective* con aire acondicionado.

air conditioning *noun* aire M acondicionado.

Air Force *noun* fuerza F aérea.

air hostess *noun* azafata F; **she's an air hostess** es azafata.

airline *noun* compañía F aérea.

airmail *noun* correo M aéreo; **by airmail** por correo aéreo.

airport *noun* aeropuerto M.

aisle *noun* (*in theatre, on plane*) pasillo M.

alarm *noun* alarma F; **a fire alarm** una alarma contra incendios; **a burglar alarm** una alarma antirrobo.

alarm clock *noun* reloj M despertador.

album *noun* álbum M.

alcohol *noun* alcohol M.

alcoholic *noun* alcohólico M, alcohólica F.
adjective alcohólico/alcohólica; **alcoholic drinks** bebidas alcohólicas.

A levels *noun* selectividad F (*students take 'la selectividad' at the same age as A levels are taken in Britain; however, they are examined in many more subjects, usually around 7, and are given one overall mark out of 10*).

alike *adjective* **1** parecido/parecida; **they're all alike** son todos parecidos; **2 to look alike** parecerse [35]; **the two brothers look alike** los dos hermanos se parecen.

alive *adjective* vivo/viva.

all *adjective*, *pronoun* **1** todo/toda; **all the knives** todos los cuchillos; **all the cups** todas las tazas; **all the time** todo el tiempo; **all day** todo el día; **2 they've eaten it all** se lo han

comido todo; **after all** después de todo; **not at all** de nada (*to somebody who's said 'thank you'*); **they're all there** están todos allí; **3 it's all I have** es todo lo que tengo; **4 three all** tres iguales.
adverb completamente; **all alone** completamente solo; **she's all alone at the moment** ahora está completamente sola.

all along *adverb* desde el primer momento; **I knew it all along** lo supe desde el primer momento.

allergic *adjective* alérgico/alérgica; **to be allergic to something** ser [1] alérgico a algo.

allow *verb* **1 to allow somebody to do** permitir [19] a alguien hacer; **the teacher allowed them to go out** el maestro les permitió salir; **2** (*to do*) **I'm not allowed to go out during the week** no me dejan salir durante la semana; **they are allowed to watch TV in the evenings** les dejan ver la tele por las noches.

all right *adverb* **1** (*showing agreement*) de acuerdo; vale (*informal*); **'come round to my house around six' – 'all right'** 'ven a mi casa a eso de las seis' – 'de acuerdo', 'ven a mi casa a eso de las seis' – 'vale'; **it's all right by me** por mí de acuerdo, por mí vale (*informal*); **2** (*fine*) **is everything all right?** ¿va todo bien?; **3** (*talking about health, wellbeing*) bien; **are you all right?** ¿estás bien?; **she's all right now** ya está bien; **4** (*not bad*) **the meal was all right** la comida no estuvo mal; **5 is it all right to leave**

the door open? ¿puedo dejar la puerta abierta?

almond *noun* almendra F.

almost *adverb* casi; **almost every day** casi cada día; **almost everybody** casi todo el mundo; **she's almost five** tiene casi cinco años.

alone *adjective* **1** solo/sola; **he lives alone** vive solo; **2 leave me alone!** ¡déjame en paz!; **3 leave these papers alone!** ¡deja esos papeles!

along *preposition* **1** a lo largo de; **there are trees all along the road** hay árboles a lo largo de toda la calle; **2** (*there is often no direct translation for 'along' so the sentence has to be expressed differently*) **she lives along the road from me** vive en mi misma calle; **to go for a walk along the beach** pasear por la playa; **a bit further along** un poco más adelante.

aloud *adverb* en voz alta; **to read something aloud** leer [37] algo en voz alta.

alphabet *noun* alfabeto M.

Alps *plural noun* **the Alps** los Alpes.

already *adverb* ya; **they've already left** ya han salido; **it's six o'clock already!** ¡ya son las seis!

Alsatian *noun* pastor M alemán.

also *adverb* también; **I've also invited Karen** he invitado también a Karen.

alter *verb* cambiar [17].

alternate *adjective* **on alternate days** un día sí y otro no.

alternative noun alternativa F; **we have no alternative** no tenemos alternativa.
adjective otro/otra; **to find an alternative solution** encontrar otra solución.

alternatively adverb o bien; **alternatively, we could go together on Saturday** o bien podríamos ir juntos el sábado.

alternative medicine noun medicina F alternativa.

although conjunction aunque; **although she's ill, she's willing to help us** aunque está enferma, está dispuesta a ayudarnos.

altogether adverb 1 en total; **I've spent thirty pounds altogether** he gastado treinta libras en total; 2 (completely) totalmente; **I'm not altogether convinced** no estoy totalmente convencido.

aluminium noun aluminio M.

always adverb siempre; **I always leave at five** siempre salgo a las cinco.

am verb SEE **be**.

a.m. abbreviation de la mañana; **at 8 a.m.** a las ocho de la mañana.

amateur noun amateur M/F (plural amateurs); **amateur dramatics** teatro M de amateurs.

amaze verb sorprender [18]; **what amazes me is …** lo que me sorprende es …

amazed adjective sorprendido/sorprendida; **I was amazed to see her** me sorprendió verla; **he'll be amazed to find out** le sorprenderá enterarse.

amazing adjective increíble; **they've got an amazing house** tienen una casa increíble; **she has an amazing number of friends** tiene un número increíble de amigos.

ambassador noun embajador M, embajadora F.

ambition noun ambición F.

ambitious adjective ambicioso/ambiciosa.

ambulance noun ambulancia F.

ambulance driver noun conductor/conductora M/F de ambulancia.

amenities plural noun servicios M (plural) públicos.

America noun América F.

American noun americano M, americana F.
adjective americano/americana.

among, amongst preposition entre; **I found it amongst my books** lo encontré entre mis libros; **you can decide amongst yourselves** podéis decidirlo entre vosotros.

amount noun 1 cantidad F; **an enormous amount of bread** una enorme cantidad de pan; **a huge amount of work** una enorme cantidad de trabajo; 2 (of money) suma F; **a large amount of money** una gran suma de dinero.

amp noun 1 amperio M; 2 (amplifier) amplificador M.

amplifier *noun* amplificador M.

amuse *verb* divertir [14].

amusement arcade *noun* salón M de juegos recreativos.

amusement park *noun* parque M de atracciones.

amusing *adjective* divertido/ divertida.

an *article* SEE **a**.

anaesthetic *noun* anestesia F.

analyse *verb* analizar [22].

analysis *noun* análisis M.

ancestor *noun* antepasado M, antepasada F.

anchovy *noun* anchoa F.

ancient *adjective* 1 (*historic*) antiguo/antigua; **an ancient abbey** una antigua abadía; 2 (*very old*) viejísimo/viejísima; **an ancient pair of jeans** unos vaqueros viejísimos; 3 **ancient Greece** la Grecia antigua.

and *conjunction* 1 y; **Sean and Anna** Sean y Anna; **your shoes and socks** tus calcetines y tus zapatos; (*'y' becomes 'e' before a word that starts with 'i' or 'hi'*) **Spain and Italy** España e Italia; 2 (*with numbers*) **three hundred and six** trescientos seis; **five hundred and thirty-one** quinientos treinta y uno; 3 **fish and chips** pescado con patatas fritas; 4 **louder and louder** cada vez más alto.

Andalusia *noun* Andalucía F.

Andalusian *noun* andaluz, andaluza M/F. *adjective* andaluz/andaluza.

angel *noun* ángel M.

anger *noun* ira F.

angle *noun* ángulo M.

angrily *adverb* con enfado.

angry *adjective* **to be angry** estar [2] enfadado/enfadada; **she was angry with me** estaba enfadada conmigo; **to get angry (about something)** enfadarse [17] (por algo).

animal *noun* animal M.

ankle *noun* tobillo M; **to break your ankle** romperse [40] el tobillo.

anniversary *noun* aniversario M; **a wedding anniversary** un aniversario de boda.

announce *verb* anunciar [17].

announcement *noun* anuncio M.

annoy *verb* **to be annoyed** estar [2] enfadado/enfadada; **to get annoyed (about something)** enfadarse [17] (por algo); **she got annoyed** se enfadó.

annoying *adjective* 1 (*person*) pesado/pesada; 2 (*noise or habit*) irritante; 3 **how annoying!** ¡qué rabia!; **the whole thing's really annoying** todo es un verdadero fastidio.

annual *adjective* anual.

anorak *noun* anorak M (*plural* **anoraks**).

anorexia *noun* anorexia F.

another *adjective* otro/otra; **would you like another cup of tea?** ¿quieres otra taza de té?; **another two years** otros dos años; **we need another three chairs** necesitamos otras tres sillas; **I'll come another time** vendré en otro momento.

answer *noun* 1 respuesta F; **the right answer** la respuesta correcta; **the wrong answer** la respuesta equivocada; **2 the answer to a problem** la solución a un problema. *verb* 1 contestar [17]; **he hasn't answered our letter** no ha contestado a nuestra carta; **to answer the phone** contestar el teléfono; **2 to answer the door** abrir [46] la puerta.

answering machine *noun* contestador M automático; **to leave a message on the answering machin** dejar [17] un mensaje en el contestador.

ant *noun* hormiga F.

Antarctic *noun* la Antártida.

anthem *noun* **the national anthem** el himno nacional.

antibiotic *noun* antibiótico M.

antique *noun* **antiques** las antigüedades. *adjective* antiguo/antigua; **an antique table** una mesa antigua.

antique shop *noun* tienda F de antigüedades.

antiseptic *noun* antiséptico M.

anxious *adjective* preocupado/preocupada.

anxiously *adverb* con preocupación.

any *pronoun* 1 (*in negative sentences*) ninguno/ninguna; **I don't want any** no quiero ninguno/ninguna; **2** (*in questions*) alguno/alguna; **do you want any?** ¿quieres alguno/alguna? *adjective, adverb* 1 (*when followed by a noun 'any' is not translated*) **is there any butter?** ¿hay mantequilla? **have you got any glasses?** ¿tienes vasos?; **there isn't any flour** no hay harina; **I haven't got any glasses** no tengo vasos; **2 is there any more?** (*followed by a singular*) ¿queda más?; (*followed by a plural*) ¿quedan más?; **there isn't any more butter** no me queda más mantequilla; **I haven't got any more glasses** no me quedan más vasos; **3** (*referring to time*) **I don't go there any more** ya no voy nunca; **I used to phone her but not any more** solía llamarla, pero ya no.

anybody, anyone *pronoun* 1 (*in questions and after 'if'*) alguien; **does anybody want some tea?** ¿alguien quiere té?; **is anybody home?** ¿hay alguien en casa?; **if anybody wants some beer, it's in the fridge** si alguien quiere cerveza, está en la nevera; **2 not … anybody** no … nadie; **there isn't anybody in her office** no hay nadie en su oficina **I don't know anybody there** no conozco a nadie allí; **3** (*absolutely* *anybody*) cualquiera; **anybody can go** puede ir cualquiera.

anyhow *adverb* SEE **anyway**.

anyone *pronoun* SEE **anybody**.

anything *pronoun* **1** (*in questions*) algo; **is there anything I can do to help?** ¿puedo hacer algo para ayudar?; **2 not ... anything** no ... nada; **there isn't anything on the table** no hay nada en la mesa; **3** (*anything at all*) cualquier cosa; **anything could happen** puede pasar cualquier cosa.

anyway, anyhow *adverb* de todos modos; **anyway, I'll ring you before I leave** de todos modos te llamaré antes de salir.

anywhere *adverb* **1** (*in questions*) **have you seen my keys anywhere?** ¿has visto mis llaves por algún lado?; **are you going anywhere tomorrow?** ¿vas a algún lado mañana?; **2 not ... anywhere** por ningún lado; **I can't find my keys anywhere** no puedo encontrar mis llaves por ningún lado; **I'm not going anywhere tonight** esta noche no voy a ningún lado; **3** (*absolutely anywhere*) donde sea; **put your cases down anywhere** pon las maletas donde sea.

apart *adjective*, *adverb* **1** (*separate*) separado/separada; **we don't like being apart** no nos gusta estar separados; **they're too far apart** están demasiado separados; **2 to be two metres apart** a dos metros de distancia; **3 apart from** aparte de; **apart from Judy everybody was**

there aparte de Judy, todo el mundo estaba allí.

apartheid *noun* apartheid M.

apartment *noun* apartamento M.

apologize *verb* **1** disculparse [17]; **he apologized for his behaviour** se disculpó por su comportamiento; **2 to apologize to somebody** pedirle [57] perdón a alguien; **he apologized to Tanya** le pidió perdón a Tanya.

apology *noun* disculpa F.

apostrophe *noun* apóstrofe M.

apparent *adjective* aparente.

apparently *adverb* al parecer.

appeal *noun* **1** (*call*) **an appeal for calm** un llamamiento a la calma; **2 an appeal for help** una solicitud de ayuda.
verb **to appeal to somebody** atraer [42] a alguien; **horror films don't appeal to me** las películas de miedo no me atraen.

appear *verb* **1** aparecer [35]; **Mick appeared at the door** Mick apareció en la puerta; **2 to appear on television** salir [63] en televisión; **3** (*seem*) parecer [35]; **it appears that somebody has stolen the key** parece que alguien ha robado la llave; **he appears to be calm** parece que está tranquilo.

appendicitis *noun* apendicitis F.

appetite *noun* apetito M; **it'll spoil your appetite** te quitará el apetito.

applaud *verb* aplaudir [19].

applause *noun* aplausos M (*plural*).

apple *noun* manzana F.

apple tree *noun* manzano M.

applicant *noun* candidato M, candidata F.

application *noun* **a job application** una solicitud de trabajo.

application form *noun* (*for a job*) impreso M de solicitud.

apply *verb* **1** **to apply for a job** solicitar [17] un trabajo; **2 I've applied for the course** he solicitado que me admitan en el curso; **3 to apply to** aplicarse [31] a; **that doesn't apply to students** eso no se aplica a los estudiantes.

appointment *noun* cita F; **to make a dental appointment** pedir [57] cita en el dentista; **I've got a hair appointment at 4** tengo cita en la peluquería para las cuatro.

appreciate *verb* agradecer [35]; **I appreciate your advice** te agradezco tus consejos; **I'd appreciate it if you could tidy up afterwards** te agradecería que luego recogieses.

apprentice *noun* aprendiz M, aprendiza F.

apprenticeship *noun* aprendizaje M.

approach *verb* **1** (*come near to*) acercarse [31] a; **we were approaching Madrid** nos

acercábamos a Madrid; **2** (*tackle*) abordar [17] (*a problem, task*).

appropriate *adjective* apropiado/ apropiada.

approval *noun* aprobación F.

approve *verb* **I don't approve of her friends** no me gustan sus amigos; **I don't approve of his methods** no estoy de acuerdo con sus métodos; **does he approve of the idea?** ¿le parece bien la idea?

approximate *adjective* aproximado/aproximada.

approximately *adverb* aproximadamente; **approximately fifty people** aproximadamente cincuenta personas.

apricot *noun* albaricoque M.

apricot tree *noun* albaricoquero M.

April *noun* abril M; **in April** en abril.

April Fool *noun* inocente M/F (*see the entry for 'April Fool's Day'*).

April Fool's Day *noun* el día de los Santos Inocentes (*this is roughly the equivalent of April Fool's Day, but it is on the 28th of December*).

apron *noun* delantal M.

Aquarius *noun* acuario M; **Sharon's Aquarius** Sharon es acuario.

Arab *noun* árabe M/F.
adjective árabe; **the Arab countries** los países árabes.

arch *noun* arco M.

archaelogist *noun* arqueólogo M, arqueóloga F; **she's an archeologist** es arqueóloga.

archaeology *noun* arqueología F.

archbishop *noun* arzobispo M.

architect *noun* arquitecto M, arquitecta F; **he's an architect** es arquitecto.

architecture *noun* arquitectura F.

Arctic *noun* **the Arctic** el Ártico.

are *verb* SEE **be**.

area *noun* **1** (*part of a town*) barrio M; **a nice area** un buen barrio; **a rough area** un barrio peligroso; **2** (*region*) zona F; **in the Leeds area** en la zona de Leeds.

Argentina *noun* Argentina F.

Argentinian *noun* argentino M, argentina F.
adjective argentino/argentina.

argue *verb* discutir [19]; **there's no point in arguing** no tiene sentido discutir; **to argue about something** discutir sobre algo; **they're arguing about the result** están discutiendo sobre el resultado.

argument *noun* discusión F; **to have an argument** discutir [19].

Aries *noun* aries M; **Pauline's Aries** Pauline es aries.

arm *noun* brazo M; **he took my arm** me cogió del brazo; **to fold your arms** cruzar los brazos; **to go arm in**

arm ir [8] del brazo; **to break your arm** romperse [40] el brazo.

armchair *noun* sillón M.

armed *adjective* armado/armada.

arms *plural noun* armas F (*plural*).

army *noun* ejército M; **to join the army** alistarse en el ejército.

around *preposition, adverb* **1** (*with time*) alrededor de; **we'll be there around ten** estaremos allí alrededor de las diez; **2** (*with amounts, age*) **we need around six kilos** necesitamos unos seis quilos; **she's around fifteen** tiene unos quince años; **3** (*surrounding*) alrededor de; **the countryside around Edinburgh** el campo de alrededor de Edinburgo; **we sat around the table** nos sentamos alrededor de la mesa; **4** (*near*) por aquí; **is there a post office around here?** ¿hay una oficina de correos por aquí?; **is Phil around?** ¿está Phil por aquí?; **5** (*wrapped around*) alrededor de; **she had a scarf around her neck** tenía una bufanda alrededor del cuello; **6 around the corner** a la vuelta de la esquina; **7 to travel around the world** viajar por el mundo.

arrange *verb* **to arrange to do** quedar [17] en hacer; **we've arranged to see a film on Saturday** quedamos en ver una película el domingo.

arrest *noun* **he's under arrest** está detenido; **you're under arrest**

queda detenido.
verb arrestar [17].

arrival *noun* llegada F.

arrive *verb* llegar [17]; **they arrived at three** llegaron a las tres.

arrow *noun* flecha F.

art *noun* **1** arte M (*plural* **artes**) (*note that the plural 'artes' is feminine*); **modern art** arte moderno; **the arts** las artes; **2** (*school subject*) dibujo M; **the art class** la clase de dibujo.

art school *noun* escuela F de Bellas Artes.

artery *noun* arteria F.

art gallery *noun* (*public*) museo M de arte.

article *noun* artículo M.

artichoke *noun* alcachofa F.

artificial *adjective* artificial.

artist *noun* artista M/F; **he's an artist** es artista.

artistic *adjective* artístico/artística.

as *conjunction*, *adverb* **1** como; **as you know** como sabes; **as usual** como siempre; **as I told you** como te dije; **2** (*because*) como; **as there were no trains, we took the bus** como no había trenes, cogimos el autobús; **3** **as ... as** tan ... como; **he's as tall as his brother** es tan alto como su hermano; **you must be as tired as I am** debes estar tan cansado como yo; **I did it as quickly as I could** lo hice tan rápido como pude; **4** **as much ... as** tanto/tanta ... como; **you**

have as much time as I do tienes tanto tiempo como yo; **5** **as many ... as** tantos/tantas ... como; **we have as many problems as he does** tenemos tantos problemas como él; **6** **as long as** siempre que (*followed by the subjunctive*); **we'll go tomorrow, as long as it's a nice day** iremos mañana, siempre que haga buen tiempo; **7** **you can stay for as long as you like** puedes quedarte todo el tiempo que quieras; **8** **as soon as possible** lo más pronto posible; **9** **to work as** trabajar [17] de; **he works as a taxi driver in the evenings** trabaja de taxista por las noches.

asbestos *noun* asbestos M.

ash *noun* ceniza F.

ashamed *adjective* **to be ashamed** estar [2] avergonzado; **you should be ashamed of yourself!** ¡deberías estar avergonzado!

ashtray *noun* cenicero M.

Asia *noun* Asia F.

ask *verb* **1** (*inquire*) preguntar [17]; **you can ask at reception** puedes preguntar en recepción; **to ask somebody something** preguntarle algo a alguien; **I asked him where he lived** le pregunté dónde vivía; **2** (*request*) pedir [57]; **to ask for something** pedir algo; **I asked for three coffees** pedí tres cafés; **to ask somebody to do** pedirle a alguien que haga; (*note that 'que' is followed by subjunctive*) **ask Danny to give you a hand** pídele a Danny que te eche una mano; **3** **to ask somebody a**

question hacerle una pregunta a alguien; **I asked you a question !** ¡te he hecho una pregunta!; **4** invitar [17]; **they've asked us to a party at their house** nos han invitado a una fiesta en su casa; **5 Paul's asked Janie out on Friday** Paul invitó a Janie a salir el viernes.

asleep *adjective* dormido/dormida; **to be asleep** estar [2] dormido; **the baby's asleep** el niño está dormido; **to fall asleep** quedarse [17] dormido.

asparagus *noun* espárrago M.

aspirin *noun* aspirina F.

assignment *noun* (*at school, college*) tarea F.

assist *verb* ayudar [17].

assistance *noun* ayuda F.

assistant *noun* **1** (*at work*) ayudante M/F; **2 a shop assistant** un dependiente/una dependienta.

association *noun* asociación F.

assorted *adjective* variado/variada.

assortment *noun* surtido M.

assume *verb* suponer [11].

assure *verb* asegurar [17]; **I assure you** te lo aseguro.

asthma *noun* asma F; **she has asthma** tiene asma.

astrology *noun* astrología F.

astronaut *noun* astronauta M/F.

astronomy *noun* astronomía F.

at *preposition* **1** (*in a place*) en; **at home** en casa; **at school** en el colegio; **at my office** en mi oficina; **I'll be at work** estaré en el trabajo; **2** (*talking about the time*) a; **at eight o'clock** a las ocho; **3 at night** por la noche; **I'll be there at the weekend** estaré allí el fin de semana; **4 at Emma's house** en casa de Emma; **she's at her brother's this evening** esta noche está en casa de su hermano; **at the hairdresser's** en la peluquería; **5 at last** por fin; **he's found a job at last** por fin ha encontrado un trabajo.

athlete *noun* atleta M/F.

athletic *adjective* atlético/atlética.

athletics *noun* atletismo M.

Atlantic *noun* **the Atlantic** el Atlántico.

atlas *noun* atlas M.

atmosphere *noun* atmósfera F.

atom *noun* átomo M.

atomic *adjective* atómico/atómica.

attach *verb* **1** (*fasten*) sujetar [17]; **2** (*tie*) atar [17]; **3** (*glue*) pegar [28].

attached *adjective* **to be attached to** (*be fond of*) tenerle cariño a.

attack *noun* ataque M. *verb* atacar [31].

attempt *noun* intento M; **at the first attempt** al primer intento.

verb **to attempt to do** intentar [17] hacer.

attend *verb* asistir [19] a; **to attend a class** asistir a clase.

attention *noun* atención F; **to pay attention to** prestar atención a; **I wasn't paying atttention** no estaba prestando atención.

attic *noun* desván M.

attitude *noun* actitud F.

attract *verb* atraer [42].

attraction *noun* atracción F.

attractive *adjective* atractivo/atractiva.

aubergine *noun* berenjena F.

auction *noun* subasta F.

audience *noun* público M.

August *noun* agosto M.

aunt, auntie *noun* tía F.

au pair *noun* au pair M/F; **I'm looking for a job as an au pair** estoy buscando un trabajo de au pair.

Australia *noun* Australia F.

Australian *noun* australiano M, australiana F.
adjective australiano/australiana.

Austria *noun* Austria F.

Austrian *noun* austriaco M, austriaca F.
adjective austriaco/austriaca.

author *noun* autor M, autora F.

autobiography *noun* autobiografía F.

autograph *noun* autógrafo M.

automatic *adjective* automático/automática.

automatically *adverb* automáticamente.

autumn *noun* otoño M.

availability *noun* disponibilidad F.

available *adjective* disponible.

avenue *noun* avenida F.

average *noun* **1** media F; **above average** por encima de la media; **2 on average** como promedio.
adjective medio/media; **of average height** de estatura media.

avocado *noun* aguacate M.

avoid *verb* evitar [17]; **she avoided me** me evitó; **to avoid doing** evitar hacer; **I avoid speaking to him** evito hablar con él.

awake *adjective* **to be awake** estar [2] despierto/despierta; **is Lola awake?** ¿está Lola despierta?

award *noun* premio M; **to win an award** ganar [17] un premio.

aware *adjective* **to be aware of a noise** oír [56] un ruido; **to be aware of a problem** ser [1] consciente de un problema; **to become aware of something** darse [4] cuenta de algo; **as far as I'm aware** que yo sepa.

away *adverb* **1 to be away** estar [2] fuera; **I'll be away next week** estaré fuera la próxima semana; **2 to go away** irse [8]; **Laura's gone away for a week** Laura se ha ido por una semana; **go away!** ¡vete!; **3 to run**

away escaparse [17]; **the thieves ran away** los ladrones se escaparon; **4 the school is two kilometres away** el colegio está a dos kilómetros; **how far away is it?** ¿a qué distancia está?; **not far away** no muy lejos; **a long way away** muy lejos; **5 to put something away** guardar [17] algo; **I'll just put my books away** voy a guardar mis libros; **6 to give something away** regalar [17] algo; **she's given away all her tapes** ha regalado todas sus cintas.

away match *noun* partido M fuera de casa.

awful *adjective* **1** horrible; **the film was awful!** la película era horrible; **2 I feel awful** (*ill*) me siento fatal; **3 I feel awful about it** me siento muy culpable; **4 an awful lot of** un montón de; **5 how awful!** ¡qué horror!

awkward *adjective* **1** difícil; **it's an awkward situation** es una situación difícil; **it's a bit awkward** no es fácil; **an awkward child** un niño difícil; **2 an awkward question** una pregunta comprometida.

axe *noun* hacha F (*even though 'hacha' is a feminine noun it is used with 'el' and 'un'*).

B b

baby *noun* bebé M.

babysit *verb* hacer [7] de canguro.

babysitter *noun* canguro M/F.

babysitting *noun* hacer de canguro.

back *noun* **1** (*of a person or garment*) espalda F; **to do something behind somebody's back** hacer [7] algo a espaldas de alguien; **2** (*of an animal*) lomo M; **3** (*of a piece of paper or your hand*) dorso M; **on the back** en el dorso; **4** (*of a car, a plane, or a hall*) fondo M; **we have seats at the back** tenemos asientos al fondo; **the children are at the back of the room** los niños que están al fondo de la habitación; **5** (*of a building*) parte F de atrás; **a garden at the back of the house** un jardín en la parte de atrás de la casa; **6** (*of a chair or sofa*) respaldo M; **7** (*in football or hockey*) defensa F.
adjective **1** trasero/trasera (*a wheel or seat*); **the back seat of the car** el asiento trasero del coche; **2 the back garden** el jardín de atrás; **the back gate** la verja de atrás.
adverb **1 to go back** volver [45]; **to go back to school** volver al colegio; **Lisa's gone back to London** Lisa ha vuelto a Londres; **2 to come back** volver [45]; **they've come back from Italy** han vuelto de Italia; **she's back at work** ha vuelto al trabajo; **Sue's not back yet** Sue no ha vuelto aún; **we went by bus and walked back** fue en autobús y volvió andando; **3 to phone back** volver [45] a llamar; **I'll ring back later** te volveré a llamar más tarde; **4 to give something back to somebody** devolverle [45] algo a alguien; **I gave him back his cassettes** le devolví sus cintas; **give**

it back! ¡devuélvemelo!
verb 1 apoyar [17] (*a candidate*); 2
apostar [24] por (*a horse*);
● **to back up** (*on a computer*) **to back
up a file** hacer [7] una copia de
seguridad de un archivo.
● **to back somebody up** apoyar [17] a
alguien.

backache *noun* dolor M de espalda.

backbone *noun* columna F
vertebral.

back door *noun* 1 (*of a building*)
puerta F de atrás; 2 (*of a car*) puerta F
trasera.

backfire *verb* (*turn out badly*) salir
[63] mal.

background *noun* 1 (*of a person*)
origen M; 2 (*of events or a situation*)
contexto M; 3 (*in a picture or view*)
fondo M; **the trees in the
background** los árboles del fondo;
4 **background music** música de
fondo; **background noise** ruido de
fondo.

backhand *noun* revés M.

backing *noun* (*moral support*)
apoyo M.

backpack *noun* mochila F.
verb **to go backpacking** viajar con
mochila.

back seat *noun* asiento M trasero.

backside *noun* trasero M.

backstroke *noun* estilo M espalda;
to swim backstroke nadar a espalda.

back to front *adverb* al revés; **your
jumper's back to front** te has puesto
el jersey al revés.

backup *noun* 1 (*support*) apoyo M;
2 (*in computing*) **a backup disk** un
disco de seguridad.

backwards *adverb* (*to lean or fall*)
hacia atrás.

bacon *noun* bacon M; **bacon and
eggs** huevos con bacon.

bad *adjective* 1 (*not good*) malo/
mala; (*malo' becomes 'mal' when it
comes before a masculine singular
noun*) **a bad moment** un mal
momento; **it's bad for your health** es
malo para la salud; 2 grave (*an
accident, a mistake*); **a bad accident**
un accidente grave; 3 fuerte (*a
headache, a cold*); **a bad cold** un
resfriado fuerte; 4 (*rotten*) podrido/
podrida; **a bad apple** una manzana
podrida; **to go bad** estropearse [17];
5 (*rude*) **bad language** lenguaje
grosero; 6 (*naughty*) malo/mala;
bad dog! ¡(perro) malo!; 7 **to be bad
at something** dársele [4] algo mal a
alguien; **I'm bad at physics** se me da
mal la física; 8 **not bad** no está mal;
his new film's not bad su nueva
película no está mal; ★ **too
bad!** (*I'm sorry for you*) ¡qué rabia!; (*I
don't care*) ¡y a mí qué!

badge *noun* 1 (*pin-on*) chapa F; 2 a
policeman badge una placa de
policía.

badly *adverb* 1 mal; **he writes badly**
escribe mal; **I slept badly** dormí mal;
my exam went badly el examen me
fue mal; 2 **badly hurt** gravemente

herido; **3 the car was badly damaged** el coche quedó muy estropeado.

bad-mannered *adjective* maleducado/maleducada.

badminton *noun* bádminton M; **to play badminton** jugar al bádminton.

bad-tempered *adjective* **1** (*answer, look*) malhumorado/malhumorada; **2 to be bad-tempered** (*for a while*) estar de mal humor; (*always*) tener mal genio.

bag *noun* **1** (*plastic, paper*) bolsa F; **2** (*handbag*) bolso M.

bags *plural noun* maletas F (*plural*); **to pack your bags** hacer las maletas; ★ **to have bags under your eyes** tener ojeras.

baggage *noun* equipaje M.

baggage allowance *noun* franquicia F de equipaje.

baggage reclaim *noun* recogida F de equipaje.

bagpipes *plural noun* gaita F; **to play the bagpipes** tocar la gaita.

bake *verb* **to bake a cake** hacer [7] un pastel; **to bake potatoes** asar [17] patatas.

baked *adjective* **1** (*fruit or vegetables*) asado/asada; **baked apples** manzanas asadas; **a baked potato** una patata asada; **2** (*fish*) al horno.

baked beans *plural noun* alubias F (*plural*) en salsa de tomate.

baker *noun* panadero M, panadera F; **to go to the baker's** ir a la panadería.

bakery *noun* panadería F.

balance *noun* **1** equilibrio M; **to lose your balance** perder el equilibrio; **2** (*money in your bank account*) saldo M.

balanced *adjective* equilibrado/equilibrada.

balcony *noun* balcón M.

bald *adjective* calvo/calva.

ball *noun* **1** (*for tennis or golf*) pelota F; **2** (*for football or volleyball*) balón M; **3** (*of string or wool*) ovillo M.

ballet *noun* ballet M.

ballet dancer *noun* bailarín M de ballet; bailarina F de ballet.

ballet shoe *noun* zapatilla F de ballet.

balloon *noun* globo M.

ballot *noun* votación F.

ballpoint (pen) *noun* boli M (*informal*); bolígrafo M.

ban *noun* prohibición F; **to put a ban on smoking** prohibir fumar. *verb* prohibir [58].

banana *noun* plátano M; **a banana yoghurt** un yogur de plátano.

band *noun* **1** (*playing music*) grupo M; **a rock band** un grupo de rock; **2 a jazz band** (*big*) una orquesta de jazz; (*small*) un conjunto de jazz; **3 a brass band**

una banda de música; **4 a rubber band** una goma elástica.

bandage *noun* venda F.
verb vendar [17].

bang *noun* **1** (*noise*) estallido M; **2** (*of a window*) golpe M; **3** (*of a door*) portazo M.
verb **1** (*to hit*) golpear [17] (*a drum, for example*); **he banged his fist on the table** golpeó la mesa con el puño; **2** (*to knock*) dar [4] golpes a; **to bang on the door** dar golpes a la puerta; **I banged my head on the door** me di un golpe en la cabeza con la puerta; **I banged into the table** me choqué con la mesa; **3 to bang the door** aporrear [17] la puerta.
exclamation (*like a gun*) ¡pum!

banister(s), bannister(s) *plural noun* barandilla F (*singular*).

bank *noun* **1** (*for money*) banco M; **I'm going to the bank** voy al banco; **2** (*of a river or lake*) orilla F.

bank account *noun* cuenta F bancaria.

bank balance *noun* saldo M.

bank card *noun* tarjeta F bancaria.

bank holiday *noun* día M festivo.

banknote *noun* billete M de banco.

bank statement *noun* extracto M de cuenta.

bar *noun* **1** (*selling drinks*) bar M; **Janet works in a bar** Janet trabaja en un bar; **2** (*the counter in a bar*) barra F; **on the bar** en la barra; **3 a bar of chocolate** una tableta de chocolate; **4 a bar of soap** una

pastilla de jabón; **5** (*made of wood or metal*) barra F; **a metal bar** una barra de metal; **6** (*in music*) compás M.
verb (*to block physically*) bloquear [17]; **to bar someone's way** bloquear el paso a alguien.

barbecue *noun* barbacoa F; **there's a barbecue tonight** hay una barbacoa esta noche.
verb **to barbecue a chicken** asar [17] un pollo a la parrilla; **barbecued chicken** pollo a la parrilla.

barbed wire *noun* alambre M de púas.

bare *adjective* desnudo/desnuda.

barefoot *adjective* descalzo/descalza; **to be barefoot** estar descalzo/descalza.

bargain *noun* (*a good buy*) ganga F; **I got a bargain** conseguí una ganga; **it's a bargain!** ¡es una ganga!

barge *noun* barcaza F.

bark *noun* **1** (*of a tree*) corteza F; **2** (*of a dog*) ladrido M.
verb ladrar [17].

barmaid *noun* camarera F.

barman *noun* camarero M.

barn *noun* granero M.

barrel *noun* tonel M.

barrier *noun* barrera F.

base *noun* base F.

baseball *noun* baloncesto M.

based *adjective* **1 to be based on** estar basado en; **the film is based**

on a true story la película está basada en una historia real; **2 to be based in** (*a company*) tener su base en; (*a person*) vivir en; **he's based in Bristol** vive en Bristol.

basement *noun* sótano M; **in the basement** en el sótano.

bash *noun* **1** golpe M; **it's got a bash on the bumper** tiene un golpe en el guardabarros; **2 I'll have a bash** voy a probar.
verb **I bashed my head** me di un golpe en la cabeza.

basic *adjective* **1** básico/básica; **basic knowledge** conocimientos básicos; **2 the basic facts** los hechos fundamentales; **3 basic salary** sueldo base; **4** (*not luxurious*) sencillo/sencilla; **the flat's a bit basic** el piso es bastante sencillo.

basically *adverb*
1 fundamentalmente; **it's basically all right** fundamentalmente está bien; **2 basically, I don't really want to go** en pocas palabras, no quiero ir.

basics *noun* rudimentos M (*plural*).

basin *noun* (*washbasin*) lavabo M.

basis *noun* **1** base F; **on the basis of** en base a; **2 on a regular basis** regularmente.

basket *noun* **1** cesta F; **a shopping basket** una cesta de la compra; **a linen basket** una cesta de ropa sucia; **2 a waste-paper basket** una papelera.

basketball *noun* baloncesto M; **to play basketball** jugar al baloncesto.

bass *noun* **1** bajo M; **to play bass** tocar el bajo; **2 a double bass** un contrabajo.

bass drum *noun* bombo M.

bass guitar *noun* bajo M.

bassoon *noun* fagot M; **to play the bassoon** tocar el fagot.

bat *noun* **1** (*for cricket or baseball*) bate M; **2** (*for table tennis*) paleta F; **3** (*animal*) murciélago M.

bath *noun* **1** baño M; **I was in the bath** estaba en el baño; **2** (*bathtub*) bañera F; **the bath's pink** la bañera es rosa; **3 to have a bath** bañarse [17].

bathe *verb* **1** lavar [17] (*a wound*); **2** (*go swimming*) bañarse [17].

bathroom *noun* cuarto M de baño.

bath towel *noun* toalla F de baño.

batter *noun* **1** (*for frying*) rebozado M; **fish in batter** pescado rebozado; **2** (*for pancakes*) masa F.

battery *noun* **1** (*for a torch or radio, for example*) pila F; **2** (*for a car*) batería F.

battle *noun* batalla F.

bay *noun* bahía F.

B.C. a.de C. (*antes de Cristo*).

be *verb* **1** (*referring to permanent characteristics*) ser [1]; **it's beautiful** es precioso; **she's very tall** es muy alta; **honey is sweet** la miel es dulce; **2** (*referring to changeable emotions and situations*) estar [2]; **she's angry** está enfadada; **I'm tired** estoy cansada; **the soup is cold** la sopa está fría; **this cake is too sweet** este pastel está demasiado dulce; **3** (*in a place*) estar [2]; **Melanie is in the kitchen** Melanie está en la cocina; **¿where's the butter?** ¿dónde está la mantequilla?; **when we were in France** cuando estábamos en Francia; **4 there is** hay; **there are** hay; **there's more here** aquí hay más; **there are two children outside** hay dos niños fuera; **is there any problem?** ¿hay algún problema?; **5** (*with jobs and professions*) ser [1]; (*note that 'a' is not translated*) **she's a teacher** es profesora; **he's a taxi driver** es taxista; **6** (*marital status*) estar [2], ser [1]; **she's married** está casada; **he's single** está/es soltero; **7** (*in clock times*) ser [1]; **it's one o'clock** es la una en punto; **it's half past five** son las cinco y media; **8** (*for days of the week and dates*) ser [1]; **what day is it today?** ¿qué día es hoy?; **it's Tuesday today** hoy es martes; **it's the twentieth of May** es veinte de mayo; **9** (*talking about age*) tener [9]; **to be fifteen** tener quince años; **how old are you?** ¿cuántos años tienes?; **Samuel's two** Samuel tiene dos años; **10** (*feeling cold, hot, hungry*) tener [9]; **I'm hot** tengo calor; **I'm cold** tengo frío; **I'm hungry** tengo hambre; **11** (*talking about weather*) **it's cold today** hoy hace frío; **it's a nice day** hace buen día; **12** (*to a country or town*) estar [2]; **I've never been to Paris** nunca he estado en París; **have you been to Spain before?** ¿has estado en España antes?; **13 to be loved** ser [1] amado; (*but note that often the*

passive is translated by the third person plural) **he has been killed** lo han matado (*literally: they have killed him*).

beach *noun* playa F; **on the beach** en la playa.

bead *noun* cuenta F.

beak *noun* pico M.

beam *noun* **1** (*of light*) rayo F; **2** (*for a roof*) viga F.

bean *noun* judía F; **baked beans** alubias en salsa de tomate; **green beans** judías verdes.

bear *noun* oso M.
verb **1** soportar [17]; **I can't bear him** no puedo soportarlo; **I can't bear the idea** no puedo soportar la idea; **2 to bear something in mind** tener [9] algo en cuenta; **I'll bear it in mind** lo tendré en cuenta.

beard *noun* barba F.

bearded *adjective* barbudo/barbuda.

bearings *plural noun* **to get your bearings** orientarse [17].

beast *noun* **1** (*animal*) bestia F; **2 you beast!** ¡bruto!

beat *noun* ritmo M.
verb **1** (*defeat*) ganarle a [17]; **we beat them!** ¡les hemos ganado!; **he beat me at chess** me ganó al ajedrez; **2** (*hit repeatedly*) golpear [17]; **3** batir [19]; **to beat the eggs** batir los huevos; **4 you can't beat a good meal** no hay nada mejor que una buena comida.

● **to beat somebody up** darle [4] una paliza a alguien (*informal*).

beautiful *adjective* precioso/preciosa; **a beautiful day** un día precioso; **a beautiful girl** una chica preciosa.

beautifully *adverb* maravillosamente.

beauty *noun* belleza F.

beauty spot *noun* (*for tourists*) lugar M pintoresco.

because *conjunction* 1 porque; **because it's you** porque eres tú; **because it's cold** porque hace frío; 2 **because of** a causa de; **because of the accident** a causa del accidente.

become *verb* 1 hacerse [7]; **I became a lawyer** me hice abogado; **she became famous** se hizo famosa; **we became friends** nos hicimos amigos; 2 (*'become' with an adjective is sometimes translated by a reflexive verb in Spanish*) **to become bored** aburrirse [19]; **to become tired** cansarse [17].

bed *noun* 1 cama F; **a double bed** una cama de matrimonio; **in bed** en la cama; **to go to bed** ir a la cama; 2 (*flower bed*) macizo M.

bedclothes *plural noun* ropa F de cama (*singular*).

bedding *noun* ropa F de cama.

bedroom *noun* habitación F; **my bedroom window** la ventana de mi habitación.

bedside table *noun* mesilla F de noche.

bedsit, bedsitter *noun* habitación F amueblada de aquiler.

bedspread *noun* colcha F.

bedtime *noun* **it's bedtime** es hora de acostarse.

bee *noun* abeja F.

beech *noun* haya F.

beef *noun* carne F de vaca; **a roast of beef** un rosbif.

beefburger *noun* hamburguesa F.

beer *noun* cerveza F; **two beers please** dos cervezas, por favor; **a beer can** una lata de cerveza.

beetle *noun* escarabajo M.

beetroot *noun* remolacha F.

before *preposition* , *adverb* 1 antes de; **before Monday** antes del lunes; 2 **before somebody** antes que alguien; **he left before me** se fue antes que yo; 3 **the day before** el día anterior; **the day before the wedding** el día anterior a la boda; **the day before yesterday** anteayer; **the week before** la semana anterior; 4 (*already*) ya; **I've seen him before somewhere** ya le he visto en algún sitio; **I had seen the film before** ya había visto la película; **she'd never tried before** nunca lo había intentado antes.
conjunction 1 antes de; **before doing** antes de hacer; **I closed the windows before leaving** cerré las ventanas antes de salir; **phone before you leave** llámame antes de

salir; **2** antes de que (*followed by the subjunctive*); **phone me before they leave** llámame antes de que salgan; **oh, before I forget** … ah, antes de que se me olvide …

beforehand *adverb* antes; **phone beforehand** llama antes.

beg *verb* **1** (*ask for money*) mendigar [28]; **2** (*ask*) suplicarle a [31]; **she begged me not to leave** me suplicó que no me marchase; **I beg your pardon** perdone.

begin *verb* **1** empezar [25]; **the meeting begins at ten** la reunión empieza a las diez; **the words beginning with P** las palabras que empiezan con P; **2 to begin to do** empezar a hacer; **I'm beginning to understand** empiezo a comprender.

beginner *noun* principiante M/F.

beginning *noun* **1** principio M; **at the beginning** al principio; **at the beginning of the holidays** al principio de las vacaciones; **2** (*with 'day', 'week', 'month', 'year'*) **at the beginning of** a principios de; **at the beginning of the month** a principios de mes.

behalf *noun* **on behalf of** en nombre de.

behave *verb* **1** portarse [17]; **he behaved badly** se portó mal; **2 to behave yourself** portarse bien; **behave yourselves!** ¡portaos bien!

behaviour *noun* comportamiento M.

behind *noun* trasero M.
preposition detrás de; **behind the**

sofa detrás del sofá; **behind them** detrás de ellos.
adverb **1** detrás; **you go behind** tú vas detrás; **the car behind** el coche de detrás; **2 to leave something behind** olvidarse [17] algo; **I've left my keys behind** me he olvidado las llaves; **to stay behind** quedarse[17]; **3** (*not making progress*) **he's behind in class** va retrasado en clase.

beige *adjective* beige (*does not change*); **beige socks** calcetines beige.

Belgian *noun*, *adjective* belga M/F.

Belgium *noun* F Bélgica.

belief *noun* creencia F; **his political beliefs** sus creencias políticas.

believe *verb* **1** creer [37]; **I believe you** te creo; **they believed what I said** se creyeron lo que dije; **I don't believe you!** ¡no te creo!; **2 to believe in** creer en; **to believe in ghosts** creer en fantasmas; **to believe in God** creer en Dios.

bell *noun* **1** (*in a church*) campana F; **2** (*on a door*) timbre M; **ring the bell!** ¡toca el timbre!; **3** (*for a cat or toy*) cascabel M; ★ **that name rings a bell** ese nombre me suena.

belong *verb* **1 to belong to** ser [1] de; **that belongs to Lucy** eso es de Lucy; **2 to belong to a club** pertenecer [35] a un club; **3** (*go*) ir [8]; **that chair belongs in the study** esa silla va en el estudio; **where does this vase belong?** ¿dónde va este jarrón?

belongings *plural noun*
pertenencias F (*plural*); **all my belongings are in London** todas mis pertenencias están en Londres.

below *preposition* debajo de; **below the window** debajo de la ventana; **the flat below yours** el piso de debajo del tuyo.
adverb abajo; **shouts came from below** se oyeron gritos abajo; **the flat below** el piso de abajo.

belt *noun* cinturón M.

bench *noun* banco M.

bend *noun* (*in a road, river*) curva F.
verb **1** (*to make a bend in*) doblar [17] (*your arm or leg, or a wire*); **2** (*to curve*) (*a road or path*) torcer [41]; **the road bends to the right** la carretera tuerce a la derecha; **3 to bend down** agacharse [17]; **she bent down to look** se agachó para mirar.

beneath *preposition* bajo.

benefit *noun* **1** beneficio M; **2 unemployment benefit** subsidio M de desempleo.

bent *adjective* doblado/doblada.

beret *noun* boina F.

berth *noun* litera F.

beside *preposition* (*next to*) al lado de; **it's beside the table** está al lado de la mesa; **she was sitting beside me** estaba sentada a mi lado; ★ **that's beside the point** eso no viene al caso.

besides *adverb* además; **besides, it's too late** además, es demasiado tarde; **four dogs, and six cats**

besides cuatro perros y además seis gatos.

best *adjective* **1** mejor; **it's the best** es el mejor; **that's the best car** ese coche es el mejor; **the best song of the album** la mejor canción del álbum; **she's my best friend** es mi mejor amiga; **2 she's the best at tennis** es la mejor jugando al tenis; **he's the best at English** es el mejor en inglés; **the best thing to do is to phone them** lo mejor es llamarlos por teléfono; **its the best I can do** es lo más que puedo hacer; **I did my best to help her** hice todo lo posible para ayudarla.
adverb **1** mejor; **he plays best** es el que mejor juega; **best of all** lo mejor de todo; **2 I like Barcelona best** Barcelona es la ciudad que más me gusta.

bet *noun* apuesta F.
verb apostar [24]; **to bet on a horse** apostar por un caballo; **I bet you he'll forget!** ¡te apuesto algo a que se le olvida!

better *adjective* **1** mejor; **she's found a better flat** ha encontrado un piso mejor; **this road's better than the other one** esta calle es mejor que la otra; **this pen writes better** esta pluma escribe mejor; **2 even better** todavía mejor; **it's even better than before** es todavía mejor que antes; **3** (*less ill*) **to be better** estar [2] mejor; **to feel better** sentirse [14] mejor; **I feel better** hoy me siento mejor; **4 to get better** mejorar [17]; **my Spanish is getting better** mi español está mejorando;

I hope you get better soon espero
que te mejores pronto; **5 so much
the better** mucho mejor; **the sooner
the better** cuanto antes mejor.
adverb **you/she/etc. had better** más
vale que (*followed by the
subjunctive*); **you'd better phone at
once** más vale que llames ahora
mismo; **he'd better not go** más vale
que no vaya; **I'd better go now** más
vale que me vaya ahora.

better off *adjective* **1** (*richer*)
they're better off than us tienen
más dinero que nosotros; **2** (*more
comfortable*) mejor; **you'd be better
off in bed** estarás mejor en la cama.

between *preposition* **1** entre;
between London and Dover entre
Londres y Dover; **I'll go sometime
between Monday and Friday** iré
entre el lunes y el viernes; **between
you and me** entre tú y yo; **2 it's
closed between 2 and 5** está cerrado
de dos a cinco.

beyond *preposition* **1** (*in space and
time*) **beyond the border** más allá
de la frontera; **2 it's beyond me!** ¡no
lo entiendo!

Bible *noun* **the Bible** la Biblia.

bicycle *noun* bicicleta F; **by bicycle**
en bicicleta.

bicycle lane *noun* carril M de
bicicletas.

big *adjective* **1** grande; **a big house**
una casa grande; **big cities** ciudades
grandes; **it's too big for me** es
demasiado grande para mí; (*'grande'
becomes 'gran' when it comes before a*
singular noun) **a big
disappointment** una gran
desilusión; **2** (*older*) mayor; **my big
sister** mi hermana mayor.

bigheaded *adjective* creído/creída;
to be bigheaded ser un creído/una
creída.

big screen *noun* pantalla F grande.

big toe *noun* dedo M gordo del pie.

bike *noun* bici F (*informal*); **by bike**
en bici.

bikini *noun* bikini M.

bilingual *adjective* bilingüe.

bill *noun* **1** (*in a restaurant*)
cuenta F; **can I have the bill, please?**
¿me trae la cuenta por favor?; **2** (*for
gas, electricity, or in a hotel*)
factura F.

billiards *noun* billar M; **to play
billiards** jugar al billar.

billion *noun* mil millones M (*plural*).

bin *noun* **1** (*dustbin*) cubo M de la
basura; **2** (*wastepaper bin*)
papelera F.

binoculars *plural noun*
prismáticos M (*plural*).

biochemistry *noun* bioquímica F.

biography *noun* biografía F.

biology *noun* biología F.

bird *noun* **1** (*small*) pájaro M;
2 (*large*) ave F (*even though 'ave' is
a feminine noun, it is used with 'el'
and 'un'*).

birdwatching *noun* **to go birdwatching** ir [8] a observar pájaros.

Biro™ *noun* boli M (*informal*).

birth *noun* nacimiento M.

birth certificate *noun* certificado M de nacimiento.

birthday *noun* cumpleaños M (*does not change in the plural*); **a birthday present** un regalo de cumpleaños; **happy birthday!** ¡feliz cumpleaños!

birthday party *noun* fiesta F de cumpleaños.

biscuit *noun* galleta F.

bishop *noun* obispo M.

bit *noun* **1** (*small piece*) trozo M; **a bit of string** un trozo de cordón; **a bit of chocolate** un trozo de chocolate; **2** (*small quantity*) **a bit of** un poco de; **a bit of sugar** un poco de azúcar; **with a bit of luck** con un poco de suerte; **to have a bit of trouble with** tengo un pequeño problema con; **3** (*in a book or film, for example*) trozo M; **this bit's brilliant!** ¡este trozo es genial!; **4 to fall to bits** hacerse pedazos; **5 a bit of news** una noticia; **a bit of advice** un consejo; **6 a bit** un poco; **wait a bit!** ¡espera un poco!; **a bit hot** un poco caliente; **a bit early** un poco pronto; **7** (*for a horse*) bocado M; ★ **bit by bit** poco a poco.

bite *noun* **1** (*snack*) bocado M; **I'll just have a bite before I go** voy a tomar un bocado antes de irme; **2** (*from an insect*) picadura F; **a mosquito bite** una picadura de mosquito; **3** (*from a dog*) mordisco M; **it gave me a bite** me dio un mordisco.
verb **1** (*a person or a dog*) morder [38]; **to bite your nails** morderse las uñas; **2** (*an insect*) picar [31].

bitter *adjective* (*taste*) amargo/amarga.

black *adjective* **1** negro/negra; **my black jacket** mi chaqueta negra; **to turn black** volerse negro/negra; **2 a black man** un negro; **a black woman** una negra; **3 a black coffee** un café solo.

blackberry *noun* mora F.

blackbird *noun* mirlo M.

blackboard *noun* pizarra F.

blackcurrant *noun* grosella F negra.

black eye *noun* ojo M morado.

blade *noun* hoja F.

blame *noun* **1** culpa F; **to put the blame on somebody** echarle la culpa a alguien; **2 to take the blame for something** asumir la responsabilidad de algo.
verb culpar [17]; **to blame somebody for something** culpar a alguien de algo; **they blamed him for the accident** lo culparon por el accidente; **she is to blame for it** ella tiene la culpa; **I blame the parents!** ¡yo culpo a los padres!; **I don't blame you!** ¡no me extraña!

blank *noun* (*empty space*) espacio M en blanco (*on a form for instance*).
adjective **1** (*a page or piece of paper,*

or a cheque, or a screen) en blanco; (*a tape or disk*) virgen; **2 my mind went blank** me quedé en blanco.

blanket *noun* manta F.

blast *noun* **1** (*an explosion*) explosión F; **2** (*of air*) ráfaga F; **3 to play music at full blast** poner la música a todo volumen.

blaze *noun* incendio M.
verb arder [18].

blazer *noun* blázer M.

bleach *noun* lejía F.

bleed *verb* sangrar [17]; **my nose is bleeding** me está sangrando la nariz.

blend *noun* mezcla F.
verb mezclar [17].

blender *noun* batidora F.

bless *verb* bendecir [5]; **bless you!** (*after a sneeze*) ¡Jesús!

blind *noun* (*in a window*) persiana F.
adjective ciego/ciega; **to go blind** quedarse ciego/ciega.

blink *verb* (*a person*) pestañear [17].

blister *noun* ampolla F.

blizzard *noun* tormenta F de nieve.

block *noun* **1** bloque M; **a block of flats** un bloque de pisos; **an office block** un bloque de oficinas; **2** (*a square group of buildings*) manzana F; **to run (or drive) round the block** dar la vuelta a la manzana.
verb **1** bloquear [17]; (*an exit or a road*) **2** atascar [31] (*a drain or a hole*); **the sink's blocked** el fregadero está atascado.

blonde *adjective* rubio/rubia.

blood *noun* sangre F.

blood test *noun* análisis M de sangre.

blouse *noun* blusa F.

blow *noun* golpe M.
verb **1** (*the wind or a person*) soplar [17]; **2 to blow off/away** salir [63] volando; **my hat blew off** mi sombrero salió volando; **3** (*in an explosion*) **the bomb blew a hole in the wall** la bomba hizo un agujero en la pared; **4 to blow your nose** sonarse [24] la nariz.
● **to blow something out** (*a candle or flames*) apagar [28] algo.
● **to blow up** (*explode*) explotar [17].
● **to blow something up** inflar [17] algo (*a balloon or tyre*); hacer [7] volar algo (*a building or car*); **they blew up the president's residence** hicieron volar la residencia del presidente.

blow-dry *noun* **a cut and blow dry is thirty pounds** cortar y marcar son treinta libras.

blue *adjective* azul; **blue eyes** ojos azules.

bluebell *noun* jacinto M silvestre.

blues *plural noun* (*jazz*) blues M (*singular*).

blunder *noun* metedura F de pata.

blunt *adjective* **1** (*a knife or scissors*) desafilado/desafilada; **2** (*a pencil*) sin punta; **3** (*a person*) directo/directa.

blurred *adjective* **1** (*vision or image*) borroso/borrosa; **2** (*photo*) movido/movida.

blush *verb* ponerse [11] colorado.

board *noun* **1** (*plank*) tabla F; **2** (*blackboard*) pizarra F; **3** (*notice board*) tablón M de anuncios; **4** (*for a board game*) tablero M; **a chess board** un tablero de ajedrez; **5** (*accommodation*) **full board** pensión completa; **half board** media pensión; **board and lodging** comida y alojamiento; **6 on board** a bordo; **on board the ferry** a bordo del ferry. *verb* embarcarse [31].

boarder *noun* (*in a school*) interno M, interna F.

board game *noun* juego M de mesa.

boarding *noun* embarque M.

boarding card *noun* tarjeta F de embarque.

boarding school *noun* internado M.

boast *verb* presumir [19]; **he was boasting about his new bike** estaba presumiendo de su nueva bici.

boat *noun* **1** (*in general*) barco M; **2** (*rowing boat*) barca F.

body *noun* **1** cuerpo M; **2** (*corpse*) cadáver M.

bodybuilding *noun* culturismo M.

bodyguard *noun* guardaespaldas M/F.

boil *noun* (*swelling*) furúnculo M. *verb* **1** hervir [14]; **the water's boiling** el agua está hirviendo; **I'm**

going to boil some water voy a hervir un poco de agua; **2 to boil vegetables** cocer [41] verduras; **to boil an egg** cocer un huevo.

● **to boil over** salirse [63].

boiled egg *noun* huevo M pasado por agua.

boiler *noun* **1** (*for central heating*) caldera F; **2** (*for water*) calentador M.

boiling *adjective* **1** (*water*) hirviendo; **2 it's boiling hot today!** ¡hoy hace un calor espantoso!

Bolivia *noun* Bolivia F.

bolt *noun* **1** (*large*) cerrojo M; **2** (*small*) pestillo M. *verb* (*a door*) cerrar [29] con cerrojo.

bombing *noun* **1** (*in a war*) bombardeo M; **2** (*a terrorist attack*) atentado M terrorista.

bomb *noun* bomba F. *verb* bombardear [17].

bone *noun* **1** hueso M; **2** (*of a fish*) espina F.

bonfire *noun* hoguera F.

bonnet *noun* (*of a car*) capó M.

book *noun* **1** (*that you read*) libro M; **a book about dinosaurs** un libro sobre dinosaurios; **a biology book** un libro de biología; **2 an exercise book** un cuaderno; **3 a book of tickets** un taco de billetes; **a book of stamps** un librito de sellos. *verb* reservar [17]; **I booked a table for 8 o'clock** reservé una mesa para las ocho.

bookcase *noun* estantería F.

booking *noun* reserva F.

booking office *noun* taquilla F.

booklet *noun* folleto M.

bookshelf *noun* estante M.

bookshop *noun* librería F.

boot *noun* 1 (*item of clothing*) bota F; **walking boots** botas de montaña; **wellington boots** botas de agua; 2 (*short fashion boot*) botín M; 3 (*of a car*) maletero M.

border *noun* (*between countries*) frontera F; **at the border** en la frontera.

bore *noun* 1 (*a boring person*) pesado M, pesada F (*informal*); 2 (*a nuisance*) **what a bore!** ¡qué rollo! (*informal*).

bored *adjective* aburrido/aburrida; **to be bored** estar aburrido; **I'm bored** estoy aburrido; **to get bored** aburrirse [19].

boring *adjective* aburrido/aburrida.

born *verb* **to be born** nacer [35]; **she was born in June** nació en junio.

borrow *verb* **can I borrow your bike?** ¿me prestas tu bici?; **to borrow something from someone** pedirle algo prestado a alguien (*literally, to ask somebody for something on loan*); **I'll borrow some money from Dad** le pediré dinero prestado a papá.

Bosnia *noun* Bosnia F.

boss *noun* jefe M, jefa F.

bossy *adjective* mandón/mandona (*informal*).

both *pronoun, adjective* los/las dos; **they both came** vinieron los dos; **they're both sold** los dos están vendidos; **both sisters were there** las dos hermanas estaban allí; **both my feet** mis dos pies.
conjunction **both … and** tanto … como; **both at home and at school** tanto en casa como en colegio; **both in summer and in winter** tanto en verano como en invierno.

bother *noun* problemas F (*plural*); **I've had a lot of bother with the car** he tenido muchos problemas con el coche; **it's no bother** no es ningún problema; **without any bother** sin ningún problema; **it's too much bother** no merece la pena molestarse.
verb 1 (*disturb*) molestar [17]; **I'm sorry to bother you** siento molestarte; 2 (*worry*) preocuparse [17]; **that doesn't bother me at all** no me preocupa en absoluto; **don't bother about dinner** no te preocupes de la cena; 3 (*take the trouble*) molestarse [17]; **she didn't even bother to come** ni siquiera se molestó en venir; **don't bother!** ¡no te molestes!

bottle *noun* botella F.

bottle bank *noun* contenedor M de botellas.

bottle opener *noun*
abrebotellas M (*does not change in the plural*).

bottom *noun* 1 (*of a page, a hill, a wall, or steps*) pie M; **at the bottom of the ladder** al pie de la escalera; **at the bottom of the page** al pie de la página; 2 (*of a bag, a hole, a stretch of water, a street, or a garden*) fondo M; **at the bottom of the lake** en el fondo del lago; 3 (*of a list*) final M; 4 (*of a bottle*) culo M; 5 (*buttocks*) trasero M.
adjective 1 (*lowest*) de abajo; **the bottom shelf** el estante de abajo; 2 (*a team, or place*) último/última; 3 **the bottom sheet** la sábana bajera; **the bottom flat** el piso bajo.

bounce *verb* rebotar [17].

bouncer *noun* gorila M (*informal*).

bound *adjective* **he's bound to be late** seguro que llega tarde; **that was bound to happen** eso tenía que pasar.

boundary *noun* línea F divisoria.

bow *noun* 1 (*in a shoelace or ribbon*) lazo M; 2 (*for playing the violin or shooting arrows*) arco M.

bowl *noun* 1 (*for cereal*) bol M; 2 (*larger, for mixing*) cuenco M; 3 (*for washing up*) barreño M; 4 **a salad bowl** una ensaladera; **a fruit bowl** un frutero.
verb lanzar [22] (*a ball*).

bowling *noun* (*tenpin*) bolos M (*plural*); **to go bowling** ir a jugar a los bolos.

bow tie *noun* pajarita F.

box *noun* 1 caja F; **a box of chocolates** una caja de bombones; **a cardboard box** una caja de cartón; 2 (*of matches*) cajetilla F; 3 (*on a form*) recuadro M.

boxer *noun* 1 (*fighter*) boxeador M; 2 (*dog*) bóxer M.

boxer shorts *plural noun* calzoncillos M (*plural*).

boxing *noun* 1 boxeo M; 2 **a boxing match** un combate de boxeo.

Boxing Day *noun* fiesta del 26 de diciembre.

box office *noun* taquilla F.

boy *noun* niño M; **a little boy** un niño pequeño.

boyfriend *noun* novio M.

bra *noun* sujetador M.

brace *noun* (*for teeth*) aparato M de los dientes.

bracelet *noun* pulsera F.

bracket *noun* **in brackets** entre paréntesis.

brain *noun* cerebro M.

brainwave *noun* idea F genial.

brake *noun* freno M.
verb frenar [17].

bramble *noun* zarzamora F.

branch *noun* 1 (*of a tree*) rama F; 2 (*of a shop, company or bank*) sucursal F; **our Oxford branch** nuestra sucursal de Oxford.

brand *noun* marca F.

brand new *adjective* nuevo/nueva.

brandy *noun* coñac M.

brass *noun* 1 (*the metal*) latón M; 2 (*in an orchestra*) **the brass** los metales.
adjective de latón.

brass band *noun* banda F de música.

Brazil *noun* Brasil M.

brave *adjective* valiente.

bread *noun* pan M; **a slice of bread** una rebanada de pan.

break *noun* 1 (*a short rest*) descanso M; **a fifteen-minute break** un descanso de quince minutos; **to take a break** descansar un rato; 2 (*in school*) recreo M; 3 **the Christmas break** las vacaciones de Navidad.
verb 1 romper [40]; **he broke a glass** rompió un vaso; 2 **to break your leg** romperse una pierna; **I broke my arm** me rompí un brazo; 3 **to break your promise** romper una promesa; **to break the rules** infringir [49] las reglas; **you mustn't break the rules** no debes infringir las reglas; 4 **to break a record** batir [19] un récord; 5 **to break the news** dar [4] la noticia.
● **to break down** estropearse [17]; **the car broke down** el coche se estropeó.
● **to break in: the thief broke in through the window** el ladrón se metió en la casa por la ventana; **the**
house was broken into entraron ladrones en la casa.
● **to break out** 1 (*a fire*) declararse [17]; 2 (*a war or a storm*) estallar [17]; 3 (*a prisoner*) escaparse [17].
● **to break up** 1 (*a family*) separarse [17]; 2 (*a couple*) romper [40]; 3 (*a crowd or clouds*) dispersarse [17]; 4 (*for the holidays*) **we break up on Thursday** empezamos las vacaciones el jueves.

breakdown *noun* 1 (*of a vehicle*) avería F; **we had a breakdown on the motorway** tuvimos una avería en la autopista; 2 (*in talks or negotiations*) ruptura F; 3 (*a nervous collapse*) crisis F nerviosa; **to have a (nervous) breakdown** sufrir una crisis nerviosa.

breakdown truck *noun* grúa F de recogida en carretera.

breakfast *noun* desayuno M; **to have breakfast** desayunar [17]; **we have breakfast at eight** desayunamos a las ocho.

break-in *noun* robo M.

breast *noun* 1 (*a woman's*) pecho M; 2 (*of a chicken or other fowl*) pechuga F.

breaststroke *noun* braza F.

breath *noun* aliento M; **out of breath** sin aliento; **to get one's breath** recobrar el aliento; **to take a deep breath** respirar hondo.

breathe *verb* respirar [17].

breathing *noun* respiración F.

breed *noun* (*of animal*) raza F. *verb* **1** criar [32] (*animals*); **2** (*to have babies*) reproducirse [60]; **rabbits breed fast** los conejos se reproducen mucho.

breeze *noun* brisa F.

bribe *noun* soborno M. *verb* sobornar [17].

brick *noun* ladrillo M; **a brick wall** una pared de ladrillo.

bride *noun* novia F; **the bride and groom** los novios, el novio y la novia.

bridegroom *noun* novio M.

bridesmaid *noun* dama F de honor.

bridge *noun* **1** (*over a river*) puente M; **a bridge over the Thames** un puente sobre el Támesis; **2** (*card game*) bridge M; **to play bridge** jugar al bridge.

bridle *noun* brida F.

brief *adjective* breve.

briefcase *noun* maletín M.

briefly *adjective* brevemente.

briefs *plural noun* calzoncillos M (*plural*).

bright *adjective* **1** (*star, light*) brillante; **2** (*colour*) vivo/viva; **bright green socks** calcetines de un verde vivo; **3** **bright sunshine** un sol radiante; **4** (*clever*) inteligente; **she's not very bright** no es muy inteligente; ★ **to look on the bright side** ver el lado bueno de las cosas.

brighten up *verb* **the weather's brightening up** el tiempo está aclarando.

brilliant *adjective* **1** (*very clever*) brillante; **a brilliant surgeon** un brillante cirujano; **he's brilliant at maths** es genial para las matemáticas; **2** (*wonderful*) fenomenal (*informal*); **the party was brilliant!** ¡la fiesta estuvo fenomenal!

bring *verb* **1** traer [42]; **they brought a present** trajeron un regalo; **bring your camera** trae tu cámara; **it brings good luck** trae buena suerte; **she's bringing all the children** trae a todos los niños; **2** **to bring something back** devolver [45] algo; **3** **to bring up** criar [32] (*children*); **he was brought up by his aunt** lo crió su tía.

bristle *noun* cerda F.

Britain *noun* Gran Bretaña F.

British *plural noun* **the British** los británicos. *adjective* británico/ británica; **the British Isles** las islas británicas.

broad *adjective* (*wide*) ancho/ ancha.

broad bean *noun* haba F.

broadcast *noun* emisión F. *verb* emitir [19] (*a programme*).

broccoli *noun* brécol M.

brochure *noun* folleto M.

broke *adjective* **to be broke** (*no money*) no tener [9] un duro (*informal*).

broken *adjective* roto/rota; **the window's broken** la ventana está rota; **to have a broken leg** tener una pierna rota.

bronchitis *noun* bronquitis F.

bronze *noun* bronce M. *adjective* de bronce.

brooch *noun* broche M.

broom *noun* 1 (*for sweeping*) escoba F; 2 (*bush*) retama F.

brother *noun* hermano M; **my little brother** mi hermano pequeño; **my mother's brother** el hermano de mi madre.

brother-in-law *noun* cuñado M.

brown *adjective* 1 marrón (*never changes*); **brown shoes** zapatos marrón; 2 castaño/castaña (*hair or eyes*); 3 (*tanned in the sun*) moreno/morena; **to go brown** ponerse moreno/morena.

brown bread *noun* pan M integral.

brown sugar *noun* azúcar M/F moreno/morena.

bruise *noun* 1 (*on a person*) moratón M; 2 (*on fruit*) magulladura F.

brush *noun* 1 (*for your hair, clothes, nails, or shoes*) cepillo M; **my hair brush** mi cepillo del pelo; 2 (*for sweeping*) escoba F; 3 (*paintbrush*) brocha F. *verb* 1 cepillar [17] (*your hair or clothes*); **to brush your hair** cepillarse el pelo; **she brushed her hair** se cepilló el pelo; 2 **to brush your teeth** lavarse [17] los dientes;

I'm going to brush my teeth voy a lavarme los dientes.

Brussels *noun* Bruselas F.

Brussels sprouts *noun* coles F (*plural*) de Bruselas.

bubble *noun* burbuja F.

bubble bath *noun* gel M de baño.

bucket *noun* cubo M.

buckle *noun* hebilla F.

Buddhism *noun* budismo M.

Buddhist *noun* budista M/F.

budget *noun* presupuesto M.

budgie *noun* periquito M.

buffet *noun* 1 (*on train*) bar M; 2 (*meal*) buffet M.

buffet car *noun* coche M restaurante.

bug *noun* 1 (*insect*) bicho M (*informal*); 2 (*virus*) virus M; **a stomach bug** un virus en el estómago.

build *verb* construir [54].

builder *noun* albañil M/F.

building *noun* edificio M.

building site *noun* solar M.

built-in *adjective* empotrado/empotrada.

built-up *adjective* urbanizado/urbanizada; **a built-up area** una zona urbanizada.

bulb *noun* 1 (*for a light*) bombilla F; 2 (*that you plant*) bulbo M.

bulky *adjective* voluminoso/
voluminosa.

bull *noun* toro M.

bulldozer *noun* bulldozer M.

bullet *noun* bala F.

bulletin *noun* boletín M; **a news
bulletin** boletín de noticias.

bully *noun* bravucón M, bravucona F;
he's a bully es un bravucón.
verb intimidar [17].

bum *noun* (*bottom*) trasero M
(*informal*).

bump *noun* **1 a bump on the head**
un chichón en la cabeza; **2 a bump
in the road** un bache en la carretera;
3 (*jolt*) sacudida F; **4** (*noise*)
golpe M.
verb **1** (*bang*) darse [4] un golpe; **I
bumped my head** me di un golpe en
la cabeza; **2 to bump into
something** chocarse [31] con algo; **I
bumped into the table** me choqué
con la mesa; **3 to bump into
somebody** (*meet by chance*)
encontrarse [24] con alguien.

bumper *noun* parachoques M (*does
not change in the plural*).

bumpy *adjective* **1** lleno/llena de
baches (*road*); **2** con muchas
sacudidas (*plane landing*).

bun *noun* **1** (*for a burger*)
panecillo M; **2** (*sweet*) bollo M.

bunch *noun* **1** (*of flowers*) ramo M;
2 (*of carrots, radishes or keys*)
manojo M; **3 a bunch of grapes** un
racimo de uvas.

bundle *noun* **1** (*of clothes*) fardo M;
2 (*of papers, letters*) paquete M.

bungalow *noun* casa F de una
planta.

bunk *noun* (*on a train or boat*)
litera F.

bunk beds *plural noun* literas F
(*plural*).

bureau *noun* **1** (*agency*) agencia F;
2 (*desk*) escritorio M.

bureau de change *noun* casa F de
cambio.

burger *noun* hamburguesa F.

burglar *noun* ladrón M, ladrona F.

burglar alarm *noun* alarma F
antirrobo.

burglary *noun* robo M.

burn *noun* quemadura F.
verb quemar [17]; **I've burned the
rubbish** he quemado la basura; **she
burnt herself on the grill** se quemó
en la parrilla; **you'll burn your
finger!** ¡te vas a quemar el dedo!;
Mum's burnt her cake a mamá se le
ha quemado el pastel; **I burn
easily** (*in the sun*) me quemo
fácilmente.

burnt *adjective* quemado/quemada.

burst *verb* **1** estallar [17] (*a balloon*);
2 reventar [29]; (*a tyre or pipe*) **a
burst tyre** una rueda con un
reventón; **3 to burst out laughing**
echarse [17] a reír; **to burst into tears**
echarse [17] a llorar; **4 to burst into
flames** empezar [25] a arder.

bury *verb* enterrar [29].

bus *noun* 1 (*public transport*)
autobús M; **we'll take the bus**
cogeremos el autobús; **on the bus** en
el autobús; **a bus ticket** un billete de
autobús; **a bus stop** una parada de
autobús; 2 (*coach*) autocar M; **to go
to London by bus** ir a Londres en
autocar.

bus driver *noun* conductor/
conductora M/F de autobús.

bush *noun* arbusto M.

business *noun* 1 (*commercial
dealings*) negocios M (*plural*); **he's
in Leeds on business** está en Leeds
de viaje de negocios; **a business
letter** una carta de negocios; 2 (*firm
or company*) negocio M; **small
businesses** las pequeñas empresas;
3 **mind your own business!** ¡no te
metas en lo que no te importa!; **that's
my business!** ¡eso es asunto mío!

business class *noun* clase F
preferente.

businessman *noun* hombre M de
negocios.

business trip *noun* viaje M de
negocios.

businesswoman *noun* mujer F de
negocios.

bus pass *noun* abono M de autobús.

bus route *noun* línea F de autobús.

bus shelter *noun* marquesina F.

bus station *noun* estación F de
autobús.

bust *noun* busto M.

busy *adjective* 1 ocupado/
ocupada (*a person*); **don't disturb
him, he's busy** no lo molestes, está
ocupado; 2 ajetreado/ajetreada (*a
day or week*); **a very busy day** un día
muy ajetreado; 3 (*full of cars or
people*) muy concurrido/
concurrida (*a road*); **the shops were
busy** las tiendas estaban muy
concurridas; 4 (*phone*) **the line's
busy** está comunicando.

but *conjunction* 1 pero; **small but
strong** pequeño pero fuerte; **I'll try,
but it's difficult** lo intentaré pero es
difícil; 2 not … but … no … sino …;
not Thursday but Friday no el jueves
sino el viernes.
preposition 1 menos; **anything but
that** cualquier cosa menos eso;
everyone but Leah todos menos
Leah; 2 **the last but one** el
penúltimo.

butcher *noun* carnicero M,
carnicera F; **the butcher's** la
carnicería.

butter *noun* mantequilla F.
verb untar [17] con mantequilla.

buttercup *noun* botón M de oro.

butterfly *noun* mariposa F.

button *noun* botón M.

buttonhole *noun* ojal M.

buy *noun* **a good buy** una buena
compra; **a bad buy** una mala
compra.
verb comprar [17]; **I bought the
cinema tickets** compré las entradas
para el cine; **to buy something for**

somebody comprarle algo a alguien; **Sarah bought him a sweater** Sarah le compró un jersey; **to buy something from someone** comprarle algo a alguien; **he bought his bike from Tim** le compré a Tom su bici.

buzz *verb* (*a fly or bee*) zumbar [17].

buzzer *noun* timbre M.

by *preposition* 1 por; **by telephone** por teléfono; **the thief came in by the window** el ladrón entró por la ventana; **eaten by a dog** comido por un perro; **it's two metres by four** mide dos metros por cuatro; **by mistake** por equivocación; **they pay by the hour** pagan por hora; **written by Lorca** escrito por Lorca; 2 (*travel*) en; **to come by bus** venir en autobús; **to leave by train** salir en tren; **by bike** en bicicleta; 3 (*near*) al lado de; **by the fire** al lado del fuego; **by the sea** al lado del mar; **close by** cerca; 4 (*before*) para; **it'll be ready by Monday** estará listo para el lunes; **Kevin was back by four** Kevin estaba de vuelta para las cuatro; 5 **they should have finished by now** ya deberían haber terminado; 6 **by yourself** solo/sola; **I was by myself in the house** estaba solo en la casa; **she did it by herself** lo hizo sola; 7 **to take somebody by the hand** coger a alguien de la mano; 8 **by the way** por cierto; 9 **to go by** pasar.

bye *exclamation* adiós; **bye for now!** ¡hasta luego!

bypass *noun* carretera F de circunvalación.

C c

cab *noun* 1 taxi M; **to call a cab** llamar un taxi; 2 (*on a lorry*) cabina F.

cabbage *noun* repollo M.

cable *noun* cable M.

cable car *noun* funicular M.

cable television *noun* televisión F por cable.

cactus *noun* cactus M.

café *noun* cafetería F.

cage *noun* jaula F.

cagoule *noun* canguro M.

cake *noun* pastel M; **would you like a piece of cake?** ¿quieres un trozo de pastel?

calculate *verb* calcular [17].

calculation *noun* cálculo M.

calculator *noun* calculadora F.

calendar *noun* calendario M.

calf *noun* 1 (*animal*) ternero M, ternera F; 2 (*of your leg*) pantorrilla F.

call *noun* (*telephone*) llamada F; **I had several calls this morning;** he tenido varias llamadas esta mañana; **thank you for your call** gracias por llamar; **a phone call** una llamada de

teléfono; **to give somebody a call**
llamar [17] a alguien.
verb **1** (*telephone*) llamar [17]; **to
call a taxi** llamar un taxi; **to call the
doctor** llamar al médico; **call this
number** llama a este número; **thank
you for calling** gracias por llamar; **I'll
call you back later** te llamo más
tarde; **2** (*name*) **they've called the
baby Julie** le han puesto Julie al
bebé; **3 to be called** llamarse [17];
she has a brother called Dan tiene
un hermano que se llama Dan;
what's he called? ¿cómo se llama?

call box *noun* cabina F telefónica.

calm *adjective* calma F.
verb calmar [17].
● **to calm down** calmarse; **he's calmed
down a bit** se ha calmado un poco.
● **to calm somebody down** calmar a
alguien; **I tried to calm her down**
intenté calmarla.

calmly *adverb* con calma.

calorie *noun* caloría F.

camcorder *noun* videocámara F.

camel *noun* camello M.

camera *noun* **1** (*for photos*)
cámara F de fotos; **2** (*film or TV
camera*) cámara F.

cameraman *noun* cámara M/F.

camp *noun* campamento M.
verb acampar [17].

campaign *noun* campaña F.

camper van *noun* caravana F.

camping *noun* camping M; **to go
camping** ir de camping; **we're going**

camping in Andalucia this summer
nos vamos de camping a Andalucía
este verano.

campsite *noun* camping M.

can[1] *noun* **1** lata F; **a can of
tomatoes** una lata de tomates;
2 (*for petrol or oil*) bidón M.

can[2] *verb* **1** poder [10]; **I can't be
there before ten** no puedo estar allí
antes de las diez; **you can leave your
bag here** puedes dejar tu bolsa aquí;
can you open the door, please?
¿puedes abrir la puerta por favor?;
can I help you? ¿puedo ayudarte?;
they couldn't come no pudieron
venir; **you could ring back
tomorrow** podrías volver a llamar
mañana; **you could have told me** me
lo podrías haber dicho; **2** (*with hear,
see, remember, find, 'can' is not
translated*) **can you hear me?** ¿me
oyes?; **I can't see her** no la veo; **I
can't remember** no me acuerdo; **I
can't find my keys** no encuentro mis
llaves; **3** (*know how to*) saber [13];
she can't drive no sabe conducir;
can you play the piano? ¿sabes
tocar el piano?

Canada *noun* Canadá M.

Canadian *noun* canadiense M/F.
adjective canadiense.

canal *noun* canal M.

Canary Islands *noun* **the Canary
Islands** las Islas Canarias.

cancel *verb* cancelar [17]; **the
concert's been cancelled** han
cancelado el concierto.

cancer noun cáncer M; **to have lung cancer** tener cáncer de pulmón.

Cancer noun cáncer M; **I'm Cancer** soy cáncer.

candidate noun candidato M, candidata F.

candle noun vela F.

candlestick noun candelabro M.

candyfloss noun algodón M de azúcar.

canned adjective en lata; **canned tomatoes** tomates en lata.

cannot verb SEE can².

canoe noun piragua F.

canoeing noun piragüismo M; **to go canoeing** hacer piragüismo; **I like canoeing** me gusta hacer piragüismo.

can-opener noun abrelatas M (does not change in the plural).

canteen noun cantina F.

canvas noun 1 (fabric) lona F; 2 (painting) lienzo M.

cap noun 1 (hat) gorro M; **a baseball cap** un gorro de béisbol; 2 (on a bottle or tube) tapón M.

capable adjective capaz.

capacity noun capacidad F.

capital noun 1 (city) capital F; **Madrid is the capital of Spain** Madrid es la capital de España; 2 (letter) mayúscula F; **in capitals** en mayúsculas.

capitalism noun capitalismo M.

Capricorn noun capricornio M; **Linda's Capricorn** Linda es capricornio.

captain noun 1 (of a ship or a team) capitán M, capitana F; 2 (of a plane) comandante M/F.

capture verb capturar [17].

car noun coche M; **a car crash** un accidente de coche; **to park the car** aparcar el coche; **we're going by car** vamos en coche.

caramel noun caramelo M.

caravan noun caravana F.

card noun 1 (for a card game) carta F; **a card game** un juego de cartas; **to have a game of cards** jugar a las cartas; 2 (greetings, phone, bank) tarjeta F; **a birthday card** una tarjeta de cumpleaños.

cardboard noun cartón M.

cardigan noun rebeca F.

cardphone noun teléfono M de tarjeta.

care noun 1 cuidado M; **he took care opening it** tuvo cuidado al abrirlo; 2 **to take care to do** asegurarse [17] de hacer; 3 **to take care of somebody** cuidar a alguien; 4 **take care!** (be careful) ¡cuidado!; (when saying goodbye) ¡cuídate!
verb 1 **to care about** preocuparse [17]; **to care about pollution** preocuparse por la contaminación; 2 **she doesn't care** a ella no le

importa; **I couldn't care less!** ¡no me importa en absoluto!

career *noun* carrera F.

careful *adjective* 1 cuidadoso/cuidadosa; **try to be more careful** procura ser más cuidadoso; 2 **a careful driver** un conductor/una conductora prudente; 3 **be careful!** ¡ten cuidado!

carefully *adverb* 1 **read the instructions carefully** lea las instrucciones atentamente; **listen carefully** escuchad atentamente; 2 (*handle*) con cuidado; **she put the vase down carefully** colocó el jarrón con cuidado; 3 **drive carefully!** ¡conduce con precaución!

careless *adjective* 1 **he's very careless** no pone atención en lo que hace; 2 **this is careless work** este trabajo está hecho sin cuidado; **a careless mistake** una falta de atención; 3 **careless driving** conducción imprudente.

caretaker *noun* (*in block of flats*) portero M, portera F.

car ferry *noun* ferry M.

car hire *noun* alquiler M de coches.

Caribbean *noun* 1 **the Caribbean (Islands)** el Caribe; 2 **the Caribbean** (*sea*) el Caribe.

caricature *noun* caricatura F.

carnation *noun* clavel M.

carnival *noun* carnaval M.

car park *noun* aparcamiento M.

carpenter *noun* carpintero M, carpintera F.

carpentry *noun* carpintería F.

carpet *noun* 1 (*fitted*) moqueta F; 2 (*loose*) alfombra F.

car phone *noun* teléfono M de automóvil.

car radio *noun* radio M de coche.

carriage *noun* vagón M.

carrier bag *noun* bolsa F.

carrot *noun* zanahoria F.

carry *verb* 1 llevar [17]; **she was carrying a parcel** llevaba un paquete; 2 (*vehicle, plane*) transportar [17]; **the coach was carrying schoolchildren** el autobús transportaba colegiales.
● **to carry on** seguir [64]; **they carried on talking** siguieron hablando.

carrycot *noun* cuna F portátil.

carsick *adjective* **to be carsick** marearse [17] al viajar en coche.

carton *noun* envase M.

cartoon *noun* 1 (*a film*) dibujos M (*plural*) animados; 2 (*a comic strip*) tira F cómica; 3 (*an amusing drawing*) chiste M.

cartridge *noun* 1 (*for a pen*) recambio M; 2 (*for a gun*) cartucho M.

carve *verb* trinchar [17] (*meat*).

case[1] *noun* 1 (*suitcase*) maleta F; **to pack a case** hacer una maleta; 2 (*a large wooden box, for wine for example*) caja F; 3 (*for spectacles or small things*) estuche M.

case[2] *noun* 1 caso M; **a case of flu** un caso de gripe; **in that case** en ese caso; **that's not the case** no se trata de eso; 2 **in case** en caso; **in case he's late** en caso de que llegue tarde; **check first, just in case** asegúrate, por si acaso; 3 **in any case** de todas formas; **in any case, it's too late** de todas formas, es demasiado tarde.

cash *noun* 1 (*money in general*) dinero M; **I haven't any cash on me** no llevo dinero encima; 2 (*money rather than a cheque*) dinero M en efectivo; **to pay in cash** pagar en efectivo; **£50 in cash** cincuenta libras en efectivo.

cash card *noun* tarjeta F de cajero automático.

cash desk *noun* caja F; **pay at the cash desk** pagar en caja.

cash dispenser *noun* cajero M automático.

cashew *noun* anacardo M.

cashier *noun* cajero M, cajera F.

cash point *noun* cajero M automático.

cassette *noun* cinta F de cassette.

cassette recorder *noun* cassette M.

cast *noun* los actores M (*plural*); **the cast were on stage** los actores estaban en el escenario.

castle *noun* 1 castillo M; 2 (*in chess*) torre F.

casual *adjective* informal.

casualty *noun* 1 (*in an accident*) víctima F; 2 (*hospital department*) urgencias F (*plural*); **he's in casualty** está en urgencias.

cat *noun* gato M; (*female*) gata F; ★ **it's raining cats and dogs** está lloviendo a cántaros (*literally: it's raining in jugfuls*).

catalogue *noun* catálogo M.

catastrophe *noun* catástrofe F.

catch *noun* 1 (*on a door*) pestillo M; 2 (*a drawback*) trampa F; **what's the catch?** ¿dónde está la trampa? *verb* 1 coger [3]; **Tom caught the ball** Tom cogió la pelota; **you can't catch me!** ¡no me coges!; **can you catch hold of the branch?** ¿puedes coger la rama?; 2 **to catch somebody doing** coger [3] a alguien haciendo; **he was caught stealing money** lo cogieron robando dinero; 3 coger [3] (*a bus or plane*); **did Tim catch his bus?** ¿cogió Tim el autobús?; 4 coger [3] (*an illness*); **he's caught chickenpox** ha cogido la varicela; **I've caught a cold** he cogido un resfriado; 5 (*fishing or hunting*) **to catch a fish** pescar [31] un pez; **to catch a mouse** cazar [22] un ratón; 6 oír [56] (*what somebody says*); **I didn't catch your name** no he oído tu nombre.
● **to catch up with somebody** alcanzar [22] a alguien.

category *noun* categoría F.

catering *noun* catering M.

caterpillar *noun* oruga F.

cathedral *noun* catedral F; **Seville cathedral** la catedral de Sevilla.

Catholic *noun* católico M, católica F. *adjective* católico/católica.

cattle *plural noun* ganado M (*singular*).

cauliflower *noun* coliflor F; **cauliflower cheese** coliflor con besamel.

cause *noun* causa F; **the cause of the accident** la causa del accidente; **for a good cause** por una buena causa.
verb causar [17]; **to cause problems** causar problemas.

caution *noun* cautela F.

cautious *adjective* cauteloso/ cautelosa.

cave *noun* cueva F.

caving *noun* espeleología F; **to go caving** hacer espeleología.

CD *noun* disco M compacto, CD M.

CD player *noun* compacto M.

CD-ROM *noun* CD-ROM M.

ceiling *noun* techo M; **on the ceiling** en el techo.

celebrate *verb* celebrar [17]; **I'm celebrating my birthday** estoy celebrando mi cumpleaños.

celebrity *noun* famoso M, famosa F.

celery *noun* apio M.

cell *noun* célula F.

cellar *noun* sótano M.

cello *noun* violonchelo M; **to play the cello** tocar [31] el violonchelo.

cement *noun* cemento M.

cemetery *noun* cementerio M.

centenary *noun* centenario M.

centigrade *adjective* centígrado M; **ten degrees centigrade** diez grados centígrados.

centimetre *noun* centímetro M.

central *adjective* central; **central London** el centro de Londres; **the office is very central** la oficina está en pleno centro.

central heating *noun* calefacción F central.

centre *noun* centro M; **in the centre of** en el centro de; **in the town centre** en el centro de la ciudad; **a shopping centre** un centro comercial.

century *noun* siglo M; **in the twentieth century** en el siglo veinte; **the sixth century** el siglo seis; **the twenty-first century** el siglo veintiuno.

cereal *noun* **breakfast cereal** cereales M (*plural*) para el desayuno; **to have cereal for breakfast** desayunar cereales.

ceremony *noun* ceremonia F.

certain *adjective* **1** (*sure*) seguro/ segura; **are you certain of the**

address? ¿estás seguro de las señas?; **I'm certain of it** estoy seguro; **to be certain that ...** estar seguro de que ...; **Nicky's certain (that) you're wrong** Nicky's está segura de que estás equivocado; **nobody knows for certain** nadie lo sabe con seguridad; **2** (*particular*) cierto/ cierta; **a certain number of** un cierto número de.

certainly *adverb* **certainly!** ¡por supuesto!; **certainly not** desde luego que no.

certificate *noun* certificado M; **a birth certificate** un certificado de nacimiento.

chain cadena F.

chair *noun* **1** (*upright*) silla F; **a kitchen chair** una silla de cocina; **2** (*with arms*) butaca F.

chair lift *noun* telesilla F.

chalet *noun* **1** (*in the mountains*) chalet M; **2** (*in a holiday camp*) bungalow M.

chalk *noun* tiza F.

challenge *noun* reto M; **the exam was a real challenge** el examen fue un verdadero reto.

champion *noun* campeón/ campeona M/F; **world champion** campeón del mundo.

chance *noun* **1** (*an opportunity*) ocasión F; **to have the chance to do** tener [9] ocasión de hacer; **if you have the chance to go to New York** si tienes ocasión de ir a Nueva York; **I haven't had the chance to write to**

him no he tenido ocasión de escribirle; **2** (*likelihood*) posibilidad F; **there's a chance that she'll pass** existe la posibilidad de que apruebe (*'de que' is followed by the subjunctive*); **there's little chance of winning** hay pocas posibilidades de ganar; **3** (*luck*) **by chance** por casualidad; **do you have her address, by any chance?** ¿tienes sus señas por casualidad?

change *noun* **1** cambio M; **a change of plan** un cambio de planes; **they've made some changes to the house** han hecho algunos cambios en la casa; **it makes a change from hamburgers** por lo menos, es algo distinto a las hamburguesas; **2 a change of clothes** una muda de ropa; **3** (*cash*) cambio M; **I haven't any change** no tengo cambio; **keep the change** quédese con el cambio; **4 for a change** para variar; **for a change, let's eat out** vamos a comer fuera, para variar.
verb **1** (*transform completely*) cambiar [17]; **it changed my life** cambió mi vida; **Liz never changes** Liz no cambia; **2** (*to switch from one thing to another*) cambiar [17] de; **we changed trains at Crewe** cambiamos de tren en Crewe; **she's changed her address** ha cambiado de dirección; **to change your mind** cambiar de opinión; **to change the subject** cambiar de tema; **they changed places** se cambiaron de sitio; **to change colour** cambiar de color; **3** (*to swap one for another*) cambiar [17]; **have you changed the towels?** ¿has cambiado las

toallas?; (*in a shop*) **can I change it for the larger size?** ¿puedo cambiarlo por una talla más grande?; **4** (*to exchange in a shop*) cambiar [17]; **5** (*to change your clothes*) cambiarse [17]; **Mike's gone up to change** Mike ha ido a cambiarse; **I must change my shirt** tengo que cambiarme de camisa.

changing room *noun* **1** (*for sport or swimming*) vestuario M; **2** (*in a shop*) probador M.

channel *noun* **1** (*on TV*) canal M; **to change channels** cambiar [17] de canal; **2 the Channel** el Canal de la Mancha.

Channel Tunnel *noun* Eurotúnel M.

chaos *noun* caos M; **it was chaos!** ¡fue un caos!

chapel *noun* capilla F.

chapter *noun* capítulo M; **in chapter two** en el capítulo número dos.

character *noun* **1** (*personality*) carácter M; **a house with a lot of character** una casa con mucho carácter; **2** (*in a book, play, or film*) personaje M; **the main character** el personaje principal.

characteristic *noun* característica F.

charcoal *noun* **1** (*for burning*) carbón M vegetal; **2** (*for drawing*) carboncillo M.

charge *noun* **1** (*what you pay*) precio M; **admission charge** precio de admisión; **there's no charge** es gratis; **an extra charge** un suplemento; **2 to be in charge** ser responsable; **who's in charge?** ¿quién es el responsable?; **to be in charge of something/somebody** estar a cargo de algo/alguien; **who's in charge of these children?** ¿quién está a cargo de estos niños?; **3 to be on a charge of theft** estar acusado de robo.

verb **1** (*ask payment*) cobrar [17]; **they charge ten pounds an hour** cobran diez libras la hora; **how much do you charge for one day?** ¿cuánto cobráis por un día?; **we don't charge, it's free** no cobramos, es gratis; **they didn't charge me for the drinks** no me cobraron las bebidas; **2 to charge somebody with** acusar [17] a alguien de (*a crime*).

charity *noun* organización F benéfica.

charm *noun* encanto M.

charming *adjective* encantador/ encantadora.

chart *noun* **1** (*table*) tabla F; **2 the weather chart** el mapa del tiempo; **3 the charts** las listas de éxitos; **number one in the charts** número uno en las listas de éxitos.

charter flight *noun* vuelo M chárter.

chase *noun* persecución F; **a car chase** una persecución en coche. *verb* perseguir [64] (*a person or animal*).

chat *noun* charla F; **to have a chat with somebody** charlar con alguien.

chat show *noun* programa M de entrevistas.

chatter *verb* 1 (*talk*) cotorrear [17] (*informal*); 2 **my teeth are chattering** me castañetean los dientes.

cheap *adjective* barato/barata; **cheap shoes** zapatos baratos; **that's very cheap!** ¡eso es muy barato!

cheaply *adverb* **to buy/sell cheaply** comprar/vender barato; **to eat/dress cheaply** comer/vestir con poco dinero.

cheap-rate *adjective* tarifa F reducida; **a cheap-rate phone call** una llamada de teléfono de tarifa reducida.

cheat *noun* tramposo M, tramposa F. *verb* engañar [17].

check *noun* 1 (*in a factory or at border controls*) control M; 2 (*by a doctor*) examen M médico; 3 (*in chess*) **check!** ¡jaque! *verb* (*to make sure*) comprobar [24]; **he checked the time** comprobó la hora; **check they're all back** comprueba que ya han llegado todos; **check with your father** pregunta a tu padre.
● **to check in** facturar [17] el equipaje (*for a flight*).

check-in *noun* facturación F de equipajes.

checkout *noun* caja F; **at the checkout** en caja.

checkup *noun* chequeo M.

cheek *noun* 1 (*part of face*) mejilla F; 2 (*nerve*) **what a cheek!** ¡qué cara! (*informal*).

cheeky *adjective* 1 (*mischievous*) descarado/descarada; 2 (*rude*) impertinente.

cheer *noun* 1 **three cheers for Tom!** ¡tres hurras por Tom!; 2 (*when you have a drink*) **cheers!** ¡salud! *verb* (*to shout hurray*) vitorear [17].
● **to cheer somebody up** animar [17] a alguien; **cheer up!** ¡ánimo!

cheerful *adjective* alegre.

cheese *noun* queso M; **blue cheese** queso azul; **a cheese sandwich** un sandwich de queso.

chef *noun* chef M/F.

chemical *noun* producto M químico.

chemist *noun* 1 farmacéutico M, farmacéutica F; 2 **chemist's** farmacia F; **at the chemist's** en la farmacia; 3 (*scientist*) químico M, química F.

chemistry *noun* química F.

cheque *noun* cheque M; **to pay by cheque** pagar con cheque; **to write a cheque** extender un cheque.

chequebook *noun* talonario M de cheques.

cherry *noun* cereza F.

chess *noun* ajedrez M; **to play chess** jugar [27] al ajedrez.

chessboard *noun* tablero M de ajedrez.

chest *noun* 1 (*part of the body*) pecho M; 2 (*box*) arcón M.

chestnut *noun* castaña F.

chestnut tree *noun* castaño M.

chest of drawers *noun* cómoda F.

chew *verb* masticar [31] (*food*).

chewing gum *noun* chicle M.

chick *noun* (*of a hen*) pollito M.

chicken *noun* pollo M; **roast chicken** pollo asado; **chicken thighs** muslos de pollo.

chickenpox *noun* varicela F.

chicory *noun* endivia F.

child *noun* (*boy*) niño M; (*girl*) niña F; **Jenny's children** los niños de Jenny.

childish *adjective* infantil.

childminder *noun* niñero M, niñera F.

Chile *noun* Chile M.

chilled *adjective* (*wine*) frío/fría.

chilli *noun* chile M.

chilly *adjective* frío/fría (*a room or the weather*); **it's chilly today** hoy hace fresco.

chimney *noun* chimenea F.

chimpanzee *noun* chimpancé M.

chin *noun* barbilla F.

china *noun* porcelana F; **a china plate** un plato de porcelana.

China *noun* China F.

Chinese *noun* 1 the Chinese (*people*) los chinos; 2 (*language*) chino M. *adjective* chino/china; **a Chinese man** un chino; **a Chinese woman** una china; **a Chinese meal** una comida china.

chip *noun* 1 (*fried potato*) patata F frita; **I'd like some chips** quiero unas patatas fritas; 2 (*microchip*) chip M; 3 (*in glass or china*) desportilladura F.

chipped *adjective* desportillado/ desportillada.

chives *noun* cebollino M (*singular*).

chocolate *noun* 1 chocolate M; **a chocolate ice-cream** un helado de chocolate; **hot chocolate** chocolate caliente; **milk chocolate** chocolate con leche; **dark chocolate** chocolate sin leche; 2 **a chocolate** un bombón; **a box of chocolates** una caja de bombones.

choice *noun* elección F; **freedom of choice** libertad de elección; **it was a good choice** fue una buena elección; **you have a choice of two flights** puede elegir entre dos vuelos; **I had no choice** no tuve más remedio.

choir *noun* coro M.

choke *noun* (*on a car*) estárter M. *verb* atragantarse [17]; **she choked on a bone** se atragantó con un hueso.

choose *verb* elegir [48]; **you chose well** elegiste bien; **Cathy chose the**

red one Cathy eligió el rojo; **it's hard to choose from all these colours** es difícil elegir entre todos estos colores.

chop *noun* chuleta F; **a lamb chop** una chuleta de cordero.
verb **1** cortar [17] (*wood*); **2** cortar [17] en trozos pequeños (*vegetables or meat*); **3** picar [31] (*onion*).

chopstick *noun* palillo M para comida china.

chord *noun* acorde M.

chorus *noun* **1** (*when everybody joins in the song*) estribillo M; **2** (*a group of singers*) coro M.

Christ *noun* Cristo.

christening *noun* bautizo M.

Christian *noun*, *adjective* cristiano/ cristiana.

Christian name *noun* nombre M de pila.

Christmas *noun* Navidad F; **at Christmas** en Navidad; **Happy Christmas!** ¡Feliz Navidad!

Christmas card *noun* tarjeta F de Navidad.

Christmas carol *noun* villancico M.

Christmas Day *noun* día M de Navidad.

Christmas dinner *noun* cena F de Navidad.

Christmas Eve *noun* Nochebuena F; **on Christmas Eve** en Nochebuena.

Christmas present *noun* regalo M de Navidad.

Christmas tree *noun* árbol M de Navidad.

chunk *noun* trozo M.

church *noun* iglesia F; **to go to church** ir a la iglesia.

churchyard *noun* cementerio M.

chute *noun* (*for sliding down*) tobogán M.

cider *noun* sidra F.

cigar *noun* puro M.

cigarette *noun* cigarrillo M; **to light a cigarette** encender un cigarrillo.

cinema *noun* cine M; **to go to the cinema** ir al cine.

circle *noun* círculo M; **to sit in a circle** sentarse en círculo; **to go round in circles** dar vueltas.

circuit *noun* (*racing track*) pista F.

circular *adjective* circular.

circumstances *plural noun* **under the circumstances** en estas circunstancias.

circus *noun* circo M.

citizen *noun* ciudadano M, ciudadana F.

city *noun* ciudad F; **the city of Seville** la ciudad de Sevilla.

city centre *noun* centro M de la ciudad; **in the city centre** en el centro de la ciudad.

civilization *noun* civilización F.

civil servant *noun* funcionario M, funcionaria F; **she's a civil servant** es funcionaria.

civil war *noun* guerra F civil.

claim *verb* asegurar [17]; **he claimed to know** aseguró saberlo.

clap *verb* **1** aplaudir [19]; **everyone clapped** todo el mundo aplaudió; **2 to clap your hands** dar [4] palmadas.

clapping *noun* aplausos M (*plural*).

clarinet *noun* clarinete M; **to play the clarinet** tocar [31] el clarinete.

clash *noun* (*for example, between police and demonstrators*) choque M.
verb **1** (*rival groups*) chocar [31]; **2** (*colours*) desentonar [17]; **the curtains clash with the wallpaper** las cortinas desentonan con el papel pintado.

clasp *noun* (*of a necklace*) broche M.

class *noun* clase F; **she's in the same class as me** está en la misma clase que yo; **an art class** una clase de arte; **in class** en clase; **a social class** una clase social.

classic *adjective* clásico/clásica.

classical *adjective* clásico/clásica; **classical music** música clásica.

classroom *noun* clase F.

claw *noun* **1** (*of a cat or dog*) zarpa F; **2** (*of a crab*) pinza F.

clay *noun* **1** (*for modelling*) arcilla F; **2 a clay court** (*in tennis*) una pista de tierra batida.

clean *adjective* **1** limpio/limpia; **a clean shirt** una camisa limpia; **my hands are clean** tengo las manos limpias; **2** (*germ-free*) puro/pura (*air or water*).
verb **1** limpiar [17]; **I cleaned the whole house** limpié toda la casa; **2 to clean your teeth** lavarse [17] los dientes; **I'm going to clean my teeth** voy a lavarme los dientes.

cleaner *noun* **1** (*in a public place*) limpiador M, limpiadora F; **2** (*a cleaning lady*) señora F de la limpieza; **3 a dry cleaner's** una tintorería.

cleaning *noun* **to do the cleaning** hacer [7] la limpieza.

cleanser *noun* **1** (*for the house*) producto M de limpieza; **2** (*for your face*) crema F limpiadora.

clear *adjective* **1** (*that you can see through*) transparente; **clear glass** cristal transparente; **2** (*cloudless*) despejado/despejada; **3** (*easy to understand*) claro/clara; **clear instructions** instrucciones claras; **is that clear?** ¿está claro?; **it's clear that ...** está claro que ...
verb **1** sacar [31] (*papers, rubbish, or clothes*); **have you cleared your stuff out of your room?** ¿has sacado todas tus cosas de tu habitación?; **2** recoger [3] (*a table*); **can I clear the table?** ¿puedo recoger la mesa?; **3** despejar [17] (*a road or path*); **4** (*fog or smoke*) disiparse [17]; **and**

then the fog **cleared** y entonces la niebla se disipó; **5 to clear your throat** aclararse [17] la voz.
● **to clear something up** recoger [3]; **I'll just clear up my books** voy a recoger mis libros.

clearly adjective **1** (to think, speak, or hear) con claridad; **2** (obviously) claramente; **she was clearly worried** estaba claramente preocupada.

clementine noun clementina F.

clever adjective **1** inteligente; **their children are all very clever** todos sus hijos son muy inteligentes; **2** (ingenious) ingenioso/ingeniosa; **a clever idea** una idea ingeniosa.

client noun cliente M/F.

cliff noun acantilado M.

climate noun clima M.

climb verb **1** subir [19] (stairs); **2** escalar [17] (a hill or a tree); **we climbed Mont Blanc** escalamos el Mont Blanc.

climber noun alpinista M/F.

climbing noun alpinismo M; **they go climbing in Italy** practican el alpinismo en Italia.

clinic noun **1** (in a hospital) consultorio M; **2** (a private hospital) clínica F.

clip noun **1** (from a film) clip M; **2** (for your hair) horquilla F. verb **1** (to cut) cortar [17]; **2** (to fasten) sujetar [17] con un clip.

cloakroom noun (for coats) guardarropa M.

clock noun reloj M; **an alarm clock** un reloj despertador; **to put the clocks forward an hour** adelantar los relojes una hora; **to put the clocks back** atrasar los relojes.

clock radio noun radiodespertador M.

close¹ adjective, adverb **1** (result) reñido/reñida; **2** (relation) cercano/cercana; **3** (friend or relationship) **she's a close friend of mine** es muy amiga mía; **they are very close** están muy unidos; **4** (near) cerca; **the station's very close** la estación está muy cerca; **she lives close by** vive cerca; **not very close** no muy cerca; **close to the cinema** cerca del cine.

close² verb cerrar [29]; **close your eyes !** ¡cierra los ojos !; **she closed the door** cerró la puerta; **the post office closes at six** la oficina de correos cierra a las seis.
● **to close down** (a shop or factory) cerrar [29].

closed adjective cerrado/cerrada; **'closed on Mondays'** 'cerrado los lunes'.

closely adverb de cerca; **to examine something closely** examinar [17] algo de cerca.

closing date noun fecha F límite; **the closing date for entries** la fecha límite para inscribirse.

closing-down sale noun liquidación F por cierre de negocio.

closing time *noun* hora F de cierre.

cloth *noun* 1 (*for the floor or wiping surfaces*) bayeta F; 2 (*for polishing*) trapo M del polvo; 3 (*for drying up*) paño M de cocina; 4 (*fabric by the metre*) tela F.

clothes *plural noun* ropa F (*singular*); **to put your clothes on** ponerse [11] la ropa; **to take your clothes off** quitarse [17] la ropa; **to change your clothes** cambiarse [17] de ropa.

clothes hanger *noun* percha F.

clothes line *noun* cuerda F de tender.

clothes peg *noun* pinza F para tender.

cloud *noun* nube F.

cloudy *adjective* nublado/nublada.

clove *noun* 1 clavo M; 2 **a clove of garlic** un diente de ajo.

clown *noun* payaso M, payasa F.

club *noun* 1 (*association*) club M; **he's in the football club** está en el club de fútbol; 2 (*in cards*) trébol; **the four of clubs** el cuatro de tréboles; 3 (*golfing iron*) palo M de golf.

clue *noun* 1 pista F; **they have a few clues** tienen unas cuantas pistas; 2 (*in a crossword*) clave F; ★ **I haven't a clue** no tengo ni idea.

clumsy *adjective* torpe.

clutch *noun* (*in a car*) embrague M. *verb* **to clutch something** tener [9] algo firmemente agarrado.

coach *noun* 1 (*bus*) autobús M; **by coach** en autobús; **on the coach** en el autobús; **to travel by coach** viajar en autobús; 2 (*sports trainer*) entrenador M, entrenadora F; 3 (*railway carriage*) vagón M.

coach station *noun* estación F de autobuses.

coach trip *noun* excursión F en autobús; **to go on a coach trip** hacer una excursión en autobús.

coal *noun* carbón M.

coal mine *noun* mina F de carbón.

coal miner *noun* minero M, minera F.

coarse *adjective* basto/basta.

coast *noun* costa F; **on the east coast** en la costa este.

coat *noun* 1 (*that you wear*) abrigo M; 2 **a coat of paint** una capa de pintura.

coat hanger *noun* percha F.

cobweb *noun* telaraña F.

cockerel *noun* gallo M.

cocoa *noun* (*drink*) chocolate M; (*powder*) cacao M.

coconut *noun* coco M.

cod *noun* bacalao M.

code *noun* 1 código M; **the highway code** el código de la circulación; 2 **the dialling code for Barcelona** el prefijo de Barcelona.

coffee *noun* café M; **a cup of coffee** un café; **a black coffee, please** un café solo, por favor; **a white coffee** un café con leche.

coffee break *noun* pausa F para el café.

coffee cup *noun* taza F de café.

coffee machine *noun* 1 (*vending machine*) máquina F de café; 2 (*electric*) cafetera F eléctrica.

coffee pot *noun* cafetera F.

coffee table *noun* mesa F de centro.

coffin *noun* ataúd M.

coin *noun* moneda F; **a pound coin** una moneda de una libra.

coincidence *noun* coincidencia F.

Coke™ *noun* Coca-Cola™ F; **two Cokes please** dos Coca-Colas, por favor.

colander *noun* colador M.

cold *noun* 1 (*cold weather*) frío M; **I don't want to go out in this cold** no quiero salir con este frío; **come in out of the cold** entra, que hace frío; **she was shivering with cold** estaba temblando de frío; 2 (*illness*) resfriado M; **to have a cold** estar resfriado/resfriada; **Carol's got a cold** Carol está resfriada; **a bad cold** un fuerte resfriado.
adjective 1 frío/fría; **your hands are cold** tienes las manos frías; **cold milk** leche fría; 2 (*weather, temperature*) **it's cold today** hoy hace frío; **it's cold in the kitchen** hace frío en la cocina; 3 (*feeling*) **I'm cold** tengo frío; **he was feeling very cold** tenía mucho frío.

cold sore *noun* calentura F.

collapse *verb* 1 (*a roof or a wall*) derrumbarse [17]; 2 (*a person*) **he collapsed in his office** sufrió un desmayo en su oficina.

collar *noun* 1 (*on a garment*) cuello M; 2 (*for a dog*) collar M.

collarbone *noun* clavícula F.

colleague *noun* compañero M, compañera F.

collect *verb* 1 (*as a hobby*) coleccionar [17]; **I collect stamps** colecciono sellos; 2 recoger [3] (*a person or a thing*); **she collects the children from school** ella recoge a los niños del colegio; **to collect in the exercise books** recoger los cuadernos; 3 cobrar [17] (*fares or money*); 4 reunir [62] (*data or information*).

collection *noun* 1 (*of stamps, CDs, etc.*) colección F; 2 (*of money*) colecta F.

college *noun* 1 (*for higher education*) colegio M universitario; **to go to college** ir a la universidad; 2 (*for vocational training*) escuela F de formación profesional; 3 (*a school*) instituto M.

collie *noun* collie M/F.

collision *noun* choque M.

Colombia *noun* Colombia F.

colour *noun* color M; **what colour is your car?** ¿de qué color es tu coche?; **what colour is it?** ¿de qué color es?; **do you have it in a different colour?** ¿lo tiene en otros colores?

verb (*with paints or crayons*) colorear [17]; **to colour something red** colorear algo de rojo.

colour blind *adjective* daltónico/daltónica.

colour film *noun* (*for a camera*) carrete M de color.

colourful *adjective* de colores.

colouring book *noun* libro M para colorear.

colour supplement *noun* suplemento M a color.

column *noun* columna F.

comb *noun* peine M.
verb **to comb your hair** peinarse [17]; **I'll just comb my hair** voy a peinarme.

combine *verb* combinar [17] (*two separate things*); **they don't combine well** no combinan bien.

come *verb* venir [15]; **come quick!** ¡ven rápido!; **come and see!** ¡ven a ver!; **Nick came by bike** Nick vino en bici; **did Jess come to school yesterday?** ¿vino Jess ayer a clase?; **can you come over for a coffee?** ¿puedes venir a tomar un café?; **the bus is coming** ya viene el autobús; **come along!** ¡ven!; **coming!** ¡ya voy!
- **to come back** volver [45]; **she's coming back to collect us** volverá para recogernos.
- **to come down** bajar [17] (*the stairs or the street*).
- **to come for** venir [15] a por (*a person*); **my father's coming for me** mi padre va a venir a por mí.

- **to come from** ser [1] de; **Ian comes from Scotland** Ian es de Escocia; **the wine comes from Spain** el vino es español.
- **to come in** entrar [17]; **come in!** ¡entra!; **she came into the kitchen** entró en la cocina.
- **to come off** 1 (*a button*) desprenderse [18]; (*a handle*) soltarse [24]; 2 (*a lid*) **I can't get the lid to come off** no puedo quitar la tapa.
- **to come out** salir [63]; **they came out when I called** salieron cuando los llamé; **the CD's coming out soon** el compacto va a salir pronto; **the sun hasn't come out yet** el sol no ha salido aún.
- **to come to** 1 (*get to*) llegar [28] a; **when you come to the church turn right** gira a la derecha cuando llegues a la iglesia; 2 (*add up to*) **it comes to 300 pesetas** suma trescientas pesetas.
- **to come up** subir [19]; **can you come up a moment?** ¿puedes subir un momento?
- **to come up to somebody** acercarse [31] a alguien.

comedian *noun* cómico M, cómica F.

comedy *noun* comedia F.

comfortable *adjective* cómodo/cómoda; **this chair's really comfortable** esta silla es muy cómoda; **to feel comfortable** (*a person*) estar cómodo/cómoda; **are you comfortable there?** ¿estás cómodo ahí?

comfortably *adverb* cómodamente.

comic *noun* (*magazine*) cómic M.

comic strip *noun* tira F cómica.

comma *noun* coma F.

command *noun* orden F.

comment *noun* (*in a conversation*) comentario M; **he made some rude comments about my friends** hizo unos comentarios de muy mal gusto sobre mis amigos.

commentary *noun* crónica F; **the commentary of the match** la crónica del partido.

commentator *noun* comentarista M/F; **a sports commentator** un comentarista deportivo.

commercial *noun* anuncio M de televisión. *adjective* comercial.

commit *verb* 1 cometer [18] (*a crime*); 2 **to commit yourself** comprometerse [18].

committee *noun* comité M.

common *adjective* 1 corriente; **it's a common problem** es un problema corriente; 2 **in common** en común; **they have nothing in common** no tienen nada en común.

common sense *noun* sentido M común.

communicate *verb* comunicar [31].

communication *noun* comunicación F.

communion *noun* comunión F.

communism *noun* comunismo M.

communist *noun* comunista M/F.

community *noun* comunidad F; **the European Community** la comunidad europea.

commute *verb* **to commute between Oxford and London** viajar [17] todos los días de Oxford a Londres para ir a trabajar.

commuter *noun* **trains full of commuters** trenes llenos de personas que van a trabajar (*Spanish does not have a word for 'commuters' so it has to be explained as 'people travelling to work'*).

compact disc *noun* disco M compacto.

compact disc player *noun* compacto M.

company *noun* 1 compañía F; **an insurance company** una compañía de seguros; **she's set up a company** ha montado una compañía; **an airline company** una compañía aérea; **a theatre company** una compañía de teatro; 2 **to keep somebody company** hacer [7] compañía a alguien; **the dogs keep me company** los perros me hacen compañía.

comparatively *adverb* relativamente.

compare *verb* comparar [17]; **if you compare the Spanish with the English** si comparas los españoles con los ingleses; **our house is small**

compared with yours nuestra casa es pequeña comparada con la tuya.

comparison *noun* comparación F; **in comparison with** en comparación con.

compartment *noun* compartimento M.

compass *noun* brújula F.

compatible *adjective* (*computing*) compatible.

compete *verb* **1** **to compete in something** participar [17] en algo (*race, event*); **2** **to compete for something** competir [57] (*jobs, places*); **thirty people are competing for the job** treinta personas compiten por el puesto.

competent *adjective* competente.

competition *noun* **1** (*in a magazine or at school*) concurso M; **a poetry competition** un concurso de poesía; **2** (*in sports*) competición F; **a fishing competition** una competición de pesca; **3** (*in business*) competencia F.

competitor *noun* **1** (*in sports*) participante M/F; **2** (*in business*) competidor M, competidora F.

complain *verb* quejarse [17]; **we complained about the hotel and the meals** nos quejamos del hotel y de las comidas.

complete *adjective* completo/ completa; **the complete collection** la colección completa. *verb* (*to finish*) terminar [17].

completely *adverb* completamente.

complexion *noun* cutis M.

complicated *adjective* complicado/complicada.

complication *noun* complicación F; **there were complications** hubo complicaciones.

compliment *noun* cumplido M; **to pay somebody a compliment** hacer un cumplido a alguien.

compose *verb* componer [11]; **composed of** compuesto de.

composer *noun* compositor M, compositora F.

compulsory *adjective* obligatorio/ obligatoria.

computer *noun* ordenador M; **to work on a computer** trabajar en ordenador.

computer engineer *noun* técnico M en informática, técnica F en informática.

computer game *noun* juego M de ordenador.

computer programmer *noun* programador M, programadora F.

computer science *noun* informática F.

computing *noun* informática F.

conceited *adjective* engreído/ engreída.

concentrate *verb* concentrarse [17]; **I can't concentrate** no puedo concentrarme; **I was concentrating on the film** me estaba concentrando en la película.

concentration *noun* concentración F.

concern *noun* (*worry*) preocupación F; **there is no cause for concern** no hay razón para preocuparse.
verb **1** (*to affect*) concernir [14]; **this doesn't concern you** esto no te concierne; **2 as far as I'm concerned** por mi parte.

concert *noun* **1** concierto M; **to go to a concert** ir [8] a un concierto; **2 a concert ticket** una entrada para un concierto.

conclusion *noun* conclusión F.

concrete *noun* cemento M; **a concrete floor** un suelo de cemento.

condemn *verb* condenar [17].

condition *noun* condición F; **in good condition** en buenas condiciones; **weather conditions** condiciones meteorológicas; **the conditions of sale** las condiciones de venta; **on one condition** con una condición; **on condition that you let me pay** a condición de que me dejes pagar.

conditional *noun* condicional M.

conditioner *noun* (*for your hair*) suavizante M.

condom *noun* condón M.

conduct *noun* conducta F.
verb dirigir [49] (*an orchestra or a piece of music*).

conductor *noun* **1** (*of an orchestra*) director M de orquesta, directora F de orquesta; **2** (*on bus*) cobrador M, cobradora F.

cone *noun* **1** (*for ice cream*) cucurucho M; **2** (*for traffic*) cono M.

conference *noun* conferencia F.

confess *verb* confesar [29].

confession *noun* confesión F.

confidence *noun* **1** (*self-confidence*) seguridad F en sí mismo; **he has a lot of confidence** tiene mucha seguridad en sí mismo; **you're lacking in confidence** te falta seguridad en ti mismo; **2** (*faith in somebody else*) confianza F; **to have confidence in somebody** tener [9] confianza en alguien.

confident *adjective* **1** (*sure of yourself*) seguro de sí mismo, segura de sí misma; **you look very confident** pareces muy seguro de ti mismo; **she's a confident young woman** es una joven segura de sí misma; **2** (*sure that something will happen*) **to be confident that** estar [2] seguro de que; **I'm confident that it will work out all right** estoy seguro de que saldrá bien.

confirm *verb* confirmar [17]; **we'll confirm the date** confirmaremos la fecha.

confuse *verb* confundir [19]; **I confuse him with his brother** lo confundí con su hermano.

confused *adjective* **1** (*unclear*) confuso/confusa; **he gave us a confused story** contó una historia

muy confusa; **2** confundido/
confundida; **now I'm completely
confused** ahora estoy
completamente confundida; **I'm
confused about the holiday dates**
no estoy segura de las fechas de las
vacaciones; **3 to get confused**
confundirse [19]; **she got confused**
se confundió.

confusing *adjective* poco claro/
clara; **the instructions are confusing**
las instrucciones son poco claras.

confusion *noun* confusión F.

congratulate *verb* felicitar [17]; **I
congratulated Tim on his success**
felicité a Tim por su éxito; **we
congratulate you on winning** te
felicitamos por haber ganado.

congratulations *plural noun*
enhorabuena F; **congratulations on
the baby!** ¡enhorabuena por el bebé!

conjurer *noun* mago M, maga F.

connect *verb* (*to plug in to the
mains*) conectar [17] (*a dishwasher
or TV, for example*).

connection *noun* conexión F; **a
faulty connection** una conexión
defectuosa; **Sally missed her
connection** Sally perdió su
conexión; **there's no connection
between his letter and my decision**
no hay relación entre su carta y mi
decisión.

conscience *noun* conciencia F; **to
have a guilty conscience** no tener
la conciencia tranquila.

conscious *adjective* consciente.

consequence *noun*
consecuencia F.

consequently *adverb* por
consiguiente.

conservation *noun* (*of nature*)
protección F del medio ambiente.

conservative *noun*, *adjective*
conservador/conservadora.

conservatory *noun* jardín M de
invierno.

consider *verb* **1** (*to give thought to*)
considerar [17]; (*a suggestion or
idea*) **2** (*to think you might do*)
plantearse [17]; **we're considering
buying a flat** estamos
planteándonos comprar un piso;
3 all things considered bien
considerado.

considerate *adjective*
considerado/considerada (*a
person*).

considering *preposition* teniendo
en cuenta; **considering her age**
teniendo en cuenta su edad;
considering he did it all himself
teniendo en cuenta que lo hizo todo
él solo.

consist *verb* **to consist of** consistir
[19] en.

consonant *noun* consonante F.

constant *adjective* constante.

constantly *adverb* constantemente.

constipated *adjective* estreñido/
estreñida.

construct *verb* construir [54].

construction *noun* construcción F.

consult *verb* consultar [17].

consumer *noun* consumidor M, consumidora F.

contact *noun* contacto M; **to be in contact with somebody** estar en contacto con alguien; **we've lost contact** hemos perdido contacto; **Rob has contacts in the music business** Rob tiene contactos en el mundo de la música.
verb ponerse [11] en contacto con; **I'll contact you tomorrow** me pondré en contacto contigo mañana.

contact lens *noun* lentilla F.

contain *verb* contener [9].

container *noun* recipiente M.

contemporary *adjective* contemporáneo/contemporánea.

contents *plural noun* contenido M; **the contents of my suitcase** el contenido de mi maleta.

contest *noun* 1 concurso M; 2 (*in sport*) competición F.

contestant *noun* concursante M/F.

continent *noun* continente M; **on the Continent** en Europa continental.

continental *adjective* **a continental holiday** unas vacaciones en Europa continental.

continue *verb* 1 continuar [20]; **we continued our journey** continuamos con nuestro viaje; **'to**

be continued' 'continuará'; **2 to continue doing** seguir [64] haciendo; **Jill continued chatting** Jill siguió hablando.

continuous *adjective* continuo/continua; **continuous assessment** evaluación F continua.

contraceptive *noun* anticonceptivo M.

contract *noun* contrato M.

contradict *verb* contradecir [5].

contradiction *noun* contradicción F.

contrary *noun* **the contrary** lo contrario; **on the contrary** al contrario.

contrast *noun* contraste M.

contribute *verb* contribuir [54] (*money*).

contribution *noun* (*to charity or an appeal*) contribución F.

control *noun* (*of a crowd or animals*) control M; **the police have lost control** la policía ha perdido el control; **everything's under control** todo está bajo control.
verb 1 controlar [17] (*a crowd, animals, or a fire, for example*); **2 to control oneself** controlarse [17].

convenient *adjective* 1 práctico/práctica; **frozen vegetables are very convenient** las verduras congeladas son muy prácticas; **2 to be convenient for somebody** venirle [15] bien a alguien; **if that's convenient for you** si te va bien; **3 the house is convenient for**

shops and schools la casa está bien situada respecto a tiendas y colegios.

conventional *adjective*
1 convencional; 2 (*person*) tradicional.

conversation *noun* conversación F.

convert *verb* convertir [14]; **we're going to convert the garage into a workshop** vamos a convertir el garaje en un taller.

convince *verb* convencer [44]; **I'm convinced you're wrong** estoy convencido de que estás equivocado.

convincing *adjective* convincente.

cook *noun* cocinero M, cocinera F.
verb 1 cocinar [17]; **who's cooking tonight?** ¿quién cocina esta noche?; **I like cooking** me gusta cocinar;
2 cocer [41] (*vegetables, pasta, etc.*); **cook the carrots for five minutes** cuece las zanahorias durante cinco minutos; 3 hacer [7] (*a meal*); **Fran's busy cooking supper** Fran está haciendo la cena; 4 (*food*) hacerse [7]; **the sausages are cooking** las salchichas se están haciendo; **is the chicken cooked?** ¿está hecho el pollo?

cooker *noun* cocina F; **an electric cooker** una cocina eléctrica; **a gas cooker** una cocina de gas.

cookery *noun* cocina F.

cookery book *noun* libro M de cocina.

cooking *noun* cocina F; **Italian cooking** la cocina italiana; **home cooking** la comida casera; **to do the cooking** cocinar [17].

cool *noun* 1 (*coldness*) fresco M; **stay in the cool** quedarse [17] al fresco; 2 (*calm*) calma F; **to lose one's cool** perder [36] la calma; **he kept his cool** mantuvo la calma.
adjective 1 (*cold*) fresco/fresca; **a cool drink** una bebida fresca; **it's cool inside** dentro hace fresco;
2 (*laid-back*) tranquilo/tranquila;
3 **to be cool** (*a person*) estar en la onda (*informal*); **he's so cool** está muy en la onda (*informal*);
4 (*trendy*) molón/molona (*informal*) (*a car or a jacket*).
verb **to cool (down)** enfriarse [32].

cop *noun* poli M/F (*informal*).

cope *verb* 1 (*to manage*) defenderse [36]; **she copes well** se defiende bien; 2 **to cope with** ocuparse [17] de (*children or work*); **I'll cope with the dishes** yo me ocupo de los platos; 3 hacer [7] frente a (*problems*); **she's had a lot to cope with** ha tenido que hacer frente a muchos problemas; **he can't cope any more** ya no puede más.

copy *noun* 1 copia F; **make ten copies of this letter** haz diez copias de esta carta; 2 (*of a book*) ejemplar M.
verb copiar [17]; **I copied (down) the address** copié las señas.

cord *noun* (*for a blind, for example*) cordón M.

cordless telephone *noun* teléfono M inalámbrico.

core noun (of an apple or a pear)
corazón M.

cork noun 1 (in a bottle) tapón M;
2 (material) corcho M.

corkscrew noun sacacorchos M
(does not change in the plural).

corn noun 1 (wheat) trigo M;
2 (sweetcorn) maíz M.

corner noun 1 (of street or page)
esquina F; **at the corner of the
street** en la esquina de la calle; **it's
just round the corner** está a la vuelta
de la esquina; **in the bottom right-
hand corner of the page** en la
esquina inferior derecha de la
página; 2 (of room or cupboard)
rincón M; **in a corner of the kitchen**
en un rincón de la cocina; 3 **out of
the corner of your eye** por el rabillo
del ojo; 4 (in football) córner M.

cornflakes noun copos M (plural)
de maíz.

Cornwall noun Cornualles M.

corpse noun cadáver M.

correct adjective 1 correcto/
correcta; **the correct sum** la
cantidad total correcta; **the correct
answer** la respuesta correcta; **the
correct choice** la elección
adecuada; 2 **yes, that's correct** sí,
así es.
verb corregir [48].

correction noun corrección F.

correspond verb corresponder [18].

corridor noun pasillo M.

cosmetics plural noun
cosméticos M (plural).

cost noun coste M; **the cost of a new
computer** el coste de un nuevo
ordenador; **the cost of living** el coste
de la vida.
verb costar [24]; **how much does it
cost?** ¿cuánto cuesta?; **the tickets
cost ten pounds** las entradas
cuestan diez libras; **it costs too
much** cuesta demasiado caro.

Costa Rica noun Costa Rica M.

costume noun 1 (fancy dress)
disfraz M; 2 (for an actor) traje M.

cosy adjective (a room) acogedor/
acogedora; **it's cosy by the fire** se
está muy bien al lado del fuego.

cot noun cuna F.

cottage noun casita F en el campo.

cotton noun 1 (fabric) algodón M;
a cotton shirt una camisa de
algodón; 2 (thread) hilo M.

cotton wool noun algodón M en
rama.

couch noun sofá M.

cough noun tos F; **a nasty cough** una
tos mala; **to have a cough** tener [9]
tos.
verb toser [18].

could verb 1 poder [10]; **if he could
pay** si pudiese pagar; **I couldn't open
it** no podía abrirlo; **they couldn't**

smoke there no podían fumar allí; **she did all she could** hizo todo lo que pudo; **2** (*knew how to*) **he couldn't drive** no sabía conducir; **I couldn't swim** no sabía nadar; **3** (*with see, hear, smell, remember, or understand, 'could' is not translated*) **I could hear a police car** oí un coche de policía; **she couldn't see anything** no veía nada; **4** (*talking about a possibility*) **they could be home by now** puede que ya estén en casa; **you could be right** puede que tengas razón; **5** (*in 'if' sentences 'could' is translated by the subjunctive*) **I would buy it if I could afford it** lo compraría si pudiese; **I could have gone if I'd wanted** hubiese podido ir si hubiese querido; **6** (*asking permission or suggesting*) **could I speak to David?** ¿podría hablar con David?; **you could try telephoning** podrías intentar llamar por teléfono.

council *noun* ayuntamiento M.

count *verb* **1** (*reckon up*) contar [24]; **I counted my money** conté mi dinero; **thirty-five not counting the children** treinta y cinco sin contar a los niños; **2 to count as** considerarse [17] como; **children over twelve count as adults** los niños mayores de doce años se consideran como adultos.

counter *noun* **1** (*in a shop*) mostrador M; **2** (*in a café*) barra F; **3** (*in a post office or bank*) ventanilla F; **4** (*for board games*) ficha F.

country *noun* **1** (*Spain, England, etc.*) país M; **a foreign country** un país extranjero; **from another country** de otro país; **2** (*not town*) campo M; **to live in the country** vivir en el campo; **a country walk** un paseo por el campo; **a country road** un camino rural.

country dancing *noun* baile M folklórico.

countryside *noun* campo M.

county *noun* condado M.

couple *noun* **1** (*a pair*) pareja F; **a married couple** una pareja de casados; **2 a couple of** un par de; **a couple of times** un par de veces; **I've got a couple of things to do** tengo que hacer un par de cosas.

courage *noun* valor M.

courier *noun* **1** (*on a package holiday*) guía M/F; **2** (*delivery service*) mensajería F; **by courier** por mensajería.

course *noun* **1** (*lessons*) curso M; **a beginners' course** un curso para principiantes; **a computer course** un curso de informática; **to go on a course** asistir a un curso; **2** (*part of a meal*) plato M; **the main course** el plato principal; **3 a golf course** un campo de golf; **4 of course** claro; **yes, of course!** ¡sí, claro!; **he's forgotten, of course** se ha olvidado, claro.

court *noun* **1** (*for tennis, squash, or basketball*) cancha F; **2** (*of law*) tribunal M.

courtyard *noun* patio M.

cousin *noun* primo M, prima F; **my cousin Sonia** mi prima Sonia.

cover *noun* 1 (*for a book*) tapa F; 2 (*for a duvet or cushion*) funda F; **a duvet cover** una funda de edredón.
verb 1 cubrir [46]; **to cover the wound** cubrir la herida; **the ground was covered with snow** el suelo estaba cubierto de nieve; **he was covered in mud** estaba cubierto de barro; 2 (*your face or eyes*) cubrirse [46]; **she covered her face** se cubrió la cara.

cow *noun* vaca F; **mad cow disease** la enfermedad de las vacas locas.

coward *noun* cobarde M/F.

cowboy *noun* vaquero M.

crab *noun* cangrejo M.

crack *noun* 1 (*in a wall*) grieta F; 2 (*in a cup or plate*) raja F; 3 (*a cracking noise*) crujido M.
verb 1 (*to make a crack in*) hacer [7] una raja en (*a cup or a window*); 2 fracturar [17] (*a bone*); 3 (*break open*) cascar [31] (*a nut or an egg*); 4 (*split by itself: ice, for example*) rajarse [17]; 5 (*make a noise*) (*a twig*) crujir [19].

cracker *noun* (*biscuit*) galleta F salada.

crackle *verb* crujir [19].

craft *noun* (*at school*) trabajos M (*plural*) manuales.

cramp *noun* calambre M; **I've got cramp in my leg** tengo un calambre en la pierna.

crane *noun* grúa F.

crash *noun* 1 (*an accident*) accidente M; **a car crash** un accidente de coche; 2 (*smashing noise*) estrépito M; **a crash of broken glass** un estrépito de vasos rotos.
verb 1 (*a car or plane*) tener [9] un accidente; **the plane crashed** el avión tuvo un accidente; 2 **to crash into something** chocar [31] con algo; **the car crashed into a tree** el coche chocó con un árbol.

crash course *noun* curso M intensivo.

crash helmet *noun* casco M.

crate *noun* 1 (*for china*) cajón M para embalar; 2 (*for bottles or fruit*) caja F.

crawl *noun* (*in swimming*) crol M.
verb 1 (*a person, a baby*) ir [8] a gatas; 2 (*cars in a jam*) ir [8] muy despacio; **we were crawling along** íbamos muy despacio.

crayon *noun* 1 (*wax*) pintura F de cera; 2 (*coloured pencil*) lápiz M de color.

craze *noun* fiebre F; **the craze for computer games** la fiebre de los juegos de ordenador.

crazy *adjective* loco/loca; **to go crazy** volverse loco/loca; **to be crazy about someone** estar loco/loca por alguien; **he's crazy about football** le encanta el fútbol.

creak *verb* (*a hinge*) chirriar [32]; (*a floorboard*) crujir [19].

cream *noun* **1** (*dairy cream*) nata F;
strawberries and cream fresas con
nata; **2** (*for hands, face, etc.*) crema F.

cream cheese *noun* queso M para
untar.

crease *noun* arruga F.

creased *adjective* arrugado/
arrugada.

create *verb* crear [17].

creative *adjective* creativo/
creativa (*a person*).

creature *noun* criatura F.

creche *noun* guardería F.

credit *noun* crédito M; **to buy
something on credit** comprar algo a
crédito.

credit card *noun* tarjeta F de
crédito.

crew *noun* **1** (*on a ship or plane*)
tripulación F; **2** (*rowing or filming*)
equipo M.

crew cut *noun* corte M de pelo al
rape.

cricket *noun* **1** (*game*) críquet M;
to play cricket jugar [27] al críquet;
2 (*insect*) grillo M.

cricket bat *noun* bate M de críquet.

crime *noun* **1** delito M; **theft is a
crime** el robo es un delito;
2 (*murder*) crimen M; **3** (*within
society*) crimen M; **the fight against
crime** la lucha contra el crimen.

criminal *noun* criminal M/F.
adjective criminal.

crisis *noun* crisis F.

crisp *noun* patata F frita; **a packet o**
(potato) crisps un paquete de
patatas fritas.
adjective crujiente.

critical *adjective* **1** crítico/crítica (*a*
remark or somebody's condition);
2 decisivo/decisiva (*a moment*).

criticism *noun* crítica F.

criticize *verb* criticar [31].

Croatia *noun* Croacia F.

crockery *noun* vajilla F.

crocodile *noun* cocodrilo M.

crook *noun* (*criminal*) granuja M/F.

crop *noun* cosecha F.

cross *noun* cruz F.
adjective enfadado/enfadada; **she's
very cross** está muy enfadada; **I'm
cross with you** estoy enfadada
contigo; **to get cross** enfadarse [17].
verb **1** (*to cross over*) cruzar [22]; **to
cross the road** cruzar la calle; **2 to
cross your legs** cruzar las piernas;
3 to cross into Spain pasar [17] a
España; **4** (*to cross each other*)
cruzarse [22]; **the two roads cross
here** las dos carreteras se cruzan
aquí.
● **to cross out** tachar [17] (*a word or*
sentence).

cross-Channel *adjective* **a cross-
Channel ferry** un ferry que cruza el
Canal de la Mancha.

cross-country *noun* **1** cross M;
2 cross-country skiing esquí M de
fondo.

crossing *noun* 1 (*from one place to another*) travesía F; **a Channel crossing** una travesía por el Canal de la Mancha; 2 **a pedestrian crossing** un cruce de peatones; **a level crossing** un paso a nivel.

cross-legged *adjective* **to sit cross-legged** sentarse con las piernas cruzadas.

crossroads *noun* cruce M; **at the crossroads** en el cruce.

crossword *noun* crucigrama M; **to do the crossword** hacer el crucigrama.

crouch *verb* ponerse [11] en cuclillas.

crow *noun* cuervo M; ★ **as the crow flies** en línea recta.
verb (*a cock*) cacarear [17].

crowd *noun* multitud F; **in the crowd** en la multitud; **a crowd of 5,000** una multitud de cinco mil personas.
verb **to crowd into** (or **onto**) aglomerase [17] en (*a room or bus, for example*); **we all crowded into the train** nos aglomeramos en el tren.

crowded *adjective* lleno/llena de gente.

crown *noun* corona F.

crude *adjective* 1 (*rough and ready*) rudimentario/rudimentaria; 2 (*vulgar*) grosero/grosera.

cruel *adjective* cruel.

cruise *noun* crucero M; **to go on a cruise** ir de crucero.

crumb *noun* miga F.

crumple *verb* arrugar [28].

crunchy *adjective* crujiente.

crush *verb* aplastar [17].

crust *noun* corteza F.

crutch *noun* muleta F; **to be on crutches** andar con muletas.

cry *noun* grito M.
verb 1 (*weep*) llorar [17]; 2 (*call out*) gritar [17].

crystal *noun* cristal M.

cub *noun* 1 (*animal*) cachorro M; 2 (*scout*) lobato M.

Cuba *noun* Cuba M/F.

cube *noun* cubo M; **an ice cube** un cubito de hielo.

cubic *adjective* (*for measurements*) cúbico/cúbica; **three cubic metres** tres metros cúbicos.

cubicle *noun* 1 (*in a changing room*) vestuario M; 2 (*in a public lavatory*) cubículo M.

cuckoo *noun* cuco M.

cucumber *noun* pepino M.

cuddle *noun* **to give somebody a cuddle** dar [4] un abrazo a alguien.
verb abrazar [22].

cue *noun* (*billiards, pool, snooker*) taco M.

cuff *noun* (*on a shirt*) puño M.

cul-de-sac *noun* callejón M sin salida.

culture noun cultura F.

cunning adjective astuto/astuta.

cup noun 1 (for drinking) taza F; **a cup of tea** una taza de té; 2 (a trophy) copa F.

cupboard noun armario M; **in the kitchen cupboard** en el armario de la cocina.

cup tie noun partido M de copa.

cure noun cura F.
verb curar [17].

curiosity noun curiosidad F.

curious adjective curioso/curiosa.

curl noun rizo M.
verb rizar [22] (hair).

curly adjective rizado/rizada.

currant noun pasa F de Corinto.

currency noun moneda F; **foreign currency** moneda extranjera.

current noun (of electricity or water) corriente F.
adjective actual (a situation, for example).

current affairs noun sucesos M (plural) de actualidad.

curriculum noun 1 (national) plan M de estudios; 2 (for a single course) programa M de estudios.

curry noun curry M; **chicken curry** curry de pollo.

curtain noun cortina F.

cushion noun cojín M.

custard noun 1 (runny) natillas F (plural); 2 (baked) flan M.

custom noun costumbre M.

customer noun cliente M, clienta F.

customs plural noun aduana F; **to go through customs** pasar por la aduana.

customs hall noun aduana F.

customs officer noun agente M/F de aduana.

cut noun (injury or haircut) corte M
verb 1 cortar [17]; **I've cut the bread** he cortado el pan; **you'll cut yourself!** ¡te vas a cortar!; **Kevin's cut his finger** Kevin se ha cortado el dedo; **to cut the grass** cortar la hierba; 2 **to get your hair cut** cortarse [17] el pelo; **Ayesha's had her hair cut** Ayesha se ha cortado el pelo; 3 **to cut prices** bajar [17] los precios.
● **to cut down something** cortar [17] algo (a tree).
● **to cut down on something: to cut down on fats** consumir [19] menos grasas.
● **to cut out something** 1 recortar [17] algo (a shape, a newspaper article); 2 suprimir [19] algo (sugar, fatty food etc.).
● **to cut up something** cortar [17] algo en trocitos (food).

cute adjective mono/mona.

cutlery noun cubertería F.

CV noun currículum M vitae.

cycle noun (bike) bicicleta F.
verb montar [17] en bicicleta; **do you like cycling?** ¿te gusta montar en bicicleta?; **we cycle to school** vamos al colegio en bicicleta.

cycle lane *noun* carril M de bicicletas.

cycle race *noun* carrera F de ciclismo.

cycling *noun* ciclismo M.

cycling holiday *noun* vacaciones F (*plural*) en bicicleta.

cyclist *noun* ciclista M/F.

D d

dad *noun* 1 padre M; **Anna's dad** el padre de Anna; **my dad works in a bank** mi padre trabaja en un banco; 2 (*within the family*) papá; **Dad's not home yet** papá no ha llegado a casa aún.

daffodil *noun* narciso M.

daily *adjective* diario/diaria.

dairy products *plural noun* productos M (*plural*) lácteos.

daisy *noun* margarita F.

dam *noun* presa F.

damage *noun* daño M; **the damage is done** el daño ya está hecho; **there's no damage** no ha habido daños.
verb dañar [17].

damn *noun* **he doesn't give a damn** le importa un comino (*informal*).
exclamation **damn!** ¡maldita sea! (*informal*).

damp *noun* humedad F; **because of the damp** a causa de la humedad.
adjective húmedo/húmeda.

dance *noun* baile M; **a folk dance** un baile folklórico.
verb bailar [17]; **I like dancing** me gusta bailar.

dancer *noun* bailarín M, bailarina F.

dancing *noun* baile M; **I love dancing** me encanta bailar.

dancing class *noun* clase F de baile; **to go to dancing classes** ir a clase de baile.

dandruff *noun* caspa F.

danger *noun* peligro M; **to be in danger** estar en peligro; **out of danger** fuera de peligro.

dangerous *adjective* peligroso/peligrosa; **it's dangerous to drive so fast** es peligroso conducir tan rápido.

Danish *noun* danés M, danesa F.
adjective danés/danesa.

dare *verb* 1 atreverse [18]; **to dare to do** atreverse a hacer; **I didn't dare suggest it** no me atreví a sugerirlo; **how dare you!** ¡cómo te atreves!; 2 **don't you dare tell her I'm here!** ¡no se te ocurra decirle que estoy aquí!; 3 **I dare you!** ¡a que no te atreves¡ (*informal*); **I dare you to tell him!** ¡a que no te atreves a decírselo! (*informal*).

daring *adjective* osado/osada; **that was a bit daring!** ¡eso ha sido un poco osado!

dark *noun* **in the dark** en la oscuridad; **to be afraid of the dark**

tener miedo de la oscuridad; **after dark** de noche.
adjective **1** (*colour or room*) oscuro/oscura; **a dark blue suit** un traje azul oscuro; **she has dark brown hair** tiene el pelo castaño oscuro; **the kitchen's a bit dark** la cocina es un poco oscura; **it's dark in here** está oscuro aquí; **2 it's dark already** ya es de noche; **to get dark** oscurecer; **it gets dark around five** oscurece a eso de las cinco.

darkness *noun* oscuridad F.

darling *noun* querido M, querida F; **see you later, darling!** ¡te veo luego querido!

dart *noun* dardo M; **to play darts** jugar a los dardos.

data *noun* información F.

database *noun* base F de datos.

date *noun* **1** fecha F; **the date of the meeting** la fecha de la reunión; **to fix a date for** fijar una fecha para; **2 what's the date today?** ¿qué día es hoy?; **3** (*between friends*) **I have a date with Jerry on Sunday** he quedado para salir con Jerry el domingo; **4 out of date** (*passport, driving licence, etc.*) caducado/caducada; (*technology, method, information, etc.*) anticuado/anticuada; **5** (*fruit*) dátil M.

date of birth *noun* fecha F de nacimiento.

daughter *noun* hija F; **Tina's daughter** la hija de Tina.

daughter-in-law *noun* nuera F.

dawn *noun* amanecer M.

day *noun* **1** día M; **three days later** tres días más tarde; **it rained all day** llovió todo el día; **it's going to be a nice day tomorrow** mañana va a hacer buen día; **2 the day after** al día siguiente; **the day after the wedding** el día después de la boda; **the day after tomorrow** pasado mañana; **my sister's arriving the day after tomorrow** mi hermana llega pasado mañana; **3 the day before** el día anterior; **the day before the wedding** el día antes de la boda; **the day before yesterday** anteayer; **my sister arrived the day before yesterday** mi hermana llegó anteayer; **4 every day** todos los días

dead *adjective* muerto/muerta; **her father's dead** su padre ha muerto.
adverb (*really*) super (*informal*); **he's dead nice** es super majo; **it's dead easy** es super fácil; **it was dead good** fue genial; **you're dead right** tienes toda la razón; **she arrived dead on time** llegó justo a la hora.

dead end *noun* callejón M sin salida.

deadline *noun* fecha F límite.

deaf *adjective* sordo/sorda; **to go deaf** quedarse sordo/sorda.

deafening *adjective* ensordecedor/ensordecedora.

deal *noun* **1** (*involving money*) negocio M; **it's a good deal** es un buen negocio; **2** (*pact*) trato M; **I'll make a deal with you** voy a hacer un

trato contigo; **it's a deal!** ¡trato hecho!; **3 a great deal of** mucho/mucha; **I don't have a great deal of time** no tengo mucho tiempo; **a great deal of energy** mucha energía; **4 a great deal** mucho; **it has improved a great deal** ha mejorado mucho.
verb (*in cards*) repartir [19].
● **to deal with something** ocuparse [17] de algo; **Linda deals with the accounts** Linda se ocupa de las cuentas; **I'll deal with it as soon as possible** me ocuparé de ello tan pronto como sea posible.

dear *adjective* **1** querido/querida; **Dear Jo** Querida Jo; **2** (*expensive*) caro/cara.

death *noun* muerte F; **after his father's death** después de la muerte de su padre; ★ **you'll frighten him to death** vas a matarlo del susto; ★ **I'm bored to death** me muero de aburrimiento; ★ **I'm sick to death of his complaining** estoy harta de sus quejas.

death penalty *noun* pena F de muerte.

debate *noun* debate M.
verb debatir [19].

debt *noun* deuda F; **to get into debt** endeudarse [17].

decade *noun* década F.

decaffeinated *adjective* descafeinado/descafeinada.

deceive *verb* engañar [17].

December *noun* diciembre M.

decent *adjective* decente; **a decent salary** un sueldo decente; **a decent meal** una comida decente; **he seems a decent enough guy** parece un tipo decente.

decide *verb* decidir [19]; **to decide to do** decidir hacer; **she's decided to buy a car** ha decidido comprarse un coche; **she's decided not to buy a car** ha decidido no comprarse un coche.

decimal *adjective* decimal.

decimal point *noun* decimal M.

decision *noun* decisión F; **the right decision** la decisión acertada; **the wrong decision** la decisión errónea; **to make a decision** tomar una decisión.

deck *noun* (*on a ship*) cubierta F.

deckchair *noun* tumbona F.

declare *verb* declarar [17].

decorate *verb* **1** adornar [17]; **to decorate the Christmas tree** adornar el árbol de Navidad; **2** (*a room*) (*with paint*) pintar [17]; (*with wallpaper*) empapelar [17].

decoration *noun* **1** decoración F; **2** (*ornament*) adorno M.

decrease *noun* disminución F; **a decrease in the number of** una disminución en el número de.
verb disminuir [54].

deduct verb deducir [60].

deep adjective profundo/profunda; **a deep feeling of gratitude** un profundo sentimiento de gratitud; **the river is very deep here** aquí el río es muy profundo; **how deep is the swimming pool?** ¿qué profundidad tiene la piscina?; **a hole two metres deep** un agujero de dos metros de profundidad.

deep end noun **the deep end** la parte honda (of a swimming pool).

deep freeze noun congelador M.

deeply adverb profundamente.

deer noun ciervo M.

defeat noun derrota F. verb derrotar [17].

defect noun defecto M.

defence noun defensa F.

defend verb defender [36].

defender noun 1 (of cause) defensor M, defensora F; 2 (in football) defensa M/F.

define verb definir [19].

definite adjective 1 (clear) claro/clara; **a definite improvement** una clara mejora; **a definite advantage** una clara ventaja; **it's a definite possibility** es claramente una posibilidad; 2 (certain) seguro/segura; **it's not definite yet** aún no es seguro; 3 (exact) preciso/precisa; **a definite answer** una respuesta precisa; **I don't have a definite idea of what I want** no tengo una idea precisa de lo que quiero.

definitely adverb 1 (when giving your opinion about something) sin ninguna duda; **the blue one is definitely the biggest** el azul es sin ninguna duda el más grande; **your French is definitely better than mine** hablas francés mejor que yo sin ninguna duda; **'are you sure you like this one better?' – 'definitely'** '¿estás seguro de que te gusta más éste?' – 'segurísimo'; 2 (for certain) **she's definitely going to be there** es seguro que va a estar aquí; **I'm definitely not going** es seguro que no voy; **she definitely said she would do it** dijo que seguro que lo haría.

definition noun definición F.

degree noun 1 grado M; **thirty degrees** treinta grados; 2 **a university degree** un título universitario.

delay noun retraso M; **a two-hour delay** un retraso de dos horas. verb retrasar [17]; **the flight was delayed by bad weather** el mal tiempo retrasó el vuelo; **the decision has been delayed until Thursday** retrasaron la decisión hasta el jueves.

deliberate adjective deliberado/deliberada.

deliberately adverb a propósito; **you did it deliberately** lo hiciste a propósito; **he left it there deliberately** lo dejó allí a propósito.

delicate adjective delicado/delicada.

delicatessen *noun* charcutería F.

delicious *adjective* delicioso/
deliciosa.

delighted *adjective* encantado/
encantada; **they're delighted with
their new flat** están encantados con
su nuevo piso; **I'm delighted to hear
you can come** estoy encantado de
saber que puedes venir.

deliver *verb* **1** (*goods*) entregar [28];
**the person who delivered the
parcel** la persona que entregó el
paquete; **2** (*mail*) repartir [19].

delivery *noun* entrega F.

demand *noun* petición F.
verb exigir [49].

democracy *noun* democracia F.

democratic *adjective* democrático/
democrática.

demolish *verb* destruir [54].

demonstrate *verb* **1** demostrar
[24] (*a theory or a skill*); **2** hacer [7]
una demostración de (*a machine,
product, or technique*); **3** (*protest*)
manifestarse [29]; **to demonstrate
against something** manifestarse en
contra de algo.

demonstration *noun* **1** (*of
machine, product, technique*)
demostración F; **2** (*protest*)
manifestación F.

demonstrator *noun* (*in protest*)
manifestante M/F.

denim *noun* tela F vaquera; **a denim
jacket** una chaqueta vaquera.

Denmark *noun* Dinamarca F.

dense *adjective* denso/densa.

dent *noun* abolladura F.
verb abollar [17].

dental *adjective* **1** dental; **dental
hygiene** higiene F dental; **2 a dental
appointment** una cita con el
dentista.

dental floss *noun* hilo M dental.

dental surgeon *noun* cirujano/
cirujana M/F dentista.

dentist *noun* dentista M/F; **my
mum's a dentist** mi madre es
dentista.

deny *verb* negar [30].

deodorant *noun* desodorante M.

depart *verb* salir [63].

department *noun* **1** (*in school,
university*) departamento M; **the
language department** el
departamento de idiomas; **2** (*in a
shop*) sección F; **the men's
department** la sección de caballeros.

department store *noun* grandes
almacenes M (*plural*).

departure *noun* salida F.

departure gate *noun* puerta F de
embarque.

departure lounge *noun* sala F de
embarque.

depend *verb* **to depend on**
depender [18] de; **it depends on the
price** depende del precio; **it depends
on what you want** depende de lo que

tú quieras (*note that 'que' is followed by the subjunctive*); **it depends** depende.

deposit *noun* 1 (*when renting, hiring, or when when booking a holiday or hotel room*) depósito M; **to pay a deposit** pagar un depósito; 2 (*as first payment when buying something*) entrada F.

depressed *adjective* deprimido/ deprimida.

depressing *adjective* deprimente.

depth *noun* profundidad F.

deputy *noun* segundo M, segunda F.

deputy head *noun* subdirector M, subdirectora F.

descend *verb* descender [36].

describe *verb* describir [52].

description *noun* descripción F.

desert *noun* desierto M.

desert island *noun* isla F desierta.

deserve *verb* merecer [35].

design *noun* diseño M; **the design of the plane** el diseño del avión; **fashion design** diseño de moda; **a floral design** un diseño de flores. *verb* diseñar [17].

designer *noun* diseñador M, diseñadora F.

desire *noun* deseo M. *verb* desear [17].

desk *noun* 1 (*in office or at home*) escritorio M; 2 (*pupil's*) pupitre M; 3 **the reception desk** la recepción;

the information desk el mostrador de información.

despair *noun* desesperación F.

desperate *adjective* 1 desesperado/desesperada; **a desperate attempt** un intento desesperado; 2 **to be desperate to do** estar [2] deseando hacer; **I'm desperate to see you** estoy deseando verte.

despise *verb* despreciar [17].

dessert *noun* postre M; **what's for dessert?** ¿qué hay de postre?

destination *noun* destino M.

destroy *verb* destruir [54].

destruction *noun* destrucción F.

detached house *noun* casa F no adosada.

detail *noun* detalle M.

detailed *adjective* detallado/ detallada.

detective *noun* 1 (*police*) agente M/F; 2 **a private detective** u detective privado/una detective privada.

detective story *noun* novela F policiaca.

detention *noun* (*in school*) **to be i detention** estar [2] castigado/ castigada.

detergent *noun* detergente M.

determined *adjective* decidido/ decidida; **he's determined to leave** está decidido a irse.

etour *noun* rodeo M.

evelop *verb* **1** (*a film*) revelar [17]; **to get a film developed** revelar un carrete de fotos; **2** desarrollarse [17]; **how children develop** cómo se desarrollan los niños.

eveloping country *noun* país M en vías de desarrollo.

evelopment *noun* desarrollo M.

evil *noun* diablo M.

evoted *adjective* **1** (*couple or family*) unido/unida; **2** (*admirer*) ferviente.

iabetes *noun* diabetes F.

iabetic *noun* diabético M, diabética F.
adjective diabético/diabética; **to be diabetic** ser diabético/diabética.

iagonal *adjective* diagonal.

iagram *noun* diagrama M.

ial *verb* marcar [31]; **lift the receiver and dial 142** coge el auricular y marca 142.

ialling tone *noun* tono M de marcar.

ialogue *noun* diálogo M.

iamond *noun* **1** diamante M; **2** (*in cards*) diamonds diamantes; **the jack of diamonds** la jota de diamantes; **3** (*shape*) rombo M.

iarrhoea *noun* diarrea F; **to have diarrhoea** tener [9] diarrea.

iary *noun* **1** (*for dates*) agenda F; **I've noted the date of the meeting in my diary** he anotado la fecha de la reunión en mi agenda; **2** (*personal*) diario M íntimo; **to keep a diary** tener [9] un diario íntimo.

dice *noun* dado M; **to throw the dice** tirar [17] los dados.

dictation *noun* dictado M.

dictionary *noun* diccionario M; **to look up a word in the dictionary** buscar [31] una palabra en el diccionario.

did *verb* SEE **do**.

die *verb* **1** morir [55]; **my grannie died in January** mi abuela murió en enero; **2 to be dying to do** estar [2] deseando hacer; **I'm dying to see them!** ¡estoy deseando verlos!

diesel *noun* **1** diesel M; **2 a diesel engine** un motor diesel; **a diesel car** un diesel.

diet *noun* **1** dieta F; **to have a healthy diet** llevar una dieta saludable; **2** (*slimming or special*) régimen M; **to be on a diet** estar a régimen; **to go on a diet** ponerse a régimen; **a salt-free diet** un régimen sin sal.

difference *noun* **1** diferencia F; **I can't see any difference between the two** no puedo ver ninguna diferencia entre los dos; **what's the difference between … ?** ¿qué diferencia hay entre … ?; **2 it makes a difference** eso cambia las cosas; **it makes no difference** da lo mismo; **it makes no difference what I say** da lo mismo lo que yo diga.

different *adjective* distinto/distinta; **the two sisters are very different**

las dos hermanas son muy distintas; **she's very different from her sister** es muy distinta a su hermana.

difficult *adjective* difícil; **it's really difficult** es muy difícil; **it's difficult to decide** es difícil decidir.

difficulty *noun* 1 dificultad F; **2 I had difficulty finding your house** me resultó difícil encontrar tu casa.

dig *verb* cavar [17]; **to dig a hole** cavar [17] un agujero.

digestion *noun* digestión F.

digital *adjective* digital; **a digital watch** un reloj digital.

dignity *noun* dignidad F.

dim *adjective* 1 tenue; **a dim light** una luz tenue; **2 she's a bit dim** es un poco tonta (*informal*).

dimension *noun* dimensión F.

din *noun* ruido M; **they were making a dreadful din** estaban haciendo un ruido enorme; **stop making such a din !** ¡deja de hacer tanto ruido !

dinghy *noun* 1 **a sailing dinghy** un bote; **2 a rubber dinghy** un bote neumático.

dining room *noun* comedor M; **in the dining room** en el comedor.

dinner *noun* 1 (*evening meal*) cena F; **to have dinner** cenar [17]; **to invite somebody to dinner** invitar [17] a alguien a cenar; **2** (*midday meal*) comida F; **to have dinner** comer [18]; **to have school dinner** comer en el colegio.

dinner party *noun* cena F.

dinner time *noun* 1 (*evening*) hora F de cenar; **2** (*midday*) hora F de comer.

dinosaur *noun* dinosaurio M.

diploma *noun* diploma M.

direct *adjective* directo/directa. *verb* 1 (*a programme, film, play or traffic*) dirigir [49]; **2** (*give direction to*) indicarle [31] el camino a; **I directed them to the station** les indiqué el camino a la estación.

direction *noun* 1 dirección F; **in the direction of the church** en dirección a la iglesia; **in the other direction** en la otra dirección; **2 to ask somebody for directions** pedir a alguien que te indique el camino; **3 directions for use** instrucciones (*plural*) de uso.

directly *adverb* 1 (*to go, fly, deal or ask*) directamente; **2** (*at once*) inmediatamente; **3 directly afterwards** inmediatamente después.

director *noun* director M, directora F (*of a company, programme, film or play*).

directory *noun* guía F telefónica; **to be ex-directory** no estar en la guía telefónica.

dirt *noun* suciedad F.

dirty *adjective* sucio/sucia; **my hands are dirty** tengo las manos sucias; **to get something dirty** ensuciar [17] algo; **I got the floor dirty** ensucié el suelo; **you'll get your**

dress dirty te vas a ensuciar el vestido; **to get dirty** ensuciarse [17]; **the curtains get dirty quickly** las cortinas se ensucian rápido.

disabled *adjective* discapacitado/discapacitada; **disabled people** los discapacitados.

disadvantage *noun*
1 desventaja F; 2 **to be at a disadvantage** estar en desventaja.

disagree *verb* **I disagree** no estoy de acuerdo; **I disagree with James** no estoy de acuerdo con James.

disappear *verb* desaparecer [35].

disappearance *noun*
desaparición F.

disappointed *adjective*
decepcionado/decepcionada; **I was disappointed with my marks** mis notas me decepcionaron.

disappointment *noun*
decepción F.

disaster *noun* desastre M; **it was a complete disaster** fue un completo desastre.

disastrous *adjective* desastroso/desastrosa.

discipline *noun* disciplina F.

disc *noun* 1 **a compact disc** un disco compacto; 2 **a slipped disc** una hernia de disco.

discipline *noun* disciplina F.

disc-jockey *noun* disc-jockey M/F.

disco *noun* 1 baile M; **they're having a disco** tienen un baile; 2 (*club*) discoteca F.

discount *noun* descuento M.

discourage *verb* 1 (*depress*) desanimar [17]; 2 **to discourage somebody from doing** convencer [44] a alguien de que no haga; (*note that 'que no' is followed by the subjunctive*) **I tried to discourage her from buying it** intenté convencerla de que no lo comprase.

discover *verb* descubrir [46].

discovery *noun* descubrimiento M.

discreet *adjective* discreto/discreta.

discrimination *noun*
discriminación F; **racial discrimination** discriminación racial.

discuss *verb* 1 (*a subject or topic*) hablar [17] de; **to discuss politics** hablar de política; **I'm going to discuss it with Phil** voy a hablarlo con Phil; 2 (*a problem or plan*) discutir [19].

discussion *noun* discusión F.

disease *noun* enfermedad F.

disgraceful *adjective* vergonzoso/vergonzosa.

disguise *noun* disfraz M; **to be in disguise** ir disfrazado.
verb disfrazar [22]; **to disguise oneself as something** disfrazarse

[22] de algo; **disguised as a woman** disfrazado de mujer.

disgust *noun* **1** (*indignation*) indignación F; **2** (*physical revulsion*) asco M.

disgusted *adjective* **1** (*indignant*) indignado/indignada; **2** (*physically sick*) asqueado/asqueada.

disgusting *adjective* asqueroso/ asquerosa.

dish *noun* **1** (*plate or food*) plato M; **to do the dishes** lavar [17] los platos; **he cooked my favourite dish** cocinó mi plato favorito; **2** (*serving dish*) fuente F; **a large white dish** una fuente grande blanca.

dishcloth *noun* (*for drying up*) paño M de cocina.

dishonest *adjective* deshonesto/ deshonesta.

dishonesty *noun* falta F de honradez.

dish towel *noun* paño M de cocina.

dishwasher *noun* lavaplatos M (*does not change in the plural*).

disinfect *verb* desinfectar [17].

disinfectant *noun* desinfectante M.

disk *noun* disco M; **a floppy disk** un disquete; **the hard disk** el disco duro.

diskette *noun* disquete M.

dislike *verb* **I dislike sport** no me gusta el deporte; **he dislikes my friends** no le gustan mis amigos.

dismay *noun* consternación F.

dismiss *verb* despedir [57] (*an employee*).

disobedient *adjective* desobediente.

display *noun* **1** exposición F; **a handicrafts display** una exposición de artesanía; **to be on display** estar expuesto; **2 a window display** un escaparate; **3 a firework display** fuegos M (*plural*) artificiales. *verb* exponer [11].

disposable *adjective* desechable.

dispute *noun* polémica F.

disqualify *verb* descalificar [31].

dissolve *verb* disolver [45].

distance *noun* distancia F; **from a distance** de lejos; **in the distance** a lo lejos; **it's within walking distance** se puede ir andando.

distant *adjective* distante.

distinct *adjective* claro/clara.

distinctly *adverb* **1** claramente; **2 it's distinctly odd** es realmente raro.

distract *verb* distraer [42].

distribute *verb* distribuir [54].

distribution *noun* distribución F.

district *noun* **1** (*in town*) barrio M **a poor district of Barcelona** un barrio pobre de Barcelona; **2** (*in the country*) región F.

disturb *verb* molestar [17]; **sorry to disturb you** perdona que te moleste

ditch *noun* zanja F.
verb **to ditch somebody** plantar [17] a alguien (*informal*).

dive *noun* zambullida F.
verb tirarse [17]; **to dive into the water** tirarse al agua.

diver *noun* (*deep-sea*) submarinista M/F.

diversion *noun* (*for traffic*) desvío M.

divide *verb* dividir [19].

diving *noun* **1** (*from a board*) saltos M (*plural*) de trampolín; **2** (*from the surface of the water*) submarinismo M.

diving board *noun* trampolín M.

division *noun* división F.

divorce *noun* divorcio M.

divorced *adjective* divorciado/divorciada.

DIY *noun* bricolage M; **to do DIY** hacer [7] bricolage; **a DIY shop** una tienda de bricolage.

dizzy *adjective* **to feel dizzy** estar [2] mareado/mareada; **I feel dizzy** estoy mareado.

DJ *noun* disc-jockey M/F.

do *verb* **1** hacer [7]; **what are you doing?** ¿qué estás haciendo?; **I'm doing my homework** estoy haciendo mis deberes; **what have you done with the hammer?** ¿qué has hecho con el martillo?; **2** (*in questions, 'do' is not translated*) **did Maria go to the party?** ¿fue María a la fiesta?; **do you want some strawberries?** ¿quieres fresas?; **when does it start?** ¿cuándo empieza?; **how did you open the door?** ¿cómo has abierto la puerta?; **3** (*in negative sentences*) (*the negative in Spanish is formed adding 'no' before the verb*) **I don't like this kind of music** no me gusta este tipo de música; **Rosie doesn't like spinach** a Rosie no le gustan las espinacas; **you didn't shut the door** no has cerrado la puerta; **it doesn't matter** no importa; **4** (*when it refers back to another verb, 'do' is not translated*) **'do you live here?' – 'yes, I do'** ¿vives aquí? – 'sí'; **she has more money than I do** tiene más dinero que yo; **'I live in Oxford' – 'so do I'** 'vivo en Oxford' – 'yo también'; **'I didn't phone Gemma' – 'neither did I'** 'no he llamado a Gemma' – 'yo tampoco'; **5 don't you?, doesn't he? etc.** ¿no?; **you know Helen, don't you?** conoces a Helen, ¿no?; **she left on Thursday, didn't she?** se marchó el jueves, ¿no?; **6 that'll do** así basta; **it'll do like that** así vale.

• **to do something up 1** atar [17] (*shoes*); **I did my shoes up** me até los zapatos; **2** abrochar [17] (*cardigan, jacket*); **do your jacket up** abróchate la chaqueta; **3** arreglar [17] (*house*).

• **to do without something** arreglarse [17] sin algo; **we can do without knives** nos arreglaremos sin cuchillos.

doctor *noun* médico M/F; **her mother's a doctor** su madre es médico.

document *noun* documento M.

documentary *noun* documental M.

dodgems *plural noun* **the dodgems** los cochecitos de choque.

dog *noun* perro M, perra F.

do-it-yourself *noun* bricolage M.

dole *noun* paro M; **to be on the dole** estar en el paro.

doll *noun* muñeca F.

dollar *noun* dólar M.

dolphin *noun* delfín M.

dominate *verb* dominar [17].

domino *noun* ficha F de dominó; **to play dominoes** jugar al dominó.

donkey *noun* burro M.

don't SEE **do**.

door *noun* puerta F; **to open the door** abrir [46] la puerta; **to shut the door** cerrar [29] la puerta.

doorbell *noun* timbre M; **to ring the doorbell** tocar [31] el timbre; **there's the doorbell** llaman a la puerta.

doorstep *noun* umbral M de la puerta.

dot *noun* **1** (*written*) punto M; **2** (*on fabric*) lunar M; **3 at ten on the dot** a las diez en punto.

double *adjective, adverb* **1** doble; **a double helping** una ración doble; **a double whisky** un whisky doble; **a double room** una habitación doble; **a double bed** una cama de matrimonio; **2** el doble; **double the time** el doble de tiempo; **double the price** el doble del precio.

double bass *noun* contrabajo M; **to play the double bass** tocar [31] el contrabajo.

double-breasted *adjective* **a double-breasted jacket** una chaqueta cruzada.

double-decker bus *noun* autobús M de dos pisos.

double glazing *noun* doble ventana F.

doubles *noun* (*in tennis*) dobles M (*plural*); **to play a game of doubles** jugar un partido de dobles.

doubt *noun* duda F; **there's no doubt about it** no hay ninguna duda al respecto; **I have my doubts** tengo mis dudas.
verb **to doubt something** dudar [17] algo; **I doubt it** lo dudo; **I doubt that** dudo que (*note that 'que' is followed by the subjunctive*); **I doubt they'll do it** dudo que lo hagan.

doubtful *adjective* **1 it's doubtful that** no es seguro que (*note that 'que' is followed by the subjunctive*); **it's doubtful that she'll want to** no es seguro que quiera; **2 to be doubtful about doing** dudar [17] si hacer; **I'm doubtful about inviting them together** estoy dudando si invitarlos a los dos juntos.

dough *noun* masa F.

doughnut *noun* donut M.

down *adverb, preposition* **1** abajo; **he's down in the cellar** está abajo, en el sótano; **2 down the road** (*nearby*) un poco más allá; **there's a chemist's just down the**

road hay una farmacia un poco más allá; **3 to go down** bajar [17]; **I went down to the kitchen** bajé a la cocina; **to walk down the street** bajar la calle; **to run down the stairs** bajar corriendo la escalera; **4 to come down** bajar [17]; **she came down from her bedroom** bajó de la habitación; **5 to sit down** sentarse [29]; **she sat down on the sofa** se sentó en el sofá.

downstairs *adverb* **1** abajo; **she's downstairs in the sitting-room** está abajo en el salón; **the dog sleeps downstairs** el perro duerme abajo; **2** (*after a noun*) de abajo; **the flat downstairs** el piso de abajo; **the people downstairs** la gente de abajo.

doze *verb* dormitar [17].

dozen *noun* docena F; **a dozen eggs** una docena de huevos.

drag *noun* **what a drag!** ¡qué rollo! (*informal*); **she's a bit of a drag** es un poco pesada (*informal*).
verb arrastrar [17].

dragon *noun* dragón M.

drain *noun* (*plughole*) desagüe M.
verb escurrir [19] (*vegetables*).

drama *noun* **1** (*subject*) arte M dramático; **2 he made a big drama about it** montó una escena por eso (*informal*).

dramatic *adjective* dramático/dramática.

draught *noun* corriente F de aire.

draughts *noun* damas F (*plural*); **to play draughts** jugar a las damas.

draw *noun* **1** (*in a match*) empate M; **it was a draw** fue un empate; **2** (*lottery*) sorteo M.
verb **1** pintar [17]; **I can't draw horses** no sé pintar caballos; **she can draw really well** pinta muy bien; **2 to draw a picture** hacer [7] un dibujo; **3 to draw the curtains** correr [18] las cortinas; **4 to draw a crowd** atraer [42] a una multitud; **5** (*in a match*) empatar [17]; **we drew three all** empatamos a tres; **6 to draw lots for something** echar [17] algo a suertes.

drawback *noun* inconveniente M.

drawer *noun* cajón M.

drawing *noun* dibujo M.

drawing pin *noun* chincheta F.

dreadful *adjective* terrible.

dreadfully *adverb* **1** (*to sing or act*) espantosamente; **2 I'm dreadfully late** llego tardísimo; **I'm dreadfully sorry** lo siento muchísmo.

dream *noun* sueño M; **to have a dream** tener [9] un sueño; **I had a horrible dream last night** tuve un sueño horrible anoche.
verb soñar [24]; **to dream about something** soñar con algo.

drenched *adjective* empapado/empapada; **to get drenched** empaparse [17]; **I got drenched on the way home** me empapé yendo a casa.

dress *noun* vestido M.
verb vestir [57]; **to dress a child** vestir a un niño.

• **to dress up** disfrazarse [22]; **to dress up as a vampire** disfrazarse de vampiro.

dressed *adjective* 1 vestido/ vestida; **is Tom dressed?** ¿está Tom vestido?; **she was dressed in black trousers and a yellow shirt** iba vestida con unos pantalones negros y una blusa amarilla; 2 **to get dressed** vestirse [57].

dresser *noun* (*for dishes*) aparador M.

dressing gown *noun* bata F.

dressing table *noun* tocador M.

drier *noun* **a hair drier** un secador de pelo; **a tumble drier** una secadora.

drift *noun* **a snow drift** una ventisca de nieve.

drill *noun* 1 (*tool*) taladradora F; 2 (*in homework*) ejercicio M.

drink *noun* 1 bebida F; **a hot drink** una bebida caliente; **a cold drink** un refresco; 2 **would you like a drink?** ¿te apetece beber algo?; 3 **to go out for a drink** salir [63] a tomar una copa (*informal*).
verb beber [18]; **he drank a glass of water** bebió un vaso de agua.

drive *noun* 1 **to go for a drive** ir [8] a dar una vuelta en coche; 2 (*up to a house*) entrada F para coches.
verb 1 conducir [60]; **she drives very fast** conduce muy rápido; **to drive a car** conducir [60] un coche; **I'd like to learn to drive** me gustaría aprender a conducir; **can you drive?** ¿sabes conducir?; 2 ir [8] en coche; **we drove to Seville** fuimos en coche

a Sevilla; 3 **to drive somebody (to a place)** llevar [17] en coche a alguien (a un sitio); **Mum drove me to the station** mamá me llevó en coche a la estación; **to drive somebody home** llevar [17] a alguien a casa en coche; ★ **she drives me mad!** ¡me saca de quicio!

driver *noun* 1 (*of a car, taxi or bus*) conductor M, conductora F; 2 (*of a racing car*) piloto M/F.

driving instructor *noun* instructor M de autoescuela, instructora F de autoescuela.

driving lesson *noun* clase F de conducir.

driving licence *noun* permiso M de conducir.

driving test *noun* examen M de conducir; **to take your driving test** presentarse [17] al examen de conducir; **Jenny's passed her driving test** Jenny ha aprobado el examen de conducir.

drop *noun* gota F.
verb 1 **I dropped my glasses** se me cayeron las gafas; **careful, don't drop it!** ¡cuidado, que no se te caiga!; 2 (*a course, subject or topic*) dejar [17]; **I'm going to drop history next year** voy a dejar la historia el próximo año; 3 dejar [17] (*a person*); **could you drop me at the station?** ¿me podrías dejar en la estación?; 4 **drop it!** ¡déjalo ya!

drown *verb* ahogarse [28]; **she drowned in the lake** se ahogó en el lago.

drug *noun* 1 (*medicine*) medicina F; 2 (*illegal*) **drugs** las drogas; **to be on drugs** drogarse [28].

drug abuse *noun* consumo M de drogas.

drug addict *noun* drogadicto M, drogadicta F.

drug addiction *noun* drogadicción F.

drum *noun* 1 tambor M; 2 **drums** batería F; **to play drums** tocar [31] la batería.

drum kit *noun* batería F.

drummer *noun* batería M/F.

drunk *noun* borracho M, borracha F. *adjective* borracho/borracha.

dry *adjective* seco/seca.
verb 1 secar [31]; **to dry the dishes** secar los platos; 2 **to let something dry** dejar que algo se seque; **it took ages to dry** tardó muchísimo en secarse; 3 **to dry oneself** secarse [31]; **to dry your hair** secarse [31] el pelo; **I'm going to dry my hair** me voy a secar el pelo.

dry cleaner's *noun* tintorería F.

dryer *noun* SEE **drier**.

dubbed *adjective* **a dubbed film** una película doblada.

duck *noun* pato M, pata F.

due *adjective*, *adverb* 1 **to be due to do** tener [9] que hacer; **we're due to leave on Thursday** tenemos que salir el jueves; **Paul's due back soon** Paul tiene que volver pronto; 2 **what time is the train due?** ¿cuándo llega el

próximo tren?; 3 **due to** debido a; **the match has been cancelled due to bad weather** el partido ha sido cancelado debido al mal tiempo.

duke *noun* duque M.

dull *adjective* 1 **dull weather** tiempo gris; **it's a dull day today** hoy hace un día muy gris; 2 (*boring*) aburrido/aburrida.

dumb *adjective* 1 mudo/muda; **to be deaf and dumb** ser sordomudo/sordomuda; 2 (*stupid*) tonto/tonta; **he asked some dumb questions** hizo unas preguntas muy tontas.

dummy *noun* (*for a baby*) chupete M.

dump *verb* 1 tirar [17] (*rubbish*); 2 plantar [17] (*a person*) (*informal*); **she's dumped her boyfriend** ha plantado a su novio.

dungarees *plural noun* pantalón M de peto.

dungeon *noun* mazmorra F.

during *preposition* durante; **during the night** durante la noche; **I saw her during the holidays** la vi durante las vacaciones.

dusk *noun* anochecer M; **at dusk** al anochecer.

dust *noun* polvo M.
verb quitar [17] el polvo; **to dust the table** quitarle el polvo a la mesa.

dustbin *noun* cubo M de la basura; **to put something in the dustbin** tirar [17] algo al cubo de la basura.

dustman *noun* basurero M.

dusty *adjective* cubierto/cubierta de polvo.

Dutch *noun* **1** (*language*) holandés M; **2 the Dutch** (*people*) los holandeses.
adjective holandés/holandesa.

duty *noun* **1** deber M; **to have a duty to do** tener [9] el deber de hacer; **you have a duty to inform us** tienes el deber de informarnos; **2 to be on duty** (*a nurse or doctor*) estar [2] de guardia; (*a policeman*) estar [2] de servicio; **to be on night duty** tener [9] el turno de noche.

duty-free *adjective* libre de impuestos; **the duty-free shops** las tiendas libres de impuestos; **duty-free purchases** artículos libres de impuestos.

duvet *noun* edredón M.

duvet cover *noun* funda F de edredón.

dwarf *noun* enano M, enana F.

dye *noun* tinte M.
verb teñir [65]; **to dye your hair** teñirse [65] el pelo; **I'm going to dye my hair pink** me voy a teñir el pelo de rosa.

dynamic *adjective* dinámico/dinámica.

dyslexia *noun* dislexia F.

dyslexic *adjective* disléxico/disléxica.

E e

each *adjective* cada; **each time** cada vez; **curtains for each window** cortinas para cada ventana.
pronoun cada uno/una; **my sisters each have a computer** mis hermanas tienen un ordenador cada una; **she gave us an apple each** nos dio una manzana a cada uno; **each of you** cada uno de vosotros; **we each bought a book** cada uno de nosotros compró un libro; **the tickets cost ten pounds each** las entradas cuestan diez libras cada una.

each other *pronoun* ('*each other*' *is usually translated using a reflexive pronoun*) **they love each other** se quieren; **we know each other** nos conocemos; **do you often see each other?** ¿os veis a menudo?

eagle *noun* águila F (*even though* '*águila*' *is a feminine noun, it is used with* '*el*' *and* '*un*').

ear *noun* oreja F.

earache *noun* **to have earache** tener dolor de oídos.

earlier *adverb* **1** (*a while ago*) hace un rato; **your brother phoned earlier** tu hermano llamó hace un rato; **2** (*not as late*) más temprano; **we should have started earlier** deberíamos haber empezado más temprano; **earlier in the morning** por la mañana temprano.

early *adverb* **1** (*in the morning*) temprano; **I get up early** me levanto temprano; **it's too early** es demasiado temprano; **2** (*for an appointment*) pronto; **we're early, the train doesn't leave until ten** hemos llegado pronto, el tren no sale hasta las diez; **Grandma likes to be early** a la abuela le gusta llegar pronto.
adjective **1** (*one of the first*) primero/primera; **in the early months** en los primeros meses; **2 to have an early lunch** comer [18] temprano; **Jan's having an early night** Jan se ha acostado temprano; **we're making an early start** vamos a salir temprano; **3 in the early afternoon** a primera hora de la tarde; **in the early hours** de madrugada.

earn *verb* ganar [17] (*money*); **Richard earns four pounds an hour** Richard gana cuatro libras por hora.

earnings *plural noun* ingresos M (*plural*).

earring *noun* pendiente M.

earth *noun* tierra F; **life on earth** la vida en la tierra; ★ **what on earth are you doing?** ¿qué demonios estás haciendo?

earthquake *noun* terremoto M.

easily *adverb* **1** (*to do something*) con facilidad; **2** (*by far*) con mucho; **he's easily the best** es con mucho el mejor.

east *noun* este M; **in the east** en el este.
adjective, *adverb* **the east side** el lado este; **an east wind** un viento del este; **east of Seville** al este de Sevilla.

Easter *noun* Semana F Santa; **they're coming at Easter** vienen en Semana Santa.

Easter Day *noun* Domingo M de Pascua.

Easter egg *noun* huevo M de Pascua.

Eastern Europe *noun* Europa F del Este.

easy *adjective* fácil; **it's easy!** ¡es fácil!; **it was easy to decide** fue fácil de decidir.

eat *verb* **1** comer [18]; **he was eating a banana** estaba comiendo un plátano; **we're going to have something to eat** vamos a comer algo; **2** tomar [17] (*a meal*); **we were eating breakfast** estábamos tomando el desayuno; **3 to eat out** comer [18] fuera.

EC *noun* CE F, Comunidad F Europea.

echo *noun* eco M.
verb hacer [7] eco.

ecological *adjective* ecológico/ ecológica.

ecology *noun* ecología F.

economical *adjective* económico/ económica (*way of doing something*); **it's more economical to buy a big one** sale más económico comprar uno grande.

economics *noun* economía F.

economy *noun* economía F.

Ecuador *noun* Ecuador M.

eczema *noun* eczema M.

edge *noun* 1 (*of table, plate, or cliff*) borde M; **the edge of the table** el borde de la mesa; 2 (*of river or lake*) orilla F; **at the edge of the lake** en la orilla del lago; 3 **to be on edge** estar nervioso.

edible *adjective* comestible.

Edinburgh *noun* Edimburgo M.

edit *verb* editar [17].

editor *noun* (*of a newspaper*) redactor M, redactora F.

educate *verb* (*a teacher*) educar [31].

education *noun* educación F.

educational *adjective* educativo/educativa.

effect *noun* efecto M; **the effect of the accident** el efecto del accidente; **to have an effect on** afectar [17] a; **it had a good effect on the whole family** afectó positivamente a toda la familia; **special effects** efectos especiales.

effective *adjective* eficaz.

efficient *adjective* eficiente.

effort *noun* esfuerzo M; **to make an effort** hacer [7] un esfuerzo; **Jess made an effort to help us** Jess hizo un esfuerzo para ayudarnos; **he didn't even make the effort to apologize** ni siquiera se molestó en disculparse; **it's not worth the effort** no merece la pena.

e.g. *abbreviation* p.ej.

egg *noun* huevo M; **a dozen eggs** una docena de huevos; **a fried egg** un huevo frito; **two boiled eggs** dos huevos pasados por agua; **a hard-boiled egg** un huevo duro; **scrambled eggs** huevos revueltos.

egg-cup *noun* huevera F.

eggshell *noun* cáscara F de huevo.

egg-white *noun* clara F de huevo.

egg-yolk *noun* yema F de huevo.

eight *number* ocho M; **Rosie's eight** Rosie tiene ocho años; **it's eight o'clock** son las ocho.

eighteen *number* dieciocho; **Kate's eighteen** Kate tiene dieciocho años.

eighth *noun* 1 (*fraction*) **an eighth** una octava parte; 2 **the eighth of July** el ocho de julio.
adjective octavo/octava; **on the eighth floor** en la octava planta.

eighties *plural noun* **the eighties** los años ochenta; **in the eighties** en los años ochenta.

eighty *number* ochenta M; **she's eighty** tiene ochenta años; **eighty-five** ochenta y cinco.

Eire *noun* Irlanda M/F.

either *pronoun* 1 (*one or the other*) **choose either (of them)** elige cualquiera (de los dos); **I don't like either (of them)** no me gusta ninguno (de los dos); 2 (*both*) **either**

is possible las dos cosas son posibles.
conjunction **1 either ... or** o ... o; **you either pay or return it** o pagas o lo devuelves; **I'll phone either Thursday or Friday** llamaré o el jueves o el viernes; (*'o' becomes 'u' before a word starting with 'o' or 'ho'*) **either one or the other** o uno u otro; **2** (*with a negative*) **he doesn't want to either** él tampoco quiere; **I don't know them either** yo tampoco los conozco.

elastic *noun* elástico M.
adjective elástico/elástica.

elastic band *noun* goma F elástica.

elbow *noun* codo M.

elder *adjective* mayor; **her elder brother** su hermano mayor.

elderly *adjective* **an elderly man** un anciano; **an elderly woman** una anciana; **an elderly couple** una pareja de ancianos; **the elderly** los ancianos.

eldest *adjective* mayor; **her eldest brother** su hermano mayor.

elect *verb* elegir [48]; **she has been elected** ha sido elegida.

election *noun* elecciones F (*plural*); **in the election** en las elecciones.

electric *adjective* eléctrico/eléctrica.

electrical *adjective* eléctrico/eléctrica.

electrician *noun* electricista M/F.

electricity *noun* electricidad F; **to turn off the electricity** desconectar [17] la corriente.

electronic *adjective* electrónico/electrónica.

electronics *noun* electrónica F.

elegant *adjective* elegante.

element *noun* elemento M.

elephant *noun* elefante M.

eleven *number* once M; **Josh is eleven** Josh tiene once años; **it's eleven o'clock** son las once.

eleventh *noun* **the eleventh of May** el once de mayo.
adjective onceavo/onceava; **on the eleventh floor** en la onceava planta.

eliminate *verb* eliminar [17].

else *adverb* **1** (*in questions and negative sentences*) más; **who else?** ¿quién más?; **what else?** ¿qué más?; **nothing else** nada más; **I don't want anything else** no quiero nada más; **2 somebody else** otra persona; **somebody else must have done it** lo ha debido hacer otra persona; **3 something else** otra cosa; **would you like something else?** ¿quieres otra cosa?; **4 everybody else** todos los demás; **everything else** todo lo demás; **5 somewhere else** en otra parte; **6 or else** si no; **hurry up, or else we'll be late** date prisa, que si no vamos a llegar tarde.

e-mail *noun* correo M electrónico.

embankment *noun* 1 (*by a river*) muro M de contención; 2 (*by a railway*) terraplén M.

embarrassed *adjective* I was terribly embarrassed me daba mucha vergüenza; she feels a bit embarrassed le da un poco de vergüenza.

embarrassing *adjective* violento/violenta (*situation or silence*); how embarrasing! ¡qué vergüenza!

embassy *noun* embajada F; the Spanish Embassy la embajada española.

embroider *verb* bordar [17].

embroidery *noun* bordado M.

emergency *noun* 1 emergencia F; in an emergency, break the glass en caso de emergencia, rompa el cristal; it's an emergency! ¡es una emergencia!; 2 (*medical*) urgencia F; an emergency operation una operación de urgencia.

emergency exit *noun* salida F de emergencia.

emergency landing *noun* aterrizaje M forzoso.

emotion *noun* emoción F.

emotional *adjective* 1 (*person*) to be emotional estar [2] emocionado/emocionada; to get emotional emocionarse [17]; she got quite emotional se emocionó mucho; 2 (*a speech or an occasion*) emotivo/emotiva.

emperor *noun* emperador M.

emphasize *verb* recalcar [31]; he emphasized that it wasn't compulsory recalcó que no era obligatorio.

empire *noun* imperio M; the Roman Empire el imperio romano.

employ *verb* 1 (*have in employment*) emplear [17]; 2 (*give work to*) dar [4] un trabajo a.

employee *noun* empleado M, empleada F.

employer *noun* patrón M, patrona F.

employment *noun* empleo M.

empty *adjective* vacío/vacía; an empty bottle una botella vacía; the room was empty la habitación estaba vacía.
verb vaciar [32]; I emptied the teapot into the sink vacié la tetera en el fregadero.

enchanting *adjective* encantador/encantadora.

enclose *verb* (*in a letter*) adjuntar [17]; please find enclosed a cheque se adjunta un cheque.

encore *noun* bis M; encore! ¡otra!

encourage *verb* animar [17]; to encourage somebody to do animar a alguien a hacer; Mum encouraged me to try again mamá me animó a intentarlo otra vez.

encouragement *noun* ánimo M.

encouraging *adjective* alentador/alentadora.

encyclopedia *noun* enciclopedia F.

end *noun* 1 (*last part*) final M; **at the end of the film** al final de la película; **by the end of the day** al final del día; **in the end I went home** al final me fui a casa; 2 **at the end of the year** a finales de año; **Sally's coming at the end of June** Sally viene a finales de junio; 3 **'The End'** (*in a book or film*) 'Fin'; 4 (*of a table, garden, or stick, for example*) extremo M; **hold the other end** sujeta el otro extremo; 5 (*of a street or road*) final M; **at the end of the street** al final de la calle; 6 (*of a pitch*) lado M; **to change ends** cambiar [17] de lado.
verb 1 (*put an end to*) poner [11] fin a (*an arrangement*); **they've ended the strike** han puesto fin a la huelga; 2 (*to come to an end*) terminar [17]; **the day ended with a dinner** el día terminó con una cena.
● **to end up** terminar [17]; **we ended up taking a taxi** terminamos cogiendo un taxi; **Ross ended up in San Francisco** Ross terminó en San Francisco.

ending *noun* final M.

endless *adjective* interminable.

enemy *noun* enemigo M, enemiga F; **to make enemies** hacer [7] enemigos.

energetic *adjective* energético/energética.

energy *noun* energía F.

engaged *adjective* 1 (*to be married*) prometido/prometida; **they're engaged** están prometidos; **to get**

engaged prometerse [18]; 2 (*a phone*) comunicando; **it's engaged, I'll ring later** está comunicando, llamaré más tarde; 3 (*a toilet*) ocupado/ocupada.

engagement *noun* (*to marry*) compromiso M.

engagement ring *noun* anillo M de compromiso.

engine *noun* 1 (*in a car*) motor M; 2 (*locomotive*) locomotora F.

engineer *noun* 1 (*who comes for repairs*) técnico M/F; 2 (*who builds roads and bridges*) ingeniero M, ingeniera F.

England *noun* Inglaterra M/F; **I'm from England** soy inglés.

English *noun* 1 (*the language*) inglés M; **do you speak English?** ¿hablas inglés?; **he answered in English** contestó en inglés; 2 (*English people*) **the English** los ingleses.
adjective 1 (*of or from England*) inglés/inglesa; **the English team** el equipo inglés; 2 **an English lesson** una clase de inglés; **our English teacher** nuestro profesor de inglés.

English Channel *noun* **the English Channel** el Canal de la Mancha.

Englishman *noun* inglés M.

Englishwoman *noun* inglesa F.

enjoy *verb* 1 disfrutar [17]; **did you enjoy the party?** ¿disfrutaste de la fiesta?; **we really enjoyed the concert** disfrutamos mucho del concierto; **2 I enjoy swimming** me gusta nadar; **do you enjoy living in York?** ¿te gusta vivir en York?; **3 to enjoy youself** divertirse [14]; **we really enjoyed ourselves** nos divertimos muchísimo; **did you enjoy yourself?** ¿te divertiste?

enjoyable *adjective* agradable.

enlarge *verb* ampliar [32].

enlargement *noun* (*of a photo*) ampliación F.

enormous *adjective* enorme.

enough *adverb, pronoun*
1 suficiente; **there's enough for everyone** hay suficiente para todos; **is there enough bread?** ¿hay pan suficiente?; **there weren't enough books** no había libros suficientes; **2** (*with an adjective or adverb*) lo suficientemente; **big enough** lo suficientemente grande; **slowly enough** lo suficientemente despacio; **3 that's enough** ya basta.

enquire *verb* informarse [17]; **I'm going to enquire about the trains** voy a informarme sobre los trenes.

enquiry *noun* **to make enquiries about something** pedir [57] información sobre algo.

enrol *verb* matricularse [17]; **I want to enrol on the course** quiero matricularme en el curso.

enter *verb* **1** (*go inside*) entrar [17] en (*a room or building*); **we all entered the church** todos entramos en la iglesia; **2 to enter for** presentarse [17] a (*an exam*); tomar [17] parte en (*a race or competition*).

entertain *verb* **1** (*keep amused*) entretener [9]; **something to entertain the children** algo para entretener a los niños; **2** (*have people round*) invitar [17] a gente; **they don't entertain much** no invitan a mucha gente.

entertaining *noun* **they do a lot of entertaining** invitan a mucha gente. *adjective* entretenido/entretenida.

entertainment *noun* (*fun*) entretenimiento M; **there wasn't much entertainment in the evenings** por las noches no había mucho entretenimiento.

enthusiasm *noun* entusiasmo M.

enthusiast *noun* **to be a rugby enthusiast** ser [1] un apasionado/una apasionada del rugby.

enthusiastic *adjective* entusiasta.

entire *adjective* entero/entera; **the entire class** la clase entera.

entirely *adverb* completamente.

entrance *noun* entrada F.

entry *noun* (*the way in*) entrada F; **'no entry'** 'prohibida la entrada'.

entry phone *noun* portero M automático.

envelope *noun* sobre M.

environment *noun* medio M ambiente.

environmental *adjective* medioambiental.

environment-friendly *noun* ecológico/ecológica.

envy *noun* envidia F.

epidemic *noun* epidemia F.

epileptic *noun* epiléptico M, epiléptica F.

episode *noun* episodio M.

equal *adjective* igual; **in equal quantities** en cantidades iguales. *verb* ser [1] igual a.

equally *adjective* (*to share*) en partes iguales; **we divided it equally** lo dividimos en partes iguales.

equality *noun* igualdad F.

equator *noun* ecuador M.

cquip *verb* equipar [17]; **well equipped for the walk** bien equipado para la marcha.

equipment *noun* 1 (*for sport*) artículos M (*plural*) deportivos; 2 (*in office or lab*) material M.

equivalent *adjective* **to be equivalent to** ser [1] equivalente a.

error *noun* 1 (*in spelling or typing*) falta F; **a spelling error** una falta de ortografía; 2 (*in maths or on a computer*) error M.

escalator *noun* escalera F mecánica.

escape *noun* (*from prison*) fuga F. *verb* 1 (*a person*) fugarse [28]; 2 (*an animal*) escaparse [17].

escort *noun* escolta F; **a police escort** una escolta policial.

especially *adjective* especialmente.

essay *noun* redacción F; **an essay on pollution** una redacción sobre la contaminación.

essential *adjective* esencial; **it's essential to reply quickly** es esencial responder rápidamente.

estate *noun* 1 (*a housing estate*) urbanización F; 2 (*a big house and grounds*) propiedad F.

estate agent's *noun* agencia F inmobiliaria.

estate car *noun* coche M ranchera.

estimate *noun* 1 (*a quote for work*) presupuesto M; 2 (*a rough guess*) cálculo M aproximado. *verb* 1 calcular [17]; 2 **the estimated time of arrival** la hora prevista de llegada.

etc. *abbreviation* etc.

ethnic *adjective* étnico/étnica; **an ethnic minority** una minoría étnica.

EU *abbreviation* Unión F Europea.

Europe *noun* Europa F.

European *noun* europco M, europea F. *adjective* europeo/europea.

European Union *noun* Unión F Europea.

eve *noun* **Christmas Eve** Nochebuena F; **New year's Eve** Nochevieja F.

even[1] *adverb* 1 incluso; **even I could do it** incluso yo podría hacerlo; 2 (*in comparisons*) **even more difficult**

aún más difícil; **even faster** aún más rápido; **even more than** aún más que; **I liked the song even more than their last one** la canción me gustó aún más que la anterior; **3** (*in negative sentences or after 'without'*) ni siquiera; **even Lisa didn't like it** ni siquiera a Lisa le gustó; **without even asking** sin ni siquiera preguntar; **not even** ni siquiera; **I don't like animals, not even dogs** no me gustan los animales, ni siquiera los perros; **4 even if** incluso si; **even if they arrive** incluso si llegan; **5 even so** aun así; **even so, we had a good time** aun así lo pasamos bien; **6 even though** aunque.

even² *adjective* **1** (*a surface or layer*) plano/plana; **2** (*a number*) par; **six is an even number** seis es un número par; **3** (*with the same score*) igualado/igualada; **Lee and Tony are even** Lee y Tony están igualados.

evening *noun* **1** (*before dark*) tarde F; (*after dark*) noche F; **this evening** (*before dark*) esta tarde; (*after dark*) esta noche; **at six o'clock in the evening** a las seis de la tarde; **at ten in the evening** a las diez de la noche; **tomorrow evening** mañana por la tarde, mañana por la noche; **on Thursday evening** el jueves por la tarde, el jueves por la noche; **the evening before** la tarde anterior, la noche anterior; **every evening** cada tarde, cada noche; **good evening** buenas tardes, buenas noches; **I work in the evening(s)** trabajo por las noches; **2 the evening meal** la cena;

3 (*event*) velada F; **an evening with Pavarotti** una velada con Pavarotti.

evening class *noun* clase F nocturna.

event *noun* **1** (*a happening*) acontecimiento M; **2** (*in athletics*) prueba F; **track events** pruebas de atletismo.

eventful *adjective* lleno de incidentes.

eventually *adverb* finalmente.

ever *adverb* **1** (*at any time*) alguna vez; **have you ever been to Spain?** ¿has estado alguna vez en España?; **have you ever noticed that?** ¿lo notaste alguna vez?; **hardly ever** casi nunca; **no-one ever came** nunca vino nadie; **more slowly than ever** más despacio que nunca; **2** (*always*) siempre; **as cheerful as ever** tan contento como siempre; **the same as ever** como siempre; **3 ever since** desde entonces; **and it's been raining ever since** y ha estado lloviendo desde entonces.

every *adjective* **1** todos/todas; **every house has a garden** todas las casas tienen jardín; **every day** todos los días; **every Monday** todos los lunes; **I've seen every one of his films** he visto todas sus películas; **2** (*repetition*) cada; **every ten kilometres** cada diez kilómetros; **every time** cada vez; **3 every now and then** de vez en cuando; **every second day** un día sí y otro no.

everybody, everyone *pronoun* todo el mundo; **everybody knows**

that ... todo el mundo sabe que ...;
everyone else todos los demás.

everything *pronoun* todo;
everything's ready está todo listo;
everything's fine está todo bien;
everything else todo lo demás;
everything you said todo lo que
dijiste.

everywhere *adverb* **there was mud
everywhere** había barro por todas
partes; **everywhere she went** a todos
los sitios a los que fue; **everywhere
else is closed** todos los demás sitios
están cerrados.

evidently *adverb* obviamente.

evil *noun* mal M.
adjective malvado/malvada.

exact *adjective* exacto/exacta; **the
exact amount** la cantidad exacta;
it's the exact opposite es
exactamente lo contrario.

exactly *adverb* exactamente; **they're
exactly the same age** tienen
exactamente la misma edad; **yes,
exactly** exacto.

exaggerate *verb* exagerar [17].

exaggeration *noun* exageración F.

exam *noun* examen M; **a history
exam** un examen de historia; **to sit
an exam** presentarse [17] a un
examen; **to pass an exam** aprobar
[24] un examen; **to fail an exam**
suspender [18] un examen.

examination *noun* examen M.

examine *verb* examinar [17].

examiner *noun* examinador M,
examinadora F.

example *noun* ejemplo M; **for
example** por ejemplo; **to set a good
example** dar [4] buen ejemplo.

excellent *adjective* excelente.

except *preposition* excepto; **except
in March** excepto en marzo; **except
Tuesdays** excepto los martes;
except when it rains excepto
cuando llueve.

exception *noun* excepción F;
without exception sin excepción;
with the exception of con la
excepción de.

exchange *noun* 1 (*of information
or students*) intercambio M; **an
exchange visit** un viaje de
intercambio; 2 **in exchange for his
help** a cambio de su ayuda.
verb cambiar [17]; **can I exchange
this shirt for a smaller one?** ¿puedo
cambiar esta camisa por una más
pequeña?

exchange rate *noun* tipo M de
cambio.

excited *adjective* 1 (*happy*)
entusiasmado/entusiasmada;
**they're really excited about the
idea** están entusiasmados con la
idea; 2 (*noisy, boisterous*)
alborotado/alborotada; **the
children were too excited** los niños
estaban demasiado alborotados;
3 **to get excited** (*happy*)
entusiasmarse [17]; (*boisterous*)

alborotarse [17]; **the dogs get excited when they hear the car** los perros se alborotan cuando oyen el coche.

exciting *adjective* emocionante; **a really exciting film** una película realmente emocionante.

exclamation mark *noun* signo M de admiración.

excursion *noun* excursión F.

excuse *noun* excusa F; **Gary has a good excuse** Gary tiene una buena excusa; **that's no excuse** eso no es excusa; **to make excuses** poner [11] excusas.
verb (*apologizing*) **excuse me!** ¡perdón!

exercise *noun* ejercicio M; **a maths exercise** un ejercicio de matemáticas; **physical exercise** ejercicio físico.

exercise book *noun* cuaderno M; **my Spanish exercise book** mi cuaderno de español.

exhausted *adjective* agotado/agotada.

exhaust fumes *noun* gases M (*plural*) del tubo de escape.

exhaust (pipe) *noun* tubo M de escape.

exhibition *noun* exposición F; **the Cézanne exhibition** la exposición de Cézanne.

exist *verb* existir [19].

exit *noun* salida F.

expect *verb* **1** esperar [17] (*guests or a baby*); **we're expecting about thirty people** esperamos unas treinta personas; **2** esperarse [17] (*something to happen*); **I didn't expect that** no me esperaba eso; **I didn't expect it at all** no me lo esperaba en absoluto; **3** (*as a supposition*) suponer [11]; **I expect you're tired** supongo que estarás cansado; **I expect she'll bring her boyfriend** supongo que traerá a su novio; **yes, I expect so** supongo que sí.

expedition *noun* expedición F.

expel *verb* **to be expelled** (*from school*) ser [1] expulsado.

expenses *noun* gastos M (*plural*).

expensive *adjective* caro/cara; **those shoes are too expensive for me** esos zapatos son demasiado caros para mí; **the most expensive hotels** los hoteles más caros.

experience *noun* experiencia F.

experienced *adjective* con experiencia.

experiment *noun* experimento M; **to do an experiment** hacer [7] un experimento.

expert *noun* experto M, experta F; **he's a computer expert** es un experto en ordenadores.

expire *verb* caducar [31].

expiry date *noun* fecha F de caducidad.

explain *verb* explicar [31].

explanation *noun* explicación F.

explode *verb* explotar [17].

explore *verb* explorar [17].

explosion *noun* explosión F.

export *verb* exportar [17].

exposure *noun* (*of a film*) exposición F; **a 24-exposure film** un carrete de veinticuatro fotos.

express *noun* (*a train*) rápido M. *verb* **1** expresar [17]; **2 to express yourself** expresarse [17].

expression *noun* expresión F.

extend *verb* ampliar [32] (*a building*).

extension *noun* **1** (*to a house*) ampliación F; **2** (*telephone*) extensión F; **can I have extension 2347 please?** ¿me puede poner con la extensión veintitrés cuarenta y siete, por favor? (*note that in spoken Spanish telephone numbers are usually broken down into groups of two figures; this applies to longer numbers as well*).

extension lead *noun* alargador M.

extension number *noun* número M de extensión.

extinguish *verb* apagar [28].

extinguisher *noun* (*fire extinguisher*) extintor M.

extinct *adjective* extinto/extinta; **to become extinct** extinguirse [50].

extra *adjective*, *adverb* **1 they gave us some extra homework** nos dieron más deberes; **2 you have to pay extra** tiene que pagar un suplemento; **to charge extra for something** cobrar [17] un suplemento por algo; **wine is extra** el vino se cobra aparte; **at no extra charge** sin coste suplementario; **3 extra hot** super picante; **extra large** super grande.

extraordinary *adjective* extraordinario/extraordinaria.

extra-special *adjective* super especial.

extra time *noun* (*in football*) prórroga F.

extravagant *adjective* derrochador/derrochadora (*a person*).

extreme *noun* extremo M; **to go to extremes** llevar [17] las cosas al extremo.
adjective extremo/extrema.

extremely *adverb* **extremely difficult** dificilísimo; **extremely fast** rapidísimo.

eye *noun* ojo M; **a girl with blue eyes** una niña con ojos azules; **shut your eyes!** ¡cierra los ojos!; ★ **to keep an eye on something** vigilar [17] algo; ★ **to make eyes at somebody** hacerle [7] ojitos a alguien (*informal*).

eyebrow *noun* ceja F.

eyelash *noun* pestaña F.

eyelid *noun* párpado M.

eyeliner *noun* delineador M de ojos.

eye make-up *noun* maquillaje M de ojos.

eye shadow *noun* sombra F de ojos.

eyesight *noun* vista F.

F f

fabric *noun* tela F.

fabulous *adjective* fabuloso/ fabulosa.

face *noun* 1 (*of a person*) cara F; **on your face** en la cara; 2 **to pull a face** hacer [7] muecas; 3 (*of a clock or watch*) esfera F.
verb 1 (*a person*) enfrentarse [17] a; 2 (*to be opposite*) estar [2] frente a; **the hotel faces the sea** el hotel está frente al mar; 3 **it faces south** está orientado hacia el sur; 4 **I can't face going back** no soporto la idea de volver.

facilities *plural noun* 1 **sports facilities** instalaciones F (*plural*) deportivas; 2 **the flat has cooking facilities** el piso tiene cocina.

fact *noun* hecho M; **in fact** de hecho; **is that a fact?** ¿es eso cierto?

factory *noun* fábrica F.

fail *verb* 1 suspender [18] (*a test or exam*); **I failed my driving test** he suspendido el examen de conducir; **three students failed** tres estudiantes suspendieron; 2 **to fail to do** no hacer; **he failed to contact us** no se puso en contacto con nosotros; ★ **without fail** sin falta; **ring me without fail** llámame sin falta.

failure *noun* 1 fracaso M; **it was a terrible failure** fue un fracaso terrible; 2 **a power failure** un apagón.

faint *adjective* 1 **to feel faint** sentirse [14] mareado/mareada; 2 (*slight*) ligero/ligera; **a faint smell of gas** un ligero olor a gas; **I haven't the faintest idea** no tengo ni la más remota idea; 3 (*a voice or sound*) débil.
verb desmayarse [17]; **Lisa fainted** Lisa se desmayó.

fair *noun* feria F.
adjective 1 (*not unfair*) justo/justa; **it's not fair!** ¡no es justo!; 2 (*hair*) rubio/rubia; **he's fair-haired** tiene el pelo rubio; 3 (*skin*) blanco/blanca; 4 (*fairly good*) bastante bueno/ buena.

fairground *noun* parque M de atracciones.

fairly *adverb* (*quite*) bastante; **she's fairly happy** es bastante feliz.

fairy *noun* hada F; (*even though 'hada' is a feminine noun, it is used with 'el' and 'un'*).

fairy tale *noun* cuento M de hadas.

faith *noun* 1 (*trust*) confianza F; **to have faith in somebody** tener confianza en alguien; 2 (*religious belief*) fe F.

faithful *adjective* fiel.

faithfully *adverb* **yours faithfully** le saluda atentamente.

fall *noun* caída F; **to have a fall** sufrir [19] una caída.
verb 1 caerse [34]; **mind, you'll fall** cuidado, te vas a caer; **Tony fell off his bike** Tony se cayó de la bici; **she fell downstairs** se cayó por las escaleras; **my jacket fell on the floor** mi chaqueta se cayó al suelo; 2 (*the temperature or prices*) bajar [17]; **it fell to minus eleven last night** la temperatura bajó a once grados bajo cero anoche.

false *adjective* falso/falsa; **a false passport** un pasaporte falso; **a false alarm** una falsa alarma.

false teeth *plural noun* dentadura F (*singular*) postiza.

fame *noun* fama F.

familiar *adjective* familiar; **your face is familiar** tu cara me es familiar.

family *noun* familia F; **a family of six** una familia de seis personas; **Ben's one of the family** Ben es uno de la familia; **the Bunting family** la familia Bunting.

famous *adjective* famoso/famosa.

fan *noun* 1 (*of a pop group*) fan M/F (*informal*); **Sarah's an Oasis fan** Sarah es fan de Oasis; 2 (*of a team*) hincha M/F; **Martin's a Chelsea fan** Martin es hincha del Chelsea; 3 (*electric, for cooling*) ventilador M; 4 (*that you hold in your hand*) abanico M.

fanatic *noun* fanático M, fanática F.

fancy *noun* **the picture took his fancy** se encaprichó del cuadro. *adjective* (*equipment*) sofisticado/sofisticada; (*hotel*) de lujo. *verb* 1 (*to want*) **do you fancy a coffee?** ¿te apetece un café?; **I don't fancy going out** no me apetece salir; 2 **I really fancy him** me gusta mucho; 3 (**just**) **fancy that!** ¡imagínate!; **fancy you being here!** ¡qué casualidad que estés aquí!

fancy dress *noun* disfraz M; **in fancy dress** disfrazado/disfrazada; **a fancy-dress party** una fiesta de disfraces.

fantastic *adjective* estupendo/estupenda (*informal*); **really? that's fantastic!** ¿de verdad? ¡eso es estupendo!; **a fantastic holiday** unas vacaciones estupendas.

far *adverb*, *adjective* 1 lejos; **It's not far** no está lejos; **is it far to Cordova?** ¿está muy lejos Córdoba?; **how far is it to Granada?** ¿a qué distancia está Granada?; **he took us as far as Bilbao** nos llevó hasta Bilbao; 2 **by far** con mucho; **the prettiest by far** es con mucho la más bonita; 3 (*much*) mucho; **far better** mucho

mejor; **far faster** mucho más rápido;
4 far too many people demasiada
gente; **far too much noise**
demasiado ruido; **5 so far** hasta
ahora; **so far everything's going
well** hasta ahora todo va bien; **as far
as I know** que yo sepa.

fare *noun* precio M del billete; **half
fare** medio billete M; **full fare**
billete M entero; **the return fare to
Barcelona** el billete de ida y vuelta a
Barcelona.

Far East *noun* Lejano Oriente M.

farm *noun* granja F.

farmer *noun* agricultor M,
agricultora F.

farmhouse *noun* casa F de
labranza.

farming *noun* agricultura F.

fascinating *adjective* fascinante.

fashion *noun* moda F; **in fashion** de
moda; **out of fashion** pasado/
pasada de moda.

fashionable *adjective* de moda.

fashion model *noun* modelo M/F.

fashion show *noun* desfile M de
modas.

fast *adjective* **1** rápido/rápida; **a fast
car** un coche rápido; **2 my watch is
fast** mi reloj adelanta; **you're ten
minutes fast** vas diez minutos
adelantado.
adverb **1** rápido; **she swims very
fast** nada muy rápido; **2 to be fast
asleep** estar [2] profundamente
dormido.

fat *noun* grasa F.
adjective gordo/gorda; **a fat man** un
hombre gordo; **to get fat** engordar
[17].

fatal *adjective* (*accident*) fatal.

father *noun* padre M; **my father's
office** la oficina de mi padre.

Father Christmas *noun* Papá M
Noel.

father-in-law *noun* suegro M.

fault *noun* **1** (*responsibility*) culpa F;
it's Steve's fault es culpa de Steve;
it's not my fault no es culpa mía;
2 (*in tennis*) falta F.

favour *noun* **1** (*a kindness*) favor M;
to do somebody a favour hacerle
[7] un favor a alguien; **can you do me
a favour?** ¿puedes hacerme un
favor?; **to ask a favour of somebody**
pedirle [57] un favor a alguien; **2 to
be in favour of something** estar [2] a
favor de algo.

favourite *adjective* favorito/
favorita; **my favourite band** mi grupo
favorito.

fax *noun* fax M; **a fax machine** un fax.

fear *noun* miedo M.
verb temer [18].

feather *noun* pluma F.

feature *noun* **1** (*of your face*)
rasgo M; **to have delicate features**
tener [9] rasgos delicados; **2** (*of a
machine, product, etc.*)
característica F.

February *noun* febrero M; **in
February** en febrero.

fed up *adjective* **I'm fed up** estoy harto/harta (*informal*); **I'm fed up with working every day** estoy harta de trabajar todos los días.

feed *verb* dar [4] de comer a; **have you fed the dog?** ¿has dado de comer al perro?

feel *verb* **1** sentirse [14]; **I feel tired** me siento cansada; **I don't feel well** no me siento bien; **2** sentir [14]; **I didn't feel a thing** no sentí nada; **3 to feel afraid** tener [9] miedo; **to feel cold** tener [9] frío; **to feel thirsty** tener [9] sed; **4 I feel like some chocolate** me apetece un poco de chocolate; **do you feel like a walk?** ¿te apetece dar un paseo?; **I don't feel like it** no me apetece; **5 to feel like doing** tener [9] ganas de hacer; **I feel like going to the cinema** tengo ganas de ir al cine; **6** (*touch*) tocar [31].

feeling *noun* **1** (*in your mind*) sentimiento M; **a feeling of embarrassment** un sentimiento de vergüenza; **to show your feelings** de mostrar los sentimientos; **to hurt somebody's feelings** herir [14] los sentimientos de alguien; **2** (*in your body*) sensación F; **a dizzy feeling** una sensación de mareo; **3** (*impression*) impresión F; **I have the feeling James doesn't like me** tengo la impresión de que no le gusto a James.

felt-tip (pen) *noun* rotulador M.

female *noun* (*animal*) hembra F. *adjective* **1** femenino/

femenina (*person, population*); **2** hembra (*animal, insect*).

feminine *adjective* femenino/femenina.

feminist *noun*, *adjective* feminista M/F.

fence *noun* valla F.

fern *noun* helecho M.

ferry *noun* ferry M.

fetch *verb* ir [8] a por; **Tom's fetching the children** Tom ha ido a por los niños; **fetch me the other knife!** ¡vete a por el otro cuchillo!

fever *noun* fiebre F.

few *adjective*, *pronoun* **1** pocos/pocas; **few people think that …** pocos piensan que …; **2 a few** (*followed by a noun*) algunos/algunas; **a few weeks earlier** algunas semanas antes; **in a few minutes** dentro de algunos minutos; **3 a few** (*by itself*) unos cuantos/unas cuantas; **have you any tomatoes? we want a few for the salad** ¿tienes tomates? queremos unos cuantos para la ensalada; **a few more books** unos cuantos libros más; **4 quite a few** bastantes; **there were quite a few questions** hubo bastantes preguntas.

fewer *adjective* menos; **there are fewer tourists this year** hay menos turistas este año; **fewer than six** menos de seis.

fiction *noun* ficción F.

field *noun* campo M; **a field of wheat** un campo de trigo; **a football field** un campo de fútbol.

fifteen *number* quince M; **Lara's fifteen** Lara tiene quince años.

fifth *noun* 1 (*fraction*) **a fifth** una quinta parte; 2 **the fifth of January** el cinco de enero.
adjective quinto/quinta; **on the fifth floor** en la quinta planta.

fifties *plural noun* **the fifties** los años cincuenta; **in the fifties** en los años cincuenta.

fifty *number* cincuenta M; **she's fifty** tiene cincuenta años; **fifty-five** cincuenta y cinco.

fig *noun* higo M.

fight *noun* 1 (*a scuffle or in boxing*) pelea F; 2 (*in war or against illness or poverty*) lucha F.
verb 1 (*in war or against poverty or a disease*) luchar [17]; 2 (*to quarrel*) pelear [17]; **they're always fighting** siempre se están peleando.

figure *noun* 1 (*number*) cifra F; **a four-figure number** un número de cuatro cifras; 2 (*body shape*) figura F; 3 (*a person*) personaje M; **a public figure** un personaje público.

file *noun* 1 (*for records of a person or case*) archivo M; 2 (*in computer system*) fichero M; 3 (*ring binder*) archivador M; 4 (*cardboard folder*) carpeta F; 5 **a nail file** una lima.
verb 1 archivar [17] (*documents;*);
2 **to file your nails** limarse [17] las uñas.

fill *verb* llenar [17]; **she filled my glass** me llenó el vaso.
● **to fill in** rellenar [17] (*a form*).

film *noun* 1 (*in a cinema*) película F; **shall we go and see a film?** ¿vamos a ver una película?; **the new film about Picasso** la nueva película sobre Picasso; 2 (*for a camera*) carrete M de fotos; **a 24-exposure colour film** un carrete de color de veinticuatro fotos.

film star *noun* estrella F de cine.

filthy *adjective* asquerosa/asquerosa (*informal*).

final *noun* (*in sport*) final F.
adjective 1 (*definite*) final; **the final result** el resultado final; 2 (*last*) último/última; **the final instalment** el último plazo.

finally *adverb* finalmente.

find *verb* encontrar [24]; **did you find your passport?** ¿has encontrado tu pasaporte?; **I can't find my keys** no puedo encontrar mis llaves.
● **to find out** 1 (*to enquire*) informarse [17]; **I don't know, I'll find out** no lo sé, me informaré; 2 **to find something out** descubrir [46] algo (*the facts or an answer;*); **when Lucy found out the truth** cuando Lucy se enteró de la verdad.

fine *noun* multa F.
adjective 1 bien; **'how are you?' – 'fine, thanks'** '¿cómo estás?' – 'bien, gracias'; **ten o'clock? yes, that's fine** ¿a las diez? sí, está bien; **Friday will be fine** el viernes está bien; 2 (*very good*) muy bueno/buena; **she's a**

fine athlete es muy buena atleta;
3 (*weather or a day;*) bueno/buena;
if it's fine si hace bueno; **4** (*not coarse or thick*) fino/fina; **in fine wool** de lana fina.

finely *adjective* (*chopped or grated*) muy fino/fina.

finger *noun* dedo M; ★ **I'll keep my fingers crossed for you** te deseo suerte.

fingernail *noun* uña F.

finish *noun* **1** (*end*) final M; **2** (*in a race*) llegada F.
verb **1** terminar [17]; **wait, I haven't finished** espera, no he terminado; **when does school finish?** ¿cuándo termina el colegio?; **have you finished the book?** ¿has terminado el libro?; **2 to finish doing** terminar [17] de hacer; **have you finished telephoning?** ¿has terminado de llamar por teléfono?
● **to finish with** terminar [17] con; **have you finished with the computer?** ¿has terminado con el ordenador?

Finland *noun* Finlandia F.

Finnish *noun* **1** (*person*) finladés/finlandesa M/F; **2** (*the language*) finlandés M.
adjective finlandés/finlandesa.

fir tree *noun* abeto M.

fire *noun* **1** (*in a grate*) fuego M; **to light the fire** encender [36] el fuego; **2** (*accidental*) incendio M; **3 to catch fire** prenderse [18] fuego; **to be on fire** estar [2] ardiendo.
verb (*to shoot*) disparar [17]; **to fire at somebody** disparar a alguien.

fire alarm *noun* alarma F contra incendios.

fire brigade *noun* cuerpo M de bomberos.

fire engine *noun* coche M de bomberos.

fire escape *noun* escalera F de incendios.

fire extinguisher *noun* extintor M.

firefighter *noun* bombero M/F.

fireplace *noun* chimenea F.

fire station *noun* estación F de bomberos.

fireworks *plural noun* fuegos M (*plural*) artificiales.

firm *noun* (*business*) empresa F.
adjective firme.

first *pronoun*, *adjective*, *adverb*
1 primero/primera; **Susan's the first** Susan es la primera; **for the first time** por primera vez; **Christy got here first** Christy llegó aquí la primera; **Ben came first in the 200 metres** Ben llegó el primero en los doscientos metros; **2 the first of May** el uno de Mayo; **3** (*to begin with*) primero; **first, I'm going to make some tea** primero voy a hacer té; **first of all** en primer lugar; **4 at first** al principio; **at first he didn't want to** al principio no quería.

first aid *noun* primeros auxilios M (*plural*).

first class *adjective* de primera (*a ticket, carriage, or hotel;*); **a first-class compartment** un compartimento de primera; **he always travels first class** siempre viaja en primera.

first floor *noun* primera planta F; **on the first floor** en la primera planta.

firstly *adverb* en primer lugar.

first name *noun* nombre M de pila.

fish *noun* 1 (*as a meal*) pescado M; **do you like fish?** ¿te gusta el pescado?; 2 (*in the sea*) pez M (*plural* peces).
verb pescar [31]; **Dad was fishing for trout** papá estaba pescando truchas.

fish and chips *noun* pescado M con patatas fritas.

fisherman *noun* pescador M.

fishing *noun* pesca F; **fishing is my favourite sport** la pesca es mi deporte favorito; **I love fishing** me encanta pescar; **to go fishing** ir de pesca.

fishing rod *noun* caña F de pescar.

fishing tackle *noun* aparejos M (*plural*) de pesca.

fist *noun* puño M.

fit *noun* ataque M; **an epileptic fit** un ataque epiléptico; **I had a fit** me dio un ataque; **your dad'll have a fit when he sees your hair!** ¡a tu padre le va a dar un ataque cuando te vea el pelo!
adjective (*healthy*) en forma; **I feel really fit** me siento realmente en forma; **to keep fit** mantenerse [9] en forma.
verb 1 (*a garment or shoes*) estar [2] bien (*a person;*); **this skirt doesn't fit me** esta falda no me está bien; **does it fit you okay?** ¿te está bien?; 2 (*go into*) entrar [17] en; **will my cases all fit in the car?** ¿entrarán todas mis maletas en el coche?; 3 (*install*) poner [11].

fitted carpet *noun* moqueta F.

five *number* cinco M; **Oskar's five** Oskar tiene cinco años; **it's five o'clock** son las cinco.

fix *verb* 1 (*repair*) arreglar [17]; **Mum's fixed the computer** mamá ha arreglado el ordenador; 2 (*to decide on*) fijar [17]; **to fix a date** fijar [17] una fecha; **at a fixed price** a un precio fijo; 3 preparar [17] (*a meal*).

fizzy *adjective* con gas; **fizzy water** agua con gas.

flag *noun* bandera F.

flame *noun* llama F.

flan *noun* 1 (*savoury*) quiche M; **an onion flan** un quiche de cebolla; 2 (*sweet*) tarta F.

flap *verb* (*a flag or sail*) agitarse [17].

flash *noun* 1 **a flash of lightning** un relámpago; 2 (*of light*) destello M; 3 **to do something in a flash** hacer [7] algo a la velocidad del rayo; 4 (*on a camera*) flash M.
verb 1 (*a light*) destellar [17]; 2 **to flash by or past** pasar [17] como un rayo; 3 **to flash your headlights**

hacer [7] señas con los faros del coche.

flat *noun* piso M; **a third-floor flat** un piso en la tercera planta.
adjective 1 plano/plana; **flat shoes** zapatos planos; **a flat surface** una superficie plana; 2 (*landscape*) llano/llana; 3 **a flat tyre** una rueda pinchada.

flatmate *noun* compañero M, compañera F de piso.

flavour *noun* sabor M; **the sauce had no flavour** la salsa no tenía sabor; **what flavour of ice cream would you like?** ¿de qué sabor quieres el helado?
verb **vanilla-flavoured** con sabor a vainilla.

flea *noun* pulga F.

flight *noun* 1 vuelo M; **a charter flight** un vuelo chárter; **the flight from Moscow is delayed** el vuelo procedente de Moscú lleva retraso; 2 **a flight of stairs** un tramo de escalera; **four flights of stairs** cuatro tramos de escalera.

fling *verb* lanzar [22].

flipper *noun* (*for a swimmer*) aleta F.

flirt *verb* flirtear [17].

float *verb* flotar [17].

flood *noun* 1 (*of water*) inundación F; **the floods in the south** las inundaciones del sur; 2 (*of letters or complaints*) avalancha F; 3 **to be in floods of tears** estar [2] llorando a mares (*literally: to be weeping oceans*).
verb inundar [17].

floodlight *noun* foco M.

floor *noun* 1 suelo M; **on the floor** en el suelo; **to sweep the floor** barrer [18]; 2 (*a storey*) planta F; **on the second floor** en la segunda planta.

floppy disk *noun* disquete M.

florist's *noun* floristería F.

flour *noun* harina F.

flower *noun* flor F; **a bunch of flowers** un ramo de flores.
verb florecer [35].

flu *noun* gripe F; **to have flu** tener [9] la gripe.

fluent *adjective* **she speaks fluent Italian** habla italiano con fluidez.

fluently *adverb* con fluidez.

flush *verb* 1 (*to go red*) enrojecer [35]; 2 **to flush the lavatory** tirar [17] de la cadena.

flute *noun* flauta F; **to play the flute** tocar [30] la flauta.

fly *noun* mosca F.
verb 1 (*a bird, an insect, or a plane*) volar [24]; 2 (*in a plane*) ir [8] en avión; **we flew to Edinburgh** fuimos en avión a Edimburgo; **we flew from Gatwick** salimos desde Gatwick; 3 hacer [7] volar (*a kite;*); 4 (*to pass quickly*) (*time*) pasar [17] volando.

foam *noun* 1 (*foam rubber*) goma F espuma; **a foam mattress** un colchón de goma espuma; 2 (*on a drink*) espuma F.

focus noun **to be in focus** estar [2] enfocado; **to be out of focus** estar [2] desenfocado.
verb enfocar [31] (a camera).

fog noun niebla F.

foggy adjective **it was foggy** había niebla; **a foggy day** un día de niebla.

foil noun (kitchen foil) papel M de aluminio.

fold noun doblez M.
verb doblar [17]; **to fold something up** doblar algo.

folder noun carpeta F.

follow verb seguir [64]; **follow me!** ¡sígueme!; **followed by a dinner** seguido de una cena; **do you follow me?** ¿me sigues?

following adjective siguiente; **the following year** el año siguiente.

fond adjective 1 **to be fond of somebody:** tenerle [9] cariño a alguien; **I'm very fond of him** le tengo mucho cariño; 2 **I'm fond of dogs** me gustan los perros.

food noun comida F; **to buy food** comprar [17] comida; **I like Italian food** me gusta la comida italiana.

fool noun idiota M/F.

foot noun 1 pie M; **he stepped on my foot** me pisó el pie; **Lucy came on foot** Lucy vino a pie; **at the foot of the stairs** al pie de las escaleras; 2 (of animal) pata F.

football noun 1 (the game) fútbol M; **to play football** jugar [27] al fútbol; 2 (ball) balón M de fútbol.

footballer noun futbolista M/F.

footpath noun sendero M.

for preposition 1 para; **a present for my mother** un regalo para mi madre; **petrol for the car** gasolina para el coche; **sausages for lunch** salchichas para comer; **it's for cleaning** es para limpiar; **what's it for?** ¿para qué es?; 2 (in time expressions in the past or future, 'for' is not usually translated) **I studied Spanish for six years** estudié español cuatro años; **I'll be away for four days** estaré fuera cuatro días; **I've been waiting here for an hour** llevo esperando aquí una hora; **my brother's been living in London for three years** mi hermano lleva tres años viviendo en Londres; 3 (cost or amount) por; **I sold my bike for fifty pounds** vendí mi bicicleta por cincuenta libras; 4 **what's the Spanish for 'bee'?** ¿cómo se dice 'bee' en español?

forbid verb prohibir [58]; **to forbid somebody to do something** prohibir [58] a alguien hacer algo; **I forbid you to go out** te prohíbo que salgas.

forbidden adjective prohibido/prohibida.

force noun fuerza F.
verb forzar [26]; **to force somebody to do** forzar a alguien a hacer.

forecast noun (weather forecast) pronóstico M.

forehead noun frente F.

foreign *adjective* extranjero/extranjera; **in a foreign country** en un país extranjero.

foreigner *noun* extranjero M, extranjera F.

forest *noun* bosque M.

forever *adverb* **1** para siempre; **I'd like to stay here forever** me gustaría quedarme aquí para siempre; **2** (*non-stop*) siempre; **he's forever asking questions** siempre está preguntando.

forget *verb* olvidarse [17]; **I forget his name** se me ha olvidado su nombre; **we've forgotten the bread!** ¡se nos ha olvidado el pan!; **to forget to do** olvidarse [17] de hacer; **I forgot to phone** se me olvidó llamar por teléfono; **to forget about something** olvidarse [17] de algo.

forgetful *adjective* olvidadizo/olvidadiza.

forgive *verb* perdonar [17]; **I forgave him** lo perdoné; **to forgive somebody for doing** perdonar [17] a alguien que (*followed by subjunctive*); **I forgave her for losing my ring** la perdoné por perderme el anillo.

fork *noun* tenedor M.

form *noun* **1** formulario M; **to fill in a form** rellenar [17] un formulario; **2** (*shape or kind*) forma F; **in the form of** bajo forma de; **3 to be on form** estar [2] en forma; **4** (*school class*) clase F; **5** (*school year*) curso M.
verb formar [17].

formal *adjective* formal (*invitation, event, complaint, etc.*).

former *adjective* antiguo/antigua (*goes before the noun*); **a former pupil** un antiguo alumno.

fortnight *noun* quince días M (*plural*); **we're going to Spain for a fortnight** vamos quince días a España.

fortunately *adverb* afortunadamente.

forty *number* cuarenta M; **he's forty** tiene cuarenta años; **forty-five** cuarenta y cinco.

forward *noun* (*in sport*) delantero M/F.
adverb **a seat further forward** un asiento de más adelante; **to move forward** ir [8] hacia adelante.

foster child *noun* higo M acogido, higa F acogida.

foster family *noun* familia F de acogida.

foul *noun* (*in sport*) falta F.
adjective asqueroso/asquerosa (*smell or taste*); **the weather's foul** el tiempo es horroroso.

fountain *noun* fuente F.

fountain pen *noun* pluma F.

four *number* cuatro M; **Simon's four** Simon tiene cuatro años; **it's four o'clock** son las cuatro.

fourteen *number* catorce M; **Susie's fourteen** Susie tiene catorce años.

fourth *noun* **1** (*fraction*) **a fourth** un cuarto; **2 the fourth of July** el cuatro de julio.
adjective cuarto/cuarta; **on the fourth floor** en la cuarta planta.

fox *noun* zorro M.

fragile *adjective* frágil.

frame *noun* (*of picture or photograph*) marco M.

France *noun* Francia F.

frantic *adjective* **1** (*desperate*) desesperado/desesperada (*efforts or a search*); **2** (*very upset*) **Mum was frantic with worry** mamá estaba muerta de preocupación.

freckle *noun* peca F.

free *adjective* **1** (*when you don't pay*) gratis; **the bus is free** el autobús es gratis; **a free ticket** un billete gratis; **2** (*not occupied*) libre; **are you free on Thursday?** ¿estás libre el jueves?; **3 sugar-free** sin azúcar; **lead-free** sin plomo.
verb **1** (*a person*) poner [11] en libertad; **2** (*an animal*) soltar [24].

freedom *noun* libertad F.

free gift *noun* regalo M.

freeze *verb* **1** (*in a freezer*) congelar [17]; **frozen peas** guisantes congelados; **2** (*in cold weather*) helarse [29] (*person or ground*).

freezer *noun* congelador M.

freezing *noun* **three degrees below freezing** tres grados bajo cero.
adjective **I'm freezing** ¡estoy helado! (*informal*); **it's freezing outside!**

¡fuera hace un frío que pela! (*informal*).

French *noun* **1** (*the language*) francés M; **2** (*the people*) **the French** los franceses.
adjective francés/francesa.

French bean *noun* judía F verde.

French fries *plural noun* patatas F (*plural*) fritas.

Frenchman *noun* francés M.

French window *noun* cristalera F.

Frenchwoman *noun* francesa F.

fresh *adjective* fresco/fresca; **fresh eggs** huevos frescos; **I'm going out for some fresh air** voy fuera a tomar un poco el aire.

Friday *noun* viernes M (*plural viernes*); **last Friday** el viernes pasado; **on Friday** el viernes; **I'll phone you on Friday evening** te llamaré el viernes por la tarde; **on Fridays** los viernes; **closed on Fridays** cerrado los viernes; **every Friday** cada viernes; **Good Friday** Viernes Santo.

fridge *noun* nevera F; **put it in the fridge** ponlo en la nevera.

friend *noun* amigo M, amiga F; **a friend of mine** un amigo mío/una amiga mía; **to make friends** hacer [7] amigos; **he made friends with Danny** se hizo amigo de Danny.

friendly *adjective* **1** (*a person*) simpático/simpática; **2** (*a letter or gesture*) amable.

friendship *noun* amistad F.

fries *plural noun* patatas F (*plural*) fritas.

fright *noun* susto M; **to get a fright** asustarse [17]; **to give somebody a fright** asustar [17] a alguien; **you gave me a fright!** ¡me has asustado!

frighten *verb* asustar [17].

frightened *adjective* **to be frightened** estar [2] asustado/ asustada; **I'm frightened of asking her** me da miedo preguntarle; **Martin's frightened of snakes** a Martin le dan miedo las serpientes.

frightening *adjective* espantoso/ espantosa.

fringe *noun* flequillo M (*of hair*).

frog *noun* rana F.

from *preposition* **1** de; **a letter from Tom** una carta de Tom; **100 metres from the cinema** a cien metros del cine; **he comes from Dublin** es de Dublín; **from seven o'clock onwards** de las siete en adelante; **2 from …to …** de …a …; **from Monday to Friday** de lunes a viernes; **the train from London to Liverpool** el tren de Londres a Liverpool; **from here to the wall** de aquí a la pared; **3** (*starting from*) desde; **tickets from ten pounds** entradas desde diez libras; **from today** desde hoy; **4 two years from now** dentro de dos años; **from then on** a partir de entonces.

front *noun* **1** (*of a car, train, envelope, or queue*) parte F de delante; **sitting in the front** sentado en la parte de delante; **the address is on the front** las señas están en la parte de delante; **from the front** por delante; **2** (*of a building*) fachada F; **3** (*of a garment*) delantero M; **4 the front of the class** el frente de la clase; **5 in front of** delante de; **in front of the TV** delante de la televisión; **in front of me** delante de mí.
adjective **1** delantero/delantera; **the front seat** (*of a car*) el asiento delantero; **2 in the front row** en la fila de delante.

front door *noun* puerta F de la calle.

frontier *noun* frontera F.

frost *noun* helada F.

frosty *adjective* **1 it was frosty this morning** había helada esta mañana; **2** cubierto/cubierta de escarcha (*windscreen, grass, etc.*).

frown *verb* fruncir [66] el ceño.

frozen *adjective* (*in a freezer*) congelado/congelada; **a frozen pizza** una pizza congelada.

fruit *noun* fruta F; **fruit juice** zumo M de fruta.

fruit salad *noun* macedonia F de frutas.

fry *verb* freír [53]; **we fried the fish** freímos el pescado; **a fried egg** un huevo frito.

frying pan *noun* sartén F.

fuel *noun* (*for a vehicle or plane*) combustible M.

full *adjective* **1** lleno/llena; **this glass is full** el vaso está lleno; **the train**

was full of tourists el tren estaba lleno de turistas; **I'm full** estoy lleno; **2** completo/completa (*a hotel or flight*); **3** (*top*) **at full speed** a toda velocidad; **at full volume** a todo volumen; **4** (*complete*) todo/toda; **the full story** toda la historia; **5 to write your name out in full** escribir [52] tu nombre completo.

full stop *noun* punto M.

full-time *noun* **a full-time job** un trabajo a tiempo completo.

fully *adjective* completamente.

fun *noun* **to have fun** divertirse [14]; **have fun!** ¡que te diviertas!; **we had fun catching the ponies** nos divertimos atrapando a los poneys; **skiing is fun** esquiar es divertido; **I do it for fun** lo hago para divertirme; **to make fun of somebody** reírse [61] de alguien.

funds *noun* fondos M (*plural*).

funeral *noun* **1** (*ceremony*) funeral M; **2** (*burial*) entierro M.

funfair *noun* feria F.

funny *adjective* **1** (*when you laugh*) gracioso/graciosa; **how funny you are!** ¡qué gracioso eres!; **a funny story** una historia graciosa; **2** (*strange*) raro; **that's funny, I'm sure I paid** qué raro, estoy seguro de que pagué; **a funny noise** un ruido raro.

fur *noun* **1** (*on an animal*) pelaje M; **2** (*for a coat*) piel F; **a fur coat** un abrigo de piel.

furious *adjective* furioso/furiosa; **she was furious with Steve** estaba furiosa con Steve.

furniture *noun* muebles M (*plural*); **to buy some furniture** comprar muebles; **a piece of furniture** un mueble.

further *adverb* **further than the station** más allá de la estación; **ten kilometres further on** diez kilómetros más adelante; **further forward** más adelante; **further back** más atrás; **further in** más adentro.

fuse *noun* fusible M.

fuss *noun* escándalo M; **to make a fuss** montar [17] un escándalo; **to make a fuss about the bill** montar [17] un escándalo a causa de la factura.

fussy *adjective* **1** (*about how things are done*) quisquilloso/ quisquillosa; **to be fussy about something** ser [1] muy quisquilloso/ quisquillosa para algo; **2** (*about food*) maniático/maniática; **to be fussy about food** ser [1] muy maniático/maniática para la comida.

future *noun* futuro M; **in future** en el futuro; **in future, ask me first** en el futuro, pregúntame antes; **in the future** en el futuro.

G g

gadget *noun* aparato M.

gain *verb* ganar [17]; **in order to gain time** para ganar tiempo; **to gain weight** ganar [17] peso.

gale *noun* vendaval M.

Galicia *noun* Galicia F.

gallery *noun* **an art gallery** (*public*) un museo de pintura; (*private*) una galería de arte.

game *noun* 1 juego M; **a board game** un juego de mesa; 2 **a game of** una partida de; **a game of cards** una partida de cartas; **to play cards** jugar [27] a las cartas; 3 partido M; **a game of football** un partido de fútbol.

gang *noun* 1 panda F (*of friends*); **all the gang were there** toda la panda estaba allí; 2 banda F (*of criminals*).

gangster *noun* gángster M/F.

gap *noun* 1 (*hole*) hueco M; 2 (*in time*) intervalo M; **a two-year gap** un intervalo de dos años; 3 **an age gap** una diferencia de edad.

garage *noun* garaje M.

garden *noun* jardín M.

gardener *noun* jardinero M, jardinera F; **he's a gardener** es jardinero.

gardening *noun* jardinería F.

garlic *noun* ajo M.

garment *noun* prenda F.

gas *noun* gas M.

gas cooker *noun* cocina F de gas.

gas fire *noun* estufa F de gas.

gas meter *noun* contador M de gas.

gate *noun* 1 (*garden*) verja F; 2 (*field*) portillo M; 3 (*at the airport*) puerta F (de embarque).

gather *verb* 1 (*people*) juntarse [17]; **a crowd gathered** se juntó una multitud; 2 recoger [3] (*fruit, vegetables, flowers*); 3 **as far as I can gather** según tengo entendido.

gay *adjective* gay (*homosexual*).

gear *noun* 1 (*in a car*) marcha F; **to change gear** cambiar [17] de marcha; **in third gear** en tercera; 2 (*equipment*) equipo M; **camping gear** equipo de acampada; 3 **fishing gear** aparejos M (*plural*) de pesca; 4 (*things*) cosas F (*plural*); **I've left all my gear at Gary's** he dejado todas mis cosas en casa de Gary.

gear lever *noun* palanca F de cambio.

gel *noun* gel M; **hair gel** gel para el pelo.

Gemini *noun* géminis M (*plural*); **Steph's Gemini** Steph es géminis.

gender *noun* (*of a word*) género M; **what is the gender of 'casa'?** ¿de qué género es 'casa'?

general *adjective* general; **in general** en general.

general election *noun* elecciones F (*plural*) generales.

general knowledge *noun* cultura F general.

generally *adverb* generalmente.

generation *noun* generación F.

generous *adjective* generoso/ generosa.

genetics *noun* genética F.

genius *noun* genio M; **Lisa, you're a genius!** Lisa, ¡eres un genio!

gentle *adjective* 1 (*person, voice or nature*) dulce; 2 (*breeze, murmur, heat*) suave.

gentleman *noun* caballero M; **ladies and gentlemen** señoras y caballeros.

gently *adverb* 1 (*talk*) dulcemente; 2 (*touch*) suavemente; 3 (*handle*) con cuidado.

gents *noun* servicios M (*plural*) de caballeros; (*marked on the door*) caballeros M (*plural*); **where's the gents?** ¿dónde están los servicios de caballeros?

genuine *adjective* 1 (*real*) auténtico/auténtica; **a genuine diamond** un diamante auténtico; 2 sincero/sincera (*person*); **she's very genuine** es muy sincera.

geography *noun* geografía F.

germ *noun* germen M.

German *noun* 1 alemán M, alemana F; 2 (*language*) alemán M. *adjective* alemán/alemana.

Germany *noun* Alemania F.

get *verb* 1 (*to obtain*) **I got fifteen for my maths exam** saqué un quince en el examen de matemáticas; **where did you get that jacket?** ¿de dónde has sacado esa chaqueta?; 2 (*as a present*) **I got a bike for my birthday** me regalaron una bicicleta por mi cumpleaños; 3 (*a parcel or letter*) recibir [19]; **I got your letter yesterday** recibí tu carta ayer; 4 (*a job*) conseguir [64]; **Fred's got a job** Fred ha conseguido un trabajo; 5 (*fetch*) ir [8] a buscar; **go and get some bread** vete a buscar pan; **I'll get your bag for you** voy a buscar tu bolso; 6 (*to buy*) comprar [17]; **I got a nice shirt in the sales** compré una camisa muy bonita en las rebajas; 7 **to have got** tener [9]; **he's got lots of money** tiene mucho dinero; **she's got long hair** tiene el pelo largo; 8 **to have got to do** tener [9] que hacer; **I've got to phone before midday** tengo que llamar antes del mediodía; 9 **to get to** llegar [28] a; **when we got to London** cuando llegamos a Londres; **to get here/ there** llegar [28]; **we got here this morning** llegamos esta mañana; **what time did they get there?** ¿a qué hora llegaron?; 10 (*become*) **to get tired** cansarse [17]; **she was getting worried** se estaba preocupando; **it's getting late** se está haciendo tarde; **I'm getting hungry** me está entrando hambre; **11 to get your hair cut** cortarse [17] el pelo.

● **to get back** volver [45]; **Mum gets back at six** mamá vuelve a las seis.

● **to get something back: we got the money back** nos devolvieron el dinero; **did you get your books back?** ¿te devolvieron los libros?

● **to get into something** entrar [17] (*a vehicle*); **he got into the car** entró en el coche.

● **to get off something** bajarse [17] de; **I got off the train at Banbury** me bajé del tren en Banbury.

● **to get on: how's Amanda getting on?** ¿cómo le va a Amanda?

● **to get on something** subir [19] a (*vehicle*); **she got on the train at Reading** subió al tren en Reading.

● **to get on with somebody** llevarse [17] bien con alguien; **she doesn't get on with her brother** no se lleva bien con su hermano.

● **to get out of something** salir [63] de (*vehicle*); **Laura got out of the car** Laura salió del coche.

● **to get something out** sacar [31] algo; **Robert got his guitar out** Robert sacó la guitarra.

● **to get together** verse [16]; **we must get together soon** tenemos que vernos pronto.

● **to get up** levantarse [17]; **I get up at seven** me levanto a la siete.

ghost *noun* fantasma M.

gift *noun* **1** regalo M; **a Christmas gift** un regalo de Navidad; **2 to have a gift for something** estar [2] dotado/dotada para; **Jo has a real**

gift for languages Jo está realmente dotada para los idiomas.

gin *noun* ginebra F.

ginger *noun* jengibre M.

giraffe *noun* jirafa F.

girl *noun* **1** niña F; **three boys and four girls** tres niños y cuatro niñas; **a little girl** una niña pequeña; **when I was a little girl** cuando yo era pequeña; **2** (*a teenager or young woman*) chica F; **an eighteen-year-old girl** una chica de dieciocho años.

girlfriend *noun* **1** (*in relationship*) novia F; **Darren's girlfriend** la novia de Darren; **2** (*female friend*) amiga F; **Lizzie and her girlfriends have gone to the cinema** Lizzie y sus amigas han ido al cine.

give *verb* dar [4]; **to give something to somebody** darle [4] algo a alguien; **I'll give you my address** te daré mis señas; **give me the key** dame la llave; **I gave Sandy the books** le di los libros a Sandy; **Yasmin's dad gave her the money** el padre de Yasmin le dio el dinero.

● **to give something away** regalar [17] algo; **she's given away all her books** ha regalado sus libros.

● **to give something back to somebody** devolverle [45] algo a alguien; **I gave her back the keys** le devolví las llaves.

● **to give in** ceder [18]; **she gave in in the end** al final cedió.

● **to give up** rendirse [57]; **I give up!** ¡me rindo!

● **to give up doing** dejar [17] de hacer; **she's given up smoking** ha dejado de fumar.

glad *adjective* **to be glad to** alegrarse [17]; **I'm glad to hear he's better** me alegra saber que está mejor; **I'm glad to be back** me alegro de haber vuelto.

glass *noun* **1** (*for drinking*) vaso M; **a glass of water** un vaso de agua; **2** (*material*) cristal M; **a glass table** una mesa de cristal.

glasses *plural noun* gafas F (*plural*); **to wear glasses** llevar [17] gafas.

global *adjective* global.

global warming *noun* calentamiento M global.

globe *noun* globo M terráqueo.

glove *noun* guante M; **a pair of gloves** un par de guantes.

glue *noun* pegamento M.

go *noun* **1** (*in a game*) **whose go is it?** ¿a quién le toca?; **it's my go** me toca a mí; **2 to have a go at doing** intentar [17] hacer; **I'll have a go at mending it for you** intentaré arreglártelo.
verb **1** ir [8]; **we're going to London tomorrow** mañana vamos a Londres; **Mark's gone to the dentist's** Mark ha ido al dentista; **to go for a walk** ir [8] a dar un paseo; **to go shopping** ir [8] de compras; **2** (*with another verb*) **to go to do** ir [8] a hacer; **I'm going to make some tea** voy a hacer té; **he was going to phone me** él iba a llamarme; **3** (*leave*) irse [8]; **Pauline's already**

gone Pauline ya se ha ido; **we're going on holiday tomorrow** nos vamos de vacaciones mañana; **4** (*a train or plane*) salir [63]; **the train goes at seven** el tren sale a las siete; **5** (*time*) pasar [17]; **the time goes quickly** el tiempo pasa rápido; **6** (*an event*) ir [8]; **did the party go well?** ¿qué tal fue la fiesta?; **7** (*a pain*) pasarse [17]; **my headache's gone** se me ha pasado el dolor de cabeza.

● **to go away** irse [8]; **go away!** ¡vete!

● **to go back** volver [45]; **I'm going back to Madrid in March** vuelvo a Madrid en marzo; **I'm not going back there again!** ¡no voy a volver nunca!; **I went back home** volví a casa.

● **to go down 1** bajar [17]; **she's gone down to the kitchen** ha bajado a la cocina; **to go down the stairs** bajar las escaleras; **prices have gone down** los precios han bajado; **2** (*tyre, balloon, airbed*) desinflarse [17].

● **to go in** entrar [17]; **he went in and shut the door** entró y cerró la puerta.

● **to go into** entrar [17]; **Fran went into the kitchen** Fran entró en la cocina; **this file won't go into my bag** esta carpeta no entra en mi bolsa.

● **to go off 1** (*bomb*) estallar [17]; **2** (*alarm clock*) sonar [24]; **my alarm clock went off at six** mi despertador sonó a las seis; **3** (*fire or burglar alarm*) dispararse [17]; **the fire alarm went off** la alarma contra incendios se disparó.

● **to go on 1** pasar [17]; **what's going on?** ¿qué pasa?; **2 to go on doing** seguir [64] haciendo; **she went on talking** siguió hablando; **3 to go on about something** hablar [17] de algo;

he's always going on about his dog
siempre está hablando de su perro.

● **to go out 1** salir [63]; **I'm going out
tonight** voy a salir esta noche; **she
went out of the kitchen** salió de la
cocina; **2 to be going out with
somebody** salir [63] con alguien;
she's going out with my brother
está saliendo con mi hermano;
3 (*light, fire*) apagarse [28]; **the light
went out** la luz se apagó.

● **to go past something** pasar [17] por
algo; **we went past your house**
pasamos por tu casa.

● **to go round: to go round to
somebody's house** ir [8] a casa de
alguien; **I went round to Fred's last
night** anoche fuimos a casa de Fred.

● **to go round something 1** recorrer
[18] (*building, park, garden*);
2 visitar [17] (*museum, monument*).

● **to go through** pasar [17] por; **the
train went through York** el tren pasó
por York; **you can go through my
office** puedes pasar por mi oficina.

● **to go up** subir [19]; **she's gone up to
her room** ha subido a su habitación;
to go up the stairs subir las
escaleras; **the price of petrol has
gone up** el precio de la gasolina ha
subido.

goal *noun* gol M; **to score a goal**
marcar un gol.

goalkeeper *noun* portero M,
portera F.

goat *noun* cabra F; **goat's cheese**
queso M de cabra.

god *noun* dios M.

God *noun* Dios M; **to believe in God**
creer en Dios.

godchild *noun* ahijado M, ahijada F.

goddaughter *noun* ahijada F.

goddess *noun* diosa F.

godfather *noun* padrino M.

godmother *noun* madrina F.

godparent *noun* padrino M,
madrina F; **my godparents** mis
padrinos.

godson *noun* ahijado M.

goggles *plural noun* **swimming
goggles** gafas F (*plural*) de
natación; **skiing goggles** gafas F
(*plural*) de esquí.

go-karting *noun* karting M; **to go
go-karting** hacer karting.

gold *noun* oro M; **a gold bracelet** una
pulsera de oro.

goldfish *noun* pececito M (rojo).

golf *noun* golf M; **to play golf** jugar
[31] al golf.

golf club *noun* **1** (*place*) club M de
golf; **2** (*iron*) palo M de golf.

golf course *noun* campo M de golf.

good *noun* **to do somebody good**
irle [15] bien a alguien; **it will do you
good** te irá bien.
adjective **1** bueno/buena; (*'bueno'
becomes 'buen' before a masculine
singular noun*) **she's a good teacher**
es una buena profesora; **a good deal**
un buen negocio; **be good !** ¡sé
bueno !; **to feel good** sentirse [14]
bien; **2 to be good for you** ser [1]
bueno para la salud; **tomatoes are
good for you** los tomates son muy

buenos para la salud; **3 she's good at art** se la da bien el arte; **I'm good at cooking** se me da bien cocinar; **4** (*kind*) amable; **she's been very good to me** ha sido muy amable conmigo; **5** bien; **it smelled good** olía bien; **it tastes good** sabe bien; **his Spanish is very good** habla español muy bien; **good!** (*well done*) ¡muy bien!; **6 for good** para siempre; **I've stopped smoking for good** he dejado de fumar para siempre.

good afternoon *exclamation* buenas tardes.

goodbye *exclamation* adiós.

good evening *exclamation* **1** (*up to eight or nine*) buenas tardes; **2** (*from nine onwards*) buenas noches.

Good Friday *noun* Viernes M Santo.

good-looking *adjective* atractivo/ atractiva; **Maya's boyfriend's really good-looking** el novio de Maya es muy atractivo.

good morning *exclamation* buenos días.

goodness *exclamation* ¡Dios mío!; **for goodness sake!** ¡por Dios!

goodnight *exclamation* buenas noches.

goods *plural noun* artículos M (*plural*).

goods train *noun* tren M de mercancías.

goose *noun* ganso M.

goose pimples *noun* carne F de gallina.

gorgeous *adjective* precioso/ preciosa; **a gorgeous dress** un vestido precioso; **it's a gorgeous day** un día precioso.

gorilla *noun* gorila M.

gosh *exclamation* ¡Dios mío!

gossip *noun* **1** (*person*) cotilla M/ F; **2** (*news*) cotilleo M; **what's the latest gossip?** ¿qué hay de nuevo? *verb* cotillear [17].

government *noun* gobierno M.

grab *verb* **1** agarrar [17]; **she grabbed my arm** me agarró el brazo; **2 to grab something from somebody** arrebatarle [17] algo a alguien; **he grabbed the book from me** me arrebató el libro.

graceful *adjective* elegante.

grade *noun* (*mark*) notas F (*plural*); **to get good grades** sacar [31] buenas notas.

gradual *adjective* gradual.

gradually *adverb* poco a poco; **the weather got gradually better** el tiempo mejoró poco a poco.

graffiti *plural noun* grafitti M (*plural*).

grain *noun* grano M.

grammar *noun* gramática F.

grammar school *noun* colegio M.

grammatical *adjective* gramatical; **a grammatical error** un error gramatical.

gramme *noun* gramo M.

gran *noun* abuelita F.

grandchildren *plural noun* nietos M (*plural*).

granddad *noun* abuelito (*informal*) M.

granddaughter *noun* nieta F.

grandfather *noun* abuelo M.

grandma *noun* abuelita (*informal*) F.

grandmother *noun* abuela F.

grandpa *noun* abuelito (*informal*) M.

grandparents *plural noun* abuelos M (*plural*).

grandson *noun* nieto M (*plural*).

granny *noun* abuelita (*informal*) F.

grape *noun* a grape una uva; to buy some grapes comprar uvas; a bunch of grapes un racimo de uvas.

grapefruit *noun* pomelo M.

graph *noun* gráfico M.

grass *noun* 1 hierba F; he was sitting on the grass estaba sentado en la hierba; 2 (*lawn*) césped M; to cut the grass cortar [17] el césped.

grasshopper *noun* saltamontes M (*plural* saltamontes).

grate *verb* rallar [17]; grated cheese queso rallado.

grateful *adjective* agradecido/ agradecida.

grater *noun* rallador M.

grave *noun* tumba F.

gravel *noun* grava F.

graveyard *noun* cementerio M.

gravy *noun* salsa F del asado.

grease *noun* grasa F.

greasy *adjective* 1 (*hands or surface*) grasiento/grasienta; 2 (*hair, skin or food*) graso/grasa; to have greasy skin tener [9] la piel grasa; I hate greasy food no soporto la comida grasa.

great *adjective* 1 gran (*plural* grandes); a great poet un gran poeta; a great opportunity una gran oportunidad; great expectations grandes esperanzas; 2 (*terrific*) estupendo/estupenda; it was a great party! ¡fue una fiesta estupenda!; great! ¡estupendo!; 3 a great deal of un montón de; a great many muchos/muchas; there are a great many things still to be done aún quedan muchas cosas por hacer.

Great Britain *noun* Gran Bretaña F.

Greece *noun* Grecia F.

greedy *adjective* (*with food*) glotón/ glotona.

Greek *noun* 1 (*person*) griego M, griega F; 2 (*language*) griego M. *adjective* griego/griega.

green *noun* 1 (*colour*) verde M; a pale green un verde pálido; 2 greens (*vegetables*) verduras F (*plural*); 3 the Greens (*ecologists*) los verdes (*informal*).

adjective **1** verde; **a green door** una puerta verde; **2** ecologista; **the Green Party** el partido ecologista.

greengrocer *noun* verdulero M, verdulera F; **the greengrocer's** la verdulería.

greenhouse *noun* invernadero M.

greenhouse effect *noun* efecto M invernadero.

greetings *plural noun* **Season's Greetings** Feliz Navidad.

greetings card *noun* tarjeta F de felicitación.

grey *adjective* **1** gris; **a grey skirt** una falda gris; **2** (*hair*) canoso/canosa; **to have grey hair** tener el pelo canoso.

greyhound *noun* galgo M.

grid *noun* **1** (*grating*) parrilla F; **2** (*network*) red F.

grief *noun* dolor M.

grill *noun* (*of a cooker*) grill M.
verb **to grill something** hacer [7] algo al grill; **I grilled the sausages** hice las salchichas al grill.

grin *noun* sonrisa F.
verb sonreír [61].

grip *verb* agarrar [17].

grit *noun* (*for roads*) arenilla F.

groan *noun* **1** (*of pain*) gemido M; **2** (*of disgust, boredom*) gruñido M.
verb **1** (*in pain*) gemir [57]; **2** (*in disgust, boredom*) refunfuñar [17].

grocer *noun* tendero M, tendera F; **my dad's a grocer** mi padre es tendero.

groceries *plural noun* cosas F (*plural*) de comer; **to buy some groceries** comprar [17] cosas de comer.

grocer's *noun* tienda F de comestibles.

groom *noun* (*bridegroom*) novio M.

gross *adjective* **1 a gross injustice** una flagrante injustica; **2 a gross error** un grave error; **3** (*disgusting*) repugnante; **the food was gross!** ¡la comida era repugnante!

ground *noun* **1** suelo M; **to sit on the ground** sentarse [29] en el suelo; **to throw something on the ground** tirar [17] algo al suelo; **2** (*for sport*) campo M; **a football ground** un campo de fútbol.
adjective molido/molida; **ground coffee** café M molido.

ground floor *noun* planta F baja; **they live on the ground floor** viven en la planta baja.

group *noun* grupo M.

grow *verb* **1** (*plant, hair or person*) crecer [35]; **you hair's grown!** te ha crecido el pelo; **my little sister's grown a lot this year** mi hermana pequeña ha crecido mucho este año; **2** cultivar [17] (*fruit, vegetables*); **our neighbours grow strawberries** nuestros vecinos cultivan fresas; **3 to grow a beard** dejarse [17] barba; **4 to grow old** envejecer [35].

- **to grow up** crecer [35]; **the children are growing up** los niños están creciendo; **she grew up in Scotland** creció en Escocia.

growl *verb* gruñir [65].

grown-up *noun* adulto M, adulta F.

growth *noun* crecimiento M.

grudge *noun* **to bear a grudge against somebody** guardarle [17] rencor a alguien; **she bears me a grudge** me guarda rencor.

gruesome *adjective* horrible.

grumble *verb* refunfuñar [17]; **she's always grumbling** siempre está refunfuñando; **to grumble about something** refunfuñar por algo.

guarantee *noun* garantía F; **a year's guarantee** una garantía de un año.
verb garantizar [22].

guard *noun* **1 a prison guard** un guardia de prisiones; **2** (*on a train*) jefe M de tren; jefa F de tren; **3 a security guard** un guardia de seguridad.
verb vigilar [17].

guard dog *noun* perro M guardián.

guess *noun* **have a guess!** ¡adivina!; **it's a good guess** lo has adivinado.
verb **1** adivinar [17]; **guess who I saw last night!** ¡adivina a quién vi anoche!; **you'll never guess!** ¡no lo vas a adivinar nunca!; **guess what!** ¿sabes qué?; **2** (*suppose*) suponer [11]; **I guess so** supongo que sí.

guest *noun* **1** invitado M, invitada F; **we've got guests coming tonight** tenemos invitados esta noche; **2** (*in a hotel*) cliente M/F; **3 a paying guest** un huésped de pago.

guide *noun* **1** (*book, girl guide*) guía F; **2** (*person*) guía M/F.

guidebook *noun* guía F.

guide dog *noun* perro M lazarillo.

guideline *noun* pauta F.

guilty *adjective* culpable; **to feel guilty** sentirse [14] culpable.

guinea pig *noun* (*pet*) cobaya F; (*in an experiment*) conejillo M de indias.

guitar *noun* guitarra F; **to play the guitar** tocar [31] la guitarra; **on the guitar** a la guitarra.

gum *noun* **1** (*in mouth*) encía F; **2** (*chewing gum*) chicle M.

gun *noun* **1** pistola F; **2** (*rifle*) fusil M.

guy *noun* tipo M (*informal*); **he's a nice guy** es un tipo muy majo; **a guy from Newcastle** un tipo de Newcastle.

gym *noun* **1** (*gymnasium*) gimnasio M; **to go to the gym** ir [8] al gimnasio; **2** (*gymnastics*) gimnasia F.

gymnasium *noun* gimnasio M.

gymnast *noun* gimnasta M/F.

gymnastics *noun* gimnasia F.

gym shoe *noun* zapatilla F de gimnasia.

H h

habit *noun* costumbre F; **to have a habit of doing** tener [9] la costumbre de hacer; **it's a bad habit** es una mala costumbre.

hail *noun* granizo M.

hailstone *noun* granizo M.

hailstorm *noun* granizada F.

hair *noun* 1 pelo M; **to have short hair** tener [9] el pelo corto; **to brush your hair** cepillarse [17] el pelo; **to wash your hair** lavarse [17] el pelo; **to have your hair cut** cortarse [17] el pelo; **she's had her hair cut** se ha cortado el pelo; 2 **a hair** (*from the head*) un pelo; (*from the body*) un vello.

hairbrush *noun* cepillo M del pelo.

haircut *noun* 1 corte M de pelo; **I like your new haircut** me gusta tu nuevo corte de pelo; 2 **to have a haircut** cortarse [17] el pelo.

hairdresser *noun* peluquero M, peluquera F; **she's a hairdresser** es peluquera; **at the hairdresser's** en la peluquería.

hair drier *noun* secador M de pelo.

hair gel *noun* gel M para el cabello.

hairslide *noun* pasador M.

hairspray *noun* laca F del pelo.

hairstyle *noun* peinado M.

hairy *adjective* peludo/peluda.

half *noun*, *pronoun* 1 mitad F; **half of** la mitad de; **I gave him half of the money** le di la mitad del dinero; 2 **to cut something in half** cortar algo por la mitad; 3 (*as a fraction*) medio; **three and a half** tres y medio; **she's five and a half** tiene seis años y medio; 4 (*in time*) media; **half an hour** media hora; **an hour and a half** una hora y media; **it's half past three** son las tres y media; 5 **half a** medio/media; **half a litre** medio litro; **half an apple** media manzana; 6 **half the people** la mitad de la gente; **half the time he's not here** la mitad del tiempo no está aquí.

half hour *noun* media hora F; **every half hour** cada media hora.

half price *adjective*, *adverb* a mitad de precio; **half-price CDs** compactos a mitad de precio; **I bought it half price** lo compré a mitad de precio.

half-time *noun* descanso M; **at half-time** en el descanso.

halfway *adverb* 1 a mitad de camino; **halfway between Madrid and Barcelona** a mitad de camino entre Madrid y Barcelona; 2 **to be halfway through** ir [8] por la mitad de; **I'm halfway through my homework** voy por la mitad de los deberes.

hall *noun* 1 (*in a house*) entrada F; 2 (*public*) salón M; **the village hall** el salón de actos del pueblo; 3 **a concert hall** una sala de conciertos.

ham *noun* 1 (*cooked*) jamón M de York; 2 (*cured*) jamón M serrano.

hamburger *noun* hamburguesa F.

hammer *noun* martillo M.

hamster *noun* hámster M.

hand *noun* 1 mano F; **to have something in your hand** tener [9] algo en la mano; **to be holding hands** (*two people*) ir [8] cogidos de la mano; **they were holding hands** iban cogidos de la mano; 2 **to give somebody a hand** echar [17] una mano a alguien; **can you give me a hand to move the table?** ¿puedes echarme una mano para mover la mesa?; **do you need a hand?** ¿necesitas que te echen una mano?; 3 **on the other hand** … por otro lado …; 4 (*of a watch or clock*) manecilla F; **the hour hand** la manecilla de las horas.
verb **to hand something to somebody** pasarle [17] algo a alguien; **I handed him the keys** le pasé las llaves.

handbag *noun* bolso M.

handbrake *noun* freno M de mano.

handcuffs *plural noun* esposas F (*plural*).

handful *noun* **a handful of** un puñado de.

handkerchief *noun* pañuelo M.

handicapped *adjective* disminuido/disminuida.

handle *noun* 1 (*of a door*) picaporte M; 2 (*of a drawer*) tirador M; 3 (*on a cup or basket*) asa F; 4 (*of a knife, tool, or pan*) mango M.

verb 1 encargarse [28] de; **Gina handles the accounts** Gina se encarga de la contabilidad; 2 **she's good at handling people** se le da muy bien tratar con la gente.

handlebars *plural noun* manillar M.

hand luggage *noun* equipaje M de mano.

handsome *adjective* guapo; **he's a very handsome guy** es un tipo muy guapo.

handwriting *noun* letra F.

handy *adjective* 1 práctico/práctica; **this little knife's very handy** este cuchillito es muy práctico; 2 a mano; **I always keep a notebook handy** siempre guardo un cuaderno a mano.

hang *verb* colgar [23]; **we hung the mirror on the wall** colgamos el espejo en la pared; **there was a mirror hanging on the wall** había un espejo colgado en la pared.
● **to hang on** esperar [17]; **hang on a second!** ¡espera un poco!
● **to hang up** (*on the phone*) colgar [23]; **she hung up on me** me colgó.
● **to hang something up** colgar [23] algo; **you can hang your coat up in the hall** puedes colgar el abrigo en la entrada.

hangover *noun* resaca F; **to have a hangover** tener [9] resaca.

happen *verb* 1 pasar [17]; **what's happening?** ¿qué pasa?; **what happened to him?** ¿qué le pasó?; **it happened in June** pasó en junio; 2 **what's happened to the can-**

opener? ¿dónde se ha metido el abridor?; **3 if you happen to see Jill** si ves a Jill.

happily *adverb* **1** alegremente; **she smiled happily** sonrió alegremente; **2** (*willingly*) con mucho gusto; **I'll happily do it for you** lo haré por ti con mucho gusto.

happiness *noun* felicidad F.

happy *adjective* feliz; **a happy child** un niño feliz; **Happy Birthday!** ¡feliz cumpleaños!

harbour *noun* puerto M.

hard *adjective* **1** duro/dura; **2** (*difficult*) difícil; **a hard question** una pregunta difícil; **it's hard to know** … es difícil saber …
adverb **1 to work hard** trabajar [17] duro; **to study hard** estudiar [17] mucho; **2 to try hard** esforzarse [26] mucho.

hard disk *noun* (*in a computer*) disco M duro.

hardly *adverb* **1** apenas; **I can hardly hear him** apenas puedo oírle; **2 hardly any** casi nada; **there's hardly any milk** casi no hay nada de leche; **3 hardly ever** casi nunca; **I hardly ever see them** casi nunca los veo; **4 there was hardly anybody** no había casi nadie.

hard up *adjective* **to be hard up** estar [2] mal de dinero (*informal*).

harm *noun* **it won't do you any harm** no te va a pasar nada.
verb **to harm somebody** hacerle [7] daño a alguien; **a cup of coffee won't harm you** una taza de café no te va a hacer daño.

hat *noun* sombrero M.

hate *verb* odiar [17]; **I hate geography** odio la geografía.

hatred *noun* odio M.

have *verb* **1** tener [9]; **Anna has three brothers** Anna tiene tres hermanos; **how many sisters do you have?** ¿cuántas hermanas tienes?; **2 to have got** tener [9]; **we've got a dog** tenemos un perro; **what have you got in your hand?** ¿qué tienes en la mano?; **3** (*to form past tenses, verbs in Spanish take 'haber'*) **I've finished** he terminado; **have you seen the film?** ¿has visto la película?; **Rosie hasn't arrived yet** Rosie aún no ha llegado; **he had left** se había ido; (*in question tags "have" is not translated*) **you've done this before, haven't you?** tú has hecho esto antes ¿no?; **4 to have to do** tener [9] que hacer; **I have to phone my mum** tengo que llamar a mi madre; **5** tomar [17] (*food or drink*); **we had a coffee** tomamos un café; **what will you have?** ¿qué vais a tomar?; **I'll have an omelette** voy a tomar una tortilla; **6 to have a shower** ducharse [17]; **to have a bath** bañarse [17]; **7 to have lunch** comer [18]; **to have dinner** (*in the evening*) cenar [17]; **8 to have a party** dar [4] una fiesta; **9** (*for illnesses*) tener [9]; **he has cancer** tiene cáncer; **I had flu** tuve la gripe; **10** (*for aches*) **she has stomachache** le duele el estómago; **I had a terrible headache** me dolía mucho la cabeza; **11 I'm**

going to have my hair cut voy a cortarme el pelo; **she's had her TV repaired** ha arreglado la tele.

hay *noun* heno M.

hay fever *noun* fiebre F del heno.

hazelnut *noun* avellana F.

he *pronoun* 1 (*'he', like other subject pronouns, is generally not translated; in Spanish the form of the verb tells you whether the subject of the verb is 'he/she/it, you', they', etc., so' he' is only translated when you want to emphasize it*) **he lives in Newcastle** vive en Newcastle; **he's a student** es estudiante; **he's a very good teacher** es muy buen profesor; **here he is !** ¡aquí está!; 2 (*for emphasis*) él; **he did it** lo hizo él.

head *noun* 1 cabeza F; **he had a cap on his head** tenía un sombrero en la cabeza; **at the head of the queue** a la cabeza de la cola; 2 (*of school*) director M, directora F; 3 (*when tossing a coin*) **'heads or tails?' – 'heads'** ¿cara o cruz? – 'cara'.
● **to head for something** dirigirse [49] a; **Liz headed for the door** Liz se dirigió a la puerta.

headache *noun* **I've got a headache** me duele la cabeza.

headlight *noun* faro M.

headline *noun* titular M; **to hit the headlines** aparecer [35] en los titulares.

headmaster *noun* director M.

headmistress *noun* directora F.

headphones *plural noun* auriculares M (*plural*).

headteacher *noun* director M, directora F.

health *noun* salud F.

health centre *noun* centro M médico.

healthy *adjective* 1 (*person*) **to be healthy** estar [2] sano; 2 **a healthy diet** una dieta sana.

heap *noun* montón M; **I've got heaps of things to do** tengo montones de cosas que hacer.

hear *verb* oír [56]; **I can't hear you** no te oigo; **I can't hear anything** no oigo nada; **I hear you've bought a dog** he oído que te has comprado un perro.
● **to hear about something** enterarse [17] de algo; **have you heard about the concert?** ¿te has enterado de lo del concierto?
● **to hear from somebody: have you heard from Amanda?** ¿sabes algo de Amanda?; **I haven't heard from them** no sé nada de ellos.

heart *noun* 1 corazón M; 2 (*in cards*) corazones M (*plural*); **the jack of hearts** la jota de corazones; ★ **to learn something by heart** aprender [18] algo de memoria;

heart attack *noun* ataque M al corazón.

heat *noun* calor M.
verb 1 calentarse [29]; **the soup's**

heating la sopa se está calentando; **2 to heat something** calentar [29] algo; **I'll go and heat the soup** voy a calentar la sopa.

heater *noun* estufa F.

heating *noun* calefacción F.

heaven *noun* cielo M.

heavy *adjective* **1** pesado/pesada; **a heavy bag** una bolsa pesada; **to be heavy** pesar [17] mucho; **my rucksack's really heavy** mi mochila pesa mucho; **2** (*busy*) ocupado/ ocupada; **I've got a heavy day tomorrow** mañana tengo un día muy ocupado; **3 heavy rain** lluvia fuerte.

hectic *adjective* **a hectic day** un día muy ajetreado.

hedge *noun* seto M.

hedgehog *noun* erizo M.

heel *noun* **1** (*of foot*) talón M; **2** (*of shoe*) tacón M.

height *noun* **1** (*of a person*) estatura F; **2** (*of a building*) altura F; **3** (*of a mountain*) altitud F.

helicopter *noun* helicóptero M.

hell *noun* infierno M; **it's hell here!** ¡esto es un infierno!

hello *exclamation* **1** (*greeting*) hola; **2** (*on the telephone*) ¿diga?

helmet *noun* casco M.

help *noun* ayuda F; **do you need any help?** ¿necesitas ayuda? *verb* **1** ayudar [17]; **to help somebody to do** ayudar [17] a alguien a hacer; **can you help me**

move the table? ¿me ayudas a mover la mesa?; **2 to help yourself to something** servirse [57] algo; **help yourselves to vegetables** serviros verdura; **help yourself!** ¡sírvete!; **3 help!** ¡socorro!

hem *noun* dobladillo M.

hen *noun* gallina F.

her *pronoun* **1** la; **I know her** la conozco; **I saw her last week** la vi la semana pasada; (*with a infinitive or when telling someone to do something, 'la' joins onto the verb*) **I can hear her** puedo oírla; **listen to her!** ¡escúchala!; (*but when telling someone NOT to do something, 'la' comes before the verb*) **don't push her!** ¡no la empujes!; **2** (*to her*) le; **I gave her my address** le di mis señas; (*'le' becomes 'se' before pronouns 'lo' or 'la'*) **I lent it to her** se lo dejé; **3** (*after a preposition, in comparisons, or after the verb 'to be'*) ella; **with her** con ella; **without her** sin ella; **he's older than her** él es mayor que ella; **it was her** era ella. *adjective* **1** (*before a singular noun*) su; **her brother** su hermano; **her house** su casa; **2** (*before a plural noun*) sus; **her children** sus niños; **3** (*with parts of the body*) el, la, los, las; **she had a glass in her hand** tenía un vaso en la mano; **she's washing her hands** se está lavando las manos.

herb *noun* hierba F.

here *adverb* **1** aquí; **not far from here** no lejos de aquí; **and here they are!** ¡aquí están!; **Tom isn't here at the moment** Tom no está aquí en este momento; **2** (*giving something*) **here it is** toma; **here's my address** toma mis señas; **here you are** toma.

hero *noun* héroe M.

heroin *noun* heroína F.

heroine *noun* heroína F.

hers *pronoun* **1** (*referring to a singular noun*) el suyo/la suya; **I took my hat and she took hers** yo cogí mi sombrero y ella cogió el suyo; **I phoned my mum and Donna phoned hers** llamé a mi madre y Donna llamó a la suya; **2** (*referring to a plural noun*) los suyos/las suyas; **I've invited my parents and Karen's invited hers** yo he invitado a mis padres y Karen a los suyos; **I showed her my photos and she showed me hers** yo le enseñé mis fotos y ella me enseñó las suyas.

herself *pronoun* **1** (*as reflexive*) se; **she's hurt herself** se ha hecho daño; **she washed herself** se lavó; **2** (*for emphasis*) ella misma; **she said it herself** lo dijo ella misma; **3 she did it by herself** lo hizo ella sola.

hesitate *verb* dudar [17]; **to hesitate to do** dudar en hacer.

heterosexual *noun* heterosexual M/F.

hi *exclamation* hola.

hiccups *plural noun* **to have the hiccups** tener [9] hipo.

hidden *adjective* escondido/ escondida.

hide *verb* **1** (*person*) esconderse [18]; **she hid behind the door** se escondió

detrás de la puerta; **2 to hide something** esconder [18] algo; **who's hidden the chocolate?** ¿quién ha escondido el chocolate?

hide-and-seek *noun* **to play hide-and-seek** jugar [27] al escondite.

hi-fi *noun* equipo M de alta fidelidad.

high *adjective* **1** alto/alta; **on a high shelf** en una estantería alta; **the wall is very high** la pared es muy alta; **how high is the wall?** ¿qué altura tiene la pared?; **the wall is two metres high** la pared tiene dos metros de altura; **2** (*number, price, temperature*) alto/ alta; **food prices are very high** el precio de la comida es muy alto; **3 at high speed** a alta velocidad; **4 high winds** vientos fuertes.

high-heeled *adjective* de tacón alto; **high-heeled shoes** zapatos de tacón alto.

high jump *noun* salto M de altura.

hilarious *adjective* divertidísimo/ divertidísima.

hill *noun* **1** (*low*) colina F; (*higher*) montaña F; **2** (*sloping street or road*) **to go up the hill** subir la cuesta.

him *pronoun* **1** lo; **I know him** lo conozco; **I saw him last week** lo vi la semana pasada; (*with an infinitive or when telling someone to do something, 'lo' joins onto the verb*) **I can't hear him** no puedo oírlo; **listen to him!** ¡escúchalo!; (*but when telling someone NOT to do something, 'lo' comes before the verb*) **don't push him!** ¡no lo empujes!; **2** (*to him*) le; **I gave him my address**

le di mis señas; (*'le' becomes 'se' before pronouns 'lo' or 'la'*) **I lent it to him** se lo dejé; **3** (*after a preposition, in comparisons, or after the verb 'to be'*) él; **with him** con él; **without him** sin él; **she's older than him** ella es mayor que él; **it was him** era él.

himself *pronoun* **1** (*as a reflexive*) se; **he's hurt himself** se hizo daño; **2** (*for emphasis*) él mismo; **he said it himself** lo dijo él mismo; **3** **he did it by himself** lo hizo él solo.

hip *noun* cadera F.

hire *noun* alquiler M; **car hire** alquiler de coches; **for hire** se alquila. *verb* alquilar [17]; **we're going to hire a car** vamos a alquilar un coche.

his *adjective* **1** (*before a singular noun*) su; **his brother** su hermano; **his house** su casa; **2** (*before a plural noun*) sus; **his children** sus niños; **3** (*with parts of the body*) el, la, los, las; **he had a glass in his hand** tenía un vaso en la mano; **he's washing his hands** se está lavando las manos. *pronoun* **1** (*referring to a singular noun*) el suyo/la suya; **I took my hat and he took his** yo cogí mi sombrero y él cogió el suyo; **I phoned my mum and Danny phoned his** llamé a mi madre y Danny llamó a la suya; **2** (*referring to a plural noun*) los suyos/las suyas; **I've invited my parents and Steve's invited his** yo he invitado a mis padres y Steve a los suyos; **I showed him my photos and he showed me his** yo le enseñé mis fotos y él me enseño las suyas.

history *noun* historia F.

hit *noun* (*song*) éxito M; **their latest hit** su último éxito; **the film is a huge hit** la película es un gran éxito. *verb* **1** golpear [17]; **to hit the ball** golpear la pelota; **2** **to hit your head on something** darse [4] un golpe en la cabeza con algo; **3** chocar [31] con; **the car hit a tree** el coche chocó con el árbol; **4** **she was hit by a car** la atropelló un coche.

hitch *noun* problema M; **there's been a slight hitch** ha habido un pequeño problema. *verb* **to hitch a lift** hacer [7] dedo (*informal*).

hitchhike *verb* hacer [7] dedo (*informal*); **we hitchhiked to Valencia** hicimos dedo hasta Valencia.

hitchhiker *noun* autoestopista M/F.

HIV-negative *adjective* seronegativo/seronegativa.

HIV-positive *adjective* seropositivo/seropositiva.

hobby *noun* pasatiempo M.

hockey *noun* hockey M; **to play hockey** jugar al hockey.

hockey stick *noun* palo M de hockey.

hold *verb* **1** sostener [9]; **to hold something in your hand** sostener algo en la mano; **can you hold the torch?** ¿puedes sostener la linterna?; **2** (*contain*) contener [9]; **a jug which holds a litre** una jarra que contiene un litro; **3** **to hold a**

meeting celebrar [17] una reunión;
4 can you hold the line, please no
se retire, por favor; **5 hold
on**! (*wait*) ¡un momento!; (*on
telephone*) ¡no cuelgues!

● **to hold somebody up** (*delay*)
entretener [9] a alguien; **I don't want
to hold you up** no quiero
entretenerte; **I was held up at the
dentist's** me entretuve en el dentista.

● **to hold something up** (*raise*)
levantar [17]; **he held up his glass**
levantó su vaso.

hold-up noun 1 retraso M; 2 (*traffic
jam*) atasco M; 3 (*robbery*)
atraco M.

hole noun agujero M.

holiday noun 1 vacaciones F
(*plural*); **where are you going for
your holiday?** ¿dónde vas de
vacaciones?; **have a good holiday**!
¡que pases unas buenas vacaciones!;
to be away on holiday estar de
vacaciones; **to go on holiday** irse de
vacaciones; **the school holidays** las
vacaciones escolares; **2 a public
holiday** un día de fiesta; **Monday's a
holiday** el lunes es fiesta.

Holland noun Holanda F.

hollow adjective hueco/hueca.

holy adjective santo/santa.

home noun casa F; **I was at home**
estaba en casa; **to stay at home**
quedarse [17] en casa; **make yourself
at home** ponte cómodo.
adverb a casa; **Susie's gone home**
Susie se ha ido a casa; **I'll call in and
see you on my way home** te iré a

visitar de camino a mi casa; **to get
home** llegar [28] a casa; **we got home
at midnight** llegamos a casa a media
noche.

homeless adjective sin hogar; **the
homeless** la gente sin hogar.

homemade adjective casero/
casera; **homemade cakes** pasteles
caseros.

home match noun **to play a home
match** jugar [27] en casa.

homeopathic adjective
homeopático/homeopática.

homesick adjective **to be homesick**
tener [9] morriña.

homework noun deberes M
(*plural*); **I did my homework** hice
mis deberes; **my Spanish homework**
mis deberes de español.

homosexual noun, adjective
homosexual.

Honduras noun Honduras F.

honest adjective 1 honrado/
honrada; 2 **to be honest** … para
serte sincero …

honestly adverb sinceramente.

honesty noun honradez F.

honey noun miel F.

honeymoon noun luna F de miel.

honour noun honor M.

hood noun capucha F.

hook noun 1 (*in clothes*)
corchete M; 2 (*for fishing*)
anzuelo M; 3 (*for hanging pictures or
clothes*) gancho M; **4 to take the**

phone of the hook descolgar [23] el teléfono.

hooligan *noun* gamberro M, gamberra F.

hooray *exclamation* ¡hurra!

hoover *verb* pasar [17] la aspiradora por; **I hoovered my bedroom** pasé la aspiradora por mi habitación.

Hoover™ *noun* aspirador M, aspiradora F.

hope *noun* esperanza F; **to give up hope** perder [36] la esperanza. *verb* esperar [17]; **hoping to see you on Friday** esperando verte el domingo; **here's hoping!** ¡esperemos!; **I hope so** espero que sí; **I hope not** espero que no; **we hope you'll be able to come** esperamos que puedas venir; (*'espero que' is followed by the subjunctive*)

hopeless *adjective* **to be hopeless at something** ser [1] un negado para algo (*informal*); **I'm hopeless at geography** soy un negado para la geografía.

horn *noun* **1** (*of an animal*) cuerno M; **2** (*of a car*) bocina F; **to sound your horn** tocar [31] la bocina; **3** (*musical instrument*) trompa F; **to play the horn** tocar [31] trompa.

horoscope *noun* horóscopo M.

horrible *adjective* **1** horrible; **the weather was horrible** el tiempo era horrible; **she's really horrible!** ¡es realmente horrible!; **2 he was really horrible to me** me trató muy mal.

horror *noun* horror M.

horror film *noun* película F de terror.

horse *noun* caballo M.

hose *noun* manguera F.

hospital *noun* hospital M; **to be in hospital** estar [2] en el hospital; **to be taken into hospital** ser [1] hospitalizado.

hospitality *noun* hospitalidad F.

hostage *noun* rehén M.

hostel *noun* **youth hostel** albergue M juvenil.

hostess *noun* azafata F; **an air hostess** una azafata de vuelo.

hot *adjective* **1** caliente; **a hot drink** una bebida caliente; **be careful, the plates are hot!** ¡cuidado! los platos están calientes; **2** (*a person*) **to be hot** tener [9] calor; **I'm hot** tengo calor; **I'm very hot** tengo mucho calor; **I'm too hot** tengo demasiado calor; **3** (*the weather or temperature in a room*) **it's hot** hace calor; **it's hot today** hace calor hoy; **it's very hot in the kitchen** hace mucho calor en la cocina; **4 a hot climate** un clima cálido; **5** (*food: spicy*) picante; **the curry's too hot for me** el curry es demasiado picante para mí.

hot dog *noun* perrito M caliente.

hotel *noun* hotel M.

hour *noun* hora F; **two hours later** dos horas más tarde; **we waited for two hours** esperamos dos horas; **two hours ago** hace dos horas; **to be**

paid by the hour cobrar [17] por hora; **I earn six pounds an hour** gano seis libras por hora; **every hour** cada hora; **half an hour** media hora; **a quarter of an hour** un cuarto de hora; **an hour and a half** una hora y media.

house *noun* casa F; **I'm at Judy's house** estoy en casa de Judy; **I'm going to Judy's house tonight** voy a casa de Judy esta noche; **I phoned from Judy's house** llamé desde casa de Judy.

housework *noun* tareas F (*plural*) de la casa; **to do the housework** hacer [7] las tareas de la casa.

hovercraft *noun* aerodeslizador M.

how *adverb* **1** cómo; **how did you do it?** ¿cómo lo hiciste?; **how are you?** ¿cómo estás?; **I know how to do it** sé cómo hacerlo; **2 how was the party?** ¿qué tal fue la fiesta?; **3 how much?** ¿cuánto?; **how much money do you have?** ¿cuánto dinero tienes?; **how much is it?** ¿cuánto cuesta?; **4 how many?** ¿cuántos?; **how many brothers do you have?** ¿cuántos hermanos tienes?; **5 how old are you?** ¿cuántos años tienes?; **how heavy is it?** ¿cuánto pesa?; **6 how far is it?** ¿a qué distancia está?; **how far is it to Bilbao?** ¿a qué distancia está Bilbao?; **7 how long will it take?** ¿cuánto tardará?; **how long have you known her?** ¿cuánto tiempo hace que la conoces?; **8** (*in exclamations*) qué; **how nice!** ¡qué bonito!

however *adverb* sin embargo.

hug *noun* **to give somebody a hug** darle [4] un abrazo a alguien; **she gave me a hug** me dio un abrazo.

huge *adjective* enorme.

hum *verb* tararear [17] (*a person*).

human *adjective* humano/humana.

human being *noun* ser M humano.

humour *noun* humor M; **to have a sense of humour** tener [9] sentido del humor.

hundred *number* **1** cien; **a hundred** cien; **about a hundred** unos/unas cien; **about a hundred people** unas cien personas; **hundreds of people** cientos de personas; **2** (*for numbers 101 to 199*) ciento; **one hundred and six** ciento seis; **3** (*for numbers 200 to 999*) **two hundred** doscientos/doscientas; **two hundred and ten** doscientos diez; **six hundred** seiscientos/seiscientas.

Hungary *noun* Hungría F.

hunger *noun* hambre F (*even though 'hambre' is a feminine noun, it is used with 'el' and 'un'*).

hungry *adjective* **to be hungry** tener [9] hambre, **I'm hungry** tengo hambre.

hunt *verb* cazar [22] (*animals*).
● **hunt for** (*search for*) buscar.

hurry *noun* **to be in a hurry** tener [9] prisa; **I'm in a hurry** tengo prisa. *verb* darse [4] prisa; **I must hurry** debo darme prisa; **we hurried home**

nos dimos prisa para llegar a casa; **hurry up!** ¡date prisa!

hurt *verb* **1 to hurt somebody** hacer [7] daño a alguien; **you're hurting me!** me estás haciendo daño; **that hurts!** ¡eso hace daño!; **2 my back hurts** me duele la espalda; **my legs hurt** me duelen las piernas; **3 to hurt yourself** hacerse [7] daño; **did you hurt yourself?** ¿te has hecho daño?; **4 to hurt your hand** hacerse [7] daño en la mano; **I hurt my arm** me hice daño en el brazo.

husband *noun* marido M.

hymn *noun* himno M.

hypermarket *noun* hipermercado M.

hyphen *noun* guión M.

I i

I *pronoun* **1** (*like other subject pronouns, 'I' is generally not translated; in Spanish the form of the verb tells you whether the subject of the verb is 'I', 'we', 'they', etc., so 'I' is only translated when you want to emphasize it*) **I am Scottish** soy escocés; **I have two sisters** tengo dos hermanas; **2** (*for emphasis*) yo; **I did it** lo hice yo; **I went but Robert didn't** yo fui pero Robert no; **Tony and I** Tony y yo.

Iberia *noun* Iberia F.

Iberian *adjective* ibérico/ibérica.

ice *noun* hielo M.

ice cream *noun* helado M; **a chocolate ice cream** un helado de chocolate.

ice-cube *noun* cubito M de hielo.

ice hockey *noun* hockey M sobre hielo.

ice rink *noun* pista F de hielo.

ice-skating *noun* patinaje M sobre hielo; **to go ice-skating** ir [8] a patinar sobre hielo.

icy *adjective* **1** cubierto/cubierta de hielo (*a road*); **2** (*very cold*) helado/helada; **an icy wind** un viento helado.

idea *noun* idea F; **what a good idea!** ¡qué buena idea!; **I've no idea** no tengo ni idea.

ideal *adjective* ideal.

identity card *noun* carné F de identidad.

idiot *noun* idiota M/F.

idiotic *adjective* idiota.

i.e. (*in writing*) i.e. (*in speech*) esto es.

if *conjunction* **1** si; **if Sue's there** si Sue está allí; **if it rains** si llueve; **if not** si no; (*when talking about something that might or might not happen, 'si' is followed by the subjunctive*) **if I won the lottery** si ganase la lotería; **2 if only …** ojalá …; **if only you'd told me** ojalá me lo hubieses dicho; **3 even if** incluso si; **even if it snows** incluso si nieva; **4 if I were you …** yo que tú …; **if I were you, I'd forget it** yo que tú me olvidaría del asunto.

ignore *verb* **1** ignorar [17] (*a person*); **2** no hacer [7] caso de (*what somebody says*); **3 just ignore it** no hagas caso.

ill *adjective* enfermo/enferma; **to fall ill, to be taken ill** enfermar [17]; **to feel ill** sentirse [14] mal.

illegal *adjective* ilegal.

illness *noun* enfermedad F.

illustrated *adjective* ilustrado/ilustrada.

illustration *noun* ilustración F.

imagination *noun* imaginación F; **to show imagination** demostrar [24] imaginación.

imaginative *adjective* imaginativo/imaginativa.

imagine *verb* imaginar [17]; **imagine that you're very rich** imagina que eres muy rico; **you can't imagine how hard it was!** ¡no puedes imaginarte lo difícil que fue!

imitate *verb* imitar [17].

imitation *noun* imitación F.

immediate *adjective* inmediato/inmediata.

immediately *adverb* inmediatamente; **I rang them immediately** los llamé inmediatamente; **immediately before** justo antes; **immediately after** justo después.

immigrant *noun* inmigrante M/F.

immigration *noun* inmigración F.

impatience *noun* impaciencia F.

impatient *adjective* **1** impaciente; **2 to get impatient with somebody** impacientarse [17] con alguien.

impatiently *adverb* con impaciencia.

imperfect *noun* (*of a verb*) imperfecto M; **in the imperfect** en imperfecto.

importance *noun* importancia F.

important *adjective* importante.

impossible *adjective* imposible; **It's impossible to find a telephone** es imposible encontrar un teléfono.

impressed *adjective* impresionado/impresionada.

impression *noun* impresión F; **to make a good impression on somebody** causar [17] una buena impresión a alguien; **I got the impression he was hiding something** me dio la impresión de que estaba ocultando algo.

improve *verb* mejorar [17]; **to improve something** mejorar [17] algo; **the weather is improving** el tiempo está mejorando.

improvement *noun* **1** (*a clear change for the better*) mejora F; **2** (*gradual progress*) progreso M (*in schoolwork, for example*).

in *preposition*, *adverb* **1** en; **in Spain** en España; **in Spanish** en español; **in Barcelona** en Barcelona; **in my**

pocket en mi bolsillo; **in the newspaper** en el periódico; **in my class** en mi clase; **I was in the bath** estaba en el baño; **a house in the country** una casa en el campo; **in school** en el colegio; **in town** en la ciudad; **in the photo** en la foto; **2 in pencil** a lápiz; **in twos** de dos en dos; **3** (*wearing*) de; **the girl in the pink shirt** la chica de la falda rosa; **he was in a suit** llevaba un traje; **dressed in white** vestida de blanco; **4** (*with month, season, or year*) **in May** en mayo; **in 1998** en mil novecientos noventa y ocho; **in winter** en invierno; **5** (*with parts of the day*) **in the morning** por la mañana; **in the night** por la noche; **at eight in the morning** a las ocho de la mañana; **6 I'll phone you in ten minutes** te llamaré dentro de diez minutos; **she did it in five minutes** lo hizo en cinco minutos; **7** (*after superlative*) de; **the tallest boy in the class** el chico más alto de la clase; **the biggest city in the world** la ciudad más grande del mundo; **8 in time** con el tiempo; **9 in the sun** al sol; **in the rain** bajo la lluvia; **10 to come in** entrar [17]; **to go in** entrar [17]; **we went into the cinema** entramos en el cine; **to run in** entrar [17] corriendo; **11 to be in** (*at home, around*) estar [2]; **Mick's not in at the moment** Mick no está en este momento.

include *verb* incluir [54]; **dinner is included in the price** la cena está incluida en el precio; **service included** servicio incluido.

including *preposition* incluido; **50 pounds including VAT** cincuenta

libras IVA incluido; **everyone, including children** todo el mundo incluidos los niños; **including Sundays** incluidos los domingos; **not including Sundays** sin incluir los domingos.

income *noun* ingresos M (*plural*).

income tax *noun* impuesto M sobre la renta.

inconvenient *adjective* **1** poco conveniente (*a place or an arrangement*); **2** inoportuno/ inoportuna (*a time*).

increase *noun* aumento M (*in price, for example*).
verb aumentar [17]; **the price has increased by ten pounds** el precio ha aumentado diez libras.

incredible *adjective* increíble.

incredibly *adverb* (*very*) increíblemente; **the film's incredibly boring** la película es increíblemente aburrida.

indeed *adverb* **1** (*to emphasize*) **she's very pleased indeed** está contentísima; **I'm very hungry indeed** tengo muchísima hambre; **thank you very much indeed** muchísimas gracias; **2** (*certainly*) **'can you hear his radio?' – 'indeed I can!'** ¿oyes su radio?' – 'ya lo creo'; **'do you like it?' – 'I do indeed!'** ¿te gusta?' – 'sí, muchísimo'.

indefinite article *noun* (*in grammar*) artículo M indefinido.

independence *noun* independencia F.

independent *adjective* 1 (*a country or person*) independiente; 2 **an independent school** una escuela privada.

index *noun* índice M.

India *noun* India F.

Indian *noun* (*of India*) indio M, india F.
adjective (*of India*) indio/india.

indigestion *noun* indigestión F; **to have indigestion** tener [9] indigestión.

individual *noun* individuo M.
adjective 1 individual (*a serving or a contribution, for example*); 2 **individual tuition** clases F (*plural*) particulares.

indoor *adjective* **an indoor swimming pool** una piscina cubierta; **an indoor plant** una planta de interior.

indoors *adverb* dentro; **it's cooler indoors** hace más fresco dentro; **to go indoors** entrar [17]; **to stay indoors** quedarse [17] dentro.

industrial *adjective* industrial.

industrial estate *noun* zona F industrial.

industry *noun* industria F; **the advertising industry** la industria de la publicidad.

inevitable *adjective* inevitable.

inevitably *adverb* inevitablemente.

inexperienced *adjective* inexperto/inexperta.

infection *noun* infección F; **an eye infection** una infección de ojos; **a throat infection** anginas F (*plural*).

infectious *adjective* infeccioso/ infecciosa.

infinitive *noun* infinitivo M; **in the infinitive** en infinitivo.

inflation *noun* inflación F.

influence *noun* influencia F; **to be a good influence on somebody** ser [1] una buena influencia para alguien.

inform *verb* informar [17]; **to inform somebody that** informar a alguien de que; **they informed us that there was a problem** nos informaron de que había un problema; **to inform somebody of something** informar a alguien de algo.

informal *adjective* 1 informal (*a meal or event, for example*); 2 (*language*) familiar; **an informal expression** una expresión familiar.

information *noun* información F; **I need some information about flights to Madrid** necesito información sobre vuelos a Madrid; **a piece of information** un dato.

information desk *noun* mostrador M de información.

information office *noun* oficina F de información.

information technology, IT *noun* informática F.

infuriating *adjective* exasperante.

ingredient *noun* ingrediente M.

initials *plural noun* iniciales F (*plural*); **put your initials here** pon tus iniciales aquí.

injection *noun* inyección F; **to give somebody an injection** ponerle [11] una inyección a alguien.

injure *verb* herir [14].

injured *adjective* herido/herida.

injury *noun* herida F.

ink *noun* tinta F.

in-laws *plural noun* suegros M (*plural*).

innocent *adjective* inocente.

insane *adjective* loco/loca.

inscription *noun* inscripción F.

insect *noun* insecto M; **an insect bite** una picadura de insecto.

inside *noun* interior M; **the inside of the oven** el interior del horno. *preposition* dentro de; **inside the cinema** dentro del cine. *adverb* dentro; **she's inside, I think** creo que está dentro; **to go inside** entrar [17].

inside out *adjective*, *adverb* del revés; **your jumper's inside out** llevas el jersey del revés.

insist *verb* 1 insistir [19]; **if you insist** si insistes; **to insist on doing** insistir en hacer; **he insisted on paying** insistió en pagar; 2 **to insist that** insistir en que; **Ruth insisted I was**

wrong Ruth insistió en que yo estaba equivocada.

inspection *noun* inspección F.

inspector *noun* inspector M, inspectora F.

inspiration *noun* inspiración F.

install *verb* instalar [17].

instalment *noun* 1 (*of a TV or radio serial*) episodio M; 2 (*payment*) plazo M; **to pay by instalments** pagar [28] a plazos.

instance *noun* **for instance** por ejemplo.

instant *noun* instante M; **come here this instant!** ¡ven aquí ahora mismo! *adjective* 1 instantáneo/ instantánea (*coffee or soup*); 2 (*immediate*) inmediato/ inmediata (*an effect or a success, for example*).

instead *adverb* 1 **Ted couldn't go, so I went instead** Ted no pudo ir, así que fui yo en su lugar; **we didn't go to the concert, we went to Lucy's instead** no fuimos al concierto, fuimos a casa de Lucy; 2 **instead of** en vez de; **instead of pudding I had cheese** en vez de dulce tomé queso; **instead of playing tennis we went swimming** en vez de jugar al tenis nos fuimos a nadar.

instinct *noun* instinto M.

instruct *verb* **to instruct somebody to do** ordenar [17] a alguien que haga (*'que' is followed by the subjunctive*); **the teacher instructed us to stay**

together la profesora nos ordenó que nos quedásemos juntos.

instructions *plural noun* instrucciones F (*plural*); **follow the instructions on the packet** siga las instrucciones del paquete; **'instructions for use'** 'modo de empleo'.

instructor *noun* 1 monitor M, monitora F; **my skiing instructor** mi monitor de esquí; 2 profesor M, profesora F; **my driving instructor** mi profesor de conducir.

instrument *noun* instrumento M; **to play an instrument** tocar [31] un instrumento.

insulin *noun* insulina F.

insult *noun* insulto M.
verb insultar [17].

insurance *noun* seguro M; **travel insurance** seguro de viaje; **fire insurance** seguro contra incendios.

intelligence *noun* inteligencia F.

intelligent *adjective* inteligente.

intend *verb* 1 querer [12]; **as I intended** como yo quería; 2 **to intend to do** tener [9] pensado hacer; **we intend to spend the night in Rome** tenemos pensado pasar la noche en Roma.

intensive *adjective* intensivo/ intensiva; **an intensive course** un curso intensivo; **in intensive care** en cuidados intensivos.

intention *noun* intención F; **I have no intention of paying** no tengo ninguna intención de pagar.

interest *noun* 1 (*hobby*) afición F; **what are your interests?** ¿qué aficiones tienes?; 2 (*keenness*) interés M; **she showed interest** mostró interés.
verb interesar [17]; **that doesn't interest me** eso no me interesa.

interested *adjective* **Sean's very interested in cooking** a Sean le interesa mucho la cocina.

interesting *adjective* interesante.

interfere *verb* 1 **to interfere with something** (*to fiddle with it*) tocar [31] algo; **don't interfere with my computer!** ¡no toques mi ordenador!; 2 **to interfere in** entrometerse [18] en (*someone else's affairs*).

interior designer *noun* interiorista M/F.

international *adjective* internacional.

Internet *noun* Internet F; **on the Internet** en la Internet.

interpreter *noun* intérprete M/F.

interrupt *verb* interrumpir [19].

interruption *noun* Interrupción F.

interval *noun* intermedio M (*in a play or concert*).

interview *noun* entrevista F; **a job interview** una entrevista de trabajo; **a TV interview** una entrevista en la tele.
verb entrevistar [17] (*on TV, radio*).

interviewer *noun* entrevistador M, entrevistadora F.

into *preposition* **1** dentro; **I put the cat into his basket** puse al gato dentro de su cesta; **2 to go into** entrar [17] a; **he's gone into the bank** ha entrado al banco; **3 to get into** entrar [17] en (*car*); **we all got into the car** entramos todos en el coche; **4 to go into town** ir [8] a la ciudad; **Mum's gone into the office** mamá ha ido a la oficina; **to get into bed** irse [8] a la cama; **5 to translate into Spanish** traducir al español; **to change pounds into pesetas** cambiar libras a pesetas.

introduce *verb* presentar [17]; **she introduced me to her brother** me presentó a su hermano; **can I introduce you to my mother?** ¿te puedo presentar a mi madre?

introduction *noun* (*in a book*) introducción F.

invade *verb* invadir [19].

invalid *noun* inválido M, inválida F.

invent *verb* inventar [17].

invention *noun* invento M.

inverted commas *plural noun* comillas F (*plural*); **in inverted commas** entre comillas.

investigation *noun* investigación F; **an investigation into the fire** una investigación sobre el fuego.

invisible *adjective* invisible.

invitation *noun* invitación F; **an invitation to dinner** una invitación a cenar.

invite *verb* invitar [17]; **Kirsty invited me to lunch** Kirsty me invitó a comer; **he's invited me out on Tuesday** me ha invitado a salir el martes.

involve *verb* **1** suponer [11]; **it involves a lot of work** supone mucho trabajo; **2** (*consist in*) **what does the job involve?** ¿en qué consiste el trabajo?; **3 to be involved in** tomar [17] parte en; **I am involved in the new project** estoy tomando parte en el nuevo proyecto.

Iran *noun* Irán M.

Iraq *noun* Irak M.

Ireland *noun* Irlanda F; **the Republic of Ireland** la República Irlandesa.

iris *noun* lirio M.

Irish *noun* **1** (*the language*) irlandés M; **2** (*the people*) **the Irish** los irlandeses. *adjective* irlandés/irlandesa.

Irishman *noun* irlandés.

Irish Sea *noun* mar M de Irlanda.

Irishwoman *noun* irlandesa F.

iron *noun* **1** (*for clothes*) plancha F; **2** (*the metal*) hierro M. *verb* planchar [17].

ironing *noun* **to do the ironing** planchar [17].

ironing board *noun* tabla F de planchar.

irregular *adjective* irregular.

irritating *adjective* irritante.

Islam *noun* Islam M.

Islamic *adjective* islámico/islámica.

island *noun* isla F.

isolated *adjective* aislado/aislada.

Israel *noun* Israel M.

Israeli *noun* israelí M/F.
adjective israelí.

issue *noun* **1** (*something you discuss*) tema M; **a political issue** un tema político; **2** (*of a magazine*) número M.
verb distribuir [54].

it *pronoun* **1** (*when used as the subject of the verb, 'it' like other subject pronouns is generally not translated; in Spanish the form of the verb tells you whether the subject of the verb is he/she/it, we, they, etc.*) **'where is my bag?' – 'it's in the kitchen'** ¿dónde está mi bolso?' – 'está en la cocina'; **read this book, it's lovely** lee este libro, es precioso; **'how old is your car?' – 'it's five years old'** ¿cuántos años tiene tu coche?' – 'cinco'; **2** (*as the object of the verb*) lo/la; **where's my book? I've lost it** ¿dónde está mi libro? lo he perdido; **give me the suitcase, I'll carry it** dame la maleta, yo la llevo; (*with a verb in the infinitive or when telling somebody to do something, 'lo' or 'la' join onto the verb*) **I've finished the letter, I only have to sign it** he terminado la carta, sólo me queda firmarla; **it's your money, take it** es tu dinero, cógelo; (*but when telling somebody*

NOT to do something, 'lo' or 'la' goes before the verb) **it's an expensive vase, don't break it** es un jarrón caro, no lo rompas; **3 who is it?** ¿quién es?; **it's me** soy yo; **what is it?** ¿qué es?; **4 yes, it's true** sí, es verdad; **it doesn't matter** no importa; **5 it's raining** está lloviendo; **it's a nice day** hace buen día; **it's very cold here** hace mucho frío aquí; **it's two o'clock** son las dos; **6** (*after a preposition*) **I don't want to talk about it** no quiero hablar de ello; **the box goes behind it** la caja va detrás.

IT *noun* (*short for information technology*) informática F.

Italian *noun* **1** (*the language*) italiano M; **2** (*person*) italiano M, italiana F.
adjective **1** italiano/italiana; **Italian food** comida italiana; **2** de italiano (*a teacher or a lesson*); **my Italian class** mi clase de italiano.

italics *noun* cursiva F; **in italics** en cursiva.

Italy *noun* Italia F.

itch *verb* **1** (*a garment*) picar [31]; **this sweater itches** este jersey pica; **2** (*a part of the body*) **my back is itching** me pica la espalda; **I'm itching all over** me pica todo el cuerpo.

item *noun* artículo M.

its *adjective* **1** (*before a singular noun*) su; **its ear** su oreja; **2** (*before a plural noun*) sus; **its toys** sus juguetes.

itself *pronoun* 1 (*as a reflexive*) se; **the cat is washing itself** el gato se está lavando; 2 **by itself** solo/sola; **he left the dog by itself** dejó al perro solo.

ivy *noun* hiedra F.

J j

jack *noun* 1 (*in cards*) jota F; **the jack of clubs** la jota de tréboles; 2 (*for a car*) gato M.

jacket *noun* 1 chaqueta F; 2 (*casual*) americana F.

jail *noun* cárcel F.
verb meter [18] en la cárcel.

jam *noun* 1 (*that you eat*) mermelada F; **raspberry jam** mermelada de frambuesa; 2 **a traffic jam** un atasco (de tráfico).

January *noun* enero M.

Japan *noun* Japón M.

Japanese *noun* 1 (*the language*) japonés M; 2 (*person*) japonés M, japonesa F; **the Japanese** los japoneses.
adjective japonés/japonesa.

jar *noun* bote M; **a jar of jam** un bote de mermelada.

jazz *noun* jazz M.

jealous *adjective* celoso/celosa.

jeans *noun* vaqueros M (*plural*); **my jeans** mis vaqueros; **a pair of jeans** unos vaqueros.

jelly *noun* 1 (*clear jam*) jalea F; 2 (*dessert*) gelatina F.

jellyfish *noun* medusa F.

jersey *noun* 1 jersey M; 2 (*for football*) camiseta F.

Jesus *noun* Jesús M; **Jesus Christ** Jesucristo.

Jew *noun* judío M, judía F.

jewel *noun* joya F.

jeweller *noun* joyero M, joyera F.

jeweller's *noun* joyería F.

jewellery *noun* joyas F (*plural*).

Jewish *adjective* judío/judía.

jigsaw *noun* rompecabezas M puzzle M.

job *noun* 1 (*paid work*) trabajo M; **a job as a secretary** un trabajo de secretaria; **he's got a job** tiene un trabajo; **out of a job** sin trabajo; **what's your job?** ¿en qué trabajas?; 2 (*a task*) tarea F; **it's not an easy job** no es una tarea fácil; **she made a good job of it** lo hizo muy bien.

jobless *adjective* en paro.

jog *verb* **to go jogging** hacer [7] footing.

join *verb* 1 (*become a member of*) hacerse [7] socio de; **I've joined the judo club** me he hecho socio del club de judo; 2 (*to meet up with*) **you go ahead, I'll join you later** id vosotros, yo voy más tarde; **we are going for a meal, do you want to join us?** vamos a salir a comer, ¿quieres venirte con nosotros?; 3 **to join two**

things together unir [19] dos cosas; **4 to join a queue** ponerse [11] a la cola.

to join in 1 participar [17]; **Ruth never joins in** Ruth nunca participa; **2 to join in something** tomar [17] parte en algo; **won't you join in the game?** ¿no quieres tomar parte en el juego?

joiner *noun* carpintero M, carpintera F.

joint *noun* **1** (*of meat*) corte M; **a joint of beef** un corte de carne; **2** (*in your body*) articulación F.

joke *noun* **1** (*a funny story*) chiste M; **to tell a joke** contar [24] un chiste; **2** (*directed against somebody*) broma F; **to play a joke on somebody** gastarle [17] una broma a alguien.
verb bromear [17]; **you must be joking!** ¡estás bromeando!

joker *noun* (*in cards*) comodín M.

journalism *noun* periodismo M.

journalist *noun* periodista M/F; **Sean's a journalist** Sean es periodista.

journey *noun* viaje M; **our journey to Turkey** nuestro viaje a Turquía; **a bus journey** un viaje en autobús.

joy *noun* alegría F.

joystick *noun* (*for computer games*) mando M.

judge *noun* juez M, jueza F.
verb juzgar [28].

judo *noun* judo M; **he does judo** hace judo.

jug *noun* jarra F (*big*) jarrita F (*small*).

juice *noun* zumo M; **two orange juices please** dos zumos de naranja, por favor.

juicy *adjective* jugoso/jugosa.

jukebox *noun* máquina F de discos.

July *noun* julio M.

jumble sale *noun* mercadillo M de beneficencia.

jumbo jet *noun* jumbo M.

jump *noun* salto M; **a parachute jump** un salto en paracaídas.
verb saltar [17].

jumper *noun* jersey M.

June *noun* junio M.

jungle *noun* selva F.

junior *adjective* **a junior school** una escuela primaria; **the juniors** los alumnos de primaria.

junk *noun* **1** (*real rubbish*) basura F; **2** (*discarded things*) trastos M (*plural*) viejos.

junk food *noun* comida F basura.

jury *noun* jurado M.

just *adverb* **1** justo; **just on time** justo a tiempo; **just after the church** justo después de misa; **it's just what I need** es justo lo que necesito; **2 to have just done** acabar [17] de hacer; **Tom has just arrived** Tom acaba de llegar; **Helen had just called** Helen acaba de llamar; **3 I'm just finishing the ironing** estoy terminando de planchar; **4** (*only*) sólo; **just for fun** sólo por pasarlo bien; **he's just a**

child es sólo un niño; **there's just me and Justine** sólo estamos Justine y yo; **5 just as** igual de; **it's just as good as the other** es igual de bueno que el otro; **it's just as possible** es igualmente posible; **6 just coming!** ¡ahora mismo voy!

justice *noun* justicia F.

K k

kangaroo *noun* canguro M.

karate *noun* kárate M.

kebab *noun* brocheta F.

keen *adjective* **1** (*enthusiastic*) **you don't look too keen** no pareces muy entusiasmado; **they were keen on the idea** estaban interesados en la idea; **2** (*committed*) **he's a keen photographer** le encanta la fotografía; **3 he's not keen on fish** no le gusta el pescado.

keep *verb* **1** quedarse [17] con; **I kept the letter** me quedé con la carta; **keep the change** quédese con el cambio; **2 to keep something for someone** guardarle [17] algo a alguien; **will you keep my seat?** ¿me guardas el sitio?; **to keep a secret** guardar [17] un secreto; **3 to keep somebody waiting** hacer [7] esperar

a alguien; **4** (*to store*) guardar; **I keep my bike in the garage** guardo mi bici en el garaje; **where do you keep the saucepans?** ¿dónde guardas las cacerolas?; **5 to keep on doing** seguir [64] haciendo; **she kept on talking** siguió hablando; **keep straight on** siga todo recto; **6 to keep on doing** (*time after time*) no parar de hacer; **he keeps on ringing me up** no para [17] de llamarme; **7 keep calm!** ¡no te pongas nervioso!; **keep still!** ¡estate quieto! **keep out of the sun** no te pongas al sol; **8 to keep a promise** mantener [9] una promesa.

kerb *noun* bordillo M de la acera.

kettle *noun* hervidora F; **to put the kettle on** enchufar la hervidora (*electric*).

key *noun* **1** (*for a lock*) llave F; **a bunch of keys** un manojo de llaves; **2** (*on a piano or typewriter*) tecla F.

keyboard *noun* (*for a piano or a computer*) teclado M.

kick *noun* (*from a person or a horse*) patada F; **to give somebody a kick** darle [4] una patada a alguien; ★ **to get a kick out of doing** disfrutar [17] haciendo.
verb **to kick somebody** darle [4] una patada a alguien; **to kick the ball** darle [4] una patada al balón.
● **to kick off** empezar [25].

kick-off *noun* saque M inicial.

kid *noun* niño M, niña F (*child*); **Dad's looking after the kids** papá está cuidando de los niños.

kidnap *verb* secuestrar [17].

kidney *noun* riñón M.

kill *verb* matar [17]; **she was killed in an accident** se mató en un accidente.

killer *noun* (*murderer*) asesino M, asesina F.

kilo *noun* kilo M; **a kilo of sugar** un kilo de azúcar; **fifty pesetas a kilo** cincuenta pesetas el kilo.

kilogramme *noun* kilogramo M.

kilometre *noun* kilómetro M.

kilt *noun* falda F escocesa.

kind *noun* tipo M; **it's a kind of fruit** es un tipo de fruta; **all kinds of people** todo tipo de personas. *adjective* amable; **Marion was very kind to me** Marion fue muy amable conmigo.

kindness *noun* amabilidad F.

king *noun* rey M; **King George** el rey George; **the king of hearts** el rey de corazones.

kingdom *noun* reino M; **the United Kingdom** el Reino Unido.

kiosk *noun* 1 (*for newspapers or snacks*) quiosco M; 2 (*for a phone*) cabina F.

kiss *noun* beso M; **to give somebody a kiss** darle [4] un beso a alguien. *verb* besar [17]; **kiss me!** ¡bésame!; **to kiss somebody goodbye** darle [4] un beso de despedida a alguien; **we kissed each other** nos besamos.

kit *noun* 1 (*of tools*) **a tool kit** una caja de herramientas; **a first-aid kit** un botiquín; 2 (*clothes*) equipo M; **where's my gym kit?** ¿dónde está mi equipo de gimnasia? 3 (*for making a model, a piece of furniture, etc*) kit M.

kitchen *noun* cocina F; **the kitchen table** la mesa de la cocina.

kitchen roll *noun* papel M de cocina.

kite *noun* (*toy*) cometa F; **to fly a kite** hacer [7] volar una cometa.

kitten *noun* gatito M, gatita F.

kiwi fruit *noun* kiwi M.

knee *noun* rodilla F; **to be on your knees** estar [2] de rodillas.

kneel *verb* (*to kneel down*) arrodillarse [17] (*to be on your knees*) estar [2] de rodillas.

knickers *plural noun* bragas F (*plural*).

knife *noun* cuchillo M.

knight *noun* (*in chess*) caballo M.

knit *verb* hacer [7] punto.

knitting *noun* punto M.

knob *noun* pomo M (*on a door*); tirador M (*on a drawer*).

knock *noun* golpe M; **a knock on the head** un golpe en la cabeza; **a knock at the door** un golpe en la puerta. *verb* 1 (*to bang*) darse [4] un golpe; **I knocked my arm on the table** me di un golpe en el brazo con la mesa; 2 **to knock at the door** llamar [17] a la puerta.

● **to knock down 1** (*in a traffic accident*) atropellar [17] (*a person*); **2** (*to demolish*) derribar [17] (*an old building*).

● **to knock out 1** (*to make unconscious*) dejar [17] sin sentido; **2** (*in sport, to eliminate*) eliminar [17].

knot *noun* nudo M; **to tie a knot in something** hacer [7] un nudo a algo.

know *verb* **1** (*know a fact*) saber [13]; **do you know where Tim is?** ¿sabes dónde está Tim?; **I know they've moved house** sé que se han cambiado de casa; **he knows it by heart** se lo sabe de memoria; **yes, I know** sí, ya lo sé; **you never know!** ¡nunca se sabe!; **2** (*be personally acquainted with*) conocer [35] (*a person, place, book, or music, for example*); **do you know that song?** ¿conoces esa canción?; **all the people I know** toda la gente que conozco; **I don't know his mother** no conozco a su madre; **3 to know how to do** saber [13] hacer; **Steve knows how to make paella** Steve sabe hacer paella; **4 to know about** estar [2] al corriente de (*the latest news*); **5 to know about** saber [13] de (*a subject, machines*); **Lindy knows about computers** Lindy sabe de ordenadores.

knowledge *noun* conocimientos M (*plural*); **scientific knowledge** conocimientos científicos.

Koran *noun* Corán M.

kosher *adjective* kosher.

L l

lab *noun* laboratorio M.

label *noun* etiqueta F.

laboratory *noun* laboratorio M.

Labour *noun* los laboristas M (*plural*); **to vote for Labour** votar [17] por los laboristas; **the Labour Party** el partido laborista.

lace *noun* **1** (*for a shoe*) cordón M; **to do up your laces** atarse los cordones; **2** (*fabric*) encaje M.

lad *noun* chaval M (*informal*).

ladder *noun* **1** (*for climbing*) escalera F; **2** (*in your tights*) carrera F.

ladies *noun* (*lavatory*) servicio M de señoras; (*on a sign*) **'Ladies'** 'Señoras'.

lady *noun* señora F; **ladies and gentlemen** señoras y caballeros.

lager *noun* cerveza F rubia.

laid-back *adjective* relajado/relajada.

lake *noun* lago M.

lamb *noun* cordero M; **a leg of lamb** una pierna de cordero.

lamp *noun* lámpara F.

lamp-post *noun* farola F.

lampshade *noun* pantalla F.

land *noun* 1 tierra F; 2 (*property*) a
piece of land un terreno; he has land
tiene tierras.
verb 1 (*plane, passenger*) aterrizar
[22]; 2 (*leave a ship*) desembarcar
[31].

landing *noun* 1 (*on the stairs*)
descansillo M; 2 (*of a plane*)
aterrizaje M; 3 (*from a boat*)
desembarco M.

landlady *noun* 1 (*of rented house*)
casera F; 2 (*of pub*) dueña F.

landlord *noun* 1 (*of rented house*)
casero M; 2 (*of pub*) dueño M.

lane *noun* 1 (*a country path*)
camino M; 2 (*of a motorway or road*)
carril M; bus lane carril de
autobuses.

language *noun* 1 (*Spanish, Italian,
etc.*) idioma M; a foreign language
un idioma extranjero; 2 (*way of
speaking*) lenguaje M; scientific
language lenguaje científico; 3 bad
language palabrotas F (*plural*); to
use bad language decir [5]
palabrotas.

language lab *noun* laboratorio M
de idiomas.

lap *noun* 1 (*your knees*) rodillas F
(*plural*); on my lap en mis rodilla;
2 (*in races*) vuelta F.

laptop *noun* ordenador M portátil.

laser *noun* láser M.

last *adjective* 1 último/última; the
last time la última vez; the last thing
I did lo último que hice; 2 last week
la semana pasada; last night (*in the
evening*) ayer por la tarde (*in the
night*) anoche.
adverb 1 (*in final position*) (*to
arrive or leave*); Rob arrived last
Rob llegó el último; I came last in
the race llegué en último lugar en la
carrera; 2 (*most recently*) I last saw
him in May la última vez que lo vi fue
en mayo; 3 at last! ¡por fin!
verb durar [17]; the play lasted two
hours la obra duró dos horas.

late *adjective, adverb* 1 tarde; we're
late llegamos tarde; they arrived
late llegaron tarde; to be late for
something llegar [28] tarde a algo;
we were late for the film llegamos
tarde a la película; 2 to be late (*a
bus or train*) llegar [28] con retraso;
the train was an hour late el tren
llegó con una hora de retraso; 3 (*late
in the day*) tarde; we got up late nos
levantamos tarde; it's getting late se
está haciendo tarde; late last night
ayer por la noche ya tarde; too late!
¡demasiado tarde!

later *adverb* más tarde; I'll explain to
you later te lo explicaré más tarde;
later that same day ese mismo día
más tarde; no later than Thursday
no más tarde del jueves; see you
later! ¡hasta luego!

latest *adjective* 1 último/última; **the latest news** las últimas noticias; 2 **at the latest** a más tardar.

Latin *noun* latín M.

Latin America *noun* América F Latina.

Latin American *adjective* latinoamericano/latinoamericana.

laugh *noun* risa F; **to do something for a laugh** hacer [7] algo por divertirse.
verb 1 reírse [61]; **everybody laughed** todo el mundo se rió; 2 **to laugh at** reírse [61] de; **I tried to explain but they laughed at me** intenté explicarlo pero se rieron de mí.

launderette *noun* lavandería F.

lavatory *noun* servicio M, aseo M.

lavender *noun* lavanda F.

law *noun* 1 ley F; **it's against the law** es ilegal; 2 (*subject of study*) derecho M.

lawn *noun* césped M.

lawnmower *noun* cortacésped M.

lawyer *noun* abogado M, abogada F.

lay *verb* poner [11]; **she laid the card on the table** puso la tarjeta en la mesa; **to lay the table** poner la mesa.

lay-by *noun* área F de reposo (*even though 'área' is a feminine noun, it is used with 'el' and 'un'*); **a lay-by** un área de reposo.

layer *noun* capa F.

lazy *adjective* perezoso/perezosa.

lead *noun* 1 (*when you are ahead*) t[c] **be in the lead** llevar [17] la delantera **Sam's in the lead** Sam lleva la delantera; **we have a lead of three points** llevamos una ventaja de tres puntos; 2 (*electric*) cable M; 3 (*for a dog*) correa F; **on a lead** con correa *adjective* (*a role or a singer*) principal.
verb 1 llevar [17]; **the path leads to the sea** el sendero lleva al mar; 2 **to lead the way** ir [8] delante; 3 (*in a competition*) llevar [17] la delantera; 4 **this will lead to problems** esto traerá problemas; **to lead to an accident** causar [17] un accidente.

leader *noun* 1 (*of a gang*) cabecilla M/F; 2 (*of a political party*) líder M/F; 3 (*in a competition*) primero M, primera F.

lead-free petrol *noun* gasolina F sin plomo.

lead singer *noun* cantante M/F principal.

leaf *noun* hoja F.

leaflet *noun* folleto M.

league *noun* (*in sport*) liga F.

lean *adjective* (*meat*) magro/magra.
verb 1 **to lean on something** apoyarse [17] en algo; 2 (*prop*) apoyar [17]; **lean the ladder against the tree** apoya la escalera en el árbol; 3 (*a person*) echarse [17]; **lean forward a bit** échate para delante un

poco; **4 to lean out of the window** asomarse [17] por la ventana.

leap year *noun* año M bisiesto.

learn *verb* aprender [18]; **to learn Russian** aprender ruso; **to learn to drive** aprender a conducir.

learner driver *noun* **she's a learner driver** está aprendiendo a conducir.

least *adverb*, *adjective pronoun* **1** menos; **the least expensive hotel** el hotel menos caro; **the least expensive glasses** las gafas menos caras; **Tony has the least money** Tony es el que menos dinero tiene; **I like the blue shirt least** la camisa azul es la que menos me gusta; **2** (*slightest*) más mínimo/más mínima; **I haven't the least idea** no tengo ni la más mínima idea; **he didn't show the least interest** no mostró el más mínimo interés; **3 at least** (*at a minimum*) por lo menos; **there must be at least twenty people** debe haber por lo menos veinte personas; **4 at least** (*at any rate*) al menos; **at least, that's what I think** al menos eso creo.

leather *noun* cuero M; **a leather jacket** una chaqueta de cuero.

leave *verb* **1** (*go away*) irse [8]; **they're leaving tomorrow** se van mañana; **we left at six** se fueron a las seis; **2** (*go away from*) irse [8] de; **I left the office at five** me fui de la oficina a las cinco; **3** (*go out of*) salir [63] de; **she left the cinema at ten** salió del cine a las diez; **4** (*abandon*) dejar [17] a (*family or partner*); **he**

left his wife dejó a su mujer; **5** (*deposit*) dejar [17]; **you can leave your coats in the hall** podéis dejar los abrigos en la entrada; **6** (*forget*) dejarse [17]; **he left his umbrella on the train** se dejó el paraguas en el tren; **7 to leave school** dejar [17] los estudios; **Guy left school at sixteen** Guy dejó los estudios a los dieciséis años; **8 be left** quedar [17]; **there are two cakes left** quedan dos pasteles; **we have ten minutes left** nos quedan diez minutos; **I don't have any money left** no me queda dinero.

lecture *noun* **1** (*at university*) clase F; **2** (*public*) conferencia F.

lecturer *noun* profesor M, profesora F.

leek *noun* puerro M.

left *noun* izquierda F; **to drive on the left** conducir [60] por la izquierda; **turn left at the church** tuerce a la izquierda en la iglesia; **on my left** a mi izquierda.
adjective izquierdo/izquierda; **his left foot** su pie izquierdo.

left-hand *noun* **the left-hand side** la parte izquierda.

left-handed *adjective* zurdo/zurda.

left luggage office *noun* consigna F.

leftovers *plural noun* sobras F (*plural*).

leg *noun* **1** (*of a person*) pierna F; **my left leg** mi pierna izquierda; **to break your leg** romperse [40] una pierna; **2** (*of a table, chair, or animal*) pata F; **3** (*in cooking*) **a leg of**

chicken un muslo de pollo; **a leg of lamb** una pierna de cordero; ★ **to pull somebody's leg** tomarle [17] el pelo a alguien (*literally: to take somebody's hair*).

legal *adjective* legal.

leggings *plural noun* leggings M (*plural*).

leisure *noun* tiempo M libre; **in my leisure time** en mi tiempo libre.

lemon *noun* limón M; **a lemon yoghurt** un yogur de limón.

lemonade *noun* 1 (*made with lemons*) limonada F; 2 (*fizzy drink*) gaseosa F.

lemon juice *noun* zumo M de limón.

lend *verb* dejar [17]; **to lend something to somebody** dejarle algo a alguien; **I lent Judy my bike** le dejé mi bici a Judy; **will you lend it to me?** ¿me lo dejas?

length *noun* 1 (*of fabric, board, etc.*) largo M; 2 (*of film, play*) duración F; 3 (*of book, list*) extensión F.

lens *noun* 1 (*in a camera*) lente F; 2 (*in spectacles*) cristal M; 3 **contact lenses** lentillas F (*plural*).

Lent *noun* Cuaresma F.

lentil *noun* lenteja F.

Leo *noun* leo M; **I'm leo** soy Leo.

leotard *noun* malla F.

lesbian *noun* lesbiana F.

less *pronoun*, *adjective adverb* 1 menos; **Richard eats less** Richard come menos; **less time** menos tiempo; **less interesting** menos interesante; **less quickly than us** menos rápido que nosotros; 2 **less than** menos de; **less than a kilo** menos de un kilo; **less than three hours** menos de tres horas; 3 **less than** (*in comparisons*) menos que; **you spent less than me** gastas menos que yo.

lesson *noun* clase F; **the history lesson** la clase de historia; **a driving lesson** una clase de conducir; **to take tennis lessons** tomar [17] clases de tenis.

let[1] *verb* 1 (*allow*) dejar [17]; **will you let me go alone?** ¿me dejas ir sola?; **the police let us through** la policía me dejó pasar; **let me help you** déjame que te ayude; **she lets me borrow her bike** me deja que coja su bici prestada; **let me see** (*show me*) déjame ver; 2 (*as a suggestion or a command*) **let's go!** ¡vámonos!; **let's not talk about it** no hablemos de ello; **let's see, if Tuesday is the third** ... vamos a ver, si el martes es e tres ...; **let's eat out** vamos a comer fuera.

● **to let off** 1 tirar [17] (*fireworks*); 2 hacer [7] estallar (*a bomb*); 3 (*to excuse from*) perdonar [17] (*homework or task*); **I'll let you off doing the dishes** te perdono que no laves los platos.

let[2] *verb* (*to rent out*) alquilar [17]; **'flat to let'** 'se alquila apartamento'.

letter *noun* 1 carta F; **a letter for you from Delia** una carta de Delia para ti; 2 (*of alphabet*) letra F; **M is the**

letter after L M es la letra que viene después de L.

letterbox *noun* buzón M.

lettuce *noun* lechuga F.

leukaemia *noun* leucemia F.

level *noun* nivel M; **at street level** a nivel de la calle.
adjective **1** plano/plana (*a shelf or floor*); **2** llano/llana (*ground*).

level crossing *noun* paso M a nivel.

lever *noun* palanca F.

liar *noun* mentiroso M, mentirosa F.

liberal *adjective* liberal; **the Liberal Democrats** los demócratas liberales.

Libra *noun* libra F; **Sean's Libra** Sean es libra.

librarian *noun* bibliotecario M, bibliotecaria F; **Mark's a librarian** Mark es bibliotecario.

library *noun* biblioteca F; **the public library** la biblioteca pública.

licence *noun* **1** (*for driving or fishing*) permiso M; **a driving licence** un permiso de conducir; **2** (*for a TV*) licencia F.

lick *verb* lamer [18].

lid *noun* tapa F; **she took the lid off** quitó la tapa.

lie *noun* mentira F; **to tell lies** decir [5] mentiras.
verb **1** (*to be stretched out*) estar [2] tumbado; **Jimmy was lying on the bed** Jimmy estaba tumbado en la cama; **2 to lie down** tumbarse [17] (*for a little while*); **come and lie down in the sun** ven tumbarte al sol; **3** (*object*) estar [2]; **my coat lay on the bed** mi abrigo estaba sobre la cama; **4** (*not to tell the truth*) mentir [14].

life *noun* vida F; **all her life** toda su vida; **full of life** lleno/llena de vida; **that's life !** ¡así es la vida !

lifebelt *noun* salvavidas M (*does not change in the plural*).

lifeboat *noun* bote M salvavidas.

life jacket *noun* chaleco M salvavidas.

life-style *noun* estilo M de vida.

lift *noun* **1** ascensor M; **let's take the lift** vamos a coger el ascensor; **2** (*a ride*) **to give somebody a lift to the station** llevar [17] a alguien a la estación; **Tom gave me a lift home** Tom me llevó a casa; **can I give you a lift?** ¿me puedes llevar?
verb levantar [17].

light *noun* **1** (*electric*) luz F; **can you turn the light on?** ¿puedes encender la luz?; **to turn off the light** apagar la luz; **are your lights on?** (*on a car*) ¿tienes las luces encendidas?; **2** (*streetlight*) farola F; **3** (*on a machine*) piloto M; **4 traffic lights** semáforo M; **the lights were green** el semáforo estaba en verde; **5 have you got a light?** ¿tienes fuego?
adjective **1** (*in colour*) claro/clara; **light blue eyes** ojos azul claro; **2** (*not night*) **it gets light at six** se hace de día a las seis; **3** (*not heavy*)

ligero/ligera; **a light sweater** un jersey fino.
verb encender [36] (*the oven, the fire, a match, or a cigarette*); **we lit a fire** encendimos un fuego.

light bulb *noun* bombilla F.

lighter *noun* encendedor M.

lightning *noun* relámpago M; **a flash of lightning** un relámpago; **the tree was struck by lightning** cayó un rayo en el árbol.

light switch *noun* interruptor M de la luz.

like[1] *preposition*, *conjunction*
1 como; **like me** como yo; **like this** como esto; **like a duck** como un pato; **like I said** como dije (yo); **what's it like?** ¿cómo es?; **what was the weather like?** ¿qué tiempo hizo?; 2 **to look like** parecerse [35] a; **Cindy looks like her father** Cindy se parece a su padre.

like[2] *verb* 1 **I like fish** me gusta el pescado; **I don't like dogs** no me gustan los perros; **Mum likes travelling** a mamá le gusta viajar; **she likes my brother** le gusta mi hermano; **I like Picasso best** el que más me gusta es Picasso; 2 **I would like** quiero; **would you like a coffee?** ¿quieres un café?; **what would you like to eat?** ¿qué quieres comer?; **yes, if you like** sí, si tú quieres.

likely *adjective* probable; **it's not very likely** no es muy probable; **she's likely to phone** es probable que llame.

lime *noun* lima F (*fruit*).

limit *noun* límite M; **the speed limit** el límite de velocidad.

line *noun* 1 línea F; **a straight line** una línea recta; **to draw a line** trazar [22] una línea; 2 **a railway line** (*from one place to another*) una línea de tren; **on the railway line** (*the track*) en la vía del tren; 3 (*a queue of people or cars*) cola F; **to stand in line** hacer [7] cola; 4 (*telephone*) línea F; **the line's bad** no se oye bien; **hold the line, please** no cuelgue, por favor.

linen *noun* lino M; **a linen jacket** una chaqueta de lino.

link *noun* conexión F; **what's the link between the two?** ¿qué conexión hay entre los dos?
verb conectar [17] (*two places*); **the terminals are linked by a shuttle service** las terminales están conectadas por un servicio de enlace.

lion *noun* león M.

lip *noun* labio M.

lip-read *verb* leer [37] los labios.

lipstick *noun* lápiz M de labios.

liquid *noun* líquido M.
adjective líquido/líquida.

liquidizer *noun* licuadora F.

list *noun* lista F.

listen *verb* escuchar [17]; **I wasn't listening** no estaba escuchando; **to listen to** escuchar [17]; **listen to the music** escucha la música; **you're not**

listening to me no me estás escuchando.

literature *noun* literatura F.

litre *noun* litro M; **a litre of milk** un litro de leche.

litter *noun* (*rubbish*) basura F.

litter bin *noun* papelera F.

little *adjective, pronoun* **1** (*small*) pequeño/pequeña; **a little boy** un niño pequeño; **a little break** una pequeña pausa; **2** (*not much*) poco/poca; **we have very little time** tenemos muy poco tiempo; **3 a little** un poco; **we have a little money** tenemos un poco de dinero; **just a little, please** sólo un poco, por favor; **it's a little late** es un poco tarde; **a little more** un poco más; **a little less** un poco menos; ★ **little by little** poco a poco.

live[1] *verb* vivir [19]; **Susan lives in York** Susan vive en York; **they live at number 57** viven en el número cincuenta y siete; **they live together** viven juntos.

live[2] *adjective* **1** en directo (*a broadcast*); **a live concert** un concierto en directo; **2** (*alive*) vivo/viva.

liver *noun* hígado M.

living *noun* **to earn a living** ganarse [17] la vida.

living room *noun* salón M.

load *noun* **1** (*on a lorry*) cargamento M; **2 a bus-load of tourists** un autobús lleno de turistas; **3 loads of** un montón de (*informal*); **loads of people** un montón de gente; **they've got loads of money** tienen un montón de dinero.
verb cargar [28].

loaf *noun* **a loaf of bread** un pan; **a loaf of wholemeal bread** un pan integral.

loan *noun* préstamo M.
verb prestar [17].

lobster *noun* langosta F.

local *noun* **1** (*a pub*) **our local** el bar de nuestro barrio; **2 the locals** (*people*) la gente del lugar.
adjective **the local library** la biblioteca del barrio; **the local newspaper** el periódico local.

lock *noun* **1** (*with a key*) cerradura F; **2** (*on a canal*) esclusa F.
verb **to lock the door** cerrar [29] la puerta con llave; **the door was locked** la puerta estaba cerrada con llave.

locker *noun* armario M.

locker room *noun* vestuario M.

lodger *noun* inquilino M, inquilina F.

loft *noun* desván M.

log *noun* tronco M.

logical *adjective* lógico/lógica.

lollipop *noun* piruleta F.

London *noun* Londres M; **to London** a Londres; **the London streets** las calles de Londres.

Londoner *noun* londinense M/F.

lonely *adjective* 1 solitario/solitaria;
she has a lonely life tiene una vida
solitaria; 2 **to feel lonely** sentirse
solo.

long *adjective*, *adverb* 1 largo/larga;
a long film una película larga; **a long
illness** una enfermedad larga; **it's
five meters long** mide cinco metros
de largo; **how long is the corridor?**
¿cuánto mide el pasillo de largo?;
how long is the play? ¿cuánto dura
la obra?; **it's been a long day** ha sido
un día muy largo; 2 **a long time**
mucho tiempo; **he stayed for a long
time** se quedó mucho tiempo; **it's an
hour long** dura una hora; **I've been
here for a long time** he pasado
mucho tiempo aquí; **a long time ago**
hace mucho tiempo; **this won't take
long** esto no llevará mucho tiempo;
I won't be long no tardo mucho;
3 **how long?** ¿cuánto tiempo?; **how
long have you been here?** ¿cuánto
tiempo llevas aquí?; 4 **a long way**
muy lejos; **we're a long way from
the cinema** estamos muy lejos del
cine; 5 **all night long** toda la noche.
verb **to long to do** anhelar [17] hacer;
I'm longing to see you anhelo verte.

longer *adverb* **no longer** ya no; **he
doesn't work here any longer** ya no
trabaja aquí; **I no longer know** ya no
lo sé; **they no longer live here** ya no
viven aquí.

long jump *noun* salto M de longitud.

longlife milk *noun* leche F
uperizada.

loo *noun* váter M (*informal*).

look *noun* 1 (*a glance*) mirada F; **to
have a look at something** mirar [17]
algo; 2 **to have a look round the
town** visitar [17] la ciudad; **to have a
look round the shops** ver [16]
tiendas; 3 **to have a look for** buscar
[31] (*something you've lost*).
verb 1 mirar [17]; **I wasn't looking**
no estaba mirando; **to look out of
the window** mirar por la ventana;
2 **to look at** mirar [17]; **Andy was
looking at the photos** Andy estaba
mirando las fotos; 3 (*to seem*)
parecer [35]; **Melanie looks pleased**
Melanie parecía contenta; **you look
well** tienes buen aspecto; **he looks ill**
tiene mal aspecto; **the salad looks
delicious** la ensalada tiene un
aspecto delicioso; 4 **to look like**
parecerse [35] a; **Sally looks like her
aunt** Sally se parece a su tía; **they
look like each other** se parecen;
5 **what does the house look like?**
¿cómo es la casa?

● **to look after** cuidar [17]; **Dad's
looking after the baby** papá está
cuidando del niño; **I'll look after
your luggage** yo te cuido el equipaje.

● **to look for** buscar [31]; **I'm looking
for the keys** estoy buscando las
llaves.

● **to look forward to something: I'm
looking forward to the holidays**
estoy deseando que lleguen las
vacaciones; **she's looking
forward to the trip** está deseando ir
de viaje.

● **to look out** (*to be careful*) tener [9]
cuidado; **look out, it's hot!** ¡cuidado,
está caliente!

● **to look something up** buscar [17] (*in a dictionary or directory*); **you can look it up in the dictionary** puedes buscarlo en el diccionario.

loose *adjective* **1** (*a screw or knot*) flojo/floja; **2** (*a garment*) amplio/amplia; **3 loose change** cambio M; ★ **I'm at a loose end** no sé qué hacer.

lorry *noun* camión M.

lorry driver *noun* camionero M, camionera F.

lose *verb* **1** perder [36]; **we lost** perdimos; **we lost the match** perdimos el partido; **Sam's lost his watch** Sam ha perdido su reloj; **2 to get lost** perderse [36]; **we got lost in the woods** nos perdimos en el bosque.

loss *noun* pérdida F.

lost *adjective* perdido/perdida.

lost property *noun* objetos M (*plural*) perdidos.

lot *noun* **1 a lot** mucho; **Jason eats a lot** Jason come mucho; **I spent a lot** gasté mucho; **your house is a lot bigger than ours** tu casa es mucho más grande que la nuestra; **2 a lot of** mucho/mucha (*plural* **muchos/muchas**); **a lot of coffee** mucho café; **lots of people** mucha gente; **a lot of books** muchos libros; **'what are you doing tonight?' – 'not a lot'** '¿qué haces esta noche?' – 'no mucho'.

lottery *noun* lotería F; **to win the lottery** ganar [17] la lotería.

loud *adjective* **1** fuerte; **a loud banging** unos golpes fuertes; **a loud shout** un grito fuerte; **the radio is very loud** la radio está muy fuerte; **2 in a loud voice** en voz alta; **to say something out loud** decir algo en voz alta.

loudspeaker *noun* altavoz M.

lounge *noun* **1** (*in a house or hotel*) salón M; **2** (*in an airport*) **the departure lounge** la sala de embarque.

love *noun* **1** amor M; **to be in love with somebody** estar [2] enamorado de alguien; **she's in love with Jake** está enamorada de Jake; **2 Gina sends her love** Gina manda recuerdos; **3 with love from Charlie** con cariño de Charlie; **lots of love, Ann** con mucho cariño: Ann; **4** (*in tennis*) cero M.
verb **1** querer [12]; (*a person*) **I love you** te quiero; **2 she loves London** le encanta Londres; **I'd love to come** me encantaría venir; **I love dancing** me encanta bailar; **Wayne loves seafood** a Wayne le encanta el marisco.

lovely *adjective* **1** (*to look at*) precioso/preciosa; **a lovely house** una casa preciosa; **2 it's a lovely day** hace un día muy bueno; **we had lovely weather** tuvimos un tiempo muy bueno; **3 I had a lovely time at their house** lo pasé muy bien en su casa; **4 it's lovely to see you!** ¡qué alegría verte!; **5** (*food, meal*) riquísimo/riquísima.

low *adjective* bajo/baja; **a low table** una mesa baja; **at a low price** a un precio bajo; **in a low voice** en voz baja.

lower *adjective* (*not as high*) inferior.

luck *noun* suerte F; **good luck!** ¡buena suerte!; **bad luck!** ¡qué mala suerte!; **with a bit of luck** con un poco de suerte.

luckily *adverb* afortunadamente; **luckily for them** afortunadamente para ellos.

lucky *adjective* **1** to be lucky (*a person*) tener [9] suerte; **we were lucky** tuvimos suerte; **2** to be lucky (*bringing luck*) traer [42] suerte; **it's supposed to be lucky** se supone que trae suerte; **my lucky number** mi número de la suerte.

luggage *noun* equipaje M.

lump *noun* **1** bulto M; (*on the body*) **2** terrón M (*of sugar*); **3** trozo M (*of cheese*).

lunch *noun* comida F; **to have lunch** comer [18]; **we had lunch in Oxford** comimos en Oxford.

lunch break *noun* descanso M para comer.

lunch hour, lunch time *noun* hora F de comer.

Luxembourg *noun* Luxemburgo M.

luxurious *adjective* lujoso/lujosa.

luxury *noun* lujo M.

lyrics *plural noun* letra F.

M m

macaroni *noun* macarrones M (*plural*).

machine *noun* máquina F.

machinery *noun* maquinaria F.

mad *adjective* **1** loco/loca; **she's completely mad!** ¡está completamente loca!; **2** (*angry*) enfadado/enfadada; **to be mad with somebody** estar enfadado/enfadada con alguien; **my mum will be mad!** ¡mamá se pondrá hecha una furia! (*informal*); **3** she's mad about horses le encantan los caballos.

madam *noun* señora F.

madness *noun* locura F.

magazine *noun* revista F.

maggot *noun* gusano M.

magic *noun* magia F.
adjective **1** mágico/mágica; **a magic wand** una varita mágica; **2** (*great*) fantástico/fantástica.

magician *noun* mago M, maga F.

magnifying glass *noun* lupa F.

maiden name *noun* nombre M de soltera.

mail *noun* correo M; **e-mail** (*electronic mail*) correo M electrónico.

mail order *noun* **to buy something by mail order** comprar [17] algo por correo; **a mail order catalogue** un catálogo de venta por correo.

main *adjective* principal; **the main entrance** la entrada principal.

mainly *adverb* principalmente.

main road *noun* carretera F principal.

Majorca *noun* Mallorca F.

majority *noun* mayoría F.

make *noun* marca F; **what make is your bike?** ¿de qué marca es tu bici? *verb* **1** hacer [7]; **I made an omelette** hice una tortilla; **she made her bed** hizo su cama; **he made me wait** me hizo esperar; **she makes me laugh** me hace reír; **to make a phone call** hacer una llamada de teléfono; **I have to make a few phone calls** tengo que hacer varias llamadas de teléfono; **2** fabricar [31]; **they make computers** fabrican ordenadores; **'made in Spain'** 'fabricado en España'; **3 that makes me hungry** eso me da hambre; **it made me sleepy** me dio sueño; **4** (*sad, happy*) **to make somebody sad** poner [11] triste a alguien; **it made me sad** me puso triste; **to make somebody happy** hacer [7] feliz a alguien; **it made him really annoyed** le dio mucha rabia; **it makes me so angry** me da tanta rabia; **5** ganar [17] (*money*); **he makes forty pounds a day** gana cuarenta libras al día; **to make a living** ganarse [17] la vida; **6** (*force*) **to make somebody do** obligar [28] a alguien a hacer ; **she made him give the money back** le obligó a devolver el

dinero; **7 to make a meal** preparar [17] una comida; **8** (*add up to*) sumar [17]; **two and three make five** dos y tres suman cinco; **9 I can't make it tonight** no puedo venir esta noche.

● **to make something up 1** inventarse [17] algo; **she made up an excuse** se inventó una excusa; **2 to make it up** (*after a quarrel*) hacer [7] las paces; **they've made it up now** han hecho las paces ahora.

make-up *noun* maquillaje M; **to put on your make-up** ponerse [11] el maquillaje; **Jo's putting on her make-up** Jo se está poniendo el maquillaje; **I don't wear make-up** yo no uso maquillaje.

male *adjective* **1** macho (*animal*); **a male rat** una rata macho; **2** (*of a man*) masculino/masculina; **a male voice** una voz masculina; **3** (*sex: on a form*) varón.

male chauvinist *noun* machista M.

man *noun* hombre M.

manage *verb* **1** dirigir [49] (*business, team*); **she manages a travel agency** ella dirige una agencia de viajes; **2** (*cope*) arreglárselas [17]; **I can manage** puedo arreglármelas; **3 to manage to do** conseguir [64] hacer; **I didn't manage to get in touch with her** no conseguí ponerme en contacto con ella.

management *noun* **1** dirección F; **the management of the company** la dirección de la empresa;

2 (*management staff*) directivos M (*plural*).

manager *noun* 1 (*of a company or a bank*) director M, directora F; 2 (*of a shop or restaurant*) encargado M, encargada F; 3 (*in sport and entertainment*) manager M/F.

manageress *noun* encargada F.

mango *noun* mango M.

maniac *noun* loco M, loca F; **she drives like a maniac!** ¡conduce como una loca!

mankind *noun* humanidad F.

manner *noun* 1 **in a manner of speaking** por así decirlo; 2 **to have good manners** tener [9] buena educación; **it's bad manners to talk like that** no es de es buena educación hablar así.

mantelpiece *noun* repisa F de la chimenea.

manual *noun* manual M.

manufacture *verb* fabricar [31].

manufacturer *noun* fabricante M.

many *adjective, pronoun* 1 muchos/ muchas; **does she have many friends?** ¿tiene muchos amigos?; **there aren't many onions left** no quedan muchas cebollas; **not many** no muchos/muchas; **many of them forgot** muchos de ellos se olvidaron; **many people** mucha gente; 2 **very many** muchos/muchas; **there aren't very many glasses** no hay muchos vasos; 3 **so many** tantos/tantas; **I have so many things to do!** ¡tengo tantas cosas que hacer!; **I've never**

eaten so many cakes nunca he comido tantos pasteles; 4 **as many as** todos los que/todas las que; **you can take as many as you like** puedes llevarte todos los que quieras; 5 **too many** demasiados/demasiadas; **I've got too many things to do** tengo demasiadas cosas que hacer; **that's far too many!** ¡ésos son demasiados!; **there were too many people** había demasiada gente; 6 **how many?** ¿cuántos?/¿cuántas?; **how many are there?** ¿cuántos hay?; **how many sisters have you got?** ¿cuántas hermanas tienes?; **how many are there left?** ¿cuántos quedan?; 7 **as many as** tantos/tantas como; **there aren't as many as before** no hay tantos como antes; **she got as many points as I did** consiguió tantos puntos como yo.

map *noun* 1 mapa M; **a road map** un mapa de carreteras; 2 (*of a town*) plano M.

marathon *noun* maratón M/F.

marble *noun* 1 mármol M; **a marble fireplace** una chimenea de mármol; 2 canica F; **to play marbles** jugar [27] a las canicas.

March *noun* marzo M.

march *noun* (*demonstration*) manifestación F.
verb (*demonstrators*) manifestarse [29].

mare *noun* yegua F.

margarine *noun* margarina F.

margin *noun* margen M.

marijuana *noun* marihuana F.

material

mark noun **1** (at school) nota F; **I got a good mark for my Spanish homework** he sacado una buena nota en los deberes de español; **what mark did you get for Spanish?** ¿que nota sacaste en español?; **2** (stain) mancha F.
verb (correct) corregir [48].

market noun mercado M.

marketing noun marketing M.

marmalade noun mermelada F de naranja.

marriage noun
matrimonio M (relationship).

married adjective casado/casada; **to be married** estar [2] casado/casada; **he's married** está casado; **they've been married for twenty years** llevan casados veinte años; **a married couple** un matrimonio.

marry verb **1 to marry somebody** casarse [17] con alguien; **she married a Spaniard** se casó con un español; **2 to get married** casarse [17]; **they got married in July** se casaron en julio.

marvellous adjective maravilloso/maravillosa; **the weather's marvellous** el tiempo es maravilloso; **how marvellous!** ¡qué maravilla!

marzipan noun mazapán M.

mascara noun rímel M.

masculine noun (in Spanish and other grammars) masculino M; **in the masculine** en masculino.

mash verb triturar [17] (vegetables).

mashed potatoes noun puré M de patatas.

mask noun máscara F.

mass noun **1 a mass of** un montón de; **2 masses of** un montón de; **they've got masses of money** tienen un montón de dinero; **there's masses left over** queda un montón; **3** (religious) misa F; **to go to mass** ir [8] a misa.

massage noun masaje M.

massive adjective enorme.

mat noun **1** (doormat) felpudo M; **2** (bathmat) alfombrilla F; **3** (for hot dish) salvamanteles M (does not change in the plural).

match noun **1** cerilla F; **a box of matches** una caja de cerillas; **2** (sports) partido M; **a football match** un partido de fútbol; **to watch the match** ver [16] el partido; **to win the match** ganar [17] el partido; **to lose the match** perder [36] el partido.
verb hacer [7] juego con; **the jacket matches the skirt** la chaqueta hace juego con la falda.

mate noun amigo M, amiga F; **I'm going out with my mates tonight** voy a salir esta noche con mis amigos.

material noun **1** (fabric) tela F; **2** (information) material M; **teaching materials** material educativo; **3** (substance) materia F; **raw materials** materias primas.

mathematics *noun* matemáticas F (*plural*).

maths *noun* matemáticas F (*plural*); **I like maths** me gustan las matemáticas; **Anna's good at maths** a Anna se le dan bien las matemáticas.

matter *noun* **what's the matter?** ¿qué pasa?
verb **1** importar [17]; **the things that matter** lo que importa; **it matters a lot to me** me importa mucho; **2 it doesn't matter** no importa; **it doesn't matter if it rains** no importa que llueva; **3 it doesn't matter** (*whether one thing or another*) da lo mismo; **you can write it in Spanish or French, it doesn't matter** puedes escribirlo en español o en francés, da lo mismo.

mattress *noun* colchón M.

maximum *noun* máximo M.
adjective máximo/máxima.

May *noun* mayo M.

may *verb* **1 she may be ill** puede que esté enferma; **we may go to Spain** puede que vayamos a España; **2** (*asking permission*) **may I close the door?** ¿puedo cerrar la puerta?

maybe *adverb* quizás; **maybe not** quizás no; **maybe he's forgotten** quizás se ha olvidado; **maybe they've got lost** quizás se han perdido.

mayonnaise *noun* mayonesa F.

mayor *noun* alcalde M, alcaldesa F.

me *pronoun* **1** me; **she knows me** me conoce; **she gave me the documents** me dio los documentos; **2** (*with an infinitive or when telling someone to do something, 'me' joins onto the verb*) **can you help me, please?** ¿puedes ayudarme por favor?; **listen to me!** ¡escúchame!; **wait for me!** ¡espérame!; (*but when telling someone NOT to do something, 'me' comes before the verb*) **don't push me!** ¡no me empujes!; **3** (*after a preposition*) mí; **behind me** detrás de mí; **they left without me** se fueron sin mí; **with me** conmigo; **I took her with me** la traje conmigo; **4** (*in comparisons or after the verb 'to be'*) yo; **she's older than me** es mayor que yo; **it's me** soy yo; **me too!** ¡yo también!; **5 excuse me!** ¡perdona!

meal *noun* comida F.

mean *verb* **1** querer [12] decir; **what do you mean?** ¿qué quieres decir?; **what does that mean?** ¿qué quiere decir eso?; **that's not what I meant** eso no es lo que quería decir; **2** (*imply*) suponer [11]; **that means that I'll have to do it again** eso supone que voy a tener que hacerlo otra vez; **3 to mean to do** tener [9] la intención de; **I meant to phone my mother** tenía la intención de llamar a mi madre; **4 she was meant to be here at six** se supone que ella tenía que estar aquí a las seis; **this is meant to be easy** se supone que esto es fácil.
adjective **1** (*with money*) tacaño/tacaña; **2** (*nasty*) **she's really mean to her brother** trata muy mal a su hermano; **what a mean thing to do!** ¡qué maldad!

meaning *noun* significado M.

means *noun* **1** medio M; **a means of transport** un medio de transporte; **by means of** por medio de; **2 a means of doing** una forma de hacer; **we have no means of contacting him** no tenemos forma de contactar con él; **3 by all means** por supuesto.

meantime *adverb* **for the meantime** por ahora; **in the meantime** mientras tanto.

measles *noun* sarampión M.

measure *verb* medir [57].

measurements *plural noun* **1** (*of a room or an object*) medidas F (*plural*); **the measurements of the room** las medidas de la habitación; **2** (*of a person*) medida F; **my waist measurement** mi medida de cintura.

meat *noun* carne F.

Mecca *noun* La Meca F.

mechanic *noun* mecánico M, mecánica F; **he's a mechanic** es mecánico.

medal *noun* medalla F; **the gold medal** la medalla de oro.

media *noun* **the media** los medios de comunicación.

medical *noun* revisión F médica; **to have a medical** someterse [18] a una revisión médica. *adjective* médico/médica.

medicine *noun* **1** medicamento M; **2** (*science*) medicina F; **she's**

studying medicine está estudiando medicina; **alternative medicine** medicina alternativa.

Mediterranean *noun* **the Mediterranean** el Mediterráneo.

medium *adjective* mediano/mediana.

medium-sized *adjective* de tamaño mediano.

meet *verb* **1** (*by chance*) encontrarse [24] con; **I met Rosie outside the baker's** me encontré con Rosie en la puerta de la panadería; **2** (*by appointment*) haber [6] quedado (con); **we're meeting at six** hemos quedado a las seis; **I'm meeting him at the museum** he quedado con él en el museo; **shall we meet after work** ¿quedamos después del trabajo?; **3** (*get to know*) conocer [35] a; **I met a Spanish girl last week** conocí a una chica española la semana pasada; **have you met Oskar?** ¿conoces a Oskar?; **4 Tom, meet Ann** Tom, te presento a Ann; **pleased to meet you!** ¡encantado/encantada!; **5** (*off a train, bus, plane*) recoger [3]; **my dad's meeting me at the station** mi padre va a ir a recogerme a la estación.

meeting *noun* reunión F; **there's a meeting a ten o'clock** hay una reunión a las diez; **she's in a meeting** está en una reunión.

megabyte *noun* megabyte M.

melon *noun* melón M.

melt *verb* **1** (*snow, butter, ice cream*) derretirse [57]; **it melts in your**

mouth se derrite en la boca; **2 to melt something** derretir [57] algo; **melt the butter in a saucepan** derretir la mantequilla en una sartén.

member *noun* **1** (*of party or committee*) miembro M/F; **she's a member of the Labour Party** es miembro del partido laborista; **2** (*of club*) socio M, socia F.

Member of Parliament *noun* diputado M, diputada F.

memorial *noun* monumento M; **a war memorial** un monumento a los caídos.

memorize *verb* **to memorize something** aprender [18] algo de memoria.

memory *noun* **1** (*of a person or computer*) memoria F; **you have a good memory!** ¡tienes buena memoria!; **I have a bad memory** tengo mala memoria; **2** (*of the past*) recuerdo M; **I have good memories of my stay in Spain** tengo buenos recuerdos de mi estancia en España.

mend *verb* arreglar [17].

mental *adjective* mental; **a mental illness** una enfermedad mental; **a mental hospital** un hospital psiquiátrico.

mention *verb* mencionar [17].

menu *noun* menú M; **on the menu** en el menú.

meringue *noun* merengue M.

merit *noun* mérito M.

merry *adjective* **1** alegre; **Merry Christmas** Feliz Navidad; **2** (*from drinking*) achispado/achispada (*informal*).

merry-go-round *noun* tiovivo M.

mess *noun* desorden M; **my papers are in a mess** mis papeles están desordenados; **don't make a mess!** ¡no desordenes nada!; **what a mess!** ¡qué desastre! (*informal*).
● **to mess about** hacer [7] el tonto; **stop messing about!** ¡deja de hacer el tonto!
● **to mess about with something** jugar [27] con algo; **it's dangerous to mess about with matches** es peligroso jugar con cerillas.
● **to mess something up** desordenar [17] algo; **you've messed up all my papers** ¡me has desordenado todos mis papeles!

message *noun* mensaje M; **a telephone message** un recado.

messenger *noun* mensajero M, mensajera F.

messy *adjective* **1 it's a messy job** es un trabajo sucio; **2 he's a messy eater** se ensucia mucho comiendo; **her writing's really messy** escribe sin poner cuidado.

metal *noun* metal M.

meter *noun* **1** (*electricity, gas, taxi*) contador M; **to read the meter** leer [37] el contador; **2 a parking meter** un parquímetro.

method *noun* método M.

Methodist *noun* metodista M/F; **I'm a Methodist** soy metodista.

metre *noun* metro M.

metric *adjective* métrico/métrica.

Mexico *noun* Méjico M.

microchip *noun* microchip M.

microphone *noun* micrófono M.

microscope *noun* microscopio M.

microwave oven *noun* microondas M (*does not change in the plural*).

midday *noun* mediodía M; **at midday** al mediodía.

middle *noun* 1 medio M; **in the middle of the room** en medio de la habitación; 2 **in the middle of the night** en mitad de la noche; **in the middle of the day** alrededor del mediodía; **in the middle of the year** a mediados de año; 3 **to be in the middle of doing** estar [2] haciendo; **when she phoned I was in the middle of washing my hair** cuando llamó estaba lavándome el pelo.

middle-aged *adjective* de mediana edad; **a middle-aged woman** una mujer de mediana edad.

middle-class *adjective* de clase media; **a middle-class family** una familia de clase media.

Middle-East *noun* Oriente M Medio.

midge *noun* mosquito M pequeño.

midnight *noun* medianoche F; **at midnight** a medianoche.

Midsummer's Day *noun* la noche de San Juan.

might *verb* **I might invite Jo** puede que invite a Jo; **Amanda might know** puede que Amanda lo sepa; **he might have forgotten** puede que se haya olvidado; **'are you going to phone him?' – 'I might'** '¿vas a llamarlo?' – 'quizás'.

migraine *noun* jaqueca F.

mike *noun* micro M (*informal*).

mild *adjective* 1 suave (*soap or cheese*); 2 templado/templada (*climate*); **it's quite mild today** hoy no hace frío.

mile *noun* 1 milla F; (*Spanish people use kilometres for distances; to convert miles roughly to kilometres, multiply by 8 and divide by 5*) **the village is ten miles from Oxford** el pueblo está a dieciséis kilómetros de Oxford; 2 **it's miles better!** ¡es mil veces mejor! (*informal*).

milk *noun* leche F; **full-cream milk** leche entera; **skimmed milk** leche desnatada; **semi-skimmed milk** leche semidesnatada.
verb ordeñar [17].

milk chocolate *noun* chocolate M con leche.

milkman *noun* lechero M.

milkshake *noun* batido M.

millimetre *noun* milímetro M.

million *noun* millón M; **a million people** un millón de personas; **two million people** dos millones de personas.

millionaire *noun* millonario M, millonaria F.

mince *noun* carne F picada.

mind *noun* 1 mente F; **a logical mind** una mente lógica; 2 **it crossed my mind that ...** se me pasó por la cabeza que ...; 3 **to change your mind** cambiar [17] de opinión; **I've changed my mind** he cambiado de opinión; 4 **to make up your mind** decidirse [19]; **I can't make up my mind** no puedo decidirme.
verb 1 cuidar [17]; **can you mind my bag for me?** ¿me cuidas el bolso?; **could you mind the baby for ten minutes?** ¿puedes cuidar del niño diez minutos?; 2 **do you mind if ...?** ¿te importa que ...?; **do you mind if I close the door?** ¿te importa que cierre la puerta?; **I don't mind** no me importa; **never mind!** ¡no importa!; 3 **I don't mind the heat** no me molesta el calor; 4 **mind the step!** ¡cuidado con el escalón!

mine¹ *noun* mina F; **a coal mine** una mina de carbón.

mine² *pronoun* 1 (*referring to a singular noun*) el mío/la mía; **she took her hat and I took mine** ella cogió su sombrero y yo cogí el mío; **Tessa phoned her mum and I phoned mine** Tessa llamó a su madre y yo llamé a la mía; 2 (*referring to a plural noun*) los míos/las mías; **Karen's invited her parents and I've invited mine** Karen ha invitado a sus padres y yo a los míos; **she showed me her photos and I showed her mine** ella me enseñó sus fotos y yo le enseñé las mías.

miner *noun* minero M, minera F.

mineral water *noun* agua F mineral.

minibus *noun* microbús M.

minimum *noun* mínimo M. *adjective* mínimo/mínima; **the minimum age** la edad mínima.

miniskirt *noun* minifalda F.

minister *noun* 1 (*in government*) ministro M, ministra F; 2 (*of a church*) pastor M, pastora F.

minor *adjective* menor.

minority *noun* minoría F.

mint *noun* 1 (*herb*) menta F; 2 (*sweet*) caramelo M de menta.

minus *preposition* 1 menos; **seven minus three is four** siete menos tres es cuatro; 2 **it was minus ten this morning** esta mañana hacía diez grados bajo cero.

minute *noun* minuto M; **it's five minutes' walk from here** está a cinco minutos andando de aquí; **I'll be ready in two minutes** en dos minutos estoy lista; **just a minute!** ¡un momento!

miracle *noun* milagro M.

mirror *noun* 1 espejo M; **I looked at myself in the mirror** me miré al espejo; 2 (*rearview mirror in a car*) retrovisor M.

misbehave *verb* portarse [17] mal.

mischief *noun* **to get up to mischief** hacer [7] travesuras.

mischievous *adjective* travieso/traviesa.

miser *noun* avaro/avara.

miserable *adjective* 1 triste; **he was miserable without her** estaba triste sin ella; **I feel really miserable today** hoy tengo el ánimo por los suelos; 2 **it's miserable weather** un tiempo deprimente; 3 **she gets paid a miserable wage** le pagan un sueldo miserable.

miss *verb* 1 perder [36]; **she missed her train** perdió el tren; **I missed the film** me perdí la película; **to miss an opportunity** perder una oportunidad; 2 **the ball missed the goal** la pelota no entró en la portería; **you missed!** ¡fallaste!; 3 faltar [17] a; **he's missed several classes** ha faltado a varias clases; 4 **I miss you** te echo de menos; **she's missing her sister** echa de menos a su hermana; **I miss Madrid** echo de menos Madrid.

Miss *noun* señorita F (*usually abbreviated to 'Srta'*); **Miss Jones** la señorita Jones.

missing *adjective* 1 **the missing piece** la pieza que falta; **the missing documents** los documentos que faltan; **the missing link** el eslabón perdido; 2 faltar [17]; **there's a plate missing** falta un plato; **there are three forks missing** faltan tres tenedores; **is there anybody missing?** ¿falta alguien?; 3 **to go missing** desaparecer [35]; **several things have gone missing lately** han desaparecido varias cosas últimamente; **three people have gone missing** han desaparecido tres personas.

mist *noun* neblina F.

mistake *noun* 1 error M; **by mistake** por error; **it was my mistake** fue un error mío; 2 falta F; **a spelling mistake** una falta de ortografía; **you've made lots of mistakes** has cometido muchas faltas; 3 **to make a mistake** (*be mistaken*) cometer [18] un error; **sorry, I made a mistake** perdona, he cometido un error.
verb confundir [19]; **I mistook you for your brother** te confundí con tu hermano.

mistaken *adjective* **to be mistaken** estar [2] equivocado/equivocada; **you're mistaken** estás equivocado.

mistletoe *noun* muérdago M.

misunderstand *verb* entender [36] mal; **I misunderstood** lo entendí mal.

misunderstanding *noun* malentendido M; **there's been a misunderstanding** hay un malentendido.

mix *noun* 1 mezcla F; **a good mix of people** una buena mezcla de gente; 2 **a cake mix** un preparado para hacer un pastel.
verb 1 mezclar [17]; **mix all the ingredients together** mezclar todos los ingredientes; 2 **to mix with** tratarse [17] con; **she mixes with lots of interesting people** se trata con mucha gente interesante.
● 1 **to mix up** desordenar [17]; **you've mixed up all my papers** has desordenado todos mis papeles; 2 (*confuse*) confundir [19]; (*confuse*) **I get him mixed up with his brother** lo confundo con su hermano; **you've got it all mixed up!** ¡te has confundido!

mixed *adjective* variado/variada; **a mixed programme** un programa variado.

mixed salad *noun* ensalada F mixta.

mixture *noun* mezcla F; **it's a mixture of jazz and rock** es una mezcla de jazz y rock.

moan *verb* (*complain*) quejarse [17]; **stop moaning!** ¡deja de quejarte!

mobile home *noun* caravana F fija.

mobile phone *noun* teléfono M móvil.

mock *noun* (*mock exam*) examen M de práctica.
verb burlarse [17] de; **stop mocking me!** ¡deja de burlarte de mí!

model *noun* 1 (*type*) modelo M; **the latest model** el último modelo; 2 (*fashion model*) modelo M/F;

she's a model es modelo; 3 (*of a plane, car, etc.*) maqueta F; **he makes models** construye maquetas; **a model of Westminster Abbey** una maqueta de la abadía de Westminster.

model aeroplane *noun* aeromodelo M.

model railway *noun* ferrocarril M de juguete.

modem *noun* módem M.

moderate *adjective* moderado/moderada.

modern *adjective* moderno/moderna.

modern languages *noun* lenguas F (*plural*) modernas.

modernize *verb* modernizar [22].

moisturizer *noun* 1 (*lotion*) loción F hidratante; 2 (*cream*) crema F hidratante.

mole *noun* 1 (*animal*) topo M; 2 (*on skin*) lunar M.

moment *noun* momento M; **he'll be here in a moment** llegará en cualquier momento; **at any moment** en cualquier momento; **at the moment** en este momento; **at the right moment** en el momento preciso; **for the moment** de momento.

monarchy *noun* monarquía F.

Monday *noun* lunes M (*does not change in the plural*); **on Monday** el lunes; **I'm going out on Monday** voy a salir el lunes; **see you on Monday!**

¡te veo el lunes!; **on Mondays** los lunes; **the museum is closed on Mondays** el museo cierra los lunes; **every Monday** todos los lunes; **last Monday** el lunes pasado; **next Monday** el próximo lunes.

money *noun* dinero M; **I don't have enough money** no tengo suficiente dinero; **to make money** hacer [7] dinero; **they gave me my money back** (*in a shop*) me devolvieron el dinero.

money box *noun* hucha F.

mongrel *noun* chucho M (*informal*).

monitor *noun* (*on computer*) monitor M.

monkey *noun* 1 mono M; 2 **you little monkey!** ¡diablillo! (*informal*).

monster *noun* monstruo M.

month *noun* mes M; **in the month of May** en el mes de mayo; **this month** este mes; **next month** el próximo mes; **we're leaving next month** nos vamos el próximo mes; **last month** el mes pasado; **every month** todos los meses; **in two months' time** dentro de dos meses; **at the end of the month** a final de mes.

monthly *adjective* mensual; **a monthly payment** una mensualidad.

monument *noun* monumento M.

mood *noun* humor M; **to be in a good mood** estar [2] de buen humor; **to be in a bad mood** estar [2] de mal humor; **I'm not in the mood** no estoy de humor.

moody *adjective* temperamental.

moon *noun* luna F; **by the light of the moon** a la luz de la luna; ★ **to be over the moon** estar loco/loca de contento (*literally: to be mad with happiness*).

moonlight *noun* luz F de la luna; **by moonlight** a la luz de la luna.

moped *noun* ciclomotor M.

moral *noun* moraleja F; **the moral of the story** la moraleja de la historia. *adjective* moral.

morals *plural noun* moralidad F.

more *adverb, adjective pronoun* 1 más; **more interesting** más interesante; **more easily** más fácilmente; **a little more milk** un poco más de leche; **a few more glasses** unos cuantos vasos más; **would you like some more cake?** ¿quieres más pastel?; **we need three more** necesitamos tres más; 2 **more … than** más … que; **the book's more interesting than the film** el libro es más interesante que la película; **he eats more than me** come más que yo; 3 **more and more** cada vez más; **books are getting more and more expensive** los libros están cada vez más caros; **it takes more and more time** lleva cada vez más tiempo; 4 **more or less** más o menos; **it's more or less finished** está más o menos terminado; 5 **any more** más; **I don't want any more** no quiero más; **I don't like it any more** ya no me gusta.

morning *noun* mañana F; **this morning** esta mañana; **tomorrow morning** mañana por la mañana; **yesterday morning** ayer por la mañana; **in the morning** por la mañana; **she doesn't work in the morning** no trabaja por las mañanas; **on Friday mornings** los viernes por la mañana; **at six o'clock in the morning** a las seis de la mañana; **I spent the whole morning doing the washing-up** me pasé toda la mañana lavando los platos.

Morocco *noun* Marruecos M.

Moscow *noun* Moscú M.

Moslem *noun* musulmán M, musulmana F.

mosque *noun* mezquita F.

mosquito *noun* mosquito M; **a mosquito bite** una picadura de mosquito.

most *adjective, adverb, pronoun* **1** (*followed by a plural noun*) la mayoría de; **most children like chocolate** a la mayoría de los niños les gusta el chocolate; **most of my friends** la mayoría de mis amigos; **2** (*followed by a singular noun*) casi todo; **they've eaten most of the chocolate** se han comido casi todo el chocolate; **3 most of the time** la mayor parte del tiempo; **most of it is clear** la mayor parte está claro; **4 the most** (*followed by adjective*) más; **the most interesting film** la película más interesante; **the most exciting**

story la historia más emocionante; **the most boring books** los libros más aburridos; **5 the most** (*followed by noun*) **I've got the most time** soy el que más tiempo tiene; **6** (*after a verb*) **what I hate most is the noise** lo que más odio es el ruido.

mother *noun* madre F; **my mother** mi madre; **Kate's mother** la madre de Kate.

mother-in-law *noun* suegra F.

Mother's Day *noun* día M de la Madre (*in Spain, the first Sunday in May*).

motivated *adjective* motivado/ motivada.

motivation *noun* motivo M.

motor *noun* motor M.

motorbike *noun* motocicleta F.

motorcyclist *noun* motociclista M/ F.

motorist *noun* automovilista M/F.

motor racing *noun* carreras F (*plural*) de coches.

motorway *noun* autopista F.

mouldy *adjective* mohoso/mohosa.

mountain *noun* montaña F; **in the mountains** en las montañas.

mountain bike *noun* bicicleta F de montaña.

mountaineer *noun* montañero M, montañera F.

mountaineering *noun* montañismo M; **to go**

mountaineering hacer [7] montañismo.

mountainous *adjective* montañoso/montañosa.

mouse *noun* ratón M (*both the animal and for a computer*).

mousse *noun* mousse F; **chocolate mousse** mousse de chocolate.

moustache *noun* bigote M.

mouth *noun* boca F.

mouthful *noun* bocado M (*of food*) trago M (*of drink*).

mouth organ *noun* armónica F; **to play the mouth organ** tocar [31] la armónica.

move *noun* 1 (*to a different house*) mudanza F; 2 (*in a game*) **your move!** ¡tu turno!
verb 1 moverse [38]; **she didn't move** no se movió; 2 **move up a bit** córrete un poco; 3 (*an object*) cambiar [17] de sitio; **you've moved the picture** has cambiado el cuadro de sitio; **can you move your bag, please?** ¿puedes correr tu bolsa, por favor?; 4 mover [38] (*an object or part of the body*); **she moved her hand** movió la mano; 5 (*car, traffic*) avanzar [22]; **the traffic was moving slowly** el tráfico avanzaba lentamente; 6 **to move forward** avanzar [22]; **he moved forward a step** avanzó un paso; 7 (*move house*) mudarse [17]; **we're moving on Tuesday** nos mudamos el martes; **they've moved house** se han mudado de casa; **they've moved to Spain** se han ido a vivir a España;

8 (*emotionally*) conmover [38]; **it really moved me** me conmovió de verdad; **to be moved** estar [2] conmovido/conmovida.

movie *noun* película F; **to go to the movies** ir [8] al cine.

moving *adjective* 1 en marcha; **a moving vehicle** un vehículo en marcha; 2 (*emotionally*) conmovedor/conmovedora; **it's a very moving film** es una película muy conmovedora.

MP *noun* diputado M, diputada F; **she's an MP** es diputada.

Mr *noun* Señor (*usually abbreviated to 'Sr.'*); **Mr Angus Brown** el Sr. Angus Brown.

Mrs *noun* Señora (*usually abbreviated to 'Sra.'*); **Mrs Mary Hendry** la Sra. Mary Hendry.

Ms *noun* Señora (*usually abbreviated to 'Sra.'; note that there is no direct equivalent to 'Ms' in Spanish, but 'Señora' may be used whether the woman is married or not*).

much *adverb, pronoun, adjective* 1 mucho; **she doesn't eat much** no come mucho; **we don't go out much** no salimos mucho; **much more** mucho más; **much shorter** mucho más bajo; 2 (*followed by a noun*) mucho/mucha; **we don't have much time** no tenemos mucho tiempo; **there isn't much butter left** no queda mucha mantequilla; 3 **very much** mucho; **I don't watch television very much** no veo mucho la tele; **thank you very much** muchas gracias; **4 very much** (*followed by a noun*) mucho/mucha; **there isn't very much milk** no queda mucha leche; **5 not much** (*referring to a verb*) no mucho; **'do you go out?'** – **'not much'** '¿sales?' – 'no mucho'; **6 not much** (*referring to a noun*) no mucho/no mucha; **'did you add salt?'** – **'yes, but not much'** '¿has puesto sal?' – 'sí, pero no mucha'; **7 so much** tanto; **we liked it so much!** ¡nos gustó tanto!; **I have so much to do!** ¡tengo tanto que hacer!; **you shouldn't have given me so much** no deberías haberme dado tanto; **8 as much as** tanto como; **you can take as much as you like** puedes coger tanto como quieras; **9 too much** demasiado; **that's far too much!** ¡eso es demasiado!; **10 too much** (*followed by noun*) demasiado/demasiada; **too much ink** demasiada tinta; **11 how much?** ¿cuánto?; **how much is it?** ¿cuánto cuesta?; **how much do you want?** ¿cuánto quieres?; **12 how much?** (*followed by a noun*) ¿cuánto?/¿cuánta?; **how much milk do you want?** ¿cuánta leche quieres?

mud *noun* barro M.

muddle *noun* desorden M; **to be in a muddle** estar [2] todo desordenado.

muddy *adjective* lleno de barro/llena de barro; **your boots are all muddy** tus botas están llenas de barro; **a muddy road** una carretera llena de barro.

mug *noun* taza F alta; **a mug of coffee** una taza alta de café.

verb **to mug somebody** atracar [31] a alguien; **my brother was mugged in the park** atracaron a mi hermano en el parque.

mugging *noun* atraco M.

multiplication *noun* multiplicación F.

multiply *verb* multiplicar [31]; **to multiply six by four** multiplicar seis por cuatro.

mum, mummy *noun* **1** madre F; **Tom's mum** la madre de Tom; **I'll ask my mum** preguntaré a mi madre; **2** (*within the family or as a name*) mamá F; **mum's not back yet** mamá no ha vuelto todavía.

mumps *noun* paperas F (*plural*).

murder *noun* asesinato M.
verb asesinar [17].

murderer *noun* asesino M, asesina F.

muscle *noun* músculo M.

museum *noun* museo M; **to go to the museum** ir [8] al museo.

mushroom *noun* champiñón M.

music *noun* música F; **pop music** música pop; **classical music** música clásica.

musical *noun* musical M.
adjective **1 a musical instrument** un instrumento musical; **2 they're a very musical family** toda la familia tiene dotes para la música.

musician *noun* músico M, música F.

Muslim *noun* musulmán M, musulmana F.

musulmana F.

mussel *noun* mejillón M.

must *verb* 1 (*expressing obligation*) tener [9] que (*stronger*) deber [18]; **you must be there at eight** tienes que estar allí a las ocho, debes estar allí a las ocho; 2 (*expressing probability*) deber [18]; **you must be tired** debes estar cansado; **it must be five o'clock** deben ser las cinco en punto; **he must have forgotten** debe haberse olvidado.

mustard *noun* mostaza F.

my *adjective* 1 (*before a singular noun*) mi; **my book** mi libro; **my sister** mi hermana; 2 (*before a plural noun*) mis; **my children** mis hijos; 3 (*with parts of the body*) el/la/los/las; **I had a glass in my hand** tenía un vaso en la mano; **I'm washing my hands** me estoy lavando las manos.

myself *pronoun* 1 (*as a reflexive*) me; **I've hurt myself** me he hecho daño; 2 **I said it myself** lo dije yo mismo; 3 (*for emphasis*) yo; **by myself** yo solo/yo sola; **I did it by myself** lo hice yo solo/yo sola.

mysterious *adjective* misterioso/misteriosa.

mystery *noun* 1 misterio M;

N n

nail *noun* 1 (*on finger or toe*) uña F; **to bite your nails** morderse [38] las uñas; 2 (*metal*) clavo M.

nailbrush *noun* cepillo M de uñas.

nailfile *noun* lima F de uñas.

nail scissors *noun* tijeras F (*plural*) de uñas.

nail varnish *noun* esmalte M de uñas.

nail varnish remover *noun* quitaesmalte M.

name *noun* 1 nombre M; **I've forgotten her name** se me ha olvidado su nombre; **what's your name?** ¿cómo te llamas?; **my name's Lily** me llamo Lily; 2 (*of a book or film*) título M.

napkin *noun* servilleta F.

nappy *noun* pañal M.

narrow *adjective* estrecho/estrecha; **a narrow street** una calle estrecha.

nasty *adjective* 1 (*mean*) cruel; **they were nasty to him** fueron crueles con él; **that was a nasty thing to do** eso fue una crueldad; 2 (*unpleasant*) desagradable; **that's a nasty job** ese es un trabajo desagradable; 3 (*bad*) repugnante; **a nasty smell** un olor repugnante.

nation *noun* nación F.

national *adjective* nacional.

national anthem *noun* himno M nacional.

nationality *noun* nacionalidad F.

national park *noun* parque M nacional.

natural *adjective* natural.

naturally *adverb* naturalmente.

nature *noun* naturaleza F.

nature reserve *noun* reserva F natural.

naughty *adjective* malo/mala.

navy *noun* marina F; **my uncle's in the navy** mi tío está en la marina.

navy-blue *adjective* azul marino. **navy-blue gloves** guantes azul marino.

near *adjective* cercano/cercana; **the nearest shop** la tienda más cercana. *adverb, preposition* **1** cerca; **they live quite near** viven bastante cerca; **to come nearer** acercarse [31]; **2 near (to)** cerca de; **near the station** cerca de la estación.

nearby *adverb* cerca; **there's a park nearby** hay un parque cerca.

nearly *adverb* casi; **nearly empty** casi vacío; **we're nearly there** ya casi hemos llegado.

neat *adjective* **1** (*well-organized*) ordenado/ordenada; **a neat desk** un pupitre ordenado; **2** arreglado/arreglada (*your clothes, or the way you look*); **she always looks very neat** siempre va muy arreglada; **3** muy cuidado/muy cuidada (*a garden*).

necessarily *adverb* **not necessarily** no necesariamente.

necessary *adjective* necesario/necesaria; **if necessary** si es necesario.

neck *noun* cuello M (*of a person or garment*).

necklace *noun* collar M.

need *noun* necesidad F; **there's no need, I've done it already** no hay necesidad, ya lo he hecho; **there's no need to wait** no hay necesidad de esperar. *verb* **1** necesitar [17]; **we need bread** necesitamos pan; **they need help** necesitan ayuda; **everything you need** todo lo que necesites; **2** (*to have to*) tener [9] que; **I need to drop in at the bank** tengo que pasarme por el banco; **she'll need to check** tendrá que comprobarlo; **3 you needn't decide today** no hace falta que decidas hoy; **you needn't wait** no hace falta que esperes.

needle *noun* aguja F.

negative *noun* (*of a photo*) negativo M.

neglected *adjective* descuidado/descuidada.

neighbour *noun* vecino M, vecina F; **we're going round to the neighbours'** vamos a casa de los vecinos.

neighbourhood *noun* barrio M; **a nice neighbourhood** un barrio agradable.

neither *conjunction* **1 neither … nor** ni … ni; **I have neither the time nor the money** no tengo ni tiempo ni dinero; **2 neither do I** yo tampoco; **'I didn't go'** – **'neither did I'** 'no fui' – 'yo tampoco'; **3** (*with 'gustar'*) **'I don't like fish'** – **'neither do I'** 'no me gusta el pescado' – 'ni a mí tampoco'; **'I didn't like the film'** – **'neither did Kirsty'** 'no me gustó la película' – 'ni a Kirsty tampoco'; **'which do you like?'** – **'neither'** '¿cuál te gusta?' – 'ninguno'.

nephew *noun* sobrino M.

nerve *noun* 1 (*in the body*) nervio M; 2 **to lose one's nerve** perder [36] el valor; 3 **you've got a nerve!** ¡vaya cara que tienes! (*informal*); ★ **he gets on my nerves** me pone los nervios de punta (*informal*).

nervous *adjective* nervioso/ nerviosa; **to feel nervous** (*before a performance or an exam*) estar nervioso.

nest *noun* nido M.

net *noun* red F.

Netherlands *noun* **the Netherlands** los Países Bajos.

nettle *noun* ortiga F.

network *noun* red F.

neutral *noun* (*in a gearbox*) punto M muerto; **to be in neutral** estar [2] en punto muerto.
adjective 1 (*impartial*) neutral; 2 (*colour*) neutro.

never *adjective* 1 nunca; **Ben never smokes** Ben no fuma nunca; **I've never seen the film** no he visto nunca la película; **'have you ever been to Spain?'** – **'no, never'** ¿has estado alguna vez en España?' – 'no, nunca'; 2 **never again!** ¡nunca jamás!; 3 **never mind** no importa.

nevertheless *adverb* sin embargo.

new *adjective* nuevo/nueva; **have you seen their new house?** ¿has visto su casa nueva?; **Debbie's new boyfriend** el nuevo novio de Debbie; **it's a new car** es un coche nuevo.

news *plural noun* 1 (*everyday gossip*) noticia F; **a piece of good news** una buena noticia; **have you heard the news?** ¿te has enterado de la noticia?; **any news?** ¿hay alguna noticia?; 2 (*on TV or radio*) noticias F (*plural*); **the midday news** las noticias del mediodía.

newsagent *noun* vendedor M de periódicos, vendedora F de periódicos; **at the newsagent's** en la tienda de periódicos.

newspaper *noun* periódico M.

newsreader *noun* presentador M, presentadora F.

New Year *noun* Año M Nuevo; **Happy New Year!** ¡Feliz Año Nuevo!

New Year's Day *noun* día M de Año Nuevo.

New Year's Eve *noun* Nochevieja F.

New Zealand *noun* Nueva Zelanda F.

next *adjective* 1 próximo/próxima; **the next train is at ten** el próximo tren sale a las diez; **next week** la próxima semana; **next Thursday** el próximo jueves; **next year** el próximo año; **the next time I see you** la próxima vez que te vea; 2 (*following*) siguiente; **the next day** el día siguiente; **at the next stop**

en la siguiente parada; **3** (*next-door*) **in the next room** en la habitación de al lado.
adverb **1** (*afterwards*) luego; **what did he say next?** ¿qué dijo luego?; **2** (*now*) ahora; **what shall we do next?** ¿qué hacemos ahora?; **3 next to** al lado de; **the girl next to Pat** la chica que está al lado de Pat; **it's next to the baker's** está al lado de la panadería.

next door *adverb* al lado; **they live next door** viven al lado; **the girl next door** la chica de al lado.

nice *adjective* **1** (*pleasant*) agradable; **we had a very nice evening** pasamos una tarde muy agradable; **Brighton's a very nice town** Brighton es una ciudad muy agradable; **have a nice time!** ¡que lo pases bien!; **2** (*attractive to look at*) bonito/bonita (*an object or place*); **that's a nice dress** ese vestido es bonito; **3** (*attractive to look at*) guapo/guapa (*a person*); **you look nice in that dress** estás muy guapa con ese vestido; **4** (*kind, friendly*) majo/maja (*informal*) (*a person*); **she's really nice** es muy majo (*informal*); **5 to be nice to somebody** ser [1] bueno/buena con alguien; **she's been very nice to me** ha sido muy buena conmigo; **6** (*tasting good*) rico/rica; **the food was really nice** la comida estaba muy rica; **7** (*weather*) **it's a nice day** hace buen día; **we had nice weather** tuvimos buen tiempo.

nick *verb* (*steal*) mangar [28] (*informal*).

nickname *noun* apodo M.

niece *noun* sobrina F.

night *noun* noche F; **what are you doing tonight?** ¿qué haces esta noche?; **see you tonight!** ¡hasta esta noche!; **I saw Greg last night** anoche vi a Greg; **it's cold at night** hace frío por la noche; **to stay the night with somebody** pasar [17] la noche con alguien.

night club *noun* club M nocturno.

nightie *noun* camisón M.

nightmare *noun* pesadilla F; **to have a nightmare** tener [9] una pesadilla.

night-time *noun* noche F.

nil *noun* cero M; **they won four-nil** ganaron cuatro a cero.

nine *number* nueve M; **Jake's nine** Jake tiene nueve años; **it's nine o'clock** son las nueve.

nineteen *number* diecinueve M; **Jonny's nineteen** Jonny tiene diecinueve años.

nineties *plural noun* **the nineties** los años noventa; **in the nineties** en los años noventa.

ninety *number* noventa M; **he's ninety** tiene noventa años; **ninety-five** noventa y cinco.

ninth *noun* **1** (*fraction*) **a ninth** una novena parte; **2 the ninth of June** el nueve de junio.
adjective noveno/novena; **on the ninth floor** en la novena planta.

no *adverb* no; **I said no** he dicho que no; **no thank you** no, gracias. *adjective* **1 we've got no bread** no tenemos pan; **no problem!** ¡sin problema!; **2** (*on a notice*) **'no smoking'** 'prohibido fumar'; **'no parking'** 'prohibido aparcar'.

nobody *pronoun* nadie; **'who's there?' – 'nobody'** '¿quién está ahí?' – 'nadie'; **there's nobody in the kitchen** no hay nadie en la cocina; **nobody knows me** nadie me conoce; **nobody answered** no contestó nadie.

nod *verb* (*to say yes*) asentir [14] con la cabeza; **he nodded** asintió con la cabeza.

noise *noun* ruido M; **to make a noise** hacer [7] ruido.

noisy *adjective* ruidoso/ruidosa.

none *pronoun* **1** (*not one*) niguno/ninguna; **'how many students failed the exam?' – 'none'** '¿cuántos estudiantes suspendieron?' – 'ninguno'; **none of the girls knows him** ninguna de las chicas lo conoce; **2 there's none left** no queda nada; **there are none left** no queda ninguno/ninguna.

nonsense *noun* tonterías F plural; **to talk nonsense** decir [5] tonterías; **nonsense! she's at least thirty!** ¡tonterías! tiene por lo menos treinta años.

non-smoker *noun* no fumador M, no fumadora F.

non-stop *adjective* directo/directa (*a train or flight*).

adverb **she talks non-stop** habla sin parar.

noodles *plural noun* fideos M (*plural*).

noon *noun* mediodía M; **at (twelve) noon** a mediodía.

no-one *pronoun* nadie; **'who's there?' – 'no-one'** '¿quién está ahí?' – 'nadie'; **there's no-one in the kitchen** no hay nadie en la cocina; **no-one knows me** nadie me conoce; **no-one answered** nadie contestó.

nor *conjunction* **1 neither … nor** ni … ni; **I have neither the time nor the money** no tengo ni tiempo ni dinero; **2 nor do I** yo tampoco; **'I didn't go' – 'nor did I'** 'no fui' – 'yo tampoco'; **3** (*with 'gustar'*) **'I don't like fish' – 'nor do I'** 'no me gusta el pescado' – 'ni a mí tampoco'; **''I didn't like the film' – 'nor did Kirsty'** 'no me gustó la película' – 'ni a Kirsty tampoco'.

normal *adjective* normal.

normally *adverb* normalmente.

north *noun* norte M; **in the north** en el norte. *adjective*, *adverb* norte (*never changes*); **the north side** la parte norte; **a north wind** un viento del norte; **north of Madrid** al norte de Madrid.

North America *noun* Norteamérica F.

northeast *noun* noreste M. *adjective* **in northeast England** en el noreste de Inglaterra.

Northern Ireland *noun* Irlanda F del Norte.

North Pole *noun* Polo M Norte.

North Sea *noun* **the North Sea** el mar del Norte.

northwest *noun* noroeste M.
adjective **in northwest England** en el noroeste de Inglaterra.

Norway *noun* Noruega F.

Norwegian *noun* **1** (*person*) noruego M, noruega F; **2** (*language*) noruego M.
adjective noruego/noruega.

nose *noun* nariz F; **to blow your nose** sonarse [24] la nariz.

nosebleed *noun* **to have a nosebleed** tener [9] una hemorragia nasal.

not *adverb* **1** no; **not on Saturdays** los sábados no; **not all alone!** ¡completamente solo no!; **not bad** no está mal; **not at all** (*in no way*) en absoluto (*after somebody says 'thank you'*) de nada; **not yet** todavía no; **of course not!** ¡por supuesto que no!; **2** (*when used with a verb*) no; **it's not my car** no es mi coche; **I don't know** no sé; **Sam didn't phone** Sam no llamó; **we decided not to wait** decidimos no esperar; **3 I hope not** espero que no.

note *noun* **1** (*a short letter*) nota F; **she left me a note** me dejó una nota; **2 to take notes** tomar [17] apuntes; **3** (*a banknote*) billete M; **a ten-pound note** un billete de diez libras; **4** (*in music*) nota F.

notebook *noun* cuaderno M.

notepad *noun* bloc M.

nothing *pronoun* **1** nada; **'what did you say?' – 'nothing'** '¿qué has dicho?' – 'nada'; **nothing new** nada nuevo; **nothing special** nada especial; **2** (*when used with a verb*) no ... nada; **she knows nothing** no sabe nada; **but there was nothing there** pero no había nada allí; **I saw nothing** no vi nada; **there's nothing happening** no está pasando nada; **there's nothing new** no hay nada nuevo; **3 they do nothing but fight** no hacen más que pelearse.

notice *noun* **1** (*a sign*) letrero M; **2 don't take any notice of her!** ¡no le hagas caso!; **3 to do something at short notice** hacer [7] algo con poca antelación.
verb notar [17]; **I didn't notice anything** no noté nada.

notice board *noun* tablón M de anuncios.

nought *noun* cero M.

noun *noun* nombre M.

novel *noun* novela F.

novelist *noun* novelista M/F.

November *noun* noviembre M.

now *adverb* **1** ahora; **where is he now?** ¿dónde está ahora?; **they live in the country now** ahora viven en el campo; **2 he's busy just now** está ocupado en este momento; **I saw her just now in the corridor** acabo de verla en el pasillo; **3 do it right now!** ¡hazlo ahora mismo!; **4 now and**

then de vez en cuando; **from now on** de ahora en adelante.

nowhere *adjective* **1** ninguna parte; **nowhere in Spain** en ninguna parte de España; **'where did she go after work?' – 'nowhere'** '¿dónde fue después del trabajo?' – 'a ninguna parte'; **2 there's nowhere to park** no hay sitio donde aparcar.

nuclear *adjective* nuclear; **a nuclear power station** una central nuclear.

nuisance *noun* **1** (*a person*) pesado/pesada; **he's a real nuisance** es un verdadero pesado; **2 it's a nuisance** es un fastidio.

number *noun* número M; **I live at number thirty-one** vivo en el número treinta y uno; **my new phone number** mi nuevo número de teléfono; **a large number of visitors** un gran número de visitantes; **the third number is a 7** el tercer número es un siete.

number plate *noun* matrícula F.

nun *noun* monja F.

nurse *noun* enfermero M, enfermera F; **Janet's a nurse** Janet es enfermera.

nursery *noun* **1** (*for children*) guardería F; **2** (*for plants*) vivero M.

nursery school *noun* jardín M de infancia.

nut *noun* **1** (*walnut*) nuez F; **2** (*almond*) almendra F; **3** (*peanut*) cacahuete M; **4** (*for a bolt*) tuerca F.

nylon *noun* nylon M.

O o

oak *noun* roble M.

oar *noun* remo M.

obedient *adjective* obediente.

obey *verb* obedecer [35] (*a person*); **to obey the rules** respetar [17] las reglas.

object *noun* objeto M. *verb* oponerse [11]; **if you don't object** si no te opones.

objection *noun* objeción F.

oboe *noun* oboe M; **to play the oboe** tocar [31] el oboe.

obsessed *adjective* obsesionado/obsesionada; **she's obsessed with her diet** está obsesionada con su dieta.

obvious *adjective* obvio/obvia.

obviously *adverb* evidentemente; **the house is obviously empty** evidentemente la casa está vacía; **'do you want to come too?' – 'obviously, but it's a bit difficult'** '¿tú quieres venir también?' – 'evidentemente, pero es un poco difícil'.

occasion *noun* ocasión F; **a special occasion** una ocasión especial.

occasionally *adverb* de vez en cuando.

occupation *noun* ocupación F.

occupied *adjective* ocupado/ocupada.

occur *verb* ocurrir [19]; **the accident occurred on Monday** el accidente ocurrió el lunes; **it never occurred to me** nunca se me había ocurrido.

ocean *noun* océano M.

o'clock *adverb* **at ten o'clock** a las diez; **it's three o'clock** son las tres; **exactly five o'clock** exactamente las cinco en punto.

October *noun* octubre M.

odd *adjective* 1 (*strange*) raro/rara; **that's odd, I'm sure I heard the phone** qué raro, estoy seguro de que he oído el teléfono; 2 (*number*) impar; **three is an odd number** el tres es un número impar.

odds and ends *plural noun* cachivaches M (*plural*).

of *preposition* 1 de (*note that 'de+el' becomes 'del'*); **a kilo of tomatoes** un kilo de tomates; **the end of my work** el final de mi trabajo; **the beginning of the concert** el principio del concierto; **the name of the flower** el nombre de la flor; **the sixth of June** el seis de junio; **a cup of tea** una taza de té; 2 **Ray has four horses but he's selling three of them** Ray tiene cuatro caballos, pero va a vender tres; **we ate a lot of it** comimos mucho; **a lot of them** muchos/muchas; **some of them** algunos/algunas; 3 **two of us** dos de nosotros; **a friend of mine** un amigo mío; 4 **a bracelet made of silver** una pulsera de plata.

off *adverb*, *adjective* *preposition* 1 (*switched off*) apagado/apagada; **is the telly off?** ¿está apagada la tele?; **to turn off the lights** apagar [28] la luz; 2 (*tap, water, gas*) cerrado/cerrada; **to turn off the tap** cerrar [29] el grifo; 3 **to be off** (*to leave*) irse [8]; **I'm off** me voy; 4 **a day off** un día libre; **Caro took three days off work** Caro se tomó tres días libres en el trabajo; **Maya's off school today** Maya no ha venido al colegio hoy; 5 **he's off sick** no ha venido al trabajo porque está enfermo; 6 (*cancelled*) suspendido/suspendida; **the match is off** el partido se ha suspendido; 7 **to be off** (*meat or fish*) estar malo/mala; **the milk's off** la leche está cortada.

offence *noun* 1 (*crime*) delito M; 2 **to take offence** ofenderse [18]; **he takes offence easily** se ofende fácilmente.

offer *noun* 1 oferta F; **a job offer** una oferta de trabajo; 2 **'on (special) offer'** 'de oferta (especial)'. *verb* 1 ofrecer [35]; (*a present, a reward, or a job*) **he offered her a chair** le ofreció una silla; 2 **to offer to do** ofrecerse [35] a hacer; **Mike offered to drive me to the station** Mike se ofreció a llevarme a la estación.

office *noun* oficina F; **he's still at the office** aún está en la oficina.

office block, office building *noun* bloque M de oficinas.

official *adjective* oficial; **the official version** la versión oficial.

off-licence *noun* tienda F de vinos y licores.

often *adverb* 1 a menudo; **he's often late** a menudo llega tarde; **I'd like to see Eric more often** me gustaría ver a Eric más a menudo; **do you go often?** ¿vas a menudo?; 2 **how often?** ¿con qué frecuencia?; **how often do you see Rosie?** ¿con qué frecuencia ves a Rosie?

oil *noun* aceite M; **olive oil** aceite de oliva; **suntan oil** aceite bronceador.

oil painting *noun* ólco M (*picture*).

ointment *noun* pomada F.

okay *adjective* 1 (*showing agreement*) vale; **okay, tomorrow at ten** vale, mañana a las diez; 2 (*asking or giving permission*) **is it okay to use the phone?** ¿puedo usar el teléfono?; **is it okay with you if I don't come till Friday?** ¿te va bien si no vengo hasta el viernes?; **it's okay if you don't want to do it** no pasa nada si no quieres hacerlo; 3 (*person*) majo/maja (*informal*); **Daisy's okay** Daisy es maja; 4 (*nothing special*) **the film was okay** la película no estuvo mal; 5 (*not ill*) **are you okay?** ¿estás bien?; **I've been ill but I'm okay now** he estado enferma, pero ahora estoy bien.

old *adjective* 1 (*not young, not new*) viejo/vieja; **an old man** un hombre viejo; **an old lady** una mujer vieja; **bring some old clothes** trae ropa vieja; **an old friend of mine** un viejo amigo mío; **old people** los ancianos; 2 (*previous*) antiguo/antigua; **our old car was a Rover** nuestro antiguo coche era un Rover; **their old address** su antigua dirección; 3 (*talking about age*) **how old are you?** ¿cuántos años tienes?; **James is ten years old** James tiene diez años; **a three-year-old child** un niño de tres años; 4 **my older sister** mi hermana mayor; **she's older than me** es mayor que yo; **he's a year older than me** es un año mayor que yo.

old age *noun* vejez F.

old age pensioner *noun* pensionista M/F.

old-fashioned *noun* 1 (*clothes, music, style*) pasado de moda/pasada de moda; 2 (*a person*) anticuado/anticuada; **my parents are so old-fashioned** mis padres son tan anticuados.

olive *noun* aceituna F.

olive oil *noun* aceite M de oliva.

Olympic Games, Olympics *plural noun* Juegos M (*plural*) Olímpicos.

omelette *noun* tortilla F; **a cheese omelette** una tortilla de queso.

on *preposition* 1 en; **on the desk** en el escritorio; **on the road** en la carretera; **on the beach** en la playa; 2 (*in expressions of time*) **on March 21st** el 21 de marzo; **he's arriving on Tuesday** llega el martes; **it's shut on Saturdays** cierra los sábados; **on rainy days** los días de lluvia; 3 (*for*

buses, trains, etc.) **she arrived on the bus** llegó en autobús; **I met Jackie on the bus** me encontré con Jackie en el autobús; **I slept on the plane** dormí en el avión; **let's go on our bikes!** ¡vayamos en las bicis!; **4 on TV** en la tele; **on the radio** en la radio; **on video** en vídeo; **5 on holiday** de vacacciones; **on strike** de huelga.
adjective **1** (*switched on*) **to be on** (*TV, light, oven, radio*) estar encendido/encendida; **all the lights were on** todas las luces estaban encendidas; **is the radio on?** ¿está encendida la radio?; **I've put the oven on** he encendido el horno; **2** (*machine*) **the dishwasher's on** el lavaplatos esta en marcha; **3** (*happening*) **what's on TV?** ¿qué ponen en la tele?; **what's on this week at the cinema?** ¿qué ponen en el cine esta semana?

once *adverb* **1** una vez; **I've tried once already** ya lo he intentado una vez; **try once more** inténtalo una vez más; **once a day** una vez al día; **more than once** más de una vez; **2 at once** (*immediately*) inmediatamente; **the doctor came at once** el médico vino inmediatamente; **3 at once** (*at the same time*) a la vez; **I can't do two things at once** no puedo hacer dos cosas a la vez.

one *number* **1** uno/una; **one apple** una manzana; (*note that 'uno' becomes 'un' before a masculine singular noun*) **one son** un hijo; **2 it's one o'clock** es la una.
pronoun **1** uno/una; **if you want a pen I've got one** si quieres un boli

yo tengo uno; **one of us** uno de nosotros; **one of my friends** uno de mis amigos; **one never knows** uno nunca sabe; **2 this one** éste/ésta; **I like that jumper, but this one's cheaper** me gusta ese jersey, pero éste es más barato; **do you want this red tie or this one?** ¿quieres esta corbata roja o ésta otra?; **3 that one** ése/ésa; **'which video?' – 'that one'** '¿qué vídeo?' – 'ése'; **4 which one?** ¿cuál?; **'my foot's hurting' – 'which one?'** 'me duele el pie' – '¿cuál?'; **5 another one** otro/otra; **I've already had a coffee, but I'll have another one** ya he tomado un café pero voy a tomar otro; **I liked the shirt so much that I bought another one** me gustó tanto la camisa que compré otra.

one's *adjective* **to pay for one's car** pagar su coche; **to wash one's hands** lavarse las manos.

oneself *pronoun* **1** (*as a reflexive*) se; **to wash oneself** lavarse; **to hurt oneself** hacerse daño; **2** (*for emphasis*) uno mismo/una misma; **one has to do everything oneself** lo tiene que hacer todo uno mismo.

one-way street *noun* calle F de sentido único.

onion *noun* cebolla F.

only *adjective* único/única; **the only free seat** el único sitio libre; **the only thing to do** lo único que se puede hacer; **I am an only child** soy hijo único.
adverb, conjunction **1** (*with a verb*) sólo; **they've only got two**

bedrooms sólo tienen dos habitaciones; **Anne's only free on Fridays** Anne sólo tiene libres los viernes; **there are only three left** sólo quedan tres; **'how long did they stay?' – 'only two days'** '¿cuánto tiempo se quedaron?' – 'sólo dos días'; **2** (*but*) pero; **I'd walk, only it's raining** iría andando, pero está lloviendo; **3 I've only just seen it** acabo de verlo.

onto *preposition* sobre.

open *noun* **in the open** al aire libre.
adjective **1** (*not shut*) abierto/ abierta; **the door's open** la puerta está abierta; **the baker's isn't open** la panadería no está abierta; **2 in the open air** al aire libre.
verb **1** abrir [46]; **can you open the door for me?** ¿me puedes abrir la puerta?; **Sam opened his eyes** Sam abrió los ojos; **the banks open at nine** los bancos abren a las nueve; **2** (*by itself*) abrirse [46]; **the door opened slowly** la puerta se abrió lentamente.

open-air *adjective* al aire libre; **an open-air swimming pool** una piscina al aire libre.

opera *noun* ópera F.

operation *noun* operación F; **she's had an operation** le han operado.

opinion *noun* opinión F; **in my opinion** en mi opinión.

opinion poll *noun* encuesta F de opinión.

opponent *noun* oponente M/F.

opportunity *noun* oportunidad F; **to have the opportunity of doing** tener [9] la oportunidad de hacer; **I took the opportunity to visit the museum** aproveché la oportunidad para visitar el museo.

opposite *noun* **the opposite** lo contrario; **no, quite the opposite** no, todo lo contrario.
adjective **1** opuesto/opuesta (*a direction, side, or view, for example*); **she went off in the opposite direction** se fue en la dirección opuesta; **2** (*facing*) de enfrente; **in the house opposite** en la casa de enfrente.
adverb enfrente; **they live opposite** viven enfrente.
preposition enfrente de; **opposite the station** enfrente de la estación.

optician *noun* oculista M/F.

optimistic *adjective* optimista.

or *conjunction* **1** o (*note that 'o' becomes 'u' before a word starting with 'o' or 'ho'*); **English or Spanish?** ¿inglés o español?; **yesterday or today?** ¿ayer u hoy?; **2** (*in negatives*) **I don't have a cat or a dog** no tengo ni un gato ni un perro; **not in June or July** ni en junio ni en julio; **3** (*or else*) si no; **phone Mum, or she'll worry** llama a mamá, si no se va a preocupar.

oral *noun* (*an exam*) oral M; **the Spanish oral** el oral de español.

orange *noun* (*the fruit*) naranja F;
an orange juice un zumo de
naranja.
adjective naranja (*never changes*);
my orange socks mis calcetines
naranja.

orchestra *noun* orquesta F.

order *noun* **1** (*arrangement*)
orden M; **in the right order**
ordenado/ordenada; **the books are
in the right order** los libros estan
ordenados; **in the wrong order**
desordenado/desordenada; **in
alphabetical order** en orden
alfabético; **2** (*command*) orden F;
that's an order es una orden; **3** (*in a
restaurant or café*) **can I take your
orders?** ¿les tomo la nota?; **4** '**out of
order**' 'no funciona'; **5 in order to
do** para hacer; **we hurried in order
to be on time** nos dimos prisa para
llegar a tiempo.
verb **1** (*in a restaurant or a shop*)
pedir [57]; **we ordered steaks**
pedimos filetes; **2** llamar [17] a (*a
taxi*).

ordinary *adjective* normal.

organ *noun* (*the instrument*)
órgano M; **to play the organ** tocar
[31] el órgano.

organic *adjective* biológico/
biológica (*food*).

organization *noun* organización F.

organize *verb* organizar [22].

original *adjective* original; **the
original version was better** la
versión original era mejor; **it's a
really original novel** es una novela
realmente original.

originally *adverb* al principio;
originally we wanted to take the car
al principio queríamos llevar el
coche.

Orkneys *plural noun* **the Orkneys**
las Órcadas F (*plural*).

ornament *noun* adorno M.

orphan *noun* huérfano M,
huérfana F.

other *adjective* **1** (*before a singular
noun*) otro/otra; **the other day** el
otro día; **we took the other road**
cogimos la otra carretera; **the other
one** el otro/la otra; **I don't like this
book, give me the other one** no me
gusta este libro, dame el otro; **2 the
others** los otros/las otras; **where are
the others?** ¿dónde están los otros?;
the other two cars los otros dos
coches; **3 every other week** una
semana sí y otra no; **4 somebody or
other** alguien; **something or other**
algo; **somewhere or other** en algún
sitio.

otherwise *adverb* (*in other ways*)
aparte de eso; **the flat's a bit small
but otherwise it's lovely** el piso es
pequeño, pero aparte de eso es
precioso.
conjunction (*or else*) si no; **I'll phone
home, otherwise they'll worry** voy
a llamar a casa, si no van a
preocuparse.

ought *verb* deber [18] (*'ought' is
translated by the conditional tense of
'deber'*); **I ought to go now** debería
irme ahora; **they ought to know the
address** deberían saber las señas;
you oughtn't to have any problems
no deberías tener ningún problemas.

our *adjective* **1** (*before a singular noun*) nuestro/nuestra; **our house** nuestra casa; **2** (*before a plural noun*) nuestros/nuestras; **our parents** nuestros padres; **our address** nuestras señas; **3** (*with parts of the body*) el/la/los/las; **we'll go and wash our hands** vamos a lavarnos las manos.

ours *pronoun* **1** (*referring to a singular noun*) el nuestro/la nuestra; **their garden's bigger than ours** su jardín es más grande que el nuestro; **their house is smaller than ours** su casa es más pequeña que la nuestra; **2** (*referring to a plural noun*) los nuestros/las nuestras; **they've invited their friends and we've invited ours** han invitado a sus amigos y nosotros a los nuestros; **they showed us their photos and we showed them ours** ellos nos enseñaron sus fotos y nosotros les enseñamos las nuestras.

ourselves *pronoun* **1** (*as a reflexive*) nos; **we introduced ourselves** nos presentamos; **2** (*for emphasis*) nosotros solos/nosotras solas; **in the end we did it ourselves** al final lo hicimos nosotros solos.

out *adverb* **1** (*outside*) fuera; **it's cold out there** hace frío ahí fuera; **out in the rain** bajo la lluvia; **they're out in the garden** están en el jardín; **2 to go out** salir [63]; **he went out of the room** salió de la habitación; **are you going out this evening?** ¿vas a salir esta noche?; **Alison's going out with Danny at the moment** Alison está saliendo ahora con Danny; **he's**

asked me out me ha pedido que salga con él; **3 to be out** (*absent*) no estar [2]; **my mum's out** mi madre no está; **when they were out** cuando ellos no estaban; **4** (*light, fire*) apagado/apagada; **are all the lights out?** ¿están todas las luces apagadas?; **the fire was out** el fuego estaba apagado; **5 he threw it out of the window** lo tiró por la ventana; **to drink out of a glass** beber [18] de un vaso; **she took the photo out of her bag** sacó la foto del bolso.

outing *noun* excursión F; **to go on an outing** ir [8] de excursión.

outline *noun* (*of an object*) contorno M.

out-of-date *noun* **1** (*no longer valid*) caducado/caducada; **my passport's out of date** mi pasaporte está caducado; **2** (*old-fashioned*) pasado/pasada de moda; **they played out-of-date music** tocaron música pasada de moda.

outside *noun* parte F de fuera; **it's blue on the outside** la parte de fuera es azul.
adjective exterior.
adverb fuera; **it's cold outside** hace frío fuera.
preposition fuera de; **I'll meet you outside the cinema** te veo fuera del cine.

outskirts *noun* afueras F (*plural*); **on the outskirts of York** en las afueras de York.

oven *noun* horno M; **I've put it in the oven** lo he puesto en el horno.

over *preposition, adverb* 1 (*above*) encima de; **there's a mirror over the sideboard** hay un espejo encima del aparador; 2 (*involving movement*) por encima de; **she jumped over the fence** saltó por encima de la valla; **he threw the ball over the wall** tiró la pelota por encima del muro; 3 **over here** aquí; **the drinks are over here** las bebidas están aquí; 4 **over there** allí; **she's over there talking to Julian** está allí, hablando con Julián; 5 (*more than*) más de; **it will cost over a hundred pounds** costará más de cien libras; **he's over sixty** tiene más de sesenta años; 6 (*during*) durante; **over the weekend** durante el fin de semana; **over Christmas** durante las Navidades; 7 (*finished*) **when the meeting's over** cuando la reunión haya acabado; **it's all over now** ahora todo ha acabado; 8 **over the phone** por teléfono; 9 **to ask someone over** invitar [17] a alguien; **can you come over on Saturday?** ¿puedes venir el sábado?; 10 **all over the place** por todas partes; **all over the house** por toda la casa.

overdose *noun* sobredosis F.

overdraft *noun* descubierto M.

overseas *adverb* en el extranjero; **Dave works overseas** Dave trabaja en el extranjero.

overtake *verb* adelantar [17] (*another car*).

overtime *noun* horas F (*plural*) extras; **to work overtime** trabajar [17] horas extras.

owe *verb* deber [18]; **I owe Rick ten pounds** le debo diez libras a Rick.

owing *adjective* 1 (*to pay*) a pagar; **there's five pounds owing** quedan cinco libras a pagar; 2 **owing to** debido a; **owing to the snow** debido a la nieve.

owl *noun* búho M.

own *adjective* 1 propio/propia (*goes before the noun*); **my own computer** mi propio ordenador; **I've got my own room** tengo mi propia habitación; 2 **on your own** solo/sola; **Annie did it on her own** Annie lo hizo sola.
verb tener [9].

owner *noun* dueño M, dueña F.

oxygen *noun* oxígeno M.

oyster *noun* ostra F.

ozone layer *noun* capa F de ozono.

P p

Pacific *noun* **the Pacific Ocean** el océano M Pacífico.

pack *noun* 1 paquete M; 2 **a pack of cards** baraja F.
verb 1 hacer [7] las maletas; 2 **I'll pack my case tonight** voy a hacer la maleta esta noche.

package *noun* paquete M.

package holiday,, package tour *noun* viaje M organizado.

packed lunch *noun* comida F preparada desde casa.

packet *noun* 1 paquete M; **a packet of biscuits** un paquete de galletas; 2 (*bag*) bolsa F; **a packet of crisps** una bolsa de patatas.

packing *noun* **to do your packing** hacer [7] las maletas.

pad *noun* (*of paper*) bloc M.

padlock *noun* cercado M.

page *noun* página F; **on page seven** en la página siete.

pain *noun* dolor M; **to be in pain** tener [9] dolor; **I've got a pain in my leg** me duele la pierna; ★ **Eric's a real pain (in the neck)** Eric es un verdadero pesado.

paint *noun* pintura F; **'wet paint'** 'recién pintado'.
verb pintar [17]; **to paint something pink** pintar algo de rosa.

paintbrush *noun* 1 (*for painting pictures*) pincel M; 2 (*for decorating*) brocha F.

painter *noun* pintor M, pintora F.

painting *noun* (*picture*) cuadro M; **a painting by Monet** un cuadro de Monet.

pair *noun* 1 par M; **a pair of socks** un par de calcetines; **a pair of shoes** un par de zapatos; 2 **a pair of jeans** unos vaqueros; **a pair of trousers** unos pantalones; **a pair of knickers** unas bragas; **a pair of scissors** unas tijeras; 3 (*of people*) pareja F; **to work in pairs** trabajar [17] en parejas.

Pakistan *noun* Pakistán M.

Pakistani *noun* pakistaní M/F.
adjective pakistaní.

palace *noun* palacio M.

pale *adjective* pálido/pálida; **pale green** verde pálido (*never changes*); **pale green curtains** cortinas verde pálido; **to turn pale** palidecer [35].

palm *noun* 1 (*of your hand*) palma F; 2 (*a palm tree*) palmera F.

pan *noun* 1 (*saucepan*) cacerola F; **a pan of water** una cacerola de agua; 2 (*frying-pan*) sartén F.

pancake *noun* crepe M.

panel *noun* 1 (*on radio or TV*) (*for a discussion*) panel M (*for a quiz show*) equipo M; 2 (*for a wall or a bath, for example*) panel M.

panel game *noun* concurso M por equipos.

panic *noun* pánico M.
verb dejarse [17] llevar por el pánico; **don't panic!** ¡no pierdas la calma!

pantomime *noun* pantomima F.

pants *plural noun* calzoncillos M (*plural*).

paper *noun* 1 papel M; **a sheet of paper** una hoja de papel; 2 **a paper hanky** un pañuelo de papel; 3 (*newspaper*) periódico M; **it was in the paper** salió en el periódico.

paperback *noun* libro M en rústica.

paperclip *noun* clip M.

paper towel *noun* toalla F de papel.

parachute *noun* paracaídas M (*does not change in the plural*).

parade *noun* desfile M.

paradise *noun* paraíso M.

paragraph *noun* párrafo M; **'new paragraph'** 'punto y aparte'.

parallel *adjective* paralelo/paralela.

paralysed *adjective* paralizado/paralizada.

parcel *noun* paquete M.

pardon *noun* **I beg your pardon** (*to someone you know*) perdón (*to someone you don't know or to show respect*) perdone; **pardon?** (*to someone you know*) ¿cómo dices? (*to someone you don't know or to show respect*) ¿cómo dice?

parents *noun* **my parents** mis padres; **a parents' evening** una reunión de padres.

park *noun* **1** parque M; **a theme park** un parque temático; **2 a car park** un aparcamiento.
verb **1** aparcar [31]; **you can park outside the house** puedes aparcar fuera de la casa; **2 to park a car** aparcar [31] un coche; **where did you park the car?** ¿dónde has aparcado el coche?

parking *noun* aparcamiento M; **'no parking'** 'no aparcar'.

parking meter *noun* parquímetro M.

parking space *noun* sitio M para aparcar.

parking ticket *noun* multa F.

parliament *noun* parlamento M.

parrot *noun* loro M.

parsley *noun* perejil M.

part *noun* **1** parte F; **part of the garden** parte del jardín; **the last part of the concert** la última parte del concierto; **that's part of your job** eso es parte de tu trabajo; **2 to take part in something** participar [17] en algo; **3** (*in a play*) papel M.

particular *adjective* particular; **nothing in particular** nada en particular.

particularly *adverb* especialmente; **not particularly interesting** no especialmente interesante.

partly *adverb* en parte.

partner *noun* **1** (*in a game*) pareja F; **2** (*the person you live with*) compañero M, compañera F; **3** (*in business*) socio M, socia F.

part-time *adjective*, *adverb* a tiempo parcial; **part-time work** trabajo a tiempo parcial; **to work part-time** trabajar [17] a tiempo parcial.

party *noun* **1** fiesta F; **a Christmas party** una fiesta de Navidad; **to have a birthday party** celebrar [17] una fiesta de cumpleaños; **we've been invited to a party at the Smiths'**

house estamos invitados a una fiesta en casa de los Smith; **2** (*group*) grupo M; **a party of schoolchildren** un grupo de colegiales; **a rescue party** un equipo de rescate; **3** (*in politics*) partido M; **the Labour party** el partido laborista.

pass noun **1** (*to let you in*) pase M; **2 a bus pass** un abono de autobús; **3** (*a mountain pass*) paso M; **4** (*in an exam*) aprobado M; **to get a pass in history** sacar [31] un aprobado en historia.
verb **1** (*go past*) pasar [17] por (*a place or building*); **we passed your house** pasamos por tu casa; **2** (*to overtake*) adelantar [17] (*a car*); **3** (*give*) pasar [17]; **could you pass me the paper please?** ¿me pasas el papel, por favor?; **4** (*time*) pasar [17]; **the time passed slowly** el tiempo pasaba lentamente; **5** (*in an exam*) aprobar [24]; **did you pass?** ¿aprobaste?; **to pass an exam** aprobar un examen.

passenger *noun* pasajero M, pasajera F.

passion *noun* pasión F.

passionate *adjective* apasionado/ apasionada.

passive *noun* voz F pasiva.
adjective pasivo/pasiva.

Passover *noun* Pascua F judía.

passport *noun* pasaporte M; **an EU passport** un pasaporte de la Comunidad Europea.

password *noun* contraseña F.

past *noun* pasado M; **in the past** en el pasado.
adjective **1** (*recent*) último/última (*goes before the noun*); **in the past few weeks** en las últimas semanas; **2** (*over*) **winter is past** ya ha pasado el invierno.
preposition, *adverb* **1 to walk or drive past something** pasar [17] por delante de algo; **we went past the school** pasamos por delante del colegio; **Ray went past in his new car** Ray pasó en su coche nuevo; **2** (*the other side of*) pasado/pasada; **it's just past the post office** está justo pasada la oficina de correos; **3** (*talking about time*) **ten past six** las seis y diez; **half past four** las cuatro y media; **a quarter past two** las dos y cuarto.

pasta *noun* pasta F; **I don't like pasta** no me gusta la pasta.

pasteurized *adjective* pasteurizado/pasteurizada.

pastry *noun* masa F.

path *noun* camino M (*very narrow*) sendero M.

patience *noun* **1** paciencia F; **2** (*card game*) solitario M.

patient *noun* paciente M/F.
adjective paciente.

patiently *adverb* pacientemente.

patio *noun* patio M.

patrol car *noun* coche M patrulla.

pattern *noun* **1** (*on wallpaper or fabric*) diseño M; **2** (*dressmaking*) patrón M; **3** (*knittting*) modelo M.

pavement *noun* acera F; **on the pavement** en la acera.

paw *noun* pata F.

pawn *noun* peón M.

pay *noun* sueldo M.
verb **1** pagar [28]; **I'm paying** yo pago; **to pay cash** pagar al contado; **2 to pay for something** pagar [28] algo; **Tony paid for the drinks** Tony pagó las bebidas; **it's all paid for** está todo pagado; **3 to pay by credit card** pagar [28] con tarjeta de crédito; **to pay by cheque** pagar [28] con cheque; **4 to pay somebody back** (*money*) devolverle [45] dinero a alguien; **5 to pay attention** prestar [17] atención; **6 to pay a visit to somebody** hacer [7] una visita a alguien.

payment *noun* pago M.

pay phone *noun* teléfono M público.

PC *noun* (*computer*) PC M.

pea *noun* guisante M.

peace *noun* paz F.

peaceful *adjective* tranquilo/tranquila (*day, scene*).

peach *noun* melocotón M.

peacock *noun* pavo M real.

peak *noun* (*of a mountain*) pico M.

peak period (*for holidays*) temporada F alta.

peak rate *noun* (*for phoning*) tarifa F máxima.

peak time *noun* (*for traffic*) hora F punta.

peanut *noun* cacahuete M.

peanut butter *noun* mantequilla F de cacahuete.

pear *noun* pera F.

pearl *noun* perla F.

pebble *noun* guijarro M.

pedal *noun* pedal M.
verb pedalear [17].

pedestrian *noun* peatón M, peatona F.

pedestrian crossing *noun* paso M peatonal.

pedestrian precinct *noun* zona F peatonal.

pee *noun* **to have a pee** hacer [7] pis; (*informal*)

peel *noun* **1** (*of an apple*) piel F; **2** (*of an orange*) cáscara F.
verb pelar [17] (*fruit, vegetables*).

peg *noun* **1** (*hook*) gancho M; **2 a clothes peg** una pinza de la ropa; **3 a tent peg** una piqueta.

pen *noun* **1** bolígrafo M, boli M (*informal*); **2** (*fountain pen*) pluma F; **3 a felt pen** un rotulador.

penalty *noun* **1** (*a fine*) multa F; **2** (*in football or rugby*) penalty M.

pence *plural noun* peniques M (*plural*).

pencil *noun* lápiz M; **to write in pencil** escribir [52] a lápiz.

pencil case *noun* estuche M para lápices.

pencil sharpener *noun* sacapuntas M (*does not change in the plural*).

pendant *noun* colgante M.

penfriend *noun* amigo M por correspondencia, amiga F por correspondencia; **my Spanish penfriend is called Cristina** mi amiga por correspondencia española se llama Cristina.

penis *noun* pene M.

penknife *noun* navaja F.

penny *noun* penique M.

pension *noun* pensión F.

pensioner *noun* pensionista M/F.

people *plural noun* 1 gente F (*singular*); **people round here** la gente de por aquí; **nice people** gente simpática; **people say he's very rich** la gente dice que es muy rico; 2 (*when you're counting them*) persona F; **ten people** diez personas; **several people** varias personas; **how many people have you asked?** ¿a cuántas personas has preguntado?

pepper *noun* 1 (*spice*) pimienta F; 2 (*vegetable*) pimiento M; **a green pepper** un pimiento verde.

peppermill *noun* pimentero M.

peppermint *noun* menta F; **peppermint tea** infusión F de menta.

per *preposition* por; **ten pounds per person** diez libras por persona.

per cent *adverb* por ciento; **sixty per cent of students** el sesenta por ciento de los estudiantes.

percentage *noun* porcentaje M.

percussion *noun* percusión F; **to play percussion** tocar [31] la percusión.

perfect *adjective* 1 perfecto/ perfecta; **she speaks perfect English** habla un inglés perfecto; 2 (*ideal*) ideal; **the perfect place for a picnic** el sitio ideal para un picnic.

perfectly *adverb* perfectamente.

perform *verb* 1 interpretar [17] (*a piece of music or a role*); 2 representar [17] (*a play*); 3 cantar [17] (*a song*).

performance *noun* 1 (*playing or acting*) interpretación F; **a wonderful performance of Macbeth** una maravillosa interpretación de Macbeth; 2 (*show*) espectáculo M; **the performance starts at eight** el espectáculo empieza a las ocho; 3 (*the results of a team or company*) actuación F.

performer *noun* artista M/F.

perfume *noun* perfume M.

perhaps *adverb* quizás; **perhaps he's missed the train** quizás ha perdido el tren; **perhaps it's in the drawer?** ¿a lo mejor está el cajón?

period *noun* 1 periodo M; **a two-year period** un periodo de dos años; 2 (*in school*) clase F; **a forty-five-minute period** una clase de cuarenta y cinco minutos; 3 (*menstruation*) periodo M; **to have your period** tener [9] el periodo.

perm *noun* permanente F.

permanent *adjective* permanente.

permanently *adverb* permanentemente.

permission *noun* permiso M; **to get permission to do** conseguir [64] permiso para hacer.

permit *noun* permiso M.
verb permitir [19]; **to permit somebody to do** permitir [19] a alguien hacer; **smoking is not permitted** está prohibido fumar; **weather permitting** si el tiempo lo permite.

person *noun* persona F; **there's room for one more person** hay sitio para una persona más; **in person** en persona.

personal *adjective* personal.

personality *noun* personalidad F.

personally *adverb* personalmente; **personally, I'm against it** personalmente, estoy en contra.

perspiration *noun* sudor M.

persuade *verb* convencer [44]; **to persuade somebody to do** convencer a alguien para que haga (*note that 'para que' is followed by the subjunctive*); **we persuaded Tim to wait a bit** convencimos a Tim para que esperara un poco.

pessimistic *adjective* pesimista.

pest *noun* 1 (*greenfly for example*) plaga F; 2 (*annoying person*) pesado M, pesada F.

pet *noun* 1 animal M de compañía; **do you have a pet?** ¿tienes un animal de compañía?; **a pet dog** un perro de compañía; 2 (*favourite person*) favorito M, favorita F; **Julie is teacher's pet** Julie es la favorita de la maestra.

petal *noun* pétalo M.

pet name *noun* apodo M cariñoso.

petrol *noun* gasolina F; **to fill up with petrol** llenar [17] de gasolina; **to run out of petrol** quedarse [17] sin gasolina.

petrol station *noun* gasolinera F.

pharmacy *noun* farmacia F.

pheasant *noun* faisán M.

philosophy *noun* filosofía F.

phone *noun* teléfono M; **she's on the phone** está hablando por teléfono; **I was on the phone to Sophie** estaba hablando por teléfono con Sophie; **you can book by phone** puedes reservar por teléfono.
verb 1 llamar [17] por teléfono; **while I was phoning** mientras llamaba por teléfono; 2 **to phone somebody** llamar [17] a alguien; **I'll phone you tonight** te llamaré esta noche.

phone book *noun* guía F telefónica.

phone box *noun* cabina F telefónica.

phone call *noun* llamada F telefónica; **phone calls are free** las llamadas telefónicas son gratis; **to make a phone call** hacer [7] una llamada (telefónica).

phone card *noun* tarjeta F telefónica.

phone number *noun* número M de teléfono.

photo *noun* foto F; **to take a photo** hacer [7] una foto; **to take a photo of somebody** hacerle [7] una foto a alguien; **I took a photo of their house** hice una foto de su casa.

photocopier *noun* fotocopiadora F.

photocopy *noun* fotocopia F.
verb fotocopiar [17].

photograph *noun* fotografía F; **to take a photograph** hacer [7] una fotografía; **to take a photograph of somebody** hacerle [7] una fotografía a alguien.
verb fotografiar [32].

photographer *noun* fotógrafo M, fotógrafa F.

photography *noun* fotografía F.

phrase *noun* frase F.

phrase-book *noun* manual M de conversación.

physicist *noun* físico M, física F.

physics *noun* física F.

physiotherapist *noun* fisioterapeuta M/F.

physiotherapy *noun* fisioterapia F.

pianist *noun* pianista M/F.

piano *noun* piano M; **to play the piano** tocar [31] el piano; **Steve played it on the piano** Steve lo tocó al piano; **a piano lesson** una clase de piano.

pick *noun* **take your pick!** ¡escoge!
verb **1** (*to choose*) escoge [3]; **pick a card** escoge una carta; **2** (*for a team*) seleccionar [17]; **I've been picked for Saturday** me han seleccionado para el sábado; **3** recoger [3] (*fruit*); **4** coger [3] (*flowers*).
● **to pick up 1** (*lift*) coger [3]; **he picked up the papers and went out** cogió los papeles y salió; **to pick up the phone** coger el teléfono; **2** (*from the floor*) recoger [3]; **pick up that piece of paper** recoge ese trozo de papel; **3** (*collect together*) recoger [3]; **I'll pick up the toys** voy a recoger los juguetes; **4** (*to collect*) recoger [3]; **I'll pick you up at six** te recogeré a las seis; **I'll pick up the keys tomorrow** recogeré las llaves mañana; **5** (*learn*) aprender [18]; **you'll soon pick it up** lo aprenderás pronto.

picnic *noun* picnic M; **to have a picnic** hacer [7] un picnic.

pickpocket *noun* carterista M/F.

picture *noun* **1** (*a painting*) cuadro M; **a picture by Picasso** un cuadro de Picasso; **he painted a picture of a horse** pintó un caballo; **2** (*a drawing*) dibujo M; **draw me a picture of your house** hazme un dibujo de tu casa; **3** (*in a book*) ilustración F; **a book with lots of pictures** un libro con muchas ilustraciones; **4 the pictures** el cine; **to go to the pictures** ir [8] al cine.

pie *noun* **1** (*sweet*) pastel M; **an apple pie** un pastel de manzana; **2** (*savoury*) empanada F; **a meat pie** una empanada de carne.

piece *noun* **1** (*a bit*) trozo M; **a big piece of cheese** un trozo grande de queso; **2** (*that you fit together*) pieza F; **the pieces of a jigsaw** las piezas de un rompecabezas; **to take something to pieces** desmontar [17] algo; **3 a piece of furniture** un mueble; **four pieces of luggage** cuatro maletas; **a piece of information** un dato; **that's a piece of luck!** ¡qué suerte!; **4** (*coin*) moneda F; **a 10p piece** una moneda de diez peniques.

pierced *adjective* **to have pierced ears** tener [9] agujeros en las orejas.

pig *noun* cerdo M, cerda F.

pigeon *noun* paloma F.

piggy bank *noun* hucha F.

pigtail *noun* trenza F.

pile *noun* **1** (*a neat stack*) pila F; **a pile of plates** una pila de platos; **2** (*a heap*) montón M; **a pile of dirty shirts** un montón de camisas sucias.

● **to pile something up** (*neatly*) apilar [17] algo; (*in a heap*) amontonar [17] algo.

pill *noun* pastilla F; **the pill** (*contraceptive*) la píldora.

pillow *noun* almohada F.

pilot *noun* piloto M/F.

pimple *noun* grano M.

pin *noun* **1** (*for sewing*) alfiler M; **2 a three-pin plug** un enchufe de tres clavijas.

● **to pin up 1** prender [18] con alfileres (*a hem*); **2** poner [11] (*a notice*).

PIN *noun* (*personal identification number*) PIN M.

pinball *noun* flipper M; **to play pinball** jugar [27] al flipper; **a pinball machine** un flipper.

pinch *noun* (*of salt, for example*) pellizco M.
verb **1** (*steal*) robar [17]; **somebody's pinched my bike** alguien me ha robado la bici; **2 to pinch somebody** pellizcar [31] a alguien.

pine *noun* pino M; **a pine table** una mesa de pino.

pineapple *noun* piña F.

pine cone *noun* piña F.

ping-pong *noun* ping-pong M; **to play ping-pong** jugar [27] al ping-pong.

pink *adjective* rosa (*never changes*); **my pink dress** mi vestido rosa; **pink socks** calcetines rosa.

pint *noun* pinta F.

pip *noun* pepita F.

pipe *noun* 1 (*for gas or water*) tubería F; 2 (*to smoke*) pipa F; **he smokes a pipe** fuma en pipa.

Pisces *noun* piscis M; **Amanda's Pisces** Amanda es piscis.

pit *noun* foso M.

pitch *noun* campo M; **a football pitch** un campo de fútbol.
verb **to pitch a tent** montar [17] una tienda.

pity *noun* 1 lástima F; **what a pity!** ¡qué lástima!; **it would be a pity to miss the beginning** sería una lástima perderse el principio; 2 (*for a person*) piedad F.
verb **to pity somebody** compadecer [35] a alguien.

pizza *noun* pizza F.

place *noun* 1 sitio M; **in a warm place** en un sitio caliente; **Rome is a wonderful place** Roma es un lugar maravilloso; **all over the place** por todos sitios; **a place for the car** un sitio para el coche; **will you keep my place?** ¿me guardas el sitio?; **to change places** cambiarse [17] de sitio; 2 (*in a race*) lugar M; **in first place** en primer lugar; 3 **at your place** et tu casa; **we'll go round to Zafir's place** iremos a casa de Zafir; 4 **to take place** tener [9] lugar; **the competition will take place at four** la competición tendrá lugar a las cuatro; 5 **if I was in your place …** si yo estuviese en tu lugar …
verb poner [11]; **he placed his cup on the table** puso su taza en la mesa.

plain *adjective* 1 sencillo/sencilla; **plain cooking** la cocina sencilla; 2 (*unflavoured*) natural; **a plain yoghurt** yogur natural; 3 **plain chocolate** chocolate sin leche; 4 (*not patterned*) liso/lisa; **plain curtains** cortinas lisas.

plait *noun* trenza F.

plan *noun* 1 plan M; **what are your plans for this summer?** ¿qué planes tienes para este verano?; **to go according to plan** salir [63] según el plan; **everything went according to plan** todo salió según el plan; 2 (*a map*) plano M.
verb 1 planear [17]; **Ricky's planning a trip to Italy** Ricky está planeando un viaje a Italia; **to plan to do** planear [17] hacer; **we're planning to leave at eight** planeamos salir a las ocho; 2 (*organize*) organizar [22]; **I'm planning my day** estoy organizándome el día; 3 (*to design*) diseñar [17]; (*a house or garden*) **a well-planned kitchen** una cocina bien diseñada.

plane *noun* avión M; **we went by plane** fuimos en avión.

planet *noun* planeta M.

plant *noun* planta F; **a house plant** una planta de interior.
verb plantar [17].

plaster *noun* **1** (*sticking plaster*) tirita™ F; **2** (*for walls*) yeso M; **3 to have your leg in plaster** tener [9] una pierna escayolada.

plastic *noun* plástico M; **a plastic bag** una bolsa de plástico.

plate *noun* plato M.

platform *noun* **1** (*in a station*) andén M; **the train arriving at platform six** el tren que llega al andén número seis; **2** (*for lecturing or performing*) estrado M.

play *noun* obra F; **a play by Shakespeare** una obra de Shakespeare; **our school is putting on a play** nuestro colegio está preparando una obra.
verb **1** jugar [27]; **the children were playing with a ball** los niños estaban jugando con una pelota; **to play tennis** jugar al tenis; **they were playing cards** estaban jugando a las cartas; **2** (*music or an instrument*) tocar [31]; **Helen plays the violin** Helen toca el violín; **they play all kinds of music** tocan todo tipo de música; **3** poner [11]; (*a tape, CD, or record*) **play me your new CD** ponme tu nuevo compacto; **4 who's playing Hamlet?** ¿quién hace el papel de Hamlet?

player *noun* **1** (*in sport*) jugador M, jugadora F; **a football player** un jugador de fútbol; **2** (*musician*) músico M, música F.

playground *noun* patio M de recreo.

playing field *noun* campo M de juego.

playroom *noun* cuarto M de los juguetes.

pleasant *adjective* agradable.

please *adverb* por favor; **two coffees, please** dos cafés, por favor; **could you turn the TV off, please?** ¿puedes apagar la tele, por favor?

pleased *adjective* contento/contenta; **I'm very pleased** estoy muy contento (*in the past tense 'ponerse' is used in place of 'estar'*); **I was really pleased!** ¡me puse muy contento!; **she was pleased with her present** se puso muy contenta con su regalo; **pleased to meet you!** ¡encantado de conocerte!

pleasure *noun* placer M.

plenty *pronoun* **1** (*lots*) mucho/mucha; **there's plenty of bread** hay mucho pan; **he's got plenty of experience** tiene mucha experiencia; **2** (*with a plural noun*) muchos/muchas; **there are plenty of cases** hay muchos casos; **she's got plenty of ideas** tiene muchas ideas; **there were plenty of them** había muchos; **3** (*quite enough*) más que suficiente; **we've got plenty of time for a coffee** tenemos tiempo más que suficiente para tomar un café; **thank you, that's plenty!** gracias, esto es más que suficiente.

plug *noun* **1** (*electrical*) enchufe M; **2** (*in a bath or sink*) tapón M; **to pull out the plug** quitar [17] el tapón.
● **to plug something in** enchufar [17] algo.

plum *noun* ciruela F; **a plum tart** una tarta de ciruelas.

plumber *noun* fontanero M, fontanera F; **he's a plumber** es fontanero.

plump *adjective* regordete/ regordeta.

plural *noun* plural M; **in the plural** en plural.

plus *preposition* más; **three children plus the baby** tres niños más el bebé.

p.m. *adverb* (*Spanish people usually use 'de la tarde', for times up to approximately 8 p.m. and 'de la noche' for times after approximately 8 p.m.*) **at two p.m.** a las dos de la tarde; **at nine p.m.** a las nueve de la noche.

poached egg *noun* huevo M escalfado.

pocket *noun* bolsillo M.

pocket money *noun* paga F.

poem *noun* poema M.

poet *noun* poeta M/F.

poetry *noun* poesía F.

point *noun* 1 (*tip*) punta F; **the point of a nail** la punta de un clavo; 2 (*in time*) momento M; **at that point the police arrived** en ese momento llegó la policía; 3 **to get the point** entender [36]; **I don't get the point** no lo entiendo; 4 **what's the point of waiting?** ¿qué sentido tiene esperar?; **there's no point phoning, he's out** no tiene sentido llamar, ha salido; **that's not the point** no se

trata de eso; 5 **that's a good point!** ¡es verdad!; 6 **from my point of view** desde mi punto de vista; 7 **her strong point** su punto fuerte; 8 (*in scoring*) punto M; **fifteen points to eleven** quince puntos a once; 9 (*in decimals*) (*in Spanish, a comma is used for the decimal point, so 6,4*) 6 **point 4** seis coma cuatro (*this is how you say it aloud*).
verb 1 señalar [17]; **a notice pointing to the station** un cartel señalando hacia la estación; **James pointed out the cathedral** James señaló la catedral; **he pointed at one of the children** señaló a uno de los niños; 2 **I'd like to point out that I'm paying** quisiera dejar claro que pago yo.

poison *noun* veneno M.
verb envenenar [17].

poisonous *adjective* venenoso/ venenosa.

Poland *noun* Polonia F.

polar bear *noun* oso M polar.

pole 1 (*for a tent*) mástil M; 2 **the North Pole** el Polo Norte.

Pole *noun* (*a Polish person*) polaco M, polaca F.

police *noun* **the police** la policía; **the police are coming** ya viene la policía (*note that a singular verb is used with 'la policía'*).
verb patrullar [17] (*the streets*).

police car *noun* coche M de policía.

policeman *noun* policía M.

police station *noun* comisaría F

policewoman *noun* mujer F policía.

polish *noun* 1 (*for furniture*) cera F; 2 (*for shoes*) betún M.
verb sacar [31] brillo a (*shoes or furniture*).

Polish *noun,* polaco M, polaca F.
adjective polaco/polaca.

polite *adjective* educado/educada; **to be polite to somebody** ser [1] educado/educada con alguien.

political *adjective* político/política.

politician *noun* político M, política F.

politics *noun* política F.

polluted *adjective* contaminado/contaminada.

pollution *noun* contaminación F.

polo-necked *adjective* de cuello alto; **a polo-necked jumper** un jersey de cuello alto.

polythene bag *noun* bolsa F de plástico.

pond *noun* 1 (*natural*) laguna F; 2 (*man-made*) estanque M.

pony *noun* poni M.

ponytail *noun* cola F de caballo.

poodle *noun* caniche M.

pool *noun* 1 (*swimming pool*) piscina F; 2 (*in the country*) alberca F; 3 (*puddle*) charco M;
4 (*game*) billar M americano; **to have a game of pool** jugar [27] al billar americano; 5 **the football pools** las quinielas; **to do the pools** hacer [7] las quinielas.

poor *adjective* 1 pobre; **a poor area** un zona pobre; **a poor family** una familia pobre; **poor Tanya's failed her exam** la pobre Tanya suspendió el examen; 2 (*bad*) malo/mala; **this is poor quality** esto es de mala calidad; **the weather was pretty poor** el tiempo fue bastante malo.

pop *noun* pop M; **a pop concert** un concierto de pop; **a pop star** una estrella del pop; **a pop song** una canción de pop.
● **to pop into** entrar [17] un momento a; **I'll just pop into the bank** voy a entrar un momento al banco.

popcorn *noun* palomitas F (*plural*) de maíz.

pope *noun* papa M.

poppy *noun* amapola F.

popular *adjective* popular.

population *noun* población F.

porch *noun* porche M.

pork *noun* cerdo M; **a pork chop** una chuleta de cerdo.

porridge *noun* gachas F (*plural*).

port *noun* 1 (*for ships*) puerto M; 2 (*wine*) oporto M.

porter *noun* 1 (*at a station or airport*) mozo M de las maletas; 2 (*in a hotel*) portero M.

portion *noun* (*of food*) ración F.

portrait *noun* retrato M.

Portugal *noun* Portugal M.

Portuguese *noun* 1 (*language*) portugués M; 2 (*a person*) portugués M, portuguesa F. *adjective* portugués/portuguesa.

posh *adjective* elegante; **a posh house** una casa elegante.

position *noun* posición F.

positive *adjective* 1 (*sure*) seguro/segura; **I'm positive he's left** estoy seguro de que se ha ido; 2 (*enthusiastic*) positivo/positiva; **her reaction was very positive** su reacción fue muy positiva; **try to be more positive** intenta tener una actitud más positiva.

possessions *plural noun* pertenencias F (*plural*); **all my possessions are in the flat** todas mis pertenencias están en el piso.

possibility *noun* posibilidad F.

possible *adjective* posible; **it's possible** es posible; **if possible** si es posible; **as quickly as possible** tan rápidamente como sea posible.

possibly *adverb* 1 (*maybe*) posiblemente; **'will you be at home at midday?' – 'possibly'** '¿estarás en casa a medio día?' – 'posiblemente'; 2 (*for emphasis*) **how can you possibly believe that?** pero, ¿cómo puedes creerte eso?; **I can't possibly arrive before Thursday** no puedo llegar antes del jueves de ninguna manera.

post *noun* 1 correo M; **to send something by post** mandar [17] algo por correo; 2 (*letters*) **is there any post for me?** ¿hay alguna carta para mí?; 3 (*a pole*) poste M; 4 (*a job*) puesto M. *verb* **to post a letter** echar [17] una carta al correo; **to post something to somebody** mandarle [17] algo a alguien.

postbox *noun* buzón M.

postcard *noun* postal F.

postcode *noun* código M postal.

poster *noun* 1 (*for decoration*) póster M; **I've bought an Oasis poster** he comprado un póster de Oasis; 2 (*advertising*) cartel M; **I saw a poster for the concert** vi un cartel del concierto.

postman *noun* cartero M; **has the postman been?** ¿ha venido el cartero?

post office *noun* oficina F de correos.

postpone *verb* **to postpone something** posponer [11] algo.

postwoman *noun* cartera F.

pot *noun* 1 (*jar*) tarro M; **a pot of honey** un tarro de miel; 2 (*teapot*) tetera F; **I'll make a pot of tea** voy ha hacer té; 3 **the pots and pans** los cacharros; ★ **to take pot luck** probar [24] suerte.

potato *noun* patata F; **fried potatoes** patatas fritas; **mashed potatoes** puré de patatas.

potato crisps *plural noun*
patatas F (*plural*) fritas de bolsa.

pottery *noun* cerámica F.

pound *noun* **1** (*money*) libra F;
fourteen pounds catorce libras;
how much is that in pounds?
¿cuánto es eso en libras?; **2** (*in weight*) libra F; **a pound of apples**
una libra de manzanas.

pour *verb* **1** echar [17] (*liquid*); **he poured the milk into the pan** echó
la leche en la cacerola; **2** servir [57] (*a drink*); **to pour the tea** servir el té; **I poured him a drink** le serví una
bebida; ★ **it's pouring down** (*with rain*) está lloviendo a
cántaros; (*literally: it's raining jugfuls*).

poverty *noun* pobreza F.

powder *noun* polvo M.

power *noun* **1** (*electricity*)
corriente F eléctrica; **a power cut** un
apagón; **2** (*energy*) energía F;
nuclear power energía nuclear;
3 (*over other people*) poder M; **to be in power** estar en el poder.

powerful *adjective* poderoso/
poderosa.

power point *noun* enchufe M.

power station *noun* central F
eléctrica.

practical *adjective* práctico/
práctica.

practice *noun* **1** (*for sport*)
entrenamiento M; **hockey practice**
entrenamiento de hockey; **2** (*for an instrument*) **to do your piano
practice** hacer [7] los ejercicios de
piano; **3 to be out of practice** (*for a sport*) estar desentrenado/
desentrenada; **4 in practice** en la
práctica.

practise *verb* **1** practicar
[31] (*music, language, etc.*); **a week
in Granada to practise my Spanish**
una semana en Granada para
practicar mi español; **2** (*in a sport*)
entrenar [17]; **the team practises on
Wednesdays** el equipo entrena los
miércoles.

praise *verb* **to praise somebody for
something** elogiar [17] a alguien por
algo.

pram *noun* cochecito M de bebé.

prawn *noun* gamba F.

pray *verb* rezar [22].

prayer *noun* oración F.

precious *adjective* precioso/
preciosa.

prefer *verb* preferir [14]; **I prefer
coffee to tea** prefiero el café al té;
he'd prefer not to see them
preferiría no verlos.

pregnant *adjective* embarazada.

prejudice *noun* prejuicio M; **a
prejudice** un prejuicio; **to fight
against racial prejudice** luchar [17]
contra los prejuicios raciales.

prejudiced *adjective* **to be
prejudiced** tener [9] prejuicios.

premiere *noun* estreno M (*of a play
or film*).

prep *noun* deberes M (*plural*); **my English prep** mis deberes de inglés.

preparation *noun*
1 preparación F; 2 **the preparations for** los preparativos para.

prepare *verb* 1 **to prepare for something** prepararse para algo; 2 preparar [17]; **to prepare somebody for** preparar [17] a alguien para (*a surprise or shock*); **to be prepared for the worst** estar [2] preparado para lo peor.

prepared *adjective* dispuesto/dispuesta; **I'm prepared to pay half** estoy dispuesta a pagar la mitad.

preposition *noun* preposición F.

prescription *noun* receta F; **on prescription** con receta.

present *noun* 1 (*a gift*) regalo M; **to give somebody a present** regalarle [17] algo a alguien; 2 (*the time now*) presente M; **in the present (tense)** en presente; **that's all for the present** eso es todo por ahora.
adjective 1 (*attending*) presente; **is Tracy present?** ¿está Tracy presente?; **to be present at** asistir [19] a; **fifty people were present at the funeral** cincuenta personas asistieron al funeral; 2 (*existing now*) actual; **the present situation** la situación actual; 3 **at the present time** en este momento.
verb 1 entregar [28] (*a prize*); 2 (*introduce*) presentar [17].

presenter *noun* (*on TV*) presentador M, presentadora F.

president *noun* presidente M, presidenta F.

press *noun* **the press** la prensa.
verb 1 (*to push*) empujar [17]; **press here to open** para abrir, empuje aquí; 2 apretar [29] (*a button or doorbell*); **she pressed the button** apretó el botón.

press conference *noun* conferencia F de prensa.

pressure *noun* presión F.

pressure group *noun* grupo M de presión.

pretend *verb* **to pretend to do** fingir [49] hacer; **he's pretending not to hear** está fingiendo no oír.

pretty *adjective* bonito/bonita; **a pretty dress** un vestido bonito.
adverb bastante; **it was pretty embarrassing** fue bastante vergonzoso.

prevent *verb* 1 evitar [17]; (*a war or disaster*) 2 **to prevent somebody from doing** impedir [57] a alguien hacer; **there's nothing to prevent you from leaving** no hay nada que te impida irte.

previous *adjective* anterior.

previously *adverb* antes.

price *noun* precio M; **the price per kilo** el precio por kilo; **CDs have gone up in price** los compactos han subido de precio.

price list *noun* lista F de precios.

price ticket *noun* etiqueta F del precio.

pride *noun* orgullo M.

priest *noun* sacerdote M.

primary school *noun* escuela F primaria.

prime minister *noun* primer ministro M, primera ministra F.

prince *noun* príncipe M; **Prince Charles** el príncipe Carlos.

princess *noun* princesa F; **Princess Anne** la Princesa Ana.

principal *noun* (*of a college*) rector M, rectora F.
adjective (*main*) principal.

print *noun* 1 (*letters*) letra F; **in small print** en letra pequeña; 2 (*a photo*) copia F; **a colour print** una copia a color.

printer *noun* (*machine*) impresora F.

print-out *noun* copia F en papel.

prison *noun* cárcel F; **in prison** en la cárcel.

prisoner *noun* preso M, presa F.

private *adjective* 1 privado/privada; **a private school** una escuela privada; **'private property'** 'propiedad privada'; 2 particular (*lesson*); **to have private lessons** tener [9] clases particulares.

prize *noun* premio M; **to win a prize** ganar [17] un premio.

prize-giving *noun* entrega F de premios.

prizewinner *noun* ganador M, ganadora F.

probable *adjective* probable.

probably *adverb* probablemente.

problem *noun* problema M; **it's a serious problem** es un problema grave; **no problem!** ¡no hay problema!

produce *noun* (*food*) productos M (*plural*).
verb 1 producir [60]; **it produces a lot of heat** produce mucho calor; 2 (*show*) presentar [17]; **I produced my passport** presenté mi pasaporte.

producer *noun* (*of a film or programme*) productor M, productora F.

product *noun* producto M.

production *noun* 1 (*of a film*) producción F; 2 (*of a play or opera*) puesta F en escena; **a new production of Hamlet** una nueva puesta en escena de Hamlet; 3 (*by a factory*) producción F.

profession *noun* profesión F.

professional *noun* profesional M/F; **he's a professional** es un profesional.
adjective profesional; **she's a professional singer** es cantante profesional.

professor *noun* catedrático M, catedrática F.

profit *noun* beneficios M (*plural*).

profitable *adjective* rentable.

program *noun* **a computer program** un programa de ordenador.

programme *noun* programa M.

progress *noun* 1 progreso M; **to make progress** (*in your work*) hacer [7] progresos; 2 **to be in progress** estar [2] en curso.

project *noun* 1 (*at school*) trabajo M; 2 (*a plan*) proyecto M; **a project to build a bridge** un proyecto para construir un puente.

projector *noun* proyector M.

promise *noun* promesa F; **to make a promise** hacer [7] una promesa; **to break a promise** romper [40] una promesa; **it's a promise!** ¡lo prometo!
verb **to promise to do** prometer [18] hacer; **I've promised to be home by ten** he prometido estar en casa a las diez.

promote *verb* ascender [36]; **she's been promoted** la han ascendido.

promotion *noun* ascenso M.

pronoun *noun* pronombre M.

pronounce *verb* pronunciar [17]; **it's hard to pronounce** es difícil de pronunciar.

pronunciation *noun* pronunciación F.

proof *noun* pruebas F (*plural*); **they've got proof** tienen pruebas; **there's no proof that …** no hay pruebas de que …

propaganda *noun* propaganda F.

propeller *noun* hélice F.

proper *adjective* 1 (*real, genuine*) de verdad; **I need a proper meal** necesito una comida de verdad; **a proper doctor** un médico titulado; 2 (*correct*) adecuado/adecuada; **the proper tool** la herramienta adecuada; 3 **in its proper place** en su sitio.

properly *adverb* bien; **hold it properly** sujétalo bien; **is it properly wrapped?** ¿está bien envuelto?

property *noun* (*your belongings*) propiedad F; **'private property'** 'propiedad privada'.

propose *verb* 1 (*suggest*) proponer [11]; 2 (*marriage*) **he proposed to her** le pidió que se casara con él.

protect *verb* proteger [3].

protection *noun* protección F.

protein *noun* proteína F.

protest *noun* protesta F; **in spite of their protests** a pesar de sus protestas.
verb 1 (*to grumble*) protestar [17]; **he protested, but …** él protestó, pero …; 2 (*demonstrate*) manifestarse [29].

Protestant *noun*, *adjective* protestante M/F.

protester *noun* manifestante M/F.

protest march *noun* manifestación F.

proud *adjective* orgulloso/orgullosa.

prove *verb* probar [24].

proverb *noun* refrán M.

provide *verb* proveer [37].

provided *conjunction* siempre que; **provided you do it now** siempre que tú lo hagas (*note that 'que' is followed by the subjunctive*).

prune *noun* ciruela F pasa.

psychiatrist *noun* psiquiatra M/F; **he's a psychiatrist** es psiquiatra.

psychological *adjective* psicológico/psicológica.

psychologist *noun* psicólogo M, psicóloga F; **she's a psychologist** es psicóloga.

psychology *noun* psicología F.

PTO sigue al dorso.

pub *noun* bar M.

public *noun* **the public** el público; **in public** en público.
adjective 1 público/pública; 2 **the public library** la biblioteca pública.

public address system *noun* sistema M de megafonía.

public holiday *noun* día M de fiesta; **the first of January is a public holiday** el uno de enero es fiesta.

publicity *noun* publicidad F.

public school *noun* colegio M privado.

public transport *noun* transporte M público.

publish *verb* publicar [31].

publisher *noun* editorial F.

pudding *noun* (*dessert*) postre M; **for pudding we've got strawberries** de postre tenemos fresas.

puddle *noun* charco M.

puff pastry *noun* hojaldre M.

pull *verb* tirar [17]; **pull hard!** ¡tira fuerte!; **to pull a rope** tirar de una cuerda; ★ **you're pulling my leg!** ¡me estás tomando el pelo! (*literally: you are taking my hair*).
● **to pull down** bajar [17] (*a blind*).
● **to pull in** (*at the roadside*) parar [17]
● **to pull something out** sacar [31] algo **he pulled a letter out of his pocket** sacó una carta del bolsillo.

pullover *noun* jersey M.

pump *noun* 1 bomba F; **a bicycle pump** una bomba de bicicleta; 2 **a petrol pump** un surtidor de gasolina *verb* bombear [17]; **they were pumping the water out of the cellar** estaban bombeando el agua del sótano.
● **to pump up** inflar [17] (*a tyre*).

punch *noun* 1 (*in boxing*) puñetazo M; 2 (*drink*) ponche M. *verb* 1 **to punch somebody** darle [4] un puñetazo a alguien; **he punched me** me dio un puñetazo; 2 picar [31] (*a ticket*).

punctual *adjective* puntual.

punctuation *noun* puntuación F.

punctuation mark *noun* signo M de puntuación.

puncture *noun* pinchazo M; **we had a puncture on the way** tuvimos un pinchazo en el camino.

punish *verb* castigar [28].

punishment *noun* castigo M.

pupil *noun* alumno M, alumna F.

puppet *noun* marioneta F.

puppy *noun* cachorro M (*female*), cachorra F; **a labrador puppy** un cachorro de labrador.

pure *adjective* puro/pura.

purple *adjective* morado/morada.

purpose *noun* 1 propósito M; **what was the purpose of her call?** ¿qué propósito tenía su llamada?; 2 **on purpose** a propósito; **she did it on purpose** lo hizo a propósito.

purr *verb* ronronear [17].

purse *noun* monedero M.

push *noun* empujón M; **to give something a push** dar [4] un empujón a alguien.
verb 1 empujar [17]; **he pushed me** me empujó; 2 (*to press*) apretar [29] (*a bell or button*); 3 **to push somebody to do** presionar [17] a alguien para que haga; (*note that 'que' is followed by the subjunctive*) **his teacher is pushing him to sit the exam** su profesor le está presionando para que se presente al examen.
● **to push something away** apartar [17] algo; **she pushed her plate away** apartó su plato.

pushchair *noun* sillita F de niño.

put *verb* 1 poner [11]; **you can put the cream in the fridge** puedes poner la nata en la nevera; **where did you put my bag?** ¿dónde has puesto mi bolso?; **put your suitcase here** pon tu maleta aquí; **put your address here** pon tus señas aquí; 2 (*put inside*) meter [18]; **I put it in the drawer** lo metí en el cajón.
● **to put away** guardar [17]; **I'll put the shopping away** voy a guardar la compra.
● **to put back** 1 volver [45] a poner; **I put it back in the drawer** lo volví a poner en el cajón; 2 (*postpone*) aplazar [22]; **the meeting has been put back until Thursday** han aplazado la reunión hasta el jueves.
● **to put down** poner [11]; **she put the vase down on the table** puse el jarrón en la mesa.
● **to put off** 1 (*postpone*) aplazar [22]; **he's put off my lesson till Thursday** ha aplazado mi clase hasta el jueves; 2 **it really put me off Chinese food!** ¡hizo que se me quitaran las ganas de tomar comida china!; 3 **to be put off** (*doing something*) desanimarse [17]; **don't be put off!** ¡no te desanimes!
● **to put on** 1 ponerse [11] (*clothing, make-up*); **I'll just put my shoes on** voy a ponerme los zapatos; 2 poner [11] (*TV, radio*); **shall we put on the telly?** ¿ponemos la tele?; **he's put on Oasis** ha puesto a Oasis; 3 (*switch on*) encender [36] (*a light or heating*); **could you put the lamp on?** ¿puedes encender la lámpara?; 4 montar [17] (*a play*); **we're putting**

on a Spanish play estamos
montando una obra española.

- **to put out 1** (*put outside*) sacar [31];
have you put the rubbish out? ¿has
sacado la basura?; **2** apagar [28] (*a
fire, light, or cigarette*); **I've put the
lights out** he apagado las luces; **3 to
put out your hand** extender [36] la
mano.

- **to put up 1** levantar [17] (*your
hand*); **I put up my hand** levanté la
mano; **2** poner [11]; (*picture*) **I've
put up some photos in my room** he
puesto algunas fotos en mi
habitacion; **3** colgar [23] (*a notice*);
4 subir [19] (*the price*); **they've put
up the price of the tickets** han
subido el precio de las entradas;
5 (*for the night*) **can you put me up
on Friday?** ¿puedo quedarme a
dormir en tu casa el viernes?

- **to put up with something** aguantar
[17] algo; **I don't know how she puts
up with it** no sé cómo lo aguanta.

puzzle *noun* (*jigsaw*)
rompecabezas M, puzzle M.

puzzled *adjective* confuso/confusa.

pyjamas *plural noun* pijama M; **a
pair of pyjamas** un pijama; **where
are my pyjamas?** ¿dónde está mi
pijama?

Pyrenees *noun* **the Pyrenees** los
Pirineos.

Q q

qualification *noun*
1 título M (*certificate, exam, degree*);
2 qualifications titulación F;
vocational qualifications titulación
profesional.

qualified *adjective* **1** cualificado/
cualificada; **she's a qualified ski
instructor** es una monitora de esquí
cualificada; **2** (*having a degree or a
diploma*) titulado/titulada; **a
qualified architect** un arquitecto
titulado.

qualify *verb* **1** (*to be eligible*) tener
[9] derecho a; **we don't qualify for a
reduction** no tenemos derecho a una
reducción; **2** (*in sport*) clasificarse
[31].

quality *noun* calidad F; **good quality
vegetables** verduras de buena
calidad.

quantity *noun* cantidad F.

quarantine *noun* cuarentena F.

quarrel *noun* pelea F; **to have a
quarrel** tener [9] una pelea.
verb pelearse [17]; **they're always
quarrelling** siempre se están
peleando.

quarter *noun* **1** cuarta parte F; **a
quarter of the class** una cuarta
parte de la clase; **three quarters of
the class** tres cuartas partes de la
clase; **2** (*telling the time*) cuarto M;

a quarter past ten las diez y cuarto; **a quarter to ten** las diez menos cuarto; **a quarter of an hour** un cuarto de hora; **three quarters of an hour** tres cuartos de hora; **an hour and a quarter** una hora y cuarto.

quartet *noun* cuarteto M; **a jazz quartet** un cuarteto de jazz.

quay *noun* muelle M.

queen *noun* reina F; **Queen Elizabeth** la reina Isabel; **the Queen Mother** la reina madre.

query *noun* duda F; **are there any queries?** ¿hay alguna duda?

question *noun* 1 pregunta F; **to ask a question** hacer [7] una pregunta; **I asked her a question** le hice una pregunta; 2 **it's a question of time** es una cuestión de tiempo; **it's out of the question!** ¡es completamente imposible!
verb interrogar [28].

question mark *noun* signo M de interrogación.

questionnaire *noun* cuestionario M; **to fill in a questionnaire** rellenar [17] un cuestionario.

queue *noun* 1 (*of people*) cola F; **to stand in a queue** estar [2] en la cola; 2 (*of cars*) fila F.
verb hacer [7] cola; **we were queueing for check-in** estábamos haciendo cola para facturar.

quick *adjective* 1 rápido/rápida; **a quick lunch** una comida rápida; **it's quicker on the motorway** es más rápido por la autopista; **to have a quick look at something** echarle [17] un vistazo rápido a algo; 2 **quick! there's the bus!** ¡de prisa, que viene el autobús!; **be quick!** ¡date prisa!

quickly *adverb* rápidamente; **I'll just quickly phone my mother** voy a llamar rápidamente a mi madre.

quiet *adjective* 1 (*silent*) silencioso/silenciosa; **the children are very quiet** los niños están muy silenciosos; 2 **to keep quiet** no hablar [17]; **please keep quiet** por favor, no hablen; 3 (*gentle*) suave; **some quiet music** una música suave; **in a quiet voice** en voz baja; 4 (*peaceful*) tranquilo/tranquila; **a quiet street** una calle tranquila; **a quiet day at home** un día tranquilo en casa.

quietly *adverb* 1 (*to move*) sin hacer ruido; **he got up quietly** se levantó sin hacer ruido; 2 (*speak*) en voz baja; 3 (*read or play*) en silencio.

quilt *noun* edredón M.

quite *adverb* 1 bastante; **it's quite cold outside** hace bastante frío fuera; **that's quite a good idea** es una idea bastante buena; **he sings quite well** canta bastante bien; **quite often** bastante a menudo; 2 **not quite** no … todavía; **the meal's not quite cooked** la carne no está hecha todavía; 3 **quite a lot of** bastante; **quite a lot of money** bastante dinero; **quite a few people** bastante gente; 4 **quite a lot of** (*with a plural noun*) bastantes; **we've got quite a lot of friends here** tengo bastantes amigos aquí.

quiz *noun* concurso M.

quotation *noun* (*from a book*) cita F.

quotation marks *plural noun* comillas F (*plural*); **in quotation marks** entre comillas.

quote *noun* 1 (*from a book*) cita F; 2 (*estimate*) presupuesto M; 3 **in quotes** entre comillas.
verb citar [17].

R r

rabbi *noun* rabino M, rabina F.

rabbit *noun* conejo M.

race *noun* 1 (*a sports event*) carrera F; **a cycle race** una carrera de bicicletas; **to have a race** echar [17] una carrera; 2 (*an ethnic group*) raza F.

racer *noun* (*bike*) bicicleta F de carreras.

racetrack *noun* 1 (*for horses*) pista F de carreras; 2 (*for cars*) circuito M; 3 (*for cycles*) velódromo M.

racing *noun* carreras F (*plural*).

racing car *noun* coche M de carreras.

racing driver *noun* piloto M/F de carreras.

racial *adjective* racial; **racial discrimination** discriminación racial.

racism *noun* racismo M.

racist *noun,* racista M/F.
adjective racista.

racket *noun* 1 (*for tennis*) raqueta F; 2 (*noise*) jaleo M; **what a racket!** ¡qué jaleo!

radiator *noun* radiador M.

radio *noun* radio F; **to listen to the radio** escuchar [17] la radio; **to hear something on the radio** oír [56] algo en la radio.

radio station *noun* emisora F de radio.

radish *noun* rabanito M.

rag *noun* trapo M.

rage *noun* furia F; **she's in a rage** está furiosa; ★ **it's all the rage** hace furor (*informal*).

rail *noun* 1 (*the railway*) **to go by rail** ir [8] en tren; 2 (*on a balcony or bridge*) baranda F; 3 (*on stairs*) pasamanos M; 4 (*for a train*) raíl M.

rail strike *noun* huelga F de trenes.

railing(s) *noun* verja F.

railway *noun* 1 (*the system*) ferrocarril M; **the railways** el ferrocarril; 2 **a railway line** una vía férrea (*from one place to another*); 3 **on the railway line** en la vía del tren (*the rails*).

railway carriage *noun* vagón M de tren.

railway station *noun* estación F de tren; **opposite the railway station** enfrente de la estación de tren.

rain *noun* lluvia F; **in the rain** bajo la lluvia.
verb llover [38]; **it's raining** está lloviendo; **it's going to rain** va a llover.

rainbow *noun* arco M iris.

raincoat *noun* impermeable M.

rainy *adjective* lluvioso/lluviosa.

raise *verb* 1 (*lift up*) levantar [17]; **she raised her head** levantó la cabeza; 2 (*increase*) subir [19] (*a price or a salary*); 3 **to raise money for something** recaudar [17] dinero para algo; 4 **to raise the alarm** dar [4] la alarma; 5 **to raise somebody's spirits** animar [17] a alguien.

raisin *noun* pasa F.

rally *noun* 1 (*a meeting*) concentración F; 2 (*for sport*) rally M; 3 (*in tennis*) peloteo M.

rambler *noun* excursionista M/F.

rambling *noun* **to go rambling** ir [8] de excursión.

ramp *noun* (*for a wheelchair, for example*) rampa F.

range *noun* 1 (*a choice*) gama F; **in a wide range of colours** en una amplia gama de colores; 2 (*of mountains*) cordillera F.

rap *noun* rap M (*music*).

rape *noun* violación F.
verb violar [17].

rare *adjective* 1 poco común; **a rare bird** un pájaro poco común; 2 poco hecho (*a steak*); **medium-rare** un filete poco hecho.

raspberry *noun* frambuesa F; **raspberry jam** mermelada de frambuesa; **a raspberry tart** una tarta de frambuesas.

rat *noun* rata F.

rate *noun* 1 (*a charge*) tarifa F; **what are the rates for children?** ¿cuáles son las tarifas para niños?; **reduced rates** tarifas reducidas; 2 **at any rate** en todo caso.

rather *adverb* 1 bastante; **I'm rather busy** estoy bastante ocupado; 2 **rather than** en vez de; **in summer rather than winter** en verano más que en invierno; 3 **I'd rather wait** preferiría esperar; **they'd rather come on Thursday** preferirían venir el jueves; 4 **rather a lot of** bastante; **I've got rather a lot of work** tengo bastante trabajo; 5 **rather a lot of** (*with a plural noun*) bastantes; **there are rather a lot of mistakes** hay bastantes errores.

raw *adjective* crudo/cruda.

razor *noun* máquina F de afeitar (*safety*).

razor blade *noun* cuchilla F.

RE *noun* religión F.

reach *noun* alcance M; **out of my reach** fuera de mi alcance; **within reach** (*of your hand*) al alcance; **within easy reach of the sea** cerca del mar.
verb llegar [28]; **when you reach the church** cuando llegues a la iglesia; **to reach the final** llegar [28] a la final.

read *verb* leer [37]; **what are you reading at the moment?** ¿qué estás leyendo en este momento?; **I'm reading a detective novel** estoy leyendo una novela policiaca; **he read out the list** leyó la lista.

reading noun lectura F; **I don't much like reading** no me gusta mucho la lectura; **some easy reading for the beach** lectura fácil para la playa.

ready adjective **1** preparado/preparada; **supper's not ready yet** la cena aún no está preparada; **2** (person) listo/lista; **are you ready to leave?** ¿estás listo para salir?; **3 to get ready** (meal or things) preparar [17]; **I'll get your room ready** voy a preparar tu habitación; **4 to get ready** (a person) prepararse [17]; **I'm getting ready to go out** me estoy preparando para salir; **I was getting ready for bed** estaba preparándome para irme a la cama.

real adjective verdadero/verdadera; **is that his real name?** ¿es ése su verdadero nombre?; **her real father is dead** su verdadero padre está muerto; **he's a real bore** es un verdadero pesado; **it's a real diamond** es un diamante de verdad.

realize verb darse [4] cuenta; **I hadn't realized** no me había dado cuenta; **to realize (that)** … darse cuenta de que …; **I didn't realize (that) he was French** no me di cuenta de que era francés; **do you realize what time it is?** ¿te das cuenta de la hora que es?

really adverb **1** (truly) **is it really midnight?** ¿de verdad son las doce de la noche?; **really?** ¿de verdad?; **not really** la verdad es que no;

2 (extremely) (Spanish uses the superlative of the adjective to express this sense) **the film was really good** la película fue buenísima; **3 I really don't know** realmente no lo sé.

reason noun razón F; **the reason for the delay** la razón del retraso; **the reason why I phoned** la razón por la que llamé.

reasonable adjective razonable.

receipt noun recibo M.

receive verb recibir [19].

receiver noun auricular M; **to pick up the receiver** descolgar [23] el teléfono.

recent adjective reciente; **a recent change** un cambio reciente.

recently adverb recientemente.

reception noun **1** recepción F; **he's waiting at reception** está esperando en recepción; **a big wedding reception** una gran celebración de boda; **2 to get a good reception** tener [9] buena acogida.

receptionist noun recepcionista M/F.

recipe noun receta F; **can I have the recipe for your salad?** ¿me puedes dar tu receta de la ensalada?

reckon verb creer [37]; **I reckon it's a good idea** creo que es una buena idea.

recognize verb reconocer [35].

recommend verb recomendar [29]; **can you recommend a dentist?** ¿puedes recomendarme un

dentista?; **I recommend the fish
soup** recomiendo la sopa de
pescado.

record *noun* **1** récord M; **it's a world
record** es un récord mundial; **record
sales** récord de ventas; **the hottest
summer on record** el verano más
caluroso del que se tienen datos; **2 to
keep a record of something** llevar
[17] un registro de algo; **3** (*music*)
disco M; **a Miles Davis record** un
disco de Miles Davis; **4** (*office files*)
archivo M; **I'll just check your
records** voy a mirar tu ficha; **5** (*of
attendance*) registro M.
verb (*on tape or CD*) grabar [17];
they're recording a new album
están grabando un nuevo álbum.

recorder *noun* **1** flauta F dulce; **to
play the recorder** tocar [31] la flauta
dulce; **2 a cassette recorder** un
cassette; **a video recorder** una
cámara de vídeo.

recording *noun* grabación F.

record player *noun* tocadiscos M
(*does not change in the plural*).

recover *verb* recuperarse [17]; **she's
recovered now** ya se ha recuperado.

recovery *noun* (*from an illness*)
recuperación F.

recovery vehicle *noun* grúa F.

rectangle *noun* rectángulo M.

rectangular *adjective* rectangular.

recycle *verb* reciclar [17].

red *adjective* **1** rojo/roja; **a red shirt**
una camisa roja; **a bright red car** un
coche rojo vivo; **2 to go red** ponerse

[11] colorado; **3** (*hair*) **to have red
hair** ser [1] pelirrojo.

Red Cross *noun* **the Red Cross** la
Cruz Roja.

redcurrant *noun* grosella F;
redcurrant jelly jalea de grosellas.

reduce *verb* reducir [60]; **they've
reduced the price** han reducido el
precio.

reduction *noun* rebaja F (*in price*).

redundant *adjective* **he was made
redundant** lo despidieron por
reducción de plantilla.

referee *noun* (*in sport*) árbitro M/F.

reference *noun* referencia F (*for a
job*); **she gave me a good reference**
me dio una buena referencia.

referendum *noun* referendum M.

refill *noun* **1** (*for pen*) recambio M;
2 (*for lighter*) carga F.

reflect *verb* reflejar [17].

reflection *noun* **1** (*in a mirror*)
reflejo M; **2** (*thought*) reflexión F;
on reflection pensándolo bien.

reflexive *adjective* **a reflexive verb**
un verbo reflexivo.

refreshing *adjective* refrescante.

refrigerator *noun* nevera F.

refugee *noun* refugiado M,
refugiada F.

refund *noun* reembolso M.
verb reembolsar [17].

refuse *noun* (*rubbish*)
desperdicios M (*plural*).

verb negarse [30]; **I refused** me negué; **he refuses to help** se niega a ayudar.

regards *plural noun* recuerdos M (*plural*); **'regards to your parents'** 'recuerdos a tus padres'; **Nat sends his regards** Nat manda recuerdos.

reggae *noun* reggae M.

region *noun* región F.

regional *adjective* regional.

register *noun* (*in school*) lista F. *verb* inscribirse [52].

registered letter *noun* carta F certificada.

registration number *noun* número M de matrícula (*of a vehicle*).

regret *verb* **to regret something** arrepentirse [14] de algo.

regular *adjective* **1 regular visits** visitas frecuentes; **2** habitual (*customer*).

regularly *adverb* regularmente.

regulation *noun* norma F.

rehearsal *noun* ensayo M.

rehearse *verb* ensayar [17].

rein *noun* rienda F.

reject *verb* rechazar [22].

related *adjective* **1** relacionado/relacionada; (*subject or ideas*) **2 we're not related** no somos parientes.

relation *noun* pariente M/F; **my relations** mis parientes.

relationship *noun* relación F; **we have a good relationship** tenemos una buena relación.

relative *noun* pariente M/F; **all my relatives** todos mis parientes.

relax *verb* relajarse [17]; **I'm going to relax and watch telly tonight** esta noche voy a relajarme y ver la tele.

relaxed *adjective* relajado/relajada.

relaxing *adjective* relajante.

relay race *noun* carrera F de relevos.

release *noun* **1** estreno M; **this week's new releases** los estrenos de esta semana; **2** (*of a prisoner or hostage*) puesta F en libertad. *verb* **1** sacar [31] (*a record or a video*); **2** estrenar [17] (*a film*); **3** poner [11] en libertad (*a person*).

reliable *adjective* **1** responsable (*person*); **2** fidedigno/fidedigna (*information*).

relief *noun* alivio M; **what a relief!** ¡qué alivio!

relieved *adjective* aliviado/aliviada; **I was relieved to hear you'd arrived** fue un alivio oír que habías llegado.

religion *noun* religión F.

religious *adjective* religioso/religiosa; **Jane's not religious** Jane no es religiosa.

rely *verb* **to rely on somebody** contar [24] con alguien; **I'm relying on you for Saturday** cuento contigo el para sábado.

remain *verb* permanecer [35].

remark *noun* comentario M; **to make remarks about** hacer [7] comentarios sobre.

remember *verb* **1** acordarse [24]; **I don't remember** no me acuerdo; **2 to remember something** acordarse de algo; **I can't remember the number** no me acuerdo del número; **3 to remember to do** acordarse de hacer; **remember to shut the door!** ¡acuérdate de cerrar la puerta!; **I remembered to bring the CDs** me acordé de traer los compactos.

remind *verb* **1** recordar [24]; **to remind somebody to do** recordarle a alguien que haga; (*note that 'que' is followed by the subjunctive*) **remind your mother to pick me up** recuérdale a tu madre que me recoja; **2 it reminds me of Paris** me recuerda a París; **he reminds me of Frank** me recuerda a Frank; **oh, that reminds me** ... ¡ah!, por cierto ...

remove *verb* quitar [17]; **he removed his jacket** se quitó la chaqueta; **the chairs had all been removed** habían quitado todas las sillas.

renew *verb* renovar [24] (*a passport or licence*).

rent *noun* alquiler M.
verb alquilar [17]; **Simon's rented a flat** Simon ha alquilado un piso.

repair *noun* reparación F.
verb arreglar [17]; **to get something repaired** arreglar [17] algo; **we've**

had the television repaired hemos arreglado la televisión.

repay *verb* devolver [45]; **he repaid me the money he owed me** me devolvió el dinero que me debía.

repeat *noun* repetición F (*of a programme*).
verb repetir [57].

reply *noun* contestación F; **I didn't get a reply to my letter** no recibí contestación a mi carta; **there's no reply** no contestan (*on the telephone*).
verb contestar [17]; **I still haven't replied to the letter** aún no he contestado a la carta.

report *noun* **1** (*of an event*) informe M; **2** (*school report*) boletín M de notas.
verb **1** informar [17] sobre (*a problem or accident*); **we've reported the theft** hemos denunciado el robo; **2** presentarse [17]; **I had to report to reception** tuve que presentarme en recepción.

reporter *noun* periodista M/F.

representative *noun* representante M/F.

reproach *noun* reproche M.
verb reprochar [17].

republic *noun* república F.

reputation *noun* **1** reputación F; **a good reputation** una buena reputación; **2 to have a reputation for something** tener [9] fama de algo; **she has a reputation for honesty** tiene fama de honesta.

request *noun* petición F; **on request** a solicitud.
verb pedir [57].

rescue *noun* **1** rescate M; **2 to come to somebody's rescue** acudir [19] en auxilio de alguien.
verb rescatar [17]; **they rescued the dog** rescataron al perro.

rescue party *noun* equipo M de rescate.

rescue worker *noun* socorrista M/F.

research *noun* investigación F; **for research into Aids** para la investigación sobre el sida; **to do research** investigar [28].
verb **to research into** investigar [28] sobre; **a well-researched programme** un programa bien documentado.

reservation *noun* (*a booking*) reserva F; **to make a reservation** hacer [7] una reserva.

reserve *noun* **1** reserva F; **we have some in reserve** tener [9] algo de reserva; **2 a nature reserve** una reserva natural; **3** (*for a match*) reserva M/F.
verb reservar [17]; **this table is reserved** la mesa está reservada.

resident *noun* residente M/F.

residential *adjective* residencial; **a residential area** un área residencial.

resign *verb* dimitir [19].

resignation *noun* (*from a post*) dimisión F.

resist *verb* resistir [19] (*an offer or temptation*); **I can't resist!** ¡no puedo resistirlo!

resit *verb* **to resit an exam** volver [45] a presentarse a.

resort *noun* **1** (*for holidays*) **a holiday resort** un centro turístico; **a ski resort** una estación de esquí; **a seaside resort** un centro turístico costero; **2 as a last resort** como último recurso.

respect *noun* respeto M.
verb respetar [17].

respectable *adjective* respetable.

respectful *adjective* respetuoso/respetuosa.

responsibility *noun* responsabilidad F.

responsible *adjective* responsable; **he's responsible for the delay** él es el responsable del retraso; **I'm responsible for booking the rooms** soy responsable de reservar las habitaciones; **he's not very responsible** no es muy responsable.

rest *noun* **1 the rest** el resto; **the rest of the day** el resto del día; **the rest of the bread** el resto del pan; **2** (*the others*) los otros; **the rest have gone home** los otros se han ido a casa; **3** descanso M; **ten days' complete rest** diez días de completo descanso; **to have a rest** descansar [17]; **4** (*a short break*) **to stop for a rest** parar [17] para descansar.
verb (*have a rest*) descansar [17].

restaurant *noun* restaurante M.

result *noun* 1 resultado M; **the exam results** los resultados del examen; 2 **as a result** como consecuencia de ello; **as a result we missed the ferry** como consecuencia de ello perdimos el ferry.

retire *verb* (*from work*) jubilarse [17]; **she retires in June** se jubila en junio; **for retired people** para los jubilados.

retirement *noun* jubilación F.

return *noun* 1 vuelta F; **the return journey** el viaje de vuelta; **by return of post** a vuelta de correo; 2 **in return** a cambio; **in return for his help** a cambio de su ayuda; ★ **many happy returns!** ¡muchas felicidades!
verb 1 (*come back or get home*) volver [45]; **he returned ten minutes later** volvió diez minutos más tarde; **to return from holiday** volver de vacaciones; **I'll ask her to phone as soon as she returns** le diré que te llame en cuanto vuelva; 2 (*to give back*) devolver [45]; **Gemma's never returned the video** Gemma no ha devuelto el vídeo.

return fare *noun* precio M del billete de ida y vuelta.

return ticket *noun* billete M de ida y vuelta.

reverse *verb* 1 (*in a car*) dar [4] marcha atrás; 2 **to reverse the charges** llamar [17] a cobro revertido.

review *noun* (*of a book, play, or film*) crítica F.
verb escribir [52] la crítica de; **the film was well reviewed** la película recibió buenas críticas.

revise *verb* repasar [17]; **Tessa's busy revising for her exams** Tessa está muy ocupada repasando para los exámenes.

revision *noun* repaso M.

revolting *adjective* asqueroso/asquerosa; **the sausages are revolting** las salchichas están asquerosas.

revolution *noun* revolución F; **the Fench Revolution** la Revolución Francesa.

reward *noun* recompensa F; **a 100 pound reward** una recompensa de cien libras.
verb recompensar [17].

rewarding *adjective* gratificante.

rhubarb *noun* ruibarbo M.

rhyme *noun* rima F.

rhythm *noun* ritmo M.

rib *noun* costilla F.

ribbon *noun* cinta F.

rice *noun* arroz M; **chicken and rice** pollo y arroz; **rice pudding** arroz con leche.

rich *adjective* rico/rica; **we're not very rich** no somos muy ricos; **the rich and the poor** los ricos y los pobres.

rid *adjective* **to get rid of something** deshacerse [7] de algo; **we got rid of the car** nos dehicimos del coche.

riddle *noun* adivinanza F.

ride *noun* **to go for a ride (on a bike)** ir [8] a montar en bicicleta; **to go for a ride (on a horse)** ir [8] a montar a caballo.
verb **1 to learn to ride a bike** aprender [18] a montar en bicicleta; **can you ride a bike?** ¿sabes montar en bicicleta?; **2 to learn to ride (a horse)** aprender [18] a montar a caballo; **I've never ridden a horse** nunca he montado a caballo.

ridiculous *adjective* ridículo/ ridícula.

riding *noun* equitación F; **to go riding** hacer [7] equitación.

riding school *noun* escuela F de equitación.

rifle *noun* rifle M.

right *noun* **1** (*not left*) derecha F; **on the right** a la derecha; **on my right** a mi derecha; **2** (*to do something*) derecho M; **the right to strike** el derecho a hacer huelga; **you have no right to say that** no tienes derecho a decir eso.
adjective **1** (*not left*) derecho/ derecha; **my right hand** mi mano derecha; **2** (*correct*) correcto/ correcta; **the right answer** la respuesta correcta; **the right telephone number** el teléfono correcto; **is this the right address?** ¿son éstas las señas?; **3 to be right** (*a person*) tener [9] razón; **you see, I**

was right ¿ves? tenía yo razón; **4 you were right to stay at home** hiciste bien en quedarte en casa; **he was right not to say anything** hizo bien en no decir nada; **5 it's not right to talk like that** no está bien hablar así.
adverb **1** (*direction*) derecha; **turn right at the lights** gira a la derecha en el semáforo; **2** (*correctly*) bien; **you're not doing it right** no lo estás haciendo bien; **3** (*completely*) **right at the bottom** al fondo del todo; **right now** ahora mismo; **right at the beginning** justo al principio; **right in the middle** justo en medio; **4** (*okay*) vale; **right, let's go** vale, vayamos.

right-hand *adjective* **on the right-hand side** a mano derecha.

right-handed *adjective* diestro/ diestra.

ring *noun* **1** (*on the phone*) **to give somebody a ring** llamar [17] a alguien; **2** (*for your finger*) anillo M; **3** (*circle*) círculo M; **4 there was a ring at the door** llamaron a la puerta.
verb **1** (*a bell or phone*) sonar [24]; **the phone rang** sonó el teléfono; **2** (*phone*) llamar [17]; **I'll ring you tomorrow** te llamaré mañana; **could you ring for a taxi?** ¿podrías llamar un taxi?
● **to ring back** volver [45] a llamar; **I'll ring you back later** te volveré a llamar más tarde.
● **to ring off** colgar [23].

rinse *verb* enjuagar [28].

ripe *adjective* maduro/madura; **are the tomatoes ripe?** ¿están maduros los tomates?

rip-off *noun* **it's a rip-off!** ¡es un robo!

rise *noun* **1** subida F; **a rise in price** una subida de precio; **2 a pay rise** un aumento de sueldo.
verb **1** (*the sun*) salir [63]; **when the sun rose** cuando salió el sol;
2 (*prices*) subir [19].

risk *noun* riesgo M; **to take risks** arriesgarse [28].
verb arriesgar [28] (*your life or reputation*); **she risked her life** arriesgó su vida.

river *noun* río M.

road *noun* **1** carretera F; **the road to London** la carretera de Londres;
2 (*in a town*) calle F; **on the other side of the road** al otro lado de la calle; **3 across the road** enfrente; **they live across the road from us** viven enfrente de nosotros.

road accident *noun* accidente M de carretera.

road map *noun* mapa M de carreteras.

roadside *noun* **by the roadside** al borde de la carretera.

road sign *noun* señal F de tráfico.

roadworks *plural noun* obras F (*plural*).

roast *noun* asado M.
adjective asado/asada; **roast potatoes** patatas asadas; **roast beef** rosbif M.

rob *verb* **1** robar [17] (*a person*);
2 atracar [31] (*a bank*).

robber *noun* **bank robber** atracador/atracadora M/F.

robbery *noun* atraco M; **a bank robbery** un atraco a un banco.

rock *noun* **1** (*a big stone*) roca F; **she was sitting on a rock** estaba sentada en una roca; **2** (*the material*) piedra F; **3** (*music*) rock M; **a rock band** un grupo de rock; **to dance rock and roll** bailar [17] rock and roll.

rock climbing *noun* escalada F en roca; **to go rock climbing** hacer [7] escalada.

rock star *noun* estrella F de rock.

rocket *noun* cohete M.

rocking horse *noun* caballito M de balancín.

rocky *adjective* rocoso/rocosa.

rod *noun* **a fishing rod** una caña de pescar.

role *noun* papel M; **to play the role of** interpretar [17] el papel de.

roll *noun* **1** rollo M; **a roll of fabric** un rollo de tela; **a toilet roll** un rollo de papel higiénico; **2 a bread roll** un panecillo.

rollerblades *plural noun* patines M (*plural*) en línea.

rollercoaster *noun* montaña F rusa (*literally: Russian mountains*).

roller skates *plural noun* patines M (*plural*).

Roman Catholic *noun* católico M, católica F.
adjective católico/católica.

romantic *adjective* romántico/
romántica.

roof *noun* tejado M.

roof rack *noun* baca F.

room *noun* 1 habitación F; **she's in
the other room** está en la otra
habitación; **it's the biggest room in
the house** es la habitación más
grande de la casa; **a three-room flat**
un piso de tres habitaciones; 2 (*a
person's bedroom in their home*)
habitación F; **Lola's in her room** Lola
está en su habitación; 3 (*space*)
sitio M; **enough room for two** sitio
suficiente para dos; **very little room**
muy poco sitio.

root *noun* raíz F.

rope *noun* cuerda F.

rose *noun* rosa F.

rosebush *noun* rosal M.

rot *verb* pudrirse [59].

rota *noun* lista F de turnos.

rotten *adjective* podrido/podrida.

rough *adjective* 1 (*scratchy*) áspero/
áspera; 2 (*vague*) aproximado/
aproximada; **a rough idea** una idea
aproximada; 3 (*stormy*) **a rough sea**
un mar agitado; 4 (*difficult*) **to have
a rough time** pasarlo [17] mal; 5 **to
sleep rough** dormir [51] a la
intemperie.

roughly *adjective* (*approximately*)
aproximadamente; **roughly ten per
cent** aproximadamente el diez por
ciento; **it takes roughly three hours**
lleva aproximadamente tres horas.

round *noun* 1 (*in a tournament*)
vuelta F; 2 (*of cards*) partida F; 3 **a
round of drinks** una ronda de
bebidas; **it's my round** esta ronda la
pago yo.
adjective redondo/redonda; **a round
table** una mesa redonda.
preposition 1 alrededor de; **round
the city** alrededor de la ciudad;
round my arm alrededor de mi brazo;
they were sitting round the table
estaban sentados alrededor de la
mesa; 2 **to go round the shops** ir
[8] de tiendas; **to go round a
museum** visitar [17] un museo; **it's
just round the corner** está a la vuelta
de la esquina.
adverb 1 **to go round to
somebody's house** ir [8] a casa de
alguien; **we invited Sally round for
lunch** invitamos a Sally a comer;
2 **all the year round** todo el año.

roundabout *noun* 1 (*for traffic*)
rotonda F; 2 (*in a fairground*)
tiovivo M.

route *noun* 1 (*that you plan*) ruta F;
the best route is via Leeds la mejor
ruta es a pasando por Leeds; 2 **a bus
route** el recorrido de un autobús.

row¹ *noun* 1 fila F (*of seats*); **in the
front row** en la primera fila; **in the
back row** en la última fila; 2 hilera F;
a row of huts un hilera de cabañas;
3 **four times in a row** cuatro veces
seguidas.

row² *verb* (*in a boat*) remar [17]; **it's
your turn to row** te toca remar; **we
rowed across the lake** cruzamos el
lago remando.

row³ *noun* **1** (*a quarrel*) pelea F; **to have a row** pelearse [17]; **they've had a row** se han peleado; **I had a row with my parents** me peleé con mis padres; **2** (*noise*) ruido M; **they were making a terrible row!** ¡están haciendo un ruido terrible!

rowing *noun* remo M; **to go rowing** practicar [31] el remo.

rowing boat *noun* bote M de remos.

royal *adjective* real; **the royal family** la familia real.

rub *verb* frotar [17]; **to rub your eyes** frotarse los ojos.
• **to rub something out** borrar [17] algo.

rubber *noun* **1** (*an eraser*) goma F de borrar; **2** (*material*) goma F; **rubber soles** suelas de goma.

rubber band *noun* goma F elástica.

rubbish *noun* **1** (*for the bin*) basura F; **2** (*nonsense*) estupideces F (*plural*); **you're talking rubbish!** ¡estás diciendo estupideces!
adjective **the film was rubbish** la película fue una porquería; **they're a rubbish band** es una porquería de grupo.

rubbish bin *noun* cubo M de la basura.

rucksack *noun* mochila F.

rude *adjective* **1** maleducado/maleducada; (*a person*) **2** **that's rude** eso es de mala educación; **3** **a rude joke** una broma grosera; **a rude word** una palabrota.

rug *noun* **1** alfombra F; **2** (*a blanket*) manta F de viaje.

rugby *noun* rugby M; **to play rugby** jugar [27] al rugby; **a rugby match** un partido de rugby.

ruin *noun* ruina F; **in ruins** en ruinas.
verb **1** estropear [17]; **you'll ruin your jacket** vas a estropear tu chaqueta; **2** fastidiar [17] (*informal*) (*day, holiday*); **it ruined my evening** me fastidió las vacaciones.

rule *noun* **1** regla F; **the rules of the game** las reglas del juego; **2** **the school rules** el reglamento del colegio; **3** **as a rule** como norma.

ruler *noun* regla F; **I've lost my ruler** he perdido mi regla.

rumour *noun* rumor M.

run *noun* **1** **to go for a run** ir [8] a correr; **2** (*in cricket*) carrera F; **3** **in the long run** a la larga.
verb **1** correr [18]; **I ran ten kilometres** corrí diez kilómetros; **he ran across the pitch** cruzó el campo corriendo; **Kitty ran for the bus** Kitty corrió para coger el autobús; **2** (*organize*) organizar [22]; **who's running this concert?** ¿quién organiza el concierto?; **3** dirigir [49] (*a business*); **he ran the firm for forty years** dirigió la compañía durante cuarenta años; **4** (*a train or bus*) circular [17]; **the buses don't run on Sundays** los autobuses no circulan los domingos; **5** (*to operate*); **6** **to run a bath** preparar [17] un baño.
• **to run away** huir [54].

- **to run into** chocar [31] con; **the car ran into a tree** el coche chocó con un árbol.
- **to run out of something I'm running out of money** se me está acabando el dinero.
- **to run somebody over** atropellar [17] a alguien; **you'll get run over!** ¡te van a atropellar!

runner-up noun segundo M, segunda F.

running noun **running is good exercise** correr es un buen ejercicio.

runway noun pista F.

rush noun (a hurry) **to be in a rush** tener [9] prisa; **sorry, I'm in a rush** perdona, tengo prisa.
verb **1** (hurry) darse [4] prisa; **I must rush!** ¡tengo que darme prisa!;
2 (run) **she rushed into the street** salió corriendo a la calle; **I rushed into the room** entré corriendo en la habitación; **3 Louise was rushed to hospital** llevaron a Louise corriendo al hospital.

rush hour noun hora F punta; **in the rush hour** a la hora punta.

Russia noun Rusia F.

Russian noun **1** (a person) ruso M, rusa F; **2** (the language) ruso M.
adjective ruso/rusa.

rye noun centeno M.

S s

Sabbath noun **1** (Jewish) sábado M; **2** (Christian) domingo M.

sack noun **1** saco M; **2 he got the sack** le despidieron.
verb **to sack somebody** despedir [57] a alguien.

sad adjective triste.

saddle noun silla F de montar.

saddlebag noun alforja F (on bike).

safe adjective **1** (out of danger) seguro/segura; **to feel safe** sentirse [14] seguro/segura; **2** (not dangerous) seguro/segura; **the path is safe** el camino es seguro; **it's not safe** no es seguro; **3** (unharmed) **to be safe** estar [2] sano y salvo.

safety noun seguridad F.

safety belt noun cinturón M de seguridad.

safety pin noun imperdible M.

Sagittarius noun sagitario M; **Kylie's Sagittarius** Kylie es sagitario.

sail noun vela F.

sailing noun vela F; **to go sailing** ir [8] a hacer vela; **she's does a lot of sailing** practica mucho la vela.

sailing boat *noun* bote M de vela.

sailor *noun* marinero M.

saint *noun* santo M, santa F.

sake *noun* **1 for your mother's sake** por tu madre; **2 for heaven's sake!** ¡por el amor de Dios!

salad *noun* ensalada F; **a tomato salad** una ensalada de tomate.

salad dressing *noun* aliño M para la ensalada.

salary *noun* sueldo M.

sale *noun* **1** (*selling*) venta F; **the sale of the house** la venta de la casa; **'for sale'** 'se vende'; **2 the sales** las rebajas; **I bought it in the sales** lo compré en las rebajas.

sales assistant *noun* dependiente M, dependienta F.

salesman *noun* representante M; **he's a salesman** es representante.

saleswoman *noun* representante F.

salmon *noun* salmón M.

salt *noun* sal F.

salty *adjective* salado/salada.

Salvation Army *noun* Ejército M de Salvación.

same *adjective* **1** mismo/misma; **she said the same thing** ella dijo lo mismo; **her birthday's the same day as mine** su cumpleaños es el mismo día que el mío; **at the same time** al mismo tiempo; **their car's the same as ours** su coche es el mismo que el nuestro; **2** (*with a plural noun*) mismos/mismas; **they were wearing the same shoes** llevaban los mismos zapatos; **3 to look the same** parecer iguales; **they all look the same to me** a mí todos me parecen iguales.
pronoun **the same** lo mismo; **it's not the same** no es lo mismo; **it's always the same** siempre pasa lo mismo.

sample *noun* muestra F; **a free sample** una muestra gratuita.

sand *noun* arena F.

sandal *noun* sandalia F; **a pair of sandals** un par de sandalias.

sand castle *noun* castillo M de arena.

sandpaper *noun* papel M de lija.

sandwich *noun* sándwich M; **a ham sandwich** un sándwich de jamón.

sanitary towel *noun* compresa F.

Santa Claus *noun* Papá M Noel.

sarcastic *adjective* sarcástico/sarcástica.

sardine *noun* sardina F.

satchel *noun* cartera F.

satellite *noun* satélite M.

satellite dish *noun* antena F parabólica.

satellite television *noun* televisión F por vía satélite.

satisfactory *adjective* satisfactorio/satisfactoria.

satisfied *adjective* satisfecho/satisfecha.

satisfy *verb* satisfacer [7].

satisfying *adjective* 1 (*pleasing*) satisfactorio/satisfactoria; 2 a **satisfying meal** una comida que llena.

Saturday *noun* sábado M; **on Saturday** el sábado; **I'm going out on Saturday** voy a salir el sábado; **see you on Saturday!** ¡te veo el sábado!; **on Saturdays** los sábados; **the museum is closed on Saturdays** el museo cierra los sábados; **every Saturday** todos los sábados; **last Saturday** el sábado pasado; **next Saturday** el próximo sábado; **to have a Saturday job** trabajar [17] los sábados.

sauce *noun* salsa F.

saucepan *noun* cazo M.

saucer *noun* platillo M.

sausage *noun* 1 salchicha F; 2 (*salami*) salchichón M.

save *verb* 1 (*rescue*) salvar [17]; **to save somebody's life** salvarle la vida a alguien; **the doctors saved his life** los médicos le salvaron la vida; 2 ahorrar [17] (*money or energy*); **I've saved £60** he ahorrado sesenta libras; **try to save electricity** intenta ahorrar electricidad; 3 (*put aside*) guardar [17] (*food*); **save the cake for later** guarda el pastel para luego; 4 (*avoid spending*) no gastar [17]; **I walk to school to save money** voy andando al colegio para no gastar dinero; 5 **to save time** ganar [17] tiempo; **we'll take a taxi to save time** cogeremos un taxi para ganar

tiempo; 6 (*on a computer*) guardar [17];
● **to save up** ahorrar [17]; **I'm saving up to go to Spain** estoy ahorrando para ir a España.

savings *plural noun* ahorros M (*plural*); **I've spent all my savings** me he gastado todos los ahorros.

savoury *adjective* salado/salada; **I prefer savoury things to sweet things** prefiero lo salado a lo dulce.

saw *noun* sierra F.

saxophone *noun* saxofón M; **to play the saxophone** tocar [31] el saxofón.

say *verb* 1 decir [5]; **what did you say?** ¿qué has dicho?; **she says she's tired** dice que está cansada; **he said to wait here** dijo que esperásemos aquí; **as they say** como se suele decir; **that goes without saying** eso no hace falta ni decirlo; 2 **to say something again** repetir [57] algo.

saying *noun* refrán M; **as the saying goes** como dice el refrán.

scale *noun* 1 (*size*) escala F; **on a large scale** en gran escala; **the scale of the disaster** la escala del desastre; 2 (*in music*) escala F; 3 (*of a fish*) escama F.

scales *noun* 1 balanza F; **kitchen scales** una balanza de cocina; 2 **bathroom scales** una báscula de baño.

scandal *noun* 1 escándalo M; 2 (*gossip*) chismorreo M.

Scandinavia *noun* Escandinavia F.

Scandinavian *adjective* escandinavo/escandinava.

scar *noun* cicatriz F.

scarce *adjective* escaso/escasa.

scare *noun* 1 susto M; **to give somebody a scare** darle [4] un susto a alguien; 2 **a bomb scare** una amenaza de bomba.
verb **to scare somebody** asustar [17] a alguien; **you scared me!** ¡me has asustado!

scarecrow *noun* espantapájaros M (*does not change in the plural*).

scared *adjective* **to be scared** estar [2] asustado/asustada; **I'm scared!** estoy asustado; **to be scared of** tenerle [9] miedo de; **he's scared of dogs** le tiene miedo de los perros.

scarf *noun* 1 (*long, warm*) bufanda F; 2 (*silky*) foulard M.

scary *adjective* de miedo (*book or film*).

scene *noun* 1 (*of an incident or a crime*) escena F; **the scene of the crime** la escena del crimen; 2 (*world*) mundo M; **on the music scene** el mundo de la música; 3 **scenes of violence** escenas violentas; 4 **to make a scene** montar [17] un número (*informal*).

scenery *noun* 1 (*landscape*) paisaje M; 2 (*theatrical*) decorado M.

schedule *noun* programa M.

scheduled flight *noun* vuelo M regular.

scheme *noun* plan M.

scholarship *noun* beca F.

school *noun* colegio M; **to go to school** ir [8] al colegio; **she's still at school** todavía va al colegio.

schoolbook *noun* libro M de texto.

schoolboy *noun* colegial M.

schoolchildren *plural noun* colegiales M (*plural*).

schoolfriend *noun* amigo M, amiga F del colegio.

schoolgirl *noun* colegiala F.

science *noun* ciencia F; **I like science** me gustan las ciencias; **the science teacher** el profesor de ciencias.

science fiction *noun* ciencia F ficción.

scientific *adjective* científico/científica.

scientist *noun* científico M, científica F.

scissors *plural noun* tijeras F (*plural*); **a pair of scissors** unas tijeras.

score *noun* (*in game*) resultado M; **the score was three two** el resultado fue tres a dos; **what's the score?** ¿a cómo van?
verb 1 (*goal*) marcar [31]; **Lenny scored a goal** Lenny marcó un gol; 2 (*points*) **I scored three points**

conseguí tres puntos; **3** (*keep score*) llevar [17] la puntuación; **4** (*in test or card game*) puntuación F.

Scorpio *noun* escorpio M; **Jess is Scorpio** Jess es escorpio.

Scot *noun* escocés M, escocesa F; **the Scots** los escoceses.

Scotland *noun* Escocia F; **in Scotland** en Escocia; **Pauline's from Scotland** Pauline es escocesa.

Scots *adjective* escocés/escocesa; **a Scots accent** un acento escocés.

Scotsman *noun* escocés M.

Scotswoman *noun* escocesa F.

Scottish *adjective* escocés/escocesa; **a Scottish accent** un acento escocés.

scout *noun* explorador M, exploradora F.

scrambled eggs *noun* huevos M (*plural*) revueltos.

scrap *noun* **a scrap of paper** un trocito de papel.

scrape *verb* rayar [17].

scratch *noun* **1** (*on your skin*) arañazo M; **2** (*on a surface*) rayón M; ★ **to start from scratch** empezar [25] de cero.
verb (*scratch yourself*) rascarse [31]; **to scratch your head** rascarse [31] la cabeza.

scream *noun* grito M.
verb gritar [17].

screen *noun* pantalla F; **on the screen** en la pantalla.

screw *noun* tornillo M.
verb atornillar [17].

screwdriver *noun* destornillador M.

scribble *verb* garabatear [17].

scrub *verb* **1** fregar [30] (*a saucepan*); **2** **to scrub your nails** cepillarse [17] las uñas.

sculpture *noun* escultura F.

sculptor *noun* escultor M, escultora F; **Frazer's a sculptor** Frazer es escultor.

sea *noun* mar M.

seafood *noun* marisco M.

seagull *noun* gaviota F.

seal *noun* (*animal*) foca F.
verb cerrar [29] (*envelope*).

seaman *noun* marinero M.

search *verb* **1** buscar [31]; **I've searched my desk but I can't find the letter** he buscado en mi escritorio pero no encuentro la carta; **2 to search for something** buscar [31] algo; **I've been searching everywhere for the scissors** he buscado las tijeras por todas partes.

seashell *noun* concha F de mar.

seasick *adjective* **to be seasick** estar [2] mareado/mareada; **to get seasick** marearse [17].

seaside *noun* costa F; **at the seaside** en la costa.

season *noun* temporada F; **the rugby season** la temporada de rugby; **strawberries are not in season at the moment** ahora no es temporada de fresas; **off-season prices** billetes de fuera de temporada.

season ticket *noun* abono M de temporada.

seat *noun* 1 asiento M; **the front seat** (*in a car*) el asiento delantero; **the back seat** el asiento trasero; **take a seat** toma asiento; 2 (*in a cinema, theatre, etc.*) localidad F; **to book a seat** reservar [17] una localidad; 3 **can you keep my seat?** ¿puedes guardarme el sitio?

seatbelt *noun* cinturón M de seguridad.

second *noun* 1 (*time unit*) segundo M; **can you wait a second?** ¿puedes esperar un segundo?; 2 **the second of July** el dos de julio. *adjective* segundo/segunda; **for the second time** por segunda vez; **on the second floor** en la segunda planta.

secondary school *noun* colegio M de enseñanza secundaria.

secondhand *adjective, adverb* de segunda mano; **a secondhand bike** una bicicleta de segunda mano; **I bought it secondhand** lo compré de segunda mano.

secondly *adverb* en segundo lugar.

secret *noun* secreto M; **to keep a secret** guardar [17] un secreto; **in secret** en secreto. *adjective* secreto/secreta; **a secret plan** un plan secreto.

secretarial college *noun* escuela F de secretariado.

secretary *noun* secretario M, secretaria F; **she's a secretary** es secretaria; **the secretary's office** la secretaría.

secretly *adverb* en secreto.

sect *noun* secta F.

section *noun* sección F.

security *noun* seguridad F.

security guard *noun* guarda M jurado, guarda F jurada; **he's a security guard** es guarda jurado.

see *verb* 1 ver [16]; **I saw Lindy yesterday** vi a Lindy ayer; **have you seen the film?** ¿has visto la película?; **I haven't seen her for ages** hace años que no la veo; **I'll see what I can do** veré lo que puedo hacer; **let's see** a ver; 2 **to be able to see** ver [16]; **I can't see anything** no veo nada; 3 **see you!** ¡hasta luego!; **see you on Saturday!** ¡hasta el sábado!; **see you soon!** ¡hasta pronto!; **see you tomorrow!** ¡hasta mañana!; 4 **to see somebody home** acompañar [17] a alguien a casa.

● **to see to something** ocuparse [17] de algo; **Jo's seeing to the drinks** Jo se está ocupando de las bebidas.

seed *noun* semilla F; **to plant seeds** plantar [17] semillas.

seem *verb* parecer [35]; **it seems odd to me** me parece raro; **it seems she's left** parece que se ha ido; **he seems a bit shy** parece un poco tímido; **the**

museum seems to be closed parece
que el museo está cerrado.

seesaw *noun* balancín M.

select *verb* seleccionar [17].

self-confidence *noun* confianza F
en sí mismo; **I don't have much self-
confidence** no tengo mucha
confianza en mí misma.

self-employed *noun* autónomo M,
autónoma F; **the self-employed** los
autónomos.
adjective autónomo/autónoma; **to
be self-employed** ser [1] autónomo.

selfish *adjective* egoísta.

self-service *adjective* **a self-
service restaurant** un autoservicio.

sell *verb* vender [18]; **to sell
something to somebody** venderle
algo a alguien; **I sold him my bike** le
vendí mi bici; **the house has been
sold** la casa se ha vendido; **the
concert's sold-out** se han agotado
las localidades para el concierto.

sell-by date *noun* fecha F límite de
venta.

Sellotape™ *noun* celo™ M.

semi *noun* casa F adosada; **we live in
a semi** vivimos en una casa adosada.

semicircle *noun* semicírculo M.

semicolon *noun* punto M y coma.

semi-detached house *noun*
casa F adosada.

semi-final *noun* semifinal F.

semi-skimmed milk *noun* leche F
semidesnatada.

send *verb* mandar [17]; **to send
something to somebody** mandarle
algo a alguien; **I sent her a present
for her birthday** le mandé un regalo
por su cumpleaños.
- **to send somebody back** hacer [7]
volver a alguien.
- **to send something back** devolver
[45] algo.

senior citizen *noun* persona F de
la tercera edad.

sensational *adjective* sensacional.

sense *noun* **1** sentido M; **common
sense** sentido común; **it doesn't
make sense** no tiene sentido; **it
makes sense** tiene sentido; **to have
a sense of humour** tener [9] sentido
del humor; **she has no sense of
humour** no tiene sentido del humor;
2 the sense of smell el olfato; **the
sense of touch** el tacto.

sensible *adjective* sensato/sensata;
she's very sensible es muy sensata;
it's a sensible decision es una
decisión sensata.

sensitive *adjective* sensible; **for
sensitive skin** para pieles sensibles.

sentence *noun* **1** frase F; **write a
sentence in Spanish** escribe una
frase en español; **2** (*by judge*)
sentencia F.
verb condenar [17].

sentimental *adjective* sentimental.

separate *adjective* **1** aparte; **in a
separate pile** en un montón aparte;
on a separate sheet of paper en una
hoja de papel aparte; **2** (*different*)
distinto/distinta; **that's a separate**

problem ese es un problema distinto; **3** (*individual*) separado/separada; **they have separate rooms** tienen habitaciones separadas.
verb **1** separar [17]; **2** (*a couple*) separarse [17].

separately *adverb* por separado.

separation *noun* separación F.

September *noun* septiembre M.

sequel *noun* continuación F.

serial *noun* serie F.

series *noun* serie F; **a television series** una serie de televisión.

serious *adjective* **1** serio/seria; **a serious discussion** una discusión seria; **are you serious?** ¿lo dices en serio?; **2** grave (*illness, injury, mistake, problem*); **we have a serious problem** tenemos un problema grave.

seriously *adverb* **1** en serio; **seriously, I have to go now** en serio, tengo que irme; **seriously?** ¿en serio?; **2** **to take somebody seriously** tomarse [17] en serio a alguien; **3** gravemente (*ill, injured*).

servant *noun* criado M, criada F.

serve *noun* (*in tennis*) saque M; **it's my serve** me toca sacar.
verb **1** (*in tennis*) sacar [31]; **2** servir [57]; **can you serve the vegetables, please?** ¿puedes servir la verdura, por favor?; **3** **are you being served?** ¿le atienden?; ★ **it serves him right** le está bien empleado.

service *noun* **1** (*in a restaurant, from a company, etc.*) servicio M; **the service is very slow** el servicio es muy lento; **service is included** el servicio está incluido; **2** **the emergency services** los servicios de emergencia; **3** (*church*) oficio M religioso; **4** (*of a car or machine*) revisión F.
verb hacerle [7] una revisión a (*a car or a machine*).

service charge *noun* servicio M; **what's the service charge?** ¿cuánto se cobra por el servicio?

service station *noun* estación F de servicio.

serviette *noun* servilleta F.

session *noun* sesión F.

set *noun* **1** (*for playing a game*) juego M; **a chess set** un juego de ajedrez; **2** (*of keys, tools, etc.*) juego M; **3** **a train set** un tren de juguete; **4** (*in tennis*) set M.
adjective **at a set time** a una hora determinada; **a set menu** un menú del día; **a set price** un precio fijo.
verb **1** fijar [17] (*date, time*); **2** establecer [35] (*record*); **3** **to set the table** poner [11] la mesa; **to set the alarm clock** poner [11] el despertador; **I've set my alarm for seven** he puesto el despertador para las siete; **4** **to set a watch** poner [11] el reloj en hora; **5** (*the sun*) ponerse [11].
● **to set off** salir [63]; **we're setting off at ten** salimos a las diez; **they set off for Barcelona yesterday** salieron ayer para Barcelona.

- **to set off something 1** tirar [17] (*firework*); **2** hacer [7] sonar (*alarm*).
- **to set out** salir [63]; **they set out for Seville yesterday** salieron ayer para Sevilla.

settee *noun* sofá M.

settle *verb* **1** (*a bill*) pagar [28]; **2** (*a problem*) solucionar [17].

seven *number* siete M; **Khalil's seven** Khalil tiene siete años; **it's seven o'clock** son las siete.

seventeen *number* diecisiete M; **Jason's seventeen** Jason tiene diecisiete años.

seventh *noun* **1** (*fraction*) **a seventh** una séptima parte; **2 the seventh of July** el siete de julio. *adjective* séptimo/séptima; **on the seventh floor** en la séptima planta.

seventies *plural noun* **the seventies** los años setenta; **in the seventies** en los años setenta.

seventy *number* setenta M; **he's seventy** tiene setenta años; **seventy-five** setenta y cinco.

several *adjective*, *pronoun* varios/varias; **I've seen her several times** la he visto varias veces; **I've read several of her novels** he leído varias novelas suyas; **he took several** cogió varios.

Seville *noun* Sevilla F.

sew *verb* coser [18].

sewing *noun* costura F; **I like sewing** me gusta la costura.

sewing machine *noun* máquina F de coser.

sex *noun* sexo M.

sex education *noun* educación F sexual.

sexism *noun* sexismo M.

sexist *adjective* sexista; **sexist remarks** comentarios sexistas.

sexual *adjective* sexual.

sexual harassment *noun* acoso M sexual.

sexuality *noun* sexualidad F.

sexy *adjective* sexy.

shabby *adjective* gastado/gastada.

shade *noun* **1** (*of a colour*) tono M; **a pretty shade of green** un bonito tono verde; **2 in the shade** en la sombra.

shadow *noun* sombra F.

shake *verb* **1** (*tremble*) temblar [29]; **my hands are shaking** me tiemblan las manos; **2 to shake something** agitar [17] algo; **3 to shake hands with somebody** estrecharle [17] la mano a alguien; **she shook hands with me** me dio la mano; **we shook hands** nos estrechamos la mano; **4 to shake your head** (*meaning no*) negar [30] con la cabeza.

shall *verb* **shall I come with you?** ¿voy contigo?; **shall we stop now?** ¿paramos ya?

shallow *adjective* poco profundo/poco profunda; **the water's very**

shallow here el agua es muy poco profunda aquí.

shambles *noun* caos M; **it was a total shambles!** ¡fue un caos total!

shame *noun* 1 vergüenza F; **shame on you!** ¡debería darte vergüenza!; 2 **what a shame!** ¡qué pena!; **it's a shame she can't come** ¡qué pena que no pueda venir! (*note that 'que' is followed by the subjunctive*).

shampoo *noun* champú M; **I bought some shampoo** compré champú.

shamrock *noun* trébol M.

shandy *noun* clara F; **a shandy** una clara.

shape *noun* forma F; **to be in good shape** estar en buena forma.

share *noun* 1 parte F; **your share of the money** tu parte del dinero; 2 (*in a company*) acción F.
verb compartir [19]; **I'm sharing a room with Emma** comparto una habitación con Emma.

sharp *adjective* 1 (*knife*) afilado/afilada; **this knife isn't very sharp** este cuchillo no está muy afilado; 2 **a sharp pencil** un lápiz con mucha punta; 3 **a sharp bend** una curva cerrada; 4 (*clever*) agudo/aguda.

shave *verb* 1 (*have a shave*) afeitarse [17]; **he's just shaving** se está afeitando; 2 **to shave your legs** afeitarse [17] las piernas; **to shave off your beard** afeitarse [17] la barba.

shaving cream *noun* crema F de afeitar.

shaving foam *noun* espuma F de afeitar.

she *pronoun* 1 (*'she' like other subject pronouns is generally not translated; in Spanish the form of the verb tells you whether the subject of the verb is 'he/she/it, you', 'they', etc., so 'she' is only translated when you want to emphasize it*) **she's in her room** está en su cuarto; **she's a student** es estudiante; **she's a very good teacher** es muy buena profesora; **here she is!** ¡aquí está!; 2 (*for emphasis*) ella; **she did it** lo hizo ella.

shed *noun* 1 cabaña F; 2 (*in garden*) cobertizo M.

sheep *noun* oveja F.

sheepdog *noun* perro M pastor.

sheet *noun* 1 (*for a bed*) sábana F; 2 **a sheet of paper** una hoja de papel; **a blank sheet** una hoja en blanco; 3 (*of glass or metal*) plancha F; ★ **to be as white as a sheet** estar [2] blanco como el papel.

shelf *noun* 1 (*in the home*) estante M; **a set of shelves** una estantería F; 2 (*in a shop or a fridge*) balda F.

shell *noun* 1 (*of an egg or a nut*) cáscara F; 2 (*seashell*) concha F; 3 (*explosive*) proyectil M.

shellfish *noun* marisco M.

shelter *noun* 1 refugio M; **to take shelter from the rain** refugiarse [17] de la lluvia; **in the shelter of** al abrigo de; 2 **a bus shelter** una marquesina del autobús.

sherry *noun* jerez M.

Shetland Islands *noun* islas F (*plural*) Shetland.

shield *noun* escudo M.

shift *noun* turno M; **the night shift** el turno de noche; **to be on night shift** hacer [7] el turno de noche.
verb **to shift something** mover [38] algo.

shin *noun* espinilla F.

shine *verb* brillar [17].

shiny *adjective* brillante.

ship *noun* 1 barco M; **a passenger ship** un barco de pasajeros; 2 **a sailing ship** un velero.

shirt *noun* camisa F.

shiver *verb* temblar [29].

shock *noun* 1 shock M; **it was a shock** fue un shock; **it gave me a shock** me llevé un shock; **in a state of shock** en estado de shock; 2 **an electric shock** una descarga eléctrica; **I got an electric shock** me dio una descarga eléctrica.
verb horrorizar [22].

shocked *adjective* horrorizado/horrorizada.

shocking *adjective* espantoso/espantosa.

shoe *noun* zapato M; **a pair of shoes** un par de zapatos.

shoelace *noun* cordón M de zapato

shoe polish *noun* betún M.

shoe shop *noun* zapatería F.

shoot *verb* 1 (*fire*) disparar [17]; **to shoot at somebody** disparar a alguien; **she shot him in the leg** le disparó en la pierna; **he was shot in the arm** le dispararon en el brazo; 2 (*kill*) asesinar [17] de un tiro; **he was shot by terrorists** los terroristas lo asesinaron de un tiro; 3 (*execute*) fusilar [17]; 4 (*in football, hockey*) lanzar [22]; 5 **to shoot a film** rodar [24] una película.

shop *noun* tienda F; **a record shop** una tienda de discos; **a shoe shop** una zapatería; **to go round the shops** ir [8] de tiendas.

shop assistant *noun* dependiente M, dependienta F; **Brad's a shop assistant** Brad trabaja de dependiente.

shopkeeper *noun* tendero M, tendera F.

shoplifter *noun* ladrón M, ladrona F.

shoplifting *noun* hurto M en las tiendas.

shopping *noun* compras F (*plural*); **can you put the shopping away?** ¿puedes guardar las compras?; **I've got a lot of shopping to do** tengo muchas cosas que comprar; **to go shopping** ir [8] a hacer la compra (*for fun, to buy clothes or presents*) ir [8] de compras.

shop window *noun* escaparate M.

short *adjective* 1 corto/corta; **a short dress** un vestido corto; **she has short hair** tiene el pelo corto; 2 (*person*) bajo/baja (*in height*); **he's quite short** es bastante bajo; 3 **a short break** un descanso corto; **a short visit** una visita corta; **to go for a short walk** ir [8] a dar un pequeño paseo; **it's a short walk from the station** es un pequeño paseo desde la estación; 4 **a short time ago** hace poco tiempo; 5 **to be short of** no tener mucho; **we're a bit short of money at the moment** no tenemos mucho dinero en este momento; **we're getting short of time** se nos está acabando el tiempo.

shortage *noun* escasez F.

shortbread *noun* galleta F de mantequilla.

shortcrust pastry *noun* pasta F quebrada.

short cut *noun* atajo M; **we took a short cut** tomamos un atajo.

shortly *adverb* dentro de poco.

shorts *plural noun* shorts M (*plural*); **a pair of shorts** unos shorts; **my red shorts** mis shorts rojos.

short-sighted *adjective* miope; **I'm short-sighted** soy miope.

shotgun *noun* escopeta F.

should *verb* 1 deber [18] (*'should' is translated by the conditional tense of 'deber'*); **you should ask Simon** deberías preguntar a Simon; **the potatoes should be cooked now** las patatas deberían estar hechas ya; 2 (*'should have' is translated by the past conditional tense of 'deber'*) **you should have told me** deberías habérmelo dicho; **I shouldn't have stayed** no deberías haberte quedado; 3 (*'should' meaning 'would' is translated by the conditional tense of the appropriate verb*) **I should forget it if I were you** yo en tu lugar me olvidaría del asunto; 4 **I should think** yo diría; **I should think he's forgotten** yo diría que se ha olvidado.

shoulder *noun* hombro M.

shoulder bag *noun* bolso M.

shout *noun* grito M.
verb gritar [17]; **stop shouting!** ¡deja de gritar!; **they shouted at us to come back** nos gritaron que volviésemos.

shovel *noun* pala F.

show *noun* 1 (*on stage*) espectáculo M; **we went to see a show** fuimos a ver un espectáculo; 2 (*on TV*) programa M; **he has a TV show** tiene un programa en la tele; 3 (*exhibition*) salón M; **the motor show** el salón del automóvil.
verb 1 enseñar [17]; **to show something to somebody** enseñar a alguien algo; **I'll show you my photos** te enseñaré mis fotos; **to show somebody how to do** enseñar a alguien cómo hacer; **he showed me how to make pancakes** me enseñó cómo hacer pancakes; 2 **it shows!** ¡ya se ve!

● **to show off** presumir [19]; **to show off something** presumir [19] de algo; **she wants to show off her computer** quiere presumir de su ordenador.

shower *noun* 1 (*in a bathroom*) ducha F; **to have a shower** ducharse [17]; 2 (*of rain*) chaparrón M.

show-off *noun* fanfarrón M, fanfarrona F.

shriek *verb* gritar [17].

shrimp *noun* camarón M.

shrink *verb* encoger [3].

Shrove Tuesday *noun* martes M de Carnaval.

shrug *verb* **to shrug your shoulders** encogerse [3] de hombros.

shuffle *verb* **to shuffle the cards** barajar [17] las cartas.

shut *adjective* cerrado/cerrada; **the shops are shut** las tiendas están cerradas.
verb cerrar [29]; **can you shut the door please?** ¿puedes cerrar la puerta por favor?; **the shops shut at six** las tiendas cierran a las seis.
● **to shut up** (*be quiet*) callarse [17]; **shut up!** ¡cállate!

shuttlecock *noun* volante M.

shy *adjective* tímido/tímida.

shyness *noun* timidez F.

Sicily *noun* Sicilia F.

sick *adjective* 1 (*ill*) enfermo/enferma; 2 **to be sick** (*vomit*) devolver [45]; **I was sick several**

times devolví varias veces; **to feel sick** tener [9] ganas de devolver; 3 **sick joke** una broma de mal gusto; 4 **to be sick of something** estar [2] harto/harta de algo; **I'm sick of staying at home every night** estoy harto de quedarme en casa todas las noches.

sickness *noun* enfermedad F.

side *noun* 1 lado M; **on the other side of the street** al otro lado de la calle; **on the wrong side** en el lado equivocado; **I'm on your side** (*I agree with you*) estoy de tu lado; 2 (*edge*) borde M; **at the side of the road** al borde de la carretera; **by the side of the pool** al borde de la piscina; **by the side of the river** a la orilla del río; 3 (*team*) equipo M; **she plays on our side** juega en nuestro equipo; 4 **to take sides** tomar [17] partido; 5 **side by side** uno al lado del otro.

sideboard *noun* aparador M.

sieve *noun* tamiz M.

sigh *noun* suspiro M.
verb suspirar [17].

sight *noun* 1 espectáculo M; **it was a marvellous sight** era un espectáculo maravilloso; 2 **at the sight of** a la vista de; **at first sight** a primera vista; 3 (*eyesight*) vista F; **to have poor sight** tener mala vista; **to know somebody by sight** conocer a alguien de vista; **I'd lost sight of them** los había perdido de vista; 4 **to see the sights** visitar los lugares de interés.

sightseeing *noun* **to do some sightseeing** visitar [17] los lugares de interés.

sign *noun* **1** (*notice*) letrero M; **there's a sign on the door** hay un letrero en la puerta; **2** (*trace, indication*) señal F; **3** (*of the Zodiac*) signo M; **what sign are you?** ¿de qué signo eres?
verb **1** firmar [17]; **to sign a cheque** firmar un cheque; **2** (*using sign language*) comunicarse [31] por señas.

● **to sign on** (*as unemployed*) inscribirse [17] al paro.

signal *noun* señal F.

signature *noun* firma F.

significance *noun* importancia F.

significant *adjective* importante.

sign language *noun* lenguaje M de gestos.

signpost *noun* señal F.

silence *noun* silencio M.

silent *adjective* silencioso/silenciosa.

silk *noun* seda F.
adjective de seda; **a silk shirt** una blusa de seda.

silky *adjective* sedoso/sedosa.

silly *adjective* tonto/tonta; **it was a really silly thing to do** hacer eso fue una verdadera tontería.

silver *noun* plata F.
adjective de plata; **a silver spoon** una cuchara de plata.

similar *adjective* parecido/parecida.

similarity *noun* parecido M.

simple *adjective* sencillo/sencilla.

simply *adverb* sencillamente.

sin *noun* pecado M.

since *preposition*, *adverb conjunction* **1** desde; (*notice that Spanish uses the present tense where English uses 'have done' or 'have been doing'*) **I've been in Madrid since Saturday** llevo en Madrid desde el sábado; **I've been learning Spanish since last year** llevo aprendiendo español desde el año pasado;
2 desde que; (*the same thing happens with tenses here as above*) **since I have known her** desde que la conozco; **since I've been learning Spanish** desde que estoy aprendiendo español; **3 I haven't seen her since** no la he visto desde entonces; **I haven't seen her since Monday** no la he visto desde el lunes; **since when?** ¿desde cuándo?;
4 (*because*) como; **since it was raining, the match was cancelled** como estaba lloviendo, cancelaron el partido.

sincere *adjective* sincero/sincera.

sincerely *adverb* **Yours sincerely** Atentamente.

sing *verb* cantar [17].

singer *noun* cantante M/F.

singing *noun* **1** canto M; **a singing lesson** una lección de canto; **2 I like singing** me gusta cantar.

single *noun* (*ticket*) billete M de ida; **a single to Barcelona, please** un billete de ida para Barcelona.
adjective **1** (*not married*) soltero/soltera; **2 a single room** una habitación individual; **a single bed** una cama individual; **3 not a single** ni un solo/ni una sola; **I haven't had a single reply** no he tenido ni una sola respuesta; **4 every single day** todos los días; **every single morning** todas las mañanas.

single parent *noun* **she's a single parent** es madre soltera; **a single-parent family** una familia monoparental.

singular *noun* singular M; **in the singular** en singular.

sink *noun* **1** (*in kitchen*) fregadero M; **2** (*in bathroom*) lavabo M.
verb hundirse [19].

sir *noun* señor M; **yes, sir** sí, señor.

sister *noun* hermana F; **my sister's ten** mi hermana tiene diez años.

sister-in-law *noun* cuñada F.

sit *verb* **1** sentarse [29]; **you can sit on the sofa** puedes sentarte en el sofá; **I can sit on the floor** me puedo sentar en el suelo; **2 to be sitting** estar [2] sentado; **Leila was sitting on the sofa** Leila estaba sentada en el sofá; **3 to sit an exam** presentarse [17] a un examen; **she's sitting her driving test on Thursday** se presenta al examen de conducir el jueves.

● **to sit down** sentarse [29]; **he sat down on a chair** se sentó en una silla; **do sit down** siéntate.

site *noun* **1 a building site** una obra; **2 a camping site** un camping.

sitting room *noun* salón M.

situation *noun* situación F.

six *number* seis M; **Tom's six** Tom tiene seis años; **it's six o'clock** son las seis.

sixteen *number* dieciséis M; **Hannah's sixteen** Hannah tiene dieciséis años.

sixth *noun* **1** (*fraction*) **a sixth** una sexta parte; **2 the sixth of July** el seis de julio.
adjective sexto/sexta; **on the sixth floor** en el sexto piso.

sixties *plural noun* **the sixties** los años sesenta; **in the sixties** en los años sesenta.

sixty *number* sesenta M; **she's sixty** tiene sesenta años; **sixty-five** sesenta y cinco.

size *noun* **1** tamaño M; **it depends on the size of the house** depende del tamaño de la casa; **2** (*precise measurements*) medidas F (*plural*); **what size is the window?** ¿qué medidas tiene la ventana?; **3** (*in clothes*) talla F; **what size do you take?** ¿qué talla usas?; **4** (*of shoes*) número M; **I take a size thirty-eight** calzo el número treinta y ocho.

skate *noun* **1 an ice skate** un patín de hielo; **2 a roller skate** un patín de ruedas.

verb **1** (*ice-skate*) hacer [7] patinaje sobre hielo; **2** (*roller-skate*) hacer [7] patinaje sobre ruedas.

skateboard *noun* monopatín M.

skateboarding *noun* **to go skateboarding** patinar [17] con el monopatín.

skating *noun* **1** (*ice*) patinaje M sobre hielo; **to go skating** ir [8] a patinar sobre hielo; **2** **roller-skating** patinaje M sobre ruedas; **to go roller-skating** ir [8] a patinar sobre ruedas.

skating rink *noun* pista F de patinaje.

sketch *noun* **1** (*drawing*) boceto M; **2** (*comedy routine*) sketch M.

ski *noun* esquí M.
verb esquiar [32].

ski boot *noun* bota F de esquí.

skid *verb* derrapar [17]; **the car skidded** el coche derrapó.

skiing *noun* esquí M; **to go skiing** ir [8] a esquiar.

skilful *noun* habilidoso/habilidosa.

ski lift *noun* telesquí M.

skill *noun* habilidad F; **it's not one of my skills** no es una de mis habilidades.

skimmed milk *noun* leche F desnatada.

skin *noun* piel F.

skinhead *noun* cabeza M rapada, cabeza F rapada.

skinny *adjective* flaco/flaca.

skip *noun* (*for rubbish*) contenedor M.
verb **1** saltarse [17] (*a meal, part of a book*); **I skipped a few chapters** me salté algunos capítulos; **2** **to skip a lesson** hacer [7] pellas de una clase (*informal*).

ski pants *noun* pantalones M (*plural*) de esquí.

ski suit *noun* traje M de esquí.

skirt *noun* falda F; **a long skirt** una falda larga; **a straight skirt** una falda de tubo; **a mini-skirt** una minifalda.

sky *noun* cielo M.

skyscraper *noun* rascacielos M (*does not change in the plural*).

slam *verb* cerrar [29] de un portazo; **she slammed the door** cerró la puerta de un portazo.

slang *noun* argot M.

slap *noun* **1** (*on the face*) bofetada F; **2** (*on the leg, bottom*) azote M.
verb **to slap somebody** (*on the face*) dar [4] una bofetada a alguien (*on the leg or bottom*) dar [4] un azote a alguien.

slate *noun* pizarra F.

sledge *noun* trineo M.

sledging *noun* **to go sledging** ir [8] en trineo.

sleep *noun* sueño M; **six hours' sleep** seis horas de sueño; **I had a good sleep** dormí bien; **to go to sleep** dormirse [51].
verb dormir [51]; **she's sleeping** está durmiendo.

sleeping bag *noun* saco M de dormir.

sleeping pill *noun* somnífero M.

sleepy *adjective* **to be sleepy** tener [9] sueño; **I feel sleepy** tengo sueño; **I was getting sleepy** me estaba entrando sueño.

sleeve *noun* manga F; **a long-sleeved jumper** un jersey de manga larga; **a short-sleeved shirt** una camisa de manga corta; **to roll up your sleeves** arremangarse [28].

slice *noun* 1 (*of bread, cheese*) rebanada F; 2 (*of meat*) loncha F; **a slice of ham** una loncha de jamón; 3 (*of cake*) trozo M; 4 (*a round slice: of lemon, tomato, etc.*) rodaja F.
verb **to slice something** cortar [17] algo en rebanadas (*or 'lonchas', 'trozos', etc., depending on what you are slicing: see noun translations above*).

slide *noun* 1 (*photo*) diapositiva F; 2 (*hairslide*) pasador M; 3 (*for sliding down*) tobogán M.

slight *adjective* ligero/ligera; **there's a slight problem** hay un pequeño problema.

slightly *adverb* ligeramente.

slim *adjective* delgado/delgada.
verb adelgazar [22]; **I'm slimming** estoy adelgazando.

slip *noun* 1 (*mistake*) error M; 2 (*petticoat*) combinación F.
verb 1 (*slide*) resbalarse [17]; 2 **the jar slipped out of my hands** el frasco se me resbaló de las manos; 3 **it had slipped my mind** se me olvidó completamente.

slipper *noun* zapatilla F.

slippery *adjective* resbaladizo/resbaladiza.

slope *noun* cuesta F.

slow *adjective* 1 lento/lenta; **the service is a bit slow** el servicio es un poco lento; 2 **my watch is slow** mi reloj está atrasado.
● **to slow down** reducir [60] la velocidad (*a car*).

slowly *adverb* despacio; **he got up slowly** se levantó despacio; **can you speak more slowly, please?** ¿puedes hablar más despacio, por favor?

smack *noun* 1 (*on the face*) bofetada F; 2 (*on the leg or bottom*) azote M.
verb **to smack somebody** (*on the face*) dar [4] una bofetada a alguien (*on the leg or bottom*) dar [4] un azote a alguien.

small *adjective* pequeño/pequeña; **a small dog** un perro pequeño.

smart *adjective* 1 (*well-dressed, posh*) elegante; **a smart restaurant** un restaurante elegante; 2 (*clever*) inteligente.

smash *verb* romper [40]; **they smashed the window** rompieron la ventana.

mashing *adjective* fantástico/fantástica.

mell *noun* olor M; **a nasty smell** un mal olor; **there's a smell of burning** huele a quemado.
verb 1 oler [39]; **I can't smell anything** no huelo nada; **I can smell lavender** huele a lavanda; 2 (*smell bad*) oler [39] mal; **the drains smell** las alcantarillas huelen mal.

melly *adjective* apestoso/apestosa.

mile *noun* sonrisa F.
verb sonreír [61].

moke *noun* humo M.
verb fumar [17]; **she doesn't smoke** no fuma; **he smokes a pipe** fuma en pipa.

moker *noun* fumador M, fumadora F.

smoking *noun* 'no smoking' 'prohibido fumar'; **to give up smoking** dejar [17] de fumar.

smooth *adjective* 1 (*stone or surface*) liso/lisa; **a smooth surface** una superficie lisa; 2 (*skin*) suave.

smuggle *verb* **to smuggle something** pasar [17] algo de contrabando.

smuggler *noun*
1 contrabandista M/F; 2 **a drugs smuggler** un/una traficante de drogas.

smuggling *noun* 1 contrabando M; 2 **drugs smuggling** tráfico M de drogas; **arms smuggling** tráfico M de armas.

snack *noun* tentempié M.

snail *noun* caracol M.

snake *noun* serpiente F.

snap *verb* 1 (*break*) romperse [40]; 2 **to snap your fingers** chasquear [17] los dedos.

snatch *verb* 1 arrebatar [17]; **to snatch something from somebody** arrebatar algo a alguien; **he snatched my book** me arrebató el libro; 2 (*steal*) robar [17]; **she had her bag snatched** le robaron el bolso.

sneak *verb* **to sneak in** entrar [17] a escondidas; **to sneak out** salir [63] a escondidas; **he sneaked up on me** se acercó a mí sin que yo me diese cuenta.

sneeze *verb* estornudar [17].

sniff *verb* olisquear [17].

snob *noun* esnob M/F.

snobbery *noun* esnobismo M.

snooker *noun* snooker M; **to play snooker** jugar [27] al snooker.

snore *verb* roncar [31].

snow *noun* nieve F.
verb nevar [29]; **it's snowing** está nevando; **it's going to snow** va a nevar.

snowball *noun* bola F de nieve.

snowman *noun* muñeco M de nieve.

so *conjunction, adverb* 1 tan; **he's so lazy** es tan vago; **the coffee's so hot I can't drink it** este café está tan caliente que no puedo beberlo; 2 **not**

so no tan; **our house is a bit like yours, but not so big** nuestra casa es parecida a la tuya pero no tan grande; **3 so much** (*after a verb*) tanto; **I hate it so much!** ¡lo odio tanto!; **4 so much** (*before a noun*) tanto/tanta; **I have so much work to do** tengo tanto trabajo que hacer; **5 so many** (*before a noun*) tantos/tantas; **we've got so many problems** tenemos tantos problemas; **6** (*therefore*) así que; **he got up late so he missed his train** se levantó tarde así que perdió el tren; **7** (*starting a sentence: there is no direct translation*) **so what's your name?** ¿y cómo te llamas?; **so what shall we do?** ¿y entonces qué hacemos?; **so what?** ¿y qué?; **8 so do I, so did I** yo también; **'I live in Leeds' – 'so do I'** 'vivo en Leeds' – 'yo también'; **so am I, so was I** yo también; **so do we, so did we** nosotros también; **'I have a headache' – 'so do I'** 'me duele la cabeza' – 'a mí también'; **'I like Miró' – 'so do I'** 'me gusta Miró' – 'a mí tambien'; **9 I think so** creo que sí; **I hope so** espero que sí.

soap *noun* **1** jabón M; **a cake of soap** una pastilla de jabón; **2** (*soap opera: on TV*) telenovela F.

soap powder *noun* jabón M en polvo.

sober *adjective* **to be sober** estar [2] sobrio/sobria.

soccer *noun* fútbol M; **to play soccer** jugar [27] al fútbol.

social *adjective* social.

socialism *noun* socialismo M.

socialist *noun,* socialista M/F. *adjective* socialista.

social security *noun* **1** asistencia F social; **to be on social security** recibir [19] asistencia social; **2 the social security** (*the system*) la seguridad social.

social worker *noun* asistente M/F social; **she's a social worker** es asistente social.

society *noun* sociedad F.

sociology *noun* sociología F.

sock *noun* calcetín M; **a pair of socks** un par de calcetines.

sofa *noun* sofá M.

sofa bed *noun* sofá-cama M.

soft *adjective* suave; ★ **to have a soft spot for somebody** tener [9] debilidad por alguien.

soft drink *noun* refresco M.

software *noun* software M.

soft toy *noun* muñeco M de peluche.

soil *noun* tierra F.

solar energy *noun* energía F solar.

soldier *noun* soldado M/F.

solicitor *noun* abogado M, abogada F; **she's a solicitor** es abogada.

solid *adjective* **1** macizo/maciza; **a table made of solid pine** una mesa de pino macizo; **a solid gold ring** un anillo de oro macizo; **solid silver**

plata maciza; **2** (*not flimsy*) sólido/
sólida; **a solid structure** una
estructura sólida.

solo *noun* solo M; **a guitar solo** un
solo de guitarra.
adjective, adverb en solitario; **a solo
album** un álbum en solitario; **to play
solo** tocar [31] en solitario.

soloist *noun* solista M/F.

some *adjective, adverb* **1** (*with a
singular noun*) un poco de; **would
you like some butter?** ¿quieres un
poco de mantequilla?; **may I have
some salad?** ¿puedo tomar un poco
de ensalada?; **can you lend me
some money?** ¿puedes prestarme un
poco de dinero?; **2** (*with a plural
noun*) unos/unas; **I've bought some
apples** he comprado unas
manzanas; **we picked some flowers**
cogimos unas flores; **3** (*referring to
something that has already been
mentioned, 'some' is not translated*)
**'would you like butter?' – 'thanks,
I've got some'** ¿quieres
mantequilla?' – 'gracias ya tengo';
he's eaten some of it ya ha comido
un poco; **4** (*certain*) algunos/
algunas; **some people think he's
wrong** algunas personas piensan
que él no tiene razón; **5 some day**
algún día.

somebody, someone *pronoun*
alguien; **there's somebody in the
garden** hay alguien en el jardín.

somehow *adverb* **1** de alguna
forma; **I've got to finish this essay
somehow** tengo que terminar esta
composición de alguna forma; **2 I**

somehow think they won't come no
sé por qué, pero creo que no van a
venir.

something *pronoun* algo; **I've got
something to tell you** tengo algo que
decirte; **something pretty** algo que
bonito; **something interesting** algo
interesante; **there's something
wrong** algo va mal; **their house is
really something!** ¡su casa es
increíble!; **a guy called Colin
something or other** un tipo llamado
Colin, o algo así.

sometime *adverb* un día de estos;
give me a ring sometime llámame
un día de estos; **I'll ring you
sometime next week** te llamaré un
día de la semana que viene.

sometimes *adverb* a veces; **I
sometimes take the train** a veces
cojo el tren.

somewhere *adverb* en algún sitio;
I've put my bag down somewhere
he puesto mi bolso en algún sitio; **I've
met you somewhere before** te he
visto antes en algún sitio.

son *noun* hijo M.

song *noun* canción F.

son-in-law *noun* yerno M.

soon *adverb* **1** pronto; **it will soon
be the holidays** pronto llegarán las
vacaciones; **see you soon!** ¡hasta
pronto!; **it's too soon** es demasiado
pronto; **2 as soon as** tan pronto
como; **as soon as she arrives** tan
pronto como llegue; **as soon as
possible** tan pronto como sea
posible.

sooner *adverb* **1** antes; **we should have started sooner** deberíamos haber empezado antes; **2 I'd sooner wait** prefiero esperar; ★ **sooner or later** tarde o temprano.

soprano *noun* soprano M/F.

sore *noun* llaga F.
adjective **he has a sore leg** le duele la pierna; **my arm's sore** me duele el brazo; ★ **it's a sore point** es un tema delicado.

sorry *adjective* **1 I'm really sorry** lo siento mucho; **I'm sorry I forgot your birthday** siento haberme olvidado de tu cumpleaños; **2 sorry to disturb you** perdona que te moleste; **3 sorry!** ¡perdón!; **4 sorry?** ¿cómo?; **5 to feel sorry for somebody** compadecer [35] a alguien; **6 to say you're sorry** pedir [57] perdón.

sort *noun* tipo M; **what sort of music do you like?** ¿qué tipo de música te gusta?; **all sorts of** todo tipo de; **for all sorts of reasons** por todo tipo de razones.
● **to sort something out 1** ordenar [17] algo (*room, desk, papers, possessions*); **I must sort out my room tonight** tengo que ordenar mi habitación esta noche; **2** solucionar [17] (*problem, arrangement*); **Liz is sorting it out** Liz se está ocupando de ello.

soul *noun* **1** alma F; (*even though 'alma' is a feminine noun, it takes a masculine article in the singular*) **the soul** el alma; **2** (*music*) soul M.

sound *noun* **1** (*noise*) ruido M; **the sound of voices** el ruido de voces;

2 (*volume*) volumen M; **to turn down the sound** bajar el volumen.
verb **it sounds easy** parece fácil; **it sounds as if she's happy** parece qu está contenta.

sound asleep *adjective* profundamente dormido/dormida.

sound effect *noun* efecto M sonoro.

soundtrack *noun* banda F sonora.

soup *noun* **1** (*clear*) consomé M; **2** (*thick*) sopa F; **3** (*pureed*) crema F; **mushroom soup** crema de champiñones.

soup plate *noun* plato M de sopa.

soup spoon *noun* cuchara F sopera

sour *adjective* **1** (*taste*) agrio/agria; **2 the milk's gone sour** la leche se ha cortado.

south *noun* sur M; **in the south** en el sur.
adjective, *adverb* sur (*never changes*); **the south side** la parte sur; **a south wind** un viento del sur; **south of Paris** al sur de París.

South Africa *noun* Sudáfrica F.

South America *noun* Sudamérica F.

southeast *noun* sureste M.
adjective sureste (*never changes*); **in southeast England** en el sureste de Inglaterra.

South Pole *noun* Polo M Sur.

southwest *noun* suroeste M.
adjective suroeste (*never changes*);

in southwest England en el suroeste de Inglaterra.

souvenir *noun* recuerdo M.

soya *noun* soja F.

space *noun* **1** (*room*) sitio M; **is there enough space?** ¿hay sitio suficiente?; **there's enough space for two** hay sitio suficiente para dos; **2** (*gap*) espacio M; **leave a space** deja un espacio; **3** (*outer space*) espacio M; **in space** en el espacio.

spacecraft *noun* nave F espacial.

spade *noun* **1** pala F; **2** (*in cards*) pica F; **the queen of spades** la reina de picas.

Spain *noun* España F.

Spaniard *noun* español M, española F.

spaniel *noun* spaniel M.

Spanish *noun* **1** (*language*) español M; **to speak Spanish** hablar [17] español; **say it in Spanish** dilo en español; **I'm learning Spanish** estoy aprendiendo español; **2 the Spanish** (*people*) los españoles M (*plural*).
adjective **1** español/española; **Pedro's Spanish** Pedro es español; **2** de español (*a teacher or lesson*); **the Spanish class** la clase de español.

spanner *noun* llave F inglesa.

spare *adjective* **1** (*part, battery*) de repuesto; **a spare battery** una batería de repuesto; **2** (*extra*) de más; **we have a spare ticket** tenemos una entrada de más.
verb **I can't spare the time** no tengo

tiempo para eso; **can you spare a moment?** ¿tienes un momento libre?; **I don't have any money to spare** no me sobra el dinero.

spare room *noun* habitación F de invitados.

spare time *noun* tiempo M libre; **in my spare time** en mi tiempo libre.

spare wheel *noun* rueda F de repuesto.

sparrow *noun* gorrión M.

speak *verb* **1** hablar [17]; **do you speak Spanish?** ¿hablas español?; **spoken Spanish** el español hablado; **'Spanish spoken here'** 'aquí se habla español'; **2 to speak to somebody** hablar [17] con alguien; **she's speaking to Mike** está hablando con Mike; **I've never spoken to her** nunca he hablado con ella; **I'll speak to him about it** hablaré sobre ello con él; **3 who's speaking?** (*on the phone*) ¿quién es?

speaker *noun* **1** (*on a music system*) altavoz M; **2** (*at a public lecture*) conferenciante M/F; **3** (*of a language*) **a Spanish speaker** un hablante de español; **an English speaker** un hablante de inglés.

special *adjective* especial.

specialist *noun* especialista M/F.

specialize *verb* **to specialize in** especializarse [22] en.

specially *adverb* especialmente; **not specially** no especialmente; **the poems have been specially chosen for small children** los poemas han sido escogidos especialmente para niños pequeños; **I came specially in order to see you** vine especialmente para verte.

spectacles *noun* gafas F (*plural*).

spectacular *adjective* espectacular.

spectator *noun* espectador M, espectadora F.

speech *noun* discurso M; **to make a speech** dar [4] un discurso.

speechless *adjective* **1** sin habla; **I was speechless** me quedé sin habla; **2 to be speechless with rage** quedarse [17] mudo de cólera.

speed *noun* velocidad F; **what speed was he doing?** ¿a qué velocidad iba?; **a twelve-speed bike** una bicicleta de doce marchas.
● **to speed up** acelerar [17].

speeding *noun* **he was fined for speeding** le multaron por exceso de velocidad.

speed limit *noun* límite M de velocidad.

spell *noun* **1** (*of time*) período M; **2** (*talking about weather*) **a cold spell** una ola de frío; **sunny spells** intervalos de sol.
verb **1** (*in writing*) escribir [52]; **how do you spell it?** ¿cómo se escribe?; **how do you spell your surname?** ¿cómo se escribe tu apellido?; **2** (*out loud*) deletrear [17]; **shall I spell it for you?** ¿se lo deletreo?

spelling *noun* ortografía F; **a spelling mistake** una falta de ortografía.

spend *verb* **1** gastar [17] (*money*); **I've spent all my money** me he gastado todo el dinero; **2** pasar [17] (*time*); **we spent three days in Barcelona** pasamos tres días en Barcelona; **she spends her time writing letters** pasa el tiempo escribiendo cartas.

spice *noun* especia F.

spicy *adjective* picante; **I don't like spicy food** no me gustan los platos picantes.

spider *noun* araña F.

spill *verb* derramar [17]; **I've spilled my wine on the carpet** he derramado vino en la alfombra.

spinach *noun* espinacas F (*plural*); **do you like spinach?** ¿te gustan las espinacas?

spire *noun* aguja F.

spirit *noun* **1** (*energy*) brío M; **2 get into the spirit of the occasion** entrar [17] en el ambiente.

spirits *noun* **1** (*alcohol*) bebidas F (*plural*) alcohólicas; **2 to be in good spirits** estar [2] de buen humor.

spit *verb* escupir [19]; **to spit something out** escupir algo.

spite *noun* **1 in spite of** a pesar de; **we decided to go in spite of the rain** decidimos ir a pesar de la lluvia; **2** (*nastiness*) maldad F; **to do something out of spite** hacer algo por maldad.

spiteful *adjective* 1 (*person*) malo/mala; 2 (*comment*) malicioso/maliciosa.

splash *noun* 1 (*noise*) **we heard a splash** oímos el ruido de algo que caía al agua; 2 **a splash of colour** un toque de color.
verb salpicar [31].

splendid *adjective* espléndido/espléndida.

splinter *noun* astilla F.

split *verb* 1 (*with an axe or a knife*) partir [19]; **to split a piece of wood** partir un trozo de madera; 2 (*come apart*) rajarse [17]; **the lining has split** el forro se ha rajado; 3 (*divide up*) dividirse [19]; **they split the money between them** se dividieron el dinero entre ellos.
● **to split up** 1 (*a married couple or group*) separarse [17]; 2 **she's split up with her boyfriend** ha roto con su novio.

spoil *verb* 1 arruinar [17]; **it completely spoiled the evening** arruinó la tarde completamente; **to spoil the surprise** arruinar la sorpresa; 2 malcriar [32] (*a child*).

spoiled *adjective* malcriado/malcriada; **a spoiled child** un niño malcriado.

spoilsport *noun* aguafiestas M/F (*does not change in the plural*).

spokesperson *noun* portavoz M/F.

sponge *noun* esponja F.

sponge cake *noun* bizcocho M.

sponsor *noun* patrocinador M, patrocinadora F.
verb patrocinar [17].

spooky *adjective* espeluznante.

spoon *noun* cuchara F; **a soup spoon** una cuchara sopera; **a teaspoon** una cucharilla.

spoonful *noun* (*large*) cucharada F (*small*) cucharadita F.

sport *noun* deporte M; **to be good at sport** tener [9] facilidad para los deportes; **my favourite sport** mi deporte favorito.

sports bag *noun* bolsa F de deportes.

sports car *noun* coche M deportivo.

sports centre *noun* polideportivo M.

sports club *noun* club M deportivo.

sportsman *noun* deportista M.

sportswear *noun* ropa F de deporte.

sportswoman *noun* deportista F

spot *noun* 1 (*in fabric*) lunar M; **a red tie with black spots** una corbata roja con lunares negros; 2 (*on your skin*) grano M; **I've got spots** tengo granos; **to be covered in spots** estar [2] cubierto de granos; 3 (*stain*) mancha F; 4 (*place*) sitio M; **a beautiful spot** un sitio precioso;

5 (*spotlight*) foco M; (*in the home*)
luz F direccional.
verb **1** divisar [17] (*a person or
object*); **I spotted her in the crowd**
la divisé entre la multitud;
2 encontrar [24] (*an error*).

spotlight *noun* **1** foco M; **2** (*in the
home*) luz F direccional.

spotty *adjective* (*pimply*) lleno de
granos/llena de granos.

sprain *noun* esguince M.
verb **to sprain your ankle** hacerse [7]
un esguince en el tobillo.

spray *noun* (*spray can*) espray M.

spread *verb* **1** (*news or a disease*)
propagarse [28]; **2** extender
[36] (*butter, jam, cement, glue, etc.*).

spring *noun* **1** (*the season*)
primavera F; **in the spring** en
primavera; **spring flowers** flores de
primavera; **2** (*made of metal*)
muelle M; **3** (*providing water*)
manantial M.

springtime *noun* primavera F; **in
springtime** en primavera.

spring water *noun* agua F de
manantial.

sprint *noun* esprint M.
verb correr [18] a toda velocidad.

sprout *noun* (*Brussels sprout*) col F
de Bruselas.

spy *noun* espía M/F.
verb **to spy on somebody** espiar [32]
a alguien.

spying *noun* espionaje M.

square *noun* **1** (*shape*)
cuadrado M; **2** (*in a town or village*)
plaza F; **the village square** la plaza
del pueblo; ★ **to go back to square
one** volver [45] a empezar de cero.
adjective cuadrado/cuadrada; **a
square box** una caja cuadrada;
three square metres tres metros
cuadrados; **the room is four metres
square** la habitación tiene cuatro
metros cuadrados.

squash *noun* **1** (*drink*) **lemon
squash** limonada F; **orange squash**
naranjada F; **2** (*sport*) squash M; **to
play squash** jugar [27] al squash.

squeak *verb* **1** (*door, hinge*) chirriar
[32]; **2** (*person, animal*) chillar [17].

squeeze *verb* **1** apretar
[29] (*somebody's arm, hand or a
toothpaste tube*); **2** exprimir [19] (*a
lemon or an orange*).

squirrel *noun* ardilla F.

stab *verb* apuñalar [17].

stable *noun* cuadra F.
adjective estable.

stack *noun* **1** (*pile*) montón M;
2 stacks of montones de; **she's got
stacks of CDs** tiene montones de
compactos.

stadium *noun* estadio M.

staff *noun* **1** (*of a company*)
personal M; **2** (*in a school*)
profesorado M.

stage *noun* **1** (*for a performance*)
escenario M; **on stage** en el

escenario; **2** (*phase*) etapa F; **the earlier stages of the project** las primeras etapas del proyecto; **3 at this stage it's hard to know** en este momento es difícil saberlo.

stain *noun* mancha F.
verb manchar [17].

stainless steel *noun* acero M inoxidable; **a stainless steel sink** un fregadero de acero inoxidable.

stair *noun* **1** (*step*) escalón M; **2 stairs** escaleras F (*plural*); **I met her on the stairs** me la encontré en las escaleras.

staircase *noun* escaleras F (*plural*).

stale *adjective* (*bread*) correoso/correosa.

stalemate *noun* (*in chess*) tablas F (*plural*).

stall *noun* **1** (*at a market or fair*) puesto M; **2 the stalls** (*in a theatre*) patio M de butacas.

stamp *noun* sello M.
verb **1** poner [11] sello(s) a (*a letter*); **2 to stamp your foot** dar [4] una patada en el suelo.

stamp album *noun* álbum M de sellos.

stamp collection *noun* colección F de sellos.

stand *verb* **1** estar [2] de pie; **several people were standing** varias personas estaban de pie; **2** (*when you say somebody is standing somewhere 'standing' is not usually translated*) **we were standing outside the cinema** estabamos delante del cine; **I'm standing here waiting for you** estoy aquí esperándote; **3 to stand on something** pisar [17] algo; **4** (*bear*) soportar [17]; **I can't stand her** no la soporto; **I can't stand waiting** no soporto esperar.

● **to stand for something** (*be short for*) significar [31]; **what does 'plc' stand for?** ¿qué significa 'plc'?

● **stand up** levantarse [17]; **everybody stood up** todo el mundo se levantó.

standard *noun* nivel M; **the standard of living** el nivel de vida.
adjective estándar; **the standard price** el precio estándar.

stands *noun* (*in a stadium*) tribuna F.

staple *noun* grapa F.
verb grapar [17]; **to staple the pages together** grapar las hojas.

stapler *noun* grapadora F.

star *noun* (*in the sky or rock star, etc.*) estrella F; **he's a film star** es una estrella de cine.
verb **to star in a film** protagonizar [22] una película.

stare *verb* mirar [17] fijamente; **he was staring at me** me estaba mirando fijamente; **what are you staring at?** ¿qué miras?

start *noun* **1** principio M; **at the start** al principio; **at the start of the book** al principio del libro; **from the start** desde el principio; **we knew from the start that it was dangerous** sabíamos desde el principio que era peligroso; **2 to make a start on**

something empezar [25] algo; **I've made a start on my homework** he empezado mis deberes; **3** (*of a race*) salida F.
verb **1** empezar [25]; **the film starts at eight** la película empieza a las ocho; **I've started the book** he empezado el libro; **2 to start doing** empezar [25] a hacer; **I've started learning Spanish** he empezado a aprender español; **3 to start a business** montar [17] un negocio; **4 to start a car** arrancar [31] un coche; **she started the car** arrancó el coche; **the car wouldn't start** el coche no arrancaba.

starter *noun* (*in a meal*) entrante M; **what would you like as a starter?** ¿qué quieres de entrante?

starve *verb* morirse [55] de hambre; **I'm starving!** ¡me muero de hambre!

state *noun* **1** estado M; **the house is in a very bad state** la casa está en muy mal estado; **2** (*administrative*) estado M; **the state** el estado; **3 the States** los Estados Unidos; **they live in the States** viven en los Estados Unidos.
verb **1** declarar [17] (*intention, opinion*); **2** indicar [31] (*address, income, occupation, reason, etc.*).

statement *noun* declaración F.

station *noun* **1** estación F; **the railway station** la estación de tren; **the bus station** la estación de autobús; **2 the police station** la comisaría; **3 a radio station** una emisora de radio; **a TV station** un canal de televisión.

stationer's *noun* papelería F.

statistics *noun* **1** (*subject*) estadística F; **2 the statistics** (*figures*) las estadísticas.

statue *noun* estatua F.

stay *noun* estancia F; **our stay in Paris** nuestra estancia en París; **enjoy your stay!** ¡que disfrutes de tu estancia!
verb **1** quedarse [17]; **I'll stay here** me quedaré aquí; **how long are you staying?** ¿cuánto tiempo te quedas?; **2** (*with time*) **we're going to stay in Berlin for three days** vamos a pasar tres días en Berlín; **3** (*at somebody's house*) **to stay with somebody** quedarse [17] con alguien; **I'm going to stay with my sister this weekend** me voy a quedar con mi hermana este fin de semana; **4** (*be temporarily lodged*) hospedarse [17]; **where are you staying?** ¿dónde te hospedas?
● **to stay in** no salir [63]; **I'm staying in tonight** esta noche no salgo.

steady *adjective* **1** estable; **a steady job** un trabajo estable; **2** constante; **a steady increase** un incremento constante; **3** (*hand, voice*) firme; **4 to hold something steady** sostener [9] algo firmemente.

steak *noun* filete M; **steak and chips** filete con patatas.

steal *verb* robar [17].

steam *noun* vapor M.

steam engine *noun* locomotora F de vapor.

steam iron *noun* plancha F a vapor.

steel *noun* acero M.

steep *adjective* empinado/empinada; **a steep slope** una cuesta empinada.

steeple *noun* 1 (*spire*) aguja F; 2 (*bell tower*) campanario M.

steering wheel *noun* volante M.

step *noun* 1 paso M; **to take a step forwards** dar [4] un paso hacia adelante; 2 (*stair*) escalón M; '**mind the step**' 'cuidado con el escalón'.
● **to step back** retroceder [18].
● **to step forward** avanzar [22].
● **to step into** entrar [17] en (*a lift*).

stepbrother *noun* hermanastro M.

stepdaughter *noun* hijastra F.

stepfather *noun* padrastro M.

stepladder *noun* escalera F de mano.

stepmother *noun* madrastra F.

stepsister *noun* hermanastra F.

stepson *noun* hijastro M.

stereo *noun* estéreo M.

sterling *noun* libra F esterlina; **in sterling** en libras esterlinas.

stew *noun* estofado M.

steward *noun* camarero M.

stewardess *noun* camarera F.

stick *noun* 1 palo M; 2 **a walking stick** un bastón; 3 **a hockey stick** un palo de hockey.
verb 1 (*with glue*) pegar [28];

2 (*put*) poner [11]; **stick them on my desk** ponlos en mi mesa.

sticker *noun* pegatina F.

sticky *adjective* 1 pegajoso/pegajosa; **my hands are sticky** tengo las manos pegajosas; 2 adhesivo/adhesiva; **sticky paper** papel M adhesivo.

sticky tape *noun* cinta F adhesiva.

stiff *adjective* **to feel stiff** estar [2] entumecido; **to have stiff legs** tener [9] las piernas entumecidas; **to have a stiff neck** tener [9] tortícolis; ★ **to be bored stiff** estar más aburrido que una ostra (*literally: to be more bored than an oyster*); ★ **to be scared stiff** estar muerto de miedo (*literally: to be dead from fear*).

still *adjective* 1 quieto/quieta; **sit still!** ¡siéntate quieto!; **keep still!** ¡estate quieto!; 2 **still mineral water** agua F mineral sin gas.
adverb 1 todavía, aún; **do you still live in London?**, ¿vives todavía en Londres? ¿vives aún en Londres?; **I've still not finished** todavía no he terminado, aún no he terminado; **he's still working** está trabajando todavía; **there's still a lot of beer left** todavía queda mucha cerveza; 2 **better still** todavía mejor, aún mejor.

sting *noun* aguijón M; **a wasp sting** un aguijón de avispa.
verb picar [31]; **I was stung by a bee** me picó una abeja.

stink *noun* peste F; **what a stink!**
¡qué peste!
verb apestar [17]; **it stinks of
cigarette smoke in here** aquí apesta
a tabaco.

stir *verb* remover [38].

stitch *noun* 1 (*in sewing*)
puntada F; 2 (*in knitting*) punto M;
3 (*surgical*) punto M de sutura.

stock *noun* 1 (*in a shop*) estock M;
to have something in stock tener [9]
algo en estock; 2 (*supply*) reserva F;
I always have a stock of pencils
siempre tengo una reserva de
lápices; 3 (*for cooking*) caldo M;
chicken stock caldo de pollo.
verb (*in a shop*) vender [18]; **they
don't stock dictionaries** no venden
diccionarios.

stock cube *noun* pastilla F de caldo.

stocking *noun* media F (de liguero).

stomach *noun* estómago M.

stomachache *noun* dolor M de
estómago; **to have stomachache**
tener [9] dolor de estómago.

stone *noun* 1 piedra F; **a stone wall**
una pared de piedra; **to throw a
stone** tirar [17] una piedra; 2 (*in
fruit*) hueso M.

stool *noun* taburete M.

stop *noun* parada F; **the bus stop** la
parada del autobús.
verb 1 (*person or vehicle*) parar [17];
he stopped in front of the shop paró
enfrente de la tienda; **does the train
stop in Cordova?** ¿para el tren en
Córdoba?; **the music stopped** la

música paró; 2 (*engine or machine*)
pararse [17]; 3 **to stop something/
somebody** parar [17] algo/a alguien;
she stopped me in the street me
paró en la calle; 4 **to stop doing** dejar
[17] de hacer; **he's stopped smoking**
ha dejado de fumar; **she never stops
asking questions** nunca deja de
hacer preguntas; 5 **to stop
somebody doing** impedir [57] a
alguien hacer; **there's nothing to
stop you going on your own** nada te
impide ir solo.

stopwatch *noun* cronómetro M.

store *noun* (*shop*) tienda F.
verb 1 guardar [17]; 2 (*on a
computer*) almacenar [17].

storey *noun* piso M; **a three-storey
house** una casa de tres pisos.

storm *noun* tormenta F; **a
snowstorm** una tormenta de nieve;
a rainstorm una tormenta de lluvia.

stormy *adjective* de tormenta.

story *noun* 1 historia F; **to tell a
story** contar una historia; 2 (*tale*)
cuento M.

stove *noun* (*cooker*) cocina F.

straight *adjective* 1 recto/recta; **a
straight line** una línea recta; 2 **to
have straight hair** tener [9] el pelo
liso; 3 (*not crooked*) derecho/
derecha; **the candle's not straight** la
vela no está derecha.
adverb 1 (*in direction*) recto; **go
straight ahead** sigue todo recto;
2 (*in time*) directamente; **he went
straight to the doctor's** fue

directamente al médico; **3 straight away** en seguida.

strange *adjective* extraño/extraña; **a strange situation** una situación extraña.

stranger *noun* desconocido M, desconocida F.

strangle *verb* estrangular [17].

strap *noun* **1** (*on camera or watch*) correa F; **a watchstrap** una correa de reloj; **2** (*on case or bag*) asa F; **3** (*on a garment*) tirante M; **4** (*on a shoe*) tira F.

straw *noun* paja F (*both the material and for drinking with*); **a straw hat** un sombrero de paja.

strawberry *noun* fresa F; **strawberry jam** mermelada de fresa.

stream *noun* (*small river*) arroyo M.

street *noun* calle F; **I met Simon in the street** me encontré con Simon en la calle.

streetlamp *noun* farol M.

street map *noun* plano M de la ciudad.

streetwise *adjective* avispado/avispada.

strength *noun* fuerza F.

stress *noun* **1** tensión F; **2** (*in a word*) acento M.
verb (*emphasize*) recalcar [31]; **to stress the importance of something** recalcar la importancia de algo.

stretch *verb* (*garment or shoes*) dar [4] de sí; **this jumper has stretched** este jersey ha dado de sí.

strict *adjective* estricto/estricta.

strike *noun* huelga F; **to go on strike** ponerse [11] en huelga; **to be on strike** estar [2] en huelga.
verb **1** (*hit*) golpear [17] (*a person*); **2** (*clock*) dar [4]; **the clock struck six** el reloj dio las seis; **3** (*go on strike*) ponerse [11] en huelga.

striker *noun* **1** (*in football*) delantero M, delantera F; **2** (*person on strike*) huelguista M/F.

string *noun* **1** (*for tying*) cordel M; **2** (*for a musical instrument*) cuerda F.

strip *noun* tira F.
verb (*undress*) desnudarse [17].

strip cartoon *noun* tira F cómica.

stripe *noun* raya F.

striped *adjective* de rayas.

stroke *noun* **1** (*style of swimming*) brazada F; **2** (*medical*) derrame M cerebral; **to have a stroke** sufrir [19] un derrame cerebral; ★ **a stroke of luck** un golpe de suerte.
verb acariciar [17].

strong *adjective* **1** (*person, drink, smell, taste, or feeling*) fuerte; **2** (*material*) resistente; **3** (*accent*) marcado.

struggle *noun* **1** lucha F; **the struggle for independence** la lucha por la independencia; **a power struggle** una lucha por el poder;

2 it's been a struggle ha sido muy difícil.
verb **1** (*to obtain something*) luchar [17]; **they have struggled to survive** han luchado para sobrevivir; **2** (*physically, in order to escape or get something*) forcejear [17]; **3** (*have difficulty in doing*) **I'm struggling to finish my homework** me está costando terminar mis deberes.

stubborn *adjective* terco/terca.

stuck *adjective* (*jammed*) atascado/atascada; **the drawer's stuck** el cajón está atascado.

stud *noun* **1** (*on a belt or jacket*) tachuela F; **2** (*on a boot*) taco M; **3** (*earring*) pendiente M de bolita.

student *noun* estudiante M/F.

studio *noun* estudio M.

studio flat *noun* estudio M.

study *verb* estudiar [17]; **he's busy studying for his exams** está muy ocupado estudiando para los exámenes; **she's studying medicine** estudia medicina.

stuff *noun* **1** (*things*) cosas F (*plural*); **we can put all that stuff in the attic** podemos poner todas estas cosas en el ático; **you can leave your stuff at my house** puedes dejar tus cosas en mi casa; **2** (*substance*) cosa F.
verb **1** (*shove*) meter [18]; **she stuffed some things into a suitcase** metió algunas cosas en una maleta; **2** rellenar [17] (*chicken, turkey, vegetables*); **stuffed aubergines** berenjenas rellenas.

stuffing *noun* (*for cooking*) relleno M.

stuffy *adjective* viciado/viciada; **it's very stuffy in here** aquí dentro falta aire.

stunned *adjective* (*amazed*) atónito/atónita.

stunning *adjective* sensacional.

stunt *noun* (*in a film*) escena F peligrosa.

stupid *adjective* estúpido/estúpida; **a stupid man** un hombre estúpido; **that was really stupid** eso fue una verdadera estupidez; **to do something stupid** hacer [7] una estupidez.

stutter *noun* **to have a stutter** tartamudear [17].
verb tartamudear [17].

style *noun* **1** estilo M; **a style of living** un estilo de vida; **he has his own style** tiene su propio estilo; **2** (*fashion*) moda F; **it's the latest style** es la última moda.

subject *noun* **1** tema M; **the subject of my talk** el tema de mi charla; **2** (*at school*) asignatura F; **my favourite subject is biology** mi asignatura favorita es la biología.

submarine *noun* submarino M.

subscription *noun* suscripción F; **to take out a subscription to** suscribirse [52] a.

subsidy *noun* subvención F.

substance *noun* sustancia F.

substitute *noun* (*person*) sustituto M, sustituta F. *verb* sustituir [54].

subtitled *adjective* (*film*) subtitulado/subtitulada.

subtitles *plural noun* subtítulos M (*plural*).

subtract *verb* restar [17].

suburb *noun* barrio M residencial de las afueras; **a suburb of Edinburgh** un barrio residencial de las afueras de Edimburgo; **in the suburbs of London** en los barrios residenciales de las afueras de Londres.

subway *noun* (*underpass*) paso M subterráneo.

succeed *verb* **1** lograr [17]; **to succeed in doing** lograr hacer; **we've succeeded in contacting her** hemos logrado contactar con ella; **2** (*be successful*) tener [9] éxito; **to succeed in business** tener éxito en los negocios.

success *noun* éxito M; **a great success** un gran éxito.

successful *adjective* **1** de éxito; **he's a successful writer** es un escritor de éxito; **2 to be successful in doing** lograr [17] hacer.

successfully *adverb* satisfactoriamente.

such *adjective*, *adverb* **1** tan; **they're such nice people!** ¡son gente tan agradable!; **I've had such a busy day!** ¡he tenido un día tan ocupado!; **it's such a long way** está tan lejos; **it's such a pity** es una verdadera lástima; **2** such a lot of tantos/ tantas; **I've got such a lot of things to tell you!** ¡tengo tantas cosas que contarte!; **3** such as como; **in big cities such as Glasgow** en ciudades grandes como Glasgow; **4 there's no such thing** eso no existe.

sudden *adjective* repentino/ repentina; ★ **all of a sudden** de repente.

suddenly *adverb* de repente; **he suddenly started to laugh** de repente empezó a reír; **suddenly the light went out** de repente se apagó la luz; **to die suddenly** morir [55] de repente.

suede *noun* ante M; **a suede jacket** una chaqueta de ante.

suffer *verb* sufrir [19].

sugar *noun* azúcar M or F; **would you like sugar?** ¿quieres azúcar?; **brown sugar** azúcar morena.

suggest *verb* sugerir [14]; **he suggested I should speak to you about it** sugirió que hablase contigo acerca de ello.

suggestion *noun* sugerencia F; **to make a suggestion** hacer [7] una sugerencia.

suicide *noun* suicidio M; **to commit suicide** suicidarse [17].

suit *noun* **1** (*man's*) traje M; **2** (*woman's*) traje M de chaqueta.

suitable *adjective* **1** adecuado/adecuada; **a suitable hotel** un hotel adecuado; **to be suitable for** ser [1] adecuado para; **2** (*clothing*) apropiado/apropiada; **I don't have any suitable shoes** no tengo zapatos apropiados.

suitcase *noun* maleta F.

sulk *verb* enfurruñarse [17].

sum *noun* **1** cantidad F; **a sum of money** una cantidad de dinero; **a large sum** una cantidad grande; **2** (*calculation*) suma F;
● **to sum up** resumir [19].

summarize *verb* resumir [19].

summary *noun* resumen M.

summer *noun* verano M; **in summer** en verano; **summer clothes** ropa F de verano; **the summer holidays** las vacaciones de verano.

summertime *noun* verano M; **in summertime** en verano.

summit *noun* cumbre F.

sun *noun* sol M; **in the sun** en el sol.

sunbathe *verb* tomar [17] el sol.

sunblock *noun* filtro M solar.

sunburn *noun* quemadura F solar.

sunburned *adjective* **1** (*tanned*) moreno/morena; **2 to get sunburned** (*burned*) quemarse [17].

Sunday *noun* domingo M; **on Sunday** el domingo; **I'm going out on Sunday** voy a salir el domingo; **see you on Sunday!** ¡hasta el domingo!; **on Sundays** los domingos; **the museum is closed on Sundays** el museo cierra los domingos; **every Sunday** todos los domingos; **last Sunday** el domingo pasado; **next Sunday** el próximo domingo.

sunflower *noun* girasol M; **sunflower oil** aceite M de girasol.

sunglasses *plural noun* gafas F (*plural*) de sol.

sunlight *noun* luz F del sol.

sunny *adjective* **1 it's a sunny day** hace sol; **it's going to be sunny** va ha hacer sol; **2** (*place*) soleado/soleada; **in a sunny corner of the garden** una esquina soleada del jardín.

sunrise *noun* salida F del sol; **at sunrise** al amanecer.

sunroof *noun* techo M solar.

sunset *noun* puesta F de sol; **at sunset** al atardecer.

sunshine *noun* sol M.

sunstroke *noun* insolación F; **to get sunstroke** coger [3] una insolación.

suntan *noun* bronceado M; **to get a suntan** broncearse [17].

suntan lotion *noun* loción F bronceadora.

suntan oil *noun* aceite M bronceador.

super *adjective* genial; **we had a super time!** ¡lo pasamos genial!

supermarket *noun* supermercado M.

supernatural *adjective* supernatural.

superstitious *adjective* supersticioso/supersticiosa.

supervise *verb* supervisar [17].

supper *noun* cena F; **I had supper at Sandy's** cené en casa de Sandy.

supplement *noun* suplemento M.

supplies *plural noun* (*of food*) provisiones F (*plural*).

supply *noun* 1 (*stock*) reservas F (*plural*); 2 **to be in short supply** escasear [17].
verb suministrar [17]; **the school supplies the paper** el colegio suministra el papel; **to supply somebody with something** suministrar algo a alguien.

supply teacher *noun* profesor M suplente, profesora F suplente.

support *noun* apoyo M; **he has a lot of support** tiene mucho apoyo.
verb 1 (*back up*) apoyar [17]; **her teachers have really supported her** sus profesoras la han apoyado mucho; 2 ser [1] hincha de (*a team*); **Graeme supports Liverpool** Graeme es hincha del Liverpool; 3 (*financially*) **to support a family** mantener [9] una familia.

supporter *noun* hincha M/F; **an Arsenal supporter** un hincha del Arsenal.

suppose *verb* suponer [11]; **I suppose she's forgotten** supongo que se ha olvidado.

supposed *adjective* **to be supposed to do** tener [9] que; **you're supposed to wear a helmet** tienes que usar casco; **he was supposed to be here at six** tenía que estar aquí a las seis.

sure *adjective* 1 seguro/segura; **are you sure?** ¿estás seguro?; **are you sure you've had enough to eat?** ¿seguro que has comido suficiente?; **are you sure you saw her?** ¿estás seguro de que la viste?; 2 **sure!** ¡claro!; **'can you shut the door?' – 'sure!'** '¿puedes cerrar la puerta?' – '¡claro!'.

surely *adverb* **surely she couldn't have forgotten!** ¡no es posible que se haya olvidado! (*note that 'que' is followed by the subjunctive*).

surface *noun* superficie F.

surfboard *noun* tabla F de surf.

surfing *noun* surfing M; **to go surfing** hacer [7] surfing.

surgeon *noun* cirujano M, cirujana F; **she's a surgeon** es cirujana.

surgery *noun* 1 **to have surgery** operarse [17]; 2 (*doctor's*) consultorio M; **the dentist's surgery** la consulta del dentista.

surname *noun* apellido M.

surprise *noun* sorpresa F; **what a surprise!** ¡qué sorpresa!

surprised *adjective* sorprendido/sorprendida; **I was surprised to see her** me sorprendió verla.

surprising *adjective* sorprendente.

surround *verb* 1 rodear [17]; **2 to be surrounded by** estar [2] rodeado de; **she's surrounded by friends** está rodeada de amigos.

survive *verb* sobrevivir [19].

survivor *noun* superviviente M/F.

suspect *noun* sospechoso M, sospechosa F.
adjective sospechoso/sospechosa.
verb sospechar [17].

suspend *verb* 1 (*hang*) suspender [18]; **2 to be suspended** (*from school*) ser [1] expulsado.

suspense *noun* suspense M.

suspicious *adjective* sospechoso/ sospechosa; **to be suspicious of** sospechar [17] de; **a suspicious parcel** un paquete sospechoso; **a suspicious-looking individual** un individuo de apariencia sospechosa.

swallow *noun* (*bird*) golondrina F.
verb tragar [28].

swan *noun* cisne M.

swap *verb* 1 cambiar [17]; **do you want to swap?** ¿quieres que cambiemos?; **he's swapped his bike for a computer** ha cambiado su bici por un ordenador; **2 to swap seats with somebody** cambiarse [17] de sitio con alguien.

swear *verb* (*use bad language*) decir [5] palabrotas; **he swears a lot** dice muchas palabrotas.

swearword *noun* palabrota F.

sweat *noun* sudor M.
verb sudar [17].

sweater *noun* suéter M.

Swede *noun* sueco M, sueca F.

Sweden *noun* Suecia F.

Swedish *noun* (*language*) sueco M.
adjective sueco/sueca.

sweep *verb* barrer [18].

sweet *noun* 1 caramelo M; **I bought her some sweets** le he comprado unos caramelos; **2** (*dessert*) postre M.
adjective 1 (*food or smile*) dulce; **I try not to eat sweet things** intento no comer cosas dulces; **2** (*kind*) encantador/encantadora; **she's a really sweet person** es realmente encantadora; **it was really sweet of him** ha sido un detalle encantador; **3** (*cute*) rico/rica; **he looks really sweet in that hat!** ¡está muy rico con ese sombrero!

sweetcorn *noun* maíz M tierno.

swim *noun* **to go for a swim** ir [8] a nadar.
verb nadar [17]; **can he swim?** ¿sabe nadar?; **to swim across something** cruzar [22] algo a nado.

swimmer *noun* nadador M, nadadora F; **she's a strong swimmer** es muy buena nadadora.

swimming *noun* natación F; **to go swimming** ir [8] a nadar.

swimming cap *noun* gorro M de baño.

swimming pool *noun* piscina F.

swimming trunks *noun* bañador M.

swimsuit *noun* traje M de baño.

swing *noun* columpio M.

Swiss *noun* (*person*) suizo M, suiza F; **the Swiss** los suizos. *adjective* suizo/suiza.

switch *noun* interruptor M. *verb* (*change*) cambiar [17]; **to switch places** cambiar de sitio.
● **to switch something off** apagar [28] algo.
● **to switch something on** encender [36] algo.

Switzerland *noun* Suiza F.

swollen *adjective* hinchado/ hinchada.

swop *verb* SEE **swap**.

sword *noun* espada F.

syllabus *noun* programa M; **to be on the syllabus** estar [2] en el programa.

sympathetic *adjective* comprensivo/comprensiva.

sympathize *verb* **to sympathize with somebody** compadecer [35] a alguien; **I sympathize with her** la compadezco.

sympathy *noun* compasión F.

symphony *noun* sinfonía F.

symphony orchestra *noun* orquesta F sinfónica.

symptom *noun* síntoma M.

synthesizer *noun* sintetizador M.

synthetic *adjective* sintético/ sintética.

syringe *noun* jeringa F.

system *noun* sistema M.

T t

table *noun* mesa F; **on the table** en la mesa; **to set the table** poner [11] la mesa; **to clear the table** quitar [17] la mesa.

tablecloth *noun* mantel M.

tablespoon *noun* cuchara F de servir; (*in recipes*) **a tablespoon of flour** una cucharada grande de harina.

tablet *noun* pastilla F.

table tennis *noun* ping-pong M; **to play table tennis** jugar [27] al ping-pong.

tackle *verb* **1** (*in football or hockey*) entrarle [17] a; **2** abordar [17] (*a job or problem*).

tact *noun* tacto M.

tactful *adjective* diplomático/ diplomática; **that wasn't very tactful** eso no ha sido muy diplomático.

tadpole *noun* renacuajo M.

tail *noun* **1** (*of dog, cat*) rabo M; **2** (*of horse, fish, bird*) cola F; **3** 'heads or tails?' – 'tails' '¿cara o cruz?' – 'cruz'.

take *verb* **1** coger [3]; **he took a chocolate** cogió un bombón; **take my hand** cógeme la mano; **I took the bus** cogí el autobús; **who's taken my keys?** ¿quién ha cogido mis llaves?; **to take a holiday** cogerse [3] unas vacaciones; **2** (*person or car*) llevar [17]; **I'm taking Jake to the doctor's** voy a llevar a Jake al médico; **I must take the car to the garage** debo llevar el coche al garaje; **3** (*carry away*) llevar [17]; **I'll take my camera with me** me llevaré la cámara; **4 to take something up(stairs)** subir [19] algo; **could you take these towels up?** ¿puedes subir estas toallas?; **5 to take something down(stairs)** bajar [17] algo; **Cheryl's taken the cups down** Cheryl ha bajado las tazas; **6** (*time: for a task or job*) llevar [17]; **it takes two hours** lleva dos horas; **7** (*food or medicine*) tomar [17]; **do you take sugar?** ¿tomas azúcar?; **8** aceptar [17]; (*a credit card or a cheque*) **do you take cheques?** ¿aceptan cheques?; **9** hacer [7] (*an exam*); **she's taking her driving test tomorrow** va a hacer el examen de conducir mañana; **10 what size do you take?** ¿qué talla usas?

● **to take something apart** desmontar [17] algo.

● **to take something back** devolver [45] algo.

● **to take off 1** (*a plane*) despegar [28]; **2** quitarse [17] (*clothes or shoes*); **he took off his shirt** se quitó la camisa; **3** rebajar [17] (*money*); **he took five pounds off the price** rebajó cinco libras del precio.

● **to take out 1** (*from a bag or pocket*) sacar [31]; **Eric took out his wallet** Eric sacó su cartera; **2 he's taking me out to lunch** me ha invitado a comer fuera; **she took me out to the theatre** me invitó a ir al teatro.

takeaway *noun* **1** (*a meal*) comida F para llevar; **an Indian takeaway** comida india para llevar; **2** (*where you buy it*) restaurante M que hace comida para llevar.

talent *noun* talento M; **to have a talent for something** estar [2] dotado/dotada para algo.

talented *adjective* **he's really talented** tiene mucho talento.

talk *noun* **1** (*a chat*) conversación F; **after our talk** después de nuestra conversación; **I had a talk with Rob about it** hablé con Rob acerca de ello; **2** charla F; **she's giving a talk on Hungary** va a dar una charla sobre Hungría.
verb hablar [17]; **I was talking to Jeevan about football** estuve hablando con Jeevan sobre fútbol; **what's he talking about?** ¿de qué está hablando?; **we'll talk about it later** hablaremos de ello más tarde.

talkative *adjective* hablador/habladora; **he's not exactly talkative!** ¡no es muy hablador!

tall *adjective* alto/alta; **she's very tall** es muy alta; **I'm 1.7 metres tall** mido un metro setenta; **how tall is she?** ¿cuánto mide?; **the tallest buildings**

in the city los edificios más altos de
la ciudad.

tame *adjective* domesticado/
domesticada (*an animal*).

tampon *noun* tampón M.

tan *noun* bronceado M; **to get a tan**
broncearse [17].
verb broncearse [17]; **I tan easily** me
bronceo fácilmente.

tank *noun* 1 (*for petrol or water*)
depósito M; 2 **a fish tank** una
pecera; 3 (*military*) tanque M.

tanned *adjective* bronceado/
bronceada.

tap *noun* 1 grifo M; **to turn on the
tap** abrir [46] el grifo; **to turn off the
tap** cerrar [29] el grifo; **the hot tap** el
grifo del agua caliente; 2 (*a pat*)
golpecito M.
verb dar [4] golpecitos.

tap-dancing *noun* claqué M; **to do
tap-dancing** hacer [7] claqué.

tape *noun* 1 cinta F; **my tape of the
Stones** mi cinta de los Stones; **I've
got it on tape** lo tengo en cinta;
2 **sticky tape** cinta F adhesiva.
verb grabar [17]; **I want to tape the
film** quiero grabar la película.

tape measure *noun* cinta F
métrica.

target *noun* objetivo M.

tart *noun* tarta F; **a raspberry tart**
una tarta de frambuesas.

tartan *adjective* escocés/escocesa; **a
tartan skirt** una falda escocesa.

task *noun* tarea F.

taste *noun* 1 (*flavour*) sabor M; **the
taste of onions** el sabor a cebolla;
2 (*judgement*) gusto M; **she has
good taste** tiene buen gusto; **in bad
taste** de mal gusto.
verb 1 saber [13]; **the soup tastes
horrible** la sopa sabe fatal; **to taste of**
saber a; **it tastes of strawberries**
sabe a fresas; 2 **do you want to
taste?** ¿quieres probarlo?

tasty *adjective* sabroso/sabrosa.

tattoo *noun* tatuaje M; **he's got a
tattoo on his arm** tiene un tatuaje
en el brazo.

Taurus *noun* tauro M; **Jo's Taurus** Jo
es tauro.

tax *noun* impuesto M.

taxi *noun* taxi M; **by taxi** en taxi; **to
take a taxi** coger [3] un taxi.

taxi driver *noun* taxista M/F.

taxi rank *noun* parada F de taxis.

TB *noun* tuberculosis F.

tea *noun* 1 té M; **a cup of tea** una
taza de té; **to have tea** tomar [17] té;
a herbal tea una infusión;
2 (*evening meal*) cena F.

teabag *noun* bolsita F de té.

teach *verb* 1 enseñar [17]; **she's
teaching me Italian** me está
enseñando italiano; **that'll teach
you!** ¡así aprenderás!; 2 (*working as
a teacher*) dar [4] clases de; **her mum
teaches maths** su madre da clases
de matemáticas; 3 **to teach yourself
something** aprender [18] algo por su

cuenta; **Anne taught herself Italian**
Anne ha aprendido italiano por su
cuenta.

teacher *noun* **1** (*in a secondary
school*) profesor M, profesora F; **my
mother's a teacher** mi madre es
profesora; **our biology teacher**
nuestra profesora de biología; **2** (*in
primary school*) maestro M,
maestra F; **she's a primary school
teacher** es maestra.

teaching *noun* enseñanza F.

team *noun* equipo M; **a football
team** un equipo de fútbol; **our team
won** nuestro equipo ganó.

teapot *noun* tetera F.

tear[1] *noun* (*a rip*) roto M; **I've got a
tear in my jeans** tengo un roto en los
vaqueros.
verb **1** romper [40]; **you've torn your
shirt** te has roto la camisa; **she tore
up my letter** rompió mi carta;
2 romperse [40]; **be careful, it tears
easily** cuidado, se rompe fácilmente.
● **to tear off 1** (*carefully*) recortar
[17]; **2** (*violently*) arrancar [31].
● **to tear open 1** (*carefully*) abrir [46];
2 (*violently*) rasgar [28].

tear[2] *noun* (*when you cry*) lágrima F;
to be in tears estar [2] llorando; **to
burst into tears** ponerse [11] a llorar.

teaspoon *noun* cucharita F; (*in
recipes*) **a teaspoonful of …** una
cucharadita de …

teatime *noun* hora F merendar.

tea towel *noun* paño M de cocina.

technical *adjective* técnico/técnica.

technical college *noun* escuela F
politécnica.

technician *noun* técnico M,
técnica F.

technological *adjective*
tecnológico/tecnológica.

technology *noun* tecnología F;
information technology
informática F.

teddy bear *noun* osito M de
peluche.

teenage *adjective* **1** adolescente;
they have a teenage son tienen un
hijo adolescente; **2** (*films,
magazines, etc.*) para adolescentes;
a teenage magazine una revista
para adolescentes.

teenager *noun* adolescente M/F; **a
group of teenagers** un grupo de
adolescentes.

teens *plural noun* adolescencia F;
he's in his teens es un adolescente.

tee-shirt *noun* camiseta F.

telephone *noun* teléfono M; **on the
telephone** al teléfono.
verb llamar [17] por teléfono; **I'll
telephone the bank** llamaré al
banco por teléfono.

telephone box *noun* cabina F
telefónica.

telephone call *noun* llamada F de
teléfono.

telephone directory *noun* guía F telefónica.

telephone number *noun* número M de teléfono.

television *noun* televisión F; **she was watching television** estaba viendo la televisión; **I saw it on television** lo vi en televisión.

television programme *noun* programa M de televisión.

tell *verb* **1 to tell somebody something** decirle [5] algo a alguien; **that's what she told me** eso es lo que ella me dijo; **I told him it was silly** le dije que era una tontería; **have you told Sara?** ¿se lo has dicho a Sara?; **I didn't tell anyone** no se lo dije a nadie; **2 to tell somebody to do** decirle [5] a alguien que haga; (*note that 'que' is followed by the subjunctive*) **he told me to do it myself** me dijo que lo hiciese solo; **she told me not to wait** me dijo que no esperase; **3** (*explain*) decir [5]; **can you tell me how to do it?** ¿puedes decirme cómo hacerlo?; **4** contar [24] (*a story*); **tell me about your holiday** cuéntame qué tal tus vacaciones; **5** (*to see*) notar [17]; **to tell the difference** notar la diferencia; **you can tell ...** se nota ...; **you can tell it's old** se nota que es viejo; **you can tell she's cross** se nota que está enfadada; **I can't tell them apart** no puedes distinguirlos.

telly *noun* tele F (*informal*); **to watch telly** ver [16] la tele; **I saw her on telly** la vi en la tele.

temper *noun* **to be in a temper** estar [2] de mal humor; **to lose your temper** perder [36] los estribos.

temperature *noun* **1** temperatura F; **the oven temperature** la temperatura del horno; **2 to have a temperature** tener [9] fiebre F.

temporary *adjective* temporal.

temptation *noun* tentación F.

tempted *adjective* tentado/tentada; **I'm really tempted to go** estoy realmente tentado de ir.

tempting *adjective* tentador/tentadora.

ten *number* diez M; **Harry's ten** Harry tiene diez años; **it's ten o'clock** son las diez.

tend *verb* **to tend to do** tender [36] a hacer; **he tends to talk a lot** tiende a hablar mucho.

tennis *noun* tenis M; **to play tennis** jugar [27] al tenis.

tennis ball *noun* pelota F de tenis.

tennis court *noun* cancha F de tenis.

tennis player *noun* jugador/jugadora M/F de tenis.

tennis racket *noun* raqueta F de tenis.

tenor *noun* tenor M.

tenpin bowling *noun* bolos M (*plural*); **to go tenpin bowling** jugar [27] a los bolos.

tense *noun* the present tense el presente; **in the future tense** en futuro.
adjective tenso/tensa.

tent *noun* tienda F.

tenth *noun* 1 (*fraction*) **a tenth** una décima parte; 2 **the tenth of April** el diez de abril.
adjective décimo/décima; **on the tenth floor** en la décima planta.

term *noun* 1 (*in school*) trimestre M; 2 **to be on good terms with somebody** llevarse [17] bien con alguien.

terminal *noun* terminal F; **terminal two** la terminal dos; **a computer terminal** una terminal de ordenador.

terrace *noun* 1 (*of a house or hotel*) terraza F; 2 **the terraces** (*at a stadium*) las gradas.

terrible *adjective* espantoso/ espantosa; **the weather was terrible** el tiempo fue espantoso.

terribly *adverb* 1 (*very*) muy; **not terribly clean** no muy limpio que digamos; 2 (*badly*) fatal; **I played terribly** jugué fatal.

terrific *adjective* 1 increíble; **at a terrific speed** a una velocidad increíble; **a terrific amount** una cantidad increíble; 2 **terrific!** ¡fenomenal!

terrified *adjective* aterrorizado/ aterrorizada.

terrorism *noun* terrorismo M.

terrorist *noun* terrorista M/F.

test *noun* 1 (*in school*) examen M; **we've got a maths test tomorrow** tenemos un examen de matemáticas el viennes; 2 (*of your skills or patience*) prueba F; 3 (*medical*) análisis M; **a blood test** un análisis de sangre; 4 **a driving test** un examen de conducir; **she's sitting her driving test tomorrow** va a hacer el exámen de conducir mañana; **he passed his driving test** ha aprobado el examen de conducir.
verb 1 (*in school*) examinarse [17]; 2 **to test something out** probar [24] algo.

text *noun* texto M.

textbook *noun* libro M de texto.

Thames *noun* **the Thames** el Támesis.

than *preposition*, *conjunction* 1 que; **their new album's better than the last one** su nuevo álbum es mejor que el último; **they have more money than we do** tienen más dinero que nosotros; 2 (*for quantities*) de; **more than forty** más de cuarenta; **more than thirty years** más de treinta años.

thank *verb* dar [4] las gracias.

thanks *plural noun* 1 gracias F (*plural*); **no thanks** no gracias; **thanks a lot** muchas gracias; **thanks for your letter** gracias por tu carta; 2 **thanks to** gracias a; **it was thanks to Micky** fue gracias a Micky.

thank you *adverb* gracias; **thank you very much for the cheque** muchas gracias por el cheque; **no thank you** no, gracias; **a thank-you letter** un carta de agradecimiento.

that *adjective* 1 (*before a masculine noun*) ese; **that dog** ese perro; **that blue car** ese coche azul; 2 (*before a feminine noun*) esa; **that woman** esa mujer; 3 **that one** (*referring to a masculine noun*) ése (*referring to a feminine noun*) ésa; **'which cake would you like?' – 'that one, please'** '¿qué pastel quieres?' – 'ése, por favor'; **I like all the skirts but I'm going to buy that one** me gustan todas las faldas pero voy a comprar ésa.
adverb **it's not that funny** no es tan divertido; **their house isn't that big** su casa no es tan grande.
pronoun 1 (*referring to a masculine noun*) ese (*referring to a feminine noun*) esa; **that's not his car** ese no es su coche; **is that Mandy?** ¿es esa Mandy?; **that's my bedroom** esa es mi habitación; 2 eso; **that's not what you told me** eso no es lo que tú me dijiste; **that's not true** eso no es cierto; **did you see that?** ¿has visto eso?; **what's that?** ¿qué es eso?; **who's that?** ¿quién es?; **where's that?** ¿dónde está?; 3 que; **the book that's on the table** el libro que está sobre la mesa; **the girl that I saw** la chica que yo vi; 4 (*when the verb is followed by a preposition*) (*referring to a masculine noun*) el que (*referring to a feminine noun*) la que; **the drawer that I put it in** el cajón en el que lo metí.

conjunction que; **I knew that he was wrong** sabía que no tenía razón.

the *definite article* 1 (*before a masculine noun*) el; **the cat** el gato; **the tree** el árbol; (*when 'el' follows 'de', they join to become 'del'*) **the branches of the tree** las ramas del árbol; (*when 'el' follows 'a' they join to become 'al'*) **we went to the park** fuimos al parque; 2 (*before a feminine noun*) la; **the table** la mesa; **the orange** la naranja; 3 (*before masculine plural nouns*) los; **the plates** los platos; 4 (*before feminine plural nouns*) las; **the windows** las ventanas.

theatre *noun* teatro M; **to go to the theatre** ir [8] al teatro.

theft *noun* robo M.

their *adjective* 1 (*before a singular noun*) su; **their flat** su piso; **their mother** su madre; 2 (*before a plural noun*) sus; **their presents** sus regalos; 3 (*with parts of the body*) el, la, los, las; **they had tatoos on their arms** tenían tatuajes en los brazos; **they're washing their hands** se están lavando las manos.

theirs *pronoun* 1 (*when referring to a singular noun*) el suyo/la suya; **our garden's smaller than theirs** nuestro jardín es más pequeño que el suyo; **our house is bigger than theirs** nuestra casa es más grande que la suya; 2 (*when referring to a plural noun*) los suyos/las suyas; **our shoes were newer than theirs** nuestros zapatos eran más nuevos que los suyos; **our photos were**

better that theirs nuestras fotos eran mejores que las suyas.

them *pronoun* 1 los/las; **she's got two brothers, but I don't know them** tiene dos hermanos, pero no los conozco; **remember Ann and Lisa? I saw them last week** ¿te acuerdas de Ann y Lisa? las vi la semana pasada; 2 (*with an infinitive or when telling somebody to do something 'los'/'las' join onto the verb*) **I don't want to see them** no quiero verlos; **listen to them!** ¡escúchalos!; (*but when telling someone NOT to do something, 'les' or 'las' comes before the verb*) **don't push them!** ¡no los empujes!; 3 (*to them*) les; **I gave them my address** les di mis señas; (*'le' becomes 'se' before pronouns 'lo' or 'la'*) **I lent it to them** se lo dejé; (*when giving an order 'se' joins the verb*) **give it back to them** ¡devuélveselo!; 4 (*after a preposition, in comparisons, or after the verb 'to be'*) ellos/ellas; **I'll go with them** iré con ellos/ellas; **without them** sin ellos/sin ellas; **she's older than them** es mayor que ellos; **it's them!** ¡son ellos!/¡son ellas!

theme park *noun* parque M temático.

themselves *pronoun* 1 (*as a reflexive*) se; **they've helped themselves** se sirvieron; 2 (*for emphasis*) ellos mismos/ellas mismas; **the boys can do it themselves** los chicos pueden hacerlo ellos mismos; **the girls will tell you themselves** las chicas te lo

dirán ellas mismas; 3 **by themselves** ellos solos/ellas solas.

then *adverb* 1 (*next*) luego; **wash up and then make your bed** lávate y luego haz la cama; **I went to the post office and then the bank** fui a la oficina de correos y luego al banco; 2 (*at that time*) entonces; **we were living in York then** entonces vivían en York; 3 (*in that case*) entonces; **then why worry?** entonces ¿para qué preocuparse?; **that's all right then** entonces vale; 4 **by then** para entonces; **by then it was too late** para entonces era demasiado tarde.

theory *noun* teoría F; **in theory** en teoría.

there *adverb* 1 ahí (*further away*) allí; **put it there** ponlo ahí (*further away*) ponlo allí; **stand there** ponte ahí; **they're in there** están ahí dentro; **look up there!** ¡mira ahí arriba!; 2 **over there** ahí (*further away*) allí; **she's over there talking to Mark** está ahí hablando con Mark (*further away*) está allí hablando con Mark; 3 **down there** ahí abajo (*further away*) allí abajo; **up there** ahí arriba (*further away*) allí arriba; 4 (*when there stands for somethng already mentioned, it is usually not translated*) **I've seen photos of Madrid but I've never been there** he visto fotos de Madrid, pero nunca he estado; **yes, I'm going there on Tuesday** sí, voy a ir el martes; 5 **there is/there are** hay; **there's a cat in the garden** hay un gato en el jardín; **there was no bread** no había pan; **yes, there's enough** sí, hay suficiente; **there are plenty of seats** hay muchos asientos; **6 there they are!** ¡ahí están!; **there she is!** ¡ahí está!; **there's the bus coming!** ¡ahí viene el autobús!

thermometer *noun* termómetro M.

these *adjective* **1** (*with a masculine noun*) estos; **these envelopes** estos sobres; **2** (*with a feminine noun*) estas; **these postcards** estas postales.

they *pronoun* **1** (*like other subject pronouns 'they' is generally not translated; in Spanish the form of the verb tells you whether the subject of the verb is 'we', you', 'they', etc., so 'they' is only translated when you want to emphasize it*) **'where are the knives?' – 'they're in the drawer'** '¿dónde están los cuchillos?' – 'están en el cajón'; **I bought some apples but they're not very nice** he comprado unas manzanas pero no están muy buenas; **2** (*for emphasis*) ellos/ellas; **they did it** lo hicieron ellos.

thick *adjective* grueso/gruesa; **a thick layer of butter** una capa gruesa de mantequilla.

thief *noun* ladrón M, ladrona F.

thigh *noun* muslo M.

thin *adjective* **1** delgado/delgada (*a person*); **to get thin** adelgazar [22]; **2** fino/fina (*a slice*); **3** (*too thin, skinny*) flaco/flaca; **she's terribly thin** está muy flaca.

thing *noun* **1** (*an object*) cosa F; **shops full of pretty things** tiendas llenas de cosas preciosas; **she told me some surprising things** me dijo algunas cosas sorprendentes; **2** (*a whatsit*) chisme M (*informal*); **you can use that thing to open it** puedes usar ese chisme para abrirlo; **3 things** (*belongings*) cosas F (*plural*); **you can put your things in my room** puedes poner tus cosas en mi habitación; **4 the best thing to do is …** lo mejor es …; **the thing is, I've lost her address** la cuestión es que he perdido sus señas; **5 how are things with you?** ¿qué tal te van las cosas?

think *verb* **1** pensar [29]; **I'm thinking about you** estoy pensando en ti; **Tony thinks it's silly** Tony piensa que es una tontería; **what do you think of my new jacket?** ¿qué piensas de mi chaqueta nueva?; **what do you think of that?** ¿qué piensas de eso?; **he thought for a moment** pensó un momento; **she's thinking of studying medicine** está pensando estudiar medicina; **2** (*believe*) creer [37]; **do you think they'll come?** ¿crees que vendrán?; **no, I don't think so** no, creo que no; **I think he's already left** creo que ya se ha ido; **3** (*imagine*) imaginar [17]; **just think! we'll soon be in Spain!** ¡imagínate! ¡pronto estaremos en España!; **I never thought it would be like this!** ¡nunca imaginé que sería así!

third *noun* **1** (*fraction*) **a third** un tercio; **2 the third of March** el tres de marzo.
adjective tercero/tercera; **on the third floor** en la tercera planta.

thirdly *adverb* en tercer lugar.

Third World *noun* **the Third World** el Tercer Mundo.

thirst *noun* sed F.

thirsty *adjective* **to be thirsty** tener [9] sed; **I'm thirsty** tengo sed; **we were all thirsty** todos teníamos sed.

thirteen *number* trece M; **Ahmed's thirteen** Ahmed tiene trece años.

thirty *number* treinta M; **she's thirty** tiene treinta años; **thirty-five** treinta y cinco.

this *adjective* **1** este (*before a masculine noun*); esta (*before a feminine noun*); **this paintbrush** este pincel; **this tree** este árbol; **this cup** esta taza; **this morning** esta mañana; **2 this one** (*referring to a masculine noun*) éste (*referring to a feminine noun*) ésta; **if you need a pen you can use this one** si necesitas un boli puedes usar éste; **if you want a lamp you can borrow this one** si quieres una lámpara puedes coger ésta. *pronoun* **1** (*referring to a masculine noun*) éste; **this is my car** éste es mi coche; **2** (*referring to a feminine noun*) ésta; **this is the best photo** ésta es la mejor foto; **3** esto; **can you hold this for a moment?** ¿puedes sostener esto un momento?; **what's this?** ¿qué es esto?; **4 this is Tracy speaking** (*on the phone*) soy Tracy; **5** (*in introductions*) **this is my sister Carla** te presento a mi hermana Carla.

thistle *noun* cardo M.

those *adjective* **1** (*before a masculine noun*) esos; (*before a feminine noun*) esas; **those books** esos libros; **2 those cups** esas tazas. *pronoun* (*referring to a masculine noun*) ésos (*referring to a feminine noun*) ésas; **if you want some knives you can take those** si quieres cuchillos puedes coger ésos; **if you want some cups you can take those** si quieres tazas puedes coger ésas.

though *conjunction* **1** aunque; **though it's cold** aunque hace calor; **though he's older than she is** aunque es mayor que ella; **2 it was a good idea, though** aun así era una buena idea.

thought *noun* pensamiento M.

thoughtful *adjective* **1** (*considerate*) amable; **it was really thoughtful of you** fue muy amable de tu parte; **2** (*deep in thought*) pensativo/pensativa.

thoughtless *adjective* desconsiderado/desconsiderada.

thousand *number* **1** mil M; **a thousand** mil; **a thousand pesetas** mil pesetas; **three thousand** tres mil; **2 thousands of** miles de; **there were thousands of tourists in Barcelona** había miles de turistas en Barcelona.

thread *noun* hilo M. *verb* enhebrar [17] (*a needle*).

threat *noun* amenaza F.

threaten *verb* amenazar [22]; **to threaten to do** amenazar con hacer.

three *number* tres M; **Lily's three** Lily tiene tres años.

three-quarters *noun* tres cuartos M (*plural*).

thrilled *adjective* encantado/ encantada; **I was thrilled to hear from you** me encantó tener noticias tuyas.

thriller *noun* **1** (*book*) novela F de suspense; **2** (*film*) película F de suspense.

thrilling *adjective* emocionante.

throat *noun* garganta F; **to have a sore throat** tener [9] dolor de garganta.

through *preposition* **1** (*across*) a través de; **a path through the forest** un camino a través del bosque; **to go through something** atravesar [29] algo; **we went through the park** atravesamos el parque; **2** (*by way of*) por; **the train went through Leeds** el tren fue por Leeds; **through the window** por la ventana; **3 to go through customs** pasar [17] la aduana.
adjective directo/directa (*a train or flight*).

throw *verb* tirar [17]; **I threw the letter into the bin** tiré la carta a la basura; **he threw the book on the floor** tiró el libro al suelo; **throw me the ball !** ¡tírame la pelota !; **we were throwing snowballs** estábamos tirando bolas de nieve.

- **to throw something away** tirar [17] algo; **I've thrown away the old newspapers** he tirado los periódicos viejos.
- **to throw somebody out** echar [17] a alguien.
- **to throw something out** tirar [17] algo (*rubbish*).
- **to throw up** devolver [45].

thumb *noun* pulgar M.

thunder *noun* truenos M (*plural*); **a peal of thunder** un trueno.

thunderstorm *noun* tormenta F eléctrica.

Thursday *noun* jueves M; **on Thursday** el jueves; **I'm going out on Thursday** voy a salir el jueves; **see you on Thursday !** ¡hasta el jueves !; **on Thursdays** los jueves; **the museum is closed on Thursdays** el museo cierra los jueves; **every Thursday** todos los jueves; **last Thursday** el jueves pasado; **next Thursday** el próximo jueves.

tick *verb* **1** (*tick-tock*) hacer [7] tictac; **2** (*on paper*) marcar [31].

ticket *noun* **1** entrada F; (*for an exhibition, a theatre or cinema*) **two tickets for the concert** dos entradas para el concierto; **2** (*for a plane, a train, a bus or the underground*) billete M; **a bus ticket** un billete de autobús; **3** (*for left luggage*) ticket M; **4 a parking ticket** una multa.

ticket inspector *noun* revisor M, revisora F.

ticket office *noun* **1** (*at a station*) mostrador M de venta de billetes; **2** (*at a cinema*) taquilla F.

tickle *verb* hacer [7] cosquillas.

tide *noun* marea F; **at high tide** cuando la marea está alta; **the tide is out** la marea está baja.

tidy *adjective* **1** ordenado/ ordenada (*a room*); **2** bien escrito/ bien escrita (*homework*); **3** bien arreglado/bien arreglada (*a person*). *verb* ordenar [17].

tie *noun* **1** corbata F; **a red tie** una corbata roja; **2** (*in a match*) empate M. *verb* **1** atar [17]; **to tie your shoelaces** atarse los zapatos; **2** to **tie a knot in something** hacer [7] un nudo a algo; **3** (*in a match*) **we tied two all** empatamos a dos.

tiger *noun* tigre M.

tight *adjective* **1** **to be tight** apretar [29]; **the skirt's a bit tight** la falda aprieta un poco; **these shoes are too tight** estos zapatos aprietan mucho; **2** (*close-fitting*) ceñido/ceñida; **she was wearing a tight dress** llevaba un vestido ceñido.

tighten *verb* apretar [29].

tightly *adverb* fuerte; **hold it tightly** agárralo fuerte.

tights *plural noun* medias F (*plural*); **a pair of purple tights** un par de medias moradas.

tile *noun* **1** (*on a floor or wall*) azulejo M; **2** (*on a roof*) teja F.

till[1] hasta; **they're here till Sunday** están aquí hasta el domingo; **till then** hasta entonces; **till now** hasta ahora; **she won't be back till ten** no volverá hasta las diez.

till[2] *noun* caja F; **pay at the till** pague en la caja.

time *noun* **1** (*on the clock*) hora F; **what time is it?** ¿qué hora es?; **it's time for lunch** es hora de comer; **ten o'clock Spanish time** las diez hora española; **on time** a la hora; **2** (*an amount of time*) tiempo M; **we've got lots of time** tenemos mucho tiempo; **there's not much time left** no queda mucho tiempo; **he talked for a long time** habló durante mucho tiempo; **she hasn't called me for a long time** hace mucho que no me llama; **3** (*moment*) momento M; **is this a good time to phone?** ¿es buen momento para llamar?; **any time now** en cualquier momento; **4 from time to time** de vez en cuando; **at times** a veces; **for the time being** por ahora; **5** (*in a series*) vez F (*plural* **veces**); **six times** seis veces; **the first time** la primera vez; **the first time I saw you** la primera vez que te vi; **three times a year** tres veces al año; **6** (*multiplying*) **three times two is six** tres por dos son seis; **7 to have a good time** pasárselo [17] bien; **we had a really good time** nos lo pasamos muy bien; **have a good time!** ¡pásatelo bien!

time off *noun* **1** (*free time*) tiempo M libre; **2** (*leave*) días M (*plural*) libres.

timetable *noun* horario M; **the bus timetable** el horario de los autobuses.

tin *noun* lata F; **a tin of tomatoes** una lata de tomates.

tinned *adjective* en lata; **tinned peas** guisantes en lata.

tin opener *noun* abrelatas M (*does not change in the plural*).

tiny *adjective* diminuto/diminuta.

tip *noun* 1 (*the end*) punta F; **the tip of my finger** la punta de mi dedo; 2 (*money*) propina F; 3 (*a useful hint*) consejo M.
verb 1 (*to give money to*) darle [4] una propina a; **we tipped the waiter** le dimos una propina al camarero; 2 tirar [17] (*liquid*).

tiptoe *noun* **on tiptoe** de puntillas.

tired *adjective* 1 cansado/cansada; **I'm tired** estoy cansado; **you look tired** pareces cansado; 2 **to be tired of** estar [2] harto de/harta de; **he's tired of London** está harto de Londres; **she says she's tired of watching TV** dice que está harta de ver la tele.

tiring *adjective* cansado/cansada.

tissue *noun* (*a paper hanky*) pañuelo M de papel; **do you have a tissue?** ¿tienes un pañuelo de papel?

title *noun* título M.

to *preposition* 1 (*to a place*) a; **to London** a Londres; **to Spain** a España; **she's gone to the office** se ha ido a la oficina; **to Paul's house** a casa de Paul; **from Monday to Friday** de lunes a viernes; (*note that 'a' followed by 'el' becomes 'al'*) **I'm going to school** voy al colegio; **I'm going to the dentist's tomorrow** voy al dentista mañana; 2 (*to a person*) a; **give the book to Leila** dale el libro a Leila; **who did you give it to?** ¿a quién se lo diste?; **to talk to somebody** hablar [17] con alguien; **he didn't talk to me** no habló conmigo; **I was nice to them** fui amable con ellos; 3 **we're ready to go** estamos listos para irnos; **it's easy to do** es fácil de hacer; **I have nothing to do** no tengo nada que hacer; **I have a lot of homework to do** tengo muchos deberes que hacer; 4 (*talking about the time*) **it's ten to nine** son las nueve menos diez; **it's twenty to** son menos veinte; 5 (*in order to*) para; **he gave me some money to buy a sandwich** me dio dinero para comprar un sandwich.

toast *noun* 1 pan M tostado; **a piece of toast** una tostada; **two slices of toast** dos tostadas; 2 (*to your health*) brindis M; **to drink a toast to the future** brindar [17] por el futuro.

toaster *noun* tostador M.

tobacco *noun* tabaco M.

tobacconist's *noun* estanco M.

today *adverb*, *noun* hoy; **today's her birthday** hoy es su cumpleaños.

toe *noun* dedo M del pie; **my big toe** mi dedo gordo del pie.

toffee *noun* toffee M.

together *adverb* juntos/juntas; **Kate and Lindy arrived together** Kate y Lindy llegaron juntas; **they all left together** se fueron todos juntos.

toilet *noun* 1 (*in a house*) baño M; **she's gone to the toilet** ha ido al baño; 2 (*in a public place*) servicio M; **where's the toilet?** ¿dónde está el servicio?; 3 **toilets** (*in a public place*) servicios M (*plural*); **where are the toilets?** ¿dónde están los servicios.

toilet paper *noun* papel M higiénico.

toilet roll *noun* rollo M de papel higiénico.

token *noun* 1 (*for a machine or game*) ficha F; 2 (*as a present*) cheque M regalo; **a record token** un cheque regalo para un disco.

tomato *noun* tomate M; **a tomato salad** una ensalada de tomate; **tomato sauce** salsa F de tomate.

tomorrow *adverb* mañana; **I'll do it tomorrow** lo haré mañana; **tomorrow afternoon** mañana por la tarde; **tomorrow morning** mañana por la mañana; **tomorrow night** mañana por la noche; **the day after tomorrow** pasado mañana.

tongue *noun* lengua F; **to stick your tongue out** sacar [31] la lengua; ★ **it's on the tip of my tongue** lo tengo en la punta de la lengua.

tonic *noun* tónica F; **a gin and tonic** un gin tonic.

tonight *adverb* esta noche; **I'm going out with my mates tonight** esta noche voy a salir con mis amigos.

tonsillitis *noun* anginas F (*plural*).

too *adverb* 1 demasiado/demasiada; **it's too expensive** es demasiado caro; **the tickets are too expensive** los billetes son demasiados caros; **too often** demasiado a menudo; 2 **too much** (*before a masculine noun*) demasiado (*before a feminine noun*) demasiada; **it takes too much time** lleva demasiado tiempo; **I watch too much TV** veo demasiada televisión; 3 **too much** (*before verb*) demasiado; **he eats too much** come demasiado; 4 **too many** (*before a masculine noun*) demasiados (*before a feminine noun*) demasiadas; **there are too many accidents** hay demasiados accidentes; 5 (*as well*) también; **Karen's coming too** Karen también viene; **me too!** ¡yo también¡; 6 (*very*) muy; **I'm not too convinced** no estoy muy convencida.

tool *noun* herramienta F.

tool kit *noun* juego M de herramientas.

tooth *noun* 1 diente M; **to brush your teeth** cepillarse [17] los dientes; 2 (*backtooth*) muela F.

toothache *noun* dolor M de muelas; **to have toothache** tener [9] dolor de muelas.

toothbrush *noun* cepillo M de dientes.

toothpaste *noun* pasta F de dientes.

top *noun* **1** alto M (*of a ladder, or stairs*); **at the top of the stairs** en lo alto de las escaleras; **2** (*of a page, container or box*) parte F superior; **the top of the box is red** la parte superior de la caja es roja; **3 on top of** (*a table, wardrobe, etc.*) encima de; **it's on top of the chest-of-drawers** está encima de la cómoda; **4** (*of a mountain*) cima F; **5** (*a lid, cap*) (*of a bottle*) tapón M (*of a pan or jar*) tapa F (*of a pen*) capuchón M; **6 to be at the top of the list** encabezar [22] una lista.
adjective **1** (*a step or floor*) último/última; **it's on the top floor** está en el último piso; **2** de arriba (*a bunk, drawer or shelf*); **3 in the top left-hand corner** en la esquina superior izquierda; ★ **and on top of all that** y para colmo; ★ **it was a bit over the top** fue un poco excesivo.

topic *noun* tema M.

torch *noun* linterna F.

torn *adjective* roto/rota.

tortoise *noun* tortuga F.

torture *noun* tortura F.
verb torturar [17].

Tory *noun* conservador M, conservadora F.

total *noun* total M.
adjective total.

totally *adverb* totalmente.

touch *noun* **1** (*contact*) **to get in touch with somebody** contactar [17] con alguien; **to stay in touch with somebody** mantenerse [9] en contacto con alguien; **we've lost touch** hemos perdido el contacto; **2** (*a little bit*) poco M; **a touch of vanilla** un poco de vainilla; **it was a touch embarrassing** fue un poco embarazoso.
verb **1** tocar [31]; **2** (*emotionally*) conmover [38].

tough *adjective* **1** duro/dura; **the meat's a bit tough** la carne está un poco dura; **a tough guy** un tipo duro; **you need to be tough to survive** tienes que ser duro para sobrevivir; **2** (*severe*) severo/severa; **3** (*fabric*) resistente; **4** (*question, problem or job*) difícil; **things are a bit tough at the moment** las cosas están un poco difíciles en este momento; **5 tough luck!** ¡te fastidias! (*informal*).

tour *noun* **1** visita F; **we did the tour of the castle** hicimos la visita al castillo; **a tour of the city** una visita a la ciudad; **2 a package tour** un viaje organizado; **3** (*by a band or theatre group*) gira F; **to go on tour** ir [8] de gira.

tourism *noun* turismo M.

tourist *noun* turista M/F.

tourist information office *noun* oficina F de información y turismo.

towards *adverb* hacia; **she went off towards the lake** se fue hacia el lago.

towel *noun* toalla F.

tower *noun* torre F; **the Eiffel Tower** la torre Eiffel.

tower block *noun* bloque M de apartamentos.

town *noun* ciudad F; **to go into town** ir [8] a la ciudad; (*to the centre*) ir [8] al centro.

town centre *noun* centro M de la ciudad.

town hall *noun* ayuntamiento M.

toy *noun* juguete M.

trace *noun* rastro M; **there is no trace of it** no hay rastro de ello. *verb* (*on paper*) calcar [31]; (*the reason for a problem*) descubrir [46]; (*a missing person*) localizar [22].

tracing paper *noun* papel M de calco.

track *noun* 1 (*for sport*) pista F; **a track event** una prueba de atletismo; **a racing track** (*for cars*) un circuito; 2 (*a path*) sendero M; 3 (*song*) tema M; **this is my favourite track** es mi tema favorito.

track suit *noun* chandal M.

tractor *noun* tractor M.

trade *noun* (*a profession*) oficio M.

trade union *noun* sindicato M.

tradition *noun* tradición F.

traditional *adjective* tradicional.

traffic *noun* tráfico M.

traffic jam *noun* embotellamiento M.

traffic lights *plural noun* semáforo M.

traffic warden *noun* guardia M/F municipal.

tragedy *noun* tragedia F.

tragic *adjective* trágico/trágica.

trail *noun* (*a path*) sendero M; **a nature trail** un sendero ecológico.

trailer *noun* remolque M.

train *noun* tren M; **he's coming by train** viene en tren; **I met her off the train** fui a recogerla a la estación; **the train for York** el tren para York. *verb* 1 estudiar [17] (*a student*); 2 **to train to be something** estudiar para algo; **he's training to be a nurse** está estudiando para ser enfermero; 3 (*in sport*) entrenar [17]; **the team trains on Saturdays** el equipo entrena los sábados.

train ticket *noun* billete M de tren.

train timetable *noun* horario M de trenes.

trainer *noun* 1 (*of an athlete or a horse*) entrenador M, entrenadora F; 2 (*shoe*) zapatilla F de deporte; **my new trainers** mis zapatillas de deporte nuevas.

training *noun* 1 (*for a career*) formación F; 2 (*for sport*) entrenamiento M.

tram *noun* tranvía M.

transfer *noun* (*sticker*) calcomanía F.

translate *verb* traducir [60]; **to translate something into Spanish** traducir algo al español.

translation *noun* traducción F.

translator *noun* traductor M, traductora F; **I'd like to be a translator** me gustaría ser traductora.

transparent *adjective* transparente.

transport *noun* transporte M; **air transport** transporte aéreo; **public transport** transporte público.

trap *noun* trampa F.

travel *noun* viajes M (*plural*); **foreign travel** viajes al extranjero; **a travel brochure** un folleto de viajes. *verb* viajar [17].

travel agency *noun* agencia F de viajes.

travel agent *noun* agente M/F de viajes.

traveller *noun* 1 viajero M, viajera F; 2 (*gypsy*) gitano M, gitana F.

traveller's cheque *noun* cheque M de viaje.

travelling *noun* **I like travelling** me gusta viajar.

travel-sick *noun* **to be/get travel-sick** marearse [17] en los viajes.

tray *noun* bandeja F.

tread *verb* **to tread on something** pisar [17] algo.

treasure *noun* tesoro M.

treat *noun* 1 capricho M; **to give yourself a treat** darse [4] un capricho; **it's a little treat** es un caprichito; 2 **I took them to the circus as a treat** les llevé al circo como algo especial.
verb 1 tratar [17]; **he treats his dog well** trata bien a su perro; **the doctor who treated you** el médico que te trató; 2 **to treat somebody to something** invitar [17] a alguien a algo; **I'll treat you to a drink** te invito a una copa; 3 **I treated myself to a new dress** me compré un vestido para darme un capricho.

treatment *noun* tratamiento M (*medical*).

tree *noun* árbol M.

tree trunk *noun* tronco M.

trend *noun* 1 (*a fashion*) moda F; 2 (*a tendency*) tendencia F.

trendy *adjective* de moda.

trial *noun* juicio M (*legal*).

triangle *noun* triángulo M.

trick *noun* 1 (*card or conjuring trick, knack*) truco M; **a card trick** un truco de cartas; **it doesn't work, there must be a trick to it** no funciona, debe tener truco; 2 (*a joke*) broma F; **to play a trick on somebody** gastarle [17] una broma a alguien.
verb engañar [17]; **he tricked me!** me engañó!

tricky *adjective* delicado/delicada; **it's a tricky situation** es una situación delicada.

tricycle *noun* triciclo M.

trip *noun* viaje M; **a trip to Florida** un viaje a Florida; **he's on a business**

trip está en viaje de negocios; **a day trip to France** un viaje de un día a Francia.
verb (*to stumble*) tropezar [25]; **Nicky tripped over a stone** Nicky tropezó con una piedra.

trolley *noun* carro M.

trombone *noun* trombón M; **to play the trombone** tocar [31] el trombón.

trophy *noun* trofeo M.

trouble *noun* **1** problemas M (*plural*); **we've had trouble with the car** tuvimos problemas con el coche; **Steph's in trouble** Steph tiene problemas; **to get into trouble** meterse [18] en problemas; **2 what's the trouble?** ¿cuál es el problema?; **3** (*difficulty*) **I had trouble finding a seat** me costó encontrar un sitio; **it's not worth the trouble** no merece la pena; **the trouble is, I've forgotten the number** el problema es que he olvidado el número; **it's no trouble!** ¡no es ningún problema!

trousers *plural noun* pantalones M (*plural*); **a new pair of trousers** unos pantalones nuevos, un nuevo par de pantalones.

trout *noun* trucha F.

truck *noun* camión M.

true *adjective* **a true story** una historia verídica; **to be true** ser [1] verdad; **is that true?** ¿es eso verdad?; **it's true she's absent-minded** es verdad que es despistada.

trump *noun* triunfo M; **spades are trumps** las picas son triunfo.

trumpet *noun* trompeta F; **to play the trumpet** tocar [31] la trompeta.

trunk *noun* **1** (*of a tree*) tronco M; **2** (*of an elephant*) trompa F; **3** (*a suitcase*) baúl M.

trunks *plural noun* **swimming trunks** bañador M.

trust *noun* confianza F.
verb confiar [32]; **I trust her** confío en ella.

truth *noun* verdad F; **to tell the truth, I'd completely forgottten** si quieres que te diga la verdad, me he olvidado completamente.

try *noun* intento M; **it's my first try** es mi primer intento; **to have a try** intentar [17]; **you should give it a try** deberías intentarlo.
verb **1** intentar [17]; **to try to do** intentar hacer; **I'm trying to open the door** estoy intentando abrir la puerta; **2** (*taste*) probar [24]; **try this sauce** prueba esta salsa; **to try hard to do** esforzarse [26] por hacer.
● **to try something on** probarse [26] algo (*a garment*).

T-shirt *noun* camiseta F.

tube *noun* **1** tubo M; **2 the tube** (*underground*) (*informal*) el metro.

tuberculosis *noun* tuberculosis F.

Tuesday *noun* martes M; **on Tuesday** el martes; **I'm going out on Tuesday** voy a salir el martes; **see you on Tuesday!** ¡hasta el martes!; **on Tuesdays** los martes; **the museum is closed on Tuesdays** el museo cierra los martes; **every**

Tuesday todos los martes; **last Tuesday** el martes pasado; **next Tuesday** el próximo martes.

tuition *noun* clases F (*plural*); **piano tuition** clases de piano; **private tuition** clases particulares.

tulip *noun* tulipán M.

tumble-drier *noun* secadora F.

tuna *noun* atún M.

tune *noun* melodía F.

tunnel *noun* túnel M; **the Channel Tunnel** el Eurotúnel.

turkey *noun* pavo M.

Turkey *noun* Turquía F.

Turkish *noun* turco M (*language*). *adjective* turco/turca.

turn *noun* 1 (*in a game*) turno M; **it's your turn** es tu turno; **whose turn is it?** ¿a quién le toca?; **it's Jane's turn to play** es el turno de Jane; **to take turns driving** turnarse [17] para conducir; 2 (*in a road*) curva F. *verb* 1 girar [17]; **turn your chair round** gira la silla; **turn left at the next set of lights** gira a la izquierda en el próximo semáforo; 2 dar [4] la vuelta a; (*a page or mattress*) 3 (*become*) ponerse [11]; **she turned red** se puso roja.

● **to turn back** volverse [45]; **we turned back** nos volvimos.

● **to turn off** 1 (*from a road*) girar [17]; 2 (*switch off*) apagar [28] (*a light, an oven, a TV, or radio*); cerrar [29] (*gas, electricity or a tap*).

● **to turn on** encender [36] (*a light, an oven, a TV or radio*); abrir [46] (*a tap*).

● **to turn out: 1 to turn out well** salir [63] bien; **it all turned out alright in the end** todo salió bien al final; **the holiday turned out badly** las vacaciones salieron mal; **2 it turned out that I was wrong** resultó que estaba equivocado.

● **to turn over 1** (*roll over*) darse [4] la vuelta; **2** dar [4] la vuelta a (*a page*).

● **to turn up 1** (*to arrive*) presentarse [17]; **they turned up an hour later** se presentaron con una hora de retraso; **2** abrir [46] más (*the gas*); **3** subir [19] (*the heating or volume*); **can you turn up the volume?** ¿puedes subir el volumen?

turnip *noun* nabo M.

turquoise *adjective* turquesa.

turtle *noun* tortuga F.

TV *noun* tele F; **I saw her on TV** la vi en la tele.

tweezers *noun* pinzas F (*plural*).

twelfth *noun* **the twelfth of May** el doce de mayo. *adjective* doceavo/doceava; **on the twelfth floor** en la planta duodécima.

twelve *number* doce M; **Tara's twelve** Tara tiene doce años; **it's twelve o'clock** (*midday*) son las doce de la mañana; (*midnight*) son las doce de la noche.

twenty *number* veinte; **Marie's twenty** Marie tiene veinte años;

twenty-one veintiuno; **twenty-five** veinticinco.

twice *adverb* **1** dos veces; **I've asked him twice** le he preguntado dos veces; **2 twice as much** el doble.

twig *noun* ramita F.

twin *noun* gemelo M, gemela F; **Helen and Tim are twins** Helen y Tim son gemelos; **her twin sister** su hermana gemela.
verb **Oxford is twinned with Salamanca** Oxford está hermanado con Salamanca.

twist *verb* girar [17] (*knob or cap of bottle*).

two *number* dos M; **Ben's two** Ben tiene dos años; **two by two** dos por dos.

type *noun* tipo M; **what type of computer is it?** ¿qué tipo de ordenador es?
verb (*on a typewriter*) escribir [52] a máquina; **I'm learning to type** estoy aprendiendo a escribir a máquina; **I was busy typing some letters** estaba ocupada escribiendo unas cartas a máquina.

typewriter *noun* máquina F de escribir.

typical *adjective* típico/típica.

tyre *noun* neumático M.

U u

ugly *adjective* feo/fea.

UK *noun* Reino M Unido.

Ulster *noun* el Ulster.

umbrella *noun* paraguas M (*does not change in the plural*).

umpire *noun* árbitro M, árbitra F.

UN *noun* ONU F (*short for 'Organización de las Naciones Unidas'*).

unable *adjective* **to be unable to do** no poder [10]; **he's unable to come** no puede venir.

unavoidable *adjective* inevitable.

unbearable *adjective* insoportable.

unbelievable *adjective* increíble.

uncle *noun* tío M; **my Uncle Tom** mi tío Tom.

uncomfortable *adjective* incómodo/incómoda.

unconscious *adjective* (*out cold*) sin sentido; **Tessa's still unconscious** Tessa está todavía sin sentido.

under *preposition* **1** (*underneath*) debajo de; **under the bed** debajo de la cama; **perhaps it's under there** quizás está ahí debajo; **to go under something** pasar por debajo de algo; **2** (*less than*) menos de; **under £20** menos de veinte libras; **3 children**

under five niños menores de cinco años.

under-age *noun* **to be under-age** ser [1] menor de edad.

underground *noun* (*a railway*) metro M; **shall we go by underground?** ¿vamos en metro? *adjective* subterráneo/subterránea; **an underground carpark** un parking subterráneo.

underline *verb* subrayar [17].

underneath *preposition* debajo de; **it's underneath these papers** está debajo de esos papeles. *adverb* debajo; **look underneath** mira debajo.

underpants *plural noun* calzoncillos M (*plural*); **my underpants** mis calzoncillos; **a pair of underpants** unos calzoncillos.

underpass *noun* **1** (*pedestrian*) paso M subterráneo; **2** (*for traffic*) paso M inferior.

understand *verb* entender [36]; **I don't understand** no entiendo; **I couldn't understand what he was saying** no entendí lo que estaba diciendo.

understandable *adjective* comprensible; **that's understandable** eso es comprensible.

underwear *noun* ropa F interior.

undo *verb* **1** desabrochar [17] (*a button or a garment*); **2** desatar [17] (*shoelaces*); **3** deshacer [7] (*a parcel or knot*).

undone *adjective* **to come undone** desabrocharse [17] (*a button*); desatarse [17] (*shoelaces*).

undress *verb* **to get undressed** desvestirse [57]; **I got undressed** me desvestí.

unemployed *noun* **the unemployed** los parados. *adjective* parado/parada; **she's unemployed** está parada.

unemployment *noun* paro M.

uneven *adjective* irregular.

unexpected *adjective* inesperado/ inesperada.

unexpectedly *adverb* (*to happen, arrive*) de improviso.

unfair *adjective* injusto/injusta; **it's unfair to young people** es injusto para la gente joven.

unfasten *verb* desabrochar [17].

unfold *verb* desdoblar [17].

unfortunate *adjective* desgraciado/desgraciada.

unfortunately *adverb* desgraciadamente.

unfriendly *adjective* antipático/ antipática.

ungrateful *adjective* desagradecido/desagradecida.

unhappy *adjective* **1** infeliz; **an unhappy childhood** una infancia infeliz; **2** (*discontented*) **to be unhappy** no estar [2] contento/ contenta.

uniform *noun* uniforme M; **in school uniform** con el uniforme del colegio.

union *noun* (*a trade union*) sindicato M.

Union Jack *noun* **the Union Jack** la bandera del Reino Unido.

unique *adjective* único/única.

unit *noun* **1** (*for measuring, for example*) unidad F; **2** (*in a kitchen*) módulo M; **3** (*a hospital department*) servicio M.

United Kingdom *noun* Reino M Unido.

United Nations *noun* Naciones F (*plural*) Unidas.

United States (of America) *plural noun* Estados M (*plural*) Unidos (de América).

universe *noun* universo M.

university *noun* universidad F; **to go to university** ir [8] a la universidad.

unkind *adjective* poco amable.

unknown *adjective* desconocido/ desconocida.

unleaded petrol *noun* gasolina F sin plomo.

unless *conjunction* a no ser que (*followed by subjunctive*); **unless he does it** a no ser que él lo haga; **unless you tell her** a no ser que tú se lo digas.

unlikely *adjective* poco probable; **it's unlikely** es poco probable.

unload *verb* descargar [28].

unlock *verb* **to unlock a door** abrir [46] una puerta; **the car's unlocked** el coche está abierto; **the door was unlocked** la puerta no estaba cerrada con llave.

unlucky *adjective* **1 to be unlucky** (*a person*) no tener [9] suerte; **I was unlucky, it was shut** no tuve suerte, estaba cerrado; **2 thirteen is an unlucky number** el trece trae mala suerte.

unmarried *adjective* soltero/ soltera.

unnatural *adjective* poco natural.

unnecessary *adjective* no necesario; **it's unnecessary to book** no es necesario reservar.

unpack *verb* **I unpacked my rucksack** saqué las cosas de mi mochila; **I'll just unpack and then come down** voy a deshacer las maletas y bajo.

unpaid *adjective* **1** sin pagar (*a bill*); **2** no remunerado (*work*).

unpleasant *adjective* desagradable.

unpopular *adjective* poco popular.

unreasonable *adjective* poco razonable; **he's being really unreasonable** no está siendo nada razonable.

unreliable *adjective* **1** poco fidedigno (*information*); **2 this computer is unreliable** no te puedes fiar de este ordenador; **3** informal (*person*); **he's unreliable** es informal.

unroll *verb* desenrollar [17].

unsafe *adjective* peligroso/peligrosa (*wiring, for instance*).

unscrew *verb* destornillar [17].

unsuccessful *adjective* **to be unsuccessful** fracasar [17]; **I tried, but I was unsuccessful** lo intenté pero fracasé; **an unsuccessful attempt** un intento fallido.

untidy *adjective* desordenado/desordenada; **the house is always untidy** la casa siempre está desordenada.

until *preposition* **1** hasta; **until Monday** hasta el lunes; **until the tenth** hasta el diez; **until now** hasta ahora; **until then** hasta entonces; **2** *not until* no hasta; **not until September** no hasta septiembre; **it won't be finished until Friday** no estará terminado hasta el viernes.

unusual *adjective* poco corriente; **an unusual beetle** un escarabajo poco corriente; **storms are unusual in June** las tormentas son poco corrientes en junio.

unwilling *adjective* **to be unwilling to do** no estar [2] dispuesto a hacer; **he's unwilling to wait** no está dispuesto a esperar.

unwrap *verb* desenvolver [45].

up *preposition*, *adverb* **1** (*higher up*) arriba; **hands up!** ¡manos arriba!; **up here** aquí arriba; **up there** ahí arriba; **it's just up the road** está en esta calle un poco más arriba; **up on the roof** en el tejado; **up in Glasgow** en Glasgow; **2 to go up** subir

[19]; (*stairs or road*) **we went up the road** subimos la calle; **I ran up the street** subí la calle corriendo; **I'll go up to Glasgow this weekend** voy a ir a Glasgow este fin de semana; **3** (*out of bed*) **to be up** estar [2] levantado; **Liz isn't up yet** Liz aún no está levantada; **to get up** levantarse [17]; **we got up at six** nos levantamos a las seis; **I was up late last night** me acosté tarde anoche; **she was up all night** no se acostó en toda la noche; **4** (*wrong*) **what's up?** ¿qué pasa?; **what's up with him?** ¿qué le pasa?; **5 up to** hasta; **up to here** hasta aquí; **up to fifty people** hasta cincuenta personas; **she came up to me** se acercó a mí; **6 what's she up to?** ¿qué está haciendo?; **it's up to you (to decide)** tú tienes que decidir; ★ **time's up!** ¡se acabó el tiempo!

upright *adjective* derecho/derecha; **put it upright** ponlo derecho; **to stand upright** estar [2] derecho.

upset *noun* **a stomach upset** un dolor de estómago.
adjective disgustado/disgustada; **he's upset** está disgustado.
verb **to upset somebody** disgustar [17] a alguien.

upside down *adjective* boca abajo.

upstairs *adverb* arriba; **Mum's upstairs** mamá está arriba; **to go upstairs** subir [19].

up-to-date *adjective* **1** (*in fashion*) moderno/moderna; **2** (*information*) actualizado/actualizada.

urgent *adjective* urgente.

us *pronoun* **1** nos; **she knows us** nos conoce; **they saw us** nos vieron; **he gave us a cheque** nos dio un cheque; (*when there are two pronouns, 'nos' comes first*) **they lent it to us** nos lo dejaron; **2** (*with an infinitive or when telling someone to do something, 'nos' joins onto the verb*) **can you help us, please?** ¿puedes ayudarnos por favor?, ¿nos puedes ayudar, por favor?; **listen to us!** ¡escúchanos!; **wait for us!** ¡espéranos!; (*but when telling someone NOT to do something, 'nos' comes before the verb*) **don't push us!** ¡no nos empujes!; **3** (*after a preposition, in comparisons, or after the verb 'to be'*) nosotros/nosotras; **behind us** detrás de nosotros/ nosotras; **they left without us** se fueron sin nosotros/nosotras; **with us** con nosotros/nosotras; **she's older than us** es mayor que nosotros/nosotras; **4 it's us!** ¡somos nosotros/nosotras!

US, USA *noun* EE.UU. M (*short for Estados Unidos*).

use *noun* **1** uso M; **instructions for use** instrucciones de uso; **2 it's no use** no sirve de nada; **it's no use phoning** no sirve de nada llamar.
verb usar [17]; **we use the dictionary** usamos el diccionario; **to use something to do** usar [17] algo para hacer; **I used a knife to open the parcel** usé un cuchillo para abrir el paquete.
● **to use up 1** consumir [19] todo (*food*); **2** gastar [17] todo (*money or petrol*).

used *adjective* **1 to be used to something** estar [2] acostumbrado/ acostumbrada a algo; **I'm not used to cats** no estoy acostumbrado a los gatos; **I'm not used to it!** ¡no estoy acostumbrado!; **I'm not used to eating in restaurants** no estoy acostumbrado a comer en restaurantes; **2 to get used to** acostumbrarse [17] a; **I've got used to living here** me he acostumbrado a vivir aquí; **you'll get used to it!** ¡ya te acostumbrarás!
verb **they used to live in the country** solían vivir en el campo; **she used to smoke** solía fumar.

useful *adjective* útil.

useless *adjective* **1** inútil (*person*); **you're completely useless!** ¡eres un completo inútil!; **2 this knife is useless** este cuchillo no sirve para nada.

user-friendly *adjective* fácil de usar.

usual *adjective, adverb* **1** (*time, place, problem*) de siempre; **it's the usual problem** es el problema de siempre; **2** (*method*) habitual; **3 as usual** como siempre; **4 it's colder than usual** hace más frío de lo normal.

usually *adverb* normalmente; **I usually leave at eight** normalmente salgo a las ocho.

V v

vacancy *noun* **1** (*in a hotel*)
'vacancies' 'habitaciones libres'; 'no
vacancies' 'completo'; **2** a job
vacancy una oferta de trabajo.

vacant *adjective* libre (*room or seat*).

vaccinate *verb* vacunar [17].

vaccination *noun* vacuna F.

vacuum *verb* pasar [17] la
aspiradora; I'm going to vacuum my
room voy a pasar la aspiradora por
mi habitación.

vacuum cleaner *noun*
aspiradora F.

vagina *noun* vagina F.

vague *adjective* poco preciso/poco
precisa.

vaguely *adverb* vagamente.

vain *adjective* vano/vana (*attempt*);
in vain en vano.

Valentine's Day *noun* día M de San
Valentín.

valid *adjective* válido/válida.

valley *noun* valle M.

valuable *adjective* valioso/valiosa;
to be valuable ser [1] valioso/
valiosa; that watch is very valuable
este reloj es muy valioso; he gave us
some valuable information nos dio
información muy valiosa.

value *noun* valor M.
verb valorar [17] (*somebody's help,
opinion, or friendship*).

van *noun* furgoneta F.

vandal *noun* gamberro M,
gamberra F.

vandalism *noun* gamberrismo M.

vandalize *verb* destrozar [22].

vanilla *noun* vainilla F; a vanilla ice
cream un helado de vainilla.

vanish *verb* desaparecer [35].

variety *noun* variedad F.

various *adjective* varios/varias
(*always goes before the noun*); there
are various ways of doing it hay
varias formas de hacerlo.

vary *verb* variar [32]; it varies a lot
varía mucho.

vase *noun* jarrón M.

VAT *noun* IVA M.

VCR *noun* cámara F de vídeo.

VDU *noun* monitor M.

veal *noun* ternera F.

vegetable *noun* verdura F.

vegetarian *noun* vegetariano M,
vegetariana F.
adjective vegetariano/vegetariana;
he's vegetarian es vegetariano.

vehicle *noun* vehículo M.

vein *noun* vena F.

velvet *noun* terciopelo M.

vending machine *noun*
máquina F expendedora.

verb noun verbo M.

verdict noun veredicto M.

verge noun 1 (*the roadside*) arcén M; 2 **to be on the verge of doing** estar [2] a punto de hacer; **I was on the verge of leaving** estaba a punto de irme.

version noun versión F.

versus preposition contra; **Arsenal versus Chelsea** Arsenal contra Chelsea.

vertical adjective vertical.

vertigo noun vértigo M.

very adverb 1 muy; **it's very difficult** es muy difícil; **very well** muy bien; 2 **very much** mucho; **I like it very much** me gusta mucho.
adjective 1 **the very person I need!** ¡justo la persona que necesito!; **the very thing he was looking for** justo lo que estaba buscando; 2 **in the very middle** justo en medio; **at the very end** justo al final; **at the very front** justo delante.

vest noun camiseta F.

vet noun veterinario M, veterinaria F; **she's a vet** es veterinaria.

via preposition **to go via** ir [8] por; **we're going via Dover** vamos por Dover; **we'll go via the bank** pasaremos por el banco.

vicar noun párroco M.

vicious adjective 1 fiero/fiera (*a dog*); 2 feroz (*an attack*).

victim noun víctima F.

victory noun victoria F.

video noun 1 (*film*) vídeo M; **to watch a video** ver [16] un vídeo; **I've got it on video** lo tengo en vídeo; 2 (*cassette*) cinta F de vídeo; **I bought a video** he comprado una cinta de vídeo; 3 (*video recorder*) cámara F de vídeo.
verb grabar [17]; **I'll video it for you** yo te lo grabo.

video cassette noun cinta F de vídeo.

video game noun videojuego M.

video recorder noun cámara F de vídeo.

video shop noun tienda F de vídeos.

view noun 1 vista F; **a room with a view of the lake** una habitación con vista al lago; 2 (*opinion*) opinión F; **in my view** en mi opinión; **a point of view** una opinión.

viewer noun (*on TV*) televidente M/F.

viewpoint noun punto M de vista.

vile adjective horrible.

villa noun chalet M.

village noun pueblo M.

vine noun vid F.

vinegar noun vinagre M.

vineyard noun viñedo M.

violence noun violencia F.

violent adjective violento/violenta.

violin noun violín M; **to play the violin** tocar [31] el violín.

violinist *noun* violinista M/F.

virgin *noun* virgen F.

Virgo *noun* virgo M; **Robert's Virgo** Robert es virgo.

virtual reality *noun* realidad F virtual.

virus *noun* virus M.

visa *noun* visado M.

visible *adjective* visible.

visit *noun* visita F.
verb visitar [17]; **we visited Auntie Pat at Christmas** visitamos a la tía Pat en Navidad.

visitor *noun* 1 visita F; **we've got visitors tonight** hoy tenemos visita; 2 (*a tourist*) visitante M/F.

visual *adjective* visual.

vital *adjective* muy importante; **it's vital to book** es muy importante reservar.

vitamin *noun* vitamina F.

vivid *adjective* 1 (*colour or imagination*) vivo/viva; **to have a vivid imagination** tener una imaginación muy viva; 2 (*memory or dream*) vívido/vívida.

vocabulary *noun* vocabulario M.

vocational *adjective* vocacional.

vodka *noun* vodka M.

voice *noun* voz F.

volcano *noun* volcán M.

volleyball *noun* vóleibol M; **to play volleyball** jugar [27] al vóleibol.

volume *noun* volumen M; **could you turn down the volume?** ¿puedes bajar el volumen?

voluntary *adjective* 1 (*not compulsory*) voluntario/voluntaria; 2 **to do voluntary work** trabajar [17] de voluntario.

volunteer *noun* voluntario M, voluntaria F.

vomit *verb* vomitar [17].

vote *verb* votar [17].

voucher *noun* vale M.

vowel *noun* vocal F.

vulgar *adjective* grosero/grosera (*person or speech*).

W w

waffle *noun* (*to eat*) gofre M.

wage(s) (*plural*) *noun* sueldo M.

waist *noun* cintura F.

waistcoat *noun* chaleco M.

waist measurement *noun* medida F de cintura.

wait *noun* espera F; **an hour's wait** una espera de una hora.
verb 1 esperar [17]; **they're waiting in the car** están esperando en el coche; **she kept me waiting** me tuvo esperando; 2 **to wait for** esperar algo; **wait for me!** ¡espérame!; **wait for the signal** espera la señal; 3 I

can't wait to open it! ¡estoy deseando abrirlo!

waiter *noun* camarero M.

waiting list *noun* lista F de espera.

waiting room *noun* sala F de espera.

waitress *noun* camarera F.

wake *verb* **1** despertar [29] (*somebody else*); **Jess woke me at six** Jess me despertó a las seis; **2** despertarse [29]; **I woke (up) at six** me desperté a las seis; **wake up!** ¡despiértate!

Wales *noun* País M de Gales.

walk *noun* paseo M; **to go for a walk** ir [8] a dar un paseo; **we went for a walk in the woods** fuimos a dar un paseo por el bosque; **we'll go for a little walk round the village** daremos un paseo por el pueblo; **to take the dog for a walk** sacar [31] a pasear al perro; **it's about five minutes' walk from here** está a unos cinco minutos de aquí a pie.
verb **1** andar [21]; **I like walking on sand** me gusta andar sobre la arena; **2** (*on foot rather than by car or bus*) ir [8] andando; **it's not far, we can walk** no está lejos, podemos ir andando.
• **to walk around** dar [4] una vuelta por; **we walked around the old town** dimos una vuelta por la parte vieja de la ciudad.
• **to walk with somebody** acompañar a alguien; **I'll walk to the bus stop with you** te acompaño hasta la parada del autobús.

walking *noun* (*hiking*) hacer [7] senderismo; **we're going walking in Scotland** vamos a hacer senderismo en Escocia.

walking distance *noun* **it's within walking distance of the sea** se puede ir andando hasta la playa.

walking stick *noun* bastón M.

walkman™ *noun* walkman™ M.

wall *noun* pared F.

wallet *noun* cartera F.

wallpaper *noun* papel M pintado.

walnut *noun* nuez F.

wander *verb* **to wander around town** pasear [17] por la ciudad; **to wander off** alejarse [17].

want *noun* **all our wants** todo lo que necesites.
verb querer [12]; **do you want some coffee?** ¿quieres café?; **what do you want to do?** ¿qué quieres hacer?; **I don't want to bother him** no quiero molestarlo; **I want them to help me** quiero que me ayuden (*note that 'querer que' is followed by the subjunctive*).

war *noun* guerra F.

ward *noun* sala F (*in a hospital*).

wardrobe *noun* **1** (*piece of furniture*) armario M; **2** (*clothes*) vestuario M.

warm *adjective* **1** (*water*) templado/templada (*not very hot*); **2** (*breeze*) cálido/cálida; **3** (*hot*) caliente; **a warm drink** una bebida caliente; **I'll keep your dinner warm** te tendré la

comida caliente; **a warm bath** un baño caliente; **4 it's warm today** hoy hace calorcito; **I'm warm** tengo calor; **are you warm enough?** ¿tienes frío?; **5** (*friendly*) caluroso/calurosa; **a warm welcome** una bienvenida calurosa; **a warm person** una persona cariñosa.
verb calentar [29]; **warm the plates** calentar los platos.
● **to warm up 1** (*the weather*) **it's warming up** está empezando a hacer más calor; **2** (*a person*) entrar [17] en calor; **3** (*to heat up*) calentar [29] (*food*); **I'll warm up some soup for you** te calentaré un poco de sopa.

warmth *noun* calor M.

warn *verb* advertir [14]; **I warn you, it's expensive** te lo advierto, es caro; **to warn somebody to do** advertir a alguien que haga (*note that 'que' is followed by the subjunctive*); **he warned me to lock the car** me advirtió que cerrase el coche.

warning *noun* advertencia F.

wart *noun* verruga F.

wash *noun* **to give something a wash** lavar [17] algo; **to have a wash** lavarse.
verb lavar [17]; **I've washed your jeans** he lavado tus vaqueros; **to wash your hands** lavarse las manos; **I washed my hands** me he lavado las manos; **to wash your hair** lavarse la cabeza; **I have to wash my hair** tengo que lavarme la cabeza; **to get washed** lavarse; **to wash the dishes** lavar los platos.
● **to wash up** lavar los platos.

washbasin *noun* lavabo M.

washing *noun* **1** (*dirty*) ropa F sucia; **2** (*clean*) ropa F limpia.

washing machine *noun* lavadora F.

washing powder *noun* detergente M.

washing-up *noun* platos F sucios; **to do the washing-up** lavar [17] los platos.

washing-up liquid *noun* lavavajillas M (*does not change in the plural*).

wasp *noun* avispa F.

waste *noun* **1** (*of food, money, paper*) desperdicio M; **2** (*of time*) **it's a waste of time** es una pérdida de tiempo.
verb **1** desperdiciar [17] (*food, money, paper*); **2** perder [36] (*time*); **you're wasting your time** estás perdiendo el tiempo.

waste-bin *noun* papelera F.

wastepaper-basket *noun* papelera F.

watch *noun* reloj M; **my watch is fast** mi reloj está adelantado; **my watch is slow** mi reloj está atrasado.
verb **1** (*to look at*) mirar [17]; **I was watching TV** estaba viendo la televisión; **2 to watch a film** ver [16] una película; **3** (*keep a check on*) **watch the time** estate atento al reloj; **could you watch the baby for a while?** ¿puedes cuidar al niño un rato?; **4** (*suspect*) vigilar [17]; **5** (*to be careful*) **watch you don't spill it**

ten cuidado de no tirarlo; **watch out for nettles** cuidado con las ortigas; **watch out!** ¡cuidado!

water *noun* agua F.
verb regar [30]; **to water the plants** regar las plantas.

waterfall *noun* cascada F.

watering can *noun* regadera F.

water melon *noun* sandía F.

waterproof *adjective* impermeable.

water-skiing *noun* esquí M acuático; **to go water-skiing** hacer [7] esquí acuático.

water sports *plural noun* deportes M náuticos.

wave *noun* **1** (*in the sea*) ola F; **2** (*with your hand*) (*to say hello*) saludo M; (*to say goodbye*) adiós M; **she gave him a wave from the bus** le saludó con la mano desde el autobús (*to say goodbye*) le dijo adiós con la mano desde el autobús.
verb **1** (*with your hand*) (*to say hello*) saludar [17]; (*to say goodbye*) decir [5] adiós; **2** (*flap*) agitar [17] (*your ticket or the newspaper, for example*).

wax *noun* cera F.

way *noun* **1** (*a route or road*) camino M; **the way to town** el camino a la ciudad; **we asked the way to the station** preguntamos el camino a la estación; **on the way back** en el camino de vuelta; **on the way** en camino; **'way in'** 'entrada'; **'way out'** 'salida'; **2** (*direction*) dirección F; **which way did he go?** en qué dirección se fue; **come this way** ven por aquí; **to be in the way** estorbar [17]; **3 put it the right way up** ponlo bien; **the wrong way up** boca abajo; **your jumper is the wrong way round** tu jersey está al revés; **4** (*distance*) **it's a long way** está muy lejos; **Terry went all the way to York** Terry fue hasta York; **5** (*manner*) manera F; **a way of talking** una manera de hablar; **he does it his way** lo hace a su manera; **I did it the wrong way** lo hice mal; **that's not the way to do it** no se hace así; **either way, she's wrong** sea como sea, está equivocada; **do it this way** hazlo de esta manera; **6 no way!** ¡ni hablar!; **7 by the way** por cierto.

we *pronoun* **1** (*'we' like other subject pronouns is generally not translated; in Spanish the form of the verb tells you whether the subject of the verb is 'we', you', they', etc., so' we' is only translated when you want to emphasize it*) **we live in Carlisle** vivimos en Carlisle; **we're going to the cinema tonight** vamos a ir al cine esta noche; **2** (*for emphasis*) nosotros/nosotras; **we did it** lo hicimos nosotros.

weak *adjective* **1** (*feeble*) débil; **her voice was weak** su voz era débil; **2** poco cargado/poco cargada (*coffee or tea*).

wealthy *adjective* rico/rica.

weapon *noun* arma F.

wear *noun* **children's wear** ropa F de niños; **sports wear** ropa de deporte.
verb llevar [17]; **Tamsin's wearing**

her trainers Tamsin lleva sus zapatillas de deporte; **he was wearing black trousers** llevaba pantalones negros; **she often wears red** a menudo viste de rojo; **to wear make-up** llevar maquillaje.

weather *noun* tiempo M; **what's the weather like?** ¿qué tiempo hace?; **in fine weather** cuando hace buen tiempo; **the weather was cold** hacía frío; **the weather here is terrible** aquí hace un tiempo horrible.

weather forecast *noun* pronóstico M del tiempo; **the weather forecast says it will rain** el pronóstico del tiempo dice que va a llover.

wedding *noun* boda F.

Wednesday *noun* miércoles M (*does not change in the plural*); **on Wednesday** el miércoles; **I'm going out on Wednesday** voy a salir el miércoles; **see you on Wednesday!** ¡hasta el miércoles!; **on Wednesdays** los miércoles; **the museum is closed on Wednesdays** el museo cierra los miércoles; **every Wednesday** cada miércoles; **last Wednesday** el miércoles pasado; **next Wednesday** el próximo miércoles.

weed *noun* mala hierba F.

week *noun* semana F; **last week** la semana pasada; **next week** la próxima semana; **this week** esta semana; **for weeks** durante semanas; **a week today** una semana a partir de hoy.

weekday *noun* **on weekdays** entre semana.

weekend *noun* fin M de semana; **last weekend** el fin de semana pasado; **next weekend** el próximo fin de semana; **they're coming for the weekend** vienen a pasar el fin de semana; **I'll do it at the weekend** lo haré durante el fin de semana; **have a nice weekend!** ¡que pases un buen el fin de semana!

weigh *verb* pesar [17]; **to weigh something** pesar algo; **how much do you weigh?** ¿cuánto pesas?; **I weigh 50 kilos** peso cincuenta kilos; **to weigh yourself** pesarse [17].

weight *noun* peso M; **to put on weight** engordar [17]; **to lose weight** adelgazar [22].

weird *adjective* extraño/extraña.

welcome *noun* bienvenida F; **they gave us a warm welcome** nos dieron una calurosa bienvenida. *adjective* 1 bienvenido/bienvenida; **you're welcome any time** siempre eres bienvenido; **welcome to Oxford!** ¡bienvenido a Oxford!; 2 'thank you' – 'you're welcome' 'gracias' – 'de nada'. *verb* dar [4] la bienvenida a.

well¹ *noun* pozo M.

well² *adverb* 1 bien; **to feel well** sentirse [14] bien; **I'm very well, thank you** estoy muy bien, gracias; 2 Terry played well Terry jugó bien; **the operation went well** la operación salió bien; **well done!** ¡bien hecho!; 3 **as well** también;

Kevin's coming as well Kevin también viene; **4 as well as** además de; **5 well then, what's the problem?** entonces, ¿cuál es el problema?; **6 very well then, you can go** muy bien, entonces ya puedes irte.

well-behaved *adjective* **a well behaved child** un niño que se porta bien; **be well-behaved** pórtate bien.

well-done *adjective* muy hecho/muy hecha (*a steak*).

wellington (boot) *noun* catiusca F.

well-known *adjective* conocido/conocida.

well-off *adjective* acomodado/acomodada.

Welsh *noun* **1 the Welsh** (*people*) los galeses; **2** (*language*) galés M. *adjective* galés/galesa.

Welshman *noun* galés M.

Welshwoman *noun* galesa F.

west *noun* oeste M; **in the west** al oeste.
adjective, adverb (*does not change*) **the west side** la parte oeste; **a west wind** un viento del oeste; **west of Paris** al oeste de París.

western *noun* (*a film*) película F de vaqueros.

West Indian *noun* afroantillano M, afroantillana F.
adjective afroantillano/afroantillana.

West Indies *plural noun* Antillas F; **in the West Indies** en las Antillas.

wet *adjective* **1** (*damp*) húmedo/húmeda; **the grass is wet** la hierba está húmeda; **to get wet** mojarse [17]; **we got wet** nos mojamos; **2 a wet day** un día lluvioso.

whale *noun* ballena F.

what *pronoun, adjective* **1** qué (*in questions*); **what did you say?** ¿qué has dicho?; **what's she doing?** ¿qué está haciendo?; **what did you buy?** ¿qué has comprado?; **what is it?** ¿qué es?; **what's the matter?** ¿qué pasa?; **what's happening?** ¿qué está pasando?; **2 what's your address?** ¿cuáles son sus señas?; **what country is it in?** ¿en qué país está?; **what colour is it?** ¿de qué color es?; **what make is it?** ¿de qué marca es?; **3 what's her name?** ¿cómo se llama?; **what?** ¿cómo?; **what's it like?** ¿cómo es?; **4 what for?** ¿para qué?; **what's it for?** ¿para qué sirve?; **what did you buy it for?** ¿para qué lo has comprado?; **5** lo que; **tell me what you bought** dime lo que has comprado; **she told me what had happened** me dijo lo que había pasado; **what I want is a car** lo que quiero es un coche.

wheat *noun* trigo M.

wheel *noun* rueda F; **the spare wheel** la rueda de repuesto; **the steering wheel** el volante.

wheelbarrow *noun* carretilla F.

wheelchair *noun* silla F de ruedas.

when *adverb* cuándo; **when's she arriving?** ¿cuándo llega?; **when's your birthday?** ¿cuándo es tu

cumpleaños?; **ask when the next train is leaving** pregunta cuándo sale el próximo tren.
conjunction cuando; **it was raining when I went out** estaba lloviendo cuando salí.

where *adverb* dónde; **where are the plates?** ¿dónde están los platos?; **where do you live?** ¿dónde vives?; **where are you going?** ¿dónde vas?; **I don't know where they live** no sé dónde viven.
pronoun donde; **the place where I live** el lugar donde vivo.
conjunction donde; **this is where I left it** ahí es donde lo dejé.

whether *conjunction* si; **I don't know whether he's back or not** no sé si ha vuelto o no.

which *adjective* qué; **which CD did you buy?** ¿qué compacto compraste?; **which drawer did you put it in?** ¿en qué cajón lo metiste?
pronoun 1 (*in questions*) cuál; **'I saw your brother'** – **'which one?'** 'ví a tu hermano' – '¿a cuál?'; **which of these jackets is yours?** ¿cuál de estas chaquetas es la tuya?;
2 (*relative pronoun*) que; **the lamp which is on the table** la lámpara que está en la mesa; **the book which you chose** el libro que escogiste; **the film which I told you about** el libro del que te hablé.

while *noun* **for a while** (*long time*) durante un tiempo (*short time*) durante un rato; **she worked here for a while** trabajó allí durante un tiempo; **I read for a while** leí durante un rato; **after a while** (*long time*)

después de un tiempo (*short time*) después de un rato.
conjunction mientras; **you can make some tea while I'm finishing my homework** puedes hacer un té mientras termino los deberes.

whip *noun* (*for a horse*) látigo M.
verb montar [17] (*cream*); **whipped cream** nata F montada.

whiskers *plural noun* bigotes M (*plural*).

whisky *noun* whisky M.

whisper *noun* susurro M; **to speak in a whisper** hablar [17] en susurros.
verb susurrar [17].

whistle *noun* 1 (*sound*) silbido M;
2 (*instrument*) silbato M.
verb silbar [17].

white *noun* 1 (*colour*) blanco M;
2 **an egg white** una clara de huevo.
adjective blanco/blanca; **a white shirt** una camisa blanca.

white coffee *noun* café M con leche.

Whitsun *noun* Pentecostés M.

who *pronoun* 1 (*in questions*) quién; **who wants some sweets?** ¿quién quiere caramelos?; 2 (*relative pronoun as subject of the verb*) que; **my friend who lives in Madrid** el amigo mío que vive en Madrid; 3 (*as object of the verb: referring to one person*) el que/la que; **the girl who I gave it to** la chica a la que se lo di; 4 (*as object of the verb: referring to more than one person*) los que/las que; **the friends who we invited** los amigos a los que he invitado.

whole *noun* **the whole of the class** toda la clase; **on the whole** en general.
adjective todo/toda; **the whole family** toda la familia; **the whole morning** toda la mañana; **the whole time** todo el tiempo; **the whole world** todo el mundo.

wholemeal *adjective* integral; **wholemeal bread** pan integral.

whom *pronoun* 1 (*in questions*) quién; **whom did you see?** ¿a quién viste?; 2 (*as relative pronoun*) que; **the person whom I saw** la persona que vi; 3 (*after a preposition: referring to one person*) el que/la que; **the person to whom I wrote** la persona a la que escribí; 4 (*after a preposition: referring to more than one person*) los que/las que; **the people to whom I wrote** las personas a las que escribí.

whose *pronoun*, *adjective* 1 de quién; **whose is this jacket?** ¿de quién es esta chaqueta?; **whose shoes are these?** ¿de quién son estos zapatos?; **whose is it?** ¿de quién es?; **I know whose it is** sé de quién es; 2 (*as relative: before a singular noun*) cuyo/cuya (*agree with the noun that follows*); **the man whose car has been stolen** el hombre cuyo coche había sido robado; 3 (*as relative; before a plural noun*) cuyos/cuyas (*agree with the noun that follows*); **the people whose names are on the list** las personas cuyos nombres están en la lista; **a friend whose children I give lessons to** un amigo a cuyos hijos doy clase.

why *adverb* por qué; **why did she phone?** ¿por qué llamó?; **nobody knows why he did it** nadie sabe por qué lo hizo.

wicked *adjective* 1 (*bad*) malvado/malvada; 2 (*brilliant*) genial.

wide *adjective* 1 ancho/ancha; **the Thames is very wide here** el Támesis es muy ancho por aquí; **a piece of paper 20 cm wide** un trozo de papel de veinte centímetros de ancho; **how wide is it?** ¿cuánto mide de ancho?; 2 **a wide range** una amplia gama.
adverb **the door was wide open** la puerta estaba abierta de par en par.

wide awake *adjective* completamente despierto/despierta.

widow *noun* viuda F.

widower *noun* viudo M.

width *noun* ancho M.

wife *noun* mujer F.

wig *noun* peluca F.

wild *adjective* 1 (*animal*) salvaje; (*plant*) silvestre; 2 (*idea*) disparatado/disparatada; 3 (*party*) desenfrenado/desenfrenada; 4 (*person*) loco/loca; 5 **to be wild about something** estar [2] loco por algo.

wildlife *noun* **a programme on wildlife in Africa** un programa sobre la flora y la fauna de África.

wildlife park *noun* reserva F natural.

will *verb* **1** (*if you are unsure of the future tense of a Spanish verb, you can check in the verb tables in the centre of the dictionary*) **I'll see you soon** te veré pronto; **he'll be pleased to see you** estará contento de verte; **it won't rain** no lloverá; **there won't be a problem** no habrá problemas; **2** ir [8] a hacer (*can be used for the immediate future*); **I'll phone them at once** voy a llamarlos ahora mismo; **3** (*in questions and requests*) **'will you write to me?' – 'of course I will!'** '¿me escribirás?' – '¡claro que sí!'; **will you have a drink?** ¿quieres beber algo?; **will you help me?** ¿me ayudas?; **4 he won't open the door** no puede abrir la puerta; **the car won't start** el coche no arranca; **the drawer won't open** el cajón no abre.

willing *adjective* **to be willing to do** estar [2] dispuesto/dispuesta a; **I'm willing to pay half** estoy dispuesto a pagar la mitad.

willingly *adverb* con gusto.

willow *noun* sauce M; **a weeping willow** un sauce llorón.

win *noun* victoria F; **our win over Everton** nuestra victoria sobre Everton.
verb ganar [17]; **we won!** ¡hemos ganado!; **Rovers won by two goals** Rovers ganó por dos goles.

wind[1] *noun* viento M; **the North wind** el viento del norte.

wind[2] *verb* **1** enrollar [17] (*a wire or a rope, for example*); **2** dar [4] cuerda a (*a clock*).

wind instrument *noun* instrumento M de viento.

window *noun* **1** (*in a building*) ventana F; **to look out of the window** mirar [17] por la ventana; **2** (*in a car, bus, train*) ventanilla F.

windscreen *noun* parabrisas M (*doesn't change in the plural*).

windscreen wipers *plural noun* limpiaparabrisas M (*plural*).

windy *adjective* **1** con mucho viento (*a place*); **2** de viento (*a day*); **3 it's windy today** hoy hace viento.

wine *noun* vino M; **a glass of white wine** una copa de vino blanco.

wing *noun* **1** ala F (*even though 'ala' is a feminine noun, it takes a masculine article in the singular*); **the wing** el ala; **2** (*in sport*) alero M/F.

wink *verb* **to wink at somebody** guiñar [17] el ojo a alguien.

winner *noun* ganador M, ganadora F.

winning *adjective* ganador (*team for example*).

winnings *plural noun* ganancias F (*plural*).

winter *noun* invierno M; **in winter** en invierno.

wipe *verb* limpiar [17]; **I'll just wipe the table** voy a limpiar la mesa; **to wipe your nose** limpiarse [17] la nariz.

● **to wipe up** (*dishes*) secar [17].

wire *noun* alambre M; **an electric wire** un cable.

wire netting *noun* red F de alambre.

wise *adjective* sabio/sabia.

wish *noun* **1** deseo M; **make a wish!** ¡piensa un deseo!; **2 best wishes on your birthday** nuestros mejores deseos en tu cumpleaños; **'best wishes, Ann'** 'saludos de: Ann' (*in letters*).
verb **1 I wish he were here** ojalá estuviese aquí (*note that 'ojalá' is followed by the subjunctive*); **2 I wished him happy birthday** le deseé un feliz cumpleaños.

wit *noun* ingenio M.

with *preposition* **1** con; **with James** con James; **with me** conmigo; **with them** con ellos; **with pleasure** con gusto; **beat the eggs with a fork** bate los huevos con un tenedor; **he took his umbrella with him** se llevó el paraguas; **2** (*at the house of*) **we're staying the night with Frank** nos quedamos a dormir en casa de Frank; **3** (*in descriptions*) **a man with blue eyes** un hombre de ojos azules; **the boy with the broken arm** el chico con el brazo roto; **4** de; **filled with water** lleno de agua; **covered with mud** cubierto de barro; **red with rage** rojo de ira.

without *preposition* sin; **without you** sin ti; **without sugar** sin azúcar; **without a sweater** sin un jersey; **without looking** sin mirar.

witness *noun* testigo M/F.

witty *adjective* ingenioso/ingeniosa.

wolf *noun* lobo M.

woman *noun* mujer F; **a woman friend** una amiga.

wonder *noun* **1** maravilla F; **2 it's no wonder you're tired** no es extraño que estés cansado.
verb preguntarse [17]; **I wonder why** me pregunto por qué; **I wonder where Jack is** me pregunto dónde está Jack.

wonderful *adjective* maravilloso/maravillosa.

wood *noun* madera F; **the lamp is made of wood** la lámpara está hecha de madera.

wooden *adjective* de madera.

woodwork *noun* carpintería F.

wool *noun* lana F.

word *noun* **1** palabra F; **a long word** una palabra larga; **what's the French word for 'window'?** ¿cómo se dice 'ventana' en francés?; **in other words** en otras palabras; **to have a word with somebody** hablar [17] con alguien; **2** (*promise*) **to give somebody your word** prometer [18] algo a alguien; **he broke his word** rompió su promesa; **3 the words of a song** la letra de una canción.

word processing *noun* tratamiento M de textos.

word processor *noun* procesador M de textos.

work *noun* 1 trabajo M; **Mum's at work** mamá está en el trabajo; **I've got some work to do** tengo trabajo que hacer; **he's out of work** está sin trabajo; **Ben's off work** (*sick*) Ben no ha ido a trabajar porque está enfermo; 2 **to be hard work** ser [1] difícil; **it's hard work to understand it** es difícil entenderlo.
verb 1 trabajar [17]; **she works in an office** trabaja en una oficina; **Dad works at home** papá trabaja en casa; **Ruth works in advertising** Ruth trabaja en publicidad; **he works nights** trabaja por las noches; 2 (*to operate*) hacer [7] funcionar; **can you work the video?** ¿sabes hacer funcionar el vídeo?; 3 (*function*) funcionar [17]; **the dishwasher's not working** el lavavajillas no funciona; **that worked really well!** ¡eso ha funcionado muy bien!
● **to work out** 1 (*understand*) entender [36]; **I can't work out why** no entiendo por qué; 2 (*exercise*) hacer [7] ejercicio; 3 (*a plan*) salir [63] bien; 4 (*calculate*) calcular [17]; **I'll work out how much it would cost** calcularé cuánto puede costar.

worked up *adjective* **to get worked up** ponerse [11] nervioso/nerviosa.

worker *noun* 1 (*in a factory*) trabajador M, trabajadora F; 2 (*in an office or bank*) empleado M, empleada F.

work experience *noun* prácticas F (*plural*) de trabajo; **to do work experience** hacer [7] prácticas; **to be on work experience** estar [2] haciendo prácticas.

working-class *adjective* clase F obrera; **a working-class background** un ambiente de clase obrera.

work of art *noun* obra F de arte.

workshop *noun* taller M.

workstation *noun* (*computer*) terminal F de trabajo.

world *noun* mundo M; **the best in the world** lo mejor del mundo; **the Western world** el mundo occidental.

World Cup *noun* **the World Cup** el Mundial.

world war *noun* guerra F mundial; **the Second World War** la segunda Guerra Mundial.

worm *noun* gusano M.

worn out *adjective* 1 (*a person*) agotado/agotada; 2 (*clothes or shoes*) muy gastado/muy gastada.

worried *adjective* preocupado/preocupada; **they're worried** están preocupados; **to be worried about** estar [2] preocupado/preocupada por; **we're worried about Susan** estamos preocupados por Susan.

worry *noun* preocupación F.
verb preocuparse [17]; **don't worry!** ¡no te preocupes!; **there's nothing to worry about** no hay razón para preocuparse.

worrying *adjective* preocupante.

worse *adjective* peor; **it was even worse than the last time** fue aún peor que la última vez; **to get worse** empeorar [17]; **the weather's**

getting worse el tiempo está empeorando; **things are getting worse and worse** las cosas van cada vez peor.

worst *adjective* **the worst** el peor; **it was the worst day of my life** fue el peor día de mi vida; **if the worst comes to the worst** en el peor de los casos.

worth *adjective* **1 to be worth** valer [43]; **how much is it worth?** ¿cuánto vale?; **2 to be worth doing** merecer [35] la pena hacer; **it's worth trying** merece la pena intentarlo; **it's not worth it** no merece la pena.

would *verb* **1** (*if you are unsure of the conditional tense of a Spanish verb, you can check in the verb tables in the centre of the dictionary*) **that would be a good idea** eso sería una buena idea; **if we asked her she would help us** si la preguntásemos, nos ayudaría; **2** (*expressing wishes*) **I'd like to go to the cinema** me gustaría ir al cine; **I would like an omelette** quisiera una tortilla (*the subjunctive is used when ordering something*); **3 would you like … ?** ¿quieres … ?; **would you like something to eat?** ¿quieres comer algo?; **4 would you mind … ?** ¿te importaría … ?; **would you mind closing the window?** ¿te importaría cerrar la ventana?; **5 he wouldn't answer** no contestaba; **the car wouldn't start** el coche no arrancaba.

wound *noun* herida F.
verb herir [14].

wrap *verb* envolver [45]; **I'm going to wrap (up) my presents** voy a envolver mis regalos; **could you wrap it for me please?** ¿me lo envuelve, por favor?

wrapping paper *noun* papel M de envolver.

wreck *noun* **I feel a wreck!** ¡estoy hecho/hecha polvo!
verb **1** destrozar [22] (*an object, a car*); **2** arruinar [17] (*plans, occasion*); **it completely wrecked my evening!** ¡me arruinó la tarde!

wrestler *noun* luchador M, luchadora F.

wrestling *noun* lucha F.

wrinkled *adjective* arrugado/arrugada.

wrist *noun* muñeca F.

write *verb* **1** escribir [52] (*a letter or a story*); **I'll write her a letter** le escribiré una carta; **to write to somebody** escribirle a alguien; **I wrote to Jean yesterday** ayer le escribí a Jean; **2 to write somebody a cheque** extenderle [36] un cheque a alguien.
● **to write down** anotar [17]; **I wrote down her name** anoté su nombre.

writer *noun* escritor M, escritora F.

writing *noun* escritura F.

wrong *adjective* **1** (*not correct*) equivocado/equivocada; **the wrong answer** la respuesta equivocada; **I've brought the wrong file** he traído la carpeta equivocada; **it's the wrong address** no son las señas correctas;

2 to be wrong (*mistaken*)
equivocarse [31]; **I was wrong** me
equivoqué; **I was wrong when I said
it was finished** me equivoqué
cuando dije que estaba terminado;
3 what's wrong? ¿qué pasa?; **what's
wrong with her?** ¿qué la pasa?;
something's wrong pasa algo;
4 (*false*) incorrecto/incorrecta; **the
information was wrong** la
información era incorrecta.

X x

xerox™ *noun* fotocopia F.
verb fotocopiar [17].

X-ray *noun* radiografía F; **I saw the
X-rays** vi las radiografías.
verb hacer [7] una radiografía de;
they X-rayed her ankle le hicieron
una radiografía del tobillo.

Y y

yacht *noun* **1** (*sailing boat*)
velero M; **2** (*large luxury boat*)
yate M.

yawn *verb* bostezar [22].

year *noun* año M; **six years ago** hace
seis años; **the whole year** todo el
año; **they lived in Moscow for years**
vivieron en Moscú durante años;
he's seventeen years old tiene

diecisiete años; **a two-year-old
child** un niño de dos años.

yell *verb* chillar [17].

yellow *adjective* amarillo/amarilla.

yes *adverb* **1** sí; **yes, I know** sí, ya lo
sé; **'is Tom in his room?' – 'yes, he
is'** '¿está Tom en su habitación?' –
'sí'; **2** (*answering a negative*) que sí;
**'you don't want to go, do you?' – '
yes I do !'** 'no quieres ir, ¿verdad?' –
'que sí quiero'; **'you haven't finished,
have you?' – 'yes, I have'** 'no has
terminado, ¿verdad?' – 'que sí'.

yesterday *adverb* ayer; **I saw her
yesterday** la vi ayer; **yesterday
afternoon** ayer por la tarde;
yesterday morning ayer por la
mañana; **the day before yesterday**
anteayer.

yet *adverb* **1** (*with a negative*) aún;
not yet aún no; **it's not ready yet** no
está listo aún; **2** (*in a question*) ya;
have you finished yet? ¿has
terminado ya?

yoghurt *noun* yogur M; **a banana
yoghurt** un yogur de plátano.

yolk *noun* yema F.

you *pronoun* **1** (*when used as the
subject of the verb, 'you' like other
subject pronouns is generally not
translated; in Spanish the form of the
verb tells you whether the subject of
the verb is 'you', 'we', 'they', etc., so
'you' is only translated when you want
to emphasize it*) **do you want to go
to the cinema tonight?** (*talking to
one person*) ¿quieres ir al cine esta
noche?; (*talking to more than one*

person) ¿quereis ir al cine esta noche?; **2** (*when emphasizing 'you'*) (*talking to one person*) tú; (*talking to more than one person*) vosotros/vosotras; **you said it!** ¡tú lo dijiste!; **you all saw it!** ¡todos vosotros lo vísteis!; **3** (*although 'tú', 'vosotros', and 'vosotras' are now commonly used in most situations, there are also more formal translations of 'you', which you would use in a job interview or other formal situations*) (*talking to one person*) usted; (*talking to more than one person*) ustedes; ¿es usted nuestro nuevo profesor?; **excuse me, are you Mr and Mrs Lawrence?** perdonen, ¿son ustedes los señores Lawrence?; **4** (*when used as the direct or indirect object of the verb*) (*talking to one person*) te; (*talking to more than one person*) os; **I'll lend you my bike** te presto mi bici; **I'll write to you both** os escribiré a los dos; **5** (*in formal situations*) (*talking to one person*) lo; (*talking to more than one person*) les; **I shall send you the document** le mandaré el documento; **Dear Mr and Mrs Jones, I am sending you the information you requested** Estimados señor y señora Jones, les mando la información que solicitaron; (*when used with another pronoun, 'le' and 'les' become 'se'*) **I shall send it to you on Monday** se lo mandaré el lunes; **6** (*in comparisons*) tú; (*more than one person*) vosotros/vosotras; **he's older than you** es mayor que tú, es mayor que vosotros/vosotras; **7 for you** para ti (*more than one person*) para vosotros/vosotras; **I'll go with**

you iré contigo; **8** (*in formal situations: after a preposition or in comparisons*) usted; (*talking to more than one person*) ustedes; **for you** para usted, para ustedes.

young *adjective* joven; **he's younger than me** es más joven que yo; **Tessa's two years younger than me** Tessa tiene dos años menos que yo; **young people** la gente joven.

your *adjective* **1** (*talking to one person*) (*with a singular noun*) tu; (*with a plural noun*) tus; **I like your skirt!** ¡me gusta tu falda!; **you've forgotten your CDs!** ¡te has olvidado tus compactos!; **2** (*talking to more than one person*) (*with a singular noun*) vuestro/vuestra; (*with a plural noun*) vuestros/vuestras; **your Spanish test is on Friday** vuestro examen de español es el viernes; **your rucksacks are in the dining room** vuestras mochilas están en el comedor; **3** (*although 'tu', vuestro', 'vuestra' are now commonly used in most situations, there are also more formal translations of 'your' which you would use in a job interview or other formal situation*) (*with a singular noun*) su; (*with a plural noun*) sus; **thank you for your hospitality** gracias por su hospitalidad; **4** (*with parts of the body or clothing*) (*with a singular noun*) el/la; (*with a plural noun*) los/las; **do you want to take your coat off?** ¿quieres quitarte el abrigo?; **wash your hands** lávate las manos.

yours *pronoun* **1** (*talking to one person*) (*referring to a singular noun*) el tuyo/la tuya; (*referring to a plural noun*) los tuyos/las tuyas; **my brother's younger than yours** mi hermano es más joven que el tuyo; **these aren't my glasses – are they yours?** estas gafas no son mías – ¿son tuyas?; **yours are better** los tuyos/las tuyas son mejores; **a friend of yours** un amigo tuyo/una amiga tuya; **2** (*talking to more than one person*) (*referring to a singular noun*) el vuestro/la vuestra; (*referring to a plural noun*) los vuestros/las vuestras; **our house is smaller than yours** nuestra casa es más pequeña que la vuestra; **our car is smaller than yours** nuestro coche es más pequeño que el vuestro; **our children are younger than yours** nuestros hijos son mayores que los vuestros; **a friend of yours** un amigo vuestro/una amiga vuestra; **3** (*as with 'you' and 'your' there are more formal translations for use in formal situations*) (*referring to a singular noun*) el suyo/la suya; (*referring to a plural noun*) los suyos/las suyas; (*note that here the translation is the same whether you are talking to one person or to more than one person*) **excuse me, is this book yours?** ¿perdone, es suyo este libro?; **excuse me, are these books yours?** ¿perdone, son suyos estos libros?

yourself *pronoun* **1** te; **you'll hurt yourself** te vas a hacer daño; **2** (*for emphasis*) tú mismo/tú misma; **did you do it yourself?** ¿lo hiciste tú mismo?/¿lo hiciste tú misma?; **by yourself** solo/sola; **3** (*like 'you' and 'your' there are more formal translations for 'yourself', which you would use in formal situations*) se; (*for emphasis*) usted mismo/usted misma; **as you yourself will understand** como usted mismo comprenderá.

yourselves *pronoun* **1** os; **when you have washed yourselves** cuando os hayáis lavado; (*when used with a verb in the infinitive or in commands, 'os' appears joined to the verb*) **help yourselves** serviros; **by yourselves** solos/solas; **2** (*for emphasis*) vosotros mismos/vosotras mismas; **did you do it yourselves?** ¿lo hicisteis vosotros mismos?/¿lo hicisteis vosotras mismas?; **3** (*like 'you' and 'your' there is a more formal translation for 'yourself', which you would use in formal situations*) se; (*when used with a verb in the infinitive or in commands, 'se' appears joined to the verb*) **please, help yourselves** sírvanse, por favor; (*for emphasis*) ustedes mismos/ustedes mismas; **did you do it yourselves?** ¿lo hicieron ustedes mismos?/¿lo hicieron ustedes mismas?

youth hostel *noun* hostal M juvenil.

Yugoslavia *noun* Yugoslavia F.

Z z

zany *adjective* chiflado/chiflada (*informal*).

zebra *noun* cebra F.

zebra crossing *noun* paso M de cebra.

zero *noun* cero M.

zigzag *verb* zigzaguear [17].

zip *noun* cremallera F.

zodiac *noun* zodiaco M; **the signs of the zodiac** los signos del zodiaco.

zone *noun* zona F.

zoo *noun* zoo M.

zoom lens *noun* lente F de zoom.

Beek - I\ther-veh-sa - Cerveza

MAPS

España